Britain's Prime and Britain's Decline

The British Economy 1870 – 1914

Sidney Pollard

Professor of Economic History, University of Bielefeld

Edward Arnold

A division of Hodder & Stoughton

LONDON   NEW YORK   MELBOURNE   AUCKLAND

For Helen

© 1989 Sidney Pollard

First published in Great Britain 1989

British Library Cataloguing Publication Data
Pollard, Sidney
  Britain's prime and Britain's decline:
  the British economy 1870–1914
  1. Great Britain. Economic condition:
  1870–1914
  I. Title
  330.941′081
  ISBN 0–7131–6591–X

Typeset in 10/11 pt Plantin by Colset Private Limited, Singapore
Printed and bound in Great Britain, for Edward Arnold, the educational,
academic and medical publishing division of Hodder and Stoughton
Limited, 41 Bedford Square, London WC1B 3DQ by Biddles Ltd,
Guildford and Kings Lynn

Table of Contents

	Pages
Preface	v
List of Tables	vi
Introduction	viii

1 Economic Growth and the Varied Industrial Scene — 1
  I. Macroeconomic Growth Patterns — 1
  II. Overall Industrial Growth Rates — 8
  III. Individual Industries: — 18
      Engineering and Shipbuilding — Mining and Metallurgy
      — Chemicals and Glass — Textiles and Clothing — Other
      Industries — Building and Public Utilities
  IV. Causes and Common Features of the Declining
      Performance — 49
  V. Conclusion — 55

2 The Export of Capital — 58
  I. Size and Structure of Foreign Investment — 59
  II. Preliminary Theoretical Considerations — 71
  III. The Risk Factor — 76
  IV. Capital Divisibility and Dynamics — 82
  V. Full Employment — 84
  VI. Costs of Capital Transfer — 86
  VII. Terms of Trade — 88
  VIII. The Bias of the Capital Market — 91
  IX. Taxation and Capital Exports — 100
  X. Sectors of the Capital Export Market — 100
  XI. Capital Exports and Balance of Payments — 107
  XII. Conclusion — 110

3 Education, Science and Technology — 115
  I. The Critique of Contemporaries — 116
  II. Science in the Industrial Revolution — 123
  III. Science, Education and Industrial Progress — 130

Contents

IV. German Education and Science Research 143
V. British Science, Education and Research 162
VI. The Adequacy of the British Provision 194
VII. Conclusion 204

4 The Role of the State 214
I. Assumptions in Britain and Abroad 214
II. Political Power and Economic Policy to 1870 215
III. Class and Power, 1870–1914 227
IV. Policies on Industry, 1870–1914 235
V. Some General Considerations 236

5 Some Conclusions: Maturity or Senescence? 260

Bibliography 272
List of Abbreviations 319
Index 320

Preface

The writing of this book has taken much longer than originally planned. New and varied duties and calls on my time repeatedly destroyed my time schedule and frustrated the publisher. Now that the final word had been written, it is not clear whether the delay is to be counted as gain or loss. The passage of time has certainly helped to modify my views, though mostly in the direction of increasing my doubts. The topics treated in this book seem to be of a kind which become less clear the closer one gets to them.

Many obligations have been incurred in the research and in the writing. The librarians and their staffs of the libraries of Sheffield University, Bielefeld University, the Erasmus University of Rotterdam and the European University Institute, Florence and of the LSE, and especially their Inter-Library Loan Departments, deserve the heartfelt thanks of a troublesome reader. I also have to thank the Editors of the *Economic History-Review* and of the series published by the Social History Department of Erasmus University, Rotterdam, for permission to use material first published in their pages. Colleagues at Sheffield, Bielefeld and Florence have contributed by their interest and their ideas, though they cannot be held responsible for the errors in this study. The research funds of Bielefeld University and the Sozialgeschichtlicher Arbeitskreis, Heidelberg, have made financial contributions which are gratefully acknowledged. I would particularly wish to thank the Erasmus University of Rotterdam for awarding me the tenure of the Tinbergen Chair for six months, and of the Rockefeller Foundation for granting me a month's Fellowship at their Bellagio Centre. These periods of study and thought, undisturbed by outside duties, have been valuable beyond description. I can only hope that these awarding institutions are not disappointed by the result.

To the typists who undertook the difficult task of bringing order into the chaos of my manuscript, Mrs Wilma Diekmann and Miss Angela Schenk, go my special thanks.

Nothing can exceed my obligation to my wife Helen who, while suffering long periods of loneliness without complaint not only helped in many material ways in the writing and typing of this book but kept my flagging spirits going at critical times by her constant encouragement and her infectious cheerfulness. To her this book is dedicated.

S.P.
Bielefeld, 1988

List of Tables

1.1 Annual rates of growth of GDP, in %, UK 1820–1913, at constant prices or constant factor costs 2
1.2 Annual rates of growth, in %, of output per head, UK 1820–1913, at constant prices or constant factor costs 2
1.3 Annual rates of growth of UK exports in %, 1856–1913 4
1.4 Annual growth rates in %, major economies, 1856–1913 5
1.5 Levels of output in 1910/13, selected countries 6
1.6 Annual growth rates, in %, of exports, selected countries, 1870–1913, 7
1.7 Shares in world exports in %, selected countries, 1860–1913 6
1.8 Annual rates of growth, in %, of industrial/manufacturing production, UK 1856–1913 9
1.9 Annual rates of growth, in %, of industrial output per head, UK 1856–1913, 10
1.10 Annual rates of growth, in %, of manufacturing and mining output, UK 1856–1913 10
1.11 Exports of manufactures, annual growth rates in %, UK 1853–1913 11
1.12 Prices (unit values) of manufactured exports, major countries, 1883–1913, index 1899 = 100 11
1.13 Annual growth rates in %, industry, 1860–1913, selected countries 12
1.14 UK share of world output, in %, 1860–1913 13
1.15 Index of manufacturing per head of population, 1913 13
1.16 Annual growth rates, in %, of manufactured exports, selected countries, 1871–1913 14
1.17 Shares in % in world manufactured exports, selected countries, 1871–1913 15
1.18 Share of manufactured output exported in %, three countries, 1899–1913 15
1.19 Growth of output, inputs and TFP, UK 1856–1913, in % p.a. 16
1.20 Annual rates of growth of certain industries, 1900–1913/14 18
1.21 Platt Brothers, spindles built 1880–1914 20
1.22 British trade in electrical goods, 1898–1913 22
1.23 British trade in engineering products, 1869–1913 23
1.24 British iron and steel production and trade, 1870–1914 27
1.25 Iron and steel imports into Great Britain, averages 1911–13 31
1.26 Tinplate, production and exports 31

1.27 Chemical production and exports, leading countries, 1901–1913   32
1.28 UK overseas trade in glass, 1875–1914, annual averages   35
1.29 Capacity of the British cotton industry, 1859–1913   36
1.30 British exports of cotton piece goods, percentage market shares 1865–1913   37
1.31 Ring and mule spindles (million) in main countries and areas, 1913   38
1.32 Imports and exports of woollen goods, 1870–1913 (annual averages)   41
1.33 Imports and exports of boots and shoes, 1875–1914 (annual averages)   43
2.1 Non-residential fixed capital stock, selected countries, 1870–1914   58
2.2 Area distribution of British overseas investments, in per cent, 1865–1914   60
2.3 Distribution of new British portfolio investment abroad by sector, 1865–1914   60
2.4 Net capital stock held abroad, as % of total British capital holdings, various estimates   61
2.5 Foreign investments of the leading countries, 1870–1914   62
2.6 Unrequited foreign payments, UK, 1855–1913   69
2.7 'Risk-adjusted' realized returns, aggregate indices, 1870–1913   77
2.8 Realized rates of return, in long swing highs and lows, sample of equities   79
2.9 Excess of the rates of return of certain types of foreign/empire firms over UK firms, %   79
2.10 Correlation of British trade and capital exports   103
2.11 United Kingdom balance of payments   109
3.1 Annual rates of increase per person employed (%)   131
3.2 Annual increases in %, 1856–1913   131
3.3 Estimated annual returns of achieving literacy, Great Britain 1839–73   137
3.4 Pupil numbers in German schools, 1902   151
3.5 Proportion of school boys in the Prussian population, 1822–1911 (per thousand)   151
3.6 Proportion of students taking science and technology subjects, c.1913, %   153
3.7 Expenditure on science and technology, 000 Marks, Germany and England   154
3.8 Total number of teaching staff in German universities and recognized university institutions   156
3.9 World production and consumption of Dyestuffs, 1913   159
3.10 Market shares of key chemicals   159
3.11 Graduates in science and technology, England 1870–1910   193
4.1 Membership of councils (averages of years), in %   225
4.2 The Black Country magistracy, 1836–1860   226
4.3 Social composition of the magistracy, 1841–1887   227
4.4 Shares of some major economic sectors, 1856–1913   228
4.5 Bankers' education, nineteenth century   232
4.6 Destinations of the exports of the UK, France and Germany, 1860–1910   244
4.7 Average cost of capital, 1870–1913   248

Introduction

To a nation accustomed to look upon itself as the world's leading economic power and the undisputed economic success story, the last three decades of the nineteenth century brought unwelcome and ominous signs of change. The accustomed increases in incomes and welfare, and the hitherto easy succession of structural changes based on new technologies met unwonted obstacles. To be sure, the British had become used to difficulties at home caused by cyclical recessions, though the depression which set in about 1873 was seen to be much more severe than anything experienced in the preceding 30 years. What was new was the rise of effective foreign competition, in the kind of manufacturing industries in which Britain had hitherto enjoyed undisputed competitive dominance. A spate of contemporary literature[1] bears witness to the growing unease over the rising industrial power of Germany, the United States and other countries, as well as over the signs of 'decline' in Britain herself.

The debate has continued, in one form or another, until the present day. The study presented here attempts, not to review the literature as a whole, but to come to grips with a limited number of issues which have appeared time and again in it, yet have remained controversial nonetheless. Had it attempted to deal with all of them, this book would have had to be inordinately long or unacceptably superficial. But the price to be paid for the treatment proposed here is that it is necessarily incomplete. Several important issues will not enter the discussion at all, and, as a result, any conclusions that may be drawn from this study will remain, at best, provisional.

The book consists of four essays, with a brief concluding chapter. The essays are self-contained, each tackling a particular topic, but they are interlinked, and they each contribute something to the conclusion. They are also not entirely parallel, but operate at different levels: this derives, to some extent, from the subject-matter itself.

Essentially, two separate problems are intertwined in the debate on the British economic slow-down or decline in the decades to 1914. While they may conceptually be easily kept apart, in practice they cannot be entirely treated in isolation. The first is the question whether, when and to what extent, the British economy slowed down or declined in those years. The second concerns the causes of such decline, if any.

Chapter 1 attempts to deal with the first issue, concentrating largely on the industrial sector where most observers have placed the British weakness.

[1] Much of it is listed in Heindel (1940); Hoffman (1964); Gamble (1981) among others. Also see chapter 4, note 62 below.

However, even this apparently empirical treatment is not free of the problems of causation, especially as far as the issue whether it was the 'modern', or 'science-based' sectors which declined most dangerously, is concerned. However, it is to be hoped that the attempt to locate the weak spots will help in the search for causes.

The wide-ranging discussion on causes has to date brought forth a whole range of different explanations, for the problem at issue was unusual, not to say unique. While normally the debate on lack of development concerns poor and backward countries, in this case it was the leading industrial economy, the economy which had furnished the nourishing soil for the first factory system ever, and had then managed to maintain an innovating, expansive and aggressive stance for over a century, which had failed to keep up its momentum and meet the challenge of the contemporary world. This seemed to be so unexpected that much of the debate has assumed it to have been unnecessary also, and has looked for scapegoats on whom to lay the blame.

The proffered explanations fall into two groups, though these touch and intermingle at many points. One may be subsumed under the heading of the 'early start': the effects of reaching maturity early, and getting fixed in structures and attitudes more appropriate to earlier conditions, while later comers were spared that handicap and started their industrialization in a more up-to-date environment. The second group of explanations seeks for causes in the social and political field, in peculiarities of British society, social structure and political behaviour, much of which, however, was in turn not unconnected with the early start or its consequences, among which must be included the acquisition of a huge Empire. No complete enumeration will be offered here, but the main themes deserve an introductory discussion.[2]

One cause was to be sought in the concentration in Britain on an ageing industrial structure: too much effort went into, or, as it has been termed, there was an 'overcommitment' to, industries of the heroic age which lay in the past, and which had little growth potential left for the future: cotton, iron and steel, wool, and coal were the leading examples.[3] There were here at least four interrelated problems.

The first was that since Britain's strength lay in industries developed earlier on, these could also most easily be started up by latecomers, using the latest techniques but cheap labour. Also, these industries had little potential left for further development. Secondly, because of the early shift out of agriculture, there was said to be little room for productivity gains by the redeployment of labour in Britain, although some estimates put the gain from redeployment within industries at 8% of national output between 1861 and 1911, and others estimated it as high as 12% between 1881–1907.[4] Thirdly, there was the 'inter-

---

[2] Extensive lists in, *inter alia*, Kirby (1981), 6 ff; Walker (1980), 20 ff; Aldcroft and Richardson (1969), 106 ff; Phelps Brown (1972), 189; Floud and McCloskey (1981), 313; McCloskey (1973), 4–5; Elbaum and Lazonick (1986b); Crouzet (1978), 343.

[3] Richardson (1965), 240, 253; Aldcroft and Richardson (1969), 136–7; Habakkuk (1967), esp. 220.

[4] Phelps Brown and Handfield-Jones (1952), 272, 281–2; Ashworth (1965); Ashworth (1966 a), 27; Walker (1982), 20; Musson (1959), 207–8; Jones (1933), 247–8; Rosenberg (1963), 415; Foreman-Peck (1983 b), 180; Williamson (1982), 20–1. Also see chapter 2 and note 103 below.

relatedness' problem, the cost of replacing much of a complex existing structure if innovations were to be introduced at any one point.[5] Lastly, there was the very success of British workers and industrialists in older industries using traditional methods and their consequent reluctance to change to something new.[6]

A different aspect of the early start theory was the early success in capital goods exports accompanied by capital exports, which in turn created financial intermediaries geared to channel capital abroad rather than into British industry. British manufacturers were therefore said to have been starved of capital compared with their main foreign competitors. This forms the topic of chapter 2.

Yet a third aspect was the alleged decline of entrepreneurship and management skills, as second and third generations followed the vigorous founders of the industrial revolution age. Probably no issue within our framework has been as hotly debated as the 'failure' of entrepreneurs in production[7] and overseas selling and marketing.[8] Partly for this very reason, no special chapter is devoted to this question in the present volume, but partly also because it is a matter very difficult to evaluate empirically. Put differently, entrepreneurship, making the right decisions in the given circumstances, enters every one of our chapters and cannot be debated in isolation from them.

A fourth problem within the early start syndrome was the weakness in scientific and technological training and research, compared with leading foreign countries. This was said to have derived from the earlier success of 'practical men' and the earlier social isolation of speculative thinkers and experimenters in Britain. It would affect the new, science-based industries such as chemicals and electrical engineering in particular.[9] This broad question forms the topic of chapter 3.

Another relic of the early start was wrong geographical location. Shipyards found themselves too high up the rivers for the larger modern vessels, steelworks were on ore fields which later gave out, coal pits were too closely together and therefore had to remain inefficiently small.[10] Altogether, the British climate seemed to be hostile to the giant concern and the cartel or monopoly combine which were then making their appearance elsewhere[11], though it is not clear whether this was a disadvantage or not. In turn, it may be linked to the survival of free trade in the face of rising protection elsewhere.

The debate over free trade versus protection was, of course, a major preoccupation of contemporaries. There would be little point in re-enacting the

---

[5] The issue is discussed further in chapter 1, p. 48, note 162 and chapter 2, p. 83, note 95.
[6] Lomax (1969), 14; Campbell (1980), 56.
[7] Aldcroft (1964–65), 127–34; Aldcroft (1981b) I, 18 ff; Kirby (1977), 23; Howe (1984), 290; Against this see: Matthews, Feinstein, Odling-Smee (1982), 115; McCloskey (1973); McCloskey (1971b), 285–309; Holmes (1976), 59–61; Jenkins and Ponting (1982), 268–70; Wilson (1965).
[8] Marshall (1970), 93–4; Diplomatic and Consular Officers (1899) XCVI.C.9078; Dispatch Chamberlain (1897), LX.C. 8449; Platt (1968), 105–6; Schulze-Gaevernitz (1906), 350; Davenport-Hines (1986); Nicholas (1984); Rathgen (1901), 126; Blaich (1982), 9, 13–14.
[9] See in general: Hobsbawm (1968), 151, 155; Adams (1982), 11, 66–8; Coleman (1973).
[10] See chapter 1, note 72 below.
[11] Holmes (1976), 52; Hannah (1976), 27; Rothbarth (1946), 387; Saul (1980), 26–17; Lazonick (1986a), 72–3; Kocka und Siegrist (1979), 55–122.

debate now, and it seems wisest to conclude with Alfred Marshall that the advantages and disadvantages for Britain of protection and dumping would be hard to evaluate. A recent econometric study found little correlation between tariff policies and economic growth among major economies in 1870–1913.[12] Chapter 4 refers to some of these issues.

Turning to the other group of alleged causes, namely political and social factors, possibly the most widely canvassed cause of British decline has been the aristocratic embrace, or loss of the 'industrial spirit'. As soon as they became successful, runs the argument, businessmen left their trade, settled on the land and adopted an aristocratic lifestyle, sending their sons to public schools to acquire a different ethos. A fatal haemorrhage of talent was the result. It is, according to one critic,

> difficult to avoid the conclusion that anti-commercial values among the British middle and upper classes . . . must ultimately be held to account.[13]

However, popular though this line of thought is, it would not be difficult to find counter-examples of families maintaining their business commitments over several successful generations.[14] Moreover, aristocratic ambitions could also be found in the first half of the nineteenth century, when no one accused Britain of lacking entrepreneurship, and in other contemporary economies, not least the German.[15]

The hierarchic and snobbish nature of British society was made responsible also for another retarding factor, the lack of a mass market such as was provided by the more democratic Americans. Though the industrial revolution had been built on mass production of a kind, it was said that the need for a broadly based, rather than a differentiated market structure for many new products for the purpose of standardization was being met better in the USA than in the UK. The large part of British industry working for foreign markets, for its part, also had to meet varied demands from different parts of the world, which again worked against standardization. However, this could not have applied in 1870, nor does it seem that German industry enjoyed more favourable conditions in this respect.[16]

On the face of it, the acquisition of an empire does not seem to offer grounds for industrial retardation, particularly since colonial officials and Europeanized natives were more likely to buy British than consumers in other overseas territories. It has, however, frequently been made a cause of British competitive failure that British exporters found it easy to escape the consequences of their displacement by German competition, by being able to switch to 'soft' markets, particularly in India and other parts of the Empire. Had this escape route not

---

12 Capie (1983); Marshall (1970), 631; Saul (1960a), 41, 134–5; Kindleberger (1975), 20; Bairoch (1976a); Cain (1979), 42. Also see chapter 4, note 80 and chapter 5, note 41 below.
13 Warwick (1985), 114; Wilken (1979), 99; Wiener (1981); Coleman and McLeod (1986); Marris (1979), 92; Byres (1967), 269; Kirby (1984).
14 Trebilcock (1977), 26; Boyson (1970), 89.236–7; Barker (1977).
15 Payne (1974), 35–8; L. Stone and J.C.F. Stone (1986); Church (1975a), 24–5, 71–4; Mayer (1981).
16 Saville (1961); Kindleberger (1978), 229; Kindleberger (1964), 151; Aldcroft and Richardson (1969), 115; Levine (1967), 116; Bagwell and Mingay (1970), 183–4; Zeitlin (1987), 175; Rothbarth (1946), 383–5; Holmes (1976), 26.

existed, it is suggested, then Britain would have had to put more steam behind modernizing her industry in order to survive.[17]

However, it is not immediately obvious that sales to relatively poor countries were easier than sales to one's European neighbours; nor will the allegation itself stand up to the evidence. While it is true that a much bigger proportion of British manufactured exports than those of other countries was sent to the non-developed world, this had been so for a long time, and there was no indication that the British were in any sense 'escaping' into it. In fact, the world outside Europe and North America took a growing share of the manufactures of all the major industrialized countries in that period.[18]

Lastly, there was the attitude of workers and their trade unions to innovations, which has been said to have been much less positive than in other countries. This, if true, may be an effect of the early start, for the British trade-union movement had been growing over a longer period and was thus firmer in the saddle when the major innovations in technology and company organization hit the British industries simultaneously with those of all advanced countries. Also, it accustomed the work force to slower glacial change and to hang on to their craft, whereas workers abroad experienced much more rapid technical revolutions when their countries underwent their expansion 'spurts'. At the same time it may also be taken as a consequence of the British class structure, and in particular of the employers' attitude of confrontation and of translating innovations into sackings instead of using them as a base to expand their trade with an undiminished work force. Workers and employers were more inclined here to see each other as the enemy.[19]

That trade unions elsewhere were weaker need not be doubted, but it does not mean that there were fewer strikes or that these were less destructive. Moreover, British industry was spared the revolutions, civil wars and wars of unification which interrupted the progress of the leading competitors abroad. It may even be that it was the relatively cheap British labour, measured against its relatively high efficiency, which inhibited the earlier application of more efficient capital.[20]

The political dimension is usually left out of account entirely in the Anglo-Saxon literature, with the exception of the tariff issue. It will be examined more closely in chapter 4.

A concluding chapter will return to the original question and will ask, in the light of the partial evidence produced here, whether there was failure in Britain in the period 1870–1914, or merely the natural catching-up process by later industrializing countries, and, if there was failure, where the main causes have to be sought.

[17] Matthews, Feinstein and Odling-Smee (1982), 452 ff; Walker (1982), 24; Musson (1959), 222; Kindleberger (1961–2), 296–9; Aldcroft and Richardson (1969), 15, 24; Saul (1954–5), 65; Kuczynski (1982), 32–3; Lewis (1978a).
[18] See Table 4.6. below.
[19] Platt (1973), 81–3; also Nicholas (1984), 491; Stopford (1974), 314. Chapter 1, note 110 and chapter 5, note 19.
[20] Aldcroft and Richardson (1969), 26–7; Aldcroft (1975), 209 ff; Matthews, Feinstein and Odling-Smee (1982), 114; Pratt (1904); Clark (1986), 498–500; Phelps Brown and Handfield-Jones (1952), 280–2; Elbaum and Lazonick (1986b), 6; More (1980), 18, 24.

1
Economic Growth and the Varied Industrial Scene

I Macroeconomic Growth Patterns

Economic failure could mean two different, though related things. One was the apparent loss of momentum in the British economy itself, a slowing down of the growth and development which had made the 1850s and 1860s, with all their fluctuations and disappointments, years of hope and self-confidence. The other was the relative rise of other economies, not merely catching up but in some cases moving ahead of Britain as far as technical innovation was concerned, and capturing growing shares of the world's markets. These will be examined in turn.

No satisfactory measures of total national income were available to contemporaries, and certainly none on a year-to-year basis. Several have been constructed since, and on the basis of the most recent of them, the following comparisons may be attempted (see Table 1.1).[1]

It is clear that there is here no absolute decline in the rate of growth: on the contrary, it is the stability of the growth rate, about which the different series seem to vary almost at random, which is remarkable. However, since the debate turns in part on loss of growth of efficiency or productivity, it might be more appropriate to deflate total output figures by the population or the work-force to discover signs of any possible loss of momentum. This is done in Table 1.2.[2]

Again, there seem to be remarkable differences between the estimates. However, in contrast to the first table there is here at least a modicum of agreement on a falling-off of the rate of growth, however measured, after 1890 and particularly in the new century, though there is also a strong hint that it picked up again in the last few years before the war. The period is too short to be certain that, had there been no war, the decline of the early twentieth century might not have been seen as a hiccup in a stable growth process rather than as

[1] Based on Maddison (1982), 213; Aldcroft (1974), 272–3; Feinstein (1972), T. 24–5; Greasley (1986), 429, 438–9; Lewis (1978a), 260–4. Readers who dislike statistics may skip this section and turn directly to section II of this introduction.
[2] Based on Maddison (1982), also Maddison (1979), 43; Feinstein, (1972), T.42, T.51–2; Mitchell and Deane (1962), 367–8; McCloskey (1974), 275. Also see Bairoch (1976a), 194; Aldcroft 1974, 272–3.

Economic Growth and the Varied Industrial Scene

Table 1.1. Annual rates of growth of GDP in %, UK 1820–1913, at constant prices or constant factor costs

By decades

	Maddison	Aldcroft	Feinstein[+]	Lewis[+]	Greasley
(1820–1870)	2.4	.	.	.	
1860–70		2.1	1.9	1.9	2.0
1870–80	1.9	1.9	1.7	1.7	1.8
1880–90	2.2	2.3	2.2	2.2	1.9
1890–1900	2.1	2.1	1.9	1.9	2.0
1900–10	.	1.1	1.3	1.3	1.2
1900–13	1.5	.	1.8	1.7	1.6

By cycles

	Aldcroft	Feinstein[+]	Lewis[+]	Greasley
1856–65	2.1[++]	2.0	2.0	1.9
1865–74	2.2	2.1	2.1	2.4
1874–83	1.8	1.7	1.7	1.7
1883–90	2.2	1.9	1.8	1.7
1890–1901	1.9	1.8	1.8	2.0
1901–07	1.7	1.5	1.4	1.4
1907–13	1.5	2.1	2.2	1.6

[+] Start-years and end-years are averages of three, of which they are the middle ones, except for 1913.
[++] 1859–65

Table 1.2 Annual rates of growth, in %, of output per head, UK 1820–1913, at constant prices or constant factor costs

By decades

	Maddison GDP per head	Feinstein[+] GDP per head	Mitchell/[+] Feinstein Net NI per head	Feinstein output per worker
(1820–70)	1.53	.	.	.
1860–70	.	1.12	2.23	1.38
1870–80	0.81	0.80	1.11	1.43
1880–90	1.43	1.54	3.13	0.86
1890–1900	1.14	1.11	1.39	0.99
1900–10	.	0.29	−0.17	0.46
1900–13	0.70	0.71	0.25	0.55

By cycles

	Feinstein[+] GDP per head	Mitchell/ Feinstein[+] NNI per head	Feinstein output per worker		McCloskey productivity
1856–65	1.19	1.97	0.85	1856–66	1.090
1865–74	1.42	1.26	1.53	1867–74	1.390
1874–83	0.75	0.69	1.28	1874–83	0.693
1883–90	1.52	3.52	0.90	1884–90	1.090
1890–1901	1.01	1.11	0.91	1891–1900	0.717
1901–07	0.37	0.07	0.63	1901–13	0.233
1907–13	1.18	0.76	0.53		

[+] Start-years and end-years are averages of three, of which they are the middle ones, except for 1913.

the start of its secular decline. It also seems possible that the period immediately preceding our 1870 starting date might have experienced faster growth, in which case the period as a whole might be seen as part of a longer slowing-down phase, as exemplified by the broadly based Matthews/Feinstein/Odling-Smee tabulation, which registers a clear drop in the growth rate of the GDP from 2.2% (1856–73) to 1.8% (1873–1913), and in the growth rate of GDP per man-year from 1.38% to 0.9% in the same years. In an earlier essay, Matthews measured an even sharper decline in the growth rate of GDP per man-year, from 1.1% in 1856–99, to 0.1% in 1899–1913.[3]

Contemporaries were more concerned with exports than with total output, largely because these were the only reasonably reliable statistics available to them, and also because they allowed easy international comparisons. To the actual export figures at current prices, which were published at the time, are here added estimates of changing volumes, as well as an estimate of the share of exports in the total British product (Table 1.3).[4]

Export growth rates, even when corrected for prices, show a clear dip in the 1880s and 1890s, calling forth the understandable concern for protectionism and foreign competition of those periods. There was, however, an equally clear recovery thereafter, reflected also in the share of exports in total national output, so that there could be no question of a secular decline. First impressions from the available statistics may be summed up by the statement that there was no obvious long-term decline in the rate of growth of output or of exports, though there are hints of somewhat faster growth rates in the 1860s and of some years of stagnation early in the twentieth century.

Yet it might still be the case that the British economy was growing less fast than some others. If true, this would be a different problem from a slowing of economic growth, but it would be a problem still. It is frequently referred to in contemporary discussion and it has dominated the literature since. A comparison with other major industrial economies shows the results as in Table 1.4.[5]

In spite of the variations between the different estimates, it is clear that British growth rates, both in absolute terms and in per capita terms, were falling seriously behind those of the major new emerging economic powers, Germany and the USA, especially after about 1890. The French position was comparable to 1890, but thereafter the French growth also became markedly faster than the British. Other economies were mostly to be found between these extremes.

Differences of 0.4% in annual growth rates such as appear here have very large effects when continued over 40 years or more, and it was the conscious-ness of these effects which was among the causes of the unease about the performance of the British economy in the years to 1914. They were rapidly annihilating the lead which Britain had accumulated in the preceding century: other countries were catching up on Britain. However, they were not yet

[3] See Table 1.19 and chapter 5, p. 263; also Matthews (1964–5) p. 3.
[4] Based on Kuznets (1967), 96; Mitchell and Deane (1962), 283–4, 328; Aldcroft (1968b), 13; Schlote (1976), 42. Also Bairoch (1976a), 192–3.
[5] Based on Maddison (1982), 172–3; Maddison (1962), 193; Bairoch (1976b), 286; Floud in Floud and McCloskey (1981), 8. Also Bairoch (1976a), 293; Crouzet, (1978), 332.

Table 1.3 *Annual rates of growth of UK exports in %, 1856–1913 (Start-years and end-years are averages of three, of which they are the middle ones, except for 1913, unless stated otherwise)*

	Domestic exports, current prices	Imlah/ Mitchell: export volume		Domestic exports, current prices	Aldcroft exports @	Schlote exports @	Imlah/ Mitchell: export volume		Kuznets: exports as % gross product
1856–65	4.95	2.4	1860–70	4.58	3.2	4.4	3.9	1857–65	16.1
1865–74	3.12	4.5	1870–80	0.57	2.8 }	2.1	2.6	1867–75	17.8
1874–83	0.56	3.3	1880–90	1.59	2.9 }		2.8	1877–85	16.1
1883–90	0.89	2.1	1890–1900	0.96	0.4	0.7	0.8	1887–95	14.9
1890–1901	1.08	1.3	1900–10	4.21			3.8	1897–1905	13.3
1901–7	5.50	4.8	1900–13	5.00	5.4	3.3	4.1	1909–13	18.8
1907–13	4.96	3.8							

@ Single years at beginning and end of decade

4

Table 1.4 Annual growth rates in %, Major Economies, 1865–1913

(a) By decades real GDP, Maddison 1982 (Western Europe, real GNP, Maddison 1962)

By decades	United Kingd.	Germany	France	USA	Western Europe
1870–80	1.9	1.8	2.0	4.8	(2.9)
1880–90	2.2	2.9	0.8	4.1	(2.7)
1890–1900	2.1	3.4	2.1	3.8	(2.2)
1900–13	1.5	3.0	1.7	3.9	(2.0)
By cycles					
1865–74	2.2	2.8	1.4	4.9	(2.5)
1874–83	1.8	1.1	0.8	4.3	(2.5)
1883–90	2.2	2.8	0.5	4.5	(2.3)
1890–1901	1.9	2.9	1.5	4.1	(1.6)
1901–07	1.7	3.6	1.6	4.1	(2.0)
1907–13	1.6	3.3	2.6	2.6	

Floud (output)

	UK (real GDP)	USA (real GDP)	Germany (real NDP)
1873–82	1.9 }	(6.5) }	1.3 }
1882–90	2.0 }		3.1 }
1890–1900	2.1	3.9	3.5
1900–07	1.5	5.2	2.7
1907–13	1.8	4.5	2.8

(b)

Real GDP per man-hour, Maddison 1982

	UK	Germany	France	USA
1870–80	1.6	1.5	2.4	2.3
1880–90	1.2	2.2	0.9	1.9
1890–1900	1.2	2.5	2.0	2.0
1900–13	0.9	1.4	1.8	2.0

Real GNP per capita Bairoch[+]

	UK	Germany	France
1870–80	0.8	0.4[++]	0.6[++]
1880–90	1.4	1.9	1.0
1890–1900	1.2	1.7	1.6
1900–13	0.7	1.2	1.0

[+] Start-years and end-years are the middle ones of three, except 1913

[++] 1870 at pre-war boundaries

Table 1.5 Levels of output in 1910/13, selected countries

	Per capita product, 1910 US $ of 1970 (Crafts)	GDP per Man-hour, 1913 US $ of 1970 (Maddison)	GNP per capita, 1913 US $ of 1960 (Bairoch)
USA		1.67	
UK	1302*	1.35	965
Belgium	1110	1.26	894
Netherlands	952	1.23	754
Switzerland	992	1.01	964
Germany	958	0.95	743
France	883	0.90	689
Sweden	763	0.83	680
Italy	548	0.72	441

* Great Britain

overtaking her. In absolute per capita terms, Britain was still the most successful economy in Europe in 1913, only the United States having overtaken her income and output levels, and in their case it was recognized that the resource base was very different from that of the European countries. Taking the British national product per capita as = 100, Continental Europe had been 62 in 1840, had fallen to 44 in 1890, and risen only to 50 in 1910. Individual countries are compared in Table 1.5.[6]

British growth was also slower than that of other countries, as far as exports were concerned, but it will be noted in Table 1.6 that in her final spurt to 1913 Britain regained some of the ground lost.[7]

Table 1.7 Shares in world exports in %, selected countries, 1860–1913

	UK	USA	France	Germany	Belgium	Switzerland
Maddison, exports f.o.b.:						
1870	18.9	7.9	10.5	10.7*	2.6	2.2*
1885	16.7	11.2	9.6	11.0	3.7	2.1
1900	15.0	15.0	8.4	11.6	3.9	1.7
1913	13.9	12.9	7.2	13.1	3.9	1.4
Buchheim, exports:						
1872	20.2			9.0		
1883	16.7			11.5		
1890	16.7			10.4		
1899	14.0			11.1		
1913	13.6			13.1		
Kuznets, trade:						
1860	25.1	8.3	10.8	9.2		
1870	24.0	8.8	10.8	9.7		
1880	22.4	9.8	10.2	10.3		
1891–5	18.0	10.5	9.2	11.0		
1901–5	16.4	10.5	7.6	11.6		
1913	12.2	10.5	7.4	12.3		

*1880

[6] Based on Maddison (1982), 212; Bairoch (1976b), 286, 307 and Bairoch (1976a), 292.
[7] Maddison (1982), 60, 248–9; Maddison (1979), 26; Maddison, (1962), 142, 179–81, 185–6.

Table 1.6 Annual growth rates, in %, of exports, selected countries, 1870–1913

	UK	USA	France	Germany	Belgium	Switzerland	World
By volume							
1870–90	2.9	10.4	3.4	2.4	6.3		3.4*
1880–90	1.3	1.4	2.0	2.9	3.7	4.0	3.4**
1890–1900	0.6	6.1	1.5	4.1	1.8		2.4
1900–13	4.2	2.5	3.8	6.4	4.9	3.6	4.1
Whole Period 1870–1913	2.8	4.9	2.8	4.1	4.2	3.9	3.4
By value							
1870–80	1.1	7.8	2.1		5.9		2.4
1880–90	1.7	0.1	0.8	1.3	1.7	−0.6	1.6
1890–1900	1.0	5.1	0.9	3.3	3.0	1.7	2.2
1900–13	6.1	4.1	4.0	6.2	5.2	3.9	5.3
Whole Period 1870–1913	2.3	4.2	2.1	3.7+	4.0	1.9++	3.0

* 1870–1881
** 1881–90
+ 1875–1913
++ 1880–1913

The result was that Britain was still the leading exporter in 1913, but only just ahead of Germany and the United States (Table 1.7).[8]

Given the much smaller population of Britain, and the greater dependence of Germany on commodity exports, there were here no obvious signs of British failure, but some causes for concern.

II Overall Industrial Growth Rates

It may be that total national income in its various versions is the wrong measure for our purposes. Most contemporary critics and later observers are agreed that the key to the alleged slowing down and comparative retardation of the British economy between *c.* 1870 and 1914 had to be found within the industrial, and above all the manufacturing sector:

> Whether historians date the beginning of imperial decline from about 1870 or after 1914, they associate it almost exclusively with the steady erosion of Britain's industrial supremacy.[9]

This belief rested in part on the parallel assumption that in the earlier successful years, it had similarly been Britain's industrial prowess which had been the foundation of her economic leadership. In part, it also rested on the recognition that it was the industrial sector which was ultimately responsible for the performance and the rate of change of other sectors: thus, even where there were genuine changes in productivity, in services or, for that matter, in agriculture, achieved by such things as cheaper schoolbooks or better ploughs, these were to be traced back to the efficiency of manufacturing. In any case, such service activities as did allow international comparisons, including shipping, banking and insurance,[10] remained singularly free of any accusations of relative decline. The causes of relative failure, if any, therefore had to lie in industry.

Statistics of rates of growth are obviously easier to establish and require fewer dubious assumptions in industry than in other economic sectors. Yet there are problems here also. Above all, the failure of total industrial production (or industrial production per head of population) to maintain a high rate of growth may be a sign of decline, but it may also indicate a switch of resources, including labour, from the industrial sector to the service and other sectors, which in turn may actually reflect a rise in incomes and living standards rather than a failure to grow. Something of this kind, a shift to services, as well as to goods which did not enter the official statistics, such as newspapers, sweets or cosmetics, has indeed been said to have happened in the later Victorian economy.[11] The alternative, to measure output per person employed (or per

---

[8] Maddison (1962), 179–81; Buchheim (1981), 276; Kuznets (1966) 306–7. Also see Capie (1983), 5.

[9] Cain and Hopkins (1986), 502. Also Cornwall (1977), chapter 7; but see Lee (1986). Actually, in 1907 manufacturing provided only one-quarter of national income, and if we include mining, quarrying, gas, electricity, water, building and contracting, this became 37%. Deane and Cole (1967), 175.

[10] See, p. 67, note 167 below.

[11] Wilson (1965); Ashworth, 1966, 17–33; Ashworth (1965), 62–74. Also chapter 3, note 300 below.

hour worked), in other words to measure labour productivity as an indicator of progress purely within industry, may fail to take account of the fact that expansion may mean the use of additional but less productive units, e.g. less skilled labour, which may bring down average productivity, yet represent progress. It also fails to take account of different quantities of capital and other resources used per man. Finally, there is the problem that the different series do not always include the same activities under the headings 'industry' or 'manufactures'.

Nevertheless, the statistical evidence relating to manufacture or industry in the wider sense is clearly of major interest to this enquiry. Much of this book will, in fact, concern itself with the problems of the industrial and mining sectors. A summary of some of the best estimates is collated in Table 1.8:[12]

Table 1.8 Annual rates of growth, in %, of industrial/manufacturing production, UK 1856–1913 (Start years and end years are averages of three, of which they are the middle ones, except for 1913, unless stated otherwise).

	Hilgerdt manufacturing production	Lewis manufacturing and mining	Feinstein industrial production	Lomax industrial production	Aldcroft/ Richardson industrial production incl. building[+]
By decades					
1860–70	.	2.6	2.4	.	2.9
1870–80	1.2[++]	2.1	2.3	2.1	2.3
1880–90	2.6	2.7	2.4	1.9	1.6
1890–1900	1.5	2.1	2.4	2.6	2.8
1900–10	1.0	1.2	0.8	0.9	.
1900–13	2.1	2.1	1.7	1.6	1.6
By cycles					
1856–65	.	2.6	3.2		
1865–74	.	2.9	2.5		
1874–83	1.7	2.4	2.1		
1883–90	1.7	1.8	1.9		
1890–1901	1.3	1.9	2.2		
1901–07	1.4	2.0	0.0		
1907–13	3.1	2.6	3.6		

[+] Single years, beginning and end of decades
[++] Start is average of 1870–1.

Once again, a per capita comparison would be useful, but is difficult because of the problem of isolating the labour force employed in manufacturing. Some approximations will be found in the series in Table 1.9.[13]

Here, also, there are considerable variations in the rates of change recorded by different methods, though possibly the switch from the older to the newer industries, which can be registered in different ways, contributed to the lack of

[12] Based on Hilgerdt (1945), 132–4; Lewis (1978a), 148–50, 260–3; Feinstein (1972), T. 24–5; Lomax (1969), 11, 32; Aldcroft and Richardson (1969), 105, 126; Aldcroft (1968b), 13.
[13] Based on Feinstein (1972), T. 24–5 and T. 120–1; Aldcroft and Richardson (1969), 126; Aldcroft (1968b), 13; Coppock (1956), 7. Also Ford (1969), 120–1 and Crouzet (1978), 328 ff.

Table 1.9 *Annual rates of growth, in %, of industrial output per head, UK 1856–1913, (Start-years and end-years are averages of three, of which they are the middle ones, except for 1913, unless stated otherwise)*

	Aldcroft industrial productivity per man-year*	Feinstein industrial production per head of population		Feinstein industrial production per head of population		Coppock industrial productivity**
1860–70	1.1	1.6	1856–65	2.5	1854/60–1861/5	0.6
1870–80	1.2	1.2	1865–74	1.5	1861/5 –1866/74	2.2
1880–90	0.5	1.6	1874–83	1.1	1866/74–1875–83	1.0
1890–1900	0.2	1.4	1883–90	1.1	1875/83–1884/9	0.5
1900–10		0.0	1890–1901	1.3	1884/9 –1890/9	0.1
1900–13	0.2	0.9	1901–7	−0.8	1890/9 –1900/7	0.2
			1907–13	2.9	1900/7–1908/13	−0.1

* Single years at beginning and end of decades
** Corrected for unemployment.

uniformity. As in the case of total national income, there is a hint of faster rates of growth in the years preceding 1870, and a drastic slowing down in the early years of the twentieth century, made up by very fast growth again to 1913. Whether this should be seen as part of a decline in industrial productivity, or a dip which might have been followed by an even greater rise, had the war not intervened, cannot be ascertained from these figures. However, as in the case of GDP, by choosing a suitable turning point, it is possible to show that the first part of the period had faster annual rates of growth (in %) than the second, so that a slowing down might be said to have taken place:[14]

Table 1.10 *Annual rates of growth, in %, of manufacturing and mining output, UK 1856–1913.*

	Output		Total factor productivity		Lomax industrial production
	Manufacturing	Mining, quarrying	Manufacturing	Mining, quarrying	
1856–60	2.5	4.2	1.2	2.4	
1860–65	1.7	4.4	−0.1	1.9	
1865–73	3.2	3.2	1.3	0.8	
1873–82	2.3	2.2	1.1	0.2	
1882–89	1.9	1.6	0.4	−0.3	
1889–99	2.3	2.0	1.1	0.0	
1899–1907	1.6	2.5	0.1	0.2	
1907–1913	2.0	1.2	0.3	−1.0	
1856–73	2.6	3.6	0.9	1.4	1860–77 3.0
1873–1913	2.0	1.9	0.6	−0.1	1877–1913 1.6

A similar picture emerges from the statistics of manufactured exports alone, possibly the key variable in the discussion of the failures of the British economy:[15]

[14] Matthews, Feinstein and Odling-Smee (1982), 229, 378; Lomax (1969), 12; Feinstein, Matthews and Odling-Smee (1981), 178.
[15] Based on Lewis (1978a), 148–50; Hilgerdt (1945), 158, 160.

Table 1.11 *Exports of manufacturers, annual growth rates in %, UK, 1853–1913*

| | Hilgerdt | | | Lewis | |
	Current prices	Constant prices		Manuf. exports constant prices	Manuf. exports less manuf. imports, constant prices
1871/5–1881/5	−0.45	2.06	1853–73	3.35	3.21
1881/5–1891/5	−0.58	0.44	1873–99	1.63	0.38
1891/5–1901/5	2.26	1.71	1899–1913	2.72	2.92
1901/5–1911/13	5.53	3.92			

At current prices, manufactured exports actually declined for two decades after the high point of the early 1870s, though in terms of volume they continued to grow. In all cases, the rapid growth after the dip of the Great Depression is clearly evident. Perhaps more significant still, the last column shows for 1899–1913 a faster rate of increase than the gross export figures or, in other words, the volume of manufactured exports was growing faster than the volume of manufactured imports, a truly remarkable result for a country in the process of being caught up by other industrializing nations.

It is an easy mathematical exercise to show that, had exports continued to grow at the pre-1870 rate, they would have been much larger than they actually were in 1913, and British output to sustain them would also have been much larger.[16] But even if we assume that there was no buoyancy in the home market because of the slow population growth (and ignore the possibility of rising incomes in Britain) the causation might just as easily have run the other way: that is, it was because of the failings of British industry that exports did not increase any faster, and allowed other industrial countries to muscle in on formerly British preserves. Certainly, British export prices can be shown (Table 1.12) to have risen much faster than the export prices of the main competitors:[17]

Table 1.12 *Prices (unit values) of manufactured exports, major countries, 1883–1913, index 1899 = 100*

	1883	1913
UK	112	125
USA	127	112
France	110	112
Germany	124	108

According to another calculation, British 'relative export prices' compared with other exporters rose by 0.4% p.a. between 1870 and 1914. Also in individual industries, the relative competitive decline of the British share could not be explained by tariffs or other artificial barriers.[18] In fact, as in the case of

16 Musson, 1959, 213; Lomax (1969), 13; Wulf (1968), 219.
17 Lewis (1978a), 122; Maizels (1970), 205; also Saul (1965), 10–11.
18 Brown (1965), 49; Burnham and Hoskins (1943), 61.

Table 1.13 Annual growth rates in % industry, 1860–1913, selected countries

Hilgerdt: Manufacturing production

	UK	USA	Germany	France	World
1860–80	2.1	5.4	2.9	2.0	3.3
1870–80	2.1	5.4	2.9	2.0	3.3
1880–90	1.9	5.4	5.5	2.5	4.3 }
1890–1900	1.5	3.4	5.0	2.7	3.6 }
1900–13	2.1	5.2	3.9	3.5	4.2
1900–13)**	(1.7)	(5.3)	(4.7)	(2.5)	(3.0)

Bairoch: Total industrial potential@

UK	USA	Germany	World
2.5	5.5	4.6	1.8
1.6	5.1	4.9	2.7
1.9	6.7	5.2	4.3

Lewis: industrial production++

UK	USA	Germany	France
2.3	5.7	5.9	2.6
2.5	5.6	4.6	1.9
2.1	3.1	3.9	2.3
2.1	5.4	4.4	3.3

Hilgerdt: Manufacturing output per head of population

	UK	USA	Germany	France
1871/5–1881/5	0.6	2.7	1.7	
1881/5–1896/1900	0.9	2.1	3.9	2.4
1896/1900–1911/13	0.7	3.2	2.5	3.3

Brown and Browne: Real output per occupied person in industry

	UK	USA	Germany	Sweden
1870–80	0.7*		0.7	
1880–90	3.0		1.4	
1890–1900	1.1	0.6	2.2	4.2+

@ Start-years and end-years are averages of three, of which they are the middle ones, except 1913
* starting 1871
+ starting 1892
** Aldcroft and Richardson
++ Excluding construction

Average annual growth, in %:	Industrial production	Industrial productivity
UK	2.1	0.6
Germany	4.7	1.5
USA	4.1	c.2.6
France	3.1	—

total GNP, it was by comparison with other countries that British growth appeared most disappointing:[19]

On a long-term basis, the problem was clear. Over 1870/1–1913, growth in industrial production and productivity compared as shown opposite:[20]

There was in consequence a drastic fall in the British share of the world's manufacturing output:[21]

Table 1.14 UK share of world output, in %, 1860–1913

	Manufacturing output (Bairoch)	Manufacturing product (Hilgerdt)	Industrial production (Solomou)	Industrial production (Capie)
1860	19.9			21
1870		31.8		
1872–82			18.95	
1880	22.9			
1881–5		26.6		
1882–90			18.14	
1890–9			17.83	
1896–1900		19.5		20
1900	18.5			
1899–1907			16.12	
1906–10		14.7		
1907–13			14.55	
1913	13.6	14.0		14

The basis for these four calculations may be different, but the downward tendency in each of them is unmistakable. However, here also, the European continent was far from having caught up with Britain:[22]

Table 1.15 Index of manufacturing per head of population, 1913 (USA = 100)

UK	90
Belgium	73
Germany	64
Switzerland	64
Sweden	50
France	46

Once again, what was significant for Britain was her position as an exporter in a competitive environment. The growth of manufactured exports compared as follows:[23]

It may be an indication of the significance attached to that measure that several separate estimates exist of the shares of the main exporting countries in

[19] Based on Bairoch (1982) 292; Hilgerdt (1945), 56, 132; Brown and Browne (1968), 436–449; Aldcroft and Richardson (1969), 105; Lewis (1978a), 248–50, 269, 271, 273. Also see Fremdling (1986) B.6.,45; Frankel (1957).
[20] Aldcroft (1968b), 13.
[21] Bairoch (1982), 296; Hilgerdt (1945), 13. Solomou (1986), 168; Capie (1983), 5.
[22] Lewis (1978a), 163; Crafts (1983), 389.
[23] Hilgerdt (1945), 158–61.

Table 1.16 Annual growth rates, in %, of manufactured exports, selected countries, 1871–1913

	UK	USA	France	Germany	Belgium	Switzerland
Current prices						
1871/5–1881/5	−0.5	4.4	−0.4			
1881/5–1891/5	−0.6	1.6	0.2	0.7		
1891/5–1901/5	2.3	9.7	3.1	4.9		3.3
1901/5–1913	5.7	7.7	4.8	6.6	4.9	3.8
1871/5–1913	1.6	5.9	2.0	4.1*		3.4+
Constant prices						
1871/5–1881/5	2.1	7.1	2.2			
1881/5–1891/5	0.4	2.7	1.2	1.7		
1891/5–1901/5	1.7	9.1	2.5	4.3		2.7
1901/5–1913	3.6	6.1	3.3	5.0	3.3	2.3
1871/5–1913	2.0	6.2	2.3	3.7*		2.1+

* 1881/5–1913
+ 1886/90–1913

the world's manufactured exports. They differ in detail, possibly because of differences in definitions, but all show similar trends (Table 1.17).[24]

The British share in the export of capital goods, possibly containing the products of the more advanced or progressive industries, showed an even more drastic fall (%):[25]

	UK	USA	Germany	Rest of world
1800	63.1	5.7	19.0	12.2
1899	44.4	22.2	17.2	16.1
1913	31.3	20.8	30.1	17.8

In view of the smaller British population, to continue to hold the largest share of the world's manufactured exports, though with a diminishing lead, was a not inconsiderable achievement. Moreover, because of the high level of British exports, even her lower rate of increase yielded a higher absolute increase in manufactured exports right up to the outbreak of the war when Britain was indeed still much the largest export economy among the three leading nations:[26]

The statistics presented here so far have been mostly rather crude summaries of complex and often finely differentiated series of observations. Inasfar as they are concerned with efficiency, as most of them purport to be, any conclusions to be drawn from them will be distorted, at least to some extent, by differences in resource endowment. Even if these are eliminated or of no great consequence, the measures we have been using hitherto, such as absolute or per capita levels of output, or productivity per capita or per worker or working hour, leave out at least one other important input: capital. Clearly, a country, an industry or a firm would not necessarily be less efficient when producing less with a given labour input (ignoring natural resources) if at the same time it also used less capital.

[24] Based on Hilgerdt (1945), 158–9; Tyszynski (1951), 286; Maizels (1970) 189; Kuznets (1967), 53–5; Buchheim (1981), 276; Phelps Brown (1972), 196; Lewis (1957), 579; Saul (1965), 12.
[25] Saul (1965), 16.
[26] Maizels (1970), 223.

Table 1.17 Shares in % in world manufactured exports, selected countries, 1871–1913

	UK	USA	France	Germany	'World'
Hilgerdt					
1881/5	45.4	4.9	17.3	21.2	8 countries
1891/5	40.7	5.5	16.7	21.6	11 countries
1901/5	32.8	9.0	14.6	22.4	13 countries
1913	30.9	11.0	13.3	24.6	14 countries
Saul/Tyszynski					
1880	41.4	2.8	22.2	19.3	
1890	40.7	4.6	17.1	20.1	
1899	32.5	11.2	15.8	22.2	11 countries
1913	29.9	12.6	12.9	26.4	11 countries
Maizels/Kuznets*					
1899	33.2	11.7	14.4	22.4	⎧Developed
	(34.0)	(11.9)	(14.7)	(23.0)	⎩countries
1913	30.2	13.0	12.1	26.6	⎧Developed
	(31.0)	(13.3)	(12.4)	(27.1)	⎩countries
Buchheim					
1872	45.5			12.6	
1883	36.5			18.7	
1890	34.6			18.8	
1899	29.4			21.0	
1913	26.8			24.4	
Lewis/Phelps Brown					
1883	37.1	3.4	14.6	17.2	
1890	35.8	3.9	14.5	17.2	
1899	28.4	9.8	12.6	19.5	
1913	25.4	11.0	10.6	23.0	

* Kuznets's figures in parentheses

Table 1.18 Share of manufactured output exported in %, three countries, 1899–1913

	UK	USA	Germany
1899	42	5	31
1913	45	5	31

In principle, efficiency must be a measure of total input compared with total output. To measure this in practice, the concept of total factor productivity (TFP) has been developed which correlates output with the input of land, labour and capital. If we take the first of these three as a constant, we are left with the task of tracing the variable inputs of capital as well as of labour. Unfortunately, the measures available for these factor inputs are not altogether convincing. As far as labour is concerned, we have to make allowances for the quality of the labour input, such as the educational level and the intensity of effort of the work force. For capital, the input calculation becomes even more problematical, for there is no safe or agreed way to measure the quantity of capital used up in any given output.

TFP is therefore a dubious guide at best.[27] Where attempts have been made to assess it in practice, results have remained broad and tentative. A good example is the comprehensive study by Matthews, Feinstein and Odling-Smee. Their calculations for our period show the values given in Table 1.19:[28]

Table 1.19 Growth of output, inputs and TFP, UK 1856–1913, in % p.a.

	Output	Total factor inputs		Total factor productivity	
		Gross capital	Net capital	Gross capital	Net capital
1856–73	2.2	0.8	0.7	1.4	1.5
1873–1913	1.8	1.3	1.3	0.5	0.5

Were the improvement in TFP truly measurable it would give us an accurate guide to the growth in efficiency in the broadest sense, including technology,[29] organization, economies of scale and capacity utilization, among others, having already accounted for improvements in the quality of the labour force. One could then also compare the performance of different countries over time. At the same time, however, many of these effects can be treated as inputs, quantified and thus eliminated from TFP. For the period 1873–1913, for example, such a process would leave for Britain, on the above calculation, a nil rate of growth in TFP.[30]

A second question deserves a brief mention. It concerns the turning point in Britain's economic fortunes. Assuming that there was a slow-down, did it show itself in the form of a marked turning point, or did vigorous growth imperceptibly turn into stagnation or even decline? And if there was a turning point, when did it occur? This issue has been much debated, and at least three different dates have been offered.

For Coppock, the real turning point came in the early 1870s. This was the beginning of the 'Great Depression' on a world-wide scale, and the key measures of economic well-being pointed downward in many countries, but unlike the rest of the industrial world, Britain never properly recovered her growth momentum thereafter. The relative decline set in then. This view is supported by Hoffmann's statistics of industrial growth, and appears to have found favour also with Lewis and with Aldcroft and Richardson.[31] Against this, Musson vigorously maintained that the Great Depression was cyclical, and

[27] The problem is discussed in Nadiri (1970); Nicholas (1982b), Eichengreen (1986), 33–5. For the problem of capital-saving technology, see e.g. Blaug (1960–61), Blaug (1963); Blaug (1960). Also see chapter 3, pp. 130–131, notes 49–50 below.
[28] Matthews, Feinstein and Odling-Smee, (1982), 208. Also Table 1.10 above.
[29] This is a complex issue. For an introduction to the debate, see Solow (1957); Phelps (1962), 548–67; Intriligator (1965), 65–70; Jorgenson and Griliches (1972), 65–94.
[30] Matthews, Feinstein and Odling-Smee (1982), 16.
[31] Coppock (1961); Coppock (1964–5); Aldcroft and Richardson (1969), 126–9; Lewis (1978a), chapter 5. Also Ashworth (1965), 68.

normal growth was resumed at its end, though some permanent changes were left by it.[32]

According to Phelps Brown and Handfield-Jones, the climacteric occurred in the 1890s. It was marked especially in the older industries, while the new ones were still too small to have much effect on the economy. This view was, not unnaturally, contested by Coppock who could cite numerous key statistical series in which the clear break, in the sense of a drastic slowing down of the growth rate, occurred in the 1870s.[33]

McCloskey favours a still later turning point, the early twentieth century: up to then, British productivity increases compared well with those of the USA and were not much below those of Germany. The view that the new century was the period of stagnation following on earlier growth appears to be shared also by Matthews and associates. It is vigorously contested by Aldcroft, whose statistical series break around 1890.[34] Finally, according to some observers, there is no climacteric, no visible break to be found at all.[35]

Those who have worked their way through the preceding statistical tables will not find it entirely surprising that in the *decelerando* of a complex economy, accompanied by several overlapping cycles, no agreement should emerge on a break, turning point or even change of tempo in any particular year or even group of years. Even a single agreed key variable, showing declining growth rates as first differences, would not lend itself easily to the determination of a point at which the change in tempo occurred. In our case too many factors intermingled and mostly worked to different rhythms. Thus it would be quite normal for a country like Britain undergoing structural change while being closely intertwined with the world economy, to show slow-growing or even stagnating industrial output or industrial productivity, while at the same time national income, boosted by vigorously rising returns from services or foreign investments, showed high and even rising growth rates.[36] Within manufacturing industry itself, several different methods are possible for matching declining older sectors against rising new ones, and the index number problem would affect also the change from self or family employment to paid employment, and from production in the home to production for the market, quite apart from the usual problems of changing qualities of goods masquerading under a constant name.

It will therefore be necessary to undergo the troublesome experience of more detailed sectoral investigations before being in a position to judge whether, and when, the British economy slowed down, and what meaning to attach to that phrase. To this we must now turn.

---

[32] Musson (1959), esp. 228; Musson (1962–3), 530; Musson (1964–5), 397.
[33] Phelps Brown and Handfield-Jones (1952); Brown and Browne (1968), 116–18, 190–4; Coppock (1956).
[34] McCloskey (1970); McCloskey (1974); Aldcroft (1974); Matthews, Feinstein and Odling-Smee (1982), 381–2; Feinstein, Matthews and Odling-Smee (1981), 169.
[35] Broadberry (1986).
[36] Kindleberger (1978), 233; Coppock (1964–5), 395–6; Aldcroft and Richardson (1969), 101, also see chapter 1, note 167 and chapter 5, note 16 below.

III Individual Industries

A first glance shows, not unexpectedly, that individual industries differed enormously in their rate of expansion in our period. Most published comparative statistics go back to the work of Walther Hoffmann, which, with all its faults,[37] has not been bettered as a starting point for the nineteenth century. An improved version by Lomax for the period 1900–1913/14 showed the following changes for selected industries (Table 1.20).[38]

It is evident at a glance that little can be deduced from such a comparison. Some industries may show fast growth because they are at the beginning of their development from a narrow starting point, others are slow because, though efficient, they have exhausted their technical possibilities. There is the further presumption that industries in a fast growth phase would by that very fact also show a rapid rise in productivity. Consequently there was no necessary correlation between growth and export success or success in keeping out imports.[39] Indeed, it is in the structural change of new industries taking the place of the old that much of overall growth had its origin.[40]

To arrive at some worthwhile conclusion, therefore, the major industries will have to be examined both from the point of view of their actual develop-

Table 1.20 *Annual rates of growth of certain industries, 1900–1913/14*

	Av. 1900–1913	Av. 1900–1914
Chemicals	3.1%	
Ferrous metal manufacture	2.4	
Non-ferrous metal manufacture	1.2	
(All metal manufacture	2.2)	
Mechanical engineering	1.3	
Electrical engineering		6.3%
Shipbuilding	2.6	
(All engineering and shipbuilding	2.1)	
Vehicles	3.4	
Textiles	2.5	
Leather		0.3
Clothing	0.8	
Food	3.9	
Drink	−0.1	
Tobacco		2.5
(All food, drink, tobacco	1.7)	
Timber	−0.04	
Paper and printing		3.1
All manufacturing	2.0	
Mining and quarrying	1.6	
Gas, water, electricity		4.8

[37] Hoffmann (1955); Ashworth (1965), 70–1; Musson (1978), 104.
[38] Calculated from Lomax (1968), 32–3. 1913 or 1914 have been chosen as end-years, according to which showed the higher absolute output.
[39] Aldcroft and Richardson (1969), 139–40; Musson (1964–5), 399.
[40] See Introduction, note 4.

ment and their potential, how far, in fact, they made the best use of their opportunities.

Engineering and shipbuilding

Engineering lies at the heart of the technical progress of the type which was created in Britain in the industrial revolution and then spread, with very little modification, to Europe and North America in the course of the following hundred years. Engineering provided the capital goods and the technology for the rest of industry. Within the engineering sector, two sectors, namely machine tools, that is, machines to build other machines, and the construction of prime movers, the sources of power, played a key role.

Curiously enough, it was precisely here, in engineering production, the location of strength of British industry that the first signs of foreign superiority appeared in the early 1850s. In what soon became known as the 'American system of manufacture' the innovations were, significantly enough, as much of an organizational as of a technical nature. They had two main aspects: the assembly of complex articles out of interchangeable parts; and the manufacture of components, on a mass basis, sufficiently accurate to be assembled without further adjustment. It was a major example of the transfer of skill from man to the machine.[41]

Started, presumably by Eli Whitney in the manufacture of arms early in the nineteenth century, it was found by expert British visitors in 1853–4 to have developed far beyond the British level, to the extent that Colonel Colt failed to acclimatize the method in Britain in 1852–6 because of the inability of British workers to cope with it.[42] Though recent research does not quite bear out this traditional tale of British failure and though the concept of 'interchangeability' is a matter of degree, there is no doubt that American engineering acquired a long lead over the British in the manufacture of sewing machines, typewriters, agricultural machinery, clocks and watches, as well as arms, largely because of mastering its principle earlier.[43] Not until the bicycle boom and the improved machine gun[44] did Britain take her own major steps forward in the mass production of interchangeable parts, to be soon overtaken once more by Henry Ford's motor car manufacture.

In the manufacture of machine tools themselves, where Britain appeared to have built up an unassailable lead early in the century, her comparative performance at the end was patchy at best: the low point was reached in the 1890s when large numbers of machine tools were actually imported into Britain from the United States. Thereafter some improvement took place: Britain had

[41] Rosenberg (1972) and Rosenberg (1969), 90–7; Fries (1975), 378; Habakkuk (1967), 104 ff.

[42] Burn, (1970); Buxbaum (1921), 136; Fries (1975); Inove (1984), 15; Floud (1976), 162.

[43] Woodbury (1960), 235–53; Musson (1980); Saul (1967), 114–16; Payne (1974), 39; Ames and Rosenberg (1970); Sandberg (1970), 120–46; Ames and Rosenberg (1967); Landes (1983), 283, 310, 322; Hoke (1986), 490; Mayr and Post (1981); Hounshell (1984), Hoke (1987), 322–4; Rosenberg (1963) 425–34; Rosenberg (1963), 96; Clapham (1963) III, 192–3; Saul (1967), 123–4; Musson (1978), 187.

[44] Trebilcock (1977), 7; Saul (1963), 38.

never, in fact, lost contact with best practice and had a large export surplus in machine tools throughout.[45]

This chequered history is explained, largely if not wholly, by different market structures and resources *vis-à-vis* the Americans, who were the technical leaders, rather than in terms of inferiority or superiority. In the USA, rich in enterprising, ingenious and well trained engineering designers and managers, there was much 'producer initiative', machine builders (and not only in the machine tool branch) meeting the anticipated demands of groups of producers by designing special machines for them.

In Britain, makers concentrated on general machine tools, leaving it to the 'customer initiative' of user firms rich in skilled labour, to adapt them for their special needs. At the same time, as in so many other fields, American firms were larger, yet offered fewer models, so that they had longer production runs for each. Other reasons for the American lead may be found in high wage rates in the USA and in strong worker and trade-union objections in the United Kingdom to innovation, while there were particular causes for the sudden American invasion of the 1890s.[46] The American ingenuity is shown by their lead in such specialisms as printing, typesetting and boot and shoe machines, but there was also some British pioneering, as in the precision grinding of ball bearings.

The same wide-ranging variety of experience is also found in other sectors of the engineering industries. The building of textile machinery and of steam engines remained a British *forte*. Platt Brothers of Oldham, the leading firm of cotton machinery makers, employing 2,200 lathes by the 1880s and 12,000 workers by the end of our period, supplied almost one-half of the cotton spindles installed in Britain and probably about one-third of those installed in the rest of the world. If British spinners neglected the new ring spindle, it was not for lack of building capacity:[47]

Table 1.21 *Platt Brothers, spindles built 1880–1913 (000)*

	Mules	Rings	Total
Home	20,008	1,659	21,667
Export	9,511	9,739	19,250
Total	29,519	11,398	40,917

British efficiency was also maintained in providing machinery for other textile branches, and in the early twentieth century, exports of textile machinery were almost eight times as large as imports.[48] Similarly, in the building of locomotives, appreciated abroad because of their sturdiness and

[45] Saul (1967), 121–2; Saul (1968a), 26; Floud (1976), 72; Floud (1971), 318; Habakkuk (1967), 171–2; Heindel (1940), 212, 220 ff; Saul (1960b), 23; Chapman (1904) I, 125; Buxbaum (1921), 137–8; Musson (1980), 100; Levine (1967), 35; Aldcroft (1964–5), 21; Clapham (1963) III, 123.
[46] Floud (1976), 48, 55–8, 101–5, 113; Rosenberg (1963), 420–1; Rosenberg (1972) 45–6, 101; Chapman (1904) I, 126, 132–3; Barnes in Mosely (1903), 72; Floud (1974), 65–8; Zeitlin (1983), 28–9.
[47] Farnie (1981), 84–6; also Berg (1979), 204.
[48] D.C. (1981a), 67, 85, 91, 102, 111. Tariff Commission (1904) IV, 24.

cheapness, and in the making of steam engines, British firms did well, in part by the efficient use of interchangeable parts.[49]

By contrast, in the making of agricultural machines, the British were driven out of many markets by the Americans and the Germans, though their output and sales were by no means negligible.[50] Bicycles showed a variety of experience which one might almost term typical. Dominated by the British until 1892, the industry was then led by the USA who were followed, until 1905, by Germany as the world leaders. From 1906 Britain again took the lead, exporting 150,000 by 1913, with Germany at 89,000 and others nowhere. The motor cycle balance was equally positive.[51]

The motor industry was still in its early, chaotic phase, catering for a tiny luxury market. Innumerable small firms produced uncounted models: of 393 companies of which the existence is known, 280 had failed by the outbreak of war.[52] Ford, the British branch of the American company, produced 6,100 vehicles in 1913 out of a national total of 34,000. Wolseley with 3,000 and Humber with 2,500 were next, but the average firm made under 100 vehicles. Much criticism was directed against the unions for maintaining unsuitable craft traditions, yet the labour force had risen to 100,000 by 1913. If there were few scientifically trained managers in the United Kingdom, there were few at the time in the USA also, and there as here workshop practice counted for more than formal education. In any case the men of talent frequently spread their innovations by moving from firm to firm. As in so many other areas, there was remarkable progress in the final 5 or 6 years of peace, when Britain was rapidly closing the gap on the French, then the European leaders in the industry.[53]

Electrical engineering was the sector probably most dependent on scientific understanding and technological innovation in that era. In spite of the major contributions by British scientists, from Faraday and Wheatstone to Kelvin and Hopkinson, and in spite of the skills of practical engineers like Parsons, Swan, Crompton, Merz and Ferranti,[54] early promises in the industry were not fulfilled. Among the causes for the backwardness of the industry in Britain were named adverse legislation in the 1880s,[55] overspeculation, competition by cheap gas, managerial incompetence especially by men with commercial rather than technical training, lack of capital, and the 'consulting engineer', a peculiar feature in Britain whose intervention prevented the fruitful direct collaboration between the engineering producer and the client, and tended to impose purely engineering instead of economic criteria.[56]

[49] Cummings in Mosely (1903), 82; Chapman (1904) I, 111, 114; Lenman (1977), 173; Saul (1960b), 20–1; Saul (1967), 114–17.

[50] David (1971), 145–214; Chapman (1904) I, 122; Munting (1978); Munting (1985); Tariff Commission (1904) IV, par.24; Saul (1967), 119–20; MacLean (1976).

[51] Chapman (1904) I, 125; Saul (1967), 125; Harrison (1969); Harrison (1981); Foreman-Peck (1983b), 186–7; Thoms and Donnelly (1985), 14–18, 28–30.

[52] Harrison (1981); Saul (1963), 23, 34; Campbell (1971), 245–6.

[53] Saul (1963), 24, 38–9; Saul (1967), 130; Church (1982); Overy (1976), 10–11; Trebilcock (1969), 489; Thoms and Donnelly (1985), 60, 66; Lewchuk (1986), 136–41. The American output averaged half a million vehicles in 1913–14. Rosenberg (1972), 114; Clapham (1963), 140.

[54] See chapter 3, pp. 203–4, chapter 4, p. 252 below.

[55] See chapter 4; p. 251 below.

[56] Sakamoto (1980), 62–7; Byatt (1979), 178; Hennessy (1972), 26 ff; notes 11, 157 below.

Within the sector, the British did well in manufacturing cables and pioneering radio, but lagged in electric lamps, traction and other heavy machinery, and telephone equipment. Overall, the British position was by no means hopeless:[57]

Table 1.22 *British trade in electrical goods, 1898–1913*

	Annual averages, £ mn		
	Exports (incl. re-exports)	Imports	Exports as % imports
1898–1902[+]	2,79	0.76	—
1903–6	2,83	1.52	186
1911–13	6,38	2.68	238

[+] Not stictly comparable with the later figures. Imports exclude electrical machinery.

Subdividing the last column of the table for the years 1911–13, on the same basis, we get the following ratios:

Electrical machinery   176
Electrical cables   550
Electric lamps   49

further emphasizing the enormous differences between sectors.

Even though much of this export success was due to the British branch factories of foreign firms, the productive capacity had in effect, become British. In an area where Britain's chief rivals were helped by protective tariffs, this result belies any conclusion of undifferentiated failure and emphasizes once again the unevenness of British industrial development. It also poses the question whether, in an industry in which research and development are costly and uncertain but in which the new ideas spread quickly across borders, there is not something to be said for being a taker rather than a provider of innovations.

Finally, the armaments industry may be considered. This was a highly competitive industry working for a monopsonistic buyer, the Government, who was in a position to test quality: the industry was early in the field in developing quality control. Although many of the inventors in this sector originated outside Britain (Nobel, Harvey, Gatling, Nordenfeldt and Maxim), yet here was an area in which Britain not only kept her lead, but possibly even increased it in the years before 1914. Certainly, Vickers became the dominant firm, only Krupp and possibly Bethlehem being in the same class. Here, at least, the usual position was reversed, and Britain's strength lay in the final and technically most difficult stages.[58]

Not all segments of the engineering industry have been included in this short survey, but even the limited number covered show that any generalizations about the relative decline of the industry are bound to be hazardous. Taking the industry as a whole, it may be said that while in 1870 Britain had been far and away the leading supplier of engineering products in international trade, by 1914 there was still a large export surplus, but the strongly expanding exports were now faced by a marked rise of imports:

[57] Based on Byatt (1979), 169; Byatt (1968), 246–7, 257; Saul (1960b), 35; Chapman (1904) I, 133; Balfour Report (1918) (XIII, C.9035) 14. Also Saul (1979), 117; Chapman (1904) I, 136; Weiher (1980), 28.
[58] Trebilcock (1969), 480–5, 490; Trebilcock, (1977), 1–4, 31, 46, 112 ff.; Scott (1962) 36–7; Trebilcock (1973), 256–7.

Table 1.23 British trade in engineering products, 1869–1913[59] (£ mn, annual averages)

	Imports of machinery declared values	Exports, current values		
		Machinery	Electr. goods	Vehicles and aircraft
1869–72	—	6.1	—	—
1897–1900	3.2	18.5	1.5	0.3
1910–13	6.1	32.6	3.1	4.2

Does a development of this kind represent a natural and healthy growth at a time when other countries are catching up, or does it bear witness to senile (relative) decline? One way of answering this is to look how the totals are made up. It is possible to break down the export statistics to some extent, and they show that, in general, there was a tendency for Britain to do better in older sectors, such as steam engines or textile machinery, and worse in newer sectors, such as gas and diesel engines and motor cars; but naval guns and their control mechanism, bicycles and locomotives in which Britain excelled belonged to the newer or technically more complex category. There is widespread support for the view that in comparison with the United States, Britain was backward in mass-production methods, and continued longer with high-quality, crafted products; but this may have merely been a sensible adaptation to a very different market and to cheaper skilled labour.[60] There is also a widely held view that the British 'consulting engineer' held back progress,[61] yet at the same time it has been a persistent critique of British engineering firms that they were run by commercial men rather than by technically trained directors. The faster total expansion of their markets may have allowed newer industrializing countries such as Germany or the USA, to install a greater proportion of newer equipment; yet in very new sectors, like electrical engineering, the British growth rate was also fast without leading to a hot pursuit at the technologic frontier, while some older sectors automated early.[62] Engineering may well be an example of a sector in which perhaps not even disaggregation by product, but only a firm by firm account, can establish whether Britain was falling behind, or was merely being caught up.

The associated shipbuilding and marine engineering industry showed some interesting contrasts as well as parallels with engineering. For one thing, it was undoubtedly more successful. Building 80% of the world's mercantile tonnage in the 1890s, British yards still launched 60% in 1900–14, which, if subsidized and protected tonnage is deducted, amounted still to 80% of competitively built ships, and even more of the costlier steam and steel ships. The orders from foreign shipowners alone were larger, year by year, than the total output of the USA or Germany, the nearest rivals.[63] Ships were among the technically most

[59] Mitchell and Deane (1962), 299, 304–5.

[60] Saul (1967), 111; Saul (1960b), 20–1, 37–8; Saul (1968b); Rosenberg (1976), 158; Rosenberg (1972), 48–51.

[61] Saul (1967), 129; Rosenberg (1972), 47; Aldcroft (1964–65), 122. Also see notes 56 above and 194 below.

[62] Allen (1929), 111; Musson (1980), 100.

[63] Pollard (1957), 426–8; Pollard and Robertson (1979), 25, 44–5; Lorenz and Wilkinson (1986), 109–34; MacKinnon (1921), 93–104.

complex products of the age, and British yards got the orders because their ships were cheapest and best. On a crude comparison, while the British shipyards worker produced an average of 12.5 tons annually, the figure for the USA was 6.8 t and for Germany, 3.3 t. Other countries lay far below this.[64]

Chairs in naval architecture had been founded relatively early, in Glasgow (1883), Newcastle (1890) and Liverpool (1908), and the leading makers of shipyard machinery, Bennie, and Craig & Donald, both of Glasgow, had no equals anywhere in the world.[65] Nevertheless, even here Britain showed a tendency to traditionalism in technique and capital equipment, relying on manual skill and lagging in the provision of heavy cranes and gantries, covered berths, mechanical rivetting, caulking, drilling and chipping machines, pneumatic, hydraulic and electrical power transmission and even electric light. Yet in view of the undoubted overall success of the industry, these features cannot be regarded as failings, as was the case in other industries. The question rather was how Britain managed to combine her factors of production so sensibly and economically. Wherein lay the secret of the British superiority?

One advantage lay in the scale of operations itself. Based originally on the large British merchant marine and on the technical lead in iron working, it became cumulative when foreign orders were attracted thereby, and it led in turn to efficient specialist sub-contractors for components and in some cases even of engines. As main buyers of steel in their regions the British yards made good bargains, they could draw on a large pool of labour and they could specialize: nothing raised the costs abroad as much as yards large enough to launch greyhound liners being used to build harbour tugs. Conversely, in a capital goods industry suffering exceptionally wide fluctuations, it was an advantage to have little capital and to transfer the burden of slumps onto the workforce. The sophisticated equipment installed abroad may be looked upon as a second-best solution in the absence of skilled labour and varied markets.[66]

Moreover, there was no lack of enterprise in British shipbuilding. British builders pioneered iron, then steel shipbuilding, steam engines and then double, triple and quadruple expansion, and ultimately the steam turbine. Shipping legislation and the need to get a Lloyd A1 rating led them to build safer ships than others, and to take more care over such things as the quality of the steel they used. In the last years before 1914 there was also a great increase in the design staff, in the technical training of managerial employees, and in the use of electricity after it had become reliable. A powerful amalgamation movement created huge horizontal and vertical combines in the shipbuilding industry.[67] Yet British owners were slow to order, and therefore British yards were slow to build, to new designs such as oil-fired ships and ships driven by diesel engines or turbines. Could it be that, as in several other industries, Britain was putting her money on traditional methods, now at their peak but

---

[64] Pollard (1957), 437.

[65] Lorenz and Wilkinson (1986), 125; Pollard and Robertson (1979), 58, 120–8. 143–5; Chapman (1904) I, 102–3; Harley (1973–74), 398; Hume (1976), 160–73, 197.

[66] Pollard and Robertson (1979), 46–51; 89 ff, 117 ff, 129; Lorenz and Wilkinson (1986), 3–9; Wilkie (1903), 93; Cummings in Mosely Report, 81; Pollard (1957), 439–42.

[67] R.C. (1905) Cd. 2643, Jeans QQ.4322ff; Pollard and Robertson (1979), 96 ff, 136–8; Byres (1967), 258–9; Slaven (1975), 178.

soon to be displaced by new methods, but that in this case there was a lag in the process, so that what was really a failing rearguard action looked like a rational disdain of unripe technology? Or would Britain, had the war not come, have adopted the new once it had proved itself, with the same ease with which she caught up elsewhere, having the best of all worlds, the old methods at their peak while other countries bore the development costs of the new, to pick the new methods like ripe plums when they began to pay off?

Mining and metallurgy

Coal mining was one of the major growth and export industries of the later Victorian and Edwardian economy. About 85% of the world's coal exports originated in Britain in 1900, and one half still in 1913. Output had been 52% of the world figure in 1870 and was 25% still in 1913 (or 40% of European production). In Europe, Britain had a huge lead in output and consumption per head and was exporting coal even to Germany and the Netherlands right up to the outbreak of war. To raise output from 123 million tons in 1870–74 (itself a record) to 271 m t. in 1910–13, the workforce had increased from 413,000 to 1,100,000, and the mining communities were vigorous recruiters of labour, were paid good wages and bore a general air of prosperity.[68]

Yet the industry has not escaped criticism, either by contemporaries or by those who attribute Britain's declining share of world manufacture to weaknesses in entrepreneurship and management. British superiority in overseas markets, it was said not without justification, might not be the result of British efficiency, but might depend entirely on natural endowment, having better or more accessible seams, located near cheap water transport. But this might give out, which, indeed, was beginning to happen. Measured by that crude indicator, output per man employed, the peak of British productivity had been reached in 1883, and while the actual peak year differed slightly from region to region, most showed a declining tendency in output per head from about then on. No doubt, some of this was due to a reduction in hours worked, and output per man-hour changed very much less: having risen from 0.137 tons in the 1870s to the peak of 0.144 tons in the 1880s, it then stabilized at around 0.132–0.135 tons from the 1890s to the outbreak of war. Nevertheless, the decline in output per man-year meant that German productivity, which had been 81% of the British in 1885, had caught it up by 1913, while the earlier American lead over Britain had widened impressively in the same years.[69]

Of course, some decline in productitivy per man was to be expected in an older mining industry as the best seams and those easiest to work were being worked out. The growing proportion of workers engaged in transport and in on-cost work might be a proof that this process was taking place in Britain. Much capital was being sunk into mining, fixed capital investment rising almost three times at constant prices between 1873 and 1913. Yet total factor

[68] Statistics from the latest re-worked figures in Church (1986), p. 3, 759, 772–3, 779, also 227–33. Taylor (1961–2), 63; Clapham (1963) III, 125; Jevons (1915), 676–8; Buxton (1978), 87; Taylor (1968), 38–9; Mitchell (1984), 107; Griffin (1971), 97; Taylor (1968), 43.
[69] Church (1986), 474–6; Taylor (1961–2), 55–6; Taylor (1968), 47–9; Mitchell (1984), 321; Walters (1975), 282-1; Slaven (1975), 242.

productivity – admittedly a crude measure – showed a drastic decline, especially in the 1890s and again in the last years of peace.[70] Could failure to use the best technology, or weaknesses in management, here as elsewhere, be held responsible for the declining performance?

Earlier in the century Britain had been the technical pioneer. In this period, critics have fastened particularly on the failure to adopt the mechanical cutting of coal as a sign of a widening lag. Experiments went back in Britain to before 1850, but in the event it was the United States where coal cutting machines were introduced first. In Britain about 1% of the coal was cut by machine by 1900 and 8% by 1913 (it was 22% in Scotland), as against 51% in the USA. On the continent, however, the cutting by machine was even more backward, the German proportion being 2% about 1913. British mines were also much slower than American to introduce electric power transmission, at any rate before 1904, and mechanical haulage, which was connected with mechanical cutting. In the matter of screening and washing of coal, associated with grading and preparation for particular markets, even some of the continental countries were ahead of Britain. In the coking plants which were frequently attached to coal mines, Britain stuck far longer than others to the beehive oven, instead of turning to continental types, which yielded more by-products. Even in 1913, 40% of the British ovens were still of the beehive type, and 50% of the by-product type.[71]

It was not that these new methods were unknown. Chairs of mining had been established at Newcastle (1880), Birmingham (temporarily, 1883), Sheffield (1892) and soon also in Glasgow, Cardiff, Manchester and Leeds, and the latest techniques were also widely discussed elsewhere. There might have been good reasons for their slow adoption. Mines suitable for mechanical cutters amounted to only about 25–33% of the total, so that cutting machines were in use in about one-quarter of those suitable, as against 8% of the total which is the usual but irrelevant figure quoted. British mine owners might well have been 'rational' to wait until 1904, when electricity had become safe, before introducing it underground, and had similar good reasons for delaying mechanical washing and screening. Mines were small – only 38 collieries out of 1784 employed as many as 2,500 workers each – but this was largely due to their early start and to the peculiar institution of the private royalty owner: in new areas, companies were larger. In spite of their more 'backward' techniques, British mines might have been economically as efficient as the American.[72] Poor labour relations and the problems of raw labour recruited in booms could be matched abroad. But before 1914 no solution could be found to the backward supply curve of labour, as output was cut back, or absenteeism increased, in years of higher wages.[73]

[70] Church (1986), 118–19; 480; 777; Clapham (1963) III, 69; Buxton (1978), 119.
[71] Church (1986), 314 ff; Chapman (1904) I, 38–40; Mitchell (1984), 78 ff; Carr and Taplin (1962), 210.
[72] Church (1986), 356–7, 390 ff, 429–30, 769–79; Hirsch and Hausman (1983), 154–5; Byres (1967), 254–5; Buxton (1978), 111; Berg (1979), 165; McCloskey (1971b), 292; Greasley (1982), 246–68; Taylor (1961–2), 64–6; Taylor (1968), 56.
[73] Church (1986), 9 694; Harley (1973/74), 395; Hirsch and Hausman (1983), 145–9, 152–3; Walters (1975), 292–3, 299.

The debate is usually conducted in terms of British 'entrepreneurship' or management skills, and these, in turn, are measured against the immediately available methods of profit maximization. The measure is ambiguous. By 1914, many British mine managers were indeed well trained and knowledgeable, though there were still many without formal training. But even if it could not be denied that they could usually see where their immediate advantage lay, they often failed to grasp long-term opportunities, to question structure and direction. As one mine inspector complained in 1903: 'There is a sort of *vis inertiae* that you have to overcome at a great many collieries before you can get any new system introduced.'[74] It was, moreover, a point of dubious strength for a leading industrial country to depend to such a large extent on the export success of an industry suffering natural diminishing returns which were bound to hit the early starter first, in which an irreplaceable raw material was being used up with little value added, and in which more recent industrializers were bound to improve their relative standing as time went on.

The significance which the literature attaches to the iron and steel industry derives less from its absolute size – it employed no more than 1.4% of the occupied labour force and earned 1.5% of Net National Income at the end of our period – than from its role as a driving force of expansion in the 1850s and 1860s, and its consequent acceptance as a status symbol at home and abroad. Its products were also significant among British exports, furnishing 12% of export values at the beginning falling to 10% at the end of the period studied here.[75]

Table 1.24 contains some of the most widely quoted statistics:[76]

Table 1.24 British iron and steel production and trade, 1870–1914 (annual averages; million tons unless otherwise stated)

	Pig iron		Steel		Iron and steel					Exports	
					Imports		Exports		% of	Ratios	Imports
	Out-put	% of world	Out-put	% of world	Qty.	£mn	Qty.	£mn	world	Qty.	£mn
1870–4	6.38	47.6	0.43	43.9	0.19	2.38	2.95	30.5	(80+)	26.8	12.8
1880–4	8.16	40.8	1.79	32.7	0.35	4.15	3.90	27.6	(70+)	11.1	6.7
1890–4	7.28	28.5	3.14	24.6	0.36	4.14	3.01	23.5	(60+)	8.4	5.7
1900–4	8.64	20.2	4.95	15.1	1.09	7.93	3.31	28.8	c.44	3.0	3.6
1910–4	9.50	14.9	7.2	10.8	1.79	11.99	4.42	46.5	32	2.5	3.9

There were features here which recalled those of other industries: continuous expansion in Britain, but loss of relative shares of world markets from an untenable position of dominance around 1870. Here, as elsewhere, Britain's share of the world's exports was much higher than that of production, or, in other words, she remained much more a trading and international economy than her main rivals at this stage; but after 1890 (having held up well until then) export shares also fell, except, curiously, in the last period, while import shares rose. In terms of steel tonnage produced, Britain was overtaken by the USA in

[74] Church (1986), 352.
[75] Burnham and Hoskins (1943), 283, 288; McCloskey (1973), 15.
[76] The figures have been published many times. Convenient summaries will be found in: Burnham and Hoskins (1943), 275–9; and percentage calculated on these; Carr and Taplin (1962), 166, 184, 188, 231.

1886 and by Germany in 1893; in terms of tonnage per head of population by the USA in 1899 and by Germany in 1907; in terms of tonnage exports, by Germany in 1910, but at no point by the USA, nor was Britain at any time overtaken in terms of export tonnage per head.

The differences among the leading countries were not very great at the end of our period, except that the USA, with their better resource base and their much higher need for steel in transport undertakings because of the greater distances, might be expected to show a markedly higher steel consumption per head. This once again leaves open the question whether the statistics may be interpreted to say that Britain was merely being caught up from an unsustainable lead, or whether she was actually falling behind.

One way of testing this might be to look to output per head, that is, to labour productivity, as a kind of absolute standard against which to measure performance in producing a practically homogeneous product such as pig iron. Britain still led the world in 1880, but by 1913 annual output per worker compared as follows:[77]

USA	760 tons
Belgium	470
UK (1911)	440
Germany	400
France	300

However, these differences might not reflect efficiency, but different factor costs. In any case, definitions of what, for example, might be counted as blast furnace employment, were not too exact.

As an alternative, technical progress might be compared. Here the Americans were ahead in handling equipment, greater use of electricity and the telephone, three-high continuous rolls instead of the clumsy British two-high reversible rolls, and a better lay-out of the works. Continental firms were said to practise better fuel economy and make better use of by-products. The Americans also gained 50% output increases by 'hard driving', which however demanded better blasting techniques and larger furnaces. Efficiency increased with size of furnace, and at the end of our period the average American blast furnace of 100,000 t. capacity compared with one of 30,000 t. in Britain and 49,000 t. in Germany, the other Europeans lying between those two. In Britain alone, it was said, labour productivity in the pig iron industry was stagnating.[78]

British firms were also too small, and were said to be too reluctant to join cartels. Their owners were also late in handing over to scientifically trained managers.[79] Having been sited early, they were often in the wrong location, but slow to move: thus the Scottish industry was on ore fields which by 1913 had largely given out. By contrast, it has been held as a grave fault not to have moved to the rich East Midland ore field before 1914, though American and

[77] Burnham and Hoskins (1943), 149, 194–7, 315–17; Carr and Taplin (1962), 206; Burn (1940), 133–43; Allen (1977), 609, 612.
[78] Jones (G.T.) (1933), 49, 55, 142, 219; Feldenkirchen (1980), 98; Musson (1978), 176; Levine (1967), 39–40; Burn (1940), 49, 183–4, 188–9, 343; Walls in Mosely Report (1903), 14; Cox in Mosely Report (1903), 47; Marshall (1970), 95; Webb (1980), 323.
[79] Balfour Committee Report (1918), 11; Payne (1967b) 534; Burn (1940), 213, 219–21, 334; Burnham and Hoskins (1943), 43, 205 ff.

German observers have vigorously denied any error in this regard on the part of the British entrepreneurs.[80]

Altogether, American steelmen were said to be more sanguine, and more ready to change their ways than the British. Given equal market signals, the Americans were said to be much more prepared to scrap old plant, to try new methods, and above all to enlarge their works capacity.[81] This difference in behaviour could, however, at least to some extent be blamed on the free-trade position in Britain, for while the foreign maker could safely count on gaining, behind his tariff walls, all the orders arising from the expansion of his home market, the British had to fear having to share it to an unknown extent with importers including dumpers. Moreover, the slower rate of growth of the British industry, arising from this factor as well as from having reached a much higher starting point earlier, itself not only inhibited investment in new methods, but gave the British equipment installed at any one time a higher age structure.[82]

At least some of the causes for the differences between British and other countries are to be looked for in different supply and demand conditions. Britain had switched early to the more reliable open-hearth (Siemens) steel demanded by shipowners and the Admiralty, and, relying on imported ores, could continue with acid steelmaking. Elsewhere, production mainly for rails and structural material could stay with the Bessemer process but, since expansion there took place largely after the Gilchrist–Thomas process had been perfected, could switch to basic steel. As it happened, much of the modern improved equipment was designed for Bessemer, which predominated abroad, and was not suitable for the British acid open-hearth plants which were efficient even on the smaller scale, leaving less scope for innovation here.

Similarly, because of Britain's greater dependence on a very varied export market, and also because British commercial relations had been established largely before the age of mass production, the orders for British steel works tended to be much smaller, giving shorter runs in the mills. In 1900, the USA was offering 33 different sections in their ordinary business, Germany 34 and the United Kingdom 122. This was not only itself more wasteful, but inhibited the introduction of better technology which paid off only with longer runs, such as the three-high rolling plant.[83]

In other respects also, the position was not uniformly gloomy. In special steel, Sheffield was still unbeatable and continued to supply even the USA in spite of the tariff. British metallurgists such as Mushet, Sorby and Hadfield,

[80] Slaven (1975), 169–76; Gibson (1958), 22–39; Byres (1967), 251, 289–90; Campbell (1980) 105, 125, 233, 238, 240; Campbell (1980), Payne (1979), 23–29, 104; in general see: Warren (1976), esp. 1–10, 42–3 and below p. 52, note 175; Burn (1940), 112–67; Isard (1948), 203 ff, 216; Wengenroth (1986), 270–88; McCloskey (1973), 59–64.
[81] Chapman (1904) I, 93; Carr and Taplin (1962), 205.
[82] Temin (1966b) 140–55; Burnham and Hoskins (1943), 74–6; Webb (1980), 326; Payne (1968), 78, 97; Hannah (1976), 27; Burn (1940), 272; Habakkuk (1967), 211–12; Levine (1967), 125–6, 132.
[83] Sinclair (1959), 33, 41–4; Harley (1973–74), 400–2; Kindleberger (1964), 32; Burnham and Hoskins (1943), 183; Elbaum (1986), 55, 66–7; Wengenroth (1986), 106 ff, 177 ff; R.C. (1905), Jeans QQ. 4302, 4307; Carr and Taplin (1962), 109–10; Burn (1940), 23; Payne (1968), 81–93; Payne (1979), 112–3; Levine (1967), 46.

still led at the frontier of knowledge, and others, including Gilchrist and Thomas still made the innovations. Just before the war, Harry Brearley of Sheffield discovered a method of producing stainless steel. Apart from its large exports of pig iron, noted above, Britain also recaptured much of the market in rolled goods and occupied a leading position in the making of tinplate, galvanized sheet and armour plate, and individual firms did keep abreast of technical developments, expecially in areas like Cleveland.[84]

Estimates of overall comparative efficiency differ widely. McCloskey held that on the basis of TFP the USA were merely catching up by their faster growth and at the end of the period were no more than 2–3% ahead. Webb calculated that the difference lay between 5% and 14%, while Allen thought that in steelmaking, both Germany and the USA exceeded British overall efficiency by 15% in 1907–9, and in ironmaking by 5%, an opinion shared by Berck. On Allen's figures, on the other hand, Britain was superior to Germany and France, if slightly inferior to Belgium in *c.* 1909. Orsagh calculated that Britain had measurably fallen behind.[85]

It is not easy to summarize the multiplicity of data and opinions. If the British home market for steel was saturated by 1890, inhibiting the kind of cost reductions that can come only with expansion, and if foreign markets were simultaneously being closed by tariffs, could not Britain have captured at least some of the markets secured by Germany and kept out more of the foreign imports? If traditional labour skills and union objections prevented the installation of better equipment, does not this point to a failure in management? The best techniques were known and there were, after 1900, some up-to-date plants, comparable to the best abroad, so that Britain was able to catch up very quickly in the war. If the regional dispersion was such that there was nowhere a demand gap large enough to justify a major new works, was this not an entrepreneurial fault? Could not better organization, possibly a cartel, and even a tariff, have created the conditions for a rapid displacement of inefficient plants by efficient units?[86]

There is a final consideration. In a world division of labour, in which other competent industrializing countries were approaching the technical level of the leader, some manufacturing specialism would certainly have to be conceded to them. It might well be best, in those circumstances, for Britain, with her higher wages and higher incomes generally, to allow others to concentrate on the rather cruder industries producing semi-finished material, like iron and steel, particularly since one reason for its early concentration in Britain, the local ore, was weakening as the reserves were giving out. Much of the iron and steel imports which flooded in in the last years before 1913, was indeed of semi-finished material, to be worked up in Britain into the more complex, higher-stage goods like ships, tinplate or galvanized sheet (Table 1.25).[87]

There were signs that some German finishing industries, including

[84] Chapman (1904 I), 69–91; Richardson and Bass (1965), 76, 84–8; Musson (1978), 142; Burnham and Hoskins (1943), 137 ff, 204, 331; Shadwell (1906), 309; Saul (1965), 15 ff; Warren (1970), 63, 114–15; Clapham (1963 III), 153; Tweedale (1983), 225–39.

[85] Allen (1977), 612–13; Allen (1979), 919; Allen (1983), 97; Webb (1980), 321–2; Feldenkirchen (1980), 99; Orsagh (1960–1), 216–25.

[86] Harley (1973–74), 403; Allen (1979), 935; Elbaum (1986), 60, 70, 72–5.

[87] Burnham and Hoskins (1943), 42, 326; Carr and Taplin (1962), 200–94.

Table 1.25 *Iron and steel imports into Great Britain, averages 1911–13 (000 tons)*

Country of origin	Semi-finished	Finished	Total
Germany	524	412	936
Belgium	148	250	398
France	—	21	21
USA	159	64	223

shipbuilding, were distinctly handicapped by the sale, or dumping, of cheap material by German firms into Britain. Looked at in this world perspective, there was similarly nothing inherently wrong on the part of Britain in meeting the dispersed demands of numerous small foreign markets in the only way in which these could efficiently be produced, by smaller-scale, rather less up-to-date technical methods.[88]

This, however, does not cover the cases in which Britain, in similar or comparable market conditions, actually used less efficient methods than the leading competitors. There were signs that that was happening on a significant scale also.[89]

Among the numerous minor metal industries, one may be picked out to illustrate further the mixed fortunes and achievements of British industry in that age: tin-plate making. Up to 1891, the making of tinplate, concentrated largely in South Wales, was almost a British world monopoly. Then the McKinley Tariff abruptly wrecked the American market, to be followed by the even more severe Dingley Tariff, while the USA, partly with the help of Welsh immigrants, began to make their own, and reached the level of the British output before the outbreak of war. Almost at once, the Americans began to introduce technical improvements beyond the British level, while in Britain even the simple tinning pot had had to wait several decades for acceptance because of the objections of the trade unions. Entrepreneurial failure seemed to arise directly out of the peculiar structure and location of the industry. It was highly competitive, consisting of many small units all using the same technology, but within their Welsh environment the tin-plate firms had built up a tradition in which profit maximization was frowned on and dog did not eat dog.[90] Yet, in spite of this recipe for disaster, the industry recovered marvellously after the American setback and reached the peak of its output and its exports just before the First World War. The statistics are given in Table 1.26:[91]

Table 1.26 *Tinplate, production and exports (000 tons).*

	Production	Total Exports	Of which to the USA
1872	143	118	87
1891	586	448	325
1896	450	267	103
1901	475	271	76
1912	848	481	2

[88] Payne (1968), 81; J.S. Jeans in Ashley (1907), 35.
[89] Burnham and Hoskins (1943), 61, 101, 267.
[90] Minchinton (1957), 56–8, 62–9, 77–9, and Minchinton (1954–55), and Minchinton (1969), XXV–XXVI; Crohn, (1916), 234 ff.
[91] Minchinton (1957), 29, 74, 79, 80, 261; Carr and Taplin (1962), 116, 187, 235; Warren (1970).

The industry took to the production of galvanized corrugated sheets in the 1890s with equal success.

Chemicals and glass

The chemical industry has also come in for criticism. Much of it has centred on the failure of Britain to train, and employ, graduate or other highly qualified chemists, and this aspect will be examined in greater detail in chapter 3 below. The question here must be: has this failure affected the efficiency and relative position of the British chemical industry in our period?

The comparison, inevitably, is with Germany, for it was the German chemical firms which shot forward, from relative obscurity in 1870, to undisputed world leadership in dyestuffs, synthetic drugs, photographic chemicals and several other products and processes in the next four decades. Apart from the potash deposits which Germany gained by the annexation of Alsace-Lorraine, there was nothing in Germany's resources which could have explained her technical superiority. Rather, it rested squarely on the skill of her chemists and entrepreneurs, and might easily have been matched in Britain, had Britain pursued different policies, especially since the key discovery was made by William Perkin, the British student of a German professor teaching in London.

By the early twentieth century, German dominance of the world's market for artificial dyes had become almost total: she was then responsible for 85% of the world's coal-tar dye production. As a branch requiring advanced science, the manufacture of synthetic chemicals and drugs carried, no doubt, particular significance for the future. Yet even in 1907, chemicals formed only 2.2% of German industrial employment, and in 1913 dyestuffs exports formed only 2% of German exports, while taking the chemical industry as a whole, there were no very striking differences to be discerned between Britain, Germany and the other leading nations:[92]

Table 1.27 *Chemical production and exports, leading countries, 1901–1913*

	Chemical production as % industrial production		Chem. exports % all manufactured exports	RM* per Head	
				Chemical products	Exports of chemicals
	1901	1913	1913	1913	1913
United Kingdom	6	6	14.0	28.86	11.75
Germany	5	6	11.4	35.83	12.74
USA	5	6		34.96	3.19
Belgium	6	7	15.5		23.67
France	6	6	9.2	21.36	7.79

* Reichsmark

In exports per head, indeed, the smaller countries, Belgium and Switzerland (not shown in the table) were ahead of Germany. As a percentage of the world's chemical exports, the British share fell only from 29.4% in 1880 to 21.9% in

[92] See chapter 3 p. 159 and Tables 3.9. and 3.10. below.

1913 and exports consistently rose faster than imports, while output also rose at a high rate.

These overall figures do, however, hide considerable differences in the distribution of output and exports among various branches. In particular, the British position was much more favourable, the export surplus much more pronounced, in the 'heavy' chemicals than in the 'light', more in traditional sectors than in new ones.

The Solvay ammonia-soda process may be typical. Developed in Belgium in the 1860s, it was adopted quickly abroad and in Britain by the new firm Brunner Mond in 1874 and helped it to high profits and rising output. Other firms held aloof, arguing rather doubtfully[93] that the older process yielded more by-products and might be improved, and hoping instead for monopoly gains and some rationalization by combining as the United Alkali Company in 1890. Overcapitalized, riddled with nepotism and poorly provided with only 50 chemists among 12,000 workers, this company slid into decline despite attempts at diversification.[94]

A third method of alkali production, the electrolysis process, was developed in the 1880s among others by H.Y. Castner, an American immigrant to Britain. A plant was started in 1895 in Runcorn, but the United Alkali Company turned it down, and the electrolytic process, particularly for the purifying of aluminium, was developed faster abroad.[95]

Sulphuric acid was another major product which had once been a British speciality but for which British producers continued for too long with an eighteenth-century method and by ignoring the new contact process, lost much of their world share of manufacturing. In the case of ammonium sulphate, performance was rather better, there was an early Nobel dynamite works opened in Ardreer (Ayrshire) in 1873, and, following an astonishing rise, shale oil extraction employed up to 10,000 in 1913.[96] However, it was significant that the technical and scientific breakthrough registered by Haber and Bosch in producing nitrogen fixed from the air in 1913 on an economic scale as well as the experimental production of synthetic rubber in 1912[97] would have been totally out of reach of the scientific and technical ability available in Britain at the time.

It was among fine chemicals, above all in the production of coal-tar dyes that Germany scored her greatest successes. These were based on the solid work of massed ranks of highly trained chemists working systematically on scientific lines, in contrast to the hit-or-miss methods, and individual genius, on which British and other chemical firms had relied hitherto. From synthetic dyes the

[93] Richardson (1968), 284–6; Williams (1972), 49; Warren (1980), 28 ff, 110, 147, 185; Lindert and Trace (1971), 239–83; Haber (1958), 89, 95–6, 155 ff, 189; Haber (1980), 100; Diplomatic and Consular Reports (1901), Cd. 430–16.LXXXV., 46.
[94] Reader (1970 I), 121, 227–8; Warren (1980), 153; Warren (1976), 50; Haber (1958), 182–5; Haber (1971), 10–12.
[95] Haber (1958), 92–3; Haber (1971), 12; Warren (1980), 180; Hohenberg (1967), 30–1; Reader (1970), 117–19; Williams (1972), 52.
[96] Haber (1972), 11, 101; Haber (1971), 103; Williams (1972), 58; Balfour Committee Report (1918), 20; Richardson (1968), 278; Campbell (1971), 246–7; Lenman (1977), 189; Reader (1970), 16 ff, 24–7; MacKinnon (1921), 84–6, 122; Schuster (1909).
[97] Hohenberg (1967), 30, 38; Haber (1971), 13, 144.

work was extended into synthetic drugs, photographic chemicals and others, for which, similarly, the Germans together with the Swiss had a near world monopoly.[98] Once a lead of this kind was achieved, it would be very difficult for outsiders to catch up without an equally large research programme staffed by equally competent scientists.

Here was a British failure indeed, yet even here the picture was not entirely bleak. London University, Sir Henry Roscoe in Manchester and universities elsewhere were making considerable progress in training chemists who showed both competence and originality, and Britain was to prove able to close the gaps in key chemicals which emerged in the war years, with remarkable speed. Coal-tar dyes, as noted above, formed only a small part of chemical activity and they fitted into an international division of labour in which, for a time, Britain exported coal, imported crude tar, exported distilled intermediate products and then imported the dyes, to be used in textiles which were then, in turn, exported.[99] In any case, a newly emerging industrial giant like Germany must be conceded some strong points.

There were several reasons, some of them lying outside the industry itself, why the British chemical industry should experience such a rapid decline from its world leadership between 1870 and 1914. The German patent laws favoured German firms at home, but the British law also favoured them in Britain, since they were able to block British progress by vaguely worded broad patent claims. An Act was passed in 1907 to prevent this abuse, but it was soon rendered inoperative by judicial decision. Another factor was that industrial alcohol, a vital ingredient, was taxed in Britain but untaxed in Germany, while Britain admitted all imports free of duty and Germany protected her industries. But there was also a lack of scientists, small, badly organized firms, and poor sales and service organization.[100] However, as in other industries, there were everywhere examples to be found of inventive originality or entrepreneurial brilliance in particular sectors or products.

One such sector was the soap industry. Soap was one of those commodities which, at levels reached by Britain in the later Victorian age, had an income elasticity of well above 1. Output rose from 90,000 t. a year in the 1850s to 150,000 t. in 1871 and 353,000 t. by 1907. Exports also showed satisfactory growth rates, from 47,000 t. in 1901 to 80,000 t. by 1911.[101] This was, comparatively speaking, a success story, achieved both by technical and commercial innovation.

Crosfield's were among the technical innovators, helping to transform soap-making from a practice-oriented to a science-based industry. The leading scientists in the firm were at first largely German or Swiss, but by 1907 most had been replaced by British graduates who formed a 'brilliant team' in the years before the war.[102] Commercially, however, the running in the soap

[98] Beer (1959); Marshall (1970), 101–2; Kaku (1980), 81–4.

[99] Williams (1972), 70–6; Hohenberg (1967), 27; Haber (1958), 163; Saul (1979), 116.

[100] Haber (1958), 200–6; Richardson (1962), 111–12; Lindert and Trace (1971), 66; Williams (1972), 68; Beer (1959), chapter 5. See chapter 3, p. 158, note 148 below. Miall (1931), 84–6; Commons Debates Hansard 4th ser, 172 (1907), cols. 1013 ff.

[101] Musson (1965), 86; Wilson (1954 I), 9, 115, 124, 138.

[102] Musson (1965); Musson (1978), 220–1; Wilson (1954), 13–14, 127.

industry was made by William Lever, who built up much the largest soap enterprise in the country by unprecedented advertising and marketing campaigns. In 1890, his firm was still a private company with an authorized capital of £300,000; on the eve of the war, the issued capital had risen to £13,250,000. In addition to exporting soap, Lever Brothers had in those years also set up a chain of factories in Europe, in the USA, Canada and Japan, largely to beat the tariffs in these countries. It was one of the major multinationals of the day.[103]

Another was the tyre firm of J.B. Dunlop. Rubber proofing of clothes had been invented by Charles Mackintosh in 1823, rubber 'masticating' by Thomas Hancock in London about the same time, vulcanizing had been developed by Hayward and Goodyear in the USA between 1835 and 1842, and there had been an early patent for a pneumatic tyre granted to R.W. Thomson in 1841. But it was Dunlop, 'rediscovering' the tyre in time for the cycle boom in 1888, who built on it a large firm after gathering in the other needed patents. In a matter of a few years he had founded several foreign branches, though without adequate control, so that some of them tended to spoil his reputation by poor management and workmanship. After the initial breakthrough, Dunlop's was pushed out of some markets in the early twentieth century by foreign competitors, but remained a major multinational firm.[104]

A further world leader in enterprise and technical up-to-dateness was found in the glass-making firm of Pilkington's. Theirs was one of those industries in which some handicraft techniques had survived from before the industrial revolution and in which Britain had at no time been able to replace the older centres abroad. In this period, major technical changes occurred, many firms collapsed, and only two large ones survived: Pilkington's and Chance's, but on the whole, Britain held her own:[105]

Table 1.28 *UK overseas trade in glass, 1875–1914, annual averages, £000*

	1875–9	1910–14
Imports	1,823	2,989
Exports	875	1,688
Re-exports	160	71

Pilkington's were in the forefront of the new technology. Among other innovations they introduced the patented tank furnace in 1872, the tunnel lehr, machine rolling, the Belgian Malevez patent polishing machines and the drawn cylinder process, as well as early electrification, the telephone, and mechanized transport in the works. There was also a growing complement of works chemists. Though there were weaknesses, Britain caught up very quickly in wartime. By 1917 Chance's had 125 research workers and marketed 72 types of glass, many of them previously obtainable in Germany only.[106]

103 Wilson (1954), esp. 45, 104 ff, 188 ff, 209. Inove (1984), 8.
104 Jones (1984a); Jones (1984b), 125–53; Chaloner (1964), chapter 17; Clapham (1963) III, 143; Allen (1929), 301.
105 Barker (1968), 308, 325; Barker (1977); Pilkington (1977), 442–3; Musson (1978), 225; Allen (1929), 270; Clapham (1963) III, 129; Scoville (1972), 179, 197.
106 Barker (1977), 124–30; 198–9, 216; Barker (1960), 161 ff, 189 ff; Saul (1979), 118 ff. Also see note 149 below.

Textiles and clothing

The last major industry to be examined as having been subjected to much criticism is the textile industry. Easily mechanized, cotton spinning and weaving were among the more vulnerable of British industries, though cotton manufacture as a whole remained by far the most important British export industry, its exports increasing in absolute terms throughout the period. Although it was inevitable that, starting from a position of overwhelming predominance, and using raw materials which were accessible to all with equal ease, the country found its share of world production reduced, in the event, the loss was comparatively light, and it left the industry at the end still in the position of much the strongest export industry in the world.

The relative position is indicated by the following data on productive capacity:[107]

Table 1.29 *Capacity of the British cotton industry, 1859–1913*

	British cotton spindles, mn	% world spindleage	British cotton looms, thousands
1859/61	30.4	66.4 (1861)	400
1875	37.5	55.7	463 (1874)
1895	45.4	47.2	628
1900	45.5	43.0	649
1913	55.7	38.8	787

Britain, with two-thirds of the world's cotton spindles in 1861, still had two-fifths of them in 1913, when their number had almost doubled. Output of yarn showed a similar increase.

Estimates of the production of cotton cloth are not easy to come by, but on the rough-and-ready guess of world production of 11 million quintals of cotton textiles in 1882–84, and of 1,088 million lbs in Britain in 1880/2, the British share would then have amounted to around 44%; in the period 1909–14, the British share of the world's cotton output had fallen to 20.4%.[108]

Britain, however, continued to dominate the export markets. In 1882–84 she supplied just over four-fifths of the world's exports of cotton goods; in 1910–13 this was still 60%, or three-fifths. Put the other way round, it appeared that in 1859–61 about 80% of the raw cotton imported into Britain was exported again in manufactured form, either as yarn or in the form of fabric. In 1913 85% of the piece-goods made were exported, plus 12% of the yarn: 74% of the yarn made was exported either as yarn or in fabrics.[109] Cotton was therefore overwhelmingly an export industry, maintaining itself against the competition of the rest of the world and doing so without subsidies or other special favours.

The critics maintained that these statistics of British export success were

[107] Published estimates do not all agree, but differences are minor. Farnie (1979), 280; Farnie (1981), 84; Robson (1957), 339–401; D.C. (1918a), 15; Merttens (1893–4), 128; Jones (1933), 277; Helm (1892), 737.
[108] Robson (1957), 357; Ellison (1886), 54; Helm in Ashley (1907), 87.
[109] Robson (1957), 358–9; Tyson (1968), 118; Balfour Committee (1928), 10, 156; D.C. (1918a), 8.

misleading: the continuing growth of the quantities exported hid the fact that most of them went to 'soft' markets, and particularly to India, while Britain was steadily being driven out of the 'hard' markets of other industrial countries. Table 1.30 shows the developments:[110]

Table 1.30 British exports of cotton piece-goods, percentage market shares, 1865–1913

	1865	1874	1880–4	1913
Northern Europe	5.9	8.3 ⎫		4.7
Rest of Europe (exc. Turkey)	8.2	8.2 ⎬	8.6	1.8
USA	6.0	3.1 ⎭		0.6
Latin America	19.8	17.2	17.7	14.1
Middle East and Africa	16.9	15.3	12.8	15.6
India	28.4*		41.6	40.0**
China and other countries	c.15.0	c.19.5	19.3	23.2
Total exports, mn yards	2014	3607	4516	7075

* 1870
** 1910–13

It is evident that there had indeed been a shift from Europe and North America to the less developed parts of the globe, and that British India figured exceptionally largely in the export statistics, but it is equally evident that that shift had occurred well before 1880, when there was no question of the loss of Britain's world leadership. Nor was there anything very surprising in the ability of Europe and the USA to produce their own cotton textiles, especially since most countries in these areas helped the process along by high tariffs against British imports. The remarkable development was that British exporters were able to open up, and successfully defend against others, entirely new markets and were extending old ones, so as to raise substantially the total quantities exported while one market after another was being closed to them.

No doubt the future held dangers, but contemporary Lancastrians would have argued, not without reason, that there were always new markets to be opened up. Britain, in fact, fitted into a world division of labour in which her yarn exports found their largest market in Germany, and not less than one half of them altogether went to Europe, while her piece-goods went to the less developed countries. Britain thus exported the finer yarns but the coarser and cheaper piece-goods. Moreover, as soon as a country began to produce its own cotton goods, the quality range of British exports to that country rose, and then continued rising ahead of the native ability to compete, whereas the average quality of goods sent to the non-industrialized countries tended to fall, as cheaper ranges were sent out to tap additional lower-income groups.[111] Britain did not, in other words, always go for the easiest markets, but on the contrary, took on some of the most difficult of all.

The trends in productivity are less clear. While a man-hour of spinning

[110] Balfour Committee (1928), 149; Sandberg (1974), 110, 145–6; Tyson (1968), 110; Farnie (1979), 91, 97.
[111] D.C. (1918a), 45–6; Tyson (1968), 107; Marrison (1975), 309–11, 320–1, 341–2; Schulze-Gävernitz (1892), 212; Sandberg (1968); Saxonhouse and Wright (1984a), 515.

produced 1.2 lbs of yarn in 1860 and 2.3 lbs in 1890, and the output of an hour of weaving rose similarly from 1.1 lbs to 1.4 lbs in the same years, thereafter, G.T. Jones alleged, real costs stagnated. Sandford, however, re-working Jones's figures, calculated a productivity rise of 25–30% in spinning between 1885–1914, most of it due to labour-saving improvements.[112] British output per man continued to exceed that of the continent though the latter worked longer hours, but was well below that of the United States, which also rose faster.[113] The failure to install the latest machinery in Britain was, once again, made responsible for this.

There were here two innovations in particular which were noted. In spinning, the ring spindle, a development of the throstle invented in the USA in 1831 and continually improved, had by the 1860s equalled the number of mules there, and by 1914 had virtually displaced them. Table 1.31 shows the world position in 1913:[114]

Table 1.31 *Ring and mule spindles (million) in main countries and areas, 1913.*

	Mules	Rings	Total	% Rings
United Kingdom	45.2	10.4	55.7	18.7
Germany	5.1	6.1	11.2	54.5
Rest of Europe	14.2	18.5	32.7	56.6
USA	4.1	27.4	31.5	87.0
Rest of world	2.7	9.8	12.4	79.0
World	71.3	72.2	143.5	50.3

The position of Britain was quite unique. Only two other major producers, Switzerland (21.4%) and France (46%) still had less than half their spindleage in rings, all others had more than half, whereas in Britain it was under 20%. In the last years before the war, she was almost the only major producer still to add to her mules, to the tune of 8.5 million in 1907–13, while others were changing over to the newer method.[115]

Why this loyalty to an apparently out of date technology? Was this a sign of British technical backwardness, or were there particular reasons for the preference for the mule spindle?

The ring spindle was of course known in Britain: indeed, as noted above, much of the world's spindleage was made in Britain and exported, and in 1907–14 25% of the new installations in Britain were rings.[116] But ring yarn was not a perfect substitute for mule yarn. Mule yarn was more suited to the finer fabrics, as well as to the coarse heavily sized fabrics for certain exports made in Britain, while ring yarn was more suited to the American automatic

[112] Blaug (1960–1), 365–6; Merttens (1893/94), 128, 131; Robson (1957), 342; Lee (1980), 173; Jones (1933), 115. Chapman (1904) I, 153, 163, 171; Tyson (1968), 120; Merttens (1893/4), 152, 165; Schulze-Gävernitz (1892), 121–8, 151; Clark (1987).

[113] Jones (1933), 149 ff.

[114] Robson (1957), 355.

[115] Robson (1957) and Copeland (1909), 128–32.

[116] Farnie (1979); Saxonhouse and Wright (1984a), 509; D.C. (1918a), 51; Saxonhouse and Wright (1984b), 283 and note 47 above.

loom. Mules could more easily be adjusted to work different qualities which suited the smaller British orders, they required more skilled labour, but could work with cheaper, shorter staple cotton and use more waste cotton than the rings. Thus the mule was more appropriate for Lancashire, where labour was cheaper and more skilled and where cotton was dearer, while rings were more adapted to American conditions, where the opposite prevailed. Moreover, given the separation, unique to Britain, of spinning mills round Manchester, from the weaving sheds located further north, and given that ring yarn on bobbins was very costly to transport, while the cost of conveying the mule yarn on paper cops, was low, this separation tended to perpetuate the predominance of the mule.[117] Lastly, as pointed out by Lazonick, the Brooklands Agreement of 1893 had created a special blockage to innovation. By virtually fixing piece rates for the spinners, it removed the incentive to install labour-saving machinery, for there was no way for employers to recoup the cost of capital if they were not allowed to reduce their unit labour costs. Their only chance of reducing costs was to use cheaper cotton, the cause of the notorious 'bad spinning'. This increased the burdens on the piecers, who were powerless within the trade unions, but it did not trouble the spinners too much, who were, in a manner, their employers.[118] Thus under the given circumstances the threshold at which the new rings began to pay was much lower in the USA than in Britain, and rings paid off for a smaller proportion of British spinners.

In the case of weaving there was, similarly, a significant technical innovation to emerge in the USA, which was almost entirely ignored in Britain – though in this case, also in the rest of Europe. This was the Northrop automatic loom introduced in the USA in 1894 by a British inventor who had had no encouragement at home. It greatly increased labour output, since one weaver could now supervise up to 20 looms compared with a maximum of 4 or 5 for the existing loom, though each loom worked somewhat more slowly. Some 46,000 of them had been installed in the USA in 1901 and 286,000 in 1914, representing over 40% of the total, whereas in Britain at the time there were 15,000 at most, representing less than 2%.[119] Once more, it is not difficult to find objective causes for the greater enthusiasm of American entrepreneurs than of the British for the Northrop or Draper loom. It worked best in long runs of plain cloth, while British orders were shorter and more varied; it worked best with ring yarn, of which there was more in the USA than in Britain; and it saved skilled labour, which was cheaper and in less short supply in Britain. Further, the union agreement made all labour-saving innovations less profitable in Britain; there was in any case trade-union opposition; and workers were not willing to supervise as many looms, even for higher pay, as were American workers.[120]

In the ancillary activities also, some technical innovations were taken up in

117 Tyson (1968), 122; Copeland (1909); Sandberg (1974), 33 ff; Lazonick (1981d), 33–4; Lazonick (1979b), 256–7; Saxonhouse and Wright (1984b). Debate between Lazonick, Saxonhouse and Wright (1987); Lazonick (1981c), 98 ff.
118 Lazonick (1981a); von Schulze-Gaevernitz, on the other hand attributed much of the British success to good labour relations based on long-term understandings (1892), 188–90.
119 Clapham (1963) III, 177; D.C. (1918a), 51; Sandberg (1974), 67–8; Lazonick (1981c), 90.
120 Wilkinson in Mosely (1903), 143; Sandberg (1974), 71–85.

Britain much later and much more slowly than in the USA. Finally, the organization of the British cotton industry also came in for criticism. Firms were said to be too small, though the average size was growing, and some, like the 'Oldham Limiteds', enjoyed some hidden economies of size by sharing managerial and financial resources. Amalgamations, such as Horrocks (1887) and Coats (1895–96) were rare.[122]

Even the splendid mercantile organization of the Lancashire cotton industry, including the Cotton Exchange, much envied by other countries, has also been seen as a handicap, for it perpetuated small orders, it kept producer and customer apart and prevented direct access of the company sales staff to the market.[123] The separation of much of the weaving and spinning capacity in specialist firms has already been referred to. It had some negative consequences, but it also provided greater flexibility in the search for markets at each stage.[124] Summing up, it may be said that the industry had much in common with industries such as coal mining, shipbuilding, and several engineering branches: In spite of alleged technical backwardness, its sales abroad continued to increase, and it showed reasonable profits.

Much of the debate here too is concerned with the quality of entrepreneurship. In the case of Scotland there is a fairly broad consensus to blame 'the want of enterprise and energy on the part of the millowners, carelessness on the part of workers, and a lack of friendly common interest among all concerned', which allowed spinning to become technically out of date and made the decline inevitable.[125] Elsewhere the consensus tends in the direction that entrepreneurs took the right decisions in the short run, but that they neglected the long-run view, and took the constraints of their organization and of trade-union obstructiveness to innovation too much for granted.[126] For the dangerous complacency behind the British technological sloth, the cotton industry furnishes an example which it would be difficult, if not impossible, to better:

> 'My lad', one young man was told by a manufacturer, 'never again let anybody in Lancashire hear you talk this childish stuff about foreign competition. . . . It's just twaddle. In the first place, we've got the only climate in the world where cotton piece-goods in any quantity can ever be produced. In the second place, no foreign Johnnies can ever be bred that can spin and weave like Lancashire lasses and lads. In the third place, there are more spindles in Oldham than in all the rest of the world put together. And last of all, if they had the climate and the men and the spindles – which they never can have – foreigners could never find the brains Lancashire cotton men have for the job.'[127]

---

[121] Marrison (1975), 325, 333; Turnbull (1951), 132; Copeland (1909), 113–16, 134, 141–3, 150.
[122] Farnie (1979), 194, 209–15, 290–6; Clapham (1963 III), 176; Smith (1961), esp. 33–7; Robson (1957), 136, Turnbull (1951), 125–6, 328.
[123] Tyson (1968), 125; Anonymous (1982), 50; Lazonick (1986b), 23.
[124] Farnie (1979), 318–22; Robson (1957), 103–13; Lazonick (1981d), 33–4.
[125] Quoted in Ellison (1986), 76; also Robertson (1970), 123, 128. Checkland (1977), 7; Slaven (1975), 163–4; Campbell (1980), 58–9; MacKinnon (1921), 117.
[126] Lazonick (1981c), 104–7; Lazonick (1981d), 31–3; Lazonick (1981b), 40; Tyson (1968), 124; Sandberg (1974), 65, 119, 133.
[127] Bowker (1928), 22–3; also, e.g. Ashton in Mosely (1903), 130–2, 137. Some modern observers, e.g. Clark (1987), might agree.

In retrospect, the opposite view might seem more appropriate:

'Lancashire', a former cotton man reminisced, 'produced yarn very efficiently and economically but lacked commercial skills. This was probably inevitable since the companies' management was in the hands of men of limited capacity and experience. The directors tended to be a mixed lot, leaving the paid officials to run the business,'

not realizing that many were corrupt as well as uneducated.[128]

Such quotations could easily be multiplied. Yet the fact remained that Britain was much the most successful cotton goods exporter, defeating foreign tariffs and finding ever-new profitable markets abroad while defending with ease a highly competitive market at home. She was well aware of the latest technology, producing most of the machines herself, and there is sufficient doubt over whether she would have benefited by introducing them sooner to exonerate her from the charge of incompetence in the short run at least. To be sure, other countries were catching up, but there was no sign of anyone overtaking Britain except the United States, where very different factor supplies imposed a more mechanized form of working much earlier than over here.

The other textile industries may be dealt with more quickly. Woollen and worsted output, to judge by the consumption of raw wool, appears to have doubled between 1870-74 and 1910-14,[129] but developments in foreign trade, seem at first glance to have been far less favourable than those of cotton:

Table 1.32 *Imports and exports of woollen goods, 1870–1913 (ann. averages)*

(a)	Exports				Imports, tissues, mn yards	
	Tissues mn yards			Yarn		
	Woollen	Worsted	Total	mn lbs.	Woollen	Worsted
1870–4			324	41.3		
1885–9	82.7	159.9	245.6	43.5	1.9	56.2
1900–4	52.1	101.8	153.9	54.5	4.8	68.2
1910–3	95.6	78.7	174.3	61.9	2.4	63.9

Jenkins and Ponting cite different totals, though their direction is the same:

(b)	Exports, annual averages			
	Woollen manuf. goods		Yarns	
	mn. lin. yards	£ mn	mn lbs.	£ mn
1870–4	349.1	14.1	40.1	6.05
1910–3	179.9*	25.1*	88.4	8.56

* 1910–14

Exports of manufactured goods showed a strong long-term downward trend. The precarious position of worsteds, with their sharply falling exports and simultaneously rising imports should be particularly noted, while expanding yarn exports, going largely to our direct competitors, also gave cause for

128 Anonymous (1982), 50.
129 Jenkins and Ponting (1982), 199; Clapham (1907), 10, 274; Balfour Committee (1928), 167; Hooper in Ashley (1907), 107; Sigsworth and Blackman (1968), 133.
130 Mitchell and Deane (1981), 82–5; Chapman (1904 I), 188; *Statistisches Jahrbuch* (1914), 51.

concern. However, most of the reduction in exports was due to tariffs in the importing countries, including Germany, France and the USA,[131] and unlike cotton, could not be made up by sales in the promising new markets of the tropical and subtropical zones; much of the increased demand had to come from the temperate zones, above all the home market itself and the Dominions. It was significant that the exports of the other major producers also stagnated while their output grew, the only open market for them being the United Kingdom, and accusations of dumping here were not unknown.[132]

Productivity increased substantially. It has been estimated that between 1880 and 1910 woollen spindles could double their yarn output, worsted spindles increase theirs sixfold, and looms threefold. At the same time, they could also work up shorter staples. With 30% more labour than the French, English producers worked twice the number of spindles and three times the number of looms. Some ring spindles had appeared, following the American example, and in place of the Northrop loom, an 'automatic worsted loom' was developed in 1911 by Crompton and Knowles, but was not used until after the war. Yorkshire was said to have accepted the new synthetic dyes with alacrity, but to have rejected the new River Plate wool.[133]

The major failure, and it was a costly one, was the loss of much of Bradford's worsted trade to the French. Beginning with the 1860s and 1870s there was a change of fashion towards softer wools, which Bradford was unwilling to meet, thinking it to be temporary. After several decades of this false anticipation, the market was lost for good. Among the reasons for the reluctance to change was the need to change the equipment from the then prevalent throstle to the mule, which would also have meant the change from female to male labour.[134]

In the debate on entrepreneurship, British technical education, and the attitude towards it, as well as British designs in the woollen industry have come in for much criticism, though the evidence is by no means all on one side.[135] For the question posed in this chapter, the answer seems more clear-cut. Given that many foreign markets were closed, by tariffs, by climate or by poverty, while the British home market alone was open, the industry held its own well against all comers. Despite the relatively high British wages, it still had larger exports than other countries, and there is no sign that it was technically behind, though some foreign makers may well have reacted much faster to changes in fashion, again pointing to a certain conservatism among British entrepreneurs.

The output of the linen industry changed hardly at all between 1870 and 1913. It suffered everywhere from the competition of cotton and changes in fashion and the numbers of spindles fell even more in the other major

[131] Mitchell and Deane (1981), 196–7; Balfour Committee (1928), 209; Tariff Commission (1904 II), 2, 1320, 1326, 1390; Clapham (1907), 245, 274–6, 285–6; Jenkins and Ponting (1982), 226, 242–3, 261, 294–5.
[132] Sigsworth and Blackman (1968), 134–40; Jenkins and Ponting (1982), 261; Tariff Commission (1904) II. 2, 1400 and 1510.
[133] Clapham (1907), 223; Jenkins and Ponting (1982), 169, 188, 201, 210–11, 217–18, 301–2; D.C. (1918a), 67.
[134] Jenkins and Ponting (1982), 262–5; Sigsworth and Blackman (1968), 142; D.C. (1918a), 67; Sigsworth (1958), 76, 83–92.
[135] Jenkins and Ponting (1982), 218, 253–4, 277–8, 288–9.

producing countries Germany, Austria, Belgium and France. There are no signs that the British industry was losing any ground to the others.[136] Silk, never a major British concern, held its own.[137] Among jute manufacturers, India had now become the largest producer, with Britain well ahead of the rest, but stagnating while others advanced. In 1913, 40% of Dundee's production was still exported, but others were catching up fast.[138] A similar tale might be told with regards to hosiery and other knitted goods. Particularly worrying was the fact that while in the 1860s Britain was still in the technical lead, by the end of our period most machinery was German or American.[139]

'Artificial silk', alone, did not run true to form of other textile industries. Several methods for producing fibres chemically had been patented in different parts of the world, but the British viscose process, developed by C.F. Cross, E.J. Bevan and C.H. Stearn, proved much the best. Enterprise was also found in Britain in the shape of the old silk firm of Courtauld, who bought the patent in 1904. By 1907 they solved most of the technical problems, and in 1909–10 had even begun to expand their chemical department having used their textile rather their chemical expertise up to then. By 1913 Britain made 27% of the world's artificial fibres against Germany's 32%, but Courtauld's were much the cheapest producer, and had even opened an American branch to beat the tariff.[140]

Finally, in the case of boots and shoes, the major innovations on the machines for mass-production were once again American. By the 1890s there were machines to replace hand work in virtually all stages of the manufacture. Also, the work had been transferred fully to the factory. In Britain, both outwork and handwork survived until later, in part because wages were lower, and in part because the trade unions effectively held out against machines much longer, but rising American competition ultimately forced British boot and shoe makers to follow the American example.[141]

Table 1.33 *Imports and exports of boots and shoes, 1875–1914 (000 doz. pairs) (annual averages)*

	Exports	Net imports	Export surplus
1875–9	441	81	360
1890–4	685	99	586
1900–4	710	224	486
1910–4	1304	179	1125
1914	1435	159	1276

136 Mitchell and Deane (1981), 202; Patterson in Ashley (1907); Chapman (1904) I, 203–5; D.C. (1918a), 85–6.
137 Coleman (1969) I, 158–63, 183–4; Tariff Commission (1904) IV, 3092–4; D.C. (1918a), 72, 81; Clapham (1963) III, 127; Buchheim (1986), 38, 60–78; Mitchell and Deane (1981), 207–10, 299–300, 304–5.
138 D.C. (1918a), 89–92; Musson (1978), 209; MacKinnon (1921), 115.
139 Musson (1978), 213, 215; Tariff Commission (1904) IV, 2362; Gulvin (1984), 65, 79–80; D.C. (1918a), 103 ff; Clapham (1963) III, 128, 179–80; Erickson (1959), 180.
140 Coleman (1969), 5, 9, 16–17, 55, 66, 94–7; Coleman (1977), 88–100; Robson (1957), 354.
141 Church (1970); Church (1968); Pope and Hoyle (1985), 31; Head (1968), 158–85; Brunner (1949).

The high point of the American invasion had been around 1902. Then the British industry was able, as in the case of cycles and tobacco, among others, to rally after trailing initially, and beat off the American challenge on its own terms. By 1914 exports ran at over £4 million, about five times the import bill.[142]

Far less successful was the response to the foreign challenge in the leather industry. Here a similar American lead had developed by the end of the century, based on larger firms, a better lay-out of tanneries, better equipment and better management, but also on better chemistry, as chemicals replaced traditional oak-bark tanning. As a result, while the (smaller) exports of leather from Britain rose only 2½-fold between 1870/4 and 1910/4, imports rose sixfold. British tanners alleged that the new methods produced inferior leather, and they did indeed keep the top end of the market, but most observers have considered the British response to have been inadequate. Blame is largely laid on poor entrepreneurship and poor technical and scientific training.[143] Interestingly enough, though, in the war British tanners rapidly managed to catch up.

To summarize: the experience of this group of industries, seen as a whole, is therefore not dissimilar from that of the other groups discussed above. While there was great variety, the general tendency was for British industry to lose the lead it held in 1870 and to drop behind technically, though there were significant exceptions. The weaknesses were more pronounced in newer sectors, among complex machinery and in areas requiring science rather than experience. British industry was additionally handicapped by tariffs in many cases. Yet commercially the picture was highly favourable. British sales at home and abroad tended to expand, firms made profits, and in most cases it was not at all clear that the technical innovations, particularly those originating in the United States, would have paid off in the short run under British market conditions and factor prices. In the long run, most of the innovations tended to point in the direction of the future. Nevertheless, while Britain was caught up on many occasions, she was overtaken in few, and left behind in none.

Other industries

From the wide variety of remaining industries, a small number may be picked out to illustrate our theme further. One activity of some interest is the making of clocks and watches. Here an earlier British lead was lost to the Swiss in the early nineteenth century, precisely when in other fields British industrialists were capturing one world market after another. While Britain's output stagnated around the 150,000 units a year mark between the 1790s and the 1870s, the Swiss by the early 1880s were (together with some minor Continental producers) marketing around 3.5 million units and the Americans 1.25 million units.

While the Americans had advanced by cheap mass-production methods for cheap articles, the Swiss led in fine designs, in skill, in superior organization

---

[142] Clapham (1963) III, 182; Saul (1965), 18.
[143] Church (1971); Allen (1929), 268, 310; Musson (1978), 231.

and division of labour, as well as paying low wages. The British industry by contrast has been characterized by 'high cost, conservative styling, obsolescent technique, entrepreneurial complacency, resistance to labour innovation' and these 'interacted and reinforced one another.'[144]

The failure extended all along the line. Thus Britain's makers failed to introduce the Swiss division of labour, her craftsmen refused to sully their hands with inferior work, so that Britain was driven onto the top end of the market only, and she fell behind in precision machinery. She was slow to substitute nickel for brass, to adopt the Swiss slim line, to adopt new types of movement, or to vary the relationships of accuracy and price. In the keyless watch, Britain was said to have been one or two generations behind the times.[145] All this happened, curiously, before the decline of the 1870s was said to have set in.

In the silver-plated tableware trade, in cutlery and tools, Sheffield, Birmingham and the Black Country had been the world's main providers, dominating the export markets until the 1860s. Then their position began to be undermined because of mechanization, both in the USA and in Germany. Stamping, drop forging, machine grinding advanced more slowly in Britain. Machine file cutting was introduced in the USA in the 1860s, in Sheffield in the 1880s, by which time much trade had been lost. The delay had been caused largely by trade-union opposition. Similarly, it has been shown that it was the delay in introducing machine forging which lost Sheffield its lead to Solingen in the making of knives and edge tools.[146] Britain was also slow in building new factories with better layout, in introducing the more flexible electric motor, and in replacing the outworker system. Cutlery export figures (in millions of Marks) were as follows:[147]

	1900	1906	1913
Germany	16.1	24.1	38.3
UK	12.8	14.1	16.7
France	4.2	5.4	6.3 (*1912*)
USA	1.2	2.3	4.6

British exports were driven out of the USA by tariffs, but they were driven out of much of Europe by German competition and kept their market successfully only in the Empire.

There was something in the claim that the British were able to retain their hold on the high-quality end of the market, and that the continental competition made inroads not only by lower prices (gained both by better equipment and by lower wages) or better marketing, but also by lower quality and shoddy manufacture. In some lines, like steel pens and japanned and tinplate goods, the British not only held their own but even gained markets at the expense of others.[148] Against this, an industry like optical glass making, once a British *forte*, had almost disappeared. At the outbreak of war, some 60%

---

[144] Landes (1983), 300, also 231, 276, 313; Church (1975a), 618.
[145] Church (1975b), 616, 623, 628–30; Landes (1983), 298.
[146] Boch (Diss. 1983), 191; Allen (1929) 225–7; Pollard (1959), 126–8.
[147] Boch (1985), 189, 196; Holmshaw in Mosely (1903), 103–4; Jones (1929), 114–16.
[148] Pollard (1959), 129, 202–7; Allen (1929), 224–6; Pope and Hoyle (1985), 12–16; Church (1977a); Church (1980b), 23.

of British supplies came from Germany, 30% from France and 10% from Chance's. The best that could be said was that the industry managed marvellously well to catch up in the first three years of war.[149]

There was rapid technical progress and institutional change in such industries as brewing, distilling and grain milling, which hardly entered into international competition.[150] Biscuits were a British export success, and the leading firm, Huntley & Palmer, employed over 5,000 workers at the end of the century, accounting for ¾ of the British export trade in biscuits. Yet it was said to have rested on its laurels, failing to put in new machinery, and switching from tins to packets, and to assortments and chocolate biscuits later than others. It held on to its exports, but was alleged to have shown a tendency to concentrate on 'short-term profits at the expense of long-term' and to distribute almost all its surplus, keeping back little for reserves.[151]

Printing was still largely a sheltered industry, but in the technical revolution both of typesetting and printing in that period, the innovations came almost wholly from the USA and Germany. The dominance of German colour printing was explained largely by lower wages.[152] Machine methods made slow progress in Britain, largely because the unions, with their 'obsolete, obstructive regulations' refused to allow them to be worked to best advantage, either insisting on their former piece wages, or working the machines at only half their speed. Those parts of the industry which were mobile, which in practice meant all except the daily press, moved to the provinces in search of lower wages, less obstruction and lower rents and rates.[153] It has at least been questioned whether Britain did not do well to let others bear the large development costs, taking the completed products on licence[154] and overall there was here no shining example of enterprise, but also no great failure.

Lastly, the tobacco industry throws some interesting light on British industrial performance. It was among the first to show initiative and originality in the mass-marketing of consumer goods, pioneering the branding of its product in 1871. A packing machine had come onto the market in 1880 and Williamson's air-tight tin in 1886, and exclusive rights for both were obtained by the Bristol firm of Wills & Co. The major technical breakthrough came with the Bonsack cigarette making machine, patented in the USA and in Britain in 1881. Although it was an American invention, Wills's were again the first firm to install it in 1884, ahead even of the Americans. It was a remarkable gamble to take for a firm now in its fourth generation of owners. In the event, it not only confirmed its leadership in Britain, but helped to transform the smoking habits of the public.

[149] R. and K. MacLeod (1975), 168–70; Rothstein (1904), 121; Saul (1979), 118 ff; Balfour Report (1918), 121; Schomerus (1952), 43 ff, 174.
[150] Rosenberg (1972), 10; Musson (1978), 233–5; Clapham (1963 II), 88–9, III, 185–6; Payne (1967a), 527, 530–1; Vaizey (1960), 3–10; Weir (1960), 217; Hawkins and Pass (1979), 17–22, 25–27, 40 ff; MacKinnon (1921), 129.
[151] Corley (1972), 91, 96, 156, 158–60, 163; Musson (1978), 234.
[152] Buchheim (1986), 107–8; Alford (1964–5), 107–8; Alford (1965), 7; Musson (1978), 39; Clapham (1963) III, 190.
[153] Dibblee (1902), 9, 13; Alford (1965), 8, 13–14.
[154] Alford (1965), 7–8; Dibblee (1902), 11.

Not only technical developments favoured the large firm in the tobacco trade by this time, but also the need to pre-pay the tobacco tax, which tied up much more capital than was tied up in equipment. An even bigger incentive to amalgamation came from the American attempt to break into the British market in 1901. After an epic battle, the major British companies, led by Wills, held off the invasion by forming the Imperial Tobacco Co., which with its 12 million of capital became for a time the largest British company. They also succeeded in dividing world markets by agreement with the Americans.[155] It was a remarkable tribute to British technical skill and entrepreneurial and organizational initiative.

Thus the industries and firms noted in this miscellaneous group showed much the same developments as those in the other sectors: some decline from their formerly dominant position but still an extremely strong export potential, and a wide variety of individual experience in detail. There was some tendency to a lagging adoption of the latest technology, but also some outstanding examples of technical and organizational originality and leadership.

Building and public utilities

The industries and occupations covered in this section are not normally considered to be in competition with foreign rivals. Nevertheless, some relevant comparisons can be and have been made, and the indirect competition with foreign supplies could be of importance.

Building itself is a varied activity, and comparisons are difficult because of its heterogeneous products. In his classic study, G.T. Jones observed that its efficiency, as measured by its real costs, had hardly improved at all between 1870–90 and 1900–13, and may even have worsened. In view of the enormous cyclical fluctuations in prices and costs,[156] such statements are hard to verify, but that neither technique nor efficiency in housebuilding were subject to much change in those years is plausible enough. For larger buildings, ferro-concrete and later steel construction became available, but British architects were said to be slow to use them. In bridges and similar works, the 'consulting engineer' may have had a baneful effect, strengthening the British reluctance to use standard parts which lost British firms some foreign contracts.[157]

In the provision of gas, Britain enjoyed long-standing advantages of low cost and the efficient use of by-products. Indeed, it was this very success which helped to inhibit the early development of electricity as well as steering legislation towards the concept of local urban supplies, sensible for gas and for tramways but not, as it turned out, for electric power.

Some of the 'deplorable' effects of the Electric Lighting Act of 1882 are noted elsewhere in this book.[158] Its provisions were determined in part by the fear of monopoly, expressed clearly by the expert committee of 1879, and by the

[155] Alford (1973), 139–43, 155–9, 301–4; Alford (1977), 49–68; Heindel (1940), 141.
[156] Jones (1933), 82, 89 ff, 245; Saul (1962–3); Cooney (1972), 220–35; Habakkuk (1962).
[157] Clapham (1963) III, 196–7; Chapman (1904) I, 121; Rothstein (1904), 214; Cummings in Mosely (1903), 83.
[158] See note 55 above and chapter 4, p. 251 below.

predilection on the part of the Board of Trade and its President, Joseph Chamberlain, for municipal enterprise. The powers of compulsory purchase after 21 years at knock-down prices by local authorities killed all interest by private companies, especially after the disastrous experience of the speculative boom of 1880–82, when 147 new companies raised £23 million for purposes connected with electricity supply and lost most of it. The local authorities themselves were reluctant to take up electricity supply, not least because of their own gas interests, so that, in the end, despite large numbers of provisional orders, not a single power station was built before the important amending Act of 1888 improved the conditions.[159]

By that time the USA and Germany had acquired a lead which it proved impossible to bridge, despite impressive technical achievements at Holborn Viaduct and Ferranti's pioneer work at Deptford.[160] In the chaos of small local-authority and private companies with their different currents and voltages, no standardization, no planning and no efficient production of equipment were possible.

Electric traction was similarly bedevilled by inept legislation and local squabbling. Britain had pioneered the first underground railway (1863), the first underground electrification (City and South London) and the Liverpool overhead railway, leased in 1887. Yet by 1900 Britain had fallen behind, and much of the equipment for the London tube extensions had to be bought from Germany or the USA. Only in the last few years before the war did a rapid process of catching-up begin, as in other industries.[161]

The railway system had been built out, as far as its main lines were concerned, well before our era opened, 15,500 route miles having been constructed by 1870, but the filling-in by local and duplicated main lines, which added another 8,000 miles by 1914, and the technical improvements available, particularly for the rolling stock, have been subject to some controversy. It was not difficult to point to the failure to adopt automatic brakes or oil axle boxes on freight trains, to the lack of standardization, and to the inefficient use of energy in the locomotives. Other alleged failings such as wagons that were too small, trains that were too short and too frequent, stopping at too many stations too close together in comparison with the American railway system, may have been explicable in terms of different geographic or traffic conditions. If in 1900 the average freight train on the London & North Western carried 68.8 t. while the average on the Pennsylvania Railroad was 486.6 t., this may not have been entirely a reflection of poor British management. Larger and certainly more efficient wagons would have meant rebuilding much of the permanent way and was thus a prime example of interrelatedness, and of the disadvantage of early construction before the full technical possibilities had become clear.[162]

It was a large part of the railways' problem that they were highly competitive while being treated by the Government as though they were a dangerous monopoly. In order to gain traffic, but possibly also to gain glory for such

[159] See chapter 4, pp. 251–2, note 103 below.
[160] Byatt (1979), 100, 218; Parsons (1939), 10 ff, 21 ff.
[161] Clapham (1963 III), 137–8; Byatt (1979), 29, 46 ff, 58–9, 187.
[162] Aldcroft (1967–8), 164–7; Pollins (1971), 89–91, 107, 114; McCloskey (1973), 8 ff.

managers as Edward Watkin and J.S. Forbes, they built an ever denser network of lines, and provided much greater comfort for passengers, greater speeds and more individual services for traders. Labour productivity may, on traditional criteria, have risen by only 0.27% a year in the 1870s and by only 0.17% a year in 1880/1–1909/10,[163] but if the additional services could have been measured as 'output', as in the case of industries producing goods, these figures would look very different. Since the Government prohibited both amalgamation and the raising of rates, the companies tried to meet their rising costs after the 1890s in part by squeezing wages, which in turn led to greater militancy on the part of labour. It is possible to argue, however, that the example of the North-Eastern Railway showed that British railways could have been managed more efficiently than in fact they were.[164] If British railways were falling behind the best practice found abroad, it was not least because of a form of organization which precluded standardization and encouraged competition as well as monopolistic collusion, both partly of the wrong kind.

IV Causes and Common Features of the Declining Performance

Possibly the outstanding conclusion from this brief survey of individual British industrial sectors is the extraordinary variety of experience. Had we segregated out individual firms rather than whole sectors, the differences would have appeared more significant still. Nevertheless, certain regularities may have appeared, to allow an approach to at least a tentative judgement as to where British weaknesses were more clearly marked, more significant or more dangerous for the future.

It is generally agreed that growth itself has a favourable effect on industrial efficiency. It offers more scope for innovation, for reorganization into larger units, and for attracting the more mobile and therefore perhaps the more flexible labour force and managerial staff. It also ensures that the average age of the capital used is lower.[165] While the American market necessarily grew faster than the British, and even in Germany population may have increased more rapidly, what mattered was purchasing power, and in this regard the growth of the British home market was unlikely to have been less in absolute terms than that achieved on the Continent. At the same time, it was impossible for the British share of the overseas market to grow as fast, given the already dominant position achieved there in 1870.

A high rate of growth may have helped certain successful British industries such as shipbuilding. The exceptionally fast increase in the consumption of electricity, on the other hand, did not enable the British electrical engineering industry to recapture its momentum. Growth rates, no doubt, matter, but they

---

[163] Aldcroft (1967–8), 159.
[164] Aldcroft (1967–8), 160–1; Gourvish (1978), 186–200; Irving (1978), 46–66. Heindel (1940), 228 ff; Pollins (1971), 99–101, 109–11, 123; Vamplew (1971a), 345–66 and see chapter 4, note 111 below.
[165] See note 82 above.

49

do not seem to have much explanatory power for the course of British industrial history, once we leave generalizations and look at individual sectors.

Related to the growth rate is the distinction between 'old' and 'new' industries. Some of the older industries may have reached the limits of their technical capabilities as well as their expansionary potential. Yet it was precisely the old ones of steel and iron making, cotton and coal mining, where the British were accused of having failed to apply the then available 'best practice'.[166] They were also particularly vulnerable to the obstructionism of the craftsmen.

An alternative explanation, favoured by the Balfour Committee, as well as by H.W. Richardson, among others, was that Britain became unduly locked onto the old staples, lagging in the newer industries. Against this it has been shown that it was by the switch to more productive sectors, including the services, that Britain achieved much of her productivity increase at the time.[167]

Another widespread view holds the low cost of labour in Britain responsible for the slow adoption of up-to-date American technology: according to this the abundance of cheap unskilled labour as well as of labour with traditional skills inhibited the installation of labour-saving machinery. 'The British economy became the victim of a "low wages" trap'.[168] There are, however, several problems with what is often known as the Habakkuk thesis. Some of the objections to the thesis relate to its faulty internal logic. Others note that it neglects the relatively abundant land in America or the fact that inasmuch as capital was also cheaper in Britain, Britain should have been more eager than the USA to install capital equipment.[169] A third problem is that while British wages were undoubtedly lower than American, Continental wages were certainly below the British, while hours were longer, yet the Continent was frequently quicker off the mark in installing the latest labour-saving devices. Nevertheless, the empirical evidence is overwhelming that the difference between British and American industry was particularly marked in labour-saving equipment.

One possible solution lies along the lines of the explanation of the Leontief Paradox: Labour costs are not necessarily measured by wages alone, but by the efficiency of labour. It might well be that British labour, though paid more per week, was so much more productive that it was cheaper than Continental, so that its replacement by machines was less urgent. Where it was not, the continentals did undersell Britain.[170] On the other side it may be that owing to the relative cheapness of material against labour, American machines tended, not only to be more wasteful of the material on which they worked, but also to be more flimsy than the British on the assumption that they would be scrapped and replaced by something more up to date sooner.[171] In the event, what were

[166] Saul (1965), 18; Zeitlin (1983), 34.
[167] Ashworth (1965); Balfour Report (1918), 23; Richardson (1965); Aldcroft (1964–65), 118; Introduction note 4.
[168] Habakkuk (1967), esp. 11–16, 23, 104 ff, 127–8, 194–8.
[169] Clarke and Summers (1980), 132; David (1975); Field (1983); Temin (1966), 277–98; Floud (1976), 106–7; Aldcroft (1964–5), 130–3; Aldcroft (1966), 130; Habakkuk (1967), 19, 54.
[170] Gulvin (1984), 80.
[171] Harley (1973–74), 392–4, 411–12; Cain and Paterson (1981); Church (1980b); Habbakuk (1967), 56–7; Kenwood and Lougheed (1982), 114–16; D.C. (1918a), 111–12; Clark (1987).

equally valid solutions, determined by different relative factor prices, then, turned out to have quite different long-term effects. The American rapid turnover of machinery, in periods of rapidly changing technology and mass production in place of the more flexible British craftsmen were much the better solution in the long run. What was once an advantage, the possession of skilled labour, became a long-term disadvantage for Britain. Examples may be found in cotton, wool, hosiery, footwear, steel, mining, and some forms of engineering, among others. In each, there may have been special factors at work; yet the phenomenon recurs too often to be put down to coincidence.

The technical changes involving labour-saving equipment were often linked to mass-production methods. In this respect, also, the British experience might differ in important ways both from that of the USA and from that of other countries in Europe.

At least three types of experience can be distinguished. In some cases, Britain became technically retarded because her varied markets or her craft traditions prevented the development of mass production. These included the steel industry, electrical engineering, motor cars, locomotives and some other forms of engineering and optical goods. There were, secondly, industries in which this flexibility was not necessarily a disadvantage, at least for the time being, but rather an effective adaptation to circumstances. The cotton industry was possibly the outstanding example.

Against this, thirdly, there were industries in which Britain led or was among the leaders in mass production, ahead of the rest of the world. These included many consumer goods industries, such as newspapers, food processing, the production of cheap household goods, cosmetics and bicycles, and, in their different ways, also rifles and small arms, ships and textile machinery.[172] Britain, it must not be forgotten, was the original fountainhead of mass production as well as being the earliest consumer society. If the British markets were more split up than others, either because of the weight of overseas sales, or because of the class character of Britain, this could also mean greater flexibility and encourage initiative.[173]

The alleged British backwardness in formal science and technology, treated at length in chapter 3 below, will have affected particularly the chemical, electrical, metallurgical, and coalmining industry, as well as such relatively craft-based industries as leather and optical glass. British design has similarly come under repeated and almost universal criticism, but at least in the case of woollen goods it was at least the equal if not the superior of that found abroad.[174]

Britain's early start was a particular handicap in the location of industrial plant, particularly where this was large and costly to move. Costs would rise where sites were fixed in relation to earlier conditions, while latecomers could choose those appropriate for the latest technology. A well-known example is found in shipbuilding, located along rivers which became increasingly constrictive as the size of ships increased. Yards located with an eye to the

[172] Saul (1967), 128; Harley (1973–74), 407; Pollard (1957); Trebilcock (1957), 486–8; Lorenz and Wilkinson (1986) 111; Supple (1977b).
[173] Lenman (1977), 204; Foreman-Peck (1983b), 181; Musson and Robinson (1969), 495–500; Marshall (1970), 580.
[174] Jenkins and Ponting (1982), 288.

market and to timber supplies, above all along the Thames, suffered most. In common with other large units, such as iron and steel works, shipyards also found expansion on their original sites difficult if not impossible because of the closely packed streets of their workers' houses around their walls. This might be considered an example of 'interrelatedness': no single extension justified the scrapping and relocation of the whole works, whereas, had the continuing process over several decades been reviewed as a whole, total relocation would have been found preferable. The most widely discussed case here is the failure to move to the East Midlands iron ore field, but it may also explain the reluctance of British firms to make use before 1914 of the freedom given by the electric motor to move out of congested inner-city sites.[175]

Industries producing largely for export have come in for particular attention and criticism, though this may be merely because sheltered home-market industries had no need to compare their performance with that of foreign suppliers. The argument has been conducted in part at the macro level, alleging that it was the failure of exports to grow as fast as the exports of other countries which slowed down Britain's overall growth rate and therefore her chance of improving her productivity.[176] There is also the related argument that Britain managed to avoid modernizing her old industries, or switching to new ones by escaping to ever new, easier markets instead of meeting her new competitors head-on in the traditional markets of Europe and North America.[177]

At the micro level it was said that British exporters were careless and incompetent in their sales methods, failing to meet the challenge of new competitors by better packaging, description, the use of local languages and measures, and active salesmanship generally.[178] At home, it was alleged, innovations proceeded only after the threat or the experience of American competition: these included the footwear, bicycle, machine tool and tobacco industries. In the case of clocks it has been argued that the easy home market allowed British producers to be lethargic about innovations, while the Swiss had to export to survive.[179] We have seen that not all these strictures will stand up to the evidence.

No doubt, much of the available entrepreneurial talent went into services, and into the mass-produced consumer goods for the home market in the development and marketing of which British entrepreneurs played a pioneering role. The tendency of the London region, as the centre of that activity, to grow while the export-oriented textile and metals regions stagnated, has also been noted.[180] For the pioneer mass-consumption society enjoying regular balance of payments surpluses because of the sale of services and the income from foreign investments, it seems not unreasonable to indulge itself in

[175] Pollard (1950), 72–89; Burnham and Hoskins (1943), 187; Payne (1968), 89; Burn (1940), 172; Allen (1929), 324 and note 80 above.
[176] Kindleberger (1961–2), 289–305; Lewis (1957), 578–587; Meyer (1964), 183–220; Levine (1967), 132–3; Wulf (1968), 227; and note 16 above.
[177] See Introduction notes 17–19.
[178] Diplomatic and Consular Reports (1901), LXXXV Cd. 430–16; Trebilcock (1977), 45 ff, 120, 124–130; Checkland (1977), 14; Introduction, note 8.
[179] Church (1975b), 630; Coleman and MacLeod (1986), 595.
[180] Lee (1981).

this way. It may, however, well have postponed and therefore ultimately endangered the necessary re-equipment of some basic British industries.

The effects of foreign tariffs – and the possible consequences of British retaliation – may well have been underrated in the literature. They were certainly at least in part responsible for the switch away from the 'hard' European and North American markets. The McKinley Tariff of 1890 in the USA, followed by the Dingley tariff seven years later, had devastating consequences for the iron and steel industry and above all for tinplate. Others suffering from foreign tariffs included the woollen and worsted industry, machine tools, the lesser textile industries, glass, alkali and other chemicals.[181] Protection abroad also encouraged monopolies and dumping policies there.[182] On the other hand, the benefit derived by industries in the later stages of production from being able to draw their raw materials and components from the cheapest sources instead of having them artificially raised by tariffs was equally significant.

Another theme which frequently recurs is the hostility of workers or their trade unions to technical innovation, and the consequent delay in introducing better techniques into British firms. The industries particularly affected would be those employing skilled and organized labour, such as shipbuilding and cotton. Precisely there, employers were also alleged to have been in the habit of fighting the men's hostility to the system, rather than inducing them to benefit from it, and to use machinery to make labour redundant rather than increase output from the same labour force. Certainly, as long as employers rushed to reduce piece rates as soon as output went up, workers were likely to oppose any innovation which raised output.[183]

Obstruction to technical progress took several forms. Few workers, and even fewer unions, opposed better machines or improved processes as such; rather they might offer passive resistance by working the new machines so slowly that no increase in. output took place, or they could attach impossible wages demands, such that the whole of the benefit should accrue to labour and none to capital for the extra capital expenditure. In other cases, it was the memory of earlier long-drawn-out troubles when new machinery was installed, which inhibited employers from even trying to reduce costs by better methods.[184]

It is frequently argued that trade-union power and relatively high wages induce innovations, either of a kind to save labour or of a kind to replace skilled by semi-killed or unskilled labour. Low wages and docile labour, by contrast, might encourage the continuation of out-of-date or wasteful equipment.[185] Indeed, high wages are generally accepted as a major factor in the mechanization of American industry. Such cases, no doubt, existed in Britain also. Yet

[181] Clapham (1907), 288; Jenkins and Ponting (1982), 226–7, 294; Tariff Commission (1904) II/2, 131 ff; Hooper in Ashley (1907), 112; Tyson (1968), 117; Warren (1980), 186–7, 192; Barker (1960), 162–3; Floud (1976), 95 ff.
[182] Carr and Taplin (1962), 293; Tariff Commission (1904) I, par. 54 ff. and this chapter note 81.
[183] Lorenz and Wilkinson (1986), 120; Gospel and Littler (1983), 58 ff, 186. Also Introduction, note 19 and this chapter notes 46, 118, 120, 141, 146, 153; Aldcroft (1981a), 26; Levine (1967), 76–8; Habakkuk (1967), 141.
[184] Rose (1986); 98; Lazonick (1979b), 256–7; Coleman and MacLeod (1986), 605–6; Berg (1979), 173; Taylor (1961–62), 60; Allen (1979), 231; Carr and Taplin (1962), 205; Lewchuk (1985), 140.
[185] Barker (1977), 190; Clark (1986), 499; Musson (1978), 165; Zeitlin (1983), 12, 27–8, 43, and note 21 above.

there is some evidence that in Britain it was the high concentration of the most skilled labour in the leading firms, where one would expect progress to originate, which allowed it both to inhibit technological progress and block ways of by-passing their obstruction.

Finally, there may have been a peculiar British weakness in large-scale organization affecting particularly industries in which capital concentration, requiring joint stock, was necessary. The joint-stock form of organization came late to Britain, and was confined to a small number of sectors only. Among the reasons for this delay were the reluctance of the formerly owning family to give up control, and therefore the limited opportunities for the professional manager; the domination of boards of directors by accountants and lawyers without technical knowledge; and the limited size of British top firms, which were frequently below the technical optimum. This last applied particularly to steel and coal mining. The monopolistic amalgamations which were found in the textile industry and also elsewhere were often poorly integrated and incompetently managed. Altogether, the share of the top 100 firms in manufacturing output has been estimated at 15% in 1909, compared with 23% in 1939 and 45–50% in 1967.[186]

There was widespread support for the view that the British were less skilful in making use of the new forms of organization than were others. There were some large capital concentrations in brewing and in transport, and there were numerous short-term price agreements. The object of mergers, however, in almost every case, was not so much to increase efficiency as to make monopoly gains.[187] At the same time it is not at all clear that size alone was of advantage. Many of the huge mergers in the USA as well as in Britain were abject failures.[188]

The British were also slow to adopt modern methods of internal management. Fordism, the thorough organization of the production process along a conveyor system and the payment of fixed, but relatively high wages, was practically unknown; the Taylor system of 'scientific management' was attacked not only by the trade unions, but denounced also by many employers as inhuman and not worth studying.[189] In all these areas, however, the Continent was scarcely more advanced than Britain.

The brief survey in this section may easily be summarized. There seems to be no single characteristic, or no particular feature, within British industry which can be made responsible for such weaknesses as appeared in the period 1870–1914. Many causes have been enumerated in the literature, but none appears to have wide validity. For almost every example there may be found

[186] Irving (1975), 162 ff; Utton (1972), 55; Jenkins and Ponting (1982), 181; Payne (1967b), 520, 526–7, 536–9; Payne (1978b), 18–20; Burn (1940), 219 ff, 256–7; Church (1977), 107–8; Farnie (1979), 192–4; Carr and Taplin (1962), 265–6. (1981), 103; Levine (1967), 53–4; Burnham and Hoskins (1943), 208; Robson (1957), 103 ff; Lazonick (1981d), 36; Hannah (1976), 216–17; Hannah (1974), 252–6; Vaizey (1974), 10.
[187] Richardson (1962), 112; Payne (1967b), 530–1; Elbaum and Lazonick (1986b), 5; Utton (1972), 52–4; Webb (1980), 326.
[188] Payne (1967b), 537; Hannah (1974), 254–6.
[189] Chapman (1904) I, 78; Cox in Mosely Report (1903), 41; Levine (1967), 60–8; Lewchuk (1983), 83–7, 136.

counter-examples. What emerges is a complex story, with ups as well as downs, and no pervasive negative effect that can safely be generalized. Splitting British industry into its many components does not help in the search for a single cause.

V Conclusion

This brief survey has necessarily brought to the fore the great variety of experience among different industries in our period. Not all industries declined relatively to comparable sectors of other countries, and hardly any declined absolutely. Several industries did very well on an international comparative basis. Some, including shipbuilding, coal mining, cotton and wool, held on to an astonishingly large, even if declining share of the world's output or export markets. Others actually increased their export markets or came to dominate them: this included bicycles, textile machinery, armaments, biscuits and tobacco goods. In others still, Britain pioneered either the technology or the market organization. This included turbines, pneumatic tyres, artificial fibres and the consumer-goods industries like soap, newspapers, chocolate, cosmetics and patent medicines, and methods of selling them.

Further, even the briefest survey shows that the industries themselves were not homogeneous: within each 'industry' there were normally some highly progressive firms, standing comparison in terms of organization and technical equipment with the best to be found abroad, while others survived by means of low wages, favourable location, traditional markets or sheer inertia. Averages or percentages, say, of the proportions of power looms installed, could therefore be misleading. This would be particularly important in considering the question whether Britain was in a position to keep up, or catch up, with the best abroad.

The critique, by contemporaries as well as in the more recent literature, concentrated very largely on features that may be derived from Britain's early start as an industrial nation supplying manufactures to the rest of the world. Its more important aspects may be summarized under the following heads.

1 Britain was concentrating unduly on the 'wrong' industries, i.e. on those which had enabled her to achieve an early lead, but which now had reached the end of their growth potential, and/or which newly industrializing countries could set up most easily in competition. By comparison, she neglected several of the new industries which had a higher growth potential and in which the level of science and technology required was too high for most low-wage countries to imitate, and in which therefore a country technically in the lead and obliged to pay high wages should have sought its comparative advantage. At the same time, the transfer of resources to newer industries with higher per capita output did contribute largely to what little British industrial output growth there was.

2 There was also a second structural fault: British firms remained small even in industries in which there were clear advantages of size. They were also

reluctant to combine even partially, for the purpose of sales cartels or market sharing. Among the causes of this were the long tradition of most family concerns and their reluctance to give up family control, either to managers or to outsiders, and the long tradition of free trade and of progress by competition. Both of these can be derived from Britain's early start.

3 Many firms and industries were wrongly located, having been established at a time when optimal location was different from that demanded by modern technology. This was particularly painful for several shipbuilding firms and for some firms in the iron and steel industry. Among other geographical disadvantages derived from the early start were coal pits that were too close together and therefore below optimal size for modern collieries, and railway tracks and tunnels unsuitable for larger, faster rolling stock than was available when they were first built.

4 Possibly most frequent was the critique that British industry was reluctant to adopt radically new methods, particularly those requiring high-level science and technology, and new forms of internal organization like 'scientific management'. British industrialists had achieved great successes and conquered overseas markets by methods which were based on skill and experience and were therefore unduly contemptuous of book learning and formally trained technical staff. They were also reluctant to scrap equipment which was still operating at a profit. At the same time, it does not follow that every technical innovation is also economically justifiable, and it has been shown in several industries, above all in iron and steel and in the cotton manufacture, that British managers may well have been sensible and rational to stick to the traditional methods, given British costs and market structures.

5 British salesmanship was also said to have become too rigidly locked onto an older pattern when Britain was the sole source of supply for many manufactured goods. The failure to send representatives inland from the comfortable coastal cities, carrying catalogues and able to speak the local languages, the failure to use local weights and measures, the failure to pack attractively and to supply attractive credit terms were frequently cited.

6 Finally, a general loss of the entrepreneurial spirit was alleged to have inhibited all innovational vigour and willingness to fight. Here the third generation syndrome, the social attractiveness of political honours or rural leisure pursuits, the low status of industrial money-making, coupled with a general idealization of pastoral bliss in British culture has been held responsible for an attitude markedly different from that of the chief rivals, Germany and the USA.

To set these criticisms in perspective, it should be emphasized that what is to be explained is not decline, but slow growth, growth moreover, which took place in spite of substantial reductions of hours and easing of working conditions in many industries. It has also to be set against an astonishing degree of domination of world markets in industrial products as well as in coal by Britain around 1870, which it would be wholly unreasonable to expect to be maintained.

The question which arises, then, is this: was Britain, herself at the technical frontier at the beginning of our period, growing more slowly because others were catching up by making up their leeway, or was she in fact being overtaken by the newcomers to be left behind ultimately, rather like the Italian cities had been in the sixteenth and seventeenth centuries?[190]

At this stage, at the end of our first chapter, it is too early to attempt an answer to this question. The favourable 'catching up' explanation may be supported by reference to the not unreasonable international division of labour, between industrial and agrarian producers, and among industrial producers themselves, among whom Britain still found herself even at the end of the period; and the ease with which Britain established even difficult industries in the years of the First World War, when she had to. For the alternative explanation it might be pointed out that Britain's weaknesses, including delay in developing industries with a high science content, the small-scale organization, and reluctance to adopt radical changes, were precisely those which would come to matter increasingly in the future. Once set on a slow-growth, traditionalist path, it might be difficult to switch over even after technical leadership had shifted elsewhere, when Britain would be put in a position of having to catch up with others.

190 Pullan (1968); Cipolla (1970), 196–214.

2

The Export of Capital

One of the most popular explanations for the slowing down of the British economy in the period 1870–1914 has been an 'excessive' export of capital. Rapid industrial progress requires frequent replacement and, most likely, expansion in absolute terms of the capital equipment used, and even a cursory glance at the statistics will show that the British rate of domestic investment was low. While the rate of saving was similar in the three leading industrial countries, Britain, Germany and the USA, fluctuating at around 11–15% of the gross national product (GNP), the proportion invested at home in Britain averaged only 5–7% of GNP in the years 1871–1913, compared with around 12% for the other two. The rest of the British savings was exported abroad.

Fixed capital per person employed, inasfar as such a difficult concept can be statistically determined, showed a strong relative decline, though still an absolute rise, in our period. While Britain was ahead of the rest in 1870, by 1890 the USA had caught up, and by 1913 they were far ahead of the United Kingdom, while Germany in turn had by then managed to catch up:[1]

Table 2.1 Non-residential fixed capital stock, selected countries, 1870–1914 (per person employed, in US$ of 1970)

	1870	1890	1913
USA	5066	6838	13147
UK	6068	6658	7999
Germany	3597	5311	7888
France	n.a.	n.a.	6481

Was 'too much' capital exported? Would some of that capital, if invested at home, have raised the growth rate and brought greater wealth and prosperity to Britain? Some of the alleged causes of the 'overinvestment' abroad were remediable, such as the structure of the London capital market which was said to have favoured foreign as against domestic investment. Could these factors, and with them the course of history, have been altered, given political will and economic understanding?

[1] Maddison (1982), 54; also Eichengreen (1982), 87; Kuznets (1961), 5, 38.

This chapter will seek to summarize critically the debate on these issues. Section I will examine the data on the actual course of capital exports. Section II will outline the extreme positions in the debate and discuss some of their assumptions. Sections III – VIII will consider some of the macro-economic issues in more detail, while Section IX will follow some of the debate at sectoral and micro-economic levels. Section X will pull together some of the theoretical and empirical points that have emerged in the preceding sections, and it will be followed by some concluding remarks.

The economic and political discussions on the effects of capital exports have ranged widely, covering aspects without direct relevance to the British economy in 1870–1914 or to our particular theme. These will be omitted here, with some regrets. Among the more important of these are (a) movements of short-term capital, except insofar as they affect long-term investments, (b) the effects of capital imports on the borrowing countries, (c) the effects of capital exports on the distribution of incomes, (d) the relationship between capital exports and the Juglar trade cycle, (e) international migration, and (f) outside factors (other than the capital exports themselves) affecting the level of savings in Britain.

Some of these exerted some effects of significance;[2] yet, to have included them, would have lengthened an already overlong chapter without adding much to the thrust of the arguments. It is hoped that by limiting ourselves to the more direct effects of foreign investment in the decades before World War I we shall be able to focus more clearly on the question of immediate interest to us: did it bear some responsibility, and if so how much, for the slowing down of the British economy?

I Size and Structure of Foreign Investment

What is remarkable at first sight is that until very recently there seems to have been little disagreement about the data. There has been a general consensus that British capital abroad had risen from an insignificant sum of *net* foreign investment at the end of the Napoleonic Wars (British investments abroad *minus* capital holdings by foreigners in Britain) to £1,000–£1,200 million by about 1875, to expand further to £4,000 million by the outbreak of the First World War.[3]

Nor has there been much disagreement about its distribution, or about the changing dimensions of the annual investment stream between *c*. 1870 and 1914. Feis's estimate for early 1914, based on Paish, may be compared with two recent estimates of the sums of the flows 1865–1914. In each case portfolio investments only appear to have been included.[4]

[2] Murphy (1960/61), 17; Tinbergen (1951), 124; Hobson (1911), 143; David and Scadding (1974).
[3] Feinstein's higher figure of £4.3 billion in 1913 seems to include short-term balances. His comparable figure for net overseas long-term assets would seem to be £4.18 billion. Feinstein (1972), T.110; Matthews, Feinstein, Odling-Smee (1982), 128. The most consistent questioning of this order of magnitude is found in Platt (1986).
[4] Feis (1965), 23; Simon (1968), 23–4; Davis and Huttenback (1986), 40, 46, 48–9; also Davis and Huttenback (1985), 66–9. United Nations (1955), 5; United Nations (1949), 3; Paish (1914), V–VI; Cairncross (1953), 185. Also p. 63, note 17 below.

The Export of Capital

Table 2.2 Area distribution of British overseas investments, in per cent. 1865–1914

	Feis 1914		Davis/Huttenback* 1865–1914		Total Investments		
	Empire	Foreign	Empire	Foreign	Feis	Simon** 1865–1914	Davis/Huttenback
Asia	10.8	3.5	8.7	5.3	14.3	14	14.0
Australasia	11.1	–	11.7	–	11.1	11	11.7
North America	13.7	20.1	12.0	21.5	33.7	34	33.5
Latin Am. Carib.	–	20.1	0.2	19.7	20.1	17	19.9
Africa	10.8	1.2	6.0	3.8	12.0	11	9.8
Europe	–	5.8	–	11.0	5.8	13	11.0
Others, Unknown	0.9	2.1			3.0		
Totals	47.3	52.8	38.6	61.3	100	100	100
Total Sums Included, £mn	1780	1983	1226	1939	3763		3165

* Minimum estimates
** Simon allocated 40% to the Empire, 60% to foreign countries

Some of the discrepancies might be dissolved on the not unreasonable assumptions of some repatriation of capital from the USA, much repatriation from Europe, and a higher rate of default in the intervening years outside the Empire than inside it.

As for the type of asset acquired, while the proportion lent to foreign governments was much reduced from the high-point of 47.4% in 1870, loans to colonial governments had increased more than 22-fold, reflecting both the astonishing rise of the overseas communities in the white dominions, and the change in the political climate – as well as the change-over of some governments from foreign to colonial status. Around 40% went on overseas railways directly, plus a proportion of the sums lent to governments. Bearing in mind the further large sums invested in other utilities and public works, very little remained for all other purposes, at least among the portfolio investments. The small though rising proportions invested in agriculture, mining and manufacturing are confirmed by Simon and by Davis and Huttenback:[5]

Table 2.3 Distribution of new British Portfolio investment abroad by sector, 1865–1914

Simon	1865–72	1909–13	Davis and Huttenback	1865–74	1910–14
Agriculture	1.7%	5.6%	Agriculture and extractive	5.6%	8.7%
Mining	5.2	9.3			
Manufacture	0.7	4.8	Manufacturing	2.0	4.0
Transportation	47.6	46.6	Transportation	39.3	38.2
Utilities	5.5	6.4	Public utilities	7.0	4.2
Public works	17.8	17.3	Finance, trade, services	7.8	7.5
Other, incl.			Unknown	0	0.4
defence	21.5	10.0	Government	38.3	37.0
	100	100		100	100

[5] Simon (1966/67), 288–9; Seagal and Simon (1961), 575; Zweig (1928/I), 275; Davis and Huttenback (1985), 59.

60

All the sources agree that the annual totals of capital exports in this period showed strongly wavelike movements about a marked upward trend. One wave of foreign lending which had begun in 1861 reached its peak in 1872, and a second peaked in 1890. The third wave rose to unprecedented heights in the final nine years before the war, 1906–14, topping £200 million a year in the last three full years of peace, 1911–13. Since this last wave was cut off in full spate by the outbreak of the war, it must forever remain unknown whether it was exceptional, or whether it would have become one phase of an ever-rising trend, had world peace continued. It might even have overcome the cyclical tendency altogether; the cycles had been far less marked, and had had a different frequency, before 1870 and might not have continued after 1914.

An idea of the size and impact of this level of investment may be gained by reflecting that net investment abroad actually exceeded the funds devoted to the home economy even if we include house building and the physical increases of stocks in the peak years 1870–74 and again in 1886–90, while from 1907 onwards it left domestic capital formation far behind, to rise to double the domestic values in the last years of our period.[6] Since, averaged out over the whole period, the annual rate of foreign investment came to approximate that of home investment while the stock of home capital was much larger at its beginning, the ratio of capital abroad to the total capital owned by British citizens was bound to rise. On varying definitions, it changed as follows:[7]

Table 2.4 Net capital stock held abroad, as % of total British capital holdings, various estimates

	1870	1873	1875	1885	1913/14
Hobson (1914)/Feis (1930)				13.0	28.0
Cairncross (1953)			22.0		43.4
Kuznets (1961)				19.2	29.1
Edelstein (1982), including bullion	17.5				33.2
Edelstein (1982), excluding bullion	14.2				30.9
Edelstein (1982), outstanding securities	37.2				47.7
Matthews, Feinstein, Odling-Smee (1982)		18.2			34.0

The proportion of British wealth held abroad by 1913–14 was thus about one-third of the total and still growing.

Finally, capital exports may be expressed as a proportion of national income. On that basis, net foreign investment formed 4.5% of the gross domestic product (GDP) in 1855–73 and rose to an average of 5.0% in 1874–90 and again in 1891–1913; however, in the years 1905–13 it reached 7% and in 1911–13 it approached 9%, actually exceeding that ratio in 1913. At those levels, the sums spent on investment abroad ran at well over one-quarter of the annual value of the whole of British exports and in the last years around one-half. The proportion of new income derived from these foreign investments rose from 2.8% of GDP (1855–73) to 5.4% (1874–90) and 6.8% (1891–1913).

[6] Feinstein (1972), VII/I, 69; T.8, 9, 14, 15, 21, 37, 38, 48.
[7] Hobson (1914), 207; Feis (1965), 14; Douglas (1929/30), 674–5; Cairncross (1953), 4; Kuznets (1959/60), 62; Edelstein (1982), 27, 48, 164 ff; Matthews, Feinstein, Odling-Smee (1982), 129.

Again, the ratio was higher in the last years of peace: it reached no less than 9.2% of gross domestic product, or more than one quarter of all incomes from property. The proportions for Scotland alone were even higher.[8]

Whether, as has frequently been claimed,[9] this implied that the British economy did indeed devote a larger proportion of its national income than any other in history to foreign investment, or whether possibly the Dutch in their golden age, or even the French and the Swiss in the nineteenth century in terms of gross investment might have equalled or exceeded it, may be debatable.[10] What was beyond dispute was the weight of the British capital supply in the world economy:[11]

Table 2.5 *Foreign investments of the leading countries, 1870–1914, in $ millions*

	c.1870	c.1900	c.1914	= %
United Kingdom	4,900	12,000	20,000	44.0 %
France	2,500	5,800	9,050	19.9
Germany		4,800	5,800	12.8
United States	,100	,500	3,500	7.8
Netherlands	,500	1,100 ⎫		
Belgium		⎬	5,500	12.1
Switzerland		⎭		
Others			1,600	3.5
World			45,450	100.1

Thus in the immediate pre-war years, well over two-fifths of the world's foreign long-term capital holdings were in British hands, and the share was rising rather than falling: in 1906–13, the British share of the top three investing countries was 62.8% of new investments, compared with at most 57.4% of the capital stock.[12]

The broad agreement of the estimates of the size of the capital export flow from the United Kingdom should not be taken as a proof of their reliability. The figures have in fact been derived from three types of evidence: (1) as a residual, year by year, of the balance of payments after all current transactions have been accounted for, (2) from the tax records on incomes arising abroad, suitably grossed up, and (3) by the laborious adding-up of all issues floated in Britain and destined for abroad. All three methods have serious weaknesses,

[8] Feinstein (1972), T.8, 37, 38, 44, 45; Matthews, Feinstein, Odling-Smee (1982), 442; Edelstein (1982), 24; Lenfant (1951), 160.
[9] Woodruff (1966), 117; Edelstein (1982), 3; Kuznets (1959/60), 5, 10–11; Hall (1968a), 1; Schumpeter (1939), 430.
[10] Bairoch (1976a), 101; Walter (1982); Landmann (1916); Goldsmith (1969), 174; Maddison (1982), 32; Sartorius von Waltershausen (1907), 374; Barbour (1976), 6; Riley (1980), 8–16, 89–96, 224–40, 253–7; Neymarck (1911), VI, ix–xi, VII, 139, 410; Fahrländer (1919), 106–15; Arndt (1915), 532–4; Lévy-Leboyer (1977a), 15–16, 29–30; Fritzsche (1913), 39–40; Mokyr (1984), 1096–7; Maddison (1982), 33, 39.
[11] Woodruff (1966), 150–5; The oft-quoted United Nations estimate gave the United Kingdom only $44,000 million, or 40.9%. United Nations (1949), 2.
[12] Bloomfield (1968), 47.

including the uncertainties regarding some items calculated for method (1),[13] the issues partially subscribed abroad or not fully subscribed under method (3), and the repatriation or naturalization of capital sent abroad in earlier years.[14] As a result of misgivings over a systematic bias in the traditional estimates, D.C.M. Platt has proposed that the figure for 1913 should be scaled down from £3.7 billion to perhaps £2.6 billion or, by a later estimate, perhaps £3.1 billion, of which £0.5 billion were 'direct' investments.[15]

These 'direct' investments deserve some further attention. Assumed to amount to no more than 10% of total overseas holdings – Paish and Feis assigned a totally arbitrary sum of £300 million for them – they have frequently been dismissed as of no great significance. They are defined in part by their method of transfer, by internal transfer within the firm instead of the capital market, and in part, or alternatively, as capital abroad of which the British investor holds a controlling share, say over 25–30%. An intermediate category, called 'associate', of 10–25% holdings, may also be distinguished. A further possible category is formed by the 'expatriate' firm financed from Britain but based on the emigration of skilled and managerial personnel.[16]

One estimate puts this type of capital as 22% of the total in our period. There has recently been an increased interest shown in the more direct expansion of firms overseas, as forming the origin of the present-day multinationals which are receiving much attention. The overall impression is that this type of investment, implying control from Britain rather than simply disdain of the London capital market, has been not only larger than assumed in the past, but also growing rapidly in the years to 1914.[17] Its neglect may seriously affect the value of theories and explanations of the phenomenon of capital exports offered in the past.

What is less in dispute is that the cyclical movement of capital exports noted above was matched to a remarkable extent by an inverse cycle of home investments. This complementary movement of home and foreign capital formation leaps to the eye[18] and has been taken as the basis of much theorizing. In particular, it is evident that if we could show that the total pool of yearly savings remained stable while only its distribution between home and foreign investments fluctuated, we could conclude quite safely either that foreign

---

[13] 'The values computed', Imlah conceded, 'can scarcely be considered to possess yearly precision. The most that can be hoped for is that quinquennial or decennial averages are fair approximations', Imlah (1952/53), 222. His important series of shipping earnings has indeed been judged most unreliable; North and Heston (1960), 265–76.

[14] Platt (1980), 4–7; Platt (1984). Also, see Chapman (1984), 83–4, 155–61, 174; Nurkse (1961), 141; Jones (1987), 66–7.

[15] Platt (1980); Platt (1984); Platt (1986). Also see Arndt (1915), 301–11, 6.

[16] Gutman (1956); Robinson (1961), 7; Heidhues (1969), 10–14; Buckley and Roberts (1982); Jenks (1951), 379, 384–5; Dorothy Adler (1970), 199–200; Paterson (1976), 5, 12, *passim*; Stopford (1974), 305–10; Jones (1987), 16–19; Chapman (1985) and Chapman (1987); Feis (1965), 23–4; Paish (1911), 187; Paish (1914), 79; Dunning (1970), 2; Stone (1977), 690–2.

[17] Dunning (1970), 6–8; Stopford (1974), 315, 326; Buckley and Roberts (1982), 36–9; Nicholas (1982a); Inoue (1984), 3–20; Jones (1984b), 125–53; Blainey (1984), 185–92; Pazos (1970), 189–91; Svedberg (1978); Bloomfield (1968), 3.

[18] Cairncross (1953), 9 ff, 187; Thomas, B. (1973), 175, *passim*; Cooney (1949), 350; Meier and Baldwin (1966), 211–12.

investment helped to stabilize the Keynesian cycles of the economy (on the assumption that there was a savings surplus),[19] or that capital exports were 'at the expense of' home investments (on the assumption that there was a scarcity of savings).

However, the data will not yield such simple correlations. For one thing, as Cooney noted, no home-investment cycle can be traced before the 1870s, the cycle lasted till the First World War only, and it had a somewhat accidental origin, so that its very cyclical nature is suspect.[20] For another, the amplitudes of the swings did not correlate perfectly, so that it is not possible to predict the quantity of home investment for any given period from the capital export.[21] In particular, the pool of savings[22] was not wholly stable, but expanded in the big investment boom of the early 1870s and again toward the very end of our period. It may also be of interest to note here that in the shorter, 'Juglar' or trade cycle, home and foreign investment moved together rather than inversely, particularly at the turning points.[23]

On the other hand, the significance of the investment cycle is much enhanced by the fact that it corresponds to an inverse cycle in the United States (and to some extent in other overseas territories also) where it has become known as the 'Kuznets cycle'. No Kuznets cycle is visible in Britain, precisely because home and foreign investments largely cancel out,[24] though it does appear in such sectoral phenomena as the building cycle or the foreign investment cycle. Plausible linkages within the 'Atlantic economy' are the association of British capital exports to the United States with high emigration from Britain, high exports, particularly of capital goods, and a building and capital-goods boom in the USA, but low building activity in Britain.[25] Although the complementarity is not perfect, as noted above, the striking inverse relationship with the USA strengthens the supposition of a possible competition for a limited joint supply of capital between the two countries.[26] More importantly, it draws attention to the major issue of impetus and motivation that will concern us later. Here we set ourselves the more limited task of following the literature to enquire whether the fluctuations themselves offer any clue as to the source of the impetus for this transfer of capital. Was it Britain or overseas? Was it pull or push?

There are some obvious pitfalls. Among them the assumption that

[19] Zimmermann-Grumbach (1953).

[20] Cooney (1960/61), 257–69; also Saul (1962–63).

[21] Stone (1971), 323; Green and Urquhart (1976), 246–52; Latham (1978), 143; Bloomfield (1968), 27 *passim*; O'Leary and Lewis (1955), 127, 142–3; Edelstein (1982), 205 ff; North (1962), 29; and pp. 65, 99 and notes 30 and 170 below.

[22] Other influences on the British propensity to save will not be followed up, as stated on page 59 above. A good introduction to the problem will be found in Edelstein (1982), 182 ff; Edelstein (1977), 289–94.

[23] Cairncross (1953), 187; Kindleberger (1968), 379 ff; Ford (1981 II), 35; O'Leary and Lewish (1955), 120–1; Stone (1971), 306–7; Brown (1965), 54.

[24] Bloomsfield (1968), 22.

[25] Cooney (1960/61), 266; Cooney (1949), 350; Thomas (1968); B. Thomas (1973); Cairncross (1953); 9, 209 ff; Habakkuk (1968), 103–4; Williamson (1968), 55–6, 80–1; Williamson (1964); Kuznets (1962); Easterlin (1966); but see Abramovitz (1968).

[26] Thomas (1968), 47–8.

correlation, even with a time lag, means causation; the assumption that, even if it can be shown that one variable 'causes' the fluctuations of another, it therefore explains its bulk; and the problem of distinguishing, in a case where the dependent variable moves well with the independent one, whether it does so because the link is close, or because the latter fluctuates very strongly.[27] Moreover, one component of the capital export figures, loans to governments for defence and similar purposes, fluctuated for non-economic reasons – though the supply of capital for them would, of course, be part of the investment cycle.[28] Finally, it should be remembered that even if the quantities of capital invested at home or abroad were obviously linked in some way, the actual capital markets were not, but on the contrary were almost completely isolated from each other.

Nevertheless, it is worth following the literature briefly into the push–pull controversy. Not all of it has been econometric; judgements were made in the earlier literature on the basis of comparisons, as it were, with the naked eye, but the results are comparable.

A part of the controversy has been concerned with the question whether within Britain it was home or foreign yields which were dominant, whether, in other words, capital exports rose because there was no profitable use for capital at home, or whether it stayed at home only when there was no profitable use for it abroad. It seems that Dunning, following the contemporary *Economist*, favours the first alternative, while Rostow, Cooney and Lythe favour the second.[29] Matthews, Feinstein and Odling-Smee see the contrast between push and pull in slightly different terms: if a high level of capital exports raised the rates of return on capital to a point at which home investment could no longer afford it, this would be an example of 'crowding out', whereas the contrary mechanism, of low home returns driving capital abroad in search of higher profits, would be a case of 'crowding in'. The capital export boom of the late 1880s would in those terms be a case of crowding in, that of 1903–13 an example of crowding out, while the home boom beginning in the late 1890s may have owed much to the low interest rates caused by low capital exports.[30]

Several authors have been impressed by the fact that waves of foreign issues frequently preceded the rise in exports by a year or two.[31] On those terms, the export of capital 'caused' the export of goods some time later, and the tendency would be to seek the driving force abroad, and to favour the 'pull' explanation. Among other authors who opted for the pull explanation, which locates the initiative outside Britain, Williamson did so largely because, as he saw it, it was the USA which managed to mesh Britain into the pre-existing American Kuznets cycle; indeed, in general, those whose interest centred on one of the receiving countries, such as the Argentine or Australia, tended to prefer the

[27] Edelstein (1974), 981.
[28] Thomas (1968), 45; Simon (1968), 35.
[29] Thomas (1968), 122, 260–5; Rostow (1948), 205; Cooney (1949), 350, 353; Lythe (1969), 48; Dunning (1970), 18.
[30] Matthews, Feinstein and Odling-Smee (1982), 354. Also see Offer (1983), 119; also see p. 108 below.
[31] E.g. Ford (1964), 27–9; Cairncross (1953), 204; Tilly (1984), 269; See page 103–4, note 191 below.

'pull' since it seemed too much of a coincidence that a flood of British capital should always be accumulated ready to reach their shores just when the receiving economy was ripe for it.[32] There is here something of the contrast, to be discussed further below, between the so-called 'autonomous' foreign investment, going for an evident opportunity, and the 'induced' investment, arising because the market has become favourable to the international transfer of resources.[33]

Among those who hold the opposite view, Habakkuk places the origins of the capital export movements in Britain because of the home building and investment cycle, while others like Beach and Zweig look to the (shorter) trade cycle in Britain as the operative mechanism. To others still the pull from overseas seems too scattered, and too dependent on separate developments in distant parts of the globe to be credited with turning into a regular cycle.[34]

Finally, there are those who believe that the location of the impetus, or indeed the mechanism that held the world capital market together, changed over the period. Thus Thomas judged that the push predominated to the 1860s, the pull later on. Edelstein believed on the contrary that the American pull was strong in 1854–71, and again in 1874–79, but weakened after that, to disappear almost entirely in the early twentieth century. This also seemed to be North's view, and Williamson, Angell and Saul may be interpreted in roughly the same way.[35] After 1900, in any case, the significance of capital exports within the interdependence of the two major Atlantic economies was much reduced.

In view of these disagreements, agnosticism seems indicated: both the push from Britain and the pull from abroad were important, perhaps at different times.

One theme within that debate, however, deserves further attention: the tendency for investment to occur in single great bursts to particular areas. With the exception of the USA, where the interest of British investors was almost continuous, our apparently single long bout of capital exports 1865–1914 consisted in fact of a sequence of totally different investment patterns for different areas.

These bursts of investments to particular regions, concentrated within a short period, had been noticeable even before 1870. First came the European governments after the Peace of 1815. There followed the investment boom of 1824–25 in the newly independent Latin American republics, most of which went into default almost at once, though ultimately many debts were acknowledged and began to yield returns. In the 1830s occurred a boom in American State and local government paper and in American railways, most of which were in default also by the end of the decade. After the home railway boom of the 1840s there came in the 1850s and 1860s large new waves of capital exports for railways in the European periphery, in the USA, in India and in

---

[32] Williamson (1968), Latham (1978), 147; Boogs (1914–15), 770 ff, 780 ff; Ford (1971), 651–4; Kelly (1965); Hall (1968b), 143–52; Butlin (1964), 33, 227, 345–6; Viner (1937), 365.

[33] Gutman (1956), 527; Bloomfield (1950), 34. This is discussed further in note 211–12 below.

[34] Habakkuk (1968), 112–13, 117, 133–6; Beach (1935), 175–7; Zweig (1928 I), 339; O'Leary and Lewis (1955), 125–7; Paterson (1974), 34.

[35] Edelstein (1974), 993–1003; and Edelstein (1982), 248; North (1956), 498 ff; Williamson (1964), 211–15; Angell (1926), 162; Saul (1965), 5–18.

some other parts of the Empire. Towards the end of the period, North American mining and Latin American Governments enjoyed renewed popularity.[36] The borrowers, it will be seen, were mostly governments and railway companies offering fixed-interest securities.

After 1870 the major investment targets, beside the American railways which never wholly lost their attraction, were Latin America, South Africa from the 1890s, and, in the last years of peace, Russia, the Far East and India. Three bursts of investment deserve special mention: those to Australia in the 1880s, to Argentina in 1884–89, and to Canada in 1900–14. They led, by 1913–14, to the highest concentrations of British capital: $387 a head in Canada, $375 in Australia and *c.* $360 in Argentina; by comparison, British capital in the USA amounted only to $72 a head.[37]

The British investors' interest in Australia began in the 1860s, but it was in the following decade that the real spurt took shape. Between 1877 and 1886 Australia was the leading target for British capital, accounting for 22.2% of all overseas issues in the early 1880s. Much of the capital went to the governments, but the largest part of this, in turn, found its way into railways and other public utilities. From 1885, investors also showed an interest in private companies. The net sums sent to Australia began to decline in the 1890s, and after 1902 there was actually some repatriation of capital. Butlin is convinced that the Australian spurt has to be explained largely in terms of conditions in the colony; Hall's, the other major study, is less certain.[38]

The Argentinian spurt was even more concentrated than the Australian. It followed a particularly favourable conjunction of circumstances, including political and monetary stabilization, the improvement in ocean transport, and the not unreasonable assumption that the fertile hinterland of the River Plate was ripe for development as a supplier of food and raw materials to the European market. Argentina's economy was tied closely to the British by its foreign trade, while many local firms were controlled by British managers and owners.

All these factors combined to unleash a railway 'mania' by British investors in the 1880s, when some £140 millions were channelled into Argentine assets: at its high-point in 1889, 40–50% of all British capital exports went to that country. The collapse of 1890, following the bad harvest of 1889 and a political coup, saw not only a classic example of overspeculation (known to history as the Baring crisis) but also of the gestation gap: for the Argentinian economy was forced, from 1889, to make large interest payments abroad on its railways before these had been completed and were capable of earning their full potential revenue. Typical was also the British export surplus to Argentina in the investment phase to 1890, and the reverse surplus after 1893, when these investments began to pay off in exports. By 1900, the British owned 88% of all Argentine railways, which represented 14.7% of that nation's capital. Once the

---

[36] Jenks (1927), 195 ff; Clarke (1878), 302, 313–18; Buer (1921), 159–79; D. Adler (1970), 7–14, 203–13; Hidy and Hidy (1960), 150–69; Select Committee Report (1875) II, 367; Spence (1958); Nash (1924), 22–3; Atkin (1977), 3–5.

[37] Bairoch (1976a), 106.

[38] Butlin (1964); Hall (1963); Wilson (1931), 7, 27–31; Iversen (1967), 400–18; Platt (1985).

success of the earlier investment was assured, a renewed capital flow began in the early twentieth century.[39]

In the case of Canada, the British were not the sole investors, but Canada was the classic example of a country receiving most of its capital from one source, the United Kingdom, while spending it on capital goods largely in another, the USA. The main investment spurt occurred in 1900–14, after an earlier smaller wave had petered out in 1894, and was associated with heavy immigration, urbanization and the development of the country's mineral riches and wheat-lands. Again it was railways (47%) and other public utilities (25%) which received most of the foreign capital. Although more heavily dependent on capital import than our other examples – 48% of her capital formation in 1901–11 came from abroad – Canada absorbed the vast sums invested, even those of the last four years of peace, and began her heavy repayments, without much strain.[40]

The fact that investment took the form of irregular bouts tells us something about the typical investor: Its bandwagon characteristics of an alternation of optimism and pessimism suggest that significant proportions of investors seemed to act in imitative emotion, driven by ignorance and the hope for a quick killing, rather than by a balancing of known marginal differences in the returns, as is assumed by theory.[41] This is rather surprising. True, Postan's 'pure' investor[42] was becoming more familiar among the middle classes in our period, and the proportion of investors in the population was rising: there may have been 300,000 of them by 1914. Nevertheless, only the very rich held a large proportion of their assets in the form of securities, and among them, in the riskier 'strategic' growth industries. About half the stock-exchange securities held at death were found in fortunes over £50,000. It appears further that the middle classes and the females had a slight preference for home firms, while elite investors (who held about half the shares) tended to opt more for foreign securities, and 'retired, deceased and unknown' for the Empire.[43] Would these people have invested at home, had capital exports been limited?

There is one final item of information which may be derived from the data. It is the tendency for an annual stream of foreign investments to set in motion a contrary movement of dividend and interest payments and loan service charges which then grow with the power of compound interest. It is not difficult to show how soon, on given assumptions as to interest rates, amortization, if any, and servicing charges, a given annual stream of foreign investments will be overtaken by the contrary stream of payments due, or, alternatively, by how much the investment stream has to grow to match or keep ahead of the reverse flow.[44] Sooner or later, unless the foreign debt is to grow to infinity, the

[39] Ferns (1960); Ferns (1950–1), 203–18; Ford (1956) and Ford (1971); Lewis (1983); Crohn (1915), 231–3, 249; Rippy (1959), 159 ff; Joslin (1963), 100; Iversen (1967), 424–58.
[40] Viner (1924); Islam (1960); Simon (1970) III, 238–54; Cairncross (1953), ch. 3; Meier (1953); Paterson (1974), 26–7; Iversen (1967), 381–400.
[41] Lewis (1957), 583 and Lewis (1978a), 180; Balogh (1982), 22–3; note 83 below.
[42] Postan (1935), 7; also p. 100 below.
[43] Hall (1963), 38–54; Michie (1981b), 147, 157; Kennedy and Britton (1984), 35; *Economist* (1.2.1868) in Platt (1984), 178; Davis and Huttenback (1982), 129; Martins (1980), 267–9; Moss (1983), 67, 69.
[44] Leary (1945), 686; Hinshaw (1945), 666–7; Mikesell (1968), 108 ff; Salant (1950), 505–7; Domar (1950), 806–8; Kindleberger (1958), 265–7 and Kindleberger (1968), 381–5, 395.

repayments will exceed the new capital raised, and – unless there is repudiation of the debt – the capital exporter will become a net capital importer, or rather a net recipient of unrequited payments.

This had, in fact, been the position reached by the United Kingdom by the beginning of our period, as is shown by the statement in Table 2.6.

Table 2.6 *Unrequited foreign payments, United Kingdom, 1855–1913[45] (£ million current or market prices. Totals for 5- or 4-year periods)*

	Net foreign lending[+]	Net funds taken by emigrants	Net property income from abroad	Property income from abroad plus taxes paid by non-residents	British transfers abroad[++]	
					A + B − C	A + B − D
	A	B	C	D	E	F
1855–9	135	7	77		65	
1860–4	106	6	104		8	
1865–9	232	8	143		87	
1870–4	392	10	227	243	175	159
1875–9	152	4	281	301	− 125	− 145
1880–4	273	10	311	334	− 28	− 51
1885–9	402	8	396	426	14	− 16
1890–4	349	5	471	506	− 117	− 152
1895–9	222	3	491	529	− 266	− 304
1900–4	172	5	544	592	− 367	− 415
1905–9	663	8	710	786	− 39	− 115
1910–3	815	10	734	819	91	6

[+] Current balance minus net additions to bullion, from Imlah
[++] A minus sign means a net inward payment

Minor items such as bullion movements, payments sent back by emigrants, or taxes paid by non-residents are not fully included but make little difference: nor would a rearrangement of the years into investment cycles rather than the rather artificial one of five years periods (*not* annual averages) adopted here. Column 'E' and 'F', representing alternative methods of calculating net capital movements, show clearly that British *net* lending came to an end after the capital export boom of the early 1870s. Before that watershed, there was still a substantial capital export in the peak phases, and only in the troughs (e.g. 1860–64) was there a rough balance. Thereafter the whole band within which the fluctuation took place shifted to the other side of the dividing line. Rough balances were achieved only in peak periods of investment abroad (1885–89 and 1905–13), while for the rest of the time the inflow regularly exceeded the outflow.

To put it another way, the United Kingdom had ceased in our period to be a net lender, and was living on the returns from earlier lendings out of which, in macro-economic terms, new loans were financed though not necessarily by the same individuals. This is sometimes referred to as a revolving fund, the sums coming in being recycled into fresh capital exports, or as 'secondary' or 'negative' capital exports, whereas 'primary' or 'positive' ones are those derived from a current trading surplus.[46] Even in the decades before 1870, a large part

[45] Based on Imlah (1958), 72–5; Feinstein (1972), T.10, 11, 37, 38; Edelstein (1982), 313–3.
[46] Ford (1962), 64; Imlah (1952/53), 222; Arndt (1915), 6–7; also p. 109 below.

of the new claims accumulated abroad had been paid for by inward flows of dividends and interest, resting on still earlier investments. If we trace the whole profitable series to its origins, we find that it started with very small sums indeed, some of which were, in fact, commercial, short-term credits to foreigners, which set the whole cumulative growth process going. Britain's rentier position at the end of Victoria's reign thus derives ultimately from the advantage of her early start in the industrialization process.

Curiously, much of the argument has ignored all this and has been conducted throughout as though it was the United Kingdom which had to find resources out of current production and sales to sustain the capital account,[47] and has therefore missed the real problems of the British economy. Others saw the issues clearly enough, especially the fact that without further foreign investment the net inward payments would have been even larger. The recipients of British capital, needless to stress, were never in any doubt that the net financial flow to them was limited in time, and was soon followed by a net outflow.[48] Moreover, while the capital received by the overseas countries depended to some extent on the capricious preferences of British investors, on the attractions of other markets, on the state of prosperity in Britain herself and on many other incalculable factors, and was therefore variable and uncertain, the income payments flowing into Britain were relatively stable, being to a large extent made up of fixed and guaranteed interest and/or amortization payments, they formed a legal obligation on the payers, and, as Table 2.6, columns C and D demonstrate, they showed a seemingly inexorable and even accelerating upward trend.

It is therefore easy to understand why the citizens of the borrowing countries felt that it was they who bore the burden of trade cycles and of other fluctuations within the British economy, which Britain could so easily transfer abroad. Others were also less impressed than was the City establishment with the gold standard, or the skill with which the Bank of England allegedly maintained it, as causes for the general equilibrium in which London found itself before 1914. They were more keenly aware that at any point in time, given the normal balance of trade and of services, the rest of the world had inescapable and regular payments to make to London, whereas British citizens had to requite these only when they deemed the circumstances favourable and these might include the British propensity to save, and investment alternatives at home. But in times of stress, 'the foreign borrower was in the first line of the Bank of England's defence'.[49] Further, in addition to the annual credits due to Britain on capital account, London derived further strength from its position as the leading market for gold, for commodities and for money, from the position of sterling as a reserve currency in third countries (though this derived in part from Britain's position as a lender), and from the monopsonistic power of Britain as a leading buyer of many goods entering international trade.

---

[47] Matthews, Feinstein and Odling-Smee (1982), 164, 356, 442, 455; Keynes (1971), 54–5; Hobson (1914), 4, 204.
[48] Nor was Great Britain in the days when she was a net borrower herself; Tucker (1960), 14. Also see Rosenberg (1961), 94 ff; Pamuk (1984), 102–5; Ford (1962), 102–5; among others.
[49] Lewis (1978a), 57, 179; de Cecco (1974), 122, 187; Keynes (1930 II), 307; Keynes (1978), XVIII, 261–2; for a contrary view see Williams (1968), 279; Ford (1958/9), 302.

Needless to stress, an overall balance for Britain did not necessarily mean a balance with every other country individually. There still had to be switches between countries with a negative capital account with Britain, and those with a positive balance,[50] but the burden of this adjustment did not fall on Britain. Even so, the capital payments in both directions formed no self-evident balancing item, and since there was no other in sight, the totals of the in-payments and out-payments could come out right, at the end of the day – or at the end of the year – seemingly only by miraculous coincidence. The mechanism by which the total balance was achieved will be discussed below.

If the gap was small, however, it might be bridged by short-term lending. The former view that Britain was a net creditor also in the area of short-term credit has recently been questioned,[51] but it is not necessary to go to the opposite extreme and assume that Britain was a permanent debtor on short-term capital account. Rather does it seem likely, especially in view of the volatile nature of the deposits of foreign banks held in London, that the balance shifted back and forth, as a truly balancing item in world trading and payments.[52] Short-term credit cannot, therefore, be said to have contributed much to the easy position of sterling among the world's currencies. The long-term capital position would seem to have been a far more consistent bulwark in that regard, and, in turn, it enjoyed that position because of the accumulated claims for interest and dividend payments on account of earlier investments, rather than because of any net 'primary' foreign investments made in our period.

II Preliminary Theoretical Considerations

It must be evident that the annual transactions on capital account of that magnitude, even if we accept Platt's downward corrections, will have had a considerable impact on the British economy. This impact will have been all the greater for the wide fluctuations in the magnitude and direction of the capital exports. Were they operating in a beneficial sense on British economic growth and welfare, or were they holding them back? Was 'too much' capital exported? The answers to these questions, it should be noted, might be given in relation to very short-term effects, for example, on the terms of trade; in relation to medium-term effects, say over five to 10 years; or in relation to long-term growth. These have sometimes been confused or conflated, and it is not impossible that the answers might differ according to which time horizon we adopt.

Much practical common-sense opinion at the time was in no doubt. It considered it to be self-evident that it was better to use capital at home, employing British labour and developing the home economy, rather than do

[50] Neisser (1929), 198; Nurkse (1961); 11; Tinbergen (1951), 84; Saul (1980), 8; Viner (1924), 280–1.
[51] This belief was held by Keynes and MacMillan Committee. Also see Tomlinson (1981), 39; Chapman (1984), Ch. 1, 2 and 7; Lindert (1969), 16–27, 37.
[52] Bloomfield (1963), 71–3; Wright (1981) suppl., 287; Edelstein (1982), 19.

the same for our competitors, who might then use cheap labour and undercut British sales. Capital exports, further, would also weaken the balance of payments.

Such sentiments were expressed during a remarkable debate in the House of Lords in 1909 by, among others, Viscount Goschen and Lords Rothschild and Revelstoke.[53] They used it as a stick with which to beat Lloyd George's budget, declaring that 'socialistic' measures were driving capital out of the country in search of a more favourable climate – no doubt to the astonishment of at least some of their listeners who were well aware that the families of these three peers had become exceedingly rich precisely by exporting British capital. The phenomenon they described was later dubbed by Keynes 'flight of capital' and became important in the inter-war years in fact and in theory. Nurkse tried to give the concept scientific clarity by describing it as the export of capital from high-yield to low-yield areas because of fears for the security of the principal.[54]

The underlying assumption was clearly that there existed an overall shortage of capital: capital was a scarce resource, and what was sent out to benefit the foreigner would be missed here. There was no need for sophisticated theory for such a view, and it was held by many practical persons.

The opposite view was also defended by Lord Rothschild. As he reminded the House, even his grandfather had believed, and had explained as early as 1815, that capital exports were fruitful, leading to the export of capital goods and returning in the form of specie and other imports.[55] Moreover, it was to be assumed that capital was sent abroad because it received a higher return there, and by finding the highest rate of return for his own capital, the investor also achieved the best return for society. Had more been invested at home, the yield would have been less, and national income lower.

This, in principle, was the view also of basic neoclassical economic theory. According to its assumptions, capital will be sent abroad if, and only if, the expected returns abroad are higher than the expected returns at home. This has even been called the 'normal' case of capital transfer, every other set of circumstances to be termed 'abnormal'.[56] If investors' expectations are realistic and the total returns from the factors of production will be increased, the export of capital will have enlarged the national cake – though there will be changes in the distribution of incomes. Private and national interests coincide. Capital exports in the period 1870–1914 were a method of enlarging the national income of the United Kingdom and/or increasing the rate of growth of the economy; on the Harvard definition of capital, they may also be said to have enlarged the national capital.[57]

Conversely, to have abstained from foreign investment would have lowered the returns on domestic capital. With an additional £3½ billion placed at home,

---

[53] Hansard (1909) IV, Lords 29.11.1909, col. 1155; 30.11.1909, col. 1277. Also Hirst (1928), 138–9; Offer (1983), 120–1.

[54] Harrod (1951), 346; Nurkse (1935), 28 ff; Fanno (1939), 49 ff; Crotty (1983), 59–65.

[55] Hansard (Lords) 1909 IV, 29.11.1909; col. 1155.

[56] Fanno (1939), 9. For literature see Caves (1960), ch. 5; also, Müller (1947), 153 ff; Iversen (1967), 157–60. The Treasury, with proper orthodoxy, considered in 1919 that the right method to stop capital being invested abroad was to raise the interest rate at home: Howson (1974), 95.

[57] Clarke (1978), 320; Gray (1972), 41–4; Pigou (1952), 662; Solow (1971a), essay 1.

argued C.K. Hobson, interest rates would have been driven down to a point at which total savings would have diminished and people would have spent more. There would therefore have been less capital altogether to benefit the nation. What, asked Russell Rea in a memorable debate in the House of Commons in 1909, would we have done with all this money?

> We have built a vast and profitable system of railways in the Argentine. Would my hon. Friend have preferred to duplicate the Great Western system? In the one case we get a good return for our money, in the other we should simply have destroyed a good property.

More recently, McCloskey has put forward the same view in almost identical terms:

> By keeping savings at home', he mocked, 'the British people could have had two Forth Bridges, two Bakerloo Lines, two London housing stocks, two Port Sunlights.[58]

The argument is overdrawn, for instead of duplicating existing utilities, the building of a Severn bridge, a Humber bridge and a Victoria line, not to mention slum clearance in London, some 60 or 70 years earlier than was in fact the case, would not have been totally wasted and might have done a great deal of good. Yet the basic idea is sound enough. Curiously, the neoclassical position is in this respect tending in the same direction as its sharpest critics, the Chamberlain imperialists on the one hand, the Marxists and the under-consumptionists of the school of J.A. Hobson on the other. Rosa Luxemburg held the Marxist view in perhaps its most extreme form, believing that without the escape route of foreign investment, the falling rate of profit in the advanced capitalist countries would have led to their early collapse.[59] Rostow and other Keynesians held a not dissimilar view, at least about the Great Depression: according to Rostow, it might be entitled 'what happened when the foreign railways were built'.[60] The underlying fear of too much capital, contained in the neoclassical approach, is however in remarkable contrast to its alleged basic philosophy, which is that of relative scarcity. It is the opposite view, that British capital exports were harmful, which rests on the notion of capital scarcity.

The neoclassical conclusion depends on a large number of assumptions:
1 All economic units are profit or income maximizers.
2 There is perfect competition in factor and product markets, and, in particular, factors are paid exactly the value of their marginal productivity.
3 Production functions are all linear and homogeneous to the first degree: there are constant costs everywhere and therefore no economies of scale.
4 There are no costs of transport.
5 Risk or uncertainty may be ignored.

[58] Hobson (1914), 37; McCloskey (1979), 539; also McCloskey (1981), 149; Hansard (Commons), 17 March 1909, col. 1164.
[59] Hobson (1911), 50, 84–5, 143 and Hobson (1968), 82–3; Luxemburg (1913); Fieldhouse (1966), 253–4; Mommsen (1979), 90, 105, 238; Parrini and Sklar (1983), 559–78.
[60] Rostow (1948), 88, also 67–85 and Rostow (1951–2), 64–6; Lewis (1978a), 30, 37, 51; Cairncross (1953), 9, 187–8.

6   A diminishing marginal product of capital is the rule. This contains the further implicit assumptions that capital is homogeneous and perfectly divisible.

7   Dynamic effects, particularly changes in technology and those derived from entrepreneurship, can be ignored. There is also the assumption that after a disturbance the system will return to a previously predictable equilibrium.

8   There is a full-employment equilibrium; this includes an invariant labour supply in the lending and borrowing country, and the assumption that the capital exported will be at the expense of home investment.

9   There are no transfer costs. The gold standard ensures stable exchange rates, there are no changes in the velocity of circulation of money and the balance of payments can be maintained without friction.

10 The terms of trade remain unchanged.

11 There is perfect knowledge. This, as we shall see, has different implication from the 'no risk' assumption 5.

12 The incidence of taxation can be ignored.

13 The debate can be conducted entirely at the macro level, without considering the type of capital investment or the country to which it goes.

In practice, of course, none of these conditions applies in full, and several are totally unrealistic. Even the first, which seems plausible, has met with some scepticism if applied to the British overseas investor in our period.[61] The next three were obviously not met. The others and their consequences will, directly or indirectly, form the subject of the remainder of this chapter. They are not without controversy and complexity, but it may be of assistance in the pages which follow, to bear two major considerations in mind which run through practically every issue: (1) Did investors act in their own best interests, at least if defined in terms of income maximization, and (2) Was the private interest identical with the social, in this case national, interest similarly defined? These are two separate questions, though they are interrelated. While these are not the only issues involved, they will help to clarify the discussion.

Before turning to that discussion, it will be best to clear three further points out of the way. The first is the widespread fallacy, that investment at home is preferable on the grounds that it furnishes incomes to British labour and perhaps land, while in investment abroad, only British capital gains an income, the wages, rents, etc. going to foreigners. Thus according to Andrew Shonfield, if we take the accepted capital-output ratio of 3 as our guide, every pound invested at home will raise national income by 33p. a year, whereas if invested abroad, at current rates, it is not likely to bring in more than 10%, or 10p. a year; unless the foreign investment could approach the 33% figure, it was less beneficial to the nation than home investment. Lewis, using late-Victorian figures, made the difference even larger: 'The capital-output ratio at home was only 3½ to 1, compared with returns of 20 to 1 for foreign investment'.[62] The fallacy rests in forgetting that the higher return at home was achieved only by

[61] Michie (1979), 158–9; Jones (1980), 152.
[62] Shonfield (1958), 111; Lewis (1957), 578; and in almost similar terms, Comments by Branco Horvat, to Kafka (1970), 235.

the co-operation of other factors of production, whose reward would have to be deducted before isolating, and arriving at the contribution of the capital alone. However, the matter is more complex than this. As Murphy noted,

there is something 'real' in the fear that when a nation's potential capital is invested abroad, the domestic factors, labour and land, are being denied something which would complement their productivity.[63]

Some of what they were being denied, the dynamic provided by new investment, is discussed below. Moreover, if we make the realistic assumption of some unemployment, then the comparison between 33% at home and 10% abroad is valid: the difference 'is the income earned by the previously under- or unused land and labour'.[64] If home unemployment had been caused in part by high wages maintained by trade unions, the gains from home investment would be particularly high.[65] Unemployment will be discussed further below, but here we might note also the widespread agreement that capital exports will keep wages down.[66]

The second point refers to a special case which works in the opposite direction. If a great deal of one country's capital is already in one country abroad, the yield on that capital will be reduced by further foreign lending, thus, unlike the home situation, benefiting only foreign labour and other cooperating factors. Nor is this case fanciful. In his famous memorandum to the Tsar in 1899, Sergei Witte reported that precisely this had happened in Russia, where 'foreign capitalists who have already obtained an advantageous place in Russian industry join in . . . heart-rending complaint (about the influence of foreign capital) and thus try and guard their monopolistic profits'. Unless the capital exporter is a monopolist who owns all the capital already abroad and will therefore take its declining returns into account, there will be a clear divergence between the private and the national interest, as the new investment, while getting its marginal return, pulls down the national average of the foreign holdings. However, if there had been unemployment abroad, the marginal returns of capital there might not be driven down by the new investment; if the capital had been unemployed at home, its export might not be at the expense of home investment, and might thus be pure gain. The actual result, as Jasay has shown in his classical study, is entirely indeterminate. There is the further consideration that even if the lending country abstains from lending abroad in order not to drive down the rate of return on the capital already there, someone else might do so, gaining all the advantages and leaving the losses to one's own investors.[67]

Our third preliminary point is a *caveat*. It would be wrong, though not entirely unreasonable[68] to see in these diametrically opposed views a clash between more or less abstract thought, theoreticians favouring large capital

[63] Murphy (1960/61), 14.
[64] Kindleberger (1964), 37.
[65] Simpson (1962), 424–5; Hobson (1911), 79–81. Also pp. 84–6 below.
[66] The modern view is the opposite: capital exports under unemployment create employment in the same way as home investment. Gutman (1956), 535; Hinshaw (1945), 661–2.
[67] Witte (1954), 69, also 71; Mikesell (1968), 220; Simpson (1962), 513; Jasay (1972), 120–7.
[68] Balogh and Streeten (1960), 213.

exports, pragmatists deploring them. The fact is that there were also numerous practical men supporting foreign investment; while as we shall see, there is large body of refined theory coming to opposite conclusions. Indeed, anything beyond the most crude schematic thought must very quickly come to recognize that any cost-benefit analysis of foreign investment in this period has to be resolved into a number of separate issues, which may yield divergent and uncertain results. To these we must now turn.

III The Risk Factor

The debate of home versus foreign investment has turned largely on the rate of return as modified by risk and possibly marketability. This section is concerned with the issue of risk, which has been subject to not a little confusion.

There is no shortage of data on returns, though some series are patchy. Much of the earlier debate used the data collected by Nash, Lehfeldt, Flux and Paish before 1914; more recently, we have had the splendid work of Edelstein and of Davis and Huttenback to draw on.[69] It is their interpretation which has caused difficulties.

A priori one would expect rates of return to bear some relation to the risk factor. Thus one would expect preference shares to pay more than debentures and ordinary shares to pay more than preference shares in the same or comparable firms, and similarly, one would expect gilt-edged securities to pay the lowest rates of all. The expected yield would be reflected in the rate at which securities would be offered to the market when new, or at which they would change hands, once they had begun to pay dividends or interest. Similarly, one would expect that foreign assets of a similar type would have to offer more than home assets to tempt the British investor, and that colonial securities would lie somewhere between the two, while foreign countries and colonies themselves would be staggered in some sort of order according to the risk factor involved.[70]

Some of these expectations were borne out by the facts. There was a gap, estimated by Lehfeldt at an average of 1.06% in 1914, between the rates at which larger firms and otherwise similar smaller firms could borrow. According to Dudley Baxter, the rates at which foreign and colonial governments might borrow in London in 1873 were as follows:

Great Britain and Denmark	3%
India, Canada, Australasia, Sweden, Netherlands, Belgium, German States	4
USA	5.1
Russia, France	5.3
Argentina	6.3
Portugal	6.7
Austria	7.5

[69] Edelstein (1982); Lehfeldt (1914), 432–5; Lehfeldt (1915), 452; Feis (1965), 4; Paish (1909); Davis and Huttenback (1982), 119–30; and Davis and Huttenback (1986).
[70] Edelstein (1982), 122 ff; Edelstein (1974), 981; Kamarck (1970), 72–3; Iversen (1967), 96–103; Mikesell (1971), 35.

Spain   16.5
Honduras   66

Honduras had evidently become the 'lemon' for which there is ultimately no market at all. Similarly, the number of years' purchase to be paid for fixed-interest state securities in 1904 ranged from 13.8 years for Greece to 35.2 for Great Britain.[71]

As these criteria, including location, risk, size and marketability to a large extent cancelled out in practice, foreign assets (high) consisting largely of Government loans or railway debentures (low), actual rates showed no neat orderly sequence. Here, for example, are returns on some investments listed in 1881:[72]

British Government and bank stock   3.67%
Home railways   4.375
Indian Government and railways   4.444
Colonial Governments   4.828
Colonial and foreign railways   5.0
Home gas and water companies   7.857
Home banks   12.0
Home insurance companies   20.0

Meaningful results could be obtained only if like were compared with like, that is to say the location factor of home and abroad would have to be compared for each type of security separately. The latest attempts to do this are those of Edelstein and of Davis and Huttenback.[73] In order to meet some of the objections raised against earlier results, Edelstein sought to eliminate the risk factor from his large sample of 566 securities after comparing their actual realized returns, price-deflated, with their market values and including capital gains and losses. The resulting 'Risk-Adjusted, Realized Returns', for all securities studied over the whole period 1870–1913 were as in Table 2.7 (in %):[74]

Table 2.7 'Risk-adjusted' realized returns, aggregate indices, 1870–1913

		Actual return	Modified by 'risk premium'	Deviation still left
A	Domestic			
	1. Equity	6.61	1.98	−1.73
	2. Preference	4.23	−1.89	−0.24
	3. Debenture	3.35	−2.03	−0.98
	Total	4.52	−0.75	−1.09
B	Nondomestic			
	1. Equity	8.66	2.06	0.24
	2. Debenture	4.49	−1.99	0.57
	Total	5.81	−1.04	0.49

[71] Platt (1984), 177; Akerlof (1970), 488–500; Lehfeldt (1915), 453; Waltershausen (1907), 38–9, also 31–2.
[72] Calculated from Nash (1881), 116; Hobson (1914), 144–5; also Imlah (1958), 61.
[73] Edelstein (1982); Davis and Huttenback (1986); Lehfeldt (1915); Cairncross (1953), 227–31; Feis (1965), 4; Salter (1951), 5; Royal Institute of International Affairs (1937), 118–19; Emmanuel (1971), 43–4.
[74] Based on Edelstein (1982), 139.

The overall average being 6.36%, home securities fetched 1.09% less than might have been expected; foreign and colonial fetched 0.49% more. This made a total difference of 1.58%, too large, according to Edelstein, to be accidental. The difference, it appears from the right-hand column, runs right across all categories. This result, confirming earlier, less sophisticated calculations,[75] allows the neoclassical school to claim that since foreign investment yielded a higher return than home, the nation profited by the foreign investment undertaken in 1870–1914.

Yet the table proves too much, for having eliminated the risk element, the neoclassics were now left with the awkward task of explaining the remaining alleged difference. Why did investors not equalize the marginal returns at home and abroad by continuing to invest abroad to the point when home and foreign yields were equal? Was it because of ignorance about the opportunities abroad, which has often been postulated[76], or irrational prejudice as expected by Ricardo or, as Edelstein offered, the tendency for foreign investment to generate more growth, or more monopoly profit than anticipated, which would be another version of ignorance? The trouble with all these explanations is that they must deny one of or other of the basic conditions of the neoclassical theorem, namely income maximization or perfect knowledge. The neoclassical claim that the historical data provide proof of the assertion that Britain benefited by investment abroad, can thus be maintained only at the price of rejecting one or other of its own key assumptions.

Moreover, there are problems in accepting the figures on capital yields themselves as they stand, even in their latest form as presented by Edelstein. To begin with, he took market values, whereas in our quest for the alternative use of capital, the appropriate sum against which to measure the returns obtained should be the capital actually invested, i.e. net issue price, plus profits ploughed back. Edelstein's principle of taking market prices abstracts from precisely the relevant relationship. White, it is interesting to note, used issue prices for France, which are a better approximation, and Davis and Huttenback used book values instead.[77]

More serious even than the capital yields used in each individual case is the problem of their averaging. The averages hide enormous differences in the returns on individual shares or bonds, not only in absolute terms, but in the direction of their movements. No one who has actually studied a number of series of returns from investments in that period can feel very confident that averages can be meaningful or, for that matter, that investors were rational.

Table 2.8 shows a typical selection of returns, being themselves already averages of many securities, and of several years in each of the main swings of cycles, which would have given each figure a strong tendency towards the middle:[78]

[75] Field (1983), 424; Nurkse (1961), 12; Richardson (1972), 99; Cottrell (1980), 182.
[76] Murphy (1960–1), 17; Kemp (1964), 201; Hobson (1914), 38; Keynes (1971), 48.
[77] Davis and Huttenback (1986), 79; White (1933), 271–2; Edelstein (1982), 114; Lewchuk (1985), 5–6.
[78] Edelstein (1982), 153; Kennedy (1973/74), 432; Lewis (1983), 199; Frankel (1965), 429; Paish (1911), 68; Viner (1924), 98; Paterson (1976), 89.

Table 2.8 Realized rates of return, in long-swing highs and lows, sample of equities

	1870–6	1877–86	1887–96	1897–1909	1910–13
Home railways	11.19	5.19	6.87	−0.83	1.51
Home electrical equipment	− 1.32	18.98	4.44	4.73	2.90
Latin American railways	5.74	18.72	3.81	8.14	1.60
Indian railways	5.46	8.22	6.46	1.48	3.94

What possible value can an averaging out of these series over the whole period (let alone of the original data of the annual returns of individual railway companies, etc.) have, to two decimal places? There is not even any consistency in these results: it will be observed that the nearest congruence is between home electrical equipment makers and Latin American railways, which common sense will reject, even if an econometric link might be 'proved'.

Moreover, there is in fact a bias in these sets of returns. For there was, not entirely surprisingly, a strong tendency for home returns to exceed the returns on similar investments abroad in the home-investment phases of the long swing, and conversely for foreign returns to exceed home yields in the capital-export phases. In the other major modern enquiry, the Davis and Huttenback study, the results worked out as follows:[79]

Table 2.9 Excess of the rates of return of certain types of foreign/empire firms over United Kingdom firms, % *

	Adjusted equity		All claims on capital	
	Foreign	Empire	Foreign	Empire
1860–4	10.0	13.9	4.2	6.7
1865–9	2.7	4.3	− 0.2	4.9
1870–4	− 0.8	− 3.2	− 0.4	1.2
1875–9	− 2.2	16.3	− 1.2	6.9
1880–4	− 5.1	− 2.2	− 2.6	0
1885–9	− 0.5	− 3.5	0.1	− 2.7
1890–4	− 4.5	− 5.3	− 2.2	− 3.2
1895–9	− 5.3	− 5.5	− 3.9	− 3.8
1900–4	− 2.7	− 4.5	− 2.1	− 3.1
1905–9	0.8	− 1.0	0.3	0.1
1910–2	5.5	− 0.9	1.3	0.4
Actual rates:				
Average	12.5	13.7	5.0	6.3
1860–84	15.1	19.9	5.8	9.7
1885–1912	10.1	8.1	5.3	3.3

* A minus sign means that the United Kingdom rate of return was higher. The percentages are on the capital, not on the rates themselves. Thus the difference between 5% at home and 6% abroad would be 1%, *not* 20%.

It is clear that there was no consistently higher yield abroad than at home, and that by choosing the right period of years, one could easily determine whether the 'average' would show that foreign investments in firms brought higher returns, or the opposite. Cairncross, in fact, using Paish's figures, concluded

[79] Davis and Huttenback (1986); Davis and Huttenback (1982), 125.

that, like for like, foreign returns were lower if Consols were omitted. In the debate following the reading of the Davis and Huttenback paper, Edelstein could do no better than throw doubt on the figures themselves, though his own study showed the same cyclical alternation of excess and deficiency on equity shares. Foreign 'debentures' always remained higher than home, but the difference had narrowed to a negligible 0.06% of the geometric mean by 1910–13.[80]

Apart from the Kuznets cycle, there was also a longer swing, known as the Kondratieff cycle in which all returns to capital fell from a peak in the early 1870s to a nadir in 1896–97 (though Lehfeldt's lowest returns actually occurred in 1901), after which they rose again to 1913. Since foreign and colonial yields tended to fluctuate more than home returns, the gap between them declined to the late 1890s and then tended to widen again.[81] This widening of the scissors, accompanied as it was by an improvement in the risk factor, or at least a greater feeling of security on the part of investors in foreign assets, led to a remarkable rise in the market value of foreign securities as against British in the years before the war, which forms part of the explanation for the foreign-investment boom of that phase. As Table 2.9 shows, all overseas returns were higher before 1884 than after.

The difficulties of disentangling risk from all the other elements that go into returns, like marketability, the methods and terms of capital repayment, etc., are thus considerable. But beyond them there still remains a doubt whether Edelstein's method of 'eliminating' risk to arrive at 'pure' return is wholly appropriate. This method, which is one favoured by several economists, measures the 'risk' by the variation of actual returns about the mean over the years.[82] In other words, the more the returns have actually varied from year to year, the 'riskier' the asset. However, there are problems with this approach.

Firstly, it is unclear whether investors considering whether, say, to buy shares in an American silver mine would look to variance in the sense of the fluctuations of year-by-year returns of any given mine, or to the variance in results, over the years, between the best and worst silver mines. Probably both should have been taken as a measure of riskiness, but were not.

Secondly, the correlation of high risks with high returns has only limited validity. Beyond a certain point, as any lottery proves, investors actually prefer high risks to the point of being willing to accept even an averaged negative return, provided the prizes for the winners are high enough. At least some observers thought the Victorian investor 'foolhardy rather than over-cautious', and Clapham has spoken of his gambling instinct.[83] There have certainly been numerous investments made abroad which can have no other explanation.

Thirdly, there is an important difference between *ex-ante* and *ex-post*, and between the private and the social return, in this context. Society will gain *ex-*

[80] Cairncross (1953), 227 and comments on Huttenback, 131–2; Edelstein (1982), 148; for a critique of Edelstein's figures see Kennedy (1976), 175.

[81] Lehfeldt (1913), 201; Edelstein (1982), 69, 327, note 2; Davis and Huttenback (1986), 121–3; Harley (1977), 70–3.

[82] Lintner (1965a), 14–16; Lintner (1965b), 588; Sharpe (1964), 428; Edelstein (1982), 131 ff; Edelstein (1976), 300–4.

[83] Michie (1981b), 156 and Michie (1981a), 249–50; Clapham (1963), III, 5. Also see p. 68, notes 41–3 above.

post by having made riskier investments if their average return, as is the assumption throughout, is higher at the end of the day than the *ex-post* average of the safer asset. Insofar as the uncertain industrial investments were mostly made at home, while the fixed-interest type of gilt-edged security prevailed abroad – Coppock's fixed 5% abroad compared with the 'real' 11% at home – there was likely to have been 'too much' foreign investment.

Fourthly, the criterion of variability, useful though it might be to a modern stockbroker, does not capture fully the uncertainties of overseas investment in our period. The risks which investors were afraid of were not so much variations about a mean, provided the mean itself was satisfactory, but the loss of the asset or of a large part of its value altogether. Edelstein does, in fact, consider defaults abroad not to have been any more prevalent than at home, and Shannon's study of joint-stock companies established in 1856–65 tends to bear him out.[84] It found that of British joint-stock companies launched there were left, after three years.

All companies:	46.1%
All colonial companies	47.1%
All foreign companies	35.6%

However, given that more overseas companies were in the more stable categories, like railways or banks, they should have shown better results, and it is likely that the Victorian investor underestimated the risks of total default abroad, especially on the part of Governments which created no real assets out of which to pay interest and amortization. The memory of earlier disasters, like the defaults by Central American states in the early 1870s soon paled, and one or two countries were disciplined, one or two even annexed in order to ensure the kind of stability that would allow the foreign investors to get their interest paid.[85] But the massive discrimination and chicanery against foreigners which became common after 1918 were not foreseen, and thus the risks of foreign investment in such countries as Turkey, Mexico and Russia were under-estimated. Once more, 'too much' was invested abroad. At the same time, as Keynes maintained, the support for colonial Government loans meant that 'too much' was invested there also.[86] Moreover, as he was to argue in 1924, in case of default, the loss abroad was total, whereas at home it was likely that the real assets such as houses, factories or the Underground system, would remain to benefit the nation even after they had bankrupted their first owners.[87] This also meant that there had been 'too much' capital exported.

To sum up: the balance of this debate on the risk element is uncertain, since several of the factors discussed here might work in either direction. Nevertheless, the general impression tends in the direction of 'too much', rather than the 'correct', quantity of foreign investment.

[84] Shannon (1932), 422; Edelstein (1982), 67, 128–30 and in Floud and McCloskey (1981), 184–5.
[85] Hobson (1914), 25; Foreman-Peck (1983a), 134.
[86] Keynes (1930), 276 and 'Foreign Investment and National Advantage' in *Collected Works*, XVIII (1981), 279; Lindert and Morton (1987).
[87] Keynes (1981), 282–3. Edelstein does not fully succeed in dealing with this effect, in Floud and McCloskey (1981), 84.

IV Capital Divisibility and Dynamics

We now turn to examine the sixth and seventh assumptions listed above, namely a diminishing marginal product together with the homogeneity and divisibility of capital, and the assumption that dynamic effects can be ignored.

Much of the debate assumes a diminishing marginal product of capital without further discussion. In Hicks' formulation:

> Other things beeing equal, the marginal efficiency of capital will be lower the greater the amount of capital goods already possessed.[88]

If true, it would mean that a substantial diversion of funds from foreign to home investment would have lowered the returns on home capital.

Capital, however, does not come in homogeneous and easily divisible form as assumed by neoclassical theory. On the contrary it tends to be highly specific and to appear in large lumps. Existing capital is, in addition, often firmly fixed to the ground. Nor can capital be 'stretched over' or combined with an infinite amount of labour. Finally, time is a key element in its valuation, while the mere effluxion of time makes existing capital technically obsolete. Any theory of capital omitting any of these characteristics is likely to miss the proper function and consequences of capital investment.[89]

It may, in fact, well be the case, as stated by Hayek in a pioneer study, that 'an increase in the current output of capital goods will frequently have the effect not of lowering but of raising the future demand for investible funds, and therefore the rate of interest'. This is evidently so for that part of gross capital expenditure going on repair and maintenance, from the proverbial 'penny-worth of tar' to a reserve of spare capacity in an incipient boom.[90]

Such circumstances act particularly powerfully in social overhead capital. In the case of a half-built railway, for example, it is obvious that its completion will not lower, but raise the returns on the existing investment. More generally, almost any productive equipment may be capable of benefiting by extensions which will allow fuller use of existing capital. This is sometimes described as breaking a bottleneck[91] or, when it is internalized, as increasing returns or economies of scale. The denial or neglect of this effect is one of the gravest weaknesses of neoclassical economic theory.[92]

Changes in capital stock supply much of the dynamic of the growth of an economy. Thus a railway may lead to a land boom; or cheaper steel may reduce the costs of building, so that building expands, raising profits in steelmaking and expanding steel capacity again.

By the same token, however, the expansion of investment at home involves governments and local authorities in providing social overhead capital which

---

[88] Hicks (1936), 249; also see Blaug (1963), 20.

[89] Lachman (1947), 114; Fisher (1969); Robinson (1975), 177–8; Nicholas (1982b), 94; Solow (1971a), 26.

[90] Hayek (1937), 174; Nurkse (1933), 112; Machlup (1932), 513; Pethick-Lawrence (1904), 61–2; Kennedy (1976), 171; Streeten (1961), 127.

[91] Dunning (1972a), 124–31; Lachman (1947), 116–18 and Lachman (1948), 699, 704; Balogh and Streeten (1960), 217.

[92] Nicholas (1982b), 90–2; Sraffa (1926), 540–3; MacDougall (1966), 201.

the investor does not take into account, and which the foreign government would have had to provide, had the investment taken place abroad.[93]

Capital investment is, in the modern world, virtually the only way in which a new technology can be installed. It alone offers a chance to engineers, skilled workers and managers to keep their skills up to date. Capital diverted abroad, therefore, amounts to a critical loss of experience necessary for real cost reductions in the future. This is particularly damaging in the present context, for it may be assumed that 'technological progress acts to offset diminishing returns to the fastest growing factor'.[94]

It may well be asked why, if these profitable opportunities for installing improved technology existed at home, more of the investors, who may be assumed to be rational, did not choose to participate in the potential home boom, but invested abroad instead? There are several answers, but they all boil down to a gap between private and social returns and between internal and external economies. If the gains accrue only when large numbers of investors act simultaneously, the chances are that no single investor will act alone, since he will expect to bear the costs without reaping the benefits. In those conditions, the investment will not take place, and the gains to the nation will be lost.

Part of the argument will be familiar from the debate on whether it was, or was not, a disadvantage for Britain to have been a pioneer country and therefore to have become burdened with obsolete equipment, as against later comers who started with green-field sites and a clean slate. Those who thought the early start a handicap, developed the concept of 'interrelatedness', which made it uneconomic for the single entrepreneur to invest in better equipment, unless the others did likewise, whereas all would have benefited had they decided to do so simultaneously. The classic example of the inefficiently small coal trucks has been referred to above, chapter 1, p. 48.[95]

But beyond this, secondly, there lies the reality of business dynamics, and of the difference between the atmosphere and opportunities of lively, progressive and expanding markets, as against stagnant and conservative ones. In the literature this factor emerges in expressions like 'dynamism', 'engine of growth' or 'a major motor for productivity gains and innovation', the 'momentum of growth', the will to innovate, and the incentive to tackle structural change and defeat rigidities.[96] On the theoretical level there is the 'Verdoorn effect', i.e. the tendency for faster growth also to show faster productivity growth; output not traceable to increases in input; the benefits of 'learning by doing'; the opportunity of bringing non-industrial regions and provinces, and their under-used resources into play; or the recognition of entrepreneurship as a fourth factor of production, beside land, labour and capital,

[93] Balogh and Streeten (1960), 215; also Young (1928), 527–42; Kindleberger (1972), 394; Johnson (1972), 450–1; Murphy (1960/61).
[94] Blaug (1960), 505; Harcourt (1969), 388 ff; Kaldor (1957), 596.
[95] There is a large literature; e.g. Frankel (1955), 296–319; Lomax (1969), 14; Richardson (1965), 260–2; Dahmen (1963), 297–8. But see Ames and Rosenberg (1967), 363–82; Jervis (1947), 112–22; Salter (1960); Lewis (1970), 345.
[96] Streeten (1961), 87; Balogh and Streeten (1960), 216–17; Fisher (1969), 575; Lachman (1948), 705; Dunning (1970), 122; Murphy (1960–1), 11.

largely because it is responsible for innovations.[97]

A third aspect concerns the relative ease with which Britain escaped her failure to maintain her share against German and other competition in the most desirable markets, by retreating to the markets of the colonies and the under-developed regions of the world. The sequence of cause and effect here may be uncertain;[98] but it is at least arguable that more investment in new industries and especially in capital-goods industries would have enabled Britain to compete in Europe rather than rely on the old staple trades for the third-world markets.

All these factors together provide at least *prime facie* support for the case that the diversion of capital from investment abroad to equipping home industry, if done on a large enough scale, might have got Britain over the hump, and imparted enough drive to transform the whole of her economic atmosphere.[99]

All of this has been disputed. It has been argued that less investment abroad would not have led to more investment at home, but to its waste, to expenditure on welfare provisions and/or to a reduction in the propensity to save, thus slowing the general growth rate. McCloskey has taken an even stronger line, believing that there was no quantity of capital that could have altered the growth rate of the British economy, since the bottleneck lay in other resources which were already stretched to the full.[100]

Whether this be so or not, it is evident that the neoclassical doctrine of an inevitable decline in the rate of return on capital as more of it is invested at home is by no means universally valid. It depends on the unrealistic assumption of homogeneous and easily divisible capital and on the absence of external economies. Additionally, the possibility cannot be excluded that a large enough wave of domestic investment, achieved by diverting much of the capital exported to home use, might have generated market conditions for an altogether different rate of economic growth.

V Full Employment

The next assumption, that of the full employment of resources or a full employment equilibrium, has been referred to several times already. Unemployment has had to be ignored or denied[101] in order to maintain the theoretical framework of the neoclassical school.

Yet sizeable and highly fluctuating unemployment was a most obtrusive characteristic of the age. The best statistics of the unemployment of labour in our period were those derived from the trade unions of skilled workers. They registered averages of around 5%, fluctuating with the Juglar cycle between a maximum of 10% and a minimum of 2%, or virtually full employment. Given that unionized labour suffered less, the general average has to be increased by

---

97 Leibenstein (1966), 396; Pratten (1972), 185; Brown (1965), 56; Arrow (1969), 155–73; Frankel (1965), 413.
98 See the discussion in the introduction, p. xv above and Table 4.6 below.
99 Kennedy (1973/74), 412–14, 436–7; and Kennedy (1976), 176.
100 McCloskey (1970), 453–4.
101 McCloskey (1970), 448; McCloskey (1981), 123, 176; McCloskey (1970–1), 146.

1–2% to give an average of 6–7% unemployment for all full-time workers before the war.[102]

This does, however, still omit large pockets of part-time employment. Apart from the Mayhew type of people, and the potters, carriers and messengers with which the pre-motor city abounded, there were also expanding modern types of under-employed men. In England and Wales alone, for example, dock workers increased from 42,500 in 1881 to 88,600 in 1901, and it was these sorts of casuals, as Stedman Jones observed, rather than those in full-time employment in industries affected by the trade cycle, who troubled the Victorian conscience when it concerned itself with the unemployed.[103]

Would this or other spare labour have been enough to match up with large quantities of capital diverted from abroad? Clapham thought not:

> a relatively small diversion of resources from foreign to home investment would soon have wiped out the few per cent of extra unemployment in the building trade, if it had been directed toward them.

But against this, Bowley and Wood, in their classic studies, found that much of the rise in real wages in this period was accounted for precisely by the shift of workers from lower-paid to higher-paid occupations rather than by the rise in incomes of any given occupation. In any case, the total population of working age was still growing rapidly and could have reacted to new employment opportunities without the pains of readjustment.[104]

It is significant that the Fair Trade movement, like earlier protectionist propaganda, placed the provision of employment very high on its list of arguments. The protectionist authors of the Minority Report of the Royal Commission on the Depression of 1886, for example, feared that one effect of tariffs abroad and free imports at home

> is to encourage and lessen the investment of capital in the development of our agriculture and manufactures . . . This directly operates to limit the employment of labour in this country.

The main thing, Joseph Chamberlain told his listeners in his famous Glasgow speech of 6 October 1903, is

> to ensure full employment, continuous employment at fair wages; and if your employment is filched from you, you will be in the long run the greatest sufferers,

and again in 1905:

> Employment . . . has been the most important question of our time . . . it includes everything.

This line of argument was generally recognized to have provided one of his most powerful sources of popular appeal.[105] This would hardly have been the

---

[102] Beveridge (1944), 72–3, 328–37; Mitchell and Deane (1962), 64–7; Glynn and Booth (1983), 331; Saville (1954), 75; Matthews, Feinstein and Odling-Smee (1982), 461; also see p. 99 note 172 below.
[103] Jones (1971), V.
[104] Introduction note 4. Clapham (1963) III, 35; Bowley (1920), 15, Wood (1909), 98; Phelps Brown and Handfield-Jones (1952), 272; Williamson (1982), 20–1.
[105] R.C., Final Report, 1886, XXIII.C. 4893, LV; Read (1964), 188; also 150; Semmel (1968), 14, 84–7, 108, 142–9, 165, 174; Harris (1972); and see discussion in chapter 4, p. 241, note 73 below.

case had the scourge of unemployment not formed one of the key problems of the age.

The contemporary agitation against the export of capital was, indeed, much concerned with employment, either by arguing that earlier capital exports had been responsible for the existing high level of unemployment, or by predicting that continuous foreign investment would increase that level. Seeing that so much capital went abroad, Hobson wrote in 1911,

> we cannot wonder at the increase in unemployment and of distress among the working classes.

At the other end of the political spectrum, it was alleged that it was Lloyd George's budget of high taxes and 'Socialism' that would aggravate the unemployment problem: 'Capital with its employment-giving power will stream abroad,' prophesied J.L. Garvin.[106]

Keynes, who took an interest in capital exports both before 1914 and in 1924–25, curiously enough discussed them largely without reference to employment. Without the multiplier, as Harrod was later to observe, it was difficult to prove that investment would give more employment if channelled to home rather than to foreign projects.[107] Early Keynesians did indeed concern themselves with the potential negative effect of foreign investment on employment,[108] but more recent theory has been unable to decide, given unemployment both at home and abroad, where the additional investment will do the most good for employment.[109] We depend on elasticities, demand and supply conditions which will differ from case to case, and we have no firm conclusions.

VI Cost of Capital Transfer

We now turn to examine the next assumption, that of a smooth, costless transfer of capital abroad. This topic has probably given rise to a more extensive literature than any other in the field.

The classical theory, known as the 'specie-flow mechanism' and its variants, which applied to the transfer of any large abnormal or unexpected payment abroad, assumed it to be covered by movements of prices and of gold such that ultimately enough goods moved to match the outward flow of the claims on the lender or provider. The reverse process would come into action when the interest and amortization payments became due.[110]

By the early twentieth century various doubts had been raised about this

---

[106] Hobson (1911), 83; Garvin (1909), 20.

[107] Harrod (1951), 346, 349, 351–3; Keynes (1981); Keynes (1930); Liberal Industrial Inquiry (1928); Keynes (1928), 45; Stein (1969), 137–41.

[108] Leary (1945), 672–4; Mikesell, in discussion following, 711; Knapp (1957), 440 and Knapp (1942/43), 115–21; Meade (1955), 484–5; Heidhues (1969), 27–9.

[109] Simpson (1962), 503–4; 523–5; Balogh and Streeten (1960), 220–1; Gutman (1956), 535; Hinshaw (1945), 161–2.

[110] Viner (1958), 197; Taussig (1927), 123–30; Schwartz (1984), 4.

model.[111] More serious than these theoretical doubts was the fact that none of the effects postulated by the theory in the different stages had in fact taken place in practice. Neither prices, nor interest rates, nor gold movements conformed to expectations, and a number of systematic studies of the capital export/import history of the United Kingdom, France, Canada and Argentina, emerged with only inconclusive or negative results.[112]

Nevertheless, economic thought still widely held on to the classical mechanism into the 1920s and much of the extensive literature on the reparations problem moved within the same framework. Reparations and capital exports had in common that in both a large payment which did not arise directly out of the current trading activities of the countries concerned, had to be made across the frontiers. Despite some important differences[113], especially the fact that reparations were not followed by dividend or interest payments, the mechanism was described in much the same terms of changing prices in the absence of gold movements leading to changes in the import and export levels, the whole helped along by appropriate interest-rate adjustments.

Cynics might care to note that since the process of reparations was activated by the fiat of foreign governments, and not by native capitalists, as were capital exports, economists suddenly discovered the adverse effects of all the necessary adjustments on home prosperity, which somehow they had missed before. Before 1914, the British had been too engrossed in admiring the smooth working of the gold standard, to notice the conflict between domestic and foreign stability, or count the cost of high interest rates, deflated employment, disruption of markets and changes of prices involved in adjusting to foreign investment. On the other hand, it might just be that they neglected these effects predicted by theory, because they could never be discovered to have occurred in fact.

In the course of the inter-war years, alternatives to the simplistic neoclassical scheme were developed in Keynesian terms. Joan Robinson's theorem was particularly interesting by its finding that, given the realistic assumption of unemployment, equilibrium becomes unpredictable and indeterminate. The balance of payments may thus remain out of equilibrium for a long time.[114]

Keynes himself had noted as early as 1930 that since the trade balance depended on relative prices, while the capital export balance depended on relative rates of return (or interest), changes in the terms of trade alone, as envisaged by traditional theory would not be enough to bring the two together:

---

[111] Hollander (1916–17), 674–90; Laughlin (1903), ch. 10; Beach (1935), 22–31; Cassel (1928b), 17–18; Wicksell (1916/17), 404–10; Taussig (1916/17b), 410–14; Ellis (1916), 26–34.

[112] Viner (1924); Williams (1920); White (1933); Angell (1928), 388 ff; Taussig (1927), 240 ff; Bordo (1984), 55–65.

[113] There is hidden here among the dissimilarities a fundamental likeness. Both in the British case before 1914, where in-payment exceeded in the capital exports, and in the German reparations case, where the in-flow of American capital exceeded the outward reparations, there were no problems at all of finding the foreign exchange; it was the inward-payers, the countries which had to meet the interest to Britain before 1914, and the American investor in the 1920s, who had the problem. One would look in vain in the contemporary literature of Britain and Germany respectively, for an appreciation of this.

[114] Robinson (1946–7), 109–11 and Robinson (1947), 136–7; Knapp (1942/43), 117–20.

incomes would have to change appropriately also. One plausible mechanism for this was described by Bachmann and Heuss.[115]

The multiplier complicated matters. A.G. Ford, who on the whole took an optimistic view of a smooth transfer for our period, believing in a healthy link between exports and capital exports, yet thought of foreign lending having to be matched, to some extent, by the reduced consumption of the lenders. According to A.J. Brown, who was more pessimistic, capital exports would tend to threaten the gold reserve and force the Bank of England to take restrictive measures to protect it, which would depress total investment and cause unemployment in the lending country. Even under a paper standard, as Gray showed, some similar mechanism was quite likely. However, here too, we find that as soon as we make the realistic assumption of some unemployment, the results become indeterminate, and equilibrium is no longer guaranteed.[116] At the same time, the increasing flow of historical data failed to confirm the luxuriant growth of theory. Thus Silverman found that price changes did not precede balance of payments changes, but fitted better when assumed to be simultaneous, while Lindert could trace no effects of bank rate on import prices in Britain in that period. It may of course be, as Viner had warned, that investment was normally a continuous process over at least several years, so that direct statistical correlations with particular branches of investment would be hard to establish.[117]

Meanwhile another line of attack questioned the realism of considering two countries in isolation, as was usually done by theory. A high bank rate, as Lindert observed, would tend to occur simultaneously in several countries and would bring gold not only to London, but also to Paris and Berlin. Similarly, it was to be expected in view of the key position of the British economy, that if Britain deflated, many others would deflate too. Both these reactions would lead to dissipation or loss of the initial impetus. If they became world-wide, they might not only affect interest rates of borrowers and lenders similarly, but even in the opposite direction from that desired.[118] Once again, in the absence of full employment, the system would be indeterminate, and on certain conditions, as Beach showed, imports drawn into the borrowing country by a loan would raise prices which would draw more imports and more specie, in a crescendo until the economy collapsed.[119] It is a sequence which completely denies the comforting doctrine of an eventual return to an equilibrium, but bears an uncanny resemblance to the indebtedness of the Third World in the early 1980s.

Almost all those who have considered these issues have been conscious of the fact that they are confronting not only the usual seamless web of history in which cause and effect are almost impossible to disentangle, but that they are investigating the mutual dependence relationships of a multilateral equilibrium, in which each individual item, whether imports or exports, short or

---

[115] Keynes (1930 I), 326–42; Bachmann and Heuss (1956); according to Angell, Cairnes had seen the connection with incomes as early as 1854, Angell (1926), 137.
[116] Ford (1965), 90–2, 96; Ford (1964), 29; Ford (1958/59), 305–7; Brown (1965), 51; Gray (1972), 54.
[117] Silverman (1931), 124; Beach (1935), 11, 173; Viner (1924), 213.
[118] Lindert (1969), 50–1; Martin (1949), 360; Triffin (1964), 3–4.
[119] Beach (1935), 9–10.

long-term loans, cash flows and gold movements, could be viewed as the cause of disturbance or as the cause of return to equilibrium. The classics, as was their wont, started with an equilibrium, disturbed by what they wanted to investigate, capital exports, but in a realistic historical situation it does not follow in the least that that is where the initiative actually rests. A theory like that of Williamson, who saw capital exports as a means of restoring the trade balance after cyclical disturbances, made them the dependent variable, while Keynes assumed that long-term capital exports would adjust themselves to the trade balance. Capital movements would then become, like gold movements for McCloskey and Zecher, not the disturbing factor, but the factor that restores equilibrium 'by satisfying the demand for money that prompted the flow in the first place'.[120]

There was also a third possibility, namely that the ultimate cause was something outside the narrow circle of factors considered here. Brinley Thomas, for example, favoured emigration as the original disturbance; it led to an increase in exports and capital exports on the part of the country losing people, while raising prices in the borrowing country, which was also the country receiving the migrants. Another possibility was that the original decision might have been one of the type to build a railway abroad in order to open up a large country.[121] But with this line of argument we have shifted the focus of our discussion on to a different plane altogether: the role of capital exports in opening up the overseas world in the long term, rather than the restoration of the balance in the short run.

The gold standard itself, though outside our direct purview, nevertheless deserves a brief mention, for its traditional picture of a smoothly operating 'automatic' system is nowadays largely discredited.[122] Faced with a loss of gold, the Bank of England would bring to bear on the London market a battery of restrictive measures, including a highly variable bank rate, which would have an adverse effect on British prosperity and growth. These costs of adjustment have of late been receiving increasing attention.[123]

The doctrine of a smooth and costless capital transfer has thus turned out to be something of a myth. There were effects of the transfer of capital abroad on the foreign exchange market, on interest rates and on economic conditions at home in general, but they remain obscure in spite of all the intellectual effort that has gone into their clarification. It is not even clear whether they are to be credited with any significant consequences after all.

VII Terms of Trade

One problem which has greatly agitated the recent debate on foreign investment, namely its effect on the balance of payments,[124] troubled the

[120] Viner (1937), 364; Seeger (1968), 13–14; Williamson (1964); McCloskey (1981), 188. Also see p. 108 note 211 below.
[121] Thomas (1968), 50; Knapp (1942/43), 117–19; Whale (1937), 25–7.
[122] Seeger (1968), 128–33; Walker (1933), 199; Triffin (1964), 3 ff.
[123] See chapter 4, p. 247, note 92–3 below.
[124] E.G. Reddaway (1967), An Interim Report and Final Report (1968); Ady (1971a), 11; Meade (1955), 473; Moffat (1967), 1.

Victorian age mercifully little. The general tendency, as we have seen, was for obligatory inward payments to Britain to exceed *ex ante* any payments due from Britain abroad, so that if any balance of payments strains appeared, they were felt abroad rather than in Britain. The question of the terms of trade, however, listed above as the tenth assumption of the neoclassical theorem, turns out to be more complex than contemporaries imagined.

The classical position, expressed perhaps with the greatest clarity by Taussig, was that the act of lending, whether accompanied by a corresponding movement of gold from lender to borrower or not, would lead to a relative rise of prices in the borrowing country and a relative fall in the lending country or, in other words, a deterioration of the terms of trade for the lender. While this would in a sense 'double' his burden, since he would not only have to export more without an immediate return, but do this against the background of a less favourable price structure than before, the fall in the lender's prices would help him to sell more of his exports to carry through the transaction.[125] The terms of trade would then perform exactly the same action in reverse when the borrower began to pay back the loan and/or made his interest payments in due course.

Unfortunately, as we have seen, this classic simplicity failed wholly to be supported by the data.[126] Various explanations for this failure have been offered. One is that even a large borrower, like the Argentine, would have all her export and virtually all her import prices determined by the world market, so that they were unaffected by the particular actions of any one lender, and this must have been even more true of smaller capital absorbers. Another possibility was that the foreign investment might be of a kind to lower the borrower's costs and prices; conversely, if the borrower bought most of his imports from the lender, he might raise his own import prices against himself; or, more subtle still, the larger exports of the lender may have raised the prices of his remaining goods. Cairncross, however, followed by others, tended to view the linkage in the opposite direction, higher prices for primary products leading to capital exports into the producing regions, so that the foreign investment followed, rather than provoked, the adverse terms of trade. Keynes believed that there would be no effects if the capital exports were balancing rather than forced, and Hobson claimed that British investors were more likely to buy foreign securities precisely when the pound sterling stood high.[127] H.G. Johnson[128] remains agnostic. The consensus is that there are many influences upon the terms of trade in income as well as price effects,[129] and there is no reason to expect that they will move to ease the transfer of the capital exports.

It might be, however, that the data failed to conform to the predictions because they were simultaneously affected by a more powerful influence: the long-term impact of British capital on the world economy. This was among

[125] Taussig (1927), 112–15, 127–31, and Taussig (1916/17a), 395 and Taussig (1925); Keynes (1971) and Keynes (1981) *Collected Works* XVIII, 329; Nurkse (1935), 72–3.
[126] See note 112 in this chapter.
[127] Ford (1962), 110–11; Robertson (1931a), 180; Whittlesay (1936), 453–4, 463–4; Maynard (1962), 82, 178–80; Södersten (1964), 89; Keynes (1981), 329; Hobson (1914), 6.
[128] Samuelson (1952), 278–304; Johnson (1958), 174–5.
[129] Also see MacDougall (1966), 204–5; Edelstein (1981), 85; Phelps-Brown and Browne (1968), 170; Morgan (1959), 1–23; Ellsworth (1956).

the most fundamental developments of the nineteenth century. It derived from the fact that the bulk of British investment after 1870 went, directly or indirectly, to open up and cheapen the production of food and raw materials overseas, and reduce the cost of their transport to Europe. In this way the prices of British imports were massively reduced, and a substantial impetus given towards the long-term improvement of the British terms of trade.[130]

It is important to stress that this improvement was not generated by monopoly power or market control, but essentially by the lowering of the real costs of production in the overseas economies which were among the main borrowers, particularly in cases where the movement of capital could be combined with a parallel migration of people. Put in more general terms, investment abroad of this type was particularly effective, and yielded more in production improvements than investment at home would have done, because it could be combined with idle or underemployed cooperating factors of production abroad.[131] So important was this, that it might have paid, *pace* the classical assumptions, even if the returns to investors had been lower than the returns at home, and if British agriculture were also harmed thereby.[132] However, it might have been better still had a competitor, like Germany, made the investment so that the capital that went into modernizing the German economy had been diverted abroad.[133]

The potential divergence between private and national interest in the case of the short-term terms of trade will be obvious, as is the significance of the difference between foreign investment which improves the efficiency of competing industries abroad and that which improves the efficiency of complementary industries. Meanwhile, we are left, once again, unable to predict, *a priori*, the effects on the British economy of changes in the terms of trade induced by capital exports.

VIII The Bias of the Capital Market

We now turn to the eleventh assumption, that of perfect knowledge. In this context this need not mean perfect knowledge of the future. What it does imply, however, is that all potential investors have equal access to the available, truthful information about the potential targets for their investments, at home and abroad, in order to make their dispositions. But since that was precisely what they did not have, it is not surprising that it is on this point that the critical literature has most frequently concentrated its attack. Investors depended on the expert advice of their brokers and bankers, and they, it has been alleged, were highly motivated to provide excellent facilities for channelling funds abroad, while erecting high or even insurmountable barriers towards the provision of capital for British industry at home. Thus, according to many observers, a main, if not the chief cause of 'overinvestment' abroad to the

---

[130] Meier (1952/3), 127; Rostow (1950), 12–13.
[131] Nurkse (1961), 88; Södersten (1964), 89; Chenery (1970); Patel (1970); North (1956), 493–4.
[132] Simpson (1962), 515–18, 526; Matthews, Feinstein and Odling-Smee (1982) 454. Hughes thought this applied to 1900, but not thereafter (1971), 390.
[133] Lewis (1957), 588; Keynes (1981), 55.

detriment of domestic industry, has been the structural bias of the British capital market.

These views have been vigorously contested. The bias of the money market, the contrary argument claims, has been exaggerated, all reasonable home propositions could obtain capital from one source or another, and if a large proportion of investments did find its way abroad, this is to be explained by the fact that there was no demand, at acceptable rates, for capital from home borrowers. One result of this controversy has been the accumulation of a large literature. It has recently been well summarized by Cottrell.[134] Only the gist of it needs to be reproduced here.

It is not in dispute that the City contained a smoothly running mechanism for making investments abroad – indeed that was one of its glories in the eyes of its admirers. In the words of F.W. Paish: 'the main business of the London new issue market was foreign investment'. In consequence, as the *Economist* wrote in 1911,

> London is often more concerned with the course of events in Mexico than with what happens in the Midlands, and is more upset by a strike on the Canadian Pacific than by one in the Cambrian collieries.[135]

The reasons for this preference were largely historical. In the early days of industrialization, the sums required for fixed capital in industry in Britain were small, and could usually be raised locally or ploughed back by the firms themselves. Banks saw themselves as supplying short-term or trading capital only, and learnt to shy away from long-term commitments – a predilection strongly confirmed in the 1860s with the example of the Overend Gurney crash and the collapse of several of the investment banks formed on the continental model before their eyes. By contrast, the leading institutions for channelling the public's savings into long-term investments, the issue houses and merchant banks,[136] had begun by financing overseas trade, and had learnt to prefer safe, standardized and large issues in which the turn of the market could be expected to be narrow; these characteristics were most clearly found in loans to foreign governments, municipalities, railways or other public utilities. Once started on their course, their own specialization and knowledge reinforced the original tendencies towards overseas finance.[137]

The results speak for themselves. Thus of the £350 million net investment in Britain in a typical pre-war year, according to Paish, £200 million went abroad, almost all of it by means of long-term issues in the London money market. By contrast, of the remaining £150–200 million which were invested at home, only £30 million were channelled through the capital market.[138]

This referred to new issues. Sales of existing securities showed a similar bias.

[134] Cottrell (1980), 184; Cottrell (1975), 55–6. See also Chapman (1984), 98–102.

[135] Paish (1951), 2; *Economist*, 20 May 1911, p. 1059.

[136] Of £3,636 million issued in the period, Merchant Banks launched 37.2%, overseas banks and agencies 15.4%, the companies themselves 20.5% and official agencies of official loans, 9.8%, leaving only 17.1% for all other sources. Cottrell (1975), 31.

[137] Hall (1963), 57; Mock (1982), 282; O'Hagan (1929) I; Kennedy (1984), 109–41; *Economist*, 15 Dec. 1866, 1451.

[138] Lavington (1921), 194, 205; Paish (1951), 2; Offer (1983), 132 ff.

In 1913, the nominal value of foreign stocks and shares quoted in London reached 60% of the value of all quoted securities. The values traded showed a similar distribution, 43% in home securities, 57% overseas; among the home securities, less than 8% related to mining, manufacture and domestic transport together.[139]

The London capital market was simply not interested in industry in Britain. What little connection there had been between local banks and industrialists before the 1870s was severed by the absorption of private and country banks by national banking companies and for other reasons, including the failure of the City of Glasgow Bank in 1878. Such links as remained could usually be explained by foreign involvement, as in the case of Rothschild and Vickers, needing finance for warship sales to foreign customers, or were in the form of short-term overdrafts. At the most, banks would support firms which had overseas contracts. While Hall was of the opinion that involvement with home industry, limited though it was, increased in our period, at least one contemporary believed the change to have been in the opposite direction, and that the offers from British undertakings 'became feebler and feebler, reflecting thus that state of the public mind which shows an inclination to avoid investments within the United Kingdom'.[140]

Some indications exist to show that it was industry which ignored the City, rather than the other way about. First, only a tiny minority of joint-stock companies turned to it for support. Thus Lavington found that of 6,542 companies established in 1911–13, 5,423, or 82, 9%, were private, only 378 (5.8%) issued a prospectus, and of these only 165 (2.5%) asked for special settlement on the London Stock Exchange. The nominal volume of the capital asked for by these 378 companies was only £9.5 million.[141]

Secondly, much of what appeared to be issued remained with the vendors, only a fraction of the capital being offered to the public. Thirdly, most issues were for conversions or extensions of existing firms, not for new foundations.[142] And lastly, most of the companies that did find their way to the stock exchange were active in finance, commerce or transport; only a few sectors of manufacturing were covered. Thus in 1914 the 8% of the securities traded on the London Stock Exchange which were those of British industry were hardly turned over at all. According to one estimate only ½% of the trading on the London Stock Exchange was in home industrials.[143]

Altogether, most estimates of the immediate pre-war years agree that while British industry needed around £50 million additional capital a year, the total raised through the London capital market for home industrials was only £15–20 million, of which two-thirds was for conversions. The genuine new capital therefore amounted to only around £5–7 million, or 10% of the capital needed every year for expansion;[144] it is the equivalent of 3% of what was sent

[139] Wieser (1919), 131; Williams (1968), 269; Morgan and Thomas (1962), 97.
[140] Hall (1963), 37, 46–7; Anonymous (1909); 613; Harris and Thane (1984), 221; Michie (1979), 168 ff; Thane in Jeremy (1984), 606–7; Wieser (1919), 13–2, 137–8, 315, 358–61; Scott (1962), 44.
[141] Lavington (1921), 202; Cairncross (1953), 96.
[142] Cairncross (1958), 144. For details of one industry, see Harrison (1981).
[143] Wieser (1919), 358; Hall (1963), 20; Morgan and Thomas (1962), 132; Cairncross (1953), 9; Cottrell (1975), 54.
[144] Cairncross (1953) and Cairncross (1958), 145.

abroad annually in new investments. In view of this, it is rather remarkable that the authorities chose to give further incentives to capital exports by the Colonial Stocks Acts of 1877–1900, which gave trustee status to certain official colonial stocks, though their effect was probably only marginal.[145]

People who saw the world through London eyes were sometimes inclined to blame the industrial provinces from keeping really promising schemes out of the capital's hands: 'Yorkshire and Lancashire take care not to send anything really profitable to London', opined *The Economist* in 1911, and this was echoed by F.W. Hirst, its one-time editor in 1932:

> A really good thing from Glasgow or Yorkshire or Lancashire, or the Midlands seldom comes to London to be floated on the public. The insiders naturally keep it to themselves and their friends.[146]

This may comfort those who hold that industry was not starved of capital; but it will confirm others in their belief in the prejudice of London capital against provincial manufacture.

The majority of signs do indeed seem to point in the direction of the City as the source of the lack of interest. Thus one cause of its inability to help industry was alleged to have been the fact that the typical industrial issue was too small for a London house to handle. Here the investment trust, which began in London in the 1860s but took more permanent form with foundations in Dundee (1873) and Edinburgh (1874), might have been expected to fill the gap. However, far from supporting home industry, the investment trusts like the 'investment syndicates' for American securities saw their task as reducing the risks while obtaining the gains of higher returns in foreign investments, by spreading their larger resources among numerous foreign assets. In 1890, following a boom in such trusts, it was estimated that only 12½% of their funds were in British assets, while £50 million had been placed abroad. In any case, these were negligible sums among £8,000 million traded securities,[147] and even smaller sums were invested by the insurance companies before 1914. Meanwhile, Scots solicitors and accountants, who had control over another substantial stream of blind capital, channelled it into the colonies and into foreign countries, often in the form of short-term loans. Individual companies with large temporary surplus funds seemed to do the same.[148]

Large companies, it is true, were not wholly excluded from the capital market at home. In the 1850s and 1860s substantial firms whose growth exceeded their capacity for self-finance, especially in iron, steel and coal, had no difficulty in raising capital. George Chadwick, the most successful company promoter of the age, launched several such, largely on northern capital, and he boasted the suspiciously round number of 5,000 potential investors on his books for such issues. Even in his case, however, the smallest company he launched (with some odd exceptions) had a capital of £100,000. Altogether he claimed to have

---

[145] Baster (1933), 602–8; Schumpeter (1939 I), 430; Atkin (1970), 324; Atkin (1977), 22; Davis and Huttenback (1986), 168.

[146] *Economist* 20. May, 1911, 1060; Hirst (1932), 175.

[147] Buckley and Roberts (1982), 4; Gilbert (1939); Chapman (1984), 98–9; Davies (1927), 158 ff; Nash (1924), 93 ff; Burton and Corner (1968), 15 ff.

[148] Hall (1963a), 53; Davis (1966), 263; Bailey (1959–60); 2–79; Barker (1977), 238–9.

raised £40 million in his career. Sir Arthur Wheeler played a similar role a little later. Later on, large firms in some other sectors, like banking and insurance, railways, cotton and textile amalgamations, power stations and brewing (a specialism of that other well-known promoter, H. Osbourne O'Hagan), and individual giants like Brunner Mond, United Alkali, Vickers and Lever could still raise capital from the market,[149] but they had to be large indeed, if the public were not to make excessive demands regarding returns. Lehfeldt found in his 1914 list that even those which he considered 'medium-sized firms' with the substantial capital of £200,000 – £900,000, had to offer considerably higher returns than larger firms in order to attract capital. Moreover, launching costs were quite disproportionally heavy for small companies. According to Lowenfeld, in London they would be at least £2,000 and could easily rise to £10,000.[150] Provincial launches however were cheaper.

One alternative open to manufacturing industry was the provincial stock exchanges. However, the resources they commanded were limited, shares moved only slowly, so that the 'turn' was high, launchings were frequently unsuccessful and it was part of the functions of provincial brokers to channel local savings to London, to buy national or overseas securities. Even by 1914 provincial exchanges would not have provided more than 10–15% of the needs of industrial capital.[151] In a few cases industries created their own capital markets: the 'Oldham Limiteds' in the cotton industry are well known. They tapped local savings, acted almost as local savings banks and ensured, at least in good times, that shares remained highly marketable.[152]

The firm with a local or regional reputation only, was therefore in the main thrown back on its own resources if it wanted to grow: ploughed-back profits, mortgaged land, the entrepreneur's own savings and those of his family and friends, or taking in moneyed partners, disliked especially by go-ahead and individualistic entrepreneurs.[153] All this might be particularly inhibiting in new, and therefore risky but promising and innovative sectors of the economy.

The gap in the provision of capital to British industry had not gone unnoticed by the less scrupulous members of the London capital market. 'Promoters' of various degrees of fraudulence cashed in on the unmet need for funds, taking their quick cut and getting out before the public had seen through them. They thus not only deprived the market of needed funds, but also spoilt it for the future. In Great Britain, in the view of *The Times* in 1909,

> money for industrial purposes has to be raised through an independent financier, who looks upon the 'industrial' as a means of making promotion profits . . . rather than a steady income.[154]

[149] Evidence by Chadwick, Select Committee on Companies Acts, 1862a and 1867, Report, including Minutes of Evidence, B PP.1977.VIII 365.QQ.2000–5, 2079; Cottrell in Jeremy (1984); Kidner in Jeremy (1984) I, 485; Chapman (1984), 102; Michie (1981a), 105, 151, 233 and Michie (1979), 228; Hannah (1979), 41; O'Hagan (1929); Trebilcock (1977), 157; Thane (1986), 85.
[150] Lehfeldt (1915), 453; Lowenfeld (1909), 174–5; Lavington (1921), 219; Nash (1924), 62.
[151] W.A. Thomas (1973), 122; Killick and Thomas (1970), 96–111; Cottrell (1980), 149–53; Cairncross (1953), 96; but see Michie (1985).
[152] W.A. Thomas (1973), 145 ff; Wieser (1919), 399 ff; Smith (1961), 33–53.
[153] Thomas (1978), 6; Cottrell (1980), 94, 180, 182, 263; Cottrell (1975), 54–5; Michie (1981b), 151; Eichengreen (1983), 156; Davis (1966), 257–60.
[154] *The Times Financial and Commercial Supplement*, 8. Oct. 1909, 'The Need for Industrial Banks'; O'Hagan (1929), 376 ff.

Some of the victims of this process could no doubt be found among the frighteningly high proportion of new joint-stock companies that turned out to be 'abortive' or short-lived. It was the age of such as E.T. Hooley and Horatio Bottomley.[155]

In order to show that this gap in finance was not inevitable, the critics pointed to Germany, where the joint-stock banks were said to have developed into 'universal' or investment banks performing precisely the functions missing in Britain. These banks have attracted a large literature, much of which concerns itself also with the possible benefits which this form of banking might have brought to British industry in the critical years before 1914.[156] It needs to be summarized only briefly here.

The German universal banks saw their duties not only in providing short-term credits, but also in raising long-term capital for their clients, which included firms in the major industries of Germany, and the major exporters. This was done in several ways, most commonly either by lending the banks' prestige to make the newly issued shares and other securities of their clients marketable to the public, or by acting as underwriters at shares issues. Most importantly, the banks continued after the launch to nurse, advise and maintain an interest in their companies, aided by the technical and market know-how accumulated by the banks' staffs (which had earlier allowed them to pick potential winners) and by their effort to prevent competition and organize collaboration, down to forming cartels. Interlocking directorships further strengthened the links between bank and customer. According to one tabulation, the leading German banks held the following numbers of seats on the board of customer firms in 1911:[157]

Deutsche Bank	159
Disconto-Gesellschaft	143
Dresdner Bank	120
Darmstädter Bank	132
Berliner Handelsgesellschaft	123
Schaaffhausenscher Bankverein	148

Their influence was enhanced by specialization. Thus 55 of the seats of the Dresdner were in coal and 38 in the iron industry, while the Schaaffhausensche Bankverein had 47 in transport and 36 in food processing. The basic freedom of action was widened by the belief that, unlike the Bank of England, the Reichsbank would supply them in times of trouble.[158]

Yet the German system has not found universal approval as a model for the British. Some have pointed out that the differences have been exaggerated, and German banks were still largely concerned with short-term finance,[159] while to others the German system was not a sign of superiority, but of failure: in the absence of the much more efficient specialist firms such as existed in Britain, the joint-stock banks in Germany had to assume duties for which they were not really equipped. This, essentially, is also the gist of the well-known Gerschen-

[155] Cottrell (1980), 179–84; Houston (1925); Symons (1955); Vallance (1955).
[156] Tilly (1966); Foxwell (1919), 504 ff, 98 ff; Riesser (1910); Eistert (1970).
[157] Riesser (1910), 651–72; Whale (1930), 61.
[158] Whale (1930), 61; Born (1983), 88–9; Neuburger (1977), 195–8; D.C. (1916), 4–7.
[159] Born (1930), 46; Tipton (1976), 68.

kron thesis: German banks, according to him, only took over long-term investment in substitution for the access to capital available to British firms.[160] The more acid criticism by Neuburger and Stokes, that the German banks did actual harm by favouring heavy industry at the expense of light and thus distorting the German economic growth path, may be exaggerated, but it cannot be denied that the German banks did tend to neglect the smaller firm.[161] While most historians would still ascribe a positive role to the German banks in that country's rapid industrialization in our period, few are convinced that precisely that model would have suited conditions in Britain.

Since no clear conclusions emerge it may be useful to look at individual industries. But here also, opinions are divided. Thus the motor industry, a sector starting from scratch but with very high growth potential and important linkages, has been held by some not to have suffered by capital shortages, since firms like Daimler, Rover, Darracq, Sunbeam, Rolls Royce (only just), Wolseley and Austin managed to get large sums without difficulty as they needed them, either from the public or from individual financiers. Altogether, motor vehicles raised at least £6 million in 1896–1914 in 51 different issues, or *c.* £120,000 average per issue. As another source of capital, Armstrong–Whitworth, a wealthy established armaments firm, was willing to sink a fortune into an initially loss-making motor works. Against this Napier, Albion, Vauxhall and Standard were held back by being limited to what capital they could plough back themselves, and of these at least Vauxhall and Standard, it was said, were so badly run that financiers were wise to have held off.[162] Yet the same evidence could be read to the effect that the pre-war motor industry was retarded by lack of adequate access to capital.[163]

In electricity supply and electrical engineering, another promising new industry, majority opinion seems to be on the side of the critics though the vagaries of local control, boosted by perverse legislation, shared some of the blame for the missing spurt. Interesting here is the stress on the shortage of capacity at the onset of booms because of inadequate investment in the preceding years, a persistent failing in Britain which allowed foreign firms to come in and dominate electrical engineering.[164] However, the opposite view that there were always financiers willing to chance their arm with what was obviously an industry set for growth by carrying high risks also has its defenders.[165]

Other industries for which capital shortages have been alleged[166] and as

[160] Gerschenkron (1966), esp. 15, 21, 89, 139; Kaelble (1982), B.9., 51–3, Böhme (1974), 442.
[161] Neuburger and Stokes (1974), 710–31; Fremdling and Tilly (1976), 416–24; Sylla (1977); Komlos (1978a), 476–9 and debate following, 480–6.
[162] Saul (1963), 22–44; Saul (1968b), 235; Irving (1975), Zeitlin (1983), 36; Church (1982), 8–9; Michie (1981b), 153; Lewchuk (1985), 7; Lewchuk (1986), 140–2; Harrison (1981), 167–9, 178.
[163] Kennedy (1976), 172–3 and Kennedy (1973/74), 439; Richardson (1965), 245–6; McLauchlin (1954); Thomas and Donnelly (1985), 55, *passim.*
[164] See chapter 1, p. 48, note 159 above.
[165] Michie (1981b), 153–4; Reader in Jeremy (1984), 434; Hughes (1962), 34.
[166] Foxwell (1919), 128 ff; Cairncross (1958), 145; Burn (1940), 250–4, 262; Payne (1980), 52; Whipp (1983), 49; Head (1968), 169; Lewis (1957), 585; Hatton (1982), 751–2; Beer (1959), 4, 43; Carr and Taplin (1962), 290–1; Saul (1962/63), 133; Boyce (1986), 497; Robertson (1970), 124–4; Habakkuk (1972), 265; Church (1986), 156–8, 166–70.

vigorously denied[167] included steelmaking, coalmining, building, ship-building, engineering contracting, the Scottish cotton industry, the Birmingham trades and chemicals. Marshall's typically judicious statement perhaps fits the evidence best:

> it seems to have been fully established that prompt and strong assistance is not always to be had for such inventions and other new ideas, as are in the minds of men whose financial position is not always strong: and who do not know their way about the City of London.

to which might be added Kindleberger's pithy: 'potentially successful frustrated borrowers leave no trace'.[168] Weaknesses in any of the 'new' industries would have a particularly powerful effect on the slowing down of British economic growth.

Occasionally a flash may light up a whole scene. Such may be the case of Fred Hopper, a pioneer bicycle manufacturer of Barton, Lincolnshire.[169] He started work in 1895 and after some vicissitudes began to operate his own firm in that town from 1898. It was an unusually progressive company, using the latest machinery, going in for its own innovations, expanding from bicycles to motor cycles and ultimately, in 1912–13, also to a cycle car, and enjoying an expanding export trade. Its labour force reached 400 in 1905 and 800 in 1912, and, remarkably enough for such a volatile industry, it showed steady profits around a comfortably satisfactory level of 7½% or more. Here, if anywhere, was an object worthy of support by a capital market interested in British industry: a progressive firm in an expanding industry, reliable, competently run and profitable. Yet the firm was beset by continuing financial troubles because of lack of capital, which must have seriously affected its efficiency and which eventually caused its liquidation. It seemed that there was no one in Britain willing to risk the necessary finance.

Such capital as the firm had, derived from the partners, the profits ploughed back and from a bank overdraft, renewed with increasing reluctance and some chicanery. Beyond these, and some personal mortgages, there was simply no source open to the firm to be tapped. Twice it tried to launch itself on the London market, but both attempts were costly failures – the first time (March 1907) partly as a result of a negative assessment by the *Economist*. The firm also tried several insurance companies without success and, equally to no purpose, the Halifax Permanent Building Society (which did 'not grant advances upon works properties except under very special circumstances'). That something was saved at all out of the wreck (including, significantly, the archives with the help of which this account could be written) when the firm had to go into liquidation in 1913 was owed entirely to a fluke, namely the decision of the National Provincial Bank to break into the territory and its eagerness to capture the town's largest account for its new branch on almost any terms.

[167] Lavington (1921), 121–7; Goldsmith (1969), 407; Matthews, Feinstein and Odling-Smee (1982), 354; Edelstein in Floud and McCloskey (1981), 82; Michie (1981b), 150, 154; Payne (1967b), 526, 533; Davis (1966), 259–68; Hannah (1976), 25; Cottrell (1980), 267–70; Warren (1980), 137; Burnham and Hoskins (1943), 259.
[168] Marshall (1923), 347; Kindleberger (1964), 38.
[169] The following paragraphs are based on Harrison (1982), 3–23.

The story of Fred Hopper is a devastating reply to those who maintain that British industry could get all the capital it needed, and that therefore the capital market cannot be held responsible for the slowing down of British industry. However, we do not know whether this single case was unique, rare, or typical, and so we cannot assess its significance.

Finally, some macro-economic argument turns on the succession of different phases. The most thorough recent study on whether foreign investment 'crowded out' useful domestic capital formation, that of Matthews, Feinstein and Odling-Smee, while denying that capital exports had any adverse effect on home investment, admits that it might have affected the timing of home investment (though this might have been important) and even its quantity, if only to a small extent, or at certain times, especially in 1903–13. A reduction in capital exports would have lowered interest rates and this would indeed have led to more investment at home, though also to less saving. In any case, if more home investment had been thought desirable, it could have been found at the expense of housing and need not have diminished foreign investment.[170]

These conclusions neatly sum up most of the recent debate. Those who denied any adverse effects of foreign on home investments stressed that while home and foreign investments were indeed alternatives drawn from the same pool, their combined total was not constant; it expanded when foreign investment was high, but contracted to below the trend in the years of the home investment boom. The latter, therefore, did not suffer any scarcity for it could have raised the ceiling of savings, had it needed to do so, to the level obtaining in the export boom phase. Savings did react to interest rates, as well as to incomes, and a repatriation of capital would have cut savings, rather than increased home investments. The lack of investment opportunities was particularly acute in the Great Depression. Interest rates and returns on home investment also showed no sign of a capital shortage for home projects. If Britain suffered from inadequate investment in modern equipment and in the new industries, this must have been due to a failure of entrepreneurship and possibly of technology, and not because of a shortage of capital.[171]

The opposite view emphasizes what the other plays down, that home and foreign investment fluctuated largely at the expense of each other, that a decline of capital exports, by lowering interest rates, would have encouraged entrepreneurship, and that more capital, in the end, would have meant more growth at home. The pools of unemployed labour in home industries in periods of capital exports, and the relief afforded to the home economy in the great depression when capital export ceased, were both stressed by Rostow.[172] Beyond all this, however, the proponents of this view, like Richardson and Kennedy, tend to stress the imperfections of the capital market. The general high capital exports insured the market to lower home investments even in periods when the pull from abroad subsided, and the brokers and bankers were

170 Matthews, Feinstein and Odling-Smee (1982), 354–6, 359, 464, 536; also Mathias (1983), 304; Edelstein in Flood and McCloskey (1981), 87. Also see p. 111 below.
171 Michie (1981b), 154; Musson (1959), 204–5, 210; Lewis (1978a), 151; Davis (1966), 266, 270–1; Lenman and Donaldson (1971), 16–17; Aldcroft (1967), 316–20; and p. 64, notes 19–26 above.
172 Rostow (1951/52), 66; Robertson (1948), 296.

at all times turning the British saver towards the kind of 'safe', large-scale object that commonly meant a foreign, rather than a home destination for his capital. It was precisely the modern, innovating, pioneering enterprises at home that suffered most from this bias.[173]

Part of the question turns on the propensity to save on the part of the Victorian investor, and whether he would have continued to save even if rates of return had been lower, or if his funds had been forced into domestic destinations. Unfortunately, we can as yet be sure of very little relating to British savings habits at the time.[174] Perfect knowledge of market opportunities, as assumed by theory, was certainly absent; but to what extent, and in what way, the market influenced investors still remains unknown.

IX Taxation and Capital Exports

In the recent literature, taxation occupies a significant place in the context of capital exports. If the foreign country is a tax haven, charging a lower tax or no tax at all, or its administration is lax, capital may be exported merely because of it, depriving the home country both of capital and of tax revenue. In that divergence between private and social interest, 'too much' foreign investment is likely to take place.[175]

None of this was of much significance in the decades before the First World War. British investors paid tax at home on their foreign earnings and the only possible effect of this, as in the case of taxes on home incomes, may have been an incentive to reinvest rather than distribute the annual surplus. In any case, tax rates were very low by present-day standards.

X Sectors of the Capital Export Market

Finally, we must examine some issues which go beyond total macro-economic quantities. For a full understanding of the consequences of capital exports it is necessary to differentiate between sectors and between countries of destination.

One distinction of obvious significance is the difference between the capital devoted to overseas industries complementary with the British economy, and that which goes into competitive ones. The assumption must be that the first is beneficial to the lending country, while the second is harmful. It is because they believed that most or all the British capital exports before 1914 were of the complementary kind, that so many observers were satisfied with the high level of foreign investment at the time. Keynes was one of them. As he wrote in 1910,

> Assertions that the exported capital goes mainly, or to any important extent, either to the industries abroad which compete with ours, or to the countries which are our international rivals are untrue. Our investments have been directed towards

[173] Richardson (1965), 245, 251–2; Kennedy (1973/74), 425, 434–5; Kennedy (1976), 176; Kennedy (1984).
[174] See notes 42, 43 above.
[175] Kemp (1962), 62 and Kemp (1964), 199–201; Davies (1927), 104 ff; Mikesell (1968), 223.

developing the purchasing power of our principal customers, or to opening up and supplying with credit and the means of transport our main sources of food and raw material.[176]

In analogy with international trade theory it might be said that capital exports which widen the ratios of productivity between the two countries concerned, will increase the gain from trade for both, whereas those which reduce the disparity in productivity, and make the lender and borrower more alike, will diminish the gains from trade for both, possibly to the point that the capital export will not benefit their combined productivity. Again, as in trade, increasing specialization has its victims, and the development of the agriculture of overseas countries by British capital helped to limit the growth of agricultural output in Europe.[177]

But there is in all matters relating to capital a strong dynamic element involved. The dilemma of the capital exporter is that of machinery, too: will he not, for the sake of an immediate small sale, build up for himself a deadly rival in the long term? True, as in the case of the simple machinery export, if one country holds back, another will supply the machinery (or the capital), and meanwhile the seller enjoys the advantages of scale, of establishing links for later orders or spare parts, while still retaining the hope of keeping one step ahead of his customer by further innovations. Against this, the capital exporter must consider that his action may make the borrower's stock of machinery more up-to-date than his own.[178]

However, the division of the world into complementary and competing economies is too simple, for one has a habit of turning into the other. As Hicks observed in his inaugural lecture in a slightly different context, world development might be characterized as a sequence in which the leaders make 'export-based' improvements, which are beneficial to them; by the time that the followers have copied them and returned them to the leaders, they have become 'import-based' and harmful.[179] This, in fact, was the course of events in the earlier phases of British capital exports to the continent of Europe and to North America. The more rapidly the world developed, the more likely it was that capital exports to complementary economies might turn into support for competitors.[180] Free traders will maintain that the development of her competitors will in the end be to Britain's advantage, since the growth of their incomes and output will ultimately provide better markets for her. In Sayers's terms, the benefits of the growth of total demand will outweigh the disadvantages of alternative supplies.[181] There can, however, be no guarantee that this will happen: the developments depend on relationships that are, *a priori*, unknown.

Indeed, it is permissible to doubt whether sending capital even to

[176] Keynes (1971), 57.
[177] Whittlesey (1936), 446, 453.
[178] Kellenberger (1939/1942) III, 32; Balfour (1903), 22; Matthews, Feinstein and Odling-Smee (1982), 353.
[179] Hicks (1953), 127–30.
[180] Streeten (1961), 122–3; Matthews, Feinstein and Odling-Smee, (1982), 451; Simpson (1962), 526.
[181] Sayers (1965), 5; Hobson (1914), 18; Kreinin (1979), 388.

complementary economies is always necessarily beneficial, given possible changes in the terms of trade and in the actions of other capital exporters.[182] As soon as we leave our narrow path of discussing one assumption at a time and contemplate several simultaneously, the consequences of capital exports become at once opaque and unpredictable.

A second significant difference in the composition of capital exports arises from the division into portfolio and direct investment, discussed briefly in section I. Recent opinion has been inclined to give much greater weight than the traditional sources to direct investment within the total before 1914. Platt estimates that it may have amounted to as much as one-fifth of capital exports, compared with a mere one-tenth assumed by Paish.[183]

One widespread incentive to direct investment of this kind was the wish to get round a tariff, particularly in the case of the USA. However, far from being universally welcomed by protectionists as defeating the objects of hostile foreigners, there were those, like Balfour, who complained that this enabled some British capitalists to compete more effectively against their unprotected countrymen, or like Mackinder, that it would strengthen our potential enemies in peace and war, or that it allowed home capital to combine with cheap foreign unprotected labour.[184] Curiously enough, protectionists in the borrowing countries, as in Germany, were also opposed to the intrusion of foreign direct capital, and attempts were frequently made to freeze it out.[185]

Apart from tariffs, firms also set up branches abroad to safeguard themselves against other nationalistically inspired restrictions, including patent legislation, and to protect their markets against potential native competitors. More aggressively, they hoped to hold and expand their overseas markets by product differentiation, obtaining some monopoly profits in imperfect markets.[186] In the main, these objectives could be pursued abroad without affecting the home market.

There might be purely technical reasons for foreign direct investment. A firm might seek access to necessary raw materials; to save on transport costs and reduce delays; to be able to undertake after-sale services; to achieve scale economies or to combine with the available labour, either because it was trained, or because it might easily be trained. But most commonly 'direct investment consists of a package of capital, technology and managerial know-how', and it was the 'quasi-rent' arising from these which decided a firm on the risks and costs of expanding abroad. At times this might be incorporated in patents, but before the First World War, actual practical technical expertise tended to be more important. A typical example was the complete works erected by the British armaments makers abroad before 1914.[187]

---

[182] Balogh and Streeten (1960), 219.

[183] £500 million out of 2,600 million. Edelstein's estimate was 30% of equity capital plus capital not in the form of shares. Platt (1986), 34.

[184] Balfour (1903), 16; Semmel (1969), 317; Pares (1937), 142; Jones (1984), 38–9.

[185] Leubuscher (1917), 335; Corden (1957), 210–12; Schmitz and Helmberger (1970), 761–3; Mundell (1957), 322–5.

[186] Shepherd, Silberston and Strange (1985), 33, 84–5; Nicholas (1982), 614–15; Buckley and Roberts (1982), 2, 119.

[187] Behrman (1962), 89; Dunning (1970), 38; Falise and Lepas (1970), 103–9; Ady (1971b), 21; Stopford (1974), 311; Cordon (1967), 212 and Cordon (1985), 159; Mikesell (1961), 256; Grubel

A third important differentiation within the total foreign investment was thought to arise from the proportion of the foreign loans which was actually spent in this country. In the course of the first two-thirds of the nineteenth century, when Britain was virtually the only possible source of advanced capital goods, it could be assumed that foreign investments would lead to orders for British firms. When, however, other nations also became capable of delivering such goods, the direct links between British capital exports and British capital goods exports were put in question. In the absence of 'tying' of particular loans to particular suppliers – and the City, having no interest in industry, took care not to interfere in its lucrative capital export business by 'tying'[188] – the borrowing authorities and companies on which British citizens might or might not be represented, bought in the cheapest market, wherever that might be.

By the end of the century, 'untied' ordering seemed to become the norm. Thus the heavy British investment in Canada 1900–13, a well-known example, brought mostly orders for American firms. In Argentina, while three-quarters of the railway investment was British, German supplies were almost as large as the British in 1909–13, while in Brazil, where about half the railway capital was French, the French supplied only one-quarter of the material, and the Americans one-half. South Africa raised £15 million in London for mining between 1906 and 1911, of which only 35% was spent on mining equipment, and only half of that, in turn, in Britain. Finally, in Chinese railway building before 1914, Great Britain and France provided much of the capital, and the USA and Belgium got most of the orders.[189] Nor does the correlation of general trade with capital exports yield much better results. Table 2.10 gives Nurkse's calculation:[190]

Table 2.10 *Correlation of British trade and capital exports.*

	Percentage of British capital overseas		Percentage of British trade	
	1870	1913	1875–9	1911–13
USA	20%	20%	19%	19%
Other countries of recent settlement	10	45	8	18
Industrial Europe	50	5	21	23
All other areas	20	30	52	40

If the two correlated badly at the beginning of our period, the correlation was even worse at its end.

Yet while no clear links can be established between loans to a particular enterprise or country, and subsequent increases in British exports to it, there

and Lloyd (1975), 113; French (1987), 64–5; Buckley and Roberts (1982), 119; Trebilcock (1973), 254–72; Nicholas (1983), 676; Inoue (1984), 4–5; Kirchner (1986), 307, 316–20, 359.
[188] Silverman (1968), 24; de Cecco (1974), 38.
[189] Much of any loan would inevitably be spent locally, e.g. on labour, and another proportion might be used to finance payments on earlier loans. Angell (1926), 513–14; Ady (1971a), 78; Taussig (1927), 126; Fritzsche (1913), 103; Foreman-Peck (1983a), 143.
[190] Nurkse (1961), 286–7.

did seem to be a connection between changes in capital exports as a whole and the movements of total exports, at least on a cyclical basis. In the last great wave, 1900–13, a rise of £175 million a year in capital exports was associated with an increase of £234 million in commodity exports, though for the period as a whole, the connection is less evident.[191]

It is easy to see that, if other things remain equal, net capital exports will in the end have to be transferred in the form of real exports of goods or of services. Even if the borrowing country spends its loan in third countries or on home resources, these will lead to higher incomes and demand which, possibly via several more countries, will claim resources freed in the one area where they are now surplus, the lending country. 'Tying' a loan would thus ultimately make little difference.[192] However, Keynesians noted that there would be leakages of the purchasing power transferred by foreign investment through bringing idle resources into use in third countries before it returned ultimately as an equivalent demand for British products. In any case, there was a time lag, during which investment and income at home might wind down. Moreover, the transfer mechanism would include a fall in the exchange value of the pound, and there was no assurance that export prices of British goods would fall in the same measure, or, if they did, that the quantity sold would rise to make up to the full extent the loss of home sales caused by the original foreign investment.[193] In practice, taking into account also the interest and repayments of earlier foreign investments, it would indeed be surprising if the results of British capital exports before 1914 could be read off the export-trade statistics.

However, it does seem likely that the large exports of capital led to a shift among exports from consumer goods to capital goods, especially in the middle decades of the nineteenth century, when much of the British capital export was for railways and much of the world's railway equipment capacity was in Britain. On the other hand, the continued concentration on an out-of-date railway equipment industry because of buoyant capital exports, may have later retarded other, more modern industries in Britain.[194]

A fourth distinction may reasonably be drawn within the total of capital invested abroad, according to its destination, within the Empire or outside British jurisdiction. Beginning with Hobson and Lenin,[195] much of the literature has held that among the primary motive forces in the acquisition of Empire, especially after 1870, was the need of the advanced countries to export capital and their desire to keep the borrowing areas under their political control in order to monopolize the supply of outside capital there. However, as has often been pointed out, there was no visible relationship between British capital investment and colonial acquisition at that time. It is true that in our period a slight shift occurred in British capital exports from independent countries

[191] Mock (1982), 276; Lewis (1981), 21–3, 72–3.
[192] Taussig (1927), 124–6; Ford (1962), 52–3; Kreinin (1979), 388; Cassel (1928b), 39; Iversen (1967), 48; Mikesell (1968), 226.
[193] Harrod (1951), 347, 351–2; Lindert (1969), 63; Stein (1969), 138; Buchanan (1945), 144; Salant (1950), 494–7.
[194] Mathias (1983), 299; Mikesell (1968), 225; Hobson (1911), 101; Joslin (1963), 107–8; Clapham (1963) III, 64; Nurkse (1961), 117–18; Cottrell (1980), 182; Zweig (1929), 73–4.
[195] Hobson (1968); Lenin (1917).

towards the Empire. The Imperial part of new issues, according to Simon, rose from 35.5% in 1870–89 to 43.5% in 1890–1914, but this is more than explained by the expansion of the Empire and the substantial capital repatriation from the USA. Moreover, the increase went largely to the old-established areas of recent settlement which later became the Dominions; investment in the recently acquired tropical colonies remained low. The tropics altogether received 21% of the London issues in 1870–89, and 23% in 1890–1914. By contrast, investment in independent countries, like the Latin American states and China, expanded fast. It is doubtful if these would have received much more, or the Dominions much less from Britain, had the ones belonged to the Empire, and the others not.[196]

Some historians have attempted to get round this difficulty by coining the concept of the 'Imperialism of Free Trade', by which is meant the use of the overwhelming economic power of Britain to gain all the advantages of colonizing overseas territories without having to annex them formally. Indeed, some leading investors like Charles Morrison supported liberal constitutionalism in such countries as the Argentine in the 1860s, in the hope that their investment would flourish most in a society which developed like that of the USA. The problem is that this then leaves the growth of the Empire unexplained.[197]

However, once having become part of the Empire and therefore coming under British Governmental control, the colonies were able to borrow in London on much more favourable terms. For the 'white' colonies the difference was probably small; for the others, it may well have halved their cost of borrowing.[198] Since, in the main, the confidence of the British investor was not misplaced, this factor benefited both lenders and borrowers.

Whether investors benefited otherwise from Empire is more doubtful. Hobson and Lenin maintained that the state supported them against outside competition, and this has been echoed by the Webbs: 'if trade follows the flag, the flag has to reciprocate by following the money-lender in order that it may protect him from his disappointed and enraged creditors.' At least, it has been said, British companies were advantaged in gaining concessions.[199]

Against this, we have the well-known memorandum by Palmerston dating from 1848:

> It has hitherto been thought by successive Governments of Great Britain undesirable that British subjects should invest their capital in loans to foreign Governments instead of employing it in profitable trading ventures at home.

[196] de Cecco (1974), 36; Graham (1959) III, 488; Edelstein in Floud and McCloskey (1981), 84.
[197] Jones (1980), 154 ff; Mommsen (1974), 21–7, 38–9, *passim*; Mommsen (1979), 105; also Semmel (1968), 3, *passim*, 157; Barratt Brown (1973), 87; Hobson (1968), 55 ff; Kemmerer (1916), 2.
[198] Edelstein, in Floud and McCloskey (1981), 94–5; Mommsen (1979), 91–2; Hobson (1914), 23; Svedberg (1982), 277; Hansen (1983), 868–73. Also p. 94, note 145 above.
[199] Svedberg tried manfully to make the case, but with indifferent success. Svedberg (1981), 21–38; S. and B. Webb (1923), 151. Hobson took the much more intelligent view, that investors wanted their Government to intervene to reduce the risks and therefore increase the value of their investments. Hobson (1968), 56 and Hobson (1911), 68.

To discourage this, they have deliberately refrained from pressing their case when defaults occurred, so that the

> mistaken confidence in the good faith of foreign Governments would prove a salutary warning to others.

Almost 80 years later, in 1926, Stanley Baldwin echoed the same sentiments in the House of Commons:

> foreign trade and foreign investment must be at the risk of those who undertake them, and if their enterprises prove for any reason unsuccessful they cannot have recourse to the taxpayer for compensation.[200]

Indeed, it has not been difficult, in complete contrast to the Imperialism theory, to present the Foreign Office and the diplomatic service as frowning on foreign investment because it damaged the British economy by sending money abroad, and refusing to be dragged into quarrels with foreign governments which would interfere with their own political objectives. Even the Boer War, according to the latest researches, can hardly be called an 'investors' war', nor can the other textbook example, the annexation of Egypt, be maintained as having been undertaken in the interests or at the behest of the investors, at least from the British side.[201]

The truth is more complex. While the Foreign Office would not be drawn into unnecessary confrontations, and always refused to support one group of British investors against another, it could not stand by and see 'legitimate' British interests be trampled underfoot, or contracts broken. Moreover, there were signs of some semi-official steering, particularly by the Bank of England. While the Russian Government, for example, found it remarkably difficult to place its papers in London as long as political relations were strained, things went smoothly after 1906, and there was clearly some Government intervention in the cases of the Imperial Bank of Persia (1889), the National Bank of Turkey (1909) and the Peking group (1898), and these pressures tended to increase in the years to 1914. Foreign investment in China in 1908–20 revealed the ambiguities of the relationship between bankers and their governments particularly clearly.[202] Allegations abounded to the effect that the American, French and German governments took a much more direct hand than the British in the foreign-investment decisions of their citizens, but in fact, their position was equally ambiguous, though possibly located at a different point along the spectrum.[203]

It was the weakness of their governments' support that forced British, and other, investors, to join together in the Corporation of Foreign Bondholders, formed in 1868 and incorporated in 1873. Its influence has, however,

---

[200] Rippy (1959), 199; Cairncross (1953), 222; Hansard, Vol. 197 (July 1926), col. 1328.
[201] Mommsen (1977), 66–7, 70–3; Barratt Brown (1973), 87; Platt (1968), 13, 54 ff, 75, 154 ff; Hansen (1983).
[202] Hobson (1914), 24; Mommsen (1977), 75–7; Kent (1975); Platt (1968), 13, 30; Tomlinson (1981), 40; McLean (1976), 292–301; Davis (1982).
[203] Platt (1968), 7; Seeger (1968), 62; Zollinger (1914), 124–5; Wilson (1916), 299–302; Lenz (1922), 48–50; Laves (1977); Arndt (1912), 185–93 und Arndt (1915), 160–2.

frequently been exaggerated in the literature. Compare the following confidential views of Hambro's, the merchant bankers, in 1891:[204]

> The corporation ought to be a very useful one, but unfortunately those who know best how to treat with foreign governments are all too busy to join the board . . . Issuing houses generally find it best to negotiate themselves with defaulting governments.

It does not sound as though British government involvement was part of the expected routine.

Only in India was the Government more active, above all in providing a guarantee on railway bonds. The role of India in balancing Britain's balance of payments and ultimately supporting the gold standard gave her a particular role in the otherwise rather embryonic development of British economic colonial policy.[205]

Meanwhile the colonies burdened Britain with large parts of the costs of their defence, administration, public works, disaster relief and other items. On defence alone, the British taxpayer carried not only a heavier burden than the French or German, but a much heavier one than the colonists. A recent calculation of the average annual costs of defence per head in the period 1860–1912 arrived at the following figures:[206]

United Kingdom	£1.32
India	0.08
Other colonies	0.05
Self-governing colonies	0.11
Colonies with some representative government	0.03

Total governmental costs arising in those colonies and falling on the mother country amounted to 1.5–3.0% on the British capital there. Against this, some assets were built up, and the net cost to the taxpayer was around 0.7% a year on British capital invested in the Empire. This practically wiped out the additional returns derived by British investors from sending their capital into the colonies rather than keeping it at home – though it was borne not by them, but by the wider community. This is a further interesting example of the divergence of private from national interest leading to 'too much' capital export.

XI Capital Exports and Balance of Payments

Before turning to our conclusion, it is worth reverting once more to the mechanism of balancing the international accounts in our period. Successful capital exports on any scale, as Matthews, Feinstein and Odling-Smee noted, can arise only if at least two conditions are met: there must be an inducement to invest abroad, and there must be a payments surplus on current account to

---

[204] Quoted in Cassis (1984), 527. Also Feis (1965), 113; Walder-Heene (1918), 42; Davies (1927); Platt (1968), 34 ff; Nash (1924), 30; Lipson (1985).
[205] de Cecco (1974), 62 ff; Saul (1954–5), 64–5.
[206] Davis and Huttenback (1982), 125; also Davies and Huttenback (1986), 177, 244–5.

make it possible. But since, in Keynes's simplifying terms, one depended on relative rates of interest (or, in neo-Keynesian terms, on differences in money stocks), while the other depended on relative prices, there is no *a priori* reason why the two, in Angell's phrase, should 'just happen' to match up *ex post*,[207] while capital exports fluctuated inside the enormous range of £50 million to £200 million a year. Of course, the balance which necessarily emerged at the end did not mean 'equilibrium' in the sense of original plans having been carried out. But the question remains, which plans were modified, and how?

Let us start with the decision to invest abroad. Normally, such a decision may be assumed, as a first approximation, to derive from the expectation of higher returns, however defined. In our period, this would in the majority, but not in all cases be based on the opportunities beckoning in developing economies with favourable growth potential. Several explanations offered for capital exports in our period, and in particular for their cyclical character, begin with prospects abroad which led to investments, these would be followed in due course, by commodity exports, leading to further attractive openings for investors, and so on – until harvest failures, failures of the market, or inability to keep up the payments on earlier loans reversed the process, the impetus for the decline again orginating, in point of time, in the periphery and moving to the centre.[208]

But, as we know, commodity exports never matched capital exports directly and at once. If we assume a multiplier which reduced investments and/or consumption at home exactly in line with capital-export decisions, such that the balance of payments improved precisely to the point required by the transfer of capital, all would be well.[209] Some econometric tests do indeed suggest that home fixed-capital formation did seem to have an antecedent influence on foreign investment, as did the rate of savings: Hobson's theory of oversaving at home, causing the rate of interest to fall and foreign investment to appear more attractive, seemed to be borne out in that test. We are then, however, still left with the problem of how the 'rationing' of capital between home and foreign uses can be coordinated with the balance of payments emerging at the end of all current transactions.[210]

Should we then reverse the chain of causation? Should we stress the 'induced' or 'compensatory', rather than the 'autonomous', type of motivation on capital exports, and postulate a sequence of events in which a payments surplus, possibly caused by the running down of expenditure on consumption and investment at home, creates favourable conditions for capitalists to turn their eyes to the opportunities available abroad? Should we, with Carl Iversen, see capital exports as 'equating' or equilibrating incipient balance of payments gaps?[211]

This would be difficult to imagine, except on a very long-term basis, in which the whole constellation of markets and of attitudes to them could be affected.

---

[207] Angell (1928), 431; Matthews, Feinstein and Odling-Smee (1982), 525; Keynes (1930 I), 326; Floyd (1969), 472–92.

[208] E.g. Zweig (1929), 318, 334, 336; Rippy (1959), 197; Ford (1965), 85.

[209] Ford (1962), 67.

[210] Edelstein (1982), 229–31; Grax (1972), 21.

[211] See note 33 and 120 above. Also Musson (1959), 221–2; Heidhues (1969), 9–10; Iversen (1967), 66–79.

Did such long-term adjustments take place? In one way, we might see the whole expansionary period of British capital exports from around 1870 to 1914 as such as secular phase of the adjustment of habits. The kind of thing that one might envisage has been sketched by Martin in his account of a running down of net capital exports matched by a long-term rise in the propensity to consume and to import and a long-term fall in the propensity to save, to balance the accounts.[212] This would be necessary because, let us recall, the problem for Britain from the early 1870s onward in macro-economic terms was not how to find funds out of the trade balance to sustain net capital exports, but on the contrary how to accommodate the swelling payments surpluses arising from the inexorably growing unrequited stream of inward payments on account of earlier investments.[213] The secular adjustments that had to be made were precisely those depicted by Martin, namely a fall in *net* capital exports to ever larger negative levels.

As it happened, all this also fitted in precisely with the secular decline in Britain's role as the leading manufacturing exporter. Had she continued to be a healthy and expanding export economy, while being flooded by a growing income stream of interest and dividends from abroad inherited from a previous phase, then even with an active capital export to open up further resources for the needs of the world, she would very quickly have set up insuperable obstacles for herself in the shape of a massive 'sterling shortage'[214] for everyone else.

The nature of the problem is illustrated by Table 2.11:[215]

Table 2.11 *United Kingdom balance of payments, 1911–13 (£ million, average of three years)*

Imports	− 731.2	Exports, incl. re-exports	− 596.9
Sundries (ship sales, bullion, smuggling, emigrants, tourists, etc.)	− 27.5	Invisibles, net	− 181.6
		Inflow of dividends and interest net	− 778.5
Gap (available for foreign investment)	− 207.7		− 187.9
	− 966.4		− 966.4

It is evident that Britain could have dealt with the looming 'gap' or world sterling shortage in one or both of two ways. She could cut exports/increase imports, or she could export capital, and the history of those decades may, in the light of the Kuznets cycle, be seen as a lurch between these two options. Both had unfortunate side-effects. To cut exports/increase imports harmed British industrial growth and, by its multiplier effects, induced the kind of stagnation deplored by the critics; but to export capital created further assets abroad, which made the problem of the incoming payments even worse the next time round.

---

[212] Martin (1949), 364. Also see Müller (1947), 23–4.

[213] See Table 2.6. above.

[214] B. Thomas (1973), 47–8; Mathias (1983), 302; Nurkse (1961), 149; Lewis (1957), 580; Lewis (1970), 3555–7; Saul (1954–5), 58; Müller (1947), 156 ff.

[215] Based on Imlah (1952/53), 239; Mitchell and Deane (1962), 284. Also see Table 2.6. above.

It is not, therefore the case, as is sometimes alleged,[216] that the failure of British manufacturing forced the nation to rely increasingly on invisibles and on earnings arising abroad. Rather, British industrial stagnation may itself be seen as a direct consequence of the early manufacturing export success, which had set going that fatal sequence of capital exports leading to inexorably growing unrequited inward payments in the form of interest and dividends later. Short of letting those sums lent abroad grow into the sky, Britain had to accept ever-increasing import surpluses, and these, in turn, inhibited industrial growth. Ideally, one might have imagined a world in which only those things in which the outside world had a clear natural advantage, such as tea or wood pulp, were imported, while the British population, growing fat as the world's rentier, would continue to initiate the product cycle[217] and to specialize in those industrial sectors in which their continuing technical lead made them unbeatable. But beside the nature of the consumption function, there were inevitable structural rigidities which stood in the way, and to that limited extent, these bore part of the blame. But the market pressures also went the wrong way. Price disadvantages for British exporters because of the 'strong' pound, the desperate need of others to increase their sales to Britain or to third markets in order to meet their interest obligations, and continuing comfortable traditional sales to extra-European markets, were added to the less tangible effects of a rentier's mentality and a conviction of permanent superiority of British industry, to keep down innovatory activity in Britain while making the export of capital more attractive to British capitalists.

In practice, both factors played a part: autonomous investment based on what appeared to the investor to be the better bargain, and world market constellations 'inducing' British decisions in that direction. As far as our main quest is concerned, however, the emphasis has now shifted in a significant way. A high level of capital export may now be seen as being damaging not so much because it simply withheld capital from Britain where it might have done some good, but because it created a growing mountain of inward obligations which not only distorted the market signals so as to limit the growth of output at home, but did so in the most destructive fashion, by undermining enterprise and entrepreneurship. If the explanation of Victorian 'failure' has to be sought in the area of capital, let us remind ourselves, once again, that it will operate not so much by showing a little capital to be lacking here or there at the margin, but by showing that the pressure for massive, long-term, future-directed changes in economic structure and emphasis was fatally weakened.

XII Conclusion

It is time to draw some conclusions. The debate on foreign investment in the decades before 1914 is sometimes conducted in terms of 'rationality'. Were the later Victorians and the Edwardians reasonable in their actions in the sense of reading the signs aright, making the most of their opportunities, giving their

---

[216] E.G. Warwick (1985), 100–1. The counter-argument was put by Griffen (1899), 28.
[217] See chapter 5 note 22 below.

preferences full rein? This approach misses the core of the problem. Though no doubt there were foolish and impetuous people among the Victorian investors, as there are in any human group, the argument about the potential damage of excessive capital export does not need to rest on this kind of irrationality, nor even on the dubious assumption that British capitalists had become an effete, risk-avoiding class seeking nothing more than gentlemanly idleness and a quiet life.

The question is rather whether rational action, within the investors' own preferences and according to their own best lights, produced results of benefit to the national economy: whether, in other words, private and national interests coincided. Put differently, the issue is not whether the Victorians obeyed the rules of the game, but whether 'the rules of the game [were] actually drawn up in such a way as to ensure that individual competitive behaviour would yield, at least approximately, Pareto optimal results for the economy as a whole'.[218] It is in answering *this* question that doubts have emerged in the literature as well as in our attempt to summarize it. Empirical research, we found, has brought to light much conflicting evidence on this point. Similarly, the conclusions of neoclassical theory are put in question by monopolistic or imperfect factor and product markets, by widespread ignorance and deliberate misinformation, by the damage done by British firms to other British firms abroad, and the costs of colonial administration and defence borne by the nation but not by the investor, among other factors.

Had less been invested abroad, for one reason or another, then, it is permissible to conclude, more would have been invested at home, but also total savings would have declined, leading to lower future savings and incomes to settle at some new, lower equilibrium. This chapter has deliberately avoided a discussion of the savings function in Britain, except to note that during capital export booms total investment expanded by up to 3% of GNP. Expressed the other way round, this may be taken to mean that total savings fell by that amount when foreign opportunities were not available. At the same time the 'swing' to home investment when capital exports were less attractive amounted to rather more than this loss, providing an indication that capital export booms did withdraw some investment from the home economy. On that basis it is difficult to believe that the home economy was saturated in any absolute sense, and to hold with McCloskey that faster growth was impossible because other factors, especially skilled labour, were fully stretched.[219]

The problem is to know by how much the growth rate and the pre-war level of incomes of the British economy could have been raised, had a significant part of the sums sent abroad been invested at home. Kennedy's attempt to derive such an estimate is the most ambitious, postulating a major structural change in the economy towards the modern growth industries on the American and German models, but no improvements in technology beyond those available to Britain's rivals. On those assumptions, the British national income might be expected to have been 25–50% higher than its actual level by the outbreak of war. Crafts, on more restrictive assumptions, made it 25%. Paul Bairoch, on the basis of rather

---

218 Kennedy, Review of Cottrell (1980), 751.
219 See note 100 above.

simpler calculations, arrived at a rise of 70% over the actual level reached in 1908–12. Sir Arthur Lewis developed a model according to which a switch from foreign to home investments would in the first stage have led to a fall in exports but a rise in home production and in imports, leading in the second stage to an export boost associated with a fast growing manufacturing capacity at home.[220]

Even the more sophisticated estimates of the likely consequences of a switch away from foreign investment cannot deal with all the possible variables. Among the macro-economic assumptions discussed here and inadequately covered in the counterfactual calculations are those of infinitely divisible capital, of full employment, of a costless transfer mechanism, of neutral terms of trade, of perfect knowledge, and of neutral taxation. Taking into account the varied composition of exported capital, whether in competing and complementary industries, direct or portfolio investment, tied or untied loans, and invested within or outside the Empire, creates further uncertainties. In the end, the effects on the national economy of foreign investment undertaken for private profit remain totally unpredictable and incalculable, depending as they do on elasticities and relationships outside the actual range experienced, which are still unknown.

It would seem that the years of devoted labour on this question by countless economists and historians have brought us little concrete benefit. It may almost be said that the more refined the theory, and the more careful the calculations, the greater the uncertainties. The temptation is great to fall back on the crude, but solid tenets of the Victorians and Edwardians themselves which required neither sophisticated theory nor refined measurement. Among the more prominent of these was that capital was beneficially employed in opening up the undeveloped areas of the world, in order to lower the import prices of food and raw materials and thereby reduce British costs, whereas equipping actual or potential competitors with capital and capital goods would ultimately prove detrimental. A second belief concerned the bias in the British capital market which channelled funds more easily abroad than to the smaller manufacturing firms at home, or to those in risky new growth industries. A third tenet was to welcome the higher returns, on average, on capital invested abroad, despite the uncertainties and the additional risks involved; but to deplore the corresponding disadvantages of unemployment or underemployment of the cooperating factors of production, in particular labour, at home. All this was well enough known at the time, but the balance was no easier to strike then than now.

It might be held that one's answer would depend on one's evaluation of theory as against empirical evidence. Simple theory might tend to the optimistic solution that large capital exports were beneficial; empirical leanings were towards a pessimistic one, that the damage done to British manufacturing industry at home was only too evident. But, as we have shown, theory is not simply optimistic, nor is empirical evidence simply pessimistic. The early neoclassical inheritance has been modified in so many particulars that many of

---

[220] Kennedy (1978) and Kennedy (1973/74), 412–14, 436–7; Bairoch (1976a), 217; Lewis (1957), 586; Crafts (1979), 536.

the more recent theoretical works end on a pessimistic, or at least agnostic note, while empirical researchers like Edelstein on the contrary tend towards a positive interpretation.

> Where so many well-informed persons of goodwill differ it most unlikely that one set is wholly right, the other wholly wrong. It is much more probable that they measure against different criteria. The alternatives that leap to the eye are those discovered by the genius of Friedrich List in relation to the similarly inconclusive debate between free traders and protectionists: the quarrel in the last resort is between those whose ultimate criterion is wealth now, and those to whom the optimal policy is one that maximizes the power to create wealth in the future. On a more subtle level this might be described as the contrast between the aristocratic world view of maintaining and maximizing present and visible status, and the bourgeois virtue of thrift with a view to later expansion.[221]

This fundamental divide between those whose ultimate measuring rod was wealth now and those who looked to the power to produce wealth in the future was found also in the debate on capital exports before 1914. Those inclined to measure immediate returns would have a positive attitude to foreign investment at the time because it brought in higher yields, while those concerned with future industrial potential had misgivings about the high level of foreign investment because it reduced capital improvement, enlargement and renovation at home. It was these latter who conjured up the vision of a rich 'nation of bankers and commission agents, supporting armies of unemployed loafers', an 'England [which will be] the retreat for the age of a small aristocracy of millionaires who will have made their money where labour is cheapest and return to spend it where life is pleasantest. No productive work will be possible in England',[222] which will have become a rentier country in danger of following Italy or the Netherlands into industrial decline.

Men of both persuasions were found not only among economists and politicians,[223] but also among businessmen. It is therefore not entirely satisfactory to exonerate the Victorian businessmen on the grounds that they could do no other than react to their immediate signals, and could not have foreseen 'the trick history was about to play on them' by inveigling them into the 'wrong' investment decisions from the point of view of the future. It may well be true that 'it is so difficult to assess how far each generation should be able to anticipate the problems which will arise for the next',[224] but the fact remains that wealth now rather than strength later was a conscious choice of contemporaries, and the American and the German business community anticipated and built for the future more successfully than the British. No doubt the British government, whose role is discussed in chapter 4, contributed to that weakness; but there was something also in British business predisposing it towards short-sightedness.

---

[221] Hampson (1982), 69; see also Lewchuk (1985), 21.
[222] Lord Wyndham, quoted in Mock (1982), 323; Waltershausen (1907), 363–7, 374, 382 ff. Hobson (1891) quoted by Cain (1985); Tariff Commission, Reports (1904), vol. II, para. 1484, also see Pollard (1984), 36; Kennedy (1980), 315; Mock (1982), 117, 295, 323; Singh (1978), 127–34; Gilpin (1976), 44 ff.
[223] But see Viner (1958), 108–20, 277–305.
[224] McCloskey and Sandberg (1971/2), 102; Saul (1965), 18.

Every society makes, in some way, a choice between present and future benefits. It may well be that, on some criteria, the Victorians did right to channel such a large part of their savings abroad. It is difficult to avoid the conclusion that they must have contributed thereby, to an unknown extent, to the deterioration of the British economic growth rate.

3

Education, Science and Technology

Among the causes for the poor performance of the British economy in the late Victorian and Edwardian period, the shortcomings in education, especially as it related to science and technology, have always occupied a prominent place in the literature. All types of education have come in for criticism, starting with the elementary schools available to the industrial worker. But particular emphasis has been placed on the defective provision for the education of the industrial leaders, on the low quality of the British engineers and of British scientific and industrial research, and on the total absence of any educational system whatever so that there was no proper dovetailing between the teaching in the lower forms and the higher education at the tertiary stages. As a result, it has been alleged, it was precisely in the new industries which demanded more systematic science or technology, such as chemistry or electrical engineering, that the British performance was particularly disappointing.[1]

For these fallings, as always, Britain's early start has had to carry much of the responsibility: it made British entrepreneurs complacent and unwilling to learn from abroad; having led the world at a time when industrial leadership did indeed depend on practical tinkering and on acquired manual skill and experience, they were inclined to look with contempt on book learning and on theory even after these had become indispensable in a growing number of industrial sectors, not realizing that the 'skills, methods and knowledge which had served so well in the past' were largely irrelevant to the new world of advanced technology. Moreover, since industrialization had come to Britain before the modern school was established, little was expected from the school system in furthering the talents needed for industrial success.[2]

Beyond this, however, and more fundamentally, it has been the social structure and the attitudes associated with it, both derived from the peculiar historical development of Britain in the eighteenth and nineteenth centuries, which have been made responsible for the weaknesses in British science and technology. Aristocratic values were never defeated in Britain's early and slow progress to modernization: science, if engaged in at all, had to be gentlemanly

---

[1] Landes (1969), 344. This is still the best concise statement. For a typically simplistic recent statement, see Julia Wrigley (1986), 162–88.

[2] Saul (1979), 115; Jansen and Stone (1966–7), 230.

and non-utilitarian; mere technicians and technical knowledge as well as all professionalism were despised; and the 'social pecking order' ensured that the public schools and the ancient universities were aped at all levels, and their value systems, concentrated on the classics and other determinedly impractical subjects, permeated all educational judgement and created a philosophy 'inimical to technical progress'.[3]

It will be the object of this chapter to examine these strictures and, in particular, to contrast the evolution of education, of science and of technology in Britain with contemporary developments in Germany. The education of girls and women will be largely ignored, as it has been omitted in most of the relevant literature; so will commercial education, since the British skills in commerce and finance were not seriously questioned before 1914.

We shall consider, in the first section of this chapter, some of the criticisms made by contemporaries, followed, in the second, by a brief account of the relatively successful application of science to British industry in the century preceding our period. The third section is a digression, discussing in a more theoretical and general way the links between education, scientific research and industrial progress. In the fourth section we examine the development of German science and education in relation to the country's industrial advance, and in the fifth section this task is performed for the United Kingdom. The sixth section is devoted to providing, in the light of the foregoing, a tentative answer to the question whether education and science in Britain 'failed' the nation, in the sense of having been responsible to some extent for the slowing down of economic growth. Finally, the seventh section summarizes some of our conclusions.

I The Critique of Contemporaries

Criticism did not have to wait for the historians. On the contrary, most of the formidable array of accusations regarding the failures in scientific and technological research and education in Britain on which the more recent literature has been based rests on the work of contemporaries. It will be convenient to begin with a brief survey of their strictures.

One of the earliest occasions for unease was the series of international industrial exhibitions which began with the London Exhibition of 1851. The latter, held on home ground in the specially constructed Crystal Palace, is commonly taken to have been a triumph for British industry, and to have marked the high point of Britain's success as the 'workshop of the world'.[4] Yet even then, warning voices were heard, including those of Charles Babbage, the mathematician, Lyon Playfair, the Scottish-born scientific adviser to many Government departments, and William Fairbairn, the engineer. Much hard labour, said the latter, was being wasted and lives endangered because of the ignorance of scientific principles, and too many discoveries were made laboriously and by chance only. Britain lacked an institution where the rising

---

[3] Brittan (1982), 81; Roderick and Stephens (1978), 172; Wiener (1981), 3–4, 11 ff, 19.
[4] Chambers (1961); French (1950); Hobhouse (1950).

generation of engineers and others could be taught 'the elementary rules of their respective professions'. She needed 'a more intelligent and better educated class of foremen, managers and workmen . . . Society never stands still; . . . and if we ever become stationary, it·is easy to foresee that others will reap the harvest of our past labours, and be first in the race of national supremacy.'[5]

The Exhibition of 1862 showed that other nations were making faster progress than the British, but it was the results of the Paris Exhibition of 1867 which shocked large sections of British public opinion. While in 1851 British exhibitors had been awarded marks of excellence in almost all of the 100 sections, in Paris this was true of only 10 out of 90 divisions. Inadequate training and education in Britain were widely blamed for this poor result, and among the reactions were a Conference called by the Royal Society of Arts in 1868, the 1870 Education Act and the Technical Instruction Act of 1889. True, the competitive performance of the British at the next great occasion, the Exhibition of 1878, was considerably improved, and in later ones, until 1914, they held their own much better. Moreover, many of the best British producers stayed away because the commercial benefits of attending did not seem to warrant the expenses,[6] and it might well be argued that it was a sign of the dominance of British industry over the world's markets that it did not have to use these flamboyant occasions as much as did the others. But an effective tocsin of alarm had been sounded after 1867 nonetheless.

Apart from these widely publicized occasions for international comparison, the critique of the British science provision was maintained by numerous 'scientific lobbies' at various levels. Even before 1850, the 'Cambridge network' of scientists had pleaded for more teaching of the natural sciences in the curricula of the Universities, and in 1849, members of the British Association who were also members of the Upper or Lower Houses of Parliament had formed a Parliamentary Committee which intervened from time to time in the perceived interests of science. Perhaps the most interesting 'coterie' was the 'X-Club' of a small number of highly influential scientific leaders, which was started in 1864 and lasted for almost three decades.[7] One high point of the science agitation was reached in the years 1865–80. It was furthered not only by professional scientists, but also by a number of industrialists, including Mundella, Samuelson, William Mather, Swire Smith, Lowthian Bell and considerable numbers of other ironmasters and also some leading chemical manufacturers. The founding of *Nature* in 1869 was part of this on-going agitation. A National Association for the Promotion of Technical Education was founded in 1887, and the passing of the Technical Instruction Act of 1889 was its first major success.[8]

In the new century, a number of 'co-efficients', led by Sidney Webb as well as R.B. Haldane and other Fabians, Hegelians and imperialists, set out to restore

[5] Babbage (1968); Playfair (1972); Fairbairn (1972), 262, 265.
[6] Floud (1976), 68–71, 83–6; R.C. (1884), ev. Cunliffe-Owen, QQ.2912–3.
[7] Cannon (1978), 34; MacLeod (1970), 305–23 and MacLeod (1971); Heyck (1982), 101 ff; Foden (1970).
[8] Simon (1965), 165; Haines (1969), 723; Langan and Schwarz (1985); Brehony (1985), 259; Mack (1973), 50 ff.

'efficiency' to British society, which had its weaknesses exposed in the Boer war as well as in the world's markets. Catching up in the field of technological education stood high on the agenda. Some of the 'efficiency' men were behind the British Science League, founded in 1905 under Sir Normal Lockyer, editor of *Nature*, for the purpose of agitating for more Government resources for scientific and technological purposes.[9]

A particular achievement of the agitation was the staging and influencing of a number of official enquiries in that period. The remarkably large number of commissions and committees on educational questions which were appointed in the later part of the Victorian and in the Edwardian reign, reflected the general unease with the state of British education. The science lobby managed to insert even into the evidence and the reports of the Royal Commissions on general schooling – on elementary schools (Newcastle, 1858–60), on the great public schools (Clarendon, 1861–64), and on other secondary schools (Taunton, 1864–68 and Bryce, 1895) – demands for more science teaching or at least recommendations to copy some of the desirable practices of the German education system, and they had similar success in the numerous contemporary enquiries into the universities (Oxford 1852, Cambridge 1852–53, Oxford and Cambridge 1872, London 1889, 1894, 1910, Scotland 1878, 1900, Wales 1881, 1909 and Durham 1863). Naturally their influence was more decisive still on the enquiries specifically conducted into the state of scientific and technical education: Samuelson's Select Committee on Scientific Instruction 1867–68, which followed the agitation over the poor results at the 1867 Exhibition; the Devonshire Commission which, having been appointed on the request of the British Association, collected evidence for more than five years (1871–76); Samuelson's Royal Commission on Technical Instruction 1881–84; and yet another enquiry into the same field in 1896.

Criticism began with the general provision of elementary education and with its lack of science content. Many teachers themselves had no knowledge of Mathematics, let alone any of the natural sciences it was found, though this improved towards the end of the century.[10]

The absence of any elementary teaching in mechanical drawing, such as was found in the schools of other countries, was particularly deplored, and there is evidence that workmen were prepared to go to considerable trouble themselves to pick up that skill later in life. But, it was said, Britain lagged in the whole gamut of possible technical schooling for her skilled workmen, foremen and those above.

More severe criticism was reserved for the secondary schools of the upper and middle classes. Although there were plenty of signs that members of the commercial and industrial bourgeoisie would have preferred their sons to be taught some modern subjects, including science, the grammar schools themselves were increasingly aping the public schools with their obsession with the classics or were turning themselves in effect into public schools, while the

[9] Cardwell (1978), 49; Meadows (1972), 273 *passim*; Newton and Porter (1988), 12–5; Poole and Andrews (1972), 36–9.
[10] Armytage (1962/63), 98–9; R.C. (1861), vol. 1, 647, 661, 665, 669; R.C. (1872), xiii, xvi, xix; R.C. (1872), ev. Kennedy Q.2035; Sharpe, Q.3449, H.E. Oakley, Q.3601; Huxley, (1895), III, 412–13.

ambitious parents, eager for the social advancement of their offspring, chose the public schools, irrespective of the curriculum. The Devonshire Commission found that of 128 endowed schools investigated, one half taught no science at all, and among the rest, science was taught at best for only a few hours per week, and the tendency was to direct the weakest scholars into the science streams.[11]

As for the public schools, their record was said to be bleakest of all. Only one out of the nine investigated by Clarendon, namely Rugby, had made any attempt to introduce science teaching, and even then in a subordinate role only (science marks forming 8 out of 100 on promotion) and a second, Harrow, had made a start; all others had ignored it completely. Eton in 1884 had 28 classics masters, 6 mathematics masters, not a single master for science or modern languages, and one for history.[12] Ludwig Wiese, the man in charge of Prussian schooling in its most reactionary period after 1848, who visited England in 1850, had the feeling that the public schools had become stuck in the sixteenth century and that the European Enlightenment had passed them by, and a similar feeling was conveyed by Matthew Arnold in his report to the Taunton Commission on continental schooling.[13] One harassed Liverpool professor even preferred his students to come from elementary schools, so that at least they did not have to unlearn what they were taught at secondary school: The University College 'was turned into an establishment for secondary education. It is a hospital where the weak come to be strengthened and the sick come to be healed. One cannot possibly push them very far. Our Mathematics students leave us before they know how to use a logarithmic table'.[14]

The ancient English universities equally came under attack. While the leading reformers, like H.H. Vaughan, Mark Pattison or Benjamin Jowett, helped the campaign along indirectly by demanding a greater commitment to professional teaching, more specialist professors and a redistribution of resources from the colleges to the universities to make these changes possible, others were directly concerned to enlarge the teaching of the natural sciences. In 1872 Charles Appleton founded the Association for the Study of Academical Organization for this purpose.[15] It was noted that the best British scientists had either been educated outside the universities, like Dalton, Faraday, Huxley or Joule; or they deplored their schooling there, like Darwin and Lyall; or else they had had to go abroad, like Playfair or Tyndall.[16] From the 1870s onward the agitation became continuous and was not without effect.

[11] R.C. (1875), 1, 10. Also see p. 170, notes 185–87 below.
[12] R.C. (1864) vol. 1, 32; Report of a Committee appointed by the Council of the British Association to consider the best means for promoting Scientific Education in Schools (1867-8), in Russell and Goodman (1972), 133–4; Huxley (1895, Vol. III), 113; Wilson (1868), 241–91; Science in 'Schools' (1867), 470–2, 488. Also see note 182 below.
[13] Paulsen (1921), vol. 2, 503; Curtis (1963), 154–6; Arnold (1874), 202 ff.
[14] R.C. (1872), Ev. Humphrey, Q.4391, Latham, Q.5225.
[15] Engel (1983a), 16, 18 and Engel (1975), 312–13; Simon (1974), 84 ff; Cardwell (1957), 38; Garland (1980), 13; Heyck (1982), 70; Sparrow (1967), 121; Smith (1982), 200; R.C. (1872), ev. Pattison, QQ.3754–6, Jowett QQ.3897, 3934–5, Challis QQ.4250, 4272, Humphrey, QQ.4391–4; Roscoe (1901), 76–8. Also p. 182 below.
[16] Basalla, Coleman, Kargon (1970); Layton (1973), 29; Galton (1874), 236; Perry (1903), 207–11 (31 Dec).

Meanwhile the University of London, which had been established in part under the influence of Benthamite thinking and on the examples of the Scottish and the German universities, all of which stressed the significance of science, had become a centre for agitation for its extension. However, its colleges, as well as the provincial civic university colleges and universities, founded later in the century with an even stronger bent towards applied science and technology, were private institutions which suffered from possessing but limited funds.[17]

In the course of the nineteenth century, the notion developed in Scotland and brought to a high pitch of efficiency in Germany, that university teaching should be associated with research, also gained ground against stiff opposition.

'If the Universities should fail to recognize the duty of promoting Original Research,' the Devonshire Commission reported in 1873, 'they would be in danger of ceasing to be centres of intellectual activity, and a means of advancing science would be lost sight of which, in this country, could not easily be supplied in any other way.'

But the plea fell largely on deaf ears. British scientists were frequently gentlemen of means and only very few of them were associated with the universities. These were, in Huxley's phrase, like officers without an army; their achievements were 'almost pathologically individualistic'. The literature on British science, as Merz noted perceptively, was biography, not the record of institutions.[18] The fact was that the Victorians expected research to pay for itself.

Altogether, while the number of university full-time students was somewhat larger in Germany than in Britain, in the case of technology there was scarcely any comparison at all. There was no equivalent for the German Polytechnic Colleges, which had achieved full status as Technical Universities by 1900. Their enrolments rose from 2,129 in 1860–61 to 12,257 in 1910–11. Against this, the total number of *science* honours degrees awarded in England and Wales in the 20 years 1880–1900 was only 530. Thereafter, the numbers rose rapidly, and the numbers graduating in 1910 were 800 in Science and 431 in Technology. But then this was still a mere fraction of the German total. Even when counting in technical colleges, those studying technology in 1901–2 numbered under 3,000 in Britain compared with 10,700 in the German Technical Universities alone, and it has to be remembered that most college students (like most students at the provincial universities) were part-timers, as against the German full-time numbers.

The numbers of scientists and technologists active in the economy showed corresponding differences. Graduate scientists working in Britain around the turn of the century have been estimated at a mere 2,000, of whom a little over 400 were teaching in universities and colleges, and 225–250 were chemists employed in industry (compared with 4,000 in Germany). Engineers with higher education working in Germany around 1900 have been estimated at 45,000 rising to over 60,000 by 1914. The British numbers in all the

[17] Cardwell (1957), 80, 104, 129–30; Roderick and Stephens (1978), 124. On their entrants, see p. 119, note 14 above.
[18] R.C. 3rd Report (1873 c. 868.XXVIII), p. lvi; 'Science in Schools' (1867), 487; Berman (1975), 40; Merz (1904) I, 279; Arnold (1874), 230.

engineering Societies together amounted to only 40,000, but there were many duplications, and the large majority of them were not qualified by German standards.[19]

Those scientists active in Britain who lacked an independent income had cause to complain of their lowly status and of official neglect. There was nothing equivalent to Academies, and very little to compare with science chairs abroad. When, in the second half of the century, possibly fired by the German example, some scientists tried to turn professional,

> they were 'discouraged and hampered by the few dismal prospects open to them'. There was nothing, not even teaching, for physicists, biologists or geologists. Chemists might find jobs, but these were paid at salaries little above those of labourers.

Whereas every other profession, complained Huxley, could provide incomes for men of ability, even science professorships, until the end of the century, hardly offered proper professional careers, and the civil service discriminated scandalously against scientists in its ranks right up to 1914.[20] Recently available data, it may be noted here, bear these strictures out in part:

Average professional earnings,

1913–14:	£ p.a.
Solicitors	568
Barristers	478
General practitioners	395
Chemists (pharmacists)	314
Engineers	292
Clergy	206

Professors could count on £600 or above. This compared with the German professional average of 11,735 M (say, £586) in 1900.

Interestingly enough, in the earlier phases of the century applied science, 'mechanical and manufacturing ingenuity', had high status, much higher than that of pure research. When in 1859–60 the three leading engineers of the railway age, Robert Stephenson, Joseph Locke and I.K. Brunel, all died, the nation mourned as on the passing of kings. Stephenson had what was practically a state funeral, being buried at Westminster Abbey next to that other great engineer of the industrial revolution, Thomas Telford.[21] This would have been unthinkable in the following generation, when, at least in the world of learning, men of applied science were even less highly regarded than those who searched for abstract principles: Charles Darwin, however, was one of those who were similarly honoured, in 1882.

The natural target for criticism in all these fields was the State, for the things

[19] Cardwell (1957), 129, 157–8; Roderick and Stephens (1978), 108 and Roderick and Stephens (1981), 197–8; Argles (1964), 72; Ahlström (1982), 13, 38; MacLeod (1971b), 227–8; Edding (1958), 33; Jarausch (1983b), 13, 16, 46; Fishlow (1966), 432; also cf. p. 154, Table 3.7 and pp. 193–4 as well as notes 136, 257, 265 and 270 below. On Technical Universities see pp. 152–4 below.

[20] MacLeod (1971b), 198; R.C. (1884) III, ev. Huxley, Q.3058; Russel and Goodman (1972), 112, 200.

[21] Rolt (1970), 161; but John Dalton was given a civic funeral in Manchester, when all shops were closed and there were 40,000 in the procession. Russel (1983), 178, 254.

which were missing here had all been done in the other parts of Europe by the State. It was the State which had failed to fund elementary education, which had failed to oblige the endowed schools to teach modern subjects, which, above all, had failed to provide for universities and for research. A bare handful of official posts was available for scientists in Britain, such as the Astronomership Royal, a few Regius chairs, and, in due course, the directorship of the geological survey and the curatorships of the two science museums, and this compared badly with the lavish State patronage abroad which began with the funding of posts for the various academies of science. The Kew Observatory, the much-praised royal bounty, was handed over to the scientists only because royalty no longer wanted it, and even then private funds had to provide for its running expenses. Even the paltry £1,000 a year, made over to the Royal Society to be used for scientific research, was going to be withdrawn again after five years in 1855, and to Devonshire's proposals, the Treasury's reply was that the Oxbridge Colleges had plenty of money which might be distributed around.[22]

To what extent all these criticisms corresponded with reality, will be discussed below. Here we may merely note at least four doubts which will be raised at once in the mind of any reader who has worked through the contemporary literature. The first is that much of the agitation was clearly self-interested: it came from a lobby of scientists who wanted more status and more resources, and must on that account be suspect. The impression must be very strong that this interested lobby underrated both the work done in Britain for the economy, and the opportunities provided by comfortable posts and sinecures in the Church of England, including College fellowships, to pursue disinterested research. Secondly, it may well be that in view of the traditionally restricted role of the State as against private initiative, the comparatively less organized structure and the private funding of both education and research in Britain compared with the Continent were not necessarily signs of inferiority.[23]

Thirdly, it is notable that the science agitation was carried mainly by specialists whose field had little or nothing to do with the progress of industry and who were only too eager to emphasize this fact: astronomers, pure mathematicians, geologists, physiologists. The utility of their work, if any, applied at best to navigation and beyond it to trade and to colonial, military and naval affairs. For these, Governments were prepared to spend money, and it is that largesse that was the target of much of the propaganda. The role of geology, one of the leading British sciences in the first half of the century and an area in which British achievements were never in doubt, is particularly interesting. For while the gentlemen of the Geological Society, one of the earliest British Scientific Societies to be formed, loudly proclaimed their distance from any practical or commercial purpose, the Government was simultaneously persuaded, mainly on the initiative of (Sir) Henry de la Beche, to organize the geological survey for the benefit of the mining industry as well as of civil

---

[22] Babbage (1968), 166, 192–5; Brewster (1930), 321–3; Kleinert (1985), 223; Berman (1975), 38; R.C. (1884), ev. Huxley, Q.2997; MacLeod (1971a), 330–1 and MacLeod (1971b), 212, 225; Basalla, Coleman, Kargon (1970), 38, 65, 101; Cardwell (1957), 155.
[23] This is discussed further below, pp. 125, 138, 146.

engineers and others, and from this in turn derived the ordnance survey as well as other measures for promoting science on the part of Government in the second half of the century.[24]

Lastly, it is difficult to collate the alleged neglect of science with the known positivist optimism of the later Victorians. Natural, honest, truth-seeking science, the triumph of empiricism and of facts, has rightly been viewed as a major ideological contribution by the British Victorian bourgeoisie. Indeed, its more optimistic devotees, like Lord Kelvin, believed that virtually all the properties of matter had already been discovered. Science was truth and no barrier was set to human progress thanks to its achievements.[25] An intellectual milieu of this kind would not seem to be one in which science would be likely to be neglected.

II Science in the Industrial Revolution

The British failure to apply science and technology appeared all the more remarkable in view of the fact that in the industrial revolution of the preceding era British had led the world in technological progress. Indeed, the miracle of the breakthrough into the modern technological age had occurred in this country, and others were mere copiers, from whom, for a long time, little that was new or significant could be learnt. The question of the later Victorian decline has therefore frequently been turned round: how had Britain managed to achieve, in the century since 1770, such a uniquely successful link-up of science, technology and industrial progress?

One answer might be that the industrial revolution required very little science; that the British turned out to be a race of inspired tinkerers, even more ignorant of theory than they were to be a hundred years later. In the words of one visiting German professor of physics in 1780:

> [he] . . . could scarcely find words to describe what wretched people English artificers generally were in matters of theory. He cannot conceive how they continue so excellently to construct machines, which they nevertheless often explain and understand quite incorrectly.

He was echoed by Thomas Henry, the Manchester chemist, two years later:

> The misfortune is that few dyers are chemists and few chemists, dyers.

and by Bishop Watson about the same time:

> The artists themselves are generally illiterate, timid and bigotted . . . Being unacquainted with the learned, or modern, languages, they seldom know anything of modern discoveries, or of the methods practised in foreign countries.[26]

Views of this kind have found widespread support in the literature; but the

[24] See below, notes 249 and 253.
[25] Thompson (1965), 331–3; Heyck (1982), 56, 63, B1–3; Sussman (1968), 33–4, 166; Basalla, Coleman, Kargon (1970), 17; Houghton (1970), 33–45.
[26] Mare and Quarrell (1938), 47; Cardwell (1957), 17; Coleby (1953), 115–16; Conant (1971), 55, 58, 67, 299–300.

opposite view, that the leading inventors and innovators of the industrial revolution were in close contact with science and made use of it in their technology, has also been defended with vigour.[27]

We cannot enter here into this controversy, which is continuing, but the disagreement turns in part on the definition of 'science'. No doubt, much of what was then currently believed by scientists, later turned out to be 'wrong'; and several sciences were still at the stage of simple taxonomy, without any unifying principles. At least one leading engineer thought as late as the 1860s that the formulae on retaining walls had 'the same practical value as the weather forecast for the year in Old Moore's Almanack' and the Tay Bridge disaster was at least in part due to erroneous calculations by Sir George Airey.[28] Against this, if Watt attempted by experiment and calculation to improve his steam engine step by step, if Wedgwood read all the literature he could lay his hands on and then made hundreds or thousands of systematic experiments, inventing his own measuring instrument and employing a professional chemist, if Faraday and John Herschel helped Dollond to produce a better optical glass, or if the chemical manufacturers attempted to apply the latest discoveries, they were, in some way, using scientific methods.[29] Similarly, it was not without significance that Cambridge professors of Mathematics, of Engineering or Chemistry considered it part of their duties to learn and describe the methods in use in industry: (Bishop) Watson, on his appointment to the Chair of Chemistry there in 1764, 'decided that the application of chemistry to the arts and manufactures was the most fitting theme at that time for a University course'. Even the Royal Institution, founded 1799 largely by a group of gentlemen, had as its object 'the application of science to the common purposes of life', which to its founders meant largely scientific agricultural improvement. In its early decades, a succession of brilliant lecturers and researches, including Humphry Davy, Michael Faraday, Thomas Young and John Tyndall did not only fundamental research but also practical work mainly on subjects of interest to London, such as gas lighting, water purification, optical glassmaking, biology (for medical students), telegraphy, printing and work in Woolwich Arsenal, beside safety in mines and the preparation of evidence to official enquiries.[30]

While Britain led the world in her industrial technology in the later eighteenth and early nineteenth centuries, it was France which made the greatest progress in pure science. Why she failed to turn this into economic progress has often been discussed. Among the causes were certainly centralization of decision taking and a lack of entrepreneurship. Leblanc, typically enough, asked for a Government subsidy in 1791 to exploit his discovery of cheap soda manufacture; the factory that was built for him in 1791 was owned

[27] There is an enormous literature. See, e.g. Musson and Robinson (1969); Hardie (1972), 168–94; McKendrick (1973), 274–319; Porter (1972), 320–43.
[28] Basalla, Coleman, Kargon (1970); Roscoe (1901), 159–60, 164, 189–90; Hooykaas (1966), 1, 2, 7, 24; Rolt (1979), 168–9, 191–2; Russell (1972), 169–70; Béland (1976), 324. For a general discussion see Mayr (1976), 663–73.
[29] McKendrick (1973), 286–7, 304.
[30] Armytage (1955), 162; Harris (1976), 168, 172–9; Hilken (1967), 4–15; Buchanan (1976), 73–83; Foote (1954), 439–40; Babbage (1837), 379; Martin (1963) I, 49, 62; Berman (1978). Also see note 247 below.

by a Royal Duke, and when the latter was guillotined two years later, it had to be closed down,[31] while British manufacturers were building a chemical industry on his process. Thus it was shown that progressive science could coexist with industrial retardation; and enormous industrial strides could be made at least in part on the basis of discoveries made elsewhere.

In sum, there is no evidence that Britain's smooth upward path of pioneering new technologies was at any time held up by weaknesses in the educational field, unplanned and uncoordinated though that was. The balance and the location of the educational provisions were evidently such as to help industrial advance without wasting too much of the precious limited national resources on education which did not benefit national progress.[32]

At the lowest level, taking the widespread assumption that a literacy rate of around 40% is needed to allow industrialization to take place, that level had been comfortably reached in Britain by the mid-eighteenth century, Scotland being well ahead of England in this matter, suffering a certain brain drain as a result. If we take the ability to sign one's name, despite all the misgivings about such a test, as a proxy for at least a minimal reading ability, then 'literacy', in that sense, extended to around 60% of males in 1750, at the onset of industrialization, and to 35% of females. By 1830–40, it had reached 65–70% for males, 50–60% for females, and by 1860, some 80–90% for both. By that time, the Newcastle Commission believed, probably justly, that poverty was no longer a barrier to minimal literacy. Only 'intemperance, apathy and recklessness' on the part of the parents kept children from a basic school attendance.[33] Whether there was a decline in literacy in the first decades of the factory system, to be made good later, is controversial.

For the middle and middling classes, it goes without saying, the provision of schooling was far superior. Frequently they might be in a position to ensure that grammar schools and other older foundations would include modern subjects such as mathematics and applied mathematics, natural science and commercial subjects. The Scots were particularly successful in this respect. When Lord Eldon's judgement in the case of Leeds Grammar School blocked that path, the middle classes formed their own new schools, starting with the Liverpool Institution in 1825; the religious minorities among them founded Ackworth, Mill Hill, Kingswood and Stonyhurst among others.[34] Where industrialists were dissatisfied with any of the available schooling, which was quite common, they had their children educated at home, if they could afford it, specifying modern subjects.[35] There were specialist schools, directed towards

[31] Lilley (1973 III), 232; Gillespie (1972), 121, 126; Treue (1966), 32–3; Cardwell (1978), 36; Rosenberg (1972), 32.
[32] Sanderson (1983), 30; Pollard (1966), 11–29; West (1975), 80, 83. But see Ringer (1979), 2.
[33] This is echoed by modern observers of less developed countries. Illiteracy is not due to poverty, they say, but to 'apathy, negligence and other causes'. Bataille (1976), 13; Illiteracy in 1969 was estimated at 81.0% in Africa, 81.1% in the Arab states, 55.2% in Asia as a whole and 32.5% in Latin America; Bataille (1976), 4; R.C. (1861), vol. 1, pp. 85, 178; Cipolla (1969), 11–15; Anderson (1983a), 16; Anderson (1963), 348–9; Stone (1969), 109. Also see pp. 138 and 162–3 below.
[34] Smout (1969), 467, 473, 479; Anderson (1983a), 349; Stone (1969), 136–7.
[35] Musgrove (1959–60), 109 and Musgrove (1970), 117–25; Schofield (1963), 131, 407 ff; Edgeworth (1809); Musson and Robinson (1969), 200 ff.

particular trades, often known as 'academies', in many towns, and while the East India Company set up Haileybury, the State was not backward in forming military colleges (Woolwich 1741, also High Wycombe 1799 and Great Marlow 1802) and the Gosport Naval Academy (1791). The Portsmouth Naval College included instruction for shipbuilders and engineers.[36]

At the highest level also, the British educational system proved to be remarkably flexible in the decades of the industrial revolution. True, the ancient universities took little part, though even here the foundation of a number of chairs in the natural sciences, especially in Cambridge, and the introduction of the Mathematical Tripos there in 1747 showed some response to the new intellectual climate. The Scottish universities, however, were among the leaders of the new science, including even applied science, in Europe. Glasgow had the closest contact with industry there, and the most alumni who turned to commercial or industrial occupations.[37] In England, it was the dissenting Academies, founded originally to train nonconformist clergymen, at which science to the highest level was taught and where some of the leading scientists of the age found employment. London and other cities also had numerous science lectures by local or peripatetic lecturers.[38] In this connection the highest educational level reached by 106 of the leading cotton masters in 1830–60 may be of interest:[39]

	Father also in cotton	First generation	Total
Village dame school	–	5	5
Grammar school	11	10	21
Private school	15	5	20
Dissenting academies	13	4	17
Public school	14	3	17
University	13	3	16
Education abroad	5	–	5
Vocational education	4	1	5
	75	31	106

Lastly, there were the societies. The Royal Society of Arts (1754) and its equivalents in Edinburgh and Dublin, offered prizes and other incentives for the invention, introduction or propagation of innovations in agriculture and industry. In others, like the Lunar Society (1765–*c*. 1800) and the numerous local 'Lit. and Phils.', members read learned papers to each other and aided each other in their scientific as well as literary investigations. The 'Geological and Polytechnic Society of the West Riding' was founded at a meeting of the Coal Owners' Association and the Royal Geological Society of Cornwall was similarly established (1814) to aid local mining.[40]

Some of the higher scientific learning was made available to artisans also. In Spitalfields, a Mathematical Society for weavers had been formed as early as

---

[36]Hans (1951); O'Day (1982), 199, 208–9; Simon (1970), 113 ff; Timmons (1983), 142–5.

[37] Smout (1969), 476–8; O'Day (1982), 225 ff; Olson (1975); Christie (1975), 117–21. Also see p. 000, note 231 below.

[38] Musson and Robinson (1969), 92–3; Gibbs (1972), 197–200; Kargon (1977), 11–12.

[39] Howe (1984), 55; Gibbs (1965), 11–16.

[40] Inkster (1983), (Introduction), 23; Schofield (1963); Phillipson (1975), 445; S.C. (1867–8), vi; Orange (1973).

1717, and there were others examples in other textile towns. John Anderson's foundation of a university for mechanics in Glasgow in 1796 led to a continuous provision of lectures, on physics and chemistry and their application to the arts, as well as on mathematics, botany, and agriculture, sometimes to enthusiastic artisan audiences of several hundred, and a similar demand seems to have existed in Edinburgh for Leonard Horner's School of Arts (1821), where James Nasmyth took evening classes in mechanical philosophy, geometry, mathematics and chemistry. There are records also of lectures in Birmingham, London and elsewhere, before the foundation of Mechanics' Institutes ushered in a new era from 1823.[41]

However, the practical know-how of artisans acquired in the works was clearly of greater significance. It was that which other countries missed most, and found most difficult to transfer. Nor should the importance and quality of the extremely efficient British apprenticeship system be underrated. When the legal apprenticeship regulations were abolished in Britain in 1814, they had become sufficiently well anchored to survive this legal assault, by virtue of the power of the trade unions which enforced them even in trades to which they had not legally applied before.[42] To the skills acquired during apprenticeship were added practical experience and the intuitive understanding of the properties of materials and of the nature of mechanical action acquired at work. Some of the leading engineering entrepreneurs, including Joseph Clement, George Stephenson, Joseph Locke, James Nasmyth, Joseph Whitworth together with John Buddle, greatest of north-eastern coal viewers, were virtually untutored or they rose from the ranks, so that in one lifetime they had not only to make the transition from rags to riches, but also to absorb, and indeed create, a completely new technology. Their range was often prodigious. The same man would build steam engines and locomotives, design bridges or canals, and lay down railway tracks and tunnels. Fairbairn, starting his business from scratch as a small engineering workshop, built, largely to his own design, engines, ships, bridges and cranes, sometimes even having to work out the needed mechanical formulae for himself.[43]

If the credit for the achievements of the British industrial revolution is frequently given to the economic and political circumstances of a thrustful free society, possibly aided by natural resources and an appropriate theology, the influence of the scientific and technological culture upon the British genius should not be forgotten, either. For just as the British scientists, who, as we have seen above, were distinguished by brilliant individual forays forward without an infantry to occupy a broad territory behind them, men without schooling or 'schools', so her technological pioneers were marked by originality, by freedom and independence of thought, unaided, but also unhampered by methodical and systematic research. These were characteristics which stood them in good stead during the industrial revolution; it was not certain that they would be equally valuable a hundred years later.

[41] O'Day (1982), 24; Musson and Robinson (1969), 489 ff; Muir (1950); Inkster (1985b), 4–5.
[42] Derry (1931–2); Rule (1981) ch. 4.
[43] Buchanan (1985), 42; Musson and Robinson (1969), 38; Heesom (1981), 138–9; Argles (1964), 10–11; Musson and Robinson (1969), 487 ff; Straub (1975), 67, 71, 82.

On this basis, technological progress, and with it economic growth at an unprecedented speed were taking place in Britain. Neither the science nor the inventive ideas themselves were necessarily British, but if they originated abroad, they were still developed and put into practice in Britain first, to be re-exported as completed techniques decades later, sometimes even then viable abroad only with the aid of British specialists.

The technical leadership and superiority over the rest of the world was maintained for at least a century, and there was scarcely an industrial sector to which it did not extend. The exceptions were unimportant or doubtful: French silks or fashion goods, perhaps, German toys or American mass-produced small arms. In all the key sectors the lead was unassailable: textiles, coal mining, iron and steel production and steam engine building, applied on the iron bridges, iron steam ships and, above all, the railways.

This was so even in those sectors which by the end of the century had turned into relative failures, such as chemicals, machine tools and electrical engineering. In the chemical industry, technical knowhow, and an intuitive understanding of the properties of matter must surely have played some part of the lives of such leading manufacturers as Charles MacIntosh, who developed not only bleaching powder but also a method of waterproofing clothing, Charles Tennant, Lord Dundonald or James Muspratt. By the mid-nineteenth century, the British chemical industry still dominated the world's markets. It had the production of sulphuric acid and the decomposition of salt at its base, but coal tar and gas were also near-monopolies of Britain, and Liebig's super-phosphate fertilizer was tried out and used there first. Even in the organic section, particularly in the early development of coal-tar dyes and pharmaceuticals in which Germany took the lead, it might be noted that many of her most original scientists had spent some time in Britain to gain experience, and the Deutsche Chemische Gesellschaft, formed in 1867 with the object of bringing scientists and industry together, was established largely by chemists who had returned from Britain.[44]

In the case of machine tools, early on the British lead seemed similarly unassailable: this was an area where some of Britain's most brilliant engineers, including Maudslay and Whitworth, had made their mark. Electrical engineering, it is true, did not yet exist. But while Faraday was one of an international group of original scientists who developed the theoretical base, the final stages of turning the abstract knowledge of electro-magnetism into a workable telegraphic system were the work of W.F. Cooke and Charles Wheatsone.[45] The first long-distance line was laid by them in 1839 on the Great Western Railway (Paddington – West Drayton), and by 1855 they operated 4,500 miles in Great Britain, the nearest rival reaching only 2,200 miles. In the following period of underwater cable-laying much of the pioneering work was again done by British firms. Only the USA had a comparable record.

[44] Borscheid (1976), 91–2, 99, 122, 210; Treue (1966), 32–3, 50; Singer, Holmyard, Hall and Williams (1954–8), IV, 239, 252, 258–64; V, 254; A. und N. Clow (1972), 163–5; Haber (1958), 55, 65–6. Also p. 157 below.
[45] Dunsheath (1962), 71–6; Singer *et al.* (1954–8); vol. 4, 654–5, vol. 5, 179–80, 218, 224; Derry and Williams (1960), 625–7; Weiher (1980), 28.

Thus in spite of the alleged weakness of British scientific and technological training and research, these science-based industries held up well at least until the mid-century. Was it merely because 'science', in the proper sense, was not yet needed?

The first signs of danger of an inadequate response to technical challenges owing to an inadequate understanding of science and technology appeared in the 1850s, at a time when the British industrial leadership in general was still undisputed. Two examples might be quoted: the mass-production of steel and the development of coal-tar dyes.

Henry Bessemer's ingenuity and resourcefulness are not in doubt. Yet when his later trials of converting pig iron into steel failed in a glare of publicity, he lacked the basic training in science which might have suggested to him why they differed from his earlier spectacular successes. It was the work of Goränsson, a Swedish ironmaster, and of R.F. Mushet, a steelmaker rather than a scientific metallurgist, who put him on the right track by pointing out that, to succeed, the converter process required ores free of phosphorus and of sulphur. Equally significant was the behaviour of the large British ironmasters, the leading firms in the world in their day. Having flocked to Bessemer, eager to pay enormous licence fees when he announced his spectacular discovery, they dropped him unceremoniously after his first failure. Not one of them had enough scientific sense or even the urge to know whether something could be salvaged from so promising a start. In the end Bessemer had to set up his own works to prove that, given the right conditions, his method was both feasible and highly profitable: even then, his steel met much prejudice, especially on the part of the Admiralty and of Lloyd's, who lacked proper means of scientific testing.[46]

Siemens, the inventor of the next important process, the open-hearth method of steelmaking, was indeed himself a man trained in science; but he, too, had to set up his own works, first in Birmingham and then at Landore, before the British steelmakers were persuaded of the benefits of his innovation, though in his case also he used no scientific discovery dating from later than the 1790s. Lowthian Bell, one of the very few British ironmasters with a knowledge of science, came closest to the truth with his assertion that the great innovations in steel-making in that transition period still originated in Britain, but that they would have been applied more easily and more rapidly had there been a better understanding of science among British industrialists.[47] Of the two originators of the third great innovation in steelmaking, the basic lining, at least one, Percy Gilchrist, was a chemist (the other, Gilchrist Thomas, being a clerk and amateur scientist) while both the other men who helped the process forward, G.J. Snelus and E. Riley, were alumni of the Royal School of Mining.

Equally poignant were the developments in the coal-tar dye industry. The key discovery was made in Britain in 1856 by W.H. Perkin, who recognized its potential at once. His teacher, Professor A.W. Hofmann, was a German trained in the German scientific tradition, and there were at the time several other able

[46] Birch (1867), 319 ff; Erickson (1959), 142 ff.
[47] Lilley (1973), 237–8; Erickson (1959), 156–64; Burn (1940), 200–18; R.C. (1872), ev. Bell Q.9167; R.C. (1872), ev. Bell QQ.265–8; Carr and Taplin (1962), 98–100.

German chemists working in Britain, since it seemed to them that this was where the chemical industry had the greatest potential and where chemical science was sadly under-developed. However, within two decades all that had changed. The leading British discoverers and chemical manufacturers, Perkin, Nicholson and Greville Williams, were retiring from business, having failed to find university-trained men to carry on their innovative tradition; the great expansion in the new line was taking place in Germany; and within a short time, coal-tar chemistry became one of the major triumphs of German industry and one of the major failures of the British.[48]

Of course, it would have been unreasonable for a country like Britain to expect to keep forever the enormous industrial lead over the rest of the world built up in the first half of the century. But it was possibly significant that the early challenges came not, as one might have expected, in sectors using cheap labour or exotic resources, in which Britain might be deficient, but precisely in what would nowadays be called the high-technology industries in which the most advanced country of the day should have had its most pronounced comparative advantages.

III Science, Education and Industrial Progress

Before turning to re-examine the evidence, it will be necessary to clarify some of the issues involved in the debate and in particular, to separate out the various relationships which are frequently confounded in it. With economic growth and/or the economic performance as the dependent variable, at least two types of input have been held to have had a significant influence: scientific knowledge, and education and training. Each of these, in turn, consists of several separate components. In the case of science, there is implicit the notion that advances in pure science lead to technological invention, that invention leads to actual practical application, and that this then spreads only if the pure science or the pioneer technology had also been developed at home. As far as education is concerned, it has been held at different times that, in the case of workers, a progressive economy requires (a) literacy (b) manual skills (c) scientific knowledge and/or flexibility of mind to accept innovation. In the case of foremen and junior managers, it has been asserted that a knowledge of science and of the principles of technology have a beneficial influence. Lastly, for senior managers and owners a knowledge of science and technology has been assumed to be positively related to growth in the economy, but a case has also been made out for a flexible mental attitude to innovation and for the ability to manage the workforce.

That technical change contributes to economic growth is nowhere in doubt. In the economic literature it is sometimes treated as an unexplained extra, the 'residual', contained in increases in output after increases due to enlarged inputs of such factors as capital, labour or land have been deducted. It is expressed alternatively as a rise in total factor productivity, or that part of it remaining after economies of scale, the level of employment and other

---

[48] See below, p. 157.

influences have been accounted for.[49] In the calculations for the twentieth century, the residual has frequently been found to account for as much growth, or even for more, than is accounted for by the increase in physical input. Denison came to the following results:

Table 3.1 *Annual rates of increase per person employed (%)*[+]

	USA 1909–29	USA 1929–57	USA 1950–62	N.W. Europe 1950–62
Output/national income	1.22	1.60	2.15	3.80
Total factor input	0.65	0.67	0.79	0.73
Output per unit of input	0.56	0.93	1.36	3.07
Due to education	0.56	0.67	0.49	0.23
Due to advancement of knowledge	NA	0.58	0.75	1.30

+ The bases for these calculations are not always strictly comparable

According to another estimate of the American output growth in 1909–49, 1.2% p.a. was due to the residual, against only 1.0% for increased factors, for Norway 1900–55, the figures were 1.8% and 0.96% respectively, and for Finland in 1925–52, they were 1.2% and 1.0%.

For the later nineteenth century, a calculation for Germany in 1850–1913, allows 1.1% p.a. of the total growth rate of 2.6% p.a. to the growth in total factor productivity; if the increase in labour productivity due to better education is deducted and counted as an input instead, the 1.13% becomes 0.94% p.a. allocable to technical progress.

For Britain, for the period 1856–1913 total factor productivity accounted for much the largest part of the output increase; if improvement in the quality of labour is counted as input, however, there is little left of TFP of productivity increase; after 1900, indeed, this became negative, to average out at zero in 1873–1913:

Table 3.2 *Annual increases in %, 1856–1913*

	Output	TFP crude	TFP, less change in labour quality	Implied lab. qual.
1856–1873	2.2	1.4	0.6	0.8
1873–1913	1.8	0.5	0.0	0.5

According to another calculation, improvement in the quality of labour amounted to 1.4% in 1856–73, 0.8% in 1873–1913, and 1.0% p.a. for the period as a whole.[50]

49 Abramovitz (1956), 12–13; Solow (1957), 312–20 and Solow (1971), 209–13; Selowsky (1969), 449. Kendrick (1961), chap. 3 and 4; Denison (1967), 281 ff; Denison (1974), 80. If we adopt the method of Jorgensson and Griliches of accounting for technological or scientific improvement by re-valuing inputs, then science, technology and education become necessary inputs, which allegedly were lower in Britain than they should have been: Jorgenson and Griliches (1974); Domar (1971), 218.
50 Cf. Table 1.19; also Becker (1975), 196; Aukrust (1972), 93–6; Schmookler (1952), 224, 230; Denison (1974), 136–7; Denison (1967), 198–301; Denison (1962), 265; Denison (n.d.), 15; Griliches (1973), 67.

This approach, and in particular the surprising accuracy of its results, has not been without its critics. Among the main points of criticisms were: the assumption that factor payments are identical with their marginal productivity; the failure to see that several of the items were interrelated and could not simply be automatically isolated; the difficulties of measuring capital inputs; and the uncertainties of a residual which includes many other things beside the growth in knowledge.[51]

Historians have always recognized the importance of technical progress. In our present context, however, the question is, to what extent and in what manner, the technical changes introduced into British firms in the period before 1914 were actually affected by weaknesses in scientific research, in technical inventiveness, and in the skill in adopting the innovations of others.

Research in pure science, we have seen, has been widely judged to have been inadequate in our period in Britain. If that weakness was to have been a contributory factor to the slow growth of the economy, what is, or was, the link between the work of the pure scientist and the methods adopted by productive industry on the ground?

We have noted that the issue is controversial even within the simpler framework of the period of the industrial revolution. It then turned, in part, on whether contemporary scientific generalizations were useful, or 'wrong', and in part, on how many of the leading industrial innovators had absorbed a scientific attitude or methodology from their dabblings in science, to stand them in good stead in their practical tinkering. But in addition, we noted that although some of the greatest scientists of the day were working in France, and many of the key discoveries were made there, this did not prevent Britain taking the technological lead and France lagging behind.

A century later, in the Victorian period, scientific discoveries had greatly widened in scope and understanding. At the same time, industry had become more dependent on science and on more advanced technology. The nature of their relationship, however, remained no less controversial.

Let us begin with two issues which loom large in the debate on the progress of science but which appear, at first sight, to have no direct relevance to our own question. The first debate concerns the extent to which scientific discovery is the result of inspiration, of solitary genius frequently working along unorthodox lines, or, alternatively, the result of systematic search perhaps by groups of linked researchers, along lines indicated by existing and confirmed theory.[52] It is evident that the structure of British science, giving a great deal of freedom to the individual, but requiring something of an obsession with science and calling for a certain independence of thought, would turn out to be a favourable soil for scientific discovery if the first alternative applied, whereas the continent, with its serried ranks of well endowed academicians and university and polytechnic teachers would be favoured, if the second applied.

The other debate concerns the direction taken by scientific enquiry at any

[51] Abramovitz (1962), Abramovitz (1964), 8; Kaldor (1961), 1–4; Nicholas (1982b).

[52] The debate on this issue, as on the following one, spills over into the debate on inventions and is not easy to separate from it. Hollomon (1965), 127–8; Layton (214–15); Schmookler (1966), 189–91; Schmookler (1972), 11–12; MacLaurin (1953), 99–101; Basalla (1968), x; Hessen (1968), 36; Pfetsch (1974), 20–4.

given time. Is it determined by 'internal' factors, such as the level of knowledge reached, the current debates, as seen in the scientific literature, and the scientific paradigmata established for the time being, or is it likely to be determined by 'outside' factors, such as social demands or economic opportunities?[53] In the latter case, weaknesses in scientific research would have a more immediate ill effect on an economy, than in the former.

For our purposes, what matters is less the causes of scientific discovery than its consequences for national industry. Curiously enough, there is widespread agreement on the reverse linkage: science frequently benefited by the activities of practical technicians and technologists, especially by the collection of data, the devising of measuring instruments and the provision of appropriate formulae. A convincing study by Rosenberg and Vincenti shows how this operated in a particular case, the building of the Britannia bridge.[54]

In regard to the linkage at the centre of our interest, the contribution of science to technology, there is far less agreement. No doubt, ultimately all technologists must depend on some general scientific notions, but this by no means implies that they depend on recent scientific discoveries, still less that they depend on the discoveries of their own countrymen. Members of the science lobby, to be sure, had no doubt on that score:

> 'A nation that has to buy its science', declared Frankland roundly, 'will always be behind, and follow the lead of other countries, which I imagine, would be a commercial disadvantage',

and Lockyer was convinced that science today was real technical progress tomorrow. As practical examples, the work of Lord Kelvin, Edison's electrical inventions and the Mond Nickel process have been quoted, in which scientific discoveries might be held to have led directly to lucrative practical applications.[55] In a slightly weaker form, this claim appeared as the assertion that science could provide a technique to achieve results, to avoid or eliminate unproductive lines of approach and therefore to make the practical inventor's path easier. This essentially was the line taken by Playfair (1885), Fairbairn (1861) and Roscoe (1887) in their presidential addresses to the British Association; it was also the central message of James B. Conant's influential work, *Science and Common Sense*.[56]

Yet this has remained distinctly a minority view. Even David Brewster, in his spirited defence of science in 1830, had to admit that

> discoveries in abstract science, however rich and ample may be their blossom, do not at once bring their fruits into the national treasury. Many a winter intervenes between their spring and their harvest, and centuries often elapse before they find a practical application.

[53] E.g. S. Rose (1969), 244–5; Berman (1975), 30–1; Price (1972), 166–70, 178; Price (1965), 553–68; Schmookler (1972), 50; Schmookler (1971), 117 ff; Griliches and Schmookler (1963), 725–9; Gilfillan (1970), 61 ff; 71, 137 ff and Gilfillan (1945), 67–71.
[54] Rosenberg and Vincenti (1978), also see Rae (1960), 144.
[55] R.C. (1872) ev. Frankland Q.5883, also Bell QQ.9190–2, 9767; Lockyer (10 Sep. 1903), 445; Weiher (1980), 34; Carter and Williams (1957), 19; Pavitt with Ward (1971), 14, 54, 95–102, 131–5.
[56] Conant (1971); Basalla *et al.* (1970); Playfair (p. 78); Fairbairn (139); Roscoe (1901), 161–2.

Numerous examples could be given from practical industry to support that proposition. Nineteenth-century metallurgy, bridge-building or brewing progressed without any science worth mentioning; the telephone and radio used scientific principles known for at least half a century, and refrigeration, for which the first useful patent was taken out in England in 1856, was based on principles known since 1755. Schmookler, after studying 934 important inventions in four industries in the period 1800–1957 judged that not in a single case could a scientific discovery be said to be the initiating factor.[57] Even in the middle of the twentieth century a major enquiry by the Materials Advisory Board of the American National Academy of Science found that the occurrence of inventions could not be related to any preceding scientific discoveries. Other enquires have led to the conclusion that

> it is not known whether there is any necessary connection between the growth of scientific knowledge and the growth of technology and invention or, if there is a connection, what are its laws (Jewkes *et al.*),

and

> There is no evidence of a positive association between national research and growth. (Williams)[58]

This reference to *national* research and growth is significant, for scientific knowledge is universal and backward countries can always use the technology developed elsewhere; conversely, it has rightly been said in the case of modern less developed countries, that their problems would seldom be reduced if they merely had more scientists.[59]. In the later nineteenth century while Russia was an example of a country with some brilliantly inventive scientists, which yet had to go abroad for even the simplest technology, the USA, by contrast, which made a very poor showing in pure science before the end of the nineteenth century, became leading in the technology of one industry after another.

It would thus be hard to sustain the view that the absence of the kind of organized pure scientific research which flourished in Germany could have affected British economic growth outside a few special fields, such as coal-tar chemistry. Besides, there was no shortage of brilliance at the highest level in an unbroken tradition from Faraday, Clerk Maxwell, Kelvin, Darwin and Huxley to Rayleigh and Rutherford.

We now turn to the second link in the chain, the transformation of an invention into a workable and working practical proposition, sometimes termed an innovation. Not all innovations are of a technical nature, and, as we shall see, even technologically based innovations frequently depend on economic, managerial and other factors. However, the assertion has sometimes been made or implied that it was here, in this link, that Britain failed, and that her shortcomings in turn were due to scientific-technical weaknesses.

As in the case of inventions, much of the literature is concerned with the

[57] Brewster (1830), 332–3; Schmookler (1966), 65–7; Gilfillan (1970), 6; Roberts (1975), 459; Rosenberg (1972), 119; Epstein (1926).
[58] Jewkes *et al.* (1969), 21; Williams (1967), 3, also 57. Layton (1977), 209; Price (1965), 568; Bud and Roberts (1984), 12–13.
[59] Strassmann (1968), 226–7; Trickovic (1973), 291.

origins of technical innovation, with the question whether it is 'induced' by economic opportunity or the result of intellectual breakthrough; indeed, the differences between invention and successful application in this context are not always made clear in the debate.[60] Patents are frequently brought into the argument, for they may be subject to quantitative treatment, but patent statistics may be misleading. Not all technical innovations are patented. In Germany the laws and regulations favoured large companies, and individuals were normally not in a position to carry registration through to its conclusion; elsewhere there were other reasons for protecting oneself by secrecy rather than by patents. Moreover, patents may be of greatly differing significance: those which contributed to progress in a major way were only a small minority of the total. Above all, however, patents may represent both a first inventive idea, or a practical application, i.e. they may lie at either end of the gap between the two extremes which it is our purpose to investigate. In any case, it has been found that the time which elapsed in practice between invention and application could be as long, and as variable, as that elapsing between scientific discovery and invention, and it clearly depended on a variety of circumstances.[61]

In the twentieth century, the stage between invention and practical feasibility is frequently termed research and development, or R & D. It has been studied in great detail, and the results are inconclusive. In the words of an OECD Report: 'there is no observed correlation between the proportion of national resources devoted to R & D and rates of growth of productivity'. Probably the oft-quoted case of the steamboat was quite typical: there was no particular point of completed development, but a slow accretion of improvements over the decades.[62]

How did all this affect Britain in the decades to 1914? The evidence, as usual, is inconclusive. Possible weaknesses were the failure to build up teams of chemists on the German model, and the conservatism in the British machine-tool industry. Against this, Froude's model tank for testing ship design, the development of Parson's turbine or Marconi's wireless, showed that Britain was capable of leading precisely in the critical breakthrough phase of technological development. The case of Marconi, an Italian inventor who took his idea to Britain where British backers and British engineers helped him through to the stage of practical application, shows, incidentally, that completed processes, like scientific ideas, travel easily across the frontiers between states at fairly equal stages of development. Technology, like science, was potentially international.[63]

To sum up: the evidence for the development stage is more mixed than for the invention stage. A greater spread of scientific or technological competence, but also some risk capital and commercial skills may be required. The British record was more mixed than in the case of pure science, but by no means dismal and, in any case, the lack of home-grown innovation need not inhibit growth: it is possible to import technology in its developed stage.

[60] Jewkes *et al.* (1969); Kennedy and Thirlwall (1972), 51–3; Pavitt (1971) 11–12; Freeman (1977) 251–2; Meier and Baldwin (1966), 159–61.
[61] Mansfield (1968), 101–3; MacLaurin (1953), 102; Williams (1967), 57; Myers and Marquis (1969), 59–61; Rosenberg (1976), 69 ff.
[62] O.E.C.D. (1971), 20; Pavitt (1980), 10; Rosenberg (1972), 120.
[63] See p. 204, note 295 below.

We turn now to the third linkage: the application of a developed innovation to the whole of the industrial sector able to profit from it. It was to failure in this process of diffusion in such examples as new methods of producing steel, the Solvay process or the diesel engine in ships, that most accusations of technical retardation seem to refer.[64]

But diffusion is a complicated process. Even in modern times it can be very slow[65] and it may well depend less on technical or scientific competence than on commercial acumen or quickness of reaction to the market, at any rate in a country as close to the leaders as the UK was in this period. The issue here is entrepreneurship, not technical superiority. Thus, once more, it is not easy to relate alleged industrial retardation to failings in science and technology.

We now turn to the second line of our enquiry, the role of education. The notion that education contributes directly to economic growth enjoys a long and respectable tradition. It goes back to Petty and Adam Smith and includes Giffen, Farr and Horace Mann.

> 'The best educated community', asserted Rufus Putnam, principal of the High School at Salem, Massachusetts, in 1854, 'will *always* be the most prosperous community . . . nothing so directly tends to promote the increase of *wealth* in a community as the thorough mental traiing of its youth.'

J.S. Nicholson attempted some broad calculations on the relationship between education and wealth in 1891, and Irving Fisher developed the idea of an internal rate of return of current costs on education over future receipts as early as 1906. Since 1935, there has been a more continuous debate on this issue.[66]

In principle, two forms of approach are possible: education as a stock of knowledge, to be added to other capital, on which a rate of return may be calculated; or education as a stream of expenditure, to be compared with higher output after some lag. But simple ratios are invalidated by the fact that education is a consumption good as well as a form of investment, or at least is undertaken for reasons other than the improvement in earning power, and that there is no known way of separating out the two components.

As in the case of the contribution of technology, it has been possible to work out the contribution of 'education' to economic growth as a form of the improvement in the quality of labour. Denison, in his pioneer work, found education to have accounted for between 20% and 40% of economic growth in the USA between 1909 and 1962 (see Table 3.1 above); 10 European countries in 1950–62 showed increases in economic growth attributable to education to range between 2% and 15% of the growth rate. In Britain education has been estimated on a similar basis to have added 0.3% a year to the quality of the labour force in 1856–73, and rather more thereafter. Of the 0.3%, 0.2%, was due to general education and 0.1% to technical education. The contribution of higher education was too small to be measured.[67]

---

[64] McCloskey (1981) and McCloskey (1973); Lindert and Trace (1971), 239–74; Burn (1940), 1, 4, 10.
[65] Mansfield (1971), 284–315; Mansfield (1973); Rogers (1962), 2–3, 15–18; Griliches (1973), 60.
[66] Nicholson (1890), 95–107; Evans and Wiseman (1984), 142; Lundgreen (1973), and Lundgreen (1975a), 64; Katz (1968), 27–30; Komarov (1971), 59 ff. and Sec.VII; Vinovskis (1970), 550–71.
[67] Lundgreen (1973), esp. 76–82, 86, 95, 105, 114–16; Denison (1966), 204–15, 234, and Denison (1967), ch. 8; Matthews, Feinstein and Odling-Smee (1982), 111; Schwartzman (1968), 508; Correa (1963), 172; André (1971), 110.

However small the contribution, it seems clear that the educational level everywhere rose with national income per head. Conversely, Schultz found that in the USA in the period 1900–56 the resources committed to education rose some 3½ times faster than national income. Between those two years, elementary education rose from 5% to 9% of gross capital formation, high school education from 2% to 13%, and higher education from 2% to 12%, or in total a rise from 9% to 34%. As a result, the educational share in the total capital stock rose from 22% to 42% between those dates. On the other hand, a cross-sectional study for a group of advanced and very poor countries in 1953–54 shows that their educational expenditure as a proportion of national income did not differ very much, though of course the differences in absolute per head expenditure were enormous. It is in any case not possible to establish a 'correct' level of educational expenditure, not least because with the passage of time more things are known, and more has to be absorbed by those seeking education, at every given level of national income; there is, in other words, a temporal as well as an income determinant of the 'appropriate' amount of education.[68]

So far, the statistical work attempting to relate education to income has been mostly rather crude. Neither the years of schooling nor the days actually spent at school can be taken effectively to represent the quantity of education received. Further, the composite nature of education – its aspect as a consumption good – is ignored. Lastly, it fails to account for the differences in mix, and the 'state of the arts' which reflected in part the development of science at each point in time.[69]

These and similar misgivings led to an alternative 'human capital' approach, which takes individual incomes rather than the total national product as its base. In many countries, data exist which allow us to correlate educational levels reached by numerous individuals with their incomes achieved later in life. On the economists' assumption that incomes reflected real marginal contribution to the national product, a significant estimate of the contribution of education to the growth of national income might be constructed by the summing of individual results.

Numerous calculations for the United States have shown that the personal submission to education, even counting in the costs and the earnings foregone, has proved to be a good 'investment' for the individual, at rates of return usually around 10%–15%, or well above alternative options. In less developed economies, education seems to yield very high returns.[70] For nineteenth-century Britain, Mitch has attempted a calculation, on the same basis, of the return to the individual of achieving literacy, and here also returns were shown to have been potentially high, but with a strongly falling tendency, at least for males, as literacy became more general:

Table 3.3 *Estimated annual returns on achieving literacy, Great Britain 1839–73.*

	Males	Females
1839–43	9.0–42.5%	Under 1 — 16.5%
1869–73	5.0–20.5%	Under 1 — 18.0%

[68] Correa and Tinbergen (1962), 776–86; Vaizey (1969), 458; Blaug (1968), 26; Schultz (1960), 577, 581–2; Martin and Lewis (1956), 209, 233–4.
[69] Schwartzman (1968); Vaizey (1969), 458–9; Lundgreen (1973), 97, 108.
[70] Blaug (1968), 29; Schultz (1962), 1–8; Becker (1975), esp. 5, 6, 63; Kiker (1971b); Miller (1971); Hanoch (1971); Selowsky (1969).

Translated into national terms, however, the effort to abolish illiteracy completely would have brought but a modest return: 2% if education is assumed to have come out of capital, and 7% if it is assumed to have come out of income.[71]

The attempt to derive the national economic value of education from individual correlations of this kind is not without its difficulties, either. The first, obvious, objection is that young people of higher ability are likely to stay longer in education than others: their higher later incomes would then, to an unknown degree, be due to their innate abilities, rather than to the education received. Denison did, indeed, deduct a somewhat arbitrary 40% from his returns to allow for that factor. Beside native ability, parental drive and ambition, the conditions found in the parental home, location, better health, and the social class aspects of jobs and their rewards, might be other variables accounting for both longer stay at school and higher income achieved later, without the one of those being a cause of the other. If education is said to allow more options and higher mobility or to provide status, this might benefit the individual but hardly society as a whole. It has also been asserted that the returns on education should be compared with similar risky assets, not with Government bonds, and would then appear in a much less favourable light. Lastly, no satisfactory study exists to link education and training with competence.[72]

Indeed, the whole argument is statistical. There is, at best, a measurable correlation. What is lacking is an adequate theory, derived from economics or from other sciences, to explain the mechanism; to lay bare, in other words, why years spent at school or college should improve the economic performance of a nation, at any particular level of education or at all of them.

As far as nineteenth-century Britain was concerned, it is clear that businessmen and manufacturers, as well as most politicians, did not believe that such a linkage existed. They preferred the necessary training to be given within the works,[73] and for this they have been widely condemned. But it is, as Roderick Floud correctly observed, at least curious that historians should always have praised the 'expensive, elitist, and state-directed German system as the model which should be followed, and have rejected as insufficient and harmful the system which appears to have developed within the framework of the free market in late nineteenth-century Britain'.[74] Even if the continental system were appropriate for the followers, might it not be more sensible for the pioneer to proceed by on-the-job training, and might not contemporary entrepreneurs have known what they were doing when they ignored the self-interested pleadings of educationists and placed little value on the benefits of formal scientific and technological education on trade?

It will be useful to break up the unwieldy theme of 'education' into its component parts and examine different types of education separately and in more detail. At the lowest level, education consisted in imparting the ability to read.

[71] Borcholdt (1965), 381–2; Lundgreen (1973), 105; Mitch (1985) 560–5.
[72] Blaug (1968), 49, also 58; Schultz (1961), 11; McLelland (1966), 257–78; Becker (1975), 6,192; Weisbrod (1971), 233; Denison (1962), 68–70, and Denison (1974), 44–5; Kullmer and Krug (1967), 570; Vaizey (1962), 89; Evans and Wiseman (1984). 141, 144; Bowman (1971b), 641.
[73] See pp. 198, 200 below.
[74] Floud (1984), 11. Also pp. 151, 162 notes 121, 160, 311 below.

Even if modern development theory assumes a literacy rate of 40% to be necessary for 'takeoff', it does not follow that the standards of the twentieth century can be applied to the eighteenth. There are good grounds for believing that for the broad mass of the labour force, literacy was then not required at all. Factories certainly needed few, if any, literate workers (though they needed literate foremen). Even 'skilled artisans', it has been said, 'may function as well without being literate', Sheffield cutlers forgot their letters once they entered the works, and coal miners also found that they rarely needed to use any literary skills. In a study of Canadian lumber camps in the latter half of the nineteenth century, Graff found that, except for clerical occupations, illiteracy brought little disadvantage in terms of incomes, jobs or security: indeed, the illiterates seemed to be rather more flexible in turning to new kinds of jobs.[75]

About the middle of the nineteenth century there was possibly a change of mood. Increasingly, observers seemed to think that workers required a modicum of literacy, at least as a basis for technical education, if not for the daily workround itself. Modern opinion tends to hold that literacy is of little value at work, but necessary for consumption, health and political influence. By the 1860s, of course, the vast majority of British workers possessed an adequate level of simple literacy and by 1890, illiteracy was down to 3½% in Scotland and 7% in England and Wales.[76] The lack of literacy cannot, then, have been a significant cause of British retardation.

There are, however, two other possible ways in which formal education may have affected the economic performance of the industrial worker: the effect of education on manual skill, and the effect of education, including science education on general attitudes and on mental flexibility.

The claim has been put forward from time to time that workers with some general education were quicker on the uptake in learning new skills or understanding the nature of their work. Economists from Fawcett onwards thought that a basic education would lead to greater 'manual dexterity', or that people with more basic education were 'cheaper to train or otherwise more desirable'.[77] However, the manual skill of the British workman was never in question; it was his attitude to innovation, his adaptability, and the use he might make of pure science, which were in doubt, and the question arises how far these attributes might be affected by education.

Educators and economists had no doubts. The Mechanics' Institute movement was launched in the hope that its science teaching would succeed in 'stimulating invention and making workmen more efficient'. Charles Babbage, in 1851, went as far as to say that even an unskilled man wielding a shovel would wield it more efficiently if he had had some scientific training. As for

---

[75] Schofield (1981), 201, 213; Schofield (1968), 312; Sanderson (1972c), 84, 93, and Sanderson (1974), 102; Sanderson (1967), 10; Smith (1982), 117; Webb (1954), 107–13, and Webb (1949), 333–51; Graff (1981b); Harris (1986), 48, quoting Boulton.

[76] Haines (1969), 49; Howe (1984), 288; Hunt (1981), 111; Walker (1982), 25; West (1978), 377–9.

[77] R.C. (1872), ev. Richardson, Q.1808, also Q.1851; Evans and Wiseman (1984), 133; Nelson *et al.* (1967), 144. Whether trade practices themselves might be taught formally in schools, as had been happening for decades in Germany, Switzerland and even in Britain in trades in which the Government had an interest, was increasingly debated in the later years of the century. Cf. ev. Waterlow and others, R.C. (1882–84), Q.4525; also Bérard (1973), 277–8.

general education, Alfred Marshall thought that what was required was 'general sagacity and energy which are not specialized to any one occupation'.

> To be able to bear in mind many things at a time, to have everything ready when wanted, to act promptly and show resource when anything goes wrong, to accommodate oneself quickly to change in detail of the work done, to be steady and trustworthy, to have always a reserve of force which will come out in an emergency, these are the qualities which make a great industrial people.

Others, in recent years, have tended to stress also the mental flexibility, the ability to turn to new machines or skills, and the wider choice of occupation open to the better educated workman.[78]

Industrialists were, apart from mechanical drawing,[79] far less sanguine about the effects of general education on efficiency. Platt Brothers, it is true, found that their works school made workmen more trustworthy, so that they needed less supervision, they understood their work better, could explain it and instruct others better and were also more willing to do so and in general to collaborate with others, they would learn and pick up new skills more quickly, foresee results and errors better, have a more positive attitude to new ideas and work with more economy in material and in time.[80] But few of these alleged benefits were technical. Most had to do with attitude and motivation, and in this regard, the possible moral influence of general education among workmen, there was a more widespread consensus among contemporaries. To cite Alfred Marshall once again:

> A good education confers great indirect benefits even on the ordinary workman. It stimulates his mental activity; it fosters in him a habit of wise acquisitiveness; it makes him more intelligent, more ready, more trustworthy in his ordinary work; it raises the tone of his life in working hours and out of working hours; it is thus an important means towards the production of material wealth.[81]

John Stuart Mill believed that education would limit the 'intemperance and improvidence' of working people, and others also stressed the better health (owing to less drunkenness), steadiness and trustworthiness of the educated workman. Nicholas Wood, one of the leading coal viewers in the North East, while denying that the subject matter taught in schools helped the miners, 'their work being mainly mechanical, and there being no superior mode of doing it', yet looked with favour on education, since it made men steadier and less prone to rioting. 'Men are selected for overmen and deputies', he continued, 'not for their education, but for their general qualities'. The Royal Commission on the Depression of Trade (1886) agreed:

> We think that the careful and thorough training in habits of punctuality and order, of alacrity and diligence, and of close attention and prompt and implicit obedience to

[78] Stephens and Roderick (1972), 350, 359; Russell (1983), 161; Babbage (1968), 5–6; Marshall (1946), 206–7; Brooks (1965), 141; Musgrave (1967), 9–10; Weisbrod (1971), 231 ff; Welch (1971), 332, 348; Cipriani (1971), 360–11; Nelson, Peck, Kalachek (1967), 14; Balfour Committee (1929), 203–5.

[79] Russell (1983), 162; More (1980), 209; Bowman (1969), 446; Jenkin, ev. to R.C. (1872), QQ.1704–6.

[80] Richardson, ev. to R.C. (1872), QQ.1808, 1884, 1919.

[81] Marshall (1946), 211.

instructions, ought to occupy more of the time and thought of teachers in elementary schools.

The view was perhaps best put by Thomas Clegg in 1854:

> I have always maintained . . . that those parties who have been educated in the (Sunday) schools that I have been connected with, will always do more for the same money and do it better and with less trouble, than those that are not educated, or educated without religion.

and more shortly by Henry Ashworth in 1880: 'if they have been to school, they're obedient, they want less licking'.[82]

The view of numerous Victorians in business then was that even if general schooling was of no value for industry and was not worth paying for for the sake of the subject matter taught, it was so for the training in attitude, i.e. not for the development of cognitive, but of affective characteristics: willingness to work, order, reliability, punctuality, 'subordinacy', 'receptivity to supervision and discipline', a 'sense of discipline and peaceful order'.[83] This comes close to that of present-day critics of the Victorian school as an instrument of acculturation to bourgeois values and of social control.[84]

If the view is correct that formal education would improve the performance of industrial workers less by making them technically more competent than by making them more flexible, and by altering their attitude to their work in a positive direction, the British educational system should be judged, as far as its effect on Britain's industrial performance in this period is concerned, on quite different criteria than has been the case hitherto.

In our period the role of the foreman, like that of the technician, salesman, and other junior executives, was increasing rapidly in significance with the growth in the size of firms and the complexity of their operations. Since foremen were normally recruited from the craftsmen, and had a craftsman's education, it was necessary that they, at least, should on promotion make use of whatever was available in the way of evening classes and other schooling, to be able to read blueprints and have a basic scientific understanding of the industrial processes used. The Sheffield Chamber of Commerce, for example, believed that foremen should understand some chemistry and metallurgy.[85]

As far as the class of owners and senior managers was concerned, it would normally be assumed that they had an adequate general education: what was at

---

82 Wood, ev. to Children's Employment Commission (1842), No. 47, also Children's Employment Commmission (1842), ev. Elliot, No. 367, 642; R.C. (1886), lxiii; Joyce (1980), 173; Howe (1984), 280; Dearle (1914). 2–4, 19; Pollard and Robertson (1979), 140–1. The modern view is that education also buys more 'work satisfaction', Mottaz (1984), 985–1004; it was also the central theme of Kay (1850), and Kay (1864).

83 Mitch (1984); Roberts (1960), 173 ff, 218; Rich (1970), 78; Wiles (1951), 159; Easterlin (1981). It was also said of the Victorian Public School that it 'should train emotions and the will before attending to the brain', Wilkinson (1964), 19.

84 There is a vast literature, e.g. Johnson (1970), 96–119; Katz (1968), 46, 87–8; Sanderson (1983), 9; Flinn (1967), 14 ff; Wadsworth (1974), 101; Johnson (1976), 44–54; Shapin and Barnes (1976), 55–65.

85 R.C. (1872), ev. Wilkinson, Q.1825; Musgrave (1967), 27, 40, 54, 75, 91; Musgrave (1970d), 151–3; Musgrave (1981), 53; Ware (1901), 26 ff; Russell and Goodman (1972), 265; R.C. (1882–84), ev. Siemens, Q.1365.

issue in their case was the value of scientific or technological knowledge at a higher level. Thus it was said that owners or managers trained in science might spot or accept innovations more readily, and, conversely, would be less likely to make avoidable costly mistakes. At least one foreign critic maintained that, in their ignorance of the mechanical sciences, British engineers built machines that were ungainly and much too heavy. This was confirmed by the well-known manager of Dowlais ironworks, Menelaus, in 1881: 'He made the best guess he could as to the strength there should be, then multiplied by four, and the things never broke'.[86]

Some of this criticism undoubtedly neglected the difference between the preparation for routine management jobs, and the preparation necessary for 'the development of a smaller class of scientific pioneers'. It was by no means certain that the latter were well served by the kind of formalized technical education provided on the continent. Engineers who had come through such training tended to go by the book and were frequently less eager to improvise or innovate than British or American engineers trained in a more practical school. Technical breakthroughs, it has been noted, were often pioneered by outsiders to the industry. Even in modern Britain it has been found that firms whose leading personality was technically or scientifically trained will not necessarily be technically more progressive than the rest, while conversely, few technically trained top managers ever make much use of their expertise.[87] Top people who had received 'an upper-class education', were trained to command and to use the expertise of others, and were therefore not necessarily averse to change that might reduce the value of technically trained people, but not their own.[88] This does not mean, however, that they would not have benefited from education in scientific methodology and in the rudiments of scientific and technological knowledge.

Here once again, the best form of education would seem to depend in part on the place which a country occupies in world development. The more organized, routinized approach to technology found on the Continent was, in principle, a sensible method for countries in the process of catching up. As Lowthian Bell remarked, one main task of scientists abroad was to inform themselves of what was happening in the United Kingdom, just as their entrepreneurs needed only to consider 'defensive innovation'.[89] The leading country, however, especially when it had been quick to translate its technical superiority into higher real wages for its workers, would have, according to the product cycle theorem, to continue to pursue 'offensive innovation', to be ahead of the rest if it was to survive. The thrust for Britain therefore had to be on the new and the unconventional. For that role, the British educational system may not have been entirely unsuited, at least until such time as even innovators needed a modicum of basic science.

---

[86] R.C. (1882–84), ev. Cucco, Q.4258; Burn (1940), 215.
[87] Lowe (1983), 54; Jewkes *et al.* (1969), 58; Carter and Williams (1957), 183–4; Bauer and Cohen (1982), 451–72.
[88] Cardwell (1957), 9; Coleman (1973), 112–14; Erickson (1959), 61.
[89] R.C. (1882–84), ev. Bell, Q.274, also see p. 125 above, and pp. 162, 173, 181, and notes 160–1.

IV German Education and Science Research

We now turn to the German educational system and the German attitude to science and technology. These were the models which the British were urged by contemporaries to follow and which historians have since held to have been a major cause of Germany's industrial success.

At the centre of German science stood the German university, generally believed to have to derived its character in the nineteenth century from the ideas developed by Wilhelm von Humboldt and exemplified by the new University of Berlin (1810). We shall therefore begin with that foundation, noting at the outset that it would be hard to think of a more unpropitious beginning for an intellectual revolution that was to take Germany forward to economic leadership.

The German university of the eighteenth century reflected that country's social, political and economic backwardness in comparison with Western Europe. There were, it is true, almost 30 universities in Germany and some 40 in the German-speaking world altogether but many of them were small and their student numbers were declining. Duisburg, for example, had but 38 students around 1800 and Erfurt had 43. No fewer than 22 universities were closed between 1792 and 1818, though some new ones were opened, including Berlin.[90] Their structure was the traditional one of three senior faculties, Theology, Medicine and Law, with Arts ('Philosophy') as the subordinate faculty. The professors, 'mediocre hardworking pedants totally without originality' had to do 20–28 hours teaching per week which nevertheless left them so underpaid that they had to have second sources of income, while the mostly teenage students were ill-disciplined and not infrequently riotous.[91]

There had, indeed, been some reforms. The recent foundations of Halle (1694) and, above all, Göttingen (1734) had introduced a new humane spirit which had not remained without imitators. New technical colleges, beginning with the Freiberg mining school, 1765, made up some of the numbers of students lost by the universities after 1750. It was, in fact, the contribution of some of the teachers at these specialist institutions, together with the work of astronomers, of travellers like Alexander von Humboldt and of medical men, as much as the work in the universities which helped to keep up the reputation of German science.[92]

The role played by Humboldt in the university reforms exemplified by the University of Berlin may well have been exaggerated in the German historical consciousness: he took over the details of several of the reforms tried out earlier in France and Germany. But his central drive was propelled forward by a powerful wave of idealist philosophy, itself nurtured by the war and the humiliating defeat and crippling loss of territory on the part of Prussia. Fichte, Schelling and Hegel, the leading thinkers, directly influenced Humboldt,

90 Farrar (1975), 180; Turner (1975), 498 ff; Schelsky (1963), 21–2.
91 Schimank (1973), 207–11; Jeismann (1974), 151; Paulsen (1921), 136; König (1970), 30–1.
92 Manegold (1976a), 254–5; Manegold (1976b), 288; Riedel (1976), 305; Ringer (1969), 15, 18; Turner (1980), 120–2; McCelland (1980), 30 ff; McCelland (1976), 146–73; Paulsen (1902), 55, *passim*.

Schleiermacher and others concerned with the new foundation. They ranged themselves wholly on the side of neo-humanism and against the utilitarian aims of the Enlightenment, which, among other failings, had to bear the stigma that they might be identified with the French Revolution.

No brief summary can do justice to the power and apparent persuasiveness of German idealism in its classical phase, nor can a later generation easily recapture the mood of despair and yet also of national defiance and of patriotism which nourished it. In the most general terms, according to Schelling, all that we regard as objective arises in fact out of certain propositions we have regarding the self: the belief that the outside world exists is merely a 'prejudice'. Consequently the subjective (thought) and the objective (nature) always agree and philosophy had no need of validation by experience or experiment. Practice should be approached only by means of theory; it exists only to prove the existence of God. It follows, further, that since we control our world in our thought, we should strive to improve it and the theme of our teaching should not be what is, but what should be. In terms of the German play on words, '*Wissen ist nicht das Abbild der Wirklichkeit, sondern ihr Vorbild*'.[93] While action must be a reflection of theory, reason itself must be moral.

Education in this view thus becomes a highly moral, if not religious, activity, and this imposes a particularly significant role on the universities. Their object must be to create a class of human beings possessing '*Bildung*' – a word characteristically untranslatable in this context, but including both the concept of a rich liberal education and of moral superiority. The young graduates, thus imbued with 'eternal reason' and their spirit pervaded by ethics ('*versittlicht*'), will go out into the world to create the perfect State. According to Fichte, when perfect graduates have created the ideal State, it will have become unnecessary and will wither away.

The modern reader, even if he can be persuaded of the validity of philosophical idealism and of seeking absolute perfection in this world, is liable to become impatient with the mass of a rhetoric and verbiage contained in this corpus which nowhere makes any attempt to come down to practical details. Moreover, to see the crabbed, provincial, autocratic and backward Prussian State as the incarnation of the ideal; the pedantic Prussian professoriate, lost in specialisms and cowering before imperious state officials, as the receptacles of eternal truth; and the volatile students, crowding lecture rooms in search of social advancement and posts with fixed salaries attached, as the apostles of the great and the good, strains credulity beyond endurance.

One key idea implanted by Humboldt was that a university education should aim to create a cultured and moral human being, and since practical training for a profession might get in the way of that, it should be rigorously excluded from the Humboldtian University. Curricula designed for earning a living were given the 'noisome name of *Brotstudien* (bread and butter studies)' and were despised if they could not be totally excluded.

'The Humboldtian theory of the University', as one critic put it, 'was an uneasy amalgam of concepts from idealist philosophy and neohumanism, and it largely

[93] König (1970), 103, also *passim*. For summary accounts also see Gower (1972–73), 311; Schelsky (1963), 66, 79–81, 109 ff, 135 ff, 148–9.

ignored the professional functions of the upper faculties or treated them with suspicion.'[94]

Secondly, at the technical level, professors were to be appointed as specialists, to engage in original research, and the preferred mode of instruction was the seminar in which the professor introduced the students to his research theme and both, teacher and student, were engaged in a joint learning process. The rank of *Privatdozent* was devised to maintain an independent research impetus.

Thirdly, there was to be unfettered freedom to teach and to learn – at least as long as it did not endanger the State. Somewhat incongruously in the light of the contempt for utilitarian studies, it was held that unfettered study would serve the State best. Lastly, the universities should form part of a comprehensive educational structure. The *Abitur*, the leaving certificate of the classical *Gymnasien* (grammar schools) for which an edict of 1812 laid down common standards, would serve as the entrance qualification for universities. In Bavaria a similar rule had been introduced in 1809, in Württemberg in 1811 and in Saxony it followed in 1829.[95]

Several of these aims were thwarted almost from the beginning. The much-vaunted university freedoms were quickly circumscribed by the censorship and the restrictions imposed by a State power afraid of independent political thought of its citizens. Humboldt failed to secure financial independence from the State for the University of Berlin, while the excessive quest for separateness on the part of the professorial staff prevented the formation of a corporate power as a counterweight to the civil servants. Instead of a single grand design, there appeared a worsening fragmentation of subjects. Above all, the resolve to stick to learning for learning's sake remained a sham. Disinterested learning might be for the richer students: for the poorer, *Brotstudien* remained the norm. Universities remained overwhelmingly professional schools, cultivating nevertheless a certain snobbery towards the sciences, and preserving an unwarranted high prestige for the classics. Engineering and other useful subjects were kept out entirely.[96]

The development of the natural sciences in the German universities was held back further, in some cases by several decades, by the acceptance of that by-product of idealism known as natural philosophy (*Naturphilosophie*). According to this doctrine, which goes back to Schelling and held sway until about 1830, all sciences are interdependent and may be derived from a single correct philosophical view of the world. Experiment, experience and measurement are therefore unnecessary, since even if they conflicted with the predetermined view, it would have to be the observation that was in error, not the philosophy. *Naturphilosophie* reinforced the contempt for experimental research and for an interest in the real world prevalent in German universities. It led to a distinct

[94] Turner (1980), 110; Manegold (1970), 26–8, also 15; Blankertz (1969), 35–6; Menze (1972), 7.
[95] Turner (1971), 141, 155, also Turner (1980), 130; Jeismann (1974), 223–4; Lundgreen (1985), 81.
[96] König (1970), 167, 174–5; Schelsky (1963), 118ff, 148–9; Ben-David and Zloczower (1972), 55; Paulsen (1902), 88–91; Schiersmann (1979), 34; Lundgreen (1984), 60; Ben-David (1977), 47–9; Borscheid (1976a), 36–7, 72, 116; Feldman (1987), 261.

falling back of German academic science relative to France and Great Britain in the first third of the century.[97]

Consonant with the economic backwardness of the country, the technical schools founded at the time, which were later to become so famous as the pace-makers of German technological leadership, were mere pathetic trade schools in their beginning, and only the rudiments of mathematical and other abstract scientific teaching gave a hint of the more ambitious developments to come.[98] Even the society of *Naturforscher*, model of the British Association, was founded in the 1820s to allow personal contacts across the petty state boundaries, something no longer needed in Britain or France. A.W. Hofmann, the great chemist and pupil of Liebig, decided to come to Britain in the 1840s in part because he was excited about the prospects of working with her advanced and progressive industry, and in part because Prussian science was too abstract and academic.

Since the universities offered almost the only means for members of the lower middle classes to raise themselves out of their circumscribed lot within a hide-bound immobile society, there was an oversupply of students especially in law, which might lead to State service jobs,[99] to the chagrin of such as von Seydlitz, supporter of the Society for Promoting Useful Industry (*Verein zur Beförderung des Gewerbefleißes*):

> 'There is need in Germany', he thundered, 'to promote the exact sciences, Mathematics, Chemistry, Physics, etc., for otherwise the country will be ruined by its hordes of Arts people; the army of civil servants, lawyers, economists, fed by the State, are sucking it dry, artists and craftsmen are starving, private enterprise is declining more and more. Anyone who would allow such an abuse of his property to go on, is committing a sin against the Holy Ghost, of which I certainly would not wish to be guilty.'[100]

The position of Germany appears to have been not unlike that of the less developed countries today: a shortage of technicians coincided with an oversupply of highly educated Arts graduates crowding round the high-prestige, highly paid traditional State jobs. The universities of Germany and of the countries under her cultural influence were in fact in conflict with industrial progress, 'vehicles of a kind of cultural lag'.[101] With the exception of the 'single-minded, almost fanatical devotion to the advancement of knowledge' and pure research for its own sake, it would be hard to imagine anything less likely to put Germany into the van of European progress than her universities as they emerged after 1815.

Apart from the universities, the most remarkable feature of the German educational system was its cohesive, formalized structure, in which each level meshed in with all the others. It will therefore be useful to cast a glance at the rest of the German educational provisions and their development in the course of the nineteenth century.

[97] Ben-David (1971), 114–17, and Ben-David (1960), 834; König (1970), 91 ff, 131, 134; Merz (1904), 205–6; Gower (1972–73); Knight (1975), 161–78; Williams (1973), 3–22.
[98] Blankertz (1969), 78–9; Riedel (1976), 305–6; McCelland (1980), 207–9.
[99] O'Boyle (1970), 473–4; Brunschwig (1974), 147 ff.; Fach and Wessel (1981), 9; Lundgreen (1985), 82, 89; Turner (1980), 106–7.
[100] Quoted in Schiersmann (1979), 52.
[101] Ringer (1979), 6–7; but see Lundgreen (1981b), 262–3.

Compulsory education had become a feature of most German (and several other European) states well before 1800. In Prussia it was first introduced in 1717 and made general in 1763, when it applied to all children between 6 and 13/14 years of age. By the later nineteenth century, the elementary school had become well-nigh universal: of those alive in 1864 in Prussia, only 5.7% had never been to school. In addition to the elementary schools (*Volksschulen*) there were also smaller numbers attending higher elementary schools, which prepared, among others, intending elementary school teachers before they went to training colleges. Nevertheless, in the 1855 levy of the *Landwehr*, the Territorials, only 12% could write well, while about one-half could not write at all.[102]

One main cause of this poor result was to be found in the basic objective of the school legislation, which was not to create scholars, but obedient, religious subjects of the king, later supplemented by the task of encouraging those qualities of disciplined industriousness which might be of use to an employer.[103] Another cause was that much of the school legislation remained on paper, especially in the villages; factory children were also without education and the 1839 Prussian Factory Act remained a dead letter. Most elementary school teachers were poorly trained and so badly paid that until well into the nineteenth century they had to have a second job. Even as late as 1903, there was an *average* of 61 pupils per teacher, and in 1901, 24% of the children, mainly in the villages, were either in schools with a single class (i.e. all the years taught jointly in one room) or in part-time or half-time education. It is thus not perhaps entirely surprising that of the immigrants into the USA in 1899–1910 aged 14 and over, the proportions of those who according to their own statement could neither read nor write were as follows:[104]

Germans	5.2%
Irish	2.6
Welsh	1.9
English	1.0
Scots	0.7

It seems that admiring British observers were too often blinded by the regulations, without observing the practice in a poor, backward country. Probably at no time was the German elementary education much ahead of the British either in quality or in numbers, though if measured against a scale of economic development, the German educational effort certainly set in earlier.

Where Germany scored was in the provision of continuation schools (*Fortbildungsschulen*) , designed in part to fill the gap left by the abolition of compulsory guild membership and its apprenticeship system. Maintained largely by students' fees and by the municipalities, they received increasing State attention from the 1860s onward. They were made compulsory for apprentices in 1861, state financial help was made available from 1864 and an Act of the North German Confederation of 1869 gave local authorities the right

---

102 Lundgreen (1973), 92–3, and Lundgreen (1975a), 69–71; Cipolla (1969), 85; R.C. (1861), Pattison, 234.
103 Paulsen (1921), 503, and Paulsen (1906), 151–7; Lundgreen (1970), 85–121; Meyer (1976), 11–16; Blankertz (1969), 97.
104 Lexis (1904), Vol. III 36, 46 ff, 58–9, 240; Roberts (1960), 324; R.C. (1861), Pattison, esp. 231–4, 238–40; Sadler (1908), 215–16; Easterlin *et al.* (1982), 9.

to make attendance compulsory for all young people in work. There were 1,169 such schools in Prussia in 1903, with 177,000 pupils, of which 997 (138.000) were in townships in which they had been made compulsory.[105] The value of that teaching, apart from its remedial aspects in general school subjects has, however, been questioned: in the end, knowledge of one's trade was essentially acquired at the place of work.[106]

At a slightly higher level, provincial *Gewerbeschulen,* or industrial trade schools began to be formed in Prussia about 1820. Berlin was given a central college to which the best pupils might be sent for further training, and this college very rapidly began a process of raising its standards that would ultimately take it up to university status. The standards of many of the provincial trade schools were also gradually improved. In 1878 they were reorganized and given the option of 3-year general, or 2-year trade-oriented courses. Most schools chose the former and, by linking up with 6-year general preparatory schools, turned themselves into complete general 9-year secondary schools known as *Oberrealschulen.*[107]

In the second half of the century, a number of special trade or *Fachschulen* at about the same level were also formed in industrial cities. By 1902 there were 104 such schools in the textile trades in Germany (36 of them in Prussia), 10 in the metal trades (5), 24 in the wood trades (7) and 6 in ceramics (3), beside 61 schools for farriers (47), 53 in the building trades (22), 26 in engineering (9), and numerous others. The 11 mining schools found in Prussia also had 4–5,000 students around 1880. There were also schools attached to and run by individual works, especially in engineering, metallurgy and mining. About 70–75 of them have been counted by 1914.[108] Some of these attained levels approaching university standards. The building trade school of Stuttgart, for example, noted by the Samuelson Commission in its second report, had a staff of 28 masters and 13 assistants teaching 448 students of average age 21, in courses lasting up to three years, including sciences and theory, as well as drawing, practical fieldwork, mensuration etc. Even more impressive was the school in Chemnitz in Saxony with its 581 students in four departments, who started at the age of 15–17 and took courses to fit them to become managers and foremen. In Prussia alone, higher-level colleges, defined as those which tended to insist on a minimum age of 16 and had the power to award the coveted 'one-year voluntary' military privileges for its alumni, contained, in the engineering branches, 54 students in 1891 and 1,107 students in 1911, in textiles, 344 and 800, and in agricultural science, 544 and 1,800.[109]

[105] In Prussia in 1901, about one-quarter of their total income came from students' fees, one-quarter from the State, and the rest from Local Authorities and private funds. Howard (1907), 101; MacDonagh (1974–75), 505; R.C. (1861), Pattison, 207; R.C. (1884), Vol. I, 47, 336–9, and Vol. V, 81; Ware (1901), 118–9, 130; Blankertz (1969), 128–32; Lexis (1904), Vol. IV, 75; Thyssen (1954), 69, 87–9.

[106] Lundgreen (1975b), 10; Musgrave (1967), 43 ff; R.C. (1895), Samuelson QQ.6274–7.

[107] Lundgreen (1973), 136–42, and Lundgreen (1975b), 36, 49–51, 64–5, 86; Schiersmann (1979), 258 ff; Müller (1977), 43, 220, 227; Fessner (1986). Also p. 150 below.

[108] Lexis (1904), Vol. IV, 30–1; R.C. (1884), Vol. 1, 50 ff, 115; Ware (1901), 130; Adelmann (1979), 27.

[109] Thyssen (1954), 76, 107; Lexis (1904), Vol. IV, 30–1, 55–7; Lundgreen (1973), 152; R.C. (1884), Vol. I, 90 ff, 102 ff, Vol. V, Report by Puttkamer, 81; Musgrave (1967), 91; Visit to Germany with a View to Ascertaining the Recent Progress in Technical Education . . . in that Country (1897), 403 ff.

Altogether, it is evident that technical and trade education was neither as systematic nor as well integrated as the rest of the otherwise logical and well-structured general education system of the German states. There can, however, be no doubt as to its quantity. By 1914, after two generations of large-scale provision, there are estimated to have been 4 million skilled workers who had had technical training while in employment, in addition to all those who had received higher instruction.[110].

We now turn to secondary education. Here the glory of the German education system, in the view of many British observers, was the classical *Gymnasium*, which may be roughly translated as grammar school. After a period of decline, the *Gymnasium* was rescued by the same impetus that reformed the universities: the idealistic neo-humanism which reaffirmed the values of educating the whole man, and aimed at 'cultivating the inner self through the medium of the classics'.[111] Like the universities, it abhorred vocational training. Its university-trained teaching body was well paid and given a high status. It was to be the training ground for the learned and for the elite, and it did indeed survive into the modern era as a fortress of privilege and exclusiveness. It charged fairly high fees, and despite the fast growing need for a highly educated manpower, the pupil population rose only very slightly, in Prussia, for example, from 18 per 10,000 inhabitants in 1832 to 21 in 1860, and to a maximum of 28 in 1885, dropping back to 27 in 1903. There was also a *Pro-Gymnasium*, offering similar courses for 6 or 7 years in place of the 9 years of the full *Gymnasium*, but it was never of much significance.[112]

Like the universities, the *Gymnasien* after the heady reform years of 1808–12 met with increasing repression and censorship by the State. The curriculum was weighted heavily towards the classics, as well as some emphasis on religion. By contrast, the natural sciences were almost totally neglected, no more than a grudging two hours per week being usually reserved for them. Mathematics, however, had an important place in the curriculum from 1816.[113] Like the English public schools which the Kaiser wished them to copy, the German *Gymnasien* did their best to ensure that a large proportion of the most intelligent and most influential population looked down with contempt on science and technology, and made sure in later life that those who had specialized in them, were kept out of all important decision making bodies.[114]

The *Gymnasium*, however, was not the only type of secondary school available. As early as the mid-eighteenth century, schools teaching modern subjects to children of families in trade and industry were established and were supported by the State, at least under Frederick the Great. For, as the Minister of Education, Zedlitz declared, in the classical schools 'the boy intended for handicrafts or commerce . . . learns nothing but things he doesn't need, and not an iota of that which he does need'.[115] The neo-humanist revolution destroyed much of this, leaving in countries like Prussia the *Gymnasium* as the sole recognized State secondary school, but the citizens engaged in trade and industry

[110] MacDonagh (1974–75), 505; Floud (1984), 3; Lee (1978), 442–91.
[111] Locke (1984), 32; Ruegg (1972), 36; Ringer (1979), 33–4; Arnold (1884), esp. 19, 45, 53, 102; Paulsen (1921), 48, 288–90, and Paulsen (1906), 127.
[112] Lexis (1904), Vol. II, 185; Müller (1977), 48–9.
[113] Paulsen (1921), 292, and Paulsen (1889), 9; Borscheid (1976a), 37; Pfetsch (1974), 154.
[114] Treue (1966), 37; Messerschmidt (1980), 244; Pope (1917), 3.
[115] Quoted in Paulsen (1921), 79, also 59–60, 98–100, 114ff.

again soon began to establish and finance their own, usually through the municipal authorities. As a result, a variety of *Realschulen* emerged in the towns. The mixture of classical snobbery and social apprehension with which they were regarded by the university-*Gymnasium* lobby, is captured neatly in the following comment from Württemberg in 1830:

> No educated person worthy of the name will ever emerge from the *Realschule*, nor one whose mind will be capable of taking ideal, higher views, or of thinking above the utility principle; instead, we shall have children of our times, revolutionaries who want to improve everything but themselves. I would never send a child into a *Realschule*, not even one destined to become a nailmaker.[116]

Their role in the revolution of 1848 in Prussia made them suspect also to the authorities, and for a time their pupils were excluded even from applying to the building and mining colleges, and were discriminated against when seeking employment in the Post Office.[117] However, a new start was made in 1859, and ultimately, three types of nine-year school emerged, the classical *Gymnasium*, the *Oberrealschule* with its modern curriculum and the *Realgymnasium* as a compromise between them, each with its own shorter six-year version.

Yet the hostility of the classical schools towards the others continued unabated as they fought every inch of the way to preserve their privileges. Carried on over different issues and at different levels well into the twentieth century, the battle generated much heat and an enormous literature. Some of its flavour may be recaptured by the following extract from an official statement of the University of Berlin in 1870:

> *Realschulen* are administrative mistakes made by unlettered local politicians; if recognized, they would lead to the neo-barbarism of a generation of men dedicated to making money and giving themselves over to pleasure, but lacking the discipline to be gained by studying Greek.[118]

Having had its former access to the mining and building colleges restored, as well as the right to claim privileges in the army for its *alumni* (the so-called one-year volunteer system), the *Realschule* (*Realgymnasium*) registered its first success in 1870, called forth by a shortage of Mathematics and Science teachers, when it was permitted to send its students into the Universities. Although this applied to the study of modern subjects only, and even then merely for the teachers' certificate for the lower forms, the modern type of school never looked back after that. The price it had to pay was to absorb a large measure of the classical curriculum, as indeed did the technical universities which also gained their recognition in those years and with which the modern schools necessarily marched very closely in step. In 1882, a major reorganization and formalization of all three types of school took place in Prussia, including a wider recognition of the *Abitur* leaving certificate of the modern school. These were the new curricula:[119]

Weekly Hours: +	Gymnasium	Realgymnasium	Oberrealschule
Latin and Greek	9–16	5–8	0
French and English	2–5	5–8	8–11

---

[116] Quoted in Paulsen (1921), 440; also Blankertz (1969), 28, 36, 96; Lundgreen (1975b), 24; Turner (1980), 132.
[117] Paulsen (1921), 556–7.
[118] Quoted in Müller (1977), 210.
[119] Müller (1977), 43, 46–7.

Mathematics	3–4	4–5	5–6
Natural Sciences	2	2–5	2–7
All Others	6–11	10–12	12–14

+ Weekly hours for each year were fixed. The range arises because of differences from year to year in the progress from the first to the ninth form. The totals came to 25–30 hours per week for each type of school.

All three types of school were given complete parity of esteem in 1900 on the direct instruction of the Kaiser, only a few specialist university courses, such as Theology, remaining the preserve of the classical *Gymnasium*. Total pupil numbers in 1902 are given in Table 3.4.

Table 3.4 Pupil numbers in German grammar schools, 1902 (in 000)

	Gymnasium and Progymnasium	Realgymnasium and Realprogymnasium	Realschule and Oberrealschule	Totals
Prussia	97.7	25.6	51.2	174.5
Bavaria	19.6	1.1	13.7	34.4
Saxony	6.5	4.9	8.6	20.0
Rest of Germany	29.9	10.9	32.2	73.0
All Germany	153.7	42.5	105.7	301.9

The relative growth rate may be derived from the following Prussian figures for the ratios of schoolboys to the total male population at different dates:

Table 3.5 Proportions of Schoolboys in the Prussian Population, 1822–1911 (per thousand)

	Gymnasium and Progymnasium	All modern schools	All secondary schools
1822	(2.56)	(1.10)	3.66
1864	4.86	2.28	7.14
1891	5.28	3.85	9.13
1911	5.41	6.28	11.68

The growth, after 1891, was almost entirely in the modern school.[120]

How can we account for the early incorporation of modern subjects, above all the sciences and modern languages into the German secondary school curriculum? Three possible causes for the difference between Britain and Germany come to mind. One lies in the comparative role of the State in the education field. The opposition of the vested educational interests was just as bitter, prolonged and emotional in Germany as in Britain, but thanks to a powerful bureaucracy concerned with the progress of society as whole, backed at times by such as William II, Bismarck and the officer class,[121] industry, trade and the scientists and engineers managed to receive a fair share of the education resources. In Britain, in as far as there was any overall control over education, it was exercised not by the State, but by the Church, and the Church was in no way concerned with the utility of education to the nation at large. On the contrary, it lay in its own interest to preserve as many teaching posts as possible as sinecures for its own ordained members; to raise the status of their training by making it a compulsory element for all; and to emphasize those elements in

[120] Based on Lehmann, Appendix to Paulsen (1921), 765–7; also Lexis (1904), Vol. I, 184–5, 218; Lundgreen (1973), 153; Burchardt (1983), 13–15.
[121] E.g. Führ (1980), 193–4; Messerschmidt (1980), 242–5. Also pp. 161–2, note 160 and p. 181 below.

education that divided and differentiated society. Of course, in Britain also, the State was instrumental in forcing through some necessary reforms, in Oxford and Cambridge, and, by means of the Charity Commissioners, to attempt to channel the funds embezzled by pious school masters for generations, back to the poor students and pupils for whom they had originally been intended. However, the British state was weaker, and it was brought in later.

The second difference lies in the apparent ease by which the British industrial and commercial middle classes were persuaded to give up the quest for education useful for themselves, and accept as superior an education intended for landowners, clergymen and colonial administrators. Whether this was because of the way in which the British upper class opened itself to entry from below; because of the different social structure of Germany which awarded the highest prestige to military officers, rather than to the landed classes as such; because of more rapid industrialization and rise of the industrial classes in Germany; or because of other circumstances, cannot be pursued here.

The third possible cause for the differences in curriculum development may lie in the different role played by science and technology in the industrialization of the two countries. This, is one sense, is the major topic of this chapter and we shall return to it at its end.

The rise of the modern school was paralleled by another development in Germany for which there is virtually no British equivalent: the creation of the technical university. Its initial inspiration had come from the Parisian *École Polytechnique*, and the first German-speaking imitations, in Prague (1806) and Vienna (1815) had as their aim the catching up with the West.[122] The aim of the Berlin *Technische Schule* of 1821, re-named *Gewerbe-Institut* in 1827 was more modest. It was intended, according to Beuth, for 'craftsmen, factory workers, foremen and managers'. The minimum age at entry was set at 14 years, and the first class of 13 pupils was looked after by a teaching staff of four. The college at Karlsruhe (Baden), which was established in 1825, began with classes for 13–15-year olds. In the competitive world of German interstate rivalry, several other similar schools then followed in quick succession: Munich (Bavaria) in 1827, spawning branches in Nuremberg in 1829 and Augsburg in 1833, Dresden (Saxony, 1828), Kassel (Hesse-K., 1830), Hanover (1831), Darmstadt (Hesse-D., 1836) and Brunswick, a reorganization of an existing school, in 1835.[123]

Standards began to be raised and numbers to be increased almost at once. In Berlin the minimum age was soon raised to 16, and the course extended to two years six months in 1826, and in 1831 by a further six months to three years; by 1845 there were 101 students. Hanover changed from a 3-year to a 4-year course in 1859.[124]

Upgrading followed. Berlin was re-named 'Industrial Academy' in 1866, it was given tertiary education or college status in 1871, and in 1879 it was combined with the building academy (founded 1799) into a technical university (*Technische Hochschule*: TH). Karlsruhe was given higher status in 1865,

122 Manegold (1976), 20–1, 34 ff, and Manegold (1976a), 260 ff; Blankertz (1969), 79–83.
123 Henderson (1967), 107; Lundgreen (1973), 141; Ruske (1976), 699 ff; Treue (1964), 225–6; Nebenius (1833), 128 ff; Borscheid (1976a), 50–4; Manegold (1970), 39 ff; D.C. (1906), 9–10. See also pp. 147–8 above.
124 Lundgreen (1985), 84, and Lundgreen (1975b), 60 ff. and Lundgreen (1975a), 67.

becoming formally a TH in 1885, for Munich the dates were 1868 and 1877, for Stuttgart (Wurttemberg) 1876 and 1890, Darmstadt and Brunswick were raised in status in 1877, Aachen, newly founded in 1870, had college status from the beginning, Hanover was given it in 1875–80, Dresden raised new buildings in 1871–5, and after the turn of the century, new THs were founded in Danzig (1904) and Breslau (1910). From the 1870s onwards, the colleges began to recognize each other's courses and examinations.

In spite of the protracted opposition of the universities, which decried them as utilitarian rather than 'scientific', the THs, based largely on their high-level mathematics, chemistry and physics, but also on engineering and other applied sciences, narrowed the gap to the universities step by step, and in the 1890s the last bastions collapsed. First, the heads of the THs were allowed to call themselves *Rektor*, like the heads of universities, and the teachers, similarly, became 'professors'. In 1898, Kaiser William II called the rectors of the THs of Aachen, Berlin and Hanover to the Upper House on the same terms as the university rectors, and in 1899, finally, the cherished right of awarding degrees was granted to the THs – though as a last sop to injured pride, the degrees '*Dipl.-Ing.*' and '*Dr.-Ing.*' had to be hyphenated, to show that they had a non-humanist base, unlike the universities' equivalent of *Dr. rer. nat.* In 1900, the two types of institution came to a market-sharing agreement, the THs concentrating on the technologies, while the universities agreed to teach technical subjects at most in a subsidiary role.[125]

The rise of the relative share of the THs within the tertiary sector was remarkable. Their share of the university-level budget rose from 8–10% in 1850–80 to 25% before World War I, measured against a rapidly rising total. In absolute numbers, their student population grew from 2,928 in 1869 to 10,142 in 1899 and 16,568 in 1910; Charlottenburg alone had 1,640 in 1890, rising to 4,343 in 1900 and then falling back to 2,943 in 1910.[126]

By British standards, these were very large numbers indeed. The German provision for the study of technology at university level was not exceptional, as Table 3.6 makes clear:[127]

Table 3.6 Proportion of students taking science and technology subjects, c.1913, %

	Medicine	Science	Technology
Germany 1914	26.3	13.9	24.1
Belgium 1913–14	17.1	26.8	31.0
Netherlands 1913–14	35.1	10.0	29.8
France 1913	21.7	17.5	
USA 1911–15	26.6	13.3	3.5 (plus part of 15.4% 'others')

Colleges for commercial subjects at a higher level had in Prussia alone a total of 1,600 students in 1911. There were also at that time in Prussia 300 students in mining academies, 140 in forestry colleges and 600 in veterinary colleges,

---

[125] Just before that, in 1896, a unified examination system was agreed on by universities and THs on pressure from industry. Manegold (1970), 83, 197–8, 213, 282 ff, 300; Lundgreen (1985), 86; Lexis (1904), Vol. IV, Part 1, 269.

[126] Pfetsch (1974), 60; Lexis (1904), Vol. I, 635.

[127] Ben-David (1968), 40.

beside 4,455 in building academies and building science sections of technical universities, and 900 in academies of art and of music.[128]

In the later years of the century there were considerable numbers of foreign students to be found in the THs, ranging from 10–30% of the total. The proportion of ex-*Gymnasium* pupils also increased. In Aachen in 1903, for example, 44.4% of the students had qualified in *Gymnasien*, 16.7% in *Real-gymnasien*, 18.6% in *Oberrealschulen* and 20.3% abroad.[129] There was a strong tendency for students from industrial and commercial homes to favour the THs, while students from professional families preferred the universities. As in Britain, however, there were complaints that industry was not in every case eager to take the students trained in THs, preferring instead a more practical training. There were, in consequence, many part-time and sandwich course students, as well as considerable fluctuations from year to year in the numbers attending individual THs.[130]

Among the pressure groups which had helped the polytechnic schools ultimately to reach university status was the *Verein Deutscher Ingenieure* (VDI), the Society of German Engineers, founded in 1856. It was one of many scientific and professional societies, but in spite of vigorous growth,[131] in this field German development was lagging behind Britain. It may be that the longer tradition of voluntary association, and the absence of state-ordained examining bodies, were among the reasons for the earlier establishment of scientific-technical societies in the United Kingdom.

By contrast, Germany gave the lead in the foundation of national research laboratories: in their case, State funding was a necessity. The surviving Academies of Science in various German capitals had mostly fallen on bad days, but there were institutes for which British parallels could be found: a meteorological institute (1847), and institutes for geodesics (1868), zoology (1872) and astrophysics (1874). The first of the new institutes was the *Physikalisch-Technische Reichsanstalt* (PTR) set up in Berlin in 1887. Among its most important tasks was fundamental physical research and standardization in science-based industry, in part to fill the gap left in the research in technical universities, and even in traditional universities, as the professors were being overloaded with teaching duties. Lavishly provided with funds mainly by the State, to the tune of £5,000 a year running costs at the start, increasing to £35,000 by 1914, plus heavy capital expenditure running in some years up to £45,000 the PTR attracted some of the best physicists of the day and became a model for other countries.[132]

As an alternative solution, mobilizing funds from private industry, Professor Felix Klein founded the 'Göttingen Society for the Promotion of Applied

[128] Ringer (1969), 75; Pfetsch (1974), 142; Lexis (1904), Vol. IV, 7–8, 30–1; Lundgreen (1973), 152.

[129] Lexis (1904), Vol. IV, 187–8, also 127.

[130] Kocka (1981a), 109; Lundgreen (1975b), 141 ff, and Lundgreen (1973), 139–40; Craig (1983), 225.

[131] Manegold (1970), 58, and Manegold (1978), 139–40, 151, and Manegold (1981), 133–65; Hortleder (1970); Burchardt (1983), 10; Scholl (1981), 30 ff; König (1981), 247–51; Borscheid (1976a), 122, 160; Krätz (1973), 274–6; p. 128, note 44 above.

[132] Burchardt (1975a), 11–12, and Burchardt (1977b), 27–36; Borscheid (1976a), 161; Brocke (1980), 54; Pfetsch (1974), 126.

Physics and Mathematics' which channelled some industrial funds into technological institutes at several universities.[133] More significantly, on the initiative of the chemical industry to establish a national research institute comparable in scope with the PTR, the *Kaiser-Wilhelm-Gesellschaft* had collected almost 12 million Reichsmark on its foundation in 1910, mainly from the banks and from the chemical industry. Ultimately the State also agreed to contribute.[134]

Meanwhile, significant developments were occurring in the university sector also. It would not be too much to say that in the second half of the nineteenth century the German universities became the leading centres of formalized learning in the world, the direct models for universities elsewhere, including Britain.

For the span of at least five or six decades, the German professorial structure, coupled with the remarkable generosity of the state governments, proved ideally suited to the widening and consolidation of academic knowledge. New specialisms could develop in the care of a *Privatdozent* or an extraordinary professor until new chairs were created for them, while still leaving to the existing chair and its holder the responsibility for the original subject. Teaching and research could thus be opened up to ever new fields without damage to older fields of knowledge.

Among the areas to benefit were the natural sciences. For Germany as a whole, science students rose from around 5% in 1830–60, to 10% in 1866–90 and 15% before the war, while those in theology fell from 30% to 20% and 10%.[135] In several of the sciences, including medicine and chemistry, Germany assumed world leadership, the numbers of her journals and papers published were unmatched elsewhere, as were the laboratories and other equipment which began to appear in new and old universities.

The State, on the whole, supported this expansion with generosity. Altogether, expenditure on the German universities grew from about 2.6 million marks in 1850–55 to 14.5 million in 1876–80 and 50 million in 1911–14, or almost 20-fold in 60 years. Expenditure on science and technology rose as

Table 3.7 *Expenditure on science and technology, 000 Marks, Germany and England*

	In universities		Elsewhere		Total		% of GNP	
	Germany	England*	Germany	England	Germany	England	Germany	England
1850	789	39	—	158	789	197	0.045	0.006
1870	2,346	397	32	3,335	2,378	3,732	0.044	0.041
1900	12,313	2,012	500	7,296	12,813	9,308	0.065	0.051
1914	26,360	6,340	1,138	11,247	27,498	17,589	0.085**	0.063

* There was additional private funding in Oxford and Cambridge for which there was no German equivalent
** 1910

[133] Manegold (1970); Pfetsch (1974), 141–2; Fischer (1978), 94.
[134] Schroder-Gudehus (1977), 474; Burchardt (1983), 31, and Burchardt (1977a), 39–42, and Burchardt (1976), 792.
[135] Riese (1977), 341, 346; Paulsen (1921), 537.

shown in Table 3.7, with 'England' added for comparison.[136]

The increase in the numbers of the university teaching staff, boosted by the simultaneous upgrading of institutions like the technical universities, is shown in Table 3.8:[137]

Table 3.8 *Total number of teaching staff in German universities and recognized university institutions.*

	Total staff				Full professors only			
	1864	1880	1900	1910	1864	1880	1900	1910
Natural sciences:								
Universities	263	366	579	727	135	181	214	241
Techn. U. & Min'g.Coll's			224	307			107	129
Other				42				34
All institutions	263	366	803	1076	135	181	321	404
Of which: (Chemistry)	72	92	254	360	31	38	74	87
(Physics)	34	48	117	185	22	26	50	71
Technologies:								
Universities	4	4	3	10	1	1	1	1
Techn. U. & Min'g.Coll's			232	340			135	197
Other				7				6
All institutions	4	4	235	357	1	1	136	204
Of which: (Mech.eng'g)	1	2	54	79			41	60
(Elec.eng'g)			36	57			11	20

The enrolment of students in institutions of higher learning showed equally dramatic increases, growing more than fivefold as a proportion of the appropriate 5-year age cohorts in 50 years.

Yet, as Table 3.7 makes clear, total expenditure on science and technology in Germany was not very greatly in excess of that in Britain – or rather, it was merely some 15–20 years ahead. True, at any given point in time, and certainly for any given stage of development, there were more scientists and technologists to be found in German industry than in British, but more significant than their numbers was their concentration in certain sectors, such as dye works, engineering works and iron and steelworks, and the organized way in which the regular progression of technical training was accepted as qualification for appropriate promotion levels in industry.[138] Curiously, however, the Germans complained just like the British, that industry was not interested in scientific and academic training and research, that engineers enjoyed but a low status and failed to penetrate to the higher echelons in the works, and that in the State service it was the lawyers who held all the top jobs.[139]

The debate on the British side is dominated by one industry in which

[136] Pfetsch (1974), 83; Brocke (1980), 19; Lundgreen and Thirlwall (1976), 38–9; Geison (1978), 86; Burchardt (1975b), 271–5, 284; Hermann (1977), 55; McCelland (1980), 204–5.
[137] Ferber (1956), 197–200.
[138] R.C. (1872), 297, 326–30, 344; Musgrave (1967), 44, 40, 100; McClelland (1980), 205.
[139] Ludwig (1974), 18–19; Locke (1977), 274–5, and Locke (1984), 80; Hortleder (1970), 83–4; Manegold (1970), 77; Berg (1984), 380; Lundgreen (1975a), 73; Troitsch (1970), 305; Treue (1967), 467.

Germany was said to have solved better than any other nation the problem of the interplay of academic science and industrial growth. This was the chemical industry, and to it we must now turn.

On the face of it, there seemed originally to be very little in the study of Chemistry that would mark it out to become a major element in German industrial progress. After a varied start in the eighteenth century, Chemistry, following the Humboldt reforms, fell victim to 'Natural Philosophy' and the contempt for anything useful, and survived mainly, at a low level, as one of the pure science subjects that might be studied theoretically, or used as an auxiliary subject in the training of pharmacists and medical men. At that time, Germany was far behind France and Great Britain both in theory and practical experience.[140]

From this starting point, the rise of chemistry to the position of the German model science seems something like a fluke. If it was accidental, the explanation may lie with Justus von Liebig, not only a chemist of genius, but also a forceful organizer and editor of a leading journal. No doubt, several factors worked in Liebig's favour. Among them must be counted the strong laboratory work tradition established in Germany before his arrival; a number of other talented professors of chemistry active at the time, including Wöhler, Bunsen, Stromeyer, Erdmann and Marchand; the saturation of Arts subjects and consequent tendency towards the sciences; and the fact that chemistry happened to be exactly at the stage at which it needed broadly based work, under supervision, by chemical students of the second rank to fill in the territory mapped out by the great theoreticians.[141] But above all, the drive behind Liebig and the other chemists of the mid-century can be traced back to Germany's determination to catch up economically.

An early trigger of the Liebig revolution was the series of bad harvest years particularly in the southern German states, culminating in the Revolution year of 1848. In their distress, the governments concerned, above all that of Baden, were prepared to devote considerable resources to agricultural improvements, and were only too eager to foster Liebig's study of fertilizers, though the practical discovery of the use of superphosphates had been made earlier, in 1842, by J.H. Gilbert and J.B. Lawes in Britain. Another early achievement of Liebig was the re-cycling of sulphur for sulphuric acid after the Sicilian monopoly had raised its price. Pioneering work was also done by Bunsen in Heidelberg and by the Polytechnic School in Karlsruhe.[142]

All this gave German chemistry some international prestige, but the significant breakthrough was the discovery of coal-tar dyes by Perkin in London in 1856, under the guidance of Prof. A.W. Hofmann, a pupil of Liebig. In their first stages they were developed mainly in Britain, where there was also much the most advanced productive capacity. Yet within less than 10 years, Germany had taken the lead, to leave all other countries, with the possible exception of Switzerland, far behind.

---

[140] Schmauderer (1976), 622–7; Hufbauer (1971), 205–31; Schimank (1973), 207–12; Borscheid (1976a), 34–6, 50–4; Lundgreen (1984), 60; Ben-David (1977), 50–1, 98.

[141] E.g. Armytage (1965), 77; Pfetsch (1974), 156; Krätz (1973), 269; Howard (1907), 60.

[142] Borscheid (1976a), 16–17, 32–3, 44, 57–9, 119, and Borscheid (1976b), 82; Hohenberg (1967), 29, 126; Fischer (1978), 74; Sullivan (1985), 305.

How did Germany achieve its success? Several possible answers have been given and most of them take the teaching of high-level chemistry into account.

One extreme explanation, offered by Borscheid and Rabi, is that there was an over-supply of trained graduate chemists, and since they could not find employment, they established their own firms and set going a fast process of expansion. In a second, weaker version, the stress is laid on the fact that many of the leading chemical firms, among them BASF (established in 1865), Hoechst (1863) and AGFA (1873), beside many smaller ones, were in fact founded by trained chemists so that the decision-makers were in a position to appreciate and pick up new ideas quickly; among the giants, only Bayer (1864) was an exception.[143]

The remarkable influx of trained chemists into factory laboratories was certainly an outstanding feature of the industry, and like the size of the German chemical industry as a whole, itself became a competitive advantage in the frantic search for new dyes and new pharmaceutical products. By 1900, the leading six firms employed a total work force of 18,000, 1,360 commercial staff, 350 engineers and 500 chemists. By 1914, the number of German works chemists had risen to 9,000 and total employment in the industry to 290,000.[144]

Large firms could pay top salaries and secure first-rate chemists who compared in quality with the leading holders of university chairs. They worked together with the universities, directing the work of young PhD students as well as of the massed ranks of 'men of ordinary, plodding ability, thoroughly trained and methodically directed, that (gave) Germany . . . so commanding an advantage.'[145] It was these resources which allowed German industrial chemists to specialize, to develop something like the synthetic indigo dye, which needed 152 patents and cost 18 million Marks before it reached a commercial stage, and ultimately the even costlier hydrogenation process.[146] Technical advantages in an industry of this kind were cumulative, for they were translated quickly into drastically lowered prices and the capture of one market after another. Moreover, the big battalions in the German chemical industry made it possible for trained chemists to be assigned to sales and commercial departments, there to advise customers and further their sales.[147]

Large firms were also able to work the patent laws to their advantage. Among the peculiarities of the Prussian patent law (patents in smaller states were hardly worth fighting for), was the power of the authorities to vet patent applications before admitting them, and many were rejected, often on what seemed capricious grounds at the time. German firms could therefore make free with ideas developed abroad. In 1877, just when Germany ceased to be mainly a consumer, and began to be a producer, of patented ideas, a new law covering the Reich as a whole, removed much of the obstructive power of the authorities but still made it costly and troublesome to secure a new patent. Also, it protected not necessarily the inventor, but the petitioner, all of which favoured the large, established firm.[148]

[143] Rabi (1965), 30; Borscheid (1976a), 84, 104 ff, 168–72, 210; Pfetsch (1974), 157–9.
[144] Haber (1971), 48; Lilley (1973), 245; Miall (1931), 85–6; Beer (1959), 55, 107, 114; R.C. (1884), 223–5.
[145] Dewar, quoted in Haber (1971), 53.
[146] Beer (1959), 88–90; Schmauderer (1976), 620–1; Hughes (1969), 111.
[147] Hohenberg (1967), 90–6, 110, 128–30; Singer *et al.* (1954–58), VI, 503; Kaku (1980), 85.
[148] Sonnemann (1963); Heggen (1975), 50 ff, 86, 111, 126, 135; Treue (1964), 330 and Treue (1976), 222; Redlich (1914), 9 ff. The British Patent Act of 1907 attempted to redress the balance: Miall (1931), 92; Fleischer (1984), 79 ff; chapter 1, p. 34 above.

Among other advantages enjoyed by the German chemical industry, beside its early link with science and its phenomenal growth rate, was the raw material base, such as coal (including surplus tar products), salt and potash. With this might be combined the voracious home market provided by the agrarian sector with its exceptionally acute need for fertilizer, and the growing textile industry. The advantages of the Rhine, as a means of transport and source of water for the German and Swiss industry have also been stressed, as has the comparative late start, which meant that Germany was not tied to out-of-date processes like the Leblanc soda process and could take up innovations like the Solvay method at once.[149] Finally, the German tradition was favourable to the formation of cartels and other monopolistic structures, and the chemical industry made full use of it. The first cartel, for alizarin, was formed in 1881. By 1905, 46 of the 385 German cartels then listed were in the chemical industry; a year before, two combinations of firms had been formed, the first stages in the creation of the later giant, the I.G. Farben: Hoechst combined with Cassella, and the 'Triple Alliance' of BASF, AGFA and Bayer linked up three of the largest and most progressive firms in the industry.[150]

The result of all these factors was a remarkable growth rate, and almost unique domination of world markets by the industry of a single country. The output of synthetic dyestuffs was estimated to have grown around 25-fold in quantity between 1880 and 1914. By then, Germany was producing about 85% of the world's dyestuffs and had an even greater share of the world's exports:[151]

Table 3.9 World production and consumption of dyestuffs, 1913 (000 tons)

	Production	Consumption
Germany	135	20
Great Britain	5	23
Rest of world	22	119
World total	162	162

The German position in other chemicals, particular in the heavy non-organic sectors, was less favourable, and the British correspondingly stronger. A particular strength of the British lay in alkali production and in the production of caustic soda by an electrical process. Even as late as 1900, Britain still had the larger chemical industry, measured by output or by capital invested. Fertilizers, explosives and soap, as well as alkalis were exported, while her imports were dominated by synthetic dyestuffs and pharmaceuticals. Market shares before the war are shown on Table 3.10:

Table 3.10 Market shares of key chemicals, 1913

	Output, 000 tons				Percentages		
	UK	USA	Germany	World	UK	USA	Germany
Synthetic dyestuffs	5	3	137*	161	3	2	85
Sulphuric acid	1082	2250	1686	8300	13	27	20
Superphosphates	820	3248	1863	11750	7	28	16
Soda ash	850	120	325	1700	50	7	9
Chemical nitrogen	90	36	119	767	12	5	16

* incl. *c.*10 of subsidiaries of German firms.

149 Hohenberg (1967), 38, 51; Haber (1971), 103; Hickel (1977), 66–7; Treue (1966), 39–40.
150 Beer (1959), 117–18, 130–2.
151 Alter (1982), 129; Haber (1971), 108; Beer (1959), 96, 114; Richardson (1962), 110–11; Redlich (1914), 44 ff, 77 ff; Hohenberg (1967), 39.

Altogether, Germany's exports of chemicals exceeded her imports in 1901 by £12.6 million while the British export surplus, on the same basis, was £8.7 million.[152] The enormous success of German organic chemicals and the key role played in it by academic science, were thus wholly exceptional even within the chemical industry.

The only other industries in which scientific research and know-how was said to have given Germany a competitive advantage were optical glass and electrical engineering. Optical glass is the most plausible case, but it was but a small industry and its success depended on a single firm, Zeiss of Jena. The case for electrical engineering is much weaker, and by 1913 Germany, like the United Kingdom, had become largely dependent on American technology.[153] More interesting still is the case of the motor car. For while the key inventions had been made in Germany, by such as N.A. Otto, Gottlieb Daimler, Wilhelm Maibach, Karl Benz and Rudolf Diesel, several of whom had connections with the *Technische Hochschulen*, and while other improvements were made in France and Britain, it was in the United States that the industry developed above all. The provision of original ideas to be exploited successfully by others, was usually said to be a British failing rather than a German.

In the latter part of the nineteenth century the German university system came under considerable criticism from contemporaries, and has also been increasingly critically viewed by historians. Many of its shortcomings arose directly out of precisely those structural features which had such a favourable influence earlier on, and others were part of the price paid for success.

One problem arose out of the sheer numbers of students attracted into the universities and colleges. As the number of graduates began to exceed the jobs available, this led not only to demoralization among the student body; the student avalanche also threatened the basis of the German university teaching system itself. The seminar type of teaching, in which the students were allowed, in an indirect way, to take part in the professor's own researches, now became impossible. Moreover, since the professor was in part paid according to the numbers of students, he had a strong incentive to accept ever larger numbers of them, laying upon himself thereby a growing time-consuming burden of teaching and administration at the expense of the research which ought to have been his main interest.[154] This was an acute form of the perennial university problem that while academic recognition, employment and promotion depend on research, professors are nominally paid to teach students.

There were two other features which, having contributed to German academic productivity in the earlier decades of expansion, now became hindrances: specialization, and professorial freedom and control within a hierarchy. Earlier on, specialization had made for expertise and the development of new sciences. Now it made for specialisms of professors so esoteric that they were of little or no use to undergraduates; it also made it impossible to foster interdisciplinary

---

[152] Haber (1971), 9–11, 39, and Haber (1980), 157–8; Chapman (1904), 218–21; Williams (1972), 50; Warren (1980); R.C. (1884), 229–30. See chapter 1, esp. note 92. See p. 32 above.

[153] Howard (1907), 58–9; Spohr (1977), 127; Weiher (1980), 31, 35–7.

[154] Müller (1977), 28, 210, 274 ff; Jarausch (1983b), 18, 21, and Jarausch (1980), 130; Titze (1983), 57–88; McClelland (1983), 320; Ben-David and Zloczower (1972), 56; Farrar (1975), 189–90; Zloczower (1981).

research; and it made for professorial jealousy harmful to the young *Privat-dozent* and his chances of becoming a professor. Of the 136 physicists who became habilitated (i.e. nominally qualified for chairs) between 1890 and 1909, 44% never got a chair at all.[155]

The German universities in their conservatism had always kept out engineering which in Britain was integrated within them; the same fate now befell other novel subjects like bacteriology and psychoanalysis; sociology and similar subjects also remained suspect for long. What innovation there was had often to be forced on reluctant universities by ministerial officials like F. Althoff in Prussia. Even in their established subjects, the Humboldtian tradition led professors to avoid research in both fundamental science and in topics that might be of use to industry: instead, many lost themselves in ever more refined following-up searches of little-frequented by ways, as did their PhD students.[156] The technical universities, by contrast, were still plagued by overloaded teachers, overloaded curricula and relatively poorer equipment, and they left too little initiative to the students. The professors, according to one British critic in 1904, 'go on in exactly the same way as they have done for the last thirty years' and complain bitterly of the lack of funds.[157] Lastly, the much-vaunted freedom to teach on the part of professors was, in an autocratic and militarist environment, in many areas little more than a sham, and did not compare with the freedom enjoyed by the British professor.[158]

It may well be that the young men from Britain and America who had come to Germany to study and then returned home full of admiration for the German system, had been to the best universities, studied with the leading professors, and had, as research students, received a great deal of personal attention, without becoming aware of the disadvantages suffered by the average German students and their academic teachers.[159] Similarly, it may well by that the benfit derived by Germany from her educational provision in her drive to successful industrialization may have been generally exaggerated. Evident enough in certain sections of the chemical industry and perhaps also in the optical glass and instruments industries, the benefits are far less certain elsewhere.

That there was a difference between Germany and Britain in the educational provision, and expecially in the role of the State in it, there can be no doubt. But this may not imply German superiority, merely a different tradition and a different place in the sequence of world industrialization. The State had always played a larger role in Germany than in the United Kingdom. State initiative was believed, additionally, to be required in catching up with western Europe, which was held to be beyond the power of unaided private enterprise. Lastly the German authorities were, in our period, far more frightened of political threats from below and were more inclined than the British to see the educational system, including the universities, as a bulwark against social change. By

---

[155] Forman, Heilbron, Weart (1973), 53–5; McCormach (1974), 162; Ben-David (1968), 30–1; Paulsen (1902), 222 ff.

[156] Howarth (1922), 235; Ben-David (1968–9), 4–7, and Ben-David (1971), 130; Ringer (1969), 34 ff, 144 ff, 162 ff. But see Lundgreen (1973).

[157] D.C. (1906), ev. Brough, Q.2063; Sanderson (1972a), 22; Haber (1971) 44–5.

[158] Ben-David and Zloczower (1972), 58; Ashby (1974), 5.

[159] Ben-David (1968–69), 7, and Ben-David (1968), 36; Hollenberg (1974), 159, 294–6.

contrast, the British State saw no need to intervene on industrial grounds, since British industry had built up a position of leadership without State aid, nor was it driven by the same fear of revolution: in any case, the education provided by private institutions, above all the Churches, could be relied on to steer the young into paths of social tranquillity. The British tradition was one of self-reliance and *laissez-faire*.[160]

Given that the tightly and logically organized, as well as more generously funded German system was appropriate to German industrial needs as well as being within her political tradition, it was not without its weaknesses. It may well be that too much was invested in education, starving other social purposes; and the meticulous allocation of separate training courses for each trade and each rank – manager, foreman, skilled man – might well have created needless rigidity, especially after Germany had caught up and could no longer merely follow well-trodden paths but had to strike out on her own.[161]

A nation entering world commerce in a major way would, after all, have to have some positions of strength on Ricardian principles, and the oft-quoted significance of German absolute dominance over some parts of the world's chemical industries may easily be exaggerated: chemicals accounted for only around 2% of German employment, and 4% of Germany's exports even in the last years before the war. Similarly, in the field of education, the German lead was much less pronounced in the natural sciences other than Chemistry, including even Physics. German academic education was still only the privilege of a small minority, and was dominated by the classics. And, as we saw above in a phase of rapid expansion, British inferiority should be seen rather as a lag in years rather than a failure in capacity. Altogether, it would be hard to maintain that Germany derived much gain and much in the way of superiority over Britain as distinct from catching up, from her more lavish, more centralized expenditure on science and technology on the part of the State in our period, outside a few particular points of comparative cost advantages.

V British Science, Education and Research

Let us return now to the British educational system. How far did it correspond to the picture drawn by the critics? To what extent may it have handicapped the British economy, either overall of at least in certain key sections?

According to the traditional picture, British education was unorganized, chaotic and of an abysmally low level, as long as it was supplied by private enterprise. Some improvements were due to the religious school societies, the National and the British and Foreign, but it was not until the State intervened, with educational subsidies which began in 1833 in a very small way and culminated in the universal education provision of Forster's Act of 1870, that a satisfactory system of elementary education emerged. Scotland has generally been

---

[160] Wardle (1970), 211; Musgrove (1981), 63; Reader (1966), 114; LeClerc (1899), 59.
[161] Turner (1985), 4; Borscheid (1976a), 211; Roderick and Stephens (1981c), 247; Floud (1984), 11; Inkster (1983), 43; Nicholas (1985a), 83 ff, also Inkster (1985c), 186 ff; Lorenz (1984); Ranis (1978); also pp. 173, 182.

exempted from these strictures, having had a universal parochial system from the end of the seventeenth century onward at least.

This traditional picture has now been modified in every important respect. As noted above[162] the state of literacy was far from abysmal even in the eighteenth century, and it had greatly improved by the middle of the nineteenth, although certain areas, such as the most rapidly growing factory towns of Lancashire and Scotland, as well as the remote rural districts, had lower figures of literacy than the average. The Scottish percentages were rather better than the English throughout, though not by much, and the British ratios were not out of line with those of other countries.

Parallel with the upward revision of the state of literacy there has also been a revision of the proportion of the population which received some formal schooling. The Newcastle Commission, by assuming that children stayed at school from the age of *c*.5 to 13, which corresponds to an attendance of eight years, instead of a realistic attendance of four years only for the typical working-class child, arrived at much too low a ratio of those at school, compared with those in the appropriate age group. Similarly, calculations of how long the average child remained at school, based on its stay on one register, erred on the pessimistic side by neglecting the fact that children might move with their parents into another district and another school, or reappear later at the same school after a spell of work, of illness or of helping out at home.[163]

On the basis of various official enquiries, the total school population may be assumed to have grown as follows:

1818   478,000
1834 1,294,000
1851 2,144,000
1859 2,535,000

Of that last total, 860,000 were in private, unsupported schools. The ratio to the whole population was 1:7.7, which compared with 1:6.27 for Prussia and 1:8.11 for the Netherlands, two of Europe's leading countries.[164]

Recent revisions of the years thereafter have advanced along three not wholly unconnected lines. The first has been to look afresh at the work done by the privately run schools in comparison with the standards of those run by the religious societies and later by the public authorities. The second has been to give more weight to the independent wishes of working-class parents regarding the schooling of their children, and to the role of the Sunday Schools. The third has been to reduce the alleged gap existing between the provisions of schooling in Scotland and in England.

Much of the traditional literature has largely relied on, if not wholly emanated from, the reformers and the educational bureaucrats who wished to expand their own projects at the expense of the pre-existing private schools, and those who wished to enlarge the element of religious indoctrination. Their adverse judgement on the private schools was therefore by no means disinterested, and was not shared by the numerous parents, including those of the

[162] See pp. 125, 139, notes 33, 75–6 above.
[163] Hurt (1979), 4, 26, 43; Schofield (1968), 317; Anderson (1983b), 531; R.C. (1861), 172–3; Madoc-Jones (1977), 41–66.
[164] West (1965), 137–40; Anderson (1983b), 525; Simon (1974), 347; R.C. (1861), 53 ff, 79 ff.

working classes, who were willing to pay sizeable sums for private schooling, even though the cheaper educational provisions by the school societies and other public sources were available. After 1870, the new Board Schools could keep their fees well below those of private venture schools, thanks to the increasing financial aid they received from the State, until ultimately they were in a position to abolish all fees. It is likely that it was this process of price reduction, rather than their inherent superiority, which led to the decline of private schooling.

Of course, the quality of the teaching in 'dame schools' and other private establishments was often poor; but then, the teaching in the schools supported by the religious bodies and the State (as well as the teaching in the Prussian elementary schools), also left much to be desired. Given the low levels of income then, little better could be expected. As a proportion of the national income, expenditure on education was in fact higher in 1833 than in 1920:[165]

	1833	1920
%NNI spent on schooling:		
children of all ages	*c.* 1.00	0.70
children below 11 years	*c.* 0.80	0.58

At the point of introduction of Forster's Education Act, private expenditure on education still exceeded public expenditure; it was only thereafter that it was driven out by publicly funded competition.[166]

Once the Government had decided to provide funds for education, its expenditure grew with remarkable rapidity, from £30,000 a year in 1839 and 1840, to £100,000 in 1846 and 1847, £260,000 in 1853 and on to a temporary peak of £837,000 in 1859. Then, after a sharp drop, it climbed again to *c.* £700,000 in 1870. The total sum disbursed in the years 1839–59, was £4,378,000, of which there was spent on scientific apparatus a grand total of £4,392. Since the grants were paid out only when a certain standard had been reached and qualified teachers employed, schools in the poorest areas were generally excluded.

Together with the work of the private schools, the work of the Sunday schools has also recently been considered afresh. It is now established that in numerous cases, particularly among the dissenters, these schools became centres for genuine education, besides teaching the basic reading skills. Whether complements or substitutes for day schools, their number gave them an undoubted importance in their own right. Assuming only working-class children as their recruiting ground, they covered one-seventh of all children in 1801, one-half in 1831 and three-quarters in 1851. In absolute numbers, attendance rose from 206,000 in 1801 to 2,6 million in 1851 and to a peak of almost 6.2 million in 1906. They were much more integrated into working-class life than the schools run by the middle classes, they reacted more sensitively to working-class educational needs, and many are the tributes from men and

[165] West (1975), 62, and West (1965), 132, 168–70, and West (1971), 637–8; Laqueur (1976a), 196–200; Gardner (1984).
[166] West (1970), 86, and West (1983), 426–34, and West (1978), and West (1965), 161 ff, and West (1975), 72, 80, 87; Hurt (1971), 624–32; Mitch (1986), 371 ff; Rich (1970) 63–4; Curtis (1963), 252; Mitch (1986), 375.

women of humble origin to the educational value for their own educational development of what they learnt in the Sunday schools.[167]

Beside these, there were also factory schools, poor law schools and the ragged schools in London and Bristol to teach the children of the poor, at least their letters and sometimes something more.[168]

Thirdly, the educational provisions of Scotland, once praised as being as comprehensive and well-organized as those of the Continent, have been re-examined, and found not to have differed as much from the English as was once believed. True enough, each parish had to have a school, but in the remoter country areas, this might be accessible to only a few, with a part-time teacher, while in the burghs it might mean a middle-class school which left the lower orders without any provision whatever. In fact, the Scottish parochial schools catered for only a minority of children, 75,000 out of 310,000 in 1851. The famous 'lad o'pairts', making his way from humble beginnings with the help of education, came usually from lower middle-class rather than from working-class families.[169]

For our purposes, possibly the teaching of science (and technology) might be of greater significance than that of the basic literary skills. What contribution did the elementary schools in fact make to an understanding of science and its principles among the working part of the population?

Little is known of what went on in unaided private schools, though some few undoubtedly taught science and technical subjects. For the grant-aided schools the picture is somewhat clearer. One of the leading reformers, John Kay-Shuttleworth, who became Secretary to the Committee of the Privy Council for Education on its establishment in 1839, had from the beginning planned to introduce into the elementary schools, in addition to the 3 Rs, some science associated with the children's later occupations, as well as some knowledge of commerce. The inspiration, clearly, was utilitarian rather than religious or the training of social submissiveness.

Much of Kay-Shuttleworth's effort went into teacher training, hinged on the so-called pupil-teacher scheme introduced in 1846. Under its rules, intending teachers first underwent a five-year apprenticeship in an existing school, and could then gain a Queen's Scholarship to a recognized training college. These latter devoted a surprisingly large proportion of their efforts to scientific-industrial subjects. In their first year, training college students took mathematics as well as mechanics; in their second, beside arithmetic, they could also opt for higher mathematics and the physical sciences. A considerable number of male trainees followed these courses in the early years.[170]

For a time all went well. Some training colleges built up laboratories for chemistry. The first school inspector with a scientific background, the Rev. Henry Mosely, FRS, had been appointed in 1843 and in 1852 he devised sets for science teaching, planned to cost £10, £15 or £20 for schools, and £100, £125 and £150 for training colleges. Science books for the use of schools,

[167] Laqueur (1976a); also Laqueur (1976b); Curtis (1963), 468.
[168] Sanderson (1967), 266–79, and Sanderson (1983), 21; Frith (1977), 67–92; Roberts (1960), 322.
[169] Anderson (1985a), and Anderson (1983b), 518–25; West (1965), 115, and West (1970), 73–6.
[170] Rich (1970), 64; R.C. (1861), 22–3, 115, 119, 647; Digby and Searby (1981), 7, 41.

written by respectable authors, began to appear, and some teachers who had been through the courses began to return to the schools and to introduce topics like 'common things' and principles which might have relevance to practical trades into their classrooms.[171]

However, this first springtime lasted but a short while. It was killed effectively by Robert Lowe's 'revised code' of 1862. Its inspiration lay in the wish to cut back government expenditure, and in the dogmatic adherence to the market economy in education. Government money was henceforth to be paid to schools according to examination passes in the 3 Rs, – a form of payment by results.[172]

Few historians have had anything good to say about the revised code. Its immediate effect was to cut out the teaching of all subjects not covered, and to reduce the teaching in the 3 Rs to mechanical rote for the passing of examinations. The status of teachers, who were now totally dependent on examination results over which they had no control, was drastically reduced. Not least, the science teaching in the training colleges also withered away,[173] though some evening teaching of science and technical subjects under the Department of Science and Art remained (see below).

Forster's Education Act of 1870 marked a change of attitude on the part of the public authorities towards the schooling of the poorer children. Variously said to have been inspired by the fear of loss of industrial supremacy, by the need to educate the newly enfranchised voters, or by the battle of Sadowa,[174] the Act, intended to fill the gap left by voluntary provision and to increase the public grants payable to the religious societies, set off a phase of seemingly irresistible educational expansion.

The Act made elementary education neither compulsory nor free at first: the former became law in effect in 1880, and the latter, by stages, in 1891, 1902 and 1918. Some local authorities enforced compulsory attendance until the age of 10 from the start. That age limit was enacted nationally in 1880. By 1893 this had become 11 years, by 1899, 12 years, and there was a general trend towards the age of 14 by the outbreak of war.[175] This extension of the years spent at school was perhaps the most significant change brought about within the current general atmosphere of expansion. As early as 1882, a 'seventh standard', going beyond the regular six standards permitted up to that time, was authorized, and became the thin end of the wedge that was to lead ultimately to the provision of secondary education for broader groups of the population, beginning with the Education Act of 1902.

The actual extent to which the years of schooling were prolonged in that period has recently been calculated to have been as follows[176]:

[171] Layton (1973), 79, 95 ff; R.C. (1861), 661, 665, 669; Hurt (1979), 28.

[172] S.C. (1867–68), ev. Lingen, Q.709; Curtis (1963), 260–1; Roderick and Stephens (1981a), 57; R.C. (1872), ev. Cromwell, QQ.7904–7.

[173] R.C. (1872), xiii–xiv; Layton (1973), 119 ff, 152–6; Tropp (1970), 202.

[174] Digby and Searby (1981), 30; Simon (1974), 356–7; Gonner (1912), 123; Chapman (1914), Vol. III, 173; Ellis (1985).

[175] Rubinstein (1977b), 231; Simon (1965), 176; Wardle (1970), 36–7, 74; Nostitz (1900), 133–4, Ellis (1985), 28.

[176] Matthews, Feinstein and Odling-Smee (1982), 573, Ellis (1985), 29.

Age cohorts
Years of birth	Av. years of schooling
1862–6	5.4
1867–71	6.1
1872–6	6.6
1877–86	7.2
1887–96	8.3
1897–1901	9.1

Similarly, the schooling enjoyed by the male labour force at different dates, a form of calculation which allows the longer periods at school of those who had recently left school to be diluted by those whose school years lay many years back, has been estimated to have grown in the following manner:

1871	4.21 years of schooling
1881	4.69
1891	5.32
1901	6.02
1911	6.75

On that reckoning, the average schooling of the whole labour force was rising by 8 months every decade. It just kept pace with the equally rapid rise of schooling in the leading European countries, Prussia and Switzerland, though it was still slightly behind in absolute terms.[177]

The numbers and qualifications of the teaching body increased in line with this expansion. Numbers of certificated teachers rose from 12,000 in 1870 to 53,000 in 1895 and 62,000 in 1900. After the early blows suffered under the revised code, conditions for elementary teachers gradually improved again in this period. The teachers' status was also raised by the abolition of the crude payments-by-results scheme in 1890, the attachment of some training colleges to universities, and the increased recruitment from the secondary schools instead of from within the elementary system, though this development greatly reduced the access of working-class children to the teaching profession.[178]

After the new code of 1890 had in effect abolished payments by results, further codes of 1893 and 1896 encouraged the development of new subjects, including science and handicrafts such as woodwork and metalwork. At first, the effects of these changes were limited. By 1893, about half the schools offered additional subjects beyond the 3 Rs, and the number of science departments in schools increased from 173 in 1891 to 1,396 in 1895. It was important that teachers themselves increasingly received some training in science subjects. From 1904 onwards every training college had to have a science department, many were given good laboratories, and numbers of teachers were emerging who had developed effective methods of teaching science in elementary schools.[179]

The momentum once started, developments were soon carried beyond the limits intended by the authorities. It was found, for example, that parents of the lower middle and the artisan classes whose children did well at school wanted

[177] Rosenberg (1982), 248.
[178] Wardle (1970), 108–9; Ringer (1979), 216; Cardwell (1957), 133; Tropp (1970), 203, 210; Armytage (1955), 255.
[179] Turner (1927), 11, 149; Cardwell (1957), 331 ff; Nostitz (1900), 150.

them to stay on beyond the compulsory school age. Most school boards in the larger industrial cities, starting with Sheffield in 1878, reacted by pulling these more able children into central schools where it was easier and more economical to do work at a higher level. This was aided by the 'seventh standard' authorized. In accordance with the demands of the parents, the emphasis of almost all these central schools was on the sciences and on industry-related practical subjects.

Here was a remarkable development indeed. Once out of reach of the privileged classes with their dogmatic notions on what education was about, British education was moving in a direction dictated by social needs, in a manner similar to Britain's chief rivals, Germany and the United States. These schools generated 'an amount of enthusiasm amongst the lower middle classes and working people for a form of higher education which no one had ever suspected'; they tended to draw out the talents, hitherto neglected, of the lower orders; they also concentrated on the subjects useful to them and to society.

Despite the limitations, such as over-large classes and shortage of funds, these central schools did remarkable work. Many of them had practical equipment; Birmingham's Bridge Street School even had two steam engines, for which the pupils made parts. By 1895 there were 67 higher grade schools with 25,000 scholars, 39 being 'organized science schools' recognized by the Department of Science and Art. By 1897, the Department supported 143 schools in England and Wales and 13 in Scotland offering a fully 'organized science' curriculum.[180]

Although the legal position of these schools was dubious and they did not meet with universal approbation, it had become clear that secondary education could in future no longer be limited to the tiny privileged group which had hitherto alone enjoyed it. The Education Act passed in 1902 under the aegis of the new Board of Education ushered in a new phase of public education provision, including for the first time secondary education aided by public grants. Moreover, 25% of the places at grant-aided secondary schools had henceforth to be reserved as free places for the children of the poor.

A remarkable expansion of secondary education followed. In England and Wales, the number of such grant-aided schools rose from 575 in 1904–5, to 1,047 in 1914, while the number of scholars also doubled from 94,000 to 198,000.[181] But at the same time, the Act of 1902 throttled the promising developments foreshadowed by the central schools and drove secondary education into a different direction. Under the regulations of 1904 which reflected the views of the department's strong man, Sir Robert Morant, these and other secondary schools, which the local authorities were now entitled to manage, were turned into elite schools, emphasizing traditional subjects. A massive blow had been struck against state support for scientific and technical education. It was probably the last time that the arrogant blinkered men of 'liberal' education managed to damage so severely the contribution that education might make to the country's economic progress and well-being.

[180] Quotations from the evidence of Forsyth and Bidgood, R.C. (1895), Vol. IV, Q.8506, also R.C. (1895), Vol. II, ev. Vardy and Cooper, *passim*, and Donelly, QQ.17 309 ff, 83; Wardle (1970), 37, 129; Eaglesham (1956); Simon (1965), 178–82; R.C. (1884), Vol. I., 425, 467, and R.C. (1884), Vol. V., 152 ff; LeClerc (1899), 139, 145–6, 160, 166, 193–4; Bamford (1967), 104–5.
[181] Singer *et al.* (1954–58), VI, 144; Wardle (1970), 75, 131; Musgrave (1970b), 24.

For the middle and upper classes, a range of institutions of secondary education had been inherited from earlier centuries. With their endowments and
traditions they had almost universally inherited also a predisposition towards
classical studies, and a contempt for most other subjects, with the possible
exception of mathematics.

The obsession with the classics as the main content of secondary, and indeed
tertiary education, was common to almost the whole of Europe. Hardly anywhere else, however, had it assumed such dimensions as in Britain, and particularly in England. There were essentially three basic causes for this
phenomenon. It was linked in the top schools, to the enormous clinging mass of
privilege, sinecurism and corruption which dominated the whole educational
field from the universities and the higher dignitaries of the Church of England
at the top right down to the humblest endowed grammar school. Secondly, the
teaching profession had no competence to teach anything else. Thirdly, in the
prevailing dominance of status (or snobbery), the concentration on the classics
trickled down from the top people's schools to those of the lower orders.

The concentration on the classics was defended on the grounds that they were
irreplaceable in instilling moral, humane and liberal values. Whatever the
merit in that argument, it could scarcely be drawn on to defend the educational
practice in the classical boy's school, for even among the boys who stayed until
the end, the large majority emerged with at best only a minimal acquaintance
with classical learning:[182] they had merely wasted their best educational years
on the dead study of a dead grammar. Against this, the significance of mathematics, which beside the classics was found in the curriculum of almost every
school should not be underrated. Here was a subject which required not only
logical thought, care and accuracy, but could also form the basis of later scientific interests or industrial and commercial occupations.

In 1861–64 nine of the leading public schools were examined in great detail
by the Clarendon Commission. Among many other reforms, its Report recom-
mended a moderate provision of science. Some of its recommendations were
incorporated in the Public Schools Act of 1868, but meanwhile the public
schools had begun setting their own house in order and in 1869 they founded
the Headmasters' Conference. Before long most public schools were offering a
'modern stream' as well as a classical stream to their scholars. This was not
unconnected with the rising number of businessmen's sons among their
pupils.[183] Yet their basic hostility and contempt for science remained. The
modern stream, only part of which concentrated on science, was still looked
down on, it had few prizes to offer, and it prestige was further depressed by
headmasters who forced the weaker pupils to opt for science. In most schools,
the science masters led a lonely, despised life, engaged in an uphill struggle
against the ill-will and contempt of the other masters. As late as 1916, 34 of the
35 headmasters of the leading public schools were classicists.[184]

Earlier in the century, the middle classes, facing the recurrent dilemma of

[182] E.g. R.C. (1864), 23–4, 31; Ward (1967), 43; Ringer (1979), 231–2; Simon (1974), 309; Clarke
(1959), 86 ff.
[183] Sanderson (1983), 38–9; Coleman (1973), 105, 108–9; Wilkinson (1962), 320–30.
[184] R.C. (1872), ev. Jenkin, Q.1734; Sanderson (1983), 37–9; Bamford (1967), 94, 108–11; R.C.
(1864), 11–15, 32.

having to opt either for schools that brought prestige or schools that taught what their children needed, had for the time being turned away from the classical foundations to found schools which conformed more closely to their own aspirations. Among the better known of these schools were Mill Hill (1807), Liverpool Institute (1825) and Liverpool College (1840), King's College School (1829), University College School (1833) and the City of London School (1837). All of them taught science and other modern subjects. There then followed foundations intended for boys with middle-class and professional occupations or for the armed services, in which science and even engineering and handicraft subjects might be of value. The first three of these were Cheltenham (1841), Marlborough (1843) and Rossall (1844). Wellington, Epsom, Haileybury, Clifton, Malvern and Bath followed soon after.[185] Yet all of these, instead of shaping their own ethos, aligned themselves increasingly with the pattern of the traditional public schools in the later years of Queen Victoria.

The Taunton Commission (1864–68), following Clarendon, examined the remainder of the secondary school field. It listed 673 schools, a mixed bag, of which 152 were really elementary schools. The Devonshire Commission, sitting in the early 1870s, also circularized over 200 endowed schools in an attempt to find out the state of their science teaching and received replies from 128 of them, presumably mainly those who took science teaching seriously. Of the hundreds of schools listed by Taunton, only 18 had as many as 4 hours of science per week; only 13 had properly equipped laboratories. Devonshire, reporting but a few years later, though on a more select group, found that about half the schools which replied taught some science, but only a little more than one quarter of the boys, 2,430 out of 8,945 benefited. In Scottish secondary schools in 1866, over 10,000 scholars in 57 schools took arithmetic, plus 1,600 classed as taking mathematics; but only 487 in 8 schools took physics, 146 in 3 schools took chemistry, and 124 in 2 schools took natural history.[186]

One year after the Taunton Report, in 1869, the Endowed Schools Act was passed, setting up a body of Commissioners which was merged in 1874 with the Charity Commission. Its main task was to deal with the misappropriation of funds by the masters of hundreds of schools, but it could also influence their curricula.

In some endowed schools, particularly those in cities with large middle-class populations, reform came quickly. Manchester Grammar School, for example, had by the early 1880s created laboratory space for 70 for its modern stream, room for 180 in its drawing hall, and in 1877–81 had won 33 prizes, and 700 passes, in the Science and Art Department's examinations. King Edward VI school in Birmingham was reformed in 1883, and Hulme Grammar School, Bradford G.S., Bedford G.S. and Exeter G.S. were other older foundations which by then devoted large resources to the teaching of science. Among them, Cowper Street School in London was particularly successful. Founded in 1866, its boys were sought after by employers looking for engineering and design apprentices. It found several imitators in London and elsewhere and became

---

[185] Curtis (1963), 148; Wardle (1970), 118–22; Bamford (1967), 229.
[186] Roderick and Stephens (1972), 36; Turner (1927), 89; R.C. (1895), 42 ff, 130 ff.

the base for the later Finsbury College. In Scotland, the middle classes had far greater influence on the management of the secondary schools, and these therefore devoted more effort to modern subjects than their English counterparts.[187]

These developments took place against a background of rising standards fostered by external examinations. While the examinations proposed by the Royal College of Preceptors (1846) had little effect at first, the Civil Service examinations beginning in 1855, the Oxford Local Examinations (1857), followed by Cambridge (1858), their joint Schools Examination Board (1873) and the 'higher locals' (1869 and 1877) raised and tended to unify the standards in all school subjects, including mathematics and, for small numbers, the sciences.[188]

The picture was therefore an extremely mixed one. The old prejudices were still widespread, and the hold of the classicists over the top jobs in the civil service, in the church and in politics was unbroken. On the other hand, the sciences had made immense strides between the 1860s and 1914. Every decade had seen a further extension of their influence in the schools, and the teaching itself had much improved, in particular by using practical work in laboratories to an increasing extent. Developments were most uneven, as behoved the British tradition, but by no means abysmal any longer.

Moreover, in addition to formal schooling, there was, consonant with the British tradition, much self-help and initiative provided by a bewildering variety of overlapping, competing, incompatible and occasionally unclassifiable agencies offering teaching and research in science and technology. Possibly the best way to enter the maze is to begin with a brief account of the major sources of finance. There were three of these: The Technical Instruction Act of 1889 and the 'whisky money' of 1890; the Department of Science and Art (DScA); and the City and Guilds of London Institute.

The Act of 1889 was a part of the response to the technical challenge by other countries. It allowed borough councils and the newly formed county councils to spend the yield of a 2d rate on technical education, defined as teaching the 'principles of science and art applicable to industry', but firmly excluding training in a particular trade. In fact, little use was made of ratepayers' money. Instead, finance was largely drawn from the windfall of the 'whisky money', some £¾ million a year intended originally for publicans who had lost their licences, but made available in 1890 for technical education. It was from this source that the schools, colleges and classes in the science and technological field run by the local authorities were largely financed.

The foundation of the DScA originated in the concern for industrial design first expressed in the 1830s. In 1852, a Department of Practical Art was set up, to which was added Science in 1853. In 1856 the Department was transferred from the Board of Trade, with which it had, significantly, begun life, to the newly formed Department of Education under the Privy Council, and there it remained until the reorganization at the end of the century noted above.

Apart from looking after the two central London colleges (see below) its activities were strictly limited until 1859, when its course was abruptly

[187] LeClerc (1899); Turner (1927), 91–4, 136–7; R.C. (1884), I, 479–80, III, 164–7, 210–13, 233; R.C. (1895), ev. Q.1740; Anderson (1985b), 176–203.
[188] Roach (1971).

171

changed. A new Minute put the Department in a position to make available grants for teachers' pay in certain science subjects. At first six subjects were named, but the list was extended later, and subjects were examined at three levels, elementary, advanced and 'honours', considered equivalent to today's third/fourth form grammar school, O-level and Sixth Form level, respectively. The most popular subject, in the early days, turned out to be practical plane and solid geometry, machine construction and drawing, geology, elementary mathematics, physical geography and building construction. By 1864, 23 subjects qualified for awards. In 1870, there were 1,871 classes with 48,905 students in mathematics, physical science, engineering and similar subjects, and 343 classes with 8,960 students in the biological sciences and in geology.

The main method of subsidization chosen was a system of payment by results, in which the teachers were paid for each successful candidate. Later on the 'recognized science schools' could get a capital grant in addition, as well as an attendance grant. There were also prizes and scholarships for the best performances. The DScA was therefore soon obliged to develop an elaborate examination system and a system of inspection of courses.[189]

The original intentions behind the scheme are best made clear by the following extract from the Minute of 1859:

> It is hoped that a system of science instruction will grow up among the industrial classes which shall entail the least possible cost and interference on the part of the state.[190]

The reference to the 'industrial classes' was interpreted in practice to mean an upper income limit of £200, later £400 a year, which would certainly also include the lower middle classes, but the DScA admitted that it did not enquire too closely into the students' income. Payments went to classes in elementary and secondary schools, to training colleges, mechanics' institutes, works classes and even to senior technical colleges, without discrimination. From 1876 onward, so-called 'organized science schools' were recognized for grants, though it took about two decades before these became at all numerous.[191]

The expansion of the numbers supported was nothing short of phenomenal. They rose from 500 students at the end of the first year (1860), to 34,000 in 1870, 68,000 in 1882 and 187,000 by 1890. The numbers of candidates examined increased similarly from 16,000 in 1870 to 34,000 in 1880, 83,000 in 1890 and 151,000 in 1900. The expenditure remained remarkably modest. Until the end of the century it averaged £100,000 a year (excluding the expenditure on Art, which is here ignored), and by 1900 it had reached £200,000 a year.[192]

[189] R.C. (1872), ev. Cole Q.6, Huxley Q.285; R.C. (1873), xix; S.C. (1867–68), ev. Cole and Donnelly, QQ.42, 53, 111, 399–401; R.C. (1895), II, ev. Donnelly, Q.1107, III, Forsyth and Bidgood, QQ. 8364–5.
[190] Quoted in Roderick and Stephens (1972), 13.
[191] S.C. (1867–68), ev. Cole and Donnelly, QQ.6–10, 401, iv; R.C. (1882–84), III, ev. Donnelly, Q.2844, V., 185, 194; R.C. (1872), ev. Jarmain, QQ.8855–8, 8901; R.C. (1895), 27 ff, ev., II, Donnelly, Q.1069; Argles (1964), 21; Musgrave (1967), 114; Le Guillou (1981), 173. Also p. 168, note 180 above.
[192] R.C. (1872), xx, R.C. (1872–75), xxi, xxiii; Musgrave (1970e), 268; Roderick and Stephens (1972), 15.

All this constituted an achievement for which there was no equivalent abroad, and which the Continent was not slow to admire.[193] It was, however, generally forgotten when comparisons were made, and when the science lobby complained of the lack of formal and state-aided science education in Britain.

Given the limitations imposed on grounds of cost, it is not surprising that there were numerous complaints about the quality of the teachers and of the teaching offered. Payment by results was attacked as inducing cramming as well as stale and unimaginative teaching. There were also complaints about the absence of apparatus in many schools, and that the courses were too theoretical and too remote from practice: it took many years, for example, before the new Bessemer and Siemens-Martin processes found their way into the metallurgy curricula.[194]

However, the Continental teaching at that level was not without its weaknesses, either, and the advantages were not only on one side. The best practice was still largely found in British works so that theoretical generalizations were less important here than in other countries. A schooling system which makes attendance voluntary and requires a considerable effort, can build on a very different motivation from that of a system in which whole age groups are herded into classes laid on for them by authority. 'Adults', explained General Sir John F.D. Donelly to the Bryce Commission, 'go to the (night) school to learn what they like; they will not go through a course that is laid down for them'.[195] That freshness and the awakening of latent originality may flourish more in a voluntary, even if badly co-ordinated system, is widely agreed. Above all, the flexibility and expansionary potential of the teaching fostered by the DScA are impressive. Once the needs made themselves felt, British society had no difficulty in multiplying in a few years the classes offered and examinations taken by those within and past school age.

The Society of Arts (later Royal Society of Arts, RSA) has been founded in 1754, and after a period of somnolence had been reactivated in the middle of the nineteenth century, when it had taken part in the organization of the 1851 Great Exhibition. In 1856 it began to set examinations, largely for the Mechanics' Institutes. The RSA certificate was awarded on the basis of two subjects, plus spelling and handwriting. By 1858 there were 1,000 candidates for the first stage, and ultimately 288 of these entered the finals and 197 passed.[196]

In order to avoid overlapping with the DScA examinations, the RSA decided in 1870 to concentrate on technological subjects. The first examinations, held in 1873, attracted only 6 candidates and six years later there were only 184. The RSA had only small funds and could offer only some prizes, but no payments by results. Looking for an organization with a longer purse, it lit up the City and Guilds of London Institute, to whom it handed over its technology

---

193 Arnold (1874), 234; Floud (1984), 7; R.C. (1884), III, ev. Huxley Q.2988; LeClerc (1899), 221–3; Musgrave (1967), 91; Ware (1901), 47.

194 Musgrave (1970e), 266, 269, and Musgrave (1967), 17; R.C. (1872), xix, ev. Frankland, Q.766; Roderick and Stephens (1978), 167.

195 R.C. (1895), IV., ev. Donnelly, Q.17, 420. Also see p. 195, note 268 below.

196 R.C. (1872), ev. Foster, Q.9002; Argles (1964), 9; Hudson and Luckhurst (1954), 189–90, 237–51.

examinations in 1879, having meanwhile set up more successfully in commercial examinations subjects in 1876.

The London livery companies had over the centuries, like the older public and grammar schools, misappropriated enormous sums originally intended for the education of the children of the poor. At a time of growing concern with the British lag in technical education, this age-old embezzlement had not surprisingly come under public scrutiny.[197] As a result, some of the richer City companies decided that the best way to forestall the public interest in their affairs was to offer funds for technical education themselves. The Clothworkers were the first, giving £10,000 to the new Yorkshire College (later the University of Leeds) in 1874. By 1877 several others had agreed to form the City and Guilds of London Institute for the Advancement of Technical Education (CGLI). This, from the first, had considerable funds at its disposal, spending around £30,000 a year in its first 10 years, and well over £20,000 a year thereafter.[198].

At the outset, the CGLI decided to apply its resources for instruction 'in the principles of science and art in their application to industrial purposes' in four directions: the foundation of Finsbury Technical College, opened 1881, aimed at people at intermediate management level; the foundation of the Central Institution in South Kensington, opened 1884, to form the core of a technological university; the support of technical teaching elsewhere; and the organization of examinations in technical subjects. Of the two London institutions more will be said below. For the examinations, the CGLI was able to offer the incentive of payment by results like the DScA. Its success was comparable to that of the latter. In 1879, it had begun life by taking over 202 candidates for examination from the RSA, by 1883 there were 2,400 candidates and by 1900, there were 14,000 in 64 subjects.[199]

Some problems remained: few working-class children managed to reach the finals; only a minority of candidates strengthened their applied science knowledge by taking courses in the pure sciences also; and the number of firms which recognized the CGLI qualifications for internal promotions was distressingly small, though it was growing. But the remarkable increase in numbers and in the quality of the teaching showed that a demand for technical education of a more formal kind was being met with growing success.[200]

Among private sources of funds by far the most significant was the gift of £100,000 in 1868 by Sir Joseph Whitworth, the well-known Manchester engineer, providing £3,000 a year for 30 scholarships to allow young men of promise to be educated 'in the theory and practice of engineering and mechanical industry in this country'. These enabled generations of men, many of whom made outstanding contributions later, to study the applied sciences at the highest levels. There were also 60 Whitworth public exhibitions of £25 a

[197] E.g. *Economist*, 17.12.1870, 1515–16, 14.1.1871, 37–8, 253.1871, 345–6, 3.6.1871, 656.
[198] Musgrave (1870c), 66; LeClerc (1899), 235; Simon (1965), 129–30; Foden (1970), 130 ff, 177–9; Firth (1976).
[199] R.C. (1884), III, ev. Waterlow and others, Q.4410, also QQ.4420, 4471–3 and ev. Gee, Q.614; Cardwell (1957), 102; Jordan (1985); Argles (1964), 23.
[200] R.C. (1884), III, ev. Huxley Q.3068; Digby and Searby (1981), 32; Foden (1970), 143; Creasy (1905), 64, 164–9.

year, tenable at various university-type institutions. Another, from 1891 onwards, was the income from the surplus of the 1851 Exhibition, used for scholarships in branches of science 'the extension of which is especially important for our national industries'. Altogether, by 1914 there were 170 privately endowed fellowships in science available in 24 institutions outside Oxford and Cambridge.[201]

With these somewhat haphazard, but by no means insignificant sources of finance in mind, we may now turn to the teaching and research in the sciences and technologies provided outside the schools system.

Independent lecturers on science subject did not survive in any number after the mid-century. Only a few individuals eked out a living in the larger cities by combining teaching or lecturing with offering chemical analyses or medical treatment. One of the last was William Sturgeon, who had lectured on science at the Adelaide Gallery in the Strand (opened 1830), and who then opened the Royal Victoria Gallery in Manchester in 1839–40 for exhibitions and lectures. But he could not make a living at it. When it collapsed in 1842, he took to itinerant lecturing, fell into destitution, and, symbolically, was given a government pension.[202]

As for the institutionalized provision of science teaching, we may begin with the two colleges mentioned above which became the direct responsibility of the Government. They illustrate in a paradigmatic way the transformation of science from its close links with practical technological needs during the industrial revolution, over an arid period of few industrial interests of science, to the astonishingly vigorous expansive phase in the decades before the First World War.

The first of these colleges, the Royal College of Chemistry, was started in 1845 entirely as a private venture, 'by a number of noblemen and gentlemen for the purpose of encouraging the study of chemistry, with a view of its application to arts and manufactures'. Its most influential supporters were agriculturists impressed by Liebig's work on agricultural chemistry; others were concerned with mining, metallurgy, pharmacy and public health.[203] The head of the college, A.W. Hofmann, soon switched the interests of the college from agriculture to coal-tar derivatives, and while this tended to ignore some of the immediate British needs, he set a high standard and attracted some excellent students. However, the college was in financial straits almost from the start, and it survived only by merging with the newly established School of Mines in 1853.

This latter school, founded with government support, had its origins in the systematic geological survey of 1834 and the Museum of Economic Geology, set up in 1837. Towards the end of 1851, partly as a result of the experiences of the Great Exhibition, a Government School of Mines and Science applied to the Arts, built on these foundations, was opened in Jermyn Street. The school

[201] Argles (1964), 24; Roderick and Stephens (1982), 18, and Roderick and Stephens (1978), 69–70; S.C. (1867–68), 387–9; Cardwell (1957), 87; Sanderson (1972a), 27.
[202] Kargon (1977), 12–13, 39 ff, 86 ff; Hays (1983), 92, 98; MacLeod (1970), 206; Morrell (1971), 195; Smith (1982), 143–4.
[203] R.C. (1872), ev. Cole Q.86, Frankland QQ.5667–8; Layton (1973), 48; Basalla, Coleman and Kargon (1970), 12; Bud and Roberts (1984), 51, 74 ff.

did not have a very happy beginning. It had to set its fees higher than the other (privately financed) London colleges, 'so that there shall not be unfair competition' from this government-supported institution. Its numbers remained small: over the total period 1851–67/8 there were only 233 full-time students, plus 1,113 occasional students. Very few of them found their way into British industry. In 1853–71 an annual average of only 4 students had found employment in mining, metallurgy or the geological survey, but virtually none in British coalmining.

In the cramped quarters of Jermyn Street, the teaching staff – a brilliant, if underpaid and idiosyncratic bunch – were at loggerheads over the direction which the school should take: should it remain a specialist mining college or develop as a general science college? In 1859 the 'miners' seem to have won, and the School was renamed 'Royal School of Mines' in 1863. However, in 1872 some of the general science departments managed to move out to a more generous site on the South Kensington estate, acquired after 1851 with the surplus of the Great Exhibition funds and a special parliamentary grant. Others followed later, leaving only the mining department on the old site.

Once at South Kensington, numbers began to increase. Whereas in the years 1855–75 only 99 associateships were awarded, the number grew fourfold, to 400, in the following 20 years 1875–95; but of the 850 students of those first 40 years of which details are known, only 170 (20%) went into British industry, mostly mining and brewing.[204] Meanwhile, the departments established at South Kensington were merged, by Treasury Minute, with the so-called Normal School of Science, which had arisen out of the DScA's short-lived scheme for the training of science teachers, into the Normal School of Science and Royal School of Mines in 1881, renamed once more in 1890 as the Royal College of Science. This, in turn, was to be incorporated, together with the Royal School of Mines and the Central Technical College set up by the CGLI, into the Imperial College, a Technical University to challenge Charlottenburg, in 1907.

There were also provincial schools and colleges set up in the same period, of varying standards and with varying success. One of the more interesting institutions of this type, classified as lying between school and university level, was the Birmingham and Midland Institute founded in 1854. Beginning with evening classes, it soon added a day school, and ultimately 14 outlying stations, providing preliminary classes to bring students up to the levels required at the centre. In the 1860s there were around 1,500 students, and by the 1880s there were three full-time teachers at the centre and four–five in the branches, catering for 4,200 students in 1886, of whom 1,800 were taking science subjects, and for 5,000 students in 1889. It was estimated that about one-third of the students were intending teachers, one-third were men from the trades and industries of the area, and the remainder joined out of general interest.[205]

In Liverpool a number of institutions emerged. The so-called Queen's College with its roots in the Mechanics' Institute, lasted from 1857–81. The

---

[204] Roderick and Stephens (1978), 142, and Roderick and Stephens (1981b); Roderick (1967), 48; Sanderson (1983), 29 ff.
[205] Smith (1982), 145–7; R.C. (1884), I, 463, III, ev. Woodward QQ.4188–4201.

Liverpool School of Science (1861) survived better, on private subscriptions as well as grants from the DScA and out of the whisky money. In 1885 there was a staff of 20 and 1,100 students; in 1893 there were 2,086 students and in 1905, 1,827; considerable numbers of them were engineering apprentices and trainee analysts. In Sheridan Muspratt's College of Chemistry (1848), Liverpool also had a specialist institution. Its certificates were recognized by the University of London and the London Apothecaries' Hall, and in 1880–96 it had an average of 75 students a year. One of the students trained there, Norman Tate, started his own School of Technical Chemistry in 1870, later to be called, somewhat grandly, the Liverpool College of Science and Technology.[206]

In Manchester, the first significant development also arose out of the Mechanics' Institute, with day classes for boys, in a so-called 'Commercial and Scientific Day School' in 1857. Under the vigorous management of J.H. Reynolds it started practical classes under the CGLI scheme and others, including bleaching, dyeing and printing, cotton manufacture, calico design, modelling, mechanical engineering, iron and steel, fuel, telegraphy and carriage building. In 1883 it became the Manchester Technical School and Mechanics' Institute, and by 1889 there were 500 full-time students and 3,328 students in all, and at least the course in mechanical engineering lasted two years. Moving into a new building in 1902, it was re-named the Manchester School of Technology.[207]

Anderson's Institution in Glasgow had its origins in the eighteenth century: in 1883 there were 139 students from industry, the gas works and overseas studying chemistry there at a high level. Other institutions which did good work were the Wigan Mining College, Canon Moseley's Trade School in Bristol, the Cornwall Mining School, Chester Training College, the Manchester and Salford Building Trades Institute, and technical colleges in Edinburgh, Newcastle upon Tyne, Sheffield, Bradford, Huddersfield, Nottingham, Putney, and Leeds. Nor should the official colleges, like the School of Naval Architecture and Marine Engineering (1864), to which some private students were admitted, and the military and naval academies be forgotten.

Some schools were founded by private firms. The best known of these was the school established in the works of Platt Brothers, the Oldham machine building firm. Made over to the town, it became the Oldham School of Science and Art, which had 676 science and 110 art students in 1882. Others were the schools established by Sir William Armstrong on the Tyne and by the London and North Western Railway at Crewe, and technical classes run by the Rochdale Cooperative Society.

The Mechanics' Institutes from which some of these colleges were descended began in the 1820s. Among the motives for their foundation were the fear of foreign competition, the need to divert the rising political interest of the artisan class into innocent channels, and, above all the recognition of the importance of

[206] R.C. (1884), I, 447, V, 219; Roderick and Stephens (1982), 358; Roderick and Stephens (1972), 69–71, and Roderick and Stephens (1978), 71.
[207] Cruickshank (1974), 134–56; LeClerc (1899), 240–1; R.C. (1884), I, 430–2, III, 168–71 (Reynolds).

science for workmen in industry. The formulation of the Manchester rules adopted in 1824 is typical for most. Their institution, they said, was

> formed for the purpose of enabling Mechanics and Artisans . . . to become acquainted with such branches of science as are of practical application to the exercise of (their) trade; that they may . . . acquire a greater degree of skill in the practice of it, and be qualified to make improvements and even inventions. [It was not to teach a trade], but there is no Art which does not depend, more or less on scientific principles, and to teach what they are, and to point out their practiccal application, will form the chief object of this Institution.

To these unexceptionable hopes, Benjamin Heywood added, in his presidential address in 1827: 'to teach [the workman] how he may advance himself in the world, and to give him an honourable and delightful employment for his leisure.'[208]

The Mechanics' Institutes, it is evident, had their origins at a time when science was still seen as directly useful and applicable in practical industry; they were children of the industrial revolution in that sense. The London Institute (1823) found a widespread echo at once. There were about 100 institutes in existence in 1826, and for 1851, the total is estimated to have been around 700 for the United Kingdom and 600 for England alone, with a membership of 120,000 all told. In 1860 there were estimated to have been 200,000 members, and the numbers continued to rise until about 1875. Thereafter a decline set in, and by 1900 most Mechanics' Institutes were closed down or absorbed by other institutions.

It is widely accepted that in spite of these impressive numbers, the aims of the founders were not fulfilled. For one thing, the institutes were from the beginning run by the middle-class sponsors who provided most of the finance and left the working-class members few decision-making powers. As a result, in at least two cases, in the Andersonian Institution in Glasgow in 1823, and in Manchester in 1829, the working-class members staged secessions to found their own alternative institutions.[209] Moreover, because of the inadequate preparation of workmen for anything but the simplest science classes, many institutes found that the classes most in demand were those in the 3Rs; other classes which paid off were in commercial subjects, or individual lectures and short courses catering for general interests and entertainment. Serious science work declined rapidly after the first few years.[210]

A similar effort involving hundreds of institutes, with their tens of thousands of books, many hundreds if not thousands of paid and myriads of unpaid teachers,[211] initiated entirely by private individuals would have been unthinkable at the time in any other country. They fulfilled some purpose; but the implication must be that if the Mechanics' Institutions were not used for the purposes intended by their initial sponsors, as stressed by the science lobby and many historians since, the demand was not yet there. Surely employers and

[208] Tylecote (1957), 35–6, 131, and Tylecote (1974), 55; Singer *et al.* (1954–58), V, 777; Shapin and Barnes (1976), 55 ff; Harrison (1961), 176 ff.
[209] Tylecote (1957), 17, 137; Simon (1974), 154, 215–17.
[210] Sanderson (1983), 28; Tylecote (1957), 70–5, 98 ff, 163; Roderick and Stephens (1978), 59, and Stephens and Roderick (1972), 352.
[211] R.C. (1884), III, ev. Baines, QQ.349–52; Inkster (1985c).

ambitious workmen would have bent such ready-made institutions as the Mechanics' Institutes to their service, had they felt the need.

Of course, some did make use of them. Spurred on and aided, first by the examinations set up by the Unions of Mechanics' Institutes themselves, and later by the examinations and grants by the DScA, many skilled artisans and foremen in Yorkshire and Lancashire especially studied scientific and technical subjects and gained both in understanding, as well as by social advancement, just as the founders had hoped.[212] And, as we have seen, in Liverpool and Manchester, and indeed in other towns, the remnants of these creations of the early century were made the foundation of the more ambitious technical colleges and schools of the decades before 1914.

The evening tradition of the Mechanics' Institutes was shared by workmen's mutual improvement societies, as well as by middle-class debating societies and by the University Extension classes begun in the 1870s. Workmen were generally held to be too tired to take in hard science subjects after a day's work, but we do hear of evening schools for apprentices at such places as Backwith and Pensher collieries, Platt's at Oldham, Brunner, Mond at Widnes, miners working at managers' certificates, and evening classes in Birmingham, Sheffield, Liverpool, Birkenhead, and no doubt other towns. Their difficulties were a challenge to the motivation of those attending.[213]

Within 20 years of the passing of the 1870 Act, the demand for evening classes in the elementary 3Rs had fallen off drastically, but since a new code of 1893 extended grants for evening classes beyond 21 and greatly widened the number of subjects, which now included the sciences, much of the teaching of the 'Technical Colleges' was thereafter done in evening classes. Altogether, the number of evening scholars rose from 120,000 in 1893 to 475,000 in 1899, and 708,000 in 1911. In London in 1912, 25,000 of the 70,000 evening scholars were in science courses, and in the country as a whole 180,000 males over 16 were taking science subjects in evening classes.[214] The quality of the teachers and the levels at which science subjects were taught also rose. New regulations extended grants to technical subjects in 1906, and grouped subjects, tailored to the needs of specific trades, were encouraged and even made compulsory in 1907.[215]

London was in many respects in a class of its own. At the top it boasted the Finsbury Technical College founded, as noted above, by the CGLI. Its classes started in 1879, and it became by common consent the leading technical college in the country below university level, and the electrical engineering department in particular enjoyed an international reputation and was perhaps for a time the best in Europe. The numbers of full-time day students, in four departments: mechanical engineering, electrical engineering, applied chemistry, and applied art, staying for a two-year course (later three years) rose from 100 in 1883 to 185

---

[212] Tylecote (1957), 81, 85; Stephens and Roderick (1972), 352, 357; Cardwell (1957), 57.

[213] Childrens' Employment Commission (1842), 715, 717; Smith (1982), 223; R.C. (1884), III, ev. Perkin, QQ.218–19, White, QQ.4325–8; D.C. (1906), ev. Rankin, QQ.1040–4, 1081, 1110, 1137, 1179, Louis, Q.1552, Arnold, Q.1997; Buxton (1982), 94. Also p. 195, note 268 below.

[214] Argles (1964), 41; Curtis (1963), 291; Roderick and Stephens (1978), 19; Simon (1965), 186; Dearle (1914), 315–18; Nicholas (1985), 84; Shadwell (1906), ch. 17.

[215] Curtis (1963), 499; Argles (1964), 37; Creasey (1905).

in 1892 and 200 in 1900. Including evening students, many of whom were apprentices or were already working in industry, total numbers rose from 621 to 1,000 and 2,000 respectively in those years.[216]

Another college with a high reputation was the Government-financed Indian Engineering College on Cooper's Hill, near Staines. Established in 1871 (and closed in 1904), it followed the East India Company's Engineering College (1809–71) and offered three-year courses in general engineering and two-year courses in telegraphy, including much practical training. Though nominally designed for intending Indian civil servants, the college was open to others also.[217] Another college with a considerable reputation was the Crystal Palace School of Practical Engineering, a privately run establishment, founded in 1871. By the 1890s it had an average attendance of 100, mostly articled engineers or those about to become such.[218]

Below these was 'a plethora of institutions offering technical education of one sort or another'. 'The functions of the technical college', as George Beilby told the Association of Technical Institutes in 1909, '[was] the training of large numbers of competent craftsmen or professional men, and the development of a smaller class of scientific pioneers'. The polytechnics covered most of that spectrum, and while 'the universities are institutions for making officers; the polytechnics were intended to be institutions to make the rank and file the most capable rank and file in the world.'[219]

The pioneer was the Regent Street Polytechnic, opened by Quintin Hogg in 1881. It was a success from the start. Within twelve months there were 100 classes there with 5,000 students, some on trade courses, others studying a wide variety of subjects. It learned to tap City Companies' funds, but the newly formed London County Council took over responsibility for the polytechnics and in 1893 set up a Technical Education Board which contributed part of its whisky money and supplied much of the drive for London's technical education.

Meanwhile other polytechnics had been founded and by 1898, there were 11 colleges of this type in London alone. Their activities were varied, including recreation, but the evening and trade classes were the fastest growing sector in education altogether before the war, and they clearly filled a need. At a higher level, Sidney Webb could boast in 1904 that there were 500 polytechnic students working for a London University degree, which was a unique achievement unparalleled anywhere else.[220]

In the Council day schools themselves there were said to be 61,500 boys in 1905 (equal to 70% of those eligible) taking handicrafts such as metalwork and woodwork, their number having swelled to 74,000 (91%) in 1913. In day trade schools, run for those who had left school, there were 878 young people in 1904–5, 2,884 in 1912–13. There was a similar growth in the attendance of London's 13 'maintained institutions', from 5,097 to 9,299 in those years. Evening continuation schools were visited by 177,000 in 1912, of whom

[216] Roderick (1967), 54; Ware (1901), 102; Armytage (1965), 116; Argles (1964), 38; Jordan (1985).
[217] Reader (1966), 142; R.C. (1884), I, 413–14, V, 142–5; Berg (1984), 626; Sviedrys (1970), 134.
[218] R.C. (1884) I, 417; Musgrave (1967), 26.
[219] Quotations from Lowe (1983), 47, 54 and 43.
[220] Argles (1964), 37–9; Curtis (1963), 495; R.C. (1884) I, 411; Foden (1970), 209; Millis (1932),

127,000 earned a grant.[221] Classes for builders, carpenters and joiners, engineers and metalworkers began at the 'Artisan's Institute', St Martin's Lane, in 1874 and were later transferred to the polytechnics and other schools; in metal plating work there was an even earlier beginning, at the St James' Working Men's classes in Soho in 1867. Most interesting was the development of plumbers' courses. A national registration scheme was started in that trade in 1885, for which some polytechnics offered courses. 145 pupils from five classes sat the examination in 1884–85; by 1886, this had jumped to 403 from 18 classes.[222] Here was a motivation akin to that operating in Germany, with similar results.

It is not easy to sum up, let alone judge, the scientific, technological and technical education below university level, offered in Britain in the half-century before the First World War, and its effects. It ranged from a wide range of science subjects and handicrafts in schools at all levels, to trade schools, science colleges, technical and polytechnic colleges, and educational institutions for particular occupations, some of which reached high levels of competence. Virtually all of this was achieved with next to no help from the State, and even local authorities came in late, though when they did enter the field they did so with remarkable verve. The main contribution of the State was that provided through the grants dispensed by the DScA, a typical method by which State expenditure and decision-making were kept at a minimum, while the initiative was left to private individuals and groups and to local authorities. Funds made available from earlier charitable bequests provided much of the remainder of the finance.

The result was an educational effort which was uneven, uncertain, even chaotic. Courses did not mesh, nor was progress always secure as in more orderly systems. Some talented people, eager for education, no doubt were thwarted or given the wrong instruction. Yet the British way tapped a motivational force of its own, it made men value that which it had been hard to attain, and few resources were wasted on elaborate schemes (not unknown elsewhere and at other times) designed to employ the teachers rather than benefit the consumers, thus making more of them available for education than was genuinely wanted. Seen each part for itself, it no doubt appeared very inferior to the German. Seen as a whole, it had a not unsuccessful logic of its own.

Possibly the most outstanding feature of the British technical and scientific education system in that period was its ability to expand. The rate of expansion, when the demand from industry, the claims of new technologies, and not least, the mind of the governing classes considered the time to be ripe, was truly breathtaking. At the end of the period, many contemporaries felt that at the sub-university level, at least, Britain had caught up with Germany:[223]

'A survey of the whole field of technical education', according to a departmental commitee of 1906, 'would show that England compared not unfavourably with

25–6; Cotgrove (1958), 60 ff.
[221] Dearle (1914), 303–22; Locke (1984), 49.
[222] Millis (1932), 16–18, 25, 32, 54 ff.
[223] D.C. (1906), 9. Also see Balfour Committee (1928), 175–7; Shadwell (1906), chapter 17; Schramm (1951), 159; and below, pp. 194, 198, 204.

other countries in the provision made for what may be called the lower and inter-mediate grades of technical education, as well as for the technical training for the learned professions obtainable at many of our Universities. The principal deficiency . . . appears to lie in the sphere of the highest technical education'.

It would be difficult to quarrel with that judgement today.

The differences in the structure and internal logic between Great Britain and Germany were equally marked in the university sector. We must, inevitably, begin with Oxford and Cambridge, since they dominate the discussion and the literature. In terms of their contribution to science and technology, however, they scarcely deserved their pride of place until the very end of our period, when they, also, showed that capacity for expansion and adaptation which marked every other sector of British scientific and technological education.

In the first half of the nineteenth century it is scarcely realistic to speak of the two ancient English universities as educational institutions. They were, rather, part of the system of preferment, sinecurism and nepotism which constituted the Church of England. Teaching was neither a career, nor taken very seriously: students who wanted to pass the examinations had to go to private tutors, while the vast majority of fellows (over 90% in 1814) were non-teaching sinecurists.[224]

There were indeed professors in Oxford and Cambridge, appointed by the university as distinct from the colleges, among them professors of science subjects and of mathematics. But these were few in number, about one-tenth of the number of fellows, they were badly paid and since their courses had no connection with the examinations, few students came to them. Several of the professors stopped teaching altogether for that reason, and most had to have other jobs to survive. One, indeed, held the Archbishopric of Dublin at the same time as his chair of Political Economy at Oxford.[225]

By the mid-century, some moderate reforms had been introduced from within the two universities. Cambridge introduced a Natural Science Tripos in 1848, as well as one for the moral sciences, as an alternative to the mathematical one; Oxford followed with a natural sciences honours examination in 1850, together with two other honours schools, which might be taken in addition to the basic Lit. Hum. But this was minor tinkering, and even two Royal Commissions, one for each university, could not overcome the conservative resistance. The Oxford University Act 1854 and Cambridge University Act 1856 which followed enforced again minor changes only, including the ending of religious tests for undergraduates and the appointment of commissioners to speed reforms.[226]

However, a signal had been given, and both universities began to bestir themselves. Some new chairs were created in the sciences, a few science Fellows appointed, and science lectures organized. More significantly, an ambitious building programme created the Oxford Science Museum (1860), the Cavendish Laboratory in Cambridge (1872) and the Clarendon in Oxford

---

[224] Sparrow (1967), 86; Engel (1983a), 3,280; Sviedrys (1970), 128; Rothblatt (1968), 68.

[225] Sparrow (1967), 65; Sviedrys (1970), 128; Turner (1927), 72.

[226] Rothblatt (1968), 227, 249, *passim*; Heyck (1982), 161 ff; Bill (1973), 101, 129–44, 150–1; Engel (1968), 26, 106, 139–40, and Engel (1975), 345. Also see p. 119, note 16 above.

(1874). Colleges also built some laboratories, and Cambridge even created a chair in Engineering in 1875.

Yet student numbers in the sciences remained small, their quality poor. The reasons included, no doubt, the tendency among the students to go to London or Scotland if they were interested in science, but the low rate of response was also connected with the fact that there were so few science fellowships, awards and prizes to be won. In 1870, Oxford had four science fellowships in the natural sciences (but 28 in mathematics) against 145 in classics; Cambridge had three in science, 102 in mathematics and 67 in classics. Of scholarships, 2% were available to the sciences in Oxford in 1872 and still only 8% in 1896.[227] Moreover, an enquiry into College finances chaired by the Duke of Cleveland in 1871–73 found that of 370 Oxford fellows, only 120 did any teaching, and of 350 Cambridge fellows, also only 120.

An Act of 1877 ensured further reforms. The celibacy rule was abolished, and the colleges were told to make available more funds for university professorships and readerships, especially in the sciences. Other changes came thick and fast in the following decades. Science became generally accepted as a major field of study in its own right, and in Cambridge the mathematical tripos was adapted to absorb physical, engineering and even economic problems. Cambridge eventually also established an engineering tripos, as well as some teaching in agriculture, while Oxford got its chair in engineering in 1907, together with a diploma in the subject. Among other reforms of that astonishing age was the admission of women students to sit the tripos (though not yet to receive degrees) in Cambridge in 1881, the recognition of research degrees and of the lower degrees of other universities in 1895 and 1903, and the near success in abolishing compulsory Greek in Cambridge in 1904.[228] It was perhaps fitting that the Cavendish should receive three Nobel prizes in rapid succession: 1904 (Lord Rayleigh), 1906 (Thomson) and 1908 (Rutherford).

Even though there were still too few science posts – Oxford was said in 1900 to have only 12 science fellowships available out of 250 and Cambridge 32 out of 297, not counting mathematics – the changes in the student numbers are illustrated by the following tabulation of successful graduates:[229]

| | 1900 | | 1914 | | Overall |
	Oxford	Cambridge	Oxford	Cambridge	change
Theology	31	13	42	19	+ 39%
Classics	154	126	133	122	– 12
Nat. sciences	37	136	87	152	+ 38
Mathematics	26	82	16	112	+ 19

These figures reflect not only the increasing intellectual challenges to be found in science but also the more subtle changes within the social structure of the universities themselves. The declining share of students from landowning

[227] R.C. (1872), ev. Pattison, Q.3801, Humphry, Q.4391, Cookson, QQ.5110, 5118, Latham, QQ.5205–6, 5269–71; Sanderson (1972a), 33, and Sanderson (1983), 45; Taylor (1952), 82–112.
[228] Engel (1975), 348, and Engel (1968), 156 ff, 257–9; Annan (1969), 253; Ringer (1979), 213; Rothblatt (1968), 252–3.
[229] Roderick and Stephens (1981b), 192, and Roderick and Stephens (1978), 95, 506; Sanderson (1972a), 34–5; Engel (1968), 228.

and clerical families was matched by a fall of the proportions taking classics. The growing numbers of men from professional and business families were more likely to enter the other professions and even business. Even the dons rediscovered the merits of professional training. As a visible sign, an Appointments Association (later Board) was established in 1899 in Cambridge.[230]

Compared with the ancient English universities the long-established Scottish universities have enjoyed a much better press as far as their contribution to science and technology is concerned. This seems to have been based on the active and fertile decades of the industrial revolution period. Over much of our period that reputation was scarcely deserved, until, as everywhere else, the reforming spirit of the last peace-time years affected Scotland also.

In the first half of the nineteenth century the teaching of science had experienced a sad decline in Scotland. Science it is true, continued to be taught, but so badly, and mathematics was taught so abstractly that Scots mathematicians and others had to go to England to complete their education. The problem was, in part, that the students came so ill prepared from the schools; they entered the universities without any qualifying examination, usually at the age of 15. The broad curricula and low level of Scots universities (and lack of research there) therefore corresponded to the senior forms of secondary schools, rather than to universities elsewhere.[231] Much is made of the creation of the first British chair of engineering in Glasgow in 1840. But this chair was forced on the Senate, which refused to give the new professor either a place in the curriculum or a proper laboratory. Even the later world-famous Williams Thomson (Lord Kelvin) had to fight for four years after his appointment to the chair of physics in 1846, before he was given a laboratory, in a disused wine cellar, with equipment dating from 1740.[232]

Reform, as in the English ancient universities, had to be imposed from outside, largely by the Acts of Parliament of 1858 and 1889. The local communities helped. The Baxter family almost singlehandedly created the Dundee University College (1883), very much like English colleges at that time, with its emphasis on the sciences. Glasgow was particularly generously treated by local industry, in its move to new premises, and in founding new chairs, such as naval architecture (1883), geology (1903) and mining (1907). Scots universities, unlike the English, could also count on generous financial aid from the State, and later from Carnegie. Yet it was only in the last decades before 1914 that in Scotland, too, the foundations for science and technology useful to industry were laid and that science and engineering graduates sought jobs at home instead of overseas.

London was here also in a class by itself. The first stirrings towards a modern university arose at about the same time as those for the Mechanics' Institutes. University College, London (UCL) derived both from Scots and German

230 Ringer (1979), 236, 239; Sanderson (1972a), 38, 48–52, and Sanderson (1983), 40–1; Stone (1975b), 67, 103; Jenkins and Jones (1950), 99; Rothblatt (1968), 88, 227, 254–8; Heyck (1982), 113, 227.
231 Sviedrys (1970), 130; Morrell (1976), 53–93; Perkin (1969), 6; Davie (1961), 57–8; Anderson (1983a), 30–1; R.C. (1872), ev. Ramsay, Q.686, Jenkin, QQ.1647–8, Thomson, QQ.2684–5.
232 Musgrave (1967), 30; Turner (1927), 122–3; Ashby (1958), 55–6.

models,[233] was founded in 1826 and opened its doors in 1828. It was a private Institution, whose shareholders/proprietors subscribed the capital of £300,000, on which they received no return. There were no privileges or rights attached to the college. From the beginning science and medicine were strongly emphasized in it. When it opened its doors to its first 300 students, there were five chairs planned in science, one in engineering, eight in medicine and 13 in the arts, law and the social sciences. In the early years, about half the students were studying medicine. The college was non-denominational.[234]

The Anglicans hit back at once. In the provinces, Durham and the insignificant Lampeter were called into being; in London, King's College (KCL) was founded in 1828, also by private proprietors, and started working in 1831. In structure it was very similar to UCL, with a similar emphasis on science.[235] In 1836 a University of London was created with these two as constituent colleges, with the right to grant degrees, and the examination service was the only one to receive government funds. Other colleges could affiliate, and by 1851 there were 29 general and 60 medical schools so affiliated. By a new Act in 1858 the University of London became a mere examining body over which the original colleges had virtually no influence at all.

In 1858, also, a science degree was started and the two senior colleges were among the first in the country to have laboratories. After the doldrums which affected all education in mid-century, the London colleges responded flexibly to the needs of science and technology. They created new chairs *inter alia* in chemical technology (UCL, 1878), engineering (UCL, 1874), a second chair in engineering (KCL, 1866), metallurgy (KCL, 1879), and electrical engineering (KCL, 1890). In the last decades before the war the colleges developed close relations with the electrical engineering, the oil, aeronautical, and radio industries respectively.[236]

A federal London University was created by an Act of 1898. UCL was incorporated in it in 1905, KCL in 1908, Imperial College and East London (Queen Mary) College in 1907. Imperial, as noted above, was an amalgamation of the CGLI Central College of 1884, the Royal College of Science and the School of Mines. All told, in 1914 London University had 3 incorporated colleges, 31 'Schools' (colleges like Imperial and the LSE), 25 other institutions, and there were recognized teachers in 30 more, including Birkbeck and Goldsmith Colleges. Science student numbers were growing rapidly, but from a low base. Total honours BSc. degrees over the period 1880–1900 were 265, of which 138 came from the two constituent colleges. The DSc., the research degree, was awarded to an average of 4 candidates a year in 1858–1900, and to 7½ a year in 1900–14.[238]

Among the newer provincial universities, Durham was the first to be founded, in 1833, in part in answer to UCL. Anglican and modelled on the

---

[233] Curtis (1963), 421 ff; Bulwer (1971), 290–2; Russel (1983), 203.

[234] Simon (1974), 122; Morrell (1971), 198; Mendelson (1964), 39.

[235] Curtis (1963), 421 ff; Cardwell (1957), 33 ff, 72.

[236] Sanderson (1972b), 246–8, 260; Allen (1976), 39; Hilken (1967), 97.

[237] Pp. 175–6 above. Also see Webb (1902), 917, 924; R.C. (1884), V. 135–40; Argles (1964), 53, 81.

[238] Cardwell (1957), 129; Sanderson (1972a), 114; MacLeod (1971b), 228.

ancient universities, it remained small and limited. It was not until the
Newcastle College of Physical Science was formed in 1871 with three foundation chairs of science, to which a chair of mining was added in 1880, and to
which Durham contributed funds and the power to grant degrees, that the
North-East had a regional university.

Owen's College, Manchester, which opened in 1851, owed its existence to a
bequest of £100,000 made in 1846 by John Owen. It aimed at university level
teaching and thus began with a bias towards the arts, but students' demand
soon forced it into a science direction. By 1858 it was near collapse, but among
the factors which rescued it was the arrival of H.E. Roscoe, then 24 years old, as
professor of chemistry. He not only created one of the best chemical schools in
the country, but also built up the links with local industry and the local community which were the life-blood of the civic universities and university colleges.

The 'civic' universities, of which Manchester was the largest and richest by
1914, were in their conception defiantly not modelled on Oxford and
Cambridge; indeed, it would be more correct to say that they arose out of
despair, on the part of provincial industry and commerce, over the exclusiveness and futility of what went on in these ancient foundations. The emphasis
from the start was on science, with a tendency towards studies with practical
application, 'teaching [the people] things which would help them in their
occupations', as the Rev. J. Percival put it in Sheffield, especially intended for
the middle classes and their professional ambitions. The inspiration for some
colleges was the fear of foreign competition, and the lessons of the Paris exhibition of 1867 certainly helped to inspire Leeds and Newcastle.[239]

In as far as there was a model, it was Germany, with its professoriate and
organization by faculties. However, ironically, towards the end of our period,
when reforms were driving Oxford and Cambridge into the direction of the
civic universities, the latter increasingly tried to ape the former's traditionalism, conscious of their still overwhelming prestige.

The main dates of the English civic universities were as follows:

	Opened	Became independent university
Durham	1833	1833
Manchester	1851	1904 (from 1880 Victoria University)
Newcastle	1871	1963 (with Durham before that)
Leeds	1874	1904 (from 1887 in Victoria Univ.)
Bristol	1876	1909
Sheffield	1879	1905
Birmingham	1880	1900
Nottingham	1881	1948
Liverpool	1882	1903 (from 1884 in Victoria Univ.)
Reading	1892	1926
Exeter	1895	1955
Southampton	1902	1952 (origins in 1862)

They had much in common. With the exception of Durham with Newcastle,
they made their start by preparing for the London external degree, switching to
their own as they received their charter. Almost all of them were strengthened

239 Sanderson (1972a), 81; also Marshall (1923), 99.

in their earlier years by being able to incorporate a pre-existing local medical school.[240] What distinguishes them most of all, however, from universities elsewhere is that they had, at the start, to rely on private donations only. In consequence they were in constant financial straits, which affected the quality of their equipment and their planning. Only in 1889 did the Treasury begin to contribute, at first the derisory sum of £15,000 to be shared among all the colleges, raised to £25,000 in 1897. By comparison, Prussia alone spent £476,000 on her universities in 1900–1. By 1913–14, the Treasury contribution had risen to £170,000 – itself quite a remarkable rise for any Treasury grant, though by that time the Prussian budget was well over £700,000. Given that the State in Britain contributed little more than one quarter to the universities' budget, while the Prussian state furnished almost all, the total budgets, however, were not dissimilar.[241]

Student numbers grew as rapidly as in other institutions of learning. Between 1861 and 1911, they had grown about three-fold in Oxbridge and 11-fold in London. From 1891 to 1911, when the civics were properly established, the ancients grew by 39%, London by 275% and the civics by 48%, counting all students, including part-timers. Full-time students at the civics grew by 44% between 1893 and 1913. The number of science students grew faster than the average.[242] The quality of the students also went up. By 1914 the three-year courses had begun to resemble modern degree levels.

The civic universities were innovative in the subjects they taught. Newcastle introduced mining, metallurgy and naval architecture. Leeds had textiles, dyeing, leather from the beginning as well as engineering, biochemistry and agriculture early on; Sheffield's associateship in metallurgy was pitched at a high level, while coalmining was elementary; Liverpool had municipal and electrical engineering as well as naval architecture; Birmingham brewing, mining and metallurgy; Manchester a huge school of chemistry including organic chemistry, and engineering.[243] Much of this was financed by local industry, and the departments collaborated in many cases with local works to provide training, but also by their research and advisory activity. Prof. O. Arnold of Sheffield, an outstanding example, advised 15 of the leading Sheffield firms, 81 of the city's 252 iron and steel firms and some of the firms in the light trades. According to one estimate, between ⅙ and ½ of the graduates of the civic universities went into industry.[244]

University development in Wales, like in Scotland and Ireland but unlike England, was aided by government early on. Aberystwyth was opened in 1872, Cardiff in 1883 and Bangor in 1884, the federal University of Wales being chartered in 1893. But the student body was dominated by intending clergymen, industry took little interest, and even the mine owners preferred to set up their own mining colleges in Treforest and Crumlin and raised £250,000 for

[240] Taylor (1975), 101; Haines (1958), 226; Tolley (1981), 203–4; Armytage (1955), 169, 226.
[241] Roderick and Stephens (1981b), 194–5, and Roderick and Stephens (1978), 101. But see pp. 208–9, note 304 below.
[242] Jarausch (1983b), 45–6; Sanderson (1972a), 96; also pp. 120, 193, 196 and notes 19, 265, 270 in this chapter.
[243] Argles (1964), 50; Robertson (1974), 230; Armytage (1955), 222.
[244] Sanderson (1978), 595, and Sanderson (1972a), 84, 101.

them by 1912, rather than help to establish a department in the university.[245]

The Belfast Academical Institution, combining school and college levels, was founded in 1810 by Ulster Presbyterians. In 1845, following an enlarged grant to the catholic Maynooth College, three new colleges were set up, Queen's in Belfast, modelled on the Scottish universities, and Cork and Galway in the catholic areas. Trinity College, Dublin, which dated from the sixteenth century, meanwhile also modernized itself, being less overshadowed by Oxbridge than English Colleges: its engineering school of 1814 was one of the largest and best staffed at the time. Belfast was also early in the field with technology. In 1908, Queen's became an independent university, the two provincial colleges, together with a new college at Dublin were combined into the National University of Ireland, while Trinity went on independently.[246]

Beside the universities, there were also some specialist institutions carrying on scientific research. One of the most distinguished of these was the Royal Institution (1799). Founded by private sponsorship in the spirit of optimism and utiliatrianism fostered by the industrial revolution, it tended to distance itself in the second half of the century from applied work and to emphasize rather the amateur tradition.[247] Imitative institutions, like the Russell Institution (1808), the London Institution (1805), the Surrey Institution (1810), and others in Cornwall, Manchester, Birmingham, Liverpool and Scotland, tended to devote themselves to lecturing and the diffusion of knowledge rather than to original research.[248] The Rothamstead agricultural experimental station was also established by private means. It was set up in 1843 by Sir John Lawes, an admirer of Liebig's methods. Kew Observatory, relinquished by the Crown in 1843, was nursed by the British Association until 1872, when it was handed over to the Royal Society.

The Government made some contributions to original research, usually doled out sparingly and indirectly. They included Greenwich Observatory (1675), the geological survey (1832) and the Museum of Economic Geology (1841). A laboratory of the Inland Revenue, set up in 1843 to deal with imported perishables, ultimately developed into the Laboratory of the Government Chemist. Beside these, the Government also contributed to numerous expeditions to unknown parts of the globe.[249]

The first major involvement of the State in modern research was motivated, at least in part, by the fear of German scientific progress. The national Physical Laboratory, built in Teddington in 1899–1900, was a direct response to, and in part copy of, the PTR in Berlin. Its original budget from the Government was quite modest, but such was the strength of the British economy and its system of private funding, that by 1912, the British NPL had accumulated enough in private subscriptions to reach an annual budget of £32,000 and a staff of 150. Its original two departments, physics and mechanical engineering, had by 1918 grown to seven, the additions being metallurgy, shipbuilding, aerodynamics,

[245] Sanderson (1972a), 121–9, 136–7.
[246] Moody (1958), 90–109; R.C. (1874–75), V., 25, VII., 29.
[247] See note 30 above; Martin (1942), 4, 10, 31 ff; Basalla, Coleman and Kargon (1970), 26; Hays (1983), 105–0.
[248] Berman (1978), 94; Morrell (1971), 195; Roderick and Stephens (1978), 55; Hays (1983), 93.
[249] Alter (1982), 107; Poole and Andrews (1972), 6; Flett (1937); and see p. 190 below.

electricity and meteorology. The Medical Research Council was set up in 1913, following the National Insurance Act of 1911.[250]

It was in the formation of private and voluntary scientific societies that the special aptitude of Britain seemed to lie. They fitted the British tradition of self-help and citizen initiative; and in a country which was in the technical lead for most of the period under discussion, it was more sensible to listen to a paper or a lecture of what had just been achieved or discovered, than to get it ponderously incorporated into textbooks and curricula.

In the luxuriant proliferation of societies, associations, clubs, institutes and institutions – to list but the most commonly used designations – at least five types may be discerned. (1) The association formed out of a general cultural interest. It was exemplified by the Lit. and Phil. Societies of the industrial revolution period. (2) About the same time there also arose the first special subject societies, listening to papers, but also collaborating on common listing or classifying tasks, possibly issuing transactions, and getting reports of experiments or of the latest achievements, thus shading into the third category. (3) The genuine scientific society whose main object was to advance the frontier of its subject(s) by publishing discoveries and reports of experiments. (4) The fourth type was the society representing in various ways the interests or the hobby, of a group of scientists or technologists. (5) Lastly, and usually developing out of (3) or (4) or both, there was the association taking on the additional responsible task of examining, certifying and licensing. In practice these not only shaded into each other, but also frequently developed from one into another, or had several of these functions simultaneously. In addition, each of them also hoped to foster personal and social contacts, while our fifth group, the 'qualifying association', was connected with the professionalization of certain occupations. This involved both the demand by the community for a certain degree of competence in such occupations as those of medical advisers, ships' masters, mine managers and chemical analysts, and the desire of the practising members of these professions themselves to raise and fortify their social status.[251]

By common consent, the Medical Society (1773) and the Linnean Society (1788) were the first societies of the modern type. Because of the problems of definition, there is, however, no agreement on later numbers and later membership. According to one estimate, there were 125 scientific societies in existence in 1870; according to another, there were some 500 in 1883, which by amalgamation had fallen to 453 in 1899, excluding the numerous Naturalists' Field Clubs. The societies which affiliated to the British Association up to 1910 numbered 119. There were at least 10 local societies in Manchester in 1839 and eight in Edinburgh in 1839. Membership varied greatly in number, from a few dozen to several thousand. One estimate of the total membership of the London-based societies arrived at 5,000 in 1850 rising to 20,000 in 1910; Leone Levi estimated 45,000 members of scientific societies of all kinds in 1865 and 12,000 members of specialist scientific societies in 1869.[252]

[250] Alter (1982), 158–62, 167, and Alter (1978), 374, 377; Cardwell (1957), 137–9. Also see p. 155, note 132 above, and p. 210, note 307 below.
[251] Millerson (1964); Engel (1983a), 9 ff; Inkster (1983), 40–2; Beland (1976), 306–7.
[252] Alter (1982), 28; Morrell (1976), 54; Thackray (1974), 674, 681; Heyck (1982), 83–90.

Limiting ourselves to a selection of those societies concerned with the sciences and technologies that were of direct interest to the industrial progress of the country, we may begin with geology – a branch of science in which Britain undoubtedly played a leading part. The Geological Society of 1807, itself following the earlier Mineralogical Society of 1799–1806, appeared early on the scene and was a model for others. It was a society for gentlemen, excluding all those of a lower social order, which meant that among others it excluded William Smith, probably the most brilliant geologist of the age. It set out to map the whole geology of the British Isles, but, the task proving too great for a private society, it was handed over to the government-financed Geological Survey in 1834, as noted above. Such a systematic survey was of major benefit to coal owners and railway and canal engineers, and local societies continued at it: these included the Royal Geological Society of Cornwall (1814), the Manchester Geological Society, and the Natural History Society (1829) and the Naturalists' Field Club (1846) both of Newcastle. The Geological and Polytechnic Society of the West Riding of Yorkshire (1837) was particularly active for about 10 years: some of its members broke successfully through the magnesian limestone to the coal below, near Castleford in 1836.[253]

Chemical science could in its early days not be separated from medicine and pharmacy. The Medical (1773) and Medical and Chirurgical Societies (1805) were among the earliest. Chemistry was a required subject under the Apothecaries' Act of 1815 which gave the Apothecaries the power to license general practitioners and prohibited all others (except the members of the Royal Colleges) from practising. Consequently, some chemistry had to be taught in the provincial medical schools, as also in the Scottish universities and in the London university colleges for the same reason. In 1841 the Chemical Society was founded in London as a learned society; by 1911 it had 3,100 members. There were also numerous local societies. Following the Sale of Food and Drugs Act of 1875 a Society of Public Analysts was founded in 1875, and the Institution of Chemistry was set up in 1877. The latter was a professional body, and in 1885 it received a charter which gave it powers to grant certificates of competence. By 1902 there were 1,300 fellows and associates. In 1881, a Society of Chemical Industry was founded, mainly by Manchester scientists and manufacturers. It issued its own journal and by the early 1880s had 4,000 members.[254] Interestingly enough, a Physical Society was formed only in 1874 and an Institution of Physics only in 1918.

The engineering associations were from the beginning concerned more with practical matters than with pure technology. Theirs was one of the most rapidly growing professions, but their status was among the most uncertain. The early builders of the great public works, canals, bridges, harbours and railways, were popular heroes of their day, and the Institution of Civil Engineers (1818, royal charter 1828), certainly cashed in on the prestige of its leading members. Its

253 Weindling (1983), 120–50; Morrell (1983), 231–56; Russell (1983), 195; McKendrick (1973), 341; Kargon (1977), 24; and see pp. 123, 188 and notes 24 and 249 above.
254 Durey (1983), 256–78; Armytage (1955), 169, and Armytage (1969), 29; Roberts (1975), 447–8, 458; Williams (1972), 63; Haber (1958), 35–6; Carr-Saunders and Wilson (1933), 165–8; Russell (1983), 181, 225; Prandy (1965), 64; Budd and Roberts (1984), 158.

purpose was the general representation of the profession against the outside world, but it also existed for mutual information, and from 1841 it published its annual *Proceedings*. There was no entrance qualification, as there was no prescribed training for engineers. Though formalized somewhat in 1869, the admission procedure remained basically that of recommendation by existing members, certifying that the candidate had completed an appropriate period of apprenticeship and training. Only in 1897 did the ICE require a formal written examination for membership. In 1903 it received a government grant for its work on establishing engineering standards.[255]

The mechanical engineers – which at that time meant largely locomotive engineers – seceded from the ICE to form their own Institution of Mechanical Engineers in 1847. They also published their Transactions, and instituted an examination for membership even later than the Civils, in 1912. Their royal charter came only in 1929.[256]

The rapid technical transformation of the following half-century called into being a whole range of new specialist engineering societies. R.A. Buchanan counted 15 additional ones in existence by 1914, making a total of 17, with 40,000 members. Among the most important of these were the Institution of Electrical Engineers, founded in 1871, with 7,045 members in 1914, the Institution of Mining Engineers (1889, 3,277), and, a portent for the future, the Institution of Automobile Engineers (1906, *c.* 900).[257] With minor variations, these institutions took their cue from the two older societies, and worked increasingly for membership by examination, so that membership became a recognized and coveted qualification. This in turn, led to the addition of formal classes within the traditional apprenticeship and practical training of engineers.

Among the societies catering for science as a whole, much the oldest, and the one with the greatest prestige, was the Royal Society, founded in 1662. After its active interest in applied science and industrial and agricultural improvement in the first century of its existence, it degenerated into an amateurish club for high-born gentlemen with a few scientific members. Only when the rules for admission were changed in 1847 could internal reform begin. The proportion of full-time practising scientists (excluding medical men) in the Society rose from 41% in 1881 to 78% in 1914.[258] Apart from awarding honours and publishing papers, the Royal Society was also from time to time called upon to advise the Government on science matters, and from 1850 onwards it was given £1,000 a year to distribute in research grants. The society was also left private endowments to distribute in grants for research. Most of the grants made to individual applicants were small and altogether about 1,000 applicants were assisted between 1850–1914. By 1914 the fellowship had become a prize to be valued by the leading scientists of the day.

[255] Roderick and Stephens (1982), 45; Ahlström (1982), 86–7; Buchanan (1985).
[256] Roderick (1967), 56; Musson and Robinson (1969), 488; Carr-Saunders and Wilson (1933), 161; and preceding footnote.
[257] Buchanan (1985).
[258] MacLeod (1983), 55–80; Shapin (1983), 151–78; Stimson (1968), 191 ff, 205–16; Poole and Andrews (1972), 5–6; Berman (1975), 35; MacLeod (1971a), 325–42; Hall (1984).

The British Association for the Advancement of Science (BAAS), the other major organization to further the whole range of sciences, underwent the transition from amateurism to professionalism by a different route. Though modelled on the German society of scientists and physicians, (1822), the BAAS, formed in 1831, was a typically British creation. Among its purposes was 'to promote the intercourse of those who cultivate science in Great Britain', in the words of its founder, the Rev. Vernon Harcourt; to represent the interests of science to the public and especially the Government, and raise funds for it from the Treasury; to indicate where research was needed, and, most ambitious of all, to 'give a systematic direction to philosophical research', by steering the professional scientists into those key areas most in need of attention, while also marshalling the armies of amateur helpers to employ themselves most usefully in a common strategy.[259]

These latter aims were never achieved. Instead, the annual meetings of the BAAS, which formed the main part of its activities, became sounding boards for the wishes and views of scientists, the place where many important and at times even sensational discoveries were announced first, and the source of encouragement and usually permanent enlargement of the circle of scientists in every city and town in which the BAAS met in its annual peregrination. It made representations on behalf of science. It published the papers read at its meetings, and, with the surpluses achieved by its meetings, supported research projects. Between 1835–1921 it spent about £83,000 in this way.[260]

Founded by clerical and aristocratic patronage, the BAAS made the transition to the professional scientist as the dominant element well ahead of the Royal Society. Engineering science was given a separate section, Section G, in 1836, and papers and discussions in that section tended to be more practical, even mentioning economic problems, and less controversial than in other sections. The first research schemes which the BAAS supported were mainly concerned with such subjects as the weather and the tides, astronomy, and the wave theory of ship resistance – all of which might be considered to be useful for navigation.[261] In many ways, the BAAS was an early harbinger of the revolution in science that occurred in the later decades of Queen Victoria.

In the field of scientific publications, the French were undoubtedly in the lead in the eighteenth century and the Germans in the latter decades of the nineteenth, but it would be difficult to argue that the British scientific community was ever handicapped by lack of journals and other publications from the Royal Society's *Transactions*, dated from 1665, and its *Philosophical Magazine* (1798) onward. In the nineteenth century learned periodicals proliferated with the growth of the scientific societies. For popular consumption, the *Mechanics' Magazine*, and *Chambers' Edinburgh Journal*, which contained snippets of scientific information, became well established as widely available sources of information. In the second half of the century a number of technical journals began to appear, of which *The Engineer* was a good example. C.E. Appleton brought out *Academy* in 1869 as part of his campaign for university research, and later he edited *Endeavour of Research*, but probably the most successful

[259] Morrell and Thackray (1984), 254–5, 342–3, and Morrell and Thackray (1981), 39 ff, 347, 375–6; Orange (1972–73), 327.
[261] Mendelsohn (1964), 29; Thackray (1970), 85; Morrell and Thackray (1981), 260–5, 425, 472, 506.

scientific journal of all was Norman Lockyer's *Nature* (1869), still going strong more than 100 years later.[262]

An important source of information were the encyclopædias, such as Chambers', the *Metropolitan* and the *Britannica*. Lardner's *Cabinet Cyclopædia*, which appeared in 133 volumes in 1829–49, paid particular attention to science and technology. There was also no shortage of textbooks in science, written with less theory and more information than their continental counterparts, many by leading scientists of the age. A particular feature of the later Victorian decades was the popularizing book on science.[263]

The field of scientific and technological education and research is a wide one, then, very complex and extremely difficult to summarize. To conclude this section, we shall recall and put together some of the data on growth. Little need be said about elementary education: there is no doubt that long before the end of the century all the children up to the age of 10 were at school. In the case of secondary education, one estimate put the proportion of 14-year-olds at school at 2% in about 1870, 9% at the turn of the century; for the 17-year-olds the ratios were 1% and 2%. Rapid growth continued thereafter. Recipients of scholarships to transfer from elementary to secondary school increased from 2,500 in 1894 to 52,500 in 1912, or more than 20-fold. Perhaps most significant of all, while the number of DScA examination papers taken rose from 62,000 in 1875 to 202,000 in 1902, by 1912 it was estimated that 160,000 boys were doing science subjects in evening schools, about 7% of the age group.[264]

Equally dramatic was the rise in the number of university students. In England alone, they increased from 3,385 in 1861 to 26,414 in 1911, or almost eightfold. The number of university teaching posts in science and technology (excluding medicine) rose from 60 in 1850 to over 400 by 1900, about sevenfold. In engineering, there had perhaps been 20 honours graduates all told to 1890, but by 1910 there was a cumulative total of 1,000, with 150 graduating that year and numbers obviously expanding fast every year. A recent count of science and technology graduates arrived at the statistics in Table 3.11 (England only):[265]

Table 3.11 Graduates in science and technology, England 1870–1910

	1870	1890	1910	Increase 1870–1910
Graduating that year:				
Science	13	138	800	× 61
Technology	6	30	431	× 72
Total	19	168	1231	× 65
Cumulative total of graduates:				
Science	77	1078	10910	× 142
Technology	50	369	3420	× 68
Total	127	1447	14330	× 113

[262] Webb (1971), 68–9, 90; Harrison (1961), 28, 34; Gillespie (1969), 160–1; Jewkes *et al.* (1969), 61; Meadows (1972), 25 ff; Roberts (1975), 458.
[263] Musgrave (1970e), 266; Basalla, Coleman and Kargon (1970), 5–6; McKendrick (1973), 336.
[264] Lowe (1983), 52; Cardwell (1957), 161.
[265] Lowe (1983), 52; Cardwell (1957), 156; Roderick and Stephens (1981b), 197–8, and Roderick and Stephens (1978), 108, 136; see also pp. 120–1, note 19 above.

As an example of the growth within the census, figures for civil engineers show a rise of more than 10-fold between 1841 and 1901, only to fall back to 1911 as a re-classification excluded mining engineers, surveyors and others. Even if the figures cannot lay claim to much accuracy, they indicate the order of magnitude. It should perhaps be emphasized that at the beginning of our period, Britain held a large proportion of the world's engineers in the modern sense; the faster growth rates of other countries started from much lower initial figures.

In terms of Government expenditure, we have seen that the grants to English provincial universities rose from £15,000 in 1889 to £170,000 in 1913–14; by that time the grants to all British universities amounted to around £300,000. Total Government expenditure on science and technology has proved extremely difficult to measure, since it was hidden under several heads. One estimate of expenditure on civil science excluding education arrived at the following figures:[266]

1850–51	£	34,000, or	0.9 % of the gross budget
1869–70		271,000	2.8 % " " "
1899–1900		618,000	2.6 % " " "
1913–14	*c.*	2,000,000	3.6 % of civil expenditure

All these data, including those listed earlier in this section, emphasize an astonishing and accelerating rate of growth.

VI The Adequacy of the British Provision

Such figures alone cannot answer our more fundamental question: Was the effect adequate, or did it trail behind needs? One approach then was to compare the British effort with that of Germany, usually in order to show up the inadequacies of British education. But since the object usually was to demand more money from the British government, these comparisons were not without bias. Thus a common method was to compare 'Britain' or even England with 'Germany', ignoring the fact that the German population was considerably larger. Another, even more misleading practice was to compare the contribution of the State, and the numbers on publicly financed schools and colleges. This overlooked the fact that the British practice was to finance a great deal out of private funds: Oxford and Cambridge were almost entirely financed from their endowments, and even the civic universities drew almost three-quarters of their funds from non-state sources. Much of the British educational and research effort was not in the public sector at all.

Compared with the German educational system, the British was, indeed, chaotic. Across the gulf of their differences, British and Germans watched each other with mutual incomprehension. Some British there were, like Matthew Arnold, who wished to adopt the Prussian educational structure almost entire,[267] but most of them wondered how education could survive under a

[266] Alter (1982), 46, 81–3; Singer *et al.* (1954–58), VI, 148–9; MacLeod (1976), 116, 120–1, 161; Cardwell (1957), 155. Also see Table 3.7. above.
[267] Arnold (1884), lxxvi–lxxix.

system in which an official, or the minister, or occasionally even the Kaiser himself could decide what should be taught in each school, or which professorship should be founded; while Germans looked in vain for a system in British education and came occasionally to the conclusion that since there was no system, there could not be any proper education either.

The advantages of the German system were obvious. There was an all-embracing net which swept in everyone who might profit from formal or technical education. At each stage, the instructors could proceed from the level reached in the preceding stage instead of, as in Britain, wasting much of their time to bring ill-prepared entrants up to the required starting level. German education was geared much more closely to later occupational needs, leaving certificates at different levels having a widely understood meaning and therefore being used with confidence in licensing, admission or military exemption procedures. By contrast, British educational efforts seemed sporadic, wasteful and unable to reach the highest stages of a subject by systematic planning. While the standards of the German professions were controlled directly by the State or indirectly through the universities, in Britain the self-administration by the professions might well leave the public inadequately protected.

Yet the German system was not without its drawbacks. For one thing, it was extremely wasteful, drawing enormous numbers into its orbit in order to make sure that the relatively few who needed it, might get their necessary grounding. It tended to fix more rigidly people's later careers, and it also rigidified knowledge and allowed government to dictate, sometimes within narrow limits, what should be taught. In the words of one French critic: 'in Germany it is believed with an excessive faith that everything may be learned and that everything may be taught . . . and it is believed that one only knows that which one has well learned'. Interestingly enough, while Germany, France and other Continental countries devised firm curricula for teaching the technologies, those differed greatly from each other, showing that the postulated certainties were spurious. The British system also scored in its motivation: Britain's brilliant top amateur scientists, not tied by tradition, or by the need to appear learned or professional, or needing to bow to authority, were unbeatable in their originality; lower down, students for whom it was an effort to attend classes, were likely to value their opportunities and make more of them than those dragooned into their classes as a matter of regulation. Night-school students, said Professor J.O. Arnold of Sheffield, 'are in dreadful earnest: it is a matter of bread and butter for them, and they work very much harder than a day student, who has probably a father behind him and some money'.[268] Curiously enough, it was frequently people of German or Jewish origin – or both – and who possibly saw the best of both civilizations, who were concerned to spur on the British educational efforts in the sciences and technologies both by the Government and by providing funds most generously themselves: names like Bernard Samuelson, Philip Magnus, Ivan Levinstein, Ludwig Mond, Alfred Beit, Ernst Cassel, Julius Wernher and the Rothschilds spring to mind. Curiously, also, it was the BAAS rather than its German equivalent which set out to cover systematically

---

[268] Hauser (1917), 43–4; D.C. (1906), ev. Arnold, Q.1997; Floud (1984), 10–11; Ben-David (1968–69), 6. Also see p. 173, note 195, and p. 179, note 213 above.

195

all the sciences by a total sweep in a planned research programme.

Even towards the end of our period, after the enormous British spurt, the numbers of German scientists still greatly exceeded those of Britain. Thus in 1910, there were only 3,000 university students in Britain studying science and technology, as against 25,000 in Germany. Again, it has been estimated that in 1914 there was a maximum of 250 teachers and 400 full-time students (plus perhaps 50 in the polytechnics) engaged in research bearing on industry in Britain, whereas in Germany at the time there were 673 teachers and 3,046 students, engaged in this way.[269] The discrepancy was particularly large, and indeed was founded on, the differences in chemistry. In 1902, Sir James Dewar asserted in his presidential address to the BAAS that whereas in Germany there were 4,000 chemists working in industry, of whom 84% were university- or TH-trained, in Britain the number was 1,500 at most, of whom fewer than $^1/_6$ were graduates. An LCC report of 1906 even made it 4,500 in Germany, 500 in the United Kingdom.[270]

There was no doubt that Germany had an enormous and, for the time, unassailable lead in chemistry. But in other areas the position was less certain. Britain had easily caught up by 1914 in the numbers of elementary and secondary as well as in the more elementary stages of technical education.[271] In physics, in particular, Britain had probably overtaken Germany by 1900:

	Germany		England	
	Universities	TH	Universities	TH equiv.
Laboratories providing practical training	19	5	16	5
'Assistants'	38	24	45	15
Students being taught	1039	990	1517	780

The total expenditure on physics laboratories in 1880–1914 compared as follows (000 Marks):

	Great Britain	*Germany*
New buildings in Universities	8,070	7,335
New buildings in research institutes	1,380	1,266
Extensions etc.	703	956
	10,153	9,557

Moreover, if we consider the following figures, of the proportion of the appropriate five-year cohort in all forms of higher education:(%)

	Great Britain	*Germany*
1860–1	0.30	0.50
1910–11	1.89	2.61

[269] Singer *et al.* (1954–58), VI, 153; Sanderson (1972b), 252; Roderick and Stephens (1978), 107, 135; Blair (1904), 41.
[270] Sanderson (1972a), 23, and Sanderson (1972b), 253; Roderick and Stephens (1981a), 59, and Roderick and Stephens (1982), 23–4; Diplomatic and Consular Reports, Germany (1901), 32. Also see pp. 120–1, note 19, and p. 158, note 144 above.
[271] See p. 181, note 223 above.

it is clear that the change over time in each country is of much more importance than the difference between them; or, in other words, the country which trails is best described, not as providing less education, but as being a few years behind its rival.[272]

Not surprisingly, warnings about the remarkable British scientific prowess were sounded by German observers, both contemporary and modern, who in their turn may not have been entirely disinterested. They had admired the Mechanics' Institutes, and they now admired the new technical colleges. Others of them deplored the continuing tendency of the *Gymnasien* to concentrate on the classics, as also that their university graduates did not go into business, and that their businessmen lacked scientific training. There was nothing in Germany, in the opinion of some, to touch Cambridge in physics, Sheffield or Birmingham in metallurgy and Leeds and Manchester in textile chemistry and dyeing.[273]

Britain, clearly, had the capacity to catch up quickly if she had a mind to. This was achieved in part by private effort, but even the State was beginning to shed its reluctance to spend money on education and science. Numbers in schools, universities and technical colleges were catching up on the German proportions and the National Physical Laboratory wiped out the lead of its German rival in a few short years. The Government was devoting increasing resources to supporting secondary school and university teaching, it helped to create the enlarged Imperial College of 1907, the London School of Tropical Medicine (1899), and the Medical Research Council (1913), and promised support for agricultural research in 1909.

If any proof were needed of the potential power and inventiveness of British industry, it was the speed with which it was able to meet the demands of war, both in the case of new products and in the case of those which Germany had supplied hitherto. Examples are the expansion of the production of dyestuffs, of optical glass, and of 'dope' for aircraft frames. This was done in a matter of a few years, and in some cases it was done in months. German authors were not slow to point out that British industry had switched more rapidly, more flexibly and more successfully to a war economy than had the German.[274]

A second method to deal with the question whether scientific and technological teaching and research 'failed' the nation would be to ask whether there were any signs of unmet needs, of shortages of persons trained in science or technology, or indeed in any other subject which the educational system might have been expected to teach. Did industry express demands for trained personnel which could not be met?

The evidence is overwhelmingly to the contrary. Indeed, it was the universal complaint of the colleges and of the teachers of these subjects that their students were not wanted by British industry, which preferred the practical training in the works. Large manufacturers, T. Rees, Registrar of the School of Mines complained to the Devonshire Commission, think that

[272] Jarausch (1983b), 16; Pfetsch (1974), 329; Forman, Heilbron and Weart (1973), 92–5. But see West (1975), 80; p. 210.
[273] Sanderson (1972a), 23; Floud (1984), 7; Singer *et al.* (1954–58), VI, 150; Short (1974), 161; Lundgreen (1975a), 73; and Lundgreen (1984), 64; Pfetsch (1974), 154.
[274] R. and K. MacLeod (1975), 171 ff; Coleman (1975), 205–27; Richardson (1962), 114–15; Ballod (1916), 483; Baudis (1981), III, 49–78; Burn (1940); Fearon (1974), 236.

'their sons would derive much more advantage by studying in the working of their own works, than by coming to London. They all think,' he added significantly, that they 'can purchase their scientific aid if they want it.'

He was echoed in a report to the Technical Education Committee of the LCC in 1892:

'The chief obstacle to the scientific training of the managers of the numerous small chemical and colour works in East London and the tanneries of Bermondsey', it stated, 'is their rooted disbelief in the value of such training.' 'There was a feeling', according to a Sheffield steel manufacturer in 1904, 'that a young man having an engineering or a science degree was an indication that too much time had been spent in theory for him to have the necessary workshop experience, and it might stand in the way of his securing the position he applied for.'

And as late as 1909 the Board of Education, in its annual report, had cause to complain that

there still exists among the generality of employers a strong preference for the man trained from an early age in the works, and a prejudice against the so-called 'college-trained man'

Proofs that 'the cult of the practical man' predominated could be multiplied many times over.[275]

Employment opportunities for scientists were indeed bleak in British industry. Most went into teaching, or abroad, above all to the colonies, where pay was higher and prospects better. Only chemists and engineers might find suitable employment at home, for others there was practically nothing.[276]

Had there been a shortage of scientists, it should have shown itself in high salaries for them. In fact, their pay was abysmally low: even just before the war, salaries of 30–40 shillings a week, about the wage level of skilled artisans, were being offered to graduate chemists.[277] It is true that in the last years before the war employment opportunities improved for chemists and others, but so did the numbers of graduates. There was even then no sign of unfilled need, though there were hints that if some knowledge of scientific theory was married to practical experience, chances of employment and promotion would improve. There was also, as always, the fear that systematized knowledge would threaten the secrets of the firms' processes.[278]

Finally, it is arguable that the employers' reluctance to employ trained scien-

[275] R.C. (1872), ev. Rees, Q.475; Argles (1964), 37; Smith (1982), 224; Musgrave (1970d), 154, and Musgrave (1967), 51; Mosely Reports (1904), 29, 238, 337; Sanderson (1972b), 259, and Sanderson (1972a), 116–18; Ahlström (1982), 84–5; Phelps-Brown (1972), 193; Howarth (1922), 236; Roderick and Stephens (1978), 118, 134–5; Procter in discussion to Heathcote (1909), 174; Jenkins and Ponting (1982), 281–6; Sigsworth and Blackman (1968), 147; Sigsworth (1958), 72–3. Also p. 208, note 301 below.

[276] Meadows (1972), 88; R.C. (1872), ev. Forster, Q.7792; Rose and Rose (1969), 29, 35; D.C. (1906), ev. Tilden, Q.2590.

[277] Musgrave (1967), 36; Berman (1975), 39; Jewkes (1960), 2; Evans and Wiseman (136); Ballod (1916), 482; Roderick and Stephens (1972), 16; Musgrove (1959–60), 110; Sanderson (1972b), 529, and Sanderson (1972a), 27; Cardwell (1957), 169.

[278] Professor Arnold of Sheffield was forbidden to write textbooks for that reason. D.C. (1906), ev. QQ.1955–8. Also Smith (1982), 224; Cardwell (1957), 189; R.C. (1872), ev. Bell, Q.9164; R.C. (1884), III, ev. Bell, Q.287, Wedgwood, Q.934, Donnelly, Q.2862.

tists and technologists and their pride in their 'rule of thumb methods' were themselves the fault, and possibly a sign of the gravest failure, of British science and technology. The fact that top people's schools and universities despised science would affect above all top people. There was a 'clear conflict', in Halsey's phrase, between the academic culture of the traditional elite and the business community. Above half of the steelmakers of the second half of the nineteenth century whose educational career is known had been to boarding school, the other half to day schools, and in both science was either not taught, or it was geared to low social expectations. Very few of them had any serious science training or indeed any higher education: Lowthian Bell and J.G.N. Alleyne were very much the exceptions. The critical failure of British education, in this view, lay in the lack of the necessary scientific and technological training for the owners and managers of productive industry, which would have allowed them to recognize promising paths forward, rather than the position where 'the only research British entrepreneurs would sponsor was that which led quickly to immediate practical results'.[279]

These generalized strictures are, once again, applicable to the chemical industry, as well as to the optical glass industry. Elsewhere, however, the common British assumption that German employers, in contrast to the British, had had the benefit of first-class scientific training which was technology-based and meritocratic, does not stand up to the evidence, and is denied also by German historians themselves. It was, on the contrary, not infrequently remarked abroad that the owners of the British leading engineering firms were themselves highly competent engineers, and the status of entrepreneurs was no lower, and might have been higher, than in France or Germany.[280]

Here also, there were some industries in which Germany had the advantage, as there were others in which Britain was still firmly in the lead.

Yet a doubt remains, for British manufacturers, while shunning British graduates, seemed to be eager to employ Germans and other foreigners. This was so particularly in two spheres, chemical works and the overseas correspondence offices of commercial and financial firms. Did not this prove the deficiencies of British education?

The argument may be granted at once in the case of chemistry, optics and possibly also electrical engineering. The chemical industry had benefited enormously by immigrants like Levinstein, Ludwig Mond, Caro, and the numerous works chemists, including Frederick Hurter, the Swiss chief chemists of the United Alkali Co. In electrical engineering also, Britain relied excessively on Germans and Americans abroad and at home. Yet in both chemistry and clerical correspondence in foreign languages, the British were catching up rapidly in the years before the war.[281] Moreover, it is not clear that it would have been more sensible to train up British scientists from scratch in areas in which a foreign country was in the lead, nor was it necessarily Great

---

[279] R.C. (1884), III, ev. Siemens, QQ.1486–7; Erickson (1959), esp. 30–2, 36, 41, 177; Musgrave (1967), 28, 38, 75; Cotgrove (1958), 27–8.
[280] Erickson (1959), 58; Allen (1976), 48–9; Kaelble (1982), B9, 53; Steward (1966), 117; Pope (1917), 11.
[281] LeClerc (1899), 237; R.C. (1872), ev. Roscoe, Q.7407; Wilson (1954), 13; also pp. 181–2, 197 above, and p. 210, note 309 below.

Britain which was the loser in a process in which the German governments spent large sums to train chemists who then migrated to Britain. Neither need it necessarily be taken a sign of weakness on Britain's part. It might equally well be viewed as a sign of continued strength in general, and the first stage in catching up, and possibly leapfrogging in turn, in an area which the Germans had made peculiarly their own. Some, like the Hofmanns and the Caros, went back to Germany, perhaps to further German interests with the knowledge they picked up in Britain; but the Monds and the Levinsteins stayed, to enrich and become part of British industry.

Among the overwhelming majority of entrepreneurs in Britain, the practical training in the works was held to be greatly superior to theoretical formal schooling in science or technology. Many employers, as we have seen, even despised the men who arrived in their works with college training. Some there were, who maintained that the more organized scientific training of technicians and managers on the continent was not an advantage, but on the contrary was their only way of making up their inferiority in practical experience, on the Gerschenkron principle of substitution. F. Redtenbacher, one of the best-known teachers of technology of the mid-century, having in his own career spanned three of the most progressive colleges on the continent, in Vienna, Zurich and Karlsruhe, admitted this freely:

> We on the continent possess neither the financial power nor the breadth of experience of working in all specialized lines to be able to follow an exclusively empirical path, and we are therefore obliged to use our reason and our scientific understanding as substitutes for the lack of funds and for our limited experience.

Exactly the same point was made by Dr von Steinberg, of Wurttemberg, to the Samuelson Commission. Oliver Reynolds, professor of engineering at Owen's College (the University of Manchester), stated that their own didactic object was to apply scientific methods to problems of engineering: the students were to be left largely to observation and experiment. The *Technische Hochschulen*, by contrast, used more theory and more bookwork.

> Our course is rather to teach [the student] to understand what he sees, while theirs is to teach him to produce things he has not seen.[282]

Even in Germany it was stated as late as 1906 that

> in a modern technical enterprise of medium size we often find men of supreme technical education with academic degrees working on the same job with the same rights as self-taught men who have never been to a specialized school.[283]

In Britain, premium apprenticeship remained the most common form of training for future leaders in the engineering, ship-building, coal mining and other technical industries. This involved considerable payments of £50–£600 or even more by the young man or his father which, had they desired a more formal education, they would have been in a position to make to one of the

---

[282] Redtenbacher quoted in Treue (1964), 227, also Treue (1976), 224, 230; R.C. (1884), V, 61, 174, 175, 221; Inkster and Morrell (1983), 43. Pollard and Robertson (1979), 147. Also see notes 22 and 73 above.
[283] Manegold (1978), 151, 156.

colleges or universities desperately seeking students at the time. Since so-called premium apprentices were destined for leading positions in their industry, their training normally involved being taken through all the departments of a firm, to work with the owner or a manager or designer, and to be urged or indeed obliged in addition to attend commercial or science classes.

Virtually all the leading employers and managers in the technical industries, whether they had any formal college training or not, had been through an apprenticeship of this kind. Its value in later life depended largely on the standing of the employer with whom they had been in pupillage, and it follows that it was only the works with the highest prestige, or the most experienced professionals, who were in a position to take pupils or premium apprentices of this kind.[284] The system formed the backbone of the transmission of British technology and know-how. An enquiry by the Engineering Training Organization made in 1917 revealed that of the 226 well-known engineering firms questioned, 43 had a pupillage system, and 61 took on secondary school boys for an apprenticeship which involved part-time study.[285] In our period, additional formal training, at least on a part-time basis, was markedly on the increase. Most motor car pioneers, for example, had been to good schools and possibly Technical or University Colleges, before entering pupillage. But, by and large, employers, managers and leading technicians based their knowledge essentially on practical experience, with or without formal evening or other classes as an addition. This applied to industries in which Britain was still leading in 1914, such as shipbuilding, steam-engine making and textile machine building, as much as to industries in which she had lost ground.[286]

Were they wrong in their assumption? Were they too ignorant to see the value of what they had missed, and too inclined towards the human failing of assuming that one's own education must have been the best possible? Or are we to say rather that sometimes they were right and at other times they were wrong, but that the tendency was for their view to be increasingly dangerous and damaging?

Pupillage payments are inherently suspect: since they could amount to a considerable source of income to a small firm or an independent consultant, the oft-voiced objection to a change in the system on the part of the latter might therefore be self-interested.[287] On the other hand, the United Kingdom with her much more varied engineering industry, and more practical experience to offer in other sectors, too, than the countries on the Continent, was clearly more justified in basing its training mainly on experience. Even today practical experience plays a leading part in technical education even in the most advanced countries as well as in those at a technical level similar to that reached by Britain

---

[284] R.C. (1872), ev. Jenkin, Q.1601, Smyth, Q.2335, Brough, QQ.2534–7, Bell, QQ.9164, 9178, Armstrong, QQ.9243–6; More (1980), 45, 104–6; Musgrove (1959–60), 111; Dearle (1914), 178; S.C. (1867–68), viii; Roderick and Stephens (1978), 116–17; R.C. (1884), III, ev. Anderson, QQ.17–25, 2702; Erickson (1959), 44; Reader (1966), 118.

[285] Albu (1971), 69. Also see Nicholas (1985), 85 ff; Inkster (1985c), 191; Saul (1967), 129.

[286] R.C. (1864), III, ev. Bell, QQ.303–4, Wedgwood, QQ.926–9, Siemens, QQ.1442–3, Anderson, Q.1753. Shelby, QQ.2706–12; Marshall (1946), 209; Saul (1963), 27.

[287] R.C. (1872), III, Reynolds, 179; More (1980), 171; Musgrave (1967), 61; Lorenz (1984), 599–634.

in the last century.[288] The contrast, here also, is not so much between the educated and the ignorant, but between two different approaches to technical education then current in Britain and on the Continent.

However, sooner or later, practical experience, supplemented by a modicum of scientific knowledge would become inadequate in a world of more complex mechanization, large-scale organization, and such science-based industries as organic chemistry and electrical engineering. The transition would be slow and gradual, people having grown up in the works possibly keeping pace with new developments without science training of their own, but the younger age cohort having to rely on systematized knowledge, and probably both groups coexisting fruitfully side by side for a considerable time. Had the time come for the change-over in our period, and had Britain missed the bus by its dilatory development in scientific education?

Opinions differ widely on the crucial period of the transition. Some put it as early as 1850, or the 1860s; others believe 1870, 1880–1900 or even the last decade before the war to be the period of the technological revolution.[289] Clearly, the death knell for the rule of thumb methods would sound at different times in different industries. For gas technology and for some branches of mechanical engineering it allegedly sounded about 1860, though Joseph Whitworth, a practical man of the old school, could demonstrate to the Mechanical Engineers in 1857 the working to an accuracy of 1/100,000 inch.[290] In organic chemistry, the transition came in the 1880s at the latest and by the turn of the century in some other specialized fields, like the electrolysis of metals.[291] In most other fields the practical man held his own, since it was he who had, in fact, created much of the technology that was taught academically in a methodical and possibly simplified way in more backward countries abroad.

Next to chronology, it is also the sequence which matters. It is evident that science and systematic technology will play a different part in the progress of the pioneer and of the imitators. In the phase of British hegemony, leadership was unscientific, the followers needed systematization; in the following phase of scientific industry, it was the pioneer who needed the organized science most.

There was, in either case, no necessary long-term disadvantage in being second, as long as contact was never lost with the leader to the extent of preventing a continuous process of leapfrogging as now one, now the other country or industry moved into the lead, but both, or all, advanced more or less in line. The potential advantages of being second are well known in the case of individual firms. Costs and uncertainties are reduced, and at times entrepreneurs may even be well advised to hold back in copying an innovation even though it may be profitable, in the expectation that a still better model or

[288] E.g. Mincer (1971b), 524; Harbison and Myers (1964), 9; Tinbergen and Bos (n.d.), 147–69; Abramovitz (1962), 771; Coleman (1962), 104; Rosenberg (1976), 154–5.

[289] Schramm (1951), 159; Sanderson (1972a), 10, 25; Locke (1984), 59; Gowing (1977–78), 71; Robertson (1974), 222–3; 233; Habakkuk (1967), 188–93.

[290] Treue (1966), 47; Roderick and Stephens (1972), 76; Böhme, v.d. Daele, Krohn (1978), 237–40; R.C. (1872), ev. Frankland, Q.827, Jenkin, Q.1583; Rolt (1970), 134.

[291] E.g. Ludwig (1974), 18; Locke (1977), 276; Ballod (1916), 482.

process will become available next year. Of course, one also runs the risk thereby of losing the market.[292] In the case of a country, no such conscious choice is usually involved, but it is not clear that, given the limitation of resources, Britain did not do well to let the USA or Germany pioneer such developments as motor cars, interchangeable part engineering or certain sectors of electrical engineering, and then have foreign firms, such as Singer, Ford, Siemens or Westinghouse introduce the processes, with the snags ironed out, into Britain.

According to the Ames and Rosenberg model it is more likely that lagging countries would catch up those in the lead than that they would actually overtake them;[293] this implies a diffusion process in which the more advanced countries grow more slowly than the rest. Did this still apply to Britain, or were her scientific weaknesses such that they would lead to her being overtaken and left behind by her rivals?

Catching up would involve a mixed picture, Britain leading in some sectors, temporarily behind in others, the position changing constantly; being overtaken would mean Britain falling behind along the whole front. The survey in chapter 1 showed that the first alternative fitted much better than the second. What is of interest here is that even in areas where Britain dropped behind, it was not necessarily her scientists who were at fault.

The most interesting example, perhaps, is to be found in the electrical engineering and electronics sector, often listed as one of Britain's failures. In the generation of electricity, Charles Parson's steam turbine (1884) was perhaps the outstanding invention making use of the highest level of science and technology then available. Sebastian de Ferranti, trained in Sir William Siemens's British factory, developed the principle of high voltage distribution (1889); he has been credited also with 176 other inventions. (Sir) John Hopkinson, professor of electrical engineering at King's College, London, patented the third wire, saving 50% of copper used. Arthur Wright, of Brighton, developed the first usable meter. The first public generating station at Holborn viaduct actually beat the first American station by some weeks, though admittedly it was built by the Edison company. Other early or pioneer achievements were found in electric traction at Brighton, in the Liverpool overhead railway and the opening of the first electric tube, the City and South London in 1890.

The invention of the telephone was perfected by Graham Bell, an emigré Scotsman, in America in 1876 and the first British telephone exchange opened only one year after the first American. As early as 1877, the British Association meeting had several types of telephone demonstrated by Bell and W.H. Preece. Later, Britain helped to develop the automatic exchange. The electric incandescent lamp was invented simultaneously by Edison in America and by Swan in Britain, and was then marketed jointly.[294]

[292] Rosenberg (1982), 107, 286, and Rosenberg (1976), 317; Nelson, Peck and Kalachek (1967), 100; Mansfield (1968), 105; Carter and Williams (1957), 159. Also discussion on pp. 142, 162, and notes 89, 160-1 above, pp. 211-12 below.
[293] Ames and Rosenberg (1967).
[294] Chapter 1, pp. 31-2, notes 53-7 above; Howarth (1922), 75; Derry and Williams (1960), 827-33; Armytage (1961), 200; Scott (1958), esp. 169-72, 200-1; Neufeld (1987), 695-6.

Of all the innovations of the age the one depending most on scientific understanding was the radio. The theoretical groundwork had been laid mainly by Hertz in Germany and Clerk Maxwell in Britain. Short-distance 'wireless' transmissions were made by Sir Oliver Lodge in 1894 and by Rutherford in 1895, but neither was interested in commercial exploitation. Their potential importance was seen most clearly by an Italian, Guglielmo Marconi. Finding no interest for his ideas in Italy, he came to Britain where he met with more support, both by the chief Post Office engineer, W.H. Preece and by several academics, and the English Marconi Co. was set up in 1897. Marconi's first transmission across the Atlantic succeeded in 1901, and interest then became world-wide; but the development of viable radio was greatly helped by British ideas, such as Kelvin's principle of the condenser, Oliver Lodge's experiments of 1889 leading to the 'tuner', and J.A. Fleming's invention of the thermionic valve, the diode in 1904.[295]

Metallurgy, to cite another example, which had been much advanced by H. Sorby, saw the development of tungsten steel by Robert F. Mushet in 1868 and of manganese steel by Robert A. Hadfield in 1888. Other 'special' steels followed, including silicon steel. Special tool steels were then developed in America, but stainless steel once more came from Sheffield, discovered by Harry Brearley in 1912. The contributions of Bessemer and Gilchrist Thomas to the development of mass-produced carbon steel are of course well known. Other metallurgical improvements emerged out of the rivalry of the armaments producers, with Vickers and Armstrong in the lead. Other examples of what Saul has called this 'astonishing series of technical advances' were the development of the model ship tank by William Froude, for the scientific-mathematical principles of ship construction, the viscose process for rayon and the Dunlop pneumatic tyre.[296]

The point about all this is not merely that Britain was in the lead, or at least up among the leaders, in the whole gamut of science-based industries but that her contributions were made not only in the field of enterprise or capital, but precisely in the area of invention, technical application and pure scientific research, which allegedly were letting her down. Conversely, there were failures of scientific enterprise also among the other leading nations. Well-known examples were the failure, as late as 1881, of Werner von Siemens to take a European licence for the Edison patents, and the lack of interest shown by the major American electrical and electronic companies, including Westinghouse and General Electric in the development of radio.[297]

VII Conclusion

Let us attempt some conclusions. We have examined the widespread view that the slowing down of the British economy, and its particular weaknesses in some

[295] Derry and Williams (1960), 621, 629; Byatt (1979), 185-6; Singer *et al.* (1954-58), IV, 1093; Baker (1970), 44-5, 63.
[296] Saul (1979), 117; Miall (1931), 177; Froude (1955), 120 ff; Tweedale (1983), 225-39; Burn (1940), 214; Trebilcock (1977), 1-4, 33, 46; Carr and Taplin (1962), 157, 220-1.
[297] Derry and Williams (1960), 634; Nelson (1959), 109; MacLaurin (1950), 96.

new industries and in the modern sectors of old industries, were linked to failings in British education, and in particular in scientific and technological education and research. This view has been found to be built up of a number of separate assertions, not always clearly distinguished from each other.

In the field of education, critics have sometimes deplored the absence of a comprehensive elementary education system, allowing large numbers among the poorer classes to remain illiterate and without the kind of mental discipline which even basic schooling is believed to instil. Others have pointed to the lack of science subjects in the schools which did exist.

Much the same strictures have also been applied to the universities, above all to the largest and richest of them, Oxford and Cambridge. Secondary education has been found wanting, first, by being limited to a very small proportion of the population only, and secondly, by its neglect of, or indeed contempt for, scientific and technological subjects. Their teaching standards, as well as those of the technical colleges of various kinds, have also not escaped censure. Numbers of students at all levels of scientific and technical training were much lower than in Germany. In place of a recognized ladder from elementary to secondary and thence to higher education, with widely accepted certificates of competence at the end of each course to set the starting levels of the more advanced education, the British educational world appeared to be almost totally chaotic. Educational standards had no common measure, nor were institutions intended to dovetail into each other or form a logical whole. The higher institutions could not rely on the lower ones to prepare their students up to a certain level – indeed until the very end of the period, there was no clear distinction between higher and lower, except perhaps that given by age. Neither teachers nor pupils had to submit to any form of standardized qualifying examination (with certain important exceptions) and even many university degrees, especially in the ancient universities, were only of the most doubtful value. Many of the leading professions set their own teaching and examining standards, or indeed had no standards at all, accepting a number of years of assistantship or pupillage to a working member of the profession as sufficient proof of competence.

As far as research and related activities were concerned, critics have pointed to the absence of research as a normal occupation of university teachers, as had become standard in Germany, until the end of our period. They have also criticized the unwillingness of the State to fund scientific research, leaving science to wealthy amateurs who were increasingly unable to provide the larger funds and larger numbers of researchers required by modern scientific progress.

The lack of research and development facilities within firms has also been commented on adversely, and this, in turn, has been linked with the shortage of trained scientific personnel. Behind this lag in the employment of trained scientists and technologists in productive industry is seen the more fundamental weakness of lack of scientific understanding on the part of the owners and managers of firms who had to make the ultimate decisions.

Among the more historically minded of the critics it was held that neither the methods which had secured the achievements of the period of the industrial revolution, nor the amateur tradition of pure scientific investigation, pursued by men of means could be eternally valid. Scientific and technical progress required increasingly more systematic and more costly science, better educational preparation for it, and a technology increasingly based on scientific understanding. The suggestion was that Britain had become fatally wedded to a system which had brought uniquely impressive results in the past but was becoming increasingly unable to cope with the present and the future, while others, including Germany, having no vested interests or rigidified structures, were able to leapfrog into methods of education and research that were more directly useful to modern industry and helped to drive it forward.

There are some obvious links between many of these assertions, but they are nevertheless too varied to be dealt with by simple generalizations, and require specific treatment, item by item. Some of them may be dealt with quickly in this concluding section; others will require more detailed consideration.

Little time need be spent on basic education and literacy. Modern studies have confirmed that the extent of literacy required in the industries of countries at the state of development which Victorian Britain had reached, was very limited: 40% of adult literacy has been set as a rough and ready standard. This level had been attained in Britain long before the onset of industrialization. Moreover, recent research has also tended show that generally the schooling available to working-class children was a great deal better than the tendentious reporting of reformers and officials had led us to believe in the past. It now seems most unlikely that the educational standards of the poor and backward Prussian countryside (Germany was far less urbanized than the British Isles) were any higher than those of Great Britain. In both countries, by 1850, and certainly by 1870, illiteracy was confined to a small, underprivileged minority and could not have affected the rate of industrial progress.

The science teaching in elementary and also in secondary schools is a much more complex matter. The educational institution for the upper and ruling classes was the public school. Its object was to shape and define the elite. Inasmuch as the elite had no economic function, it required no useful subjects to be taught; inasfar as it was destined to govern, it required 'character training', training that would keep the class together and would keep it ruling. It also required a means of distinguishing its own from the rest, and for this a range of subjects without utility, on which the lower orders could not afford to spend the time, was required: the classics filled the bill admirably. By the same token, the public school had to despise and denigrate science together with all utilitarian and 'modern' subjects.[298] Because it represented the elite, the other schools took their attitude more or less from it.

This posed problems for the industrial middle and lower middle classes. On the one hand, fathers were looking for a useful education for their sons, and in the first half of the nineteenth century they used and adapted local grammar schools and founded new proprietary and boarding schools with that purpose in mind. Further progress along those lines might have provided a full Benthamite secondary and even tertiary system of education 'established on meritocratic

---

[298] Even the Rev. Harcourt, science enthusiast and founder of the British Association, did not once mention its utility to industry in his inaugural address in 1831. Basalla, Coleman and Kargon (1970), 30 ff; Gowing (1977–78), 83–4; MacDonagh (1974–75), 516; Ahlström (1982), 84; above, p. 169, note 184.

lines, which favoured science and technology and operated an aggressive search for innovation and the practical application of research'.[299] But ranged against this was the fact that for a thorough reform, especially of the endowed schools surviving from past ages, the aid of the State would have been necessary, and the middle classes feared and disliked the State – it was, after all, not theirs.

Besides, they were afraid that schooling that was too meritocratic would open the door to the claims and advancement of the lower orders. It was easier to accept the standards of the elite and to make schooling an instrument of social ascent rather than of technical competence. Perhaps things might have been different: Herbert Spencer might have won out against Matthew Arnold, the positivist optimism of a world opened up by science against the refined aestheticist withdrawal from turbulent reality. As it turned out, the forces ranged against that option were too strong. Increasingly, northern manufacturers sent their boys into the public schools helping thereby to revive them and to raise their numbers and prestige once more.

It was unfortunate that when, towards the end of the century, the School Boards in the industrial towns followed the natural desires and interests of local industry and the local lower middle and working classes and built up 'Central Schools' which favoured the scientific education of the more talented elementary school children, they not only fell foul of departmental jealousies in London, but also found that their legal position was insecure.[300] Possibly for the last time, the classics lobby managed to nip this development in the bud, and, on the basis of the 1902 Education Act, set up secondary schools in the image of the elite schools that were able to channel the more talented working-class children away from an industrial, and towards an elite pattern of education.

This is the indictment, and it is true as far as it goes. Yet the contrast with Germany can be overdrawn. There was nothing in Germany to compare with the incalculable stimulus given to science teaching at several levels, ultimately to hundreds of thousands of students, by the grants administered by the DScA and the CGLI. The classical *Gymnasium* continued to predominate in numbers and prestige, and science was a weak and neglected plant there also. More modern secondary schools also developed, it is true; but they had to fight a long and bitter battle for recognition, and it was not until the end of the nineteenth century, and even then only by the direct intervention of the emperor, that they received nominal equality of status, though even then not true parity of esteem.

The German system, because it was unitary, could react more quickly to an order from above, but the British, because it was decentralized, was more flexible, and it could experiment more easily in many directions at once. It proved capable of expanding science education in public and grammar schools, in higher elementary schools and in numerous continuation schools for the less privileged classes in so many and varied ways, as to prompt the inevitable question whether, had more science education been demanded, or had it been demanded earlier, it would not have been forthcoming equally easily. Had the public schools and most grammar schools continued to be so dominated by the classicists that no outside influence could have broken through their barriers,

[299] Fox (1985), 226–7.
[300] See above, p. 168, note 180.

would they not have been by-passed? How long would they have held out against loss of income and pupils, had these dropped off to any serious extent? How much sooner would, in that case, the recommendations of the Clarendon Commission, the Devonshire Commission and others have been implemented? Given the vested interests, there would have been delay, but there was never any sign of any inability to match demand for science or technology education with supply; indeed, the contrary seems to have been the case, supply normally running ahead of demand.

In the ancient universities also, late though the provision of science courses and degrees was, there was, once again, a demand rather than a supply deficiency.[301] They were by-passed in part by the foundation of the civic universities, many of which resembled the *Technische Hochschulen* more than they resembled traditional universities. Here also, local industrialists and other dignitaries seemed to be more eager to give money to their local university than to send students to it, but by the end of our period both supply and demand seemed to rise in a steep curve.

The German system of combining university teaching with research was adopted late, but led almost at once to some brilliant successes. It was only in the unique case of the organic chemical industry that the British lost their lead and were held back because they simply did not have the numbers of highly trained specialists that the German universities were able to supply to the chemical firms.

Meanwhile, the 'liberal' tradition of non-functional learning was at least as strong in Germany. In fact, it was the German chemist A.W. Hofmann who tried to dissuade his star pupil, W.H. Perkin, from making practical use of his path-breaking discovery of synthetic dyes. 'He appeared much annoyed and spoke in a very disparaging manner', Perkin recalled later, 'making me feel that perhaps I might be taking a false step which might ruin my future prospects.'[302]

Much of the criticism of the British performance can be reduced to criticism of the State. It was the State, or the local authorities under compulsion by the State, that should have introduced elementary education earlier and more comprehensively, and enlarged the science and practical content within it; the State should have taken over and provided more widely, secondary and technical education for the less privileged classes; and it should have given more money to the universities, and financed science research within and without them earlier and more generously.

Whether contemporary Continental countries did indeed all that for their scientific progress or not, the critics always assumed that at least Germany or Prussia did. Alfred Marshall was not alone in admiring 'Germany's strong, though harsh military-bureaucratic organization'[303] in this regard.

Current German opinion is not entirely convinced of that superiority, pointing out that part of the cost of schooling, particularly at the secondary level, had to be borne by the parents. Moreover, even if it were true that the total share of national income going to education was higher there, the greater wealth of

---

[301] Cardwell (1978), 46; Payne (1978), VII, 210–11; Inkster (1985c), 182.
[302] Russel and Goodman (1972), 67; Beer (1959), 46.
[303] Marshall (1923), 579. The role of the State is discussed at length in ch. 4.

Britain (and the much greater contribution from private sources) ensured that actual total expenditure was no lower here.[304]

There can be no doubt of the strong and tradition-based opposition of the public authorities to spending taxpayers' money on education and scientific research. The middle classes had only just, after almost a century of battle, cleansed the State apparatus from a mass of corruption and 'tax-eating'; the upper classes, in their turn, were not eager to see public funds used to make access to top jobs easier for the middle and lower orders. Moreover, the more intelligent members of the bureaucracy, who may well have wished to extend the role of the State on Benthamite principles or simply as an aspect of empire-building, were well aware of the enormous sums available for education out of gifts and endowments over the centuries – the sum of £700,000 a year was talked of for Oxford and Cambridge alone in the 1870s – and misappropriated by clerics, city alderman and others. Robert Lowe's oft-quoted dictum, made in 1869, that 'I hold it as our duty not to spend public money to do that which people can do for themselves'[305] has to be understood at least partly in that light.

Nor were all the leading scientists, especially among the comfortably-off, very eager to accept State aid. Airy was able to declare in his presidential address to the British Association in 1851, safe in his position as Astronomer Royal, the highest paid State science post, that the British preferred 'natural genius' to State patronage. There was even a Society for Opposing the Endowment of Research. Universities and schools, also, were afraid of State interference.

> 'Government may do much', declared Sir Joseph Hooker, President of the Royal Society in 1876, 'but it must always be under such vexatious restrictions that it tries a man's temper and patience, let his patriotism be what it will, to undertake the expenditure of what Government gives, and I fear it must ever be so.'

One Secretary of the Treasury, formerly of the Science and Art Department, expressed his belief in 1882 that the small annual research grant from the Treasury distributed through the Royal Society was

> probably the least mischievous form of aid, although even that implies the question 'what are you doing' and 'when may we look for results', which I believe to be more grievous than poverty with its freedom (!) to the investigator who is worth anything, and who must far oftener turn back than go forward.[306]

Possibly the critics underrated the contribution of the State to British science. This aid came under at least four headings. First, there was support for surveys, expeditions and observatories. Secondly, there was legislation, including that relating to public health, medical examinations or safety in mines, which obliged the appointment of qualified scientists in the Civil Service; its reform of 1855 may also in part be said to have been designed to aid and foster

---

[304] Borchardt (1965), 387–90; Lundgreen (1973), 64–5, 77; Brock (1976), 174. Also p. 194, note 266 above.

[305] Roderick (1967), 28; Roderick and Stephens (1981a), 6; Alter (1982), 278. Also p. 122, note 22 above.

[306] MacLeod (1971a), 340, 347, also 328–9, 342; Russel and Goodman (1972), 2; Morrell (1971), 187, 203.

educational institutions. Thirdly, there was the employment of scientists in the Governments' service itself, ranging from public analysts to railway inspectors. Fourthly, there was the direct contribution of funds to universities, to research projects and to such institutions as the National Physical Laboratory.[307]

The directions of this activity are interesting. The preoccupation with public health was forced on the government very much against its will. The expeditions and surveys benefited largely those engaged in shipping, and the coal royalty owners, classes for which British governments had always had a soft spot. There was little there to help industry. Against this, the State intervened more than once to harm most grievously the progress of key high-tech. industries in their most sensitive phase, such as electrical engineering and the motor industry.[308]

In quantitative terms, the contribution of the State was derisory at the beginning of our period, but it rose with astonishing rapidity. The provision of funds for schools has been noted above. Contributions to the expeditions, survey, etc. rose from around £34,000 at the middle of the century, to over £600,000 at its end. If anything, the growth of support for the civic universities and other projects with a scientific or technical leaning was even faster in the two decades leading up to the war. New projects, like the National Physical Laboratory, medical research, agricultural research and tropical medicine were paid for in addition. Behind them, and particularly behind the support for the Imperial College of Science and Technology, was the new belief in national 'efficiency', the fear of falling behind Germany and others, and the newly found conviction that it was national policy to further industrial progress, by fostering advanced technology.[309] It was precisely what had inspired Government support for science on the continent.

Timing is important, and the delay, of possibly a decade or two only, may have been enough to give other countries a foothold in subjects requiring science and a lead which Britain could not catch up, at least in the short run. Whether in other respects the shortcomings of the State should be given a great deal of weight is another matter. By comparing the educational systems of Britain and Germany and their influence on economic growth, we are not comparing like with like. We are comparing a country which had been industrially far in the lead of the rest of the world with a country which was bending every effort to catch up.

Britain was in many ways the odd man out in Europe: she was the first to industrialize, and the last to professionalize her science, and the two may not be unconnected.[310] In comparing her general *laissez-faire* attitude with the more regimented science and education abroad, above all in Germany, we are not justified in terming one a failed attempt to match the other. They were different solutions, because they were attempting to deal with different problems. It is

[307] Carr-Saunders and Wilson (1933), 151–2, 305–6; Brock (1976), 178; Poole and Andrews (1972), 6–9; Hughes (1962), 63–4; Rothblatt (1983), 146–7; Pollard (1952), 101–4. Also see pp. 188–9 above.

[308] See chapter 4, pp. 251–3.

[309] MacLeod (1976), 118–20; Morrell (1976), 59; Taylor (1975), 23; Hollenberg (1974), 255; also p. 199, note 281 above.

[310] Berman (1975), 42; Jarausch (1983b), 10; Sanderson (1972b), 245–6.

not immediately obvious why the educational policies adopted in one country should be admired in another country which had no need of them.[311]

Apart from the very different role of the State in Britain and on the continent, the roots of which extend far wider than the educational field, there were essentially two characteristics shaping the attitude of British managers and entrepreneurs to formal science and technology in contrast to those on the continent: their advantage of having actual experience of the latest practice at each stage, and their freedom of action within the law. As to the first, there was, in Bowker's phrase, a 'vast common stock of technological science'[312] in British industry, within the consciousness and the feel of thousands of people actually engaged in the works.

It had not yet been systematized, and much of it would not, or could not be systematized since it would lose its validity faster than academics could be apprised of it. But as long as this 'science', which included design as well as a knowledge of the market, was not available abroad, it gave the British manufacturer an immense advantage over his rival.

The freedom of action was, of course, the positive side of the *laissez-faire* coin and it had played a considerable part, and possibly the decisive part, in the industrialization of Britain and the economic lead which it had given to her. It was held widely, not least by Alfred Marshall, that the apparent chaos and unscientific nature of English education had precisely the merit that it stimulated the intellectual alertness which had created the industrial revolution, and kept the impetus going for a century. *The Times* echoed that sentiment:

> 'Self-help and spontaneous growth are better suited to Englishmen' it wrote in 1889, 'but [we are] ready to believe and willing to hope, that state initiative and socialistic science and self-conscious statesmanship may be adapted to other circumstances and other habits . . . the German is accustomed to official control, official delays and police supervision from the cradle to the grave . . . whereas . . . self-help and spontaneous growth are better suited to Englishmen.'[313]

British science and science education, including scientific technology, were also distinguished from their Continental variety by at least two particular characteristics. One was their amateur tradition; the other was, again, their freedom and lack of orthodoxy; and once more, it is not clear why these should be considered inferior to the officially fostered science and education on the Continent.

The British tradition was to give those individuals who possessed the interest, energy and ability the chance of driving themselves forward, without flattening the contours by making it too easy for all. The elitist nature of that tradition was captured by the younger Herschel when he declared that he failed to see any benefit in fostering an 'overwhelming mass of mediocrity' – by which he meant the bulk of the membership of the British Association.

> 'A thousand bad opinions do not make a good one', he continued, 'nor can a thousand eyes looking through as many Spyglasses see as well or as far as one with a first

[311] See p. 138, notes 74 and 161 above.
[312] Bowker (1928), 14.
[313] Marshall (1923), 96; *Times*, (19.6.1899) on the occasion of the extension of Bismarck's insurance scheme; also Inkster (1983), 43.

rate telescope . . . Perfect spontaneous freedom of thought is the essence of scientific progress . . . If you want to win a race you would hardly enter half a dozen horses and harness them together.'[314]

It was a philosophy that had paid off earlier in the century. Its aptness came increasingly under question when massed groups of collaborating scientists were called for.

Of course British, and above all English, schools did not consciously train spontaneity and originality, but rather what became known as character build-ing. The subject is a controversial, and to some a highly emotional one. But it seems clear that if it were possible to encourage and foster such qualities as leadership and self-reliance, the courage of one's conviction, and willingness to back one's own judgement, what some would nowadays call inner-directedness; as well as fair dealing and a modicum of team spirit, or, as one definition has it, 'probity, orthodoxy, romantic liberalism and a strong sense of public responsibility',[315] all of which were useful to a ruling class; then such qualities, after they had trickled down to their lesser schools, would also benefit an entre-preneur or manager.

At a time when all that was known about the technology of an industry could be learnt quickly, or trained experts could be employed in specialist fields, this was perhaps not as negative a contribution to economic growth as has some-times been asserted. The pedantic acquisition of knowledge provided by the German *Gymnasium* or even *Oberrealschule* was not necessarily superior in every respect to the training provided in the English public school.

No doubt, a time would come when the British system would become a fetter on progress as science and technology became more complex and more demanding. A time would also come when organized research on a large scale, frequently with costly equipment beyond the purse of the individual, and when planned cooperation with others were necessary ingredients of technical and economic progress; though even then there would also be room for the brilliant agnostic and lone rogue elephant. This point would be reached at different times for different industries, but for any particular industry it would be extremely difficult to determine when it would have 'paid' to switch from control by tradition to control by science, and from practical tinkering to organized R & D. The point would, in any case, always come later for the leading country, with its wealth of experience and know-how of processes and markets, than for those trying to catch up. The point of change had been reached in organic chemistry well before the end of the nineteenth century, but it is doubtful if it had as yet been reached in any other sector.

The question then remains whether, when that point had been reached, the British economy would be in a position to get into gear and tackle new heights, on a new, more scientific basis. The 'British economy' is a large congeries of sectors. We have seen that the science education sector proved to be extremely, even astonishingly, flexible and capable of expansion. The vigour with which civic universities were created by private initiative and then aided increasingly

[314] Hershel to Whewell, 20.9.1831 in: Morrell and Thackray (1984), 67; also see Halsey and Trow (1971), 50–1.
[315] Barnett (1972), 43; Mack (1973), 23, 38.

212

by the State; the deliberate and successful effort that went into the making of London University and Imperial College, the massive expansion of technical education as aided by the CGLI, at various levels; the expansion of science teaching in schools and the creation of popular secondary schools; and the expansion of science research, even in Oxford and Cambridge and in Government institutions like the NPL, are but some examples of the capacity of the educational sector of the British economy to respond to challenges facing it. The skill and speed with which the needs of war were met after 1914 show the same inventiveness and physical and technical capacity, which was not inferior to anything to be found elsewhere in Europe. Britain was well placed, given the right incentives, to leapfrog technically over other economies in the twentieth century, as she proved in the 1930s and the years of World War II.

The contribution of education and science to the British slowing down before 1914 was moderate at most, and essentially of a reactive rather than causal nature. British science was still up with the leaders, retaining or recapturing its position in the van of progress in numerous fields. It had been slow to develop links with education and with modern industry and may thus have led to significant delays in some cases, but in these respects it was catching up rapidly in the years before the war. It was a not unworthy component of what was still the richest and most productive economy in Europe.

4

The Role of the State

I Assumptions in Britain and Abroad

Traditionally, very little is said in the historical literature about the role of the State in British economic growth, and less still is said of its role in its slow-down. Although there has in recent years been a growing awareness of the economic functions of the British State in the years since industrialization,[1] and references are not lacking to specific actions by the public authorities which might have affected one or other economic development, the tendency in the Anglo-Saxon literature has been to think of the State as a political force which had no business to try and influence the overall performance of the economy.

On the Continent they view these matters quite differently. While the Englishman, at any rate before 1914, will have demanded a good reason why the State should take any interest in any economic matter at all, the Frenchman and Prussian, just like the Austrian or Russian, will have required good reasons before agreeing that it should not.

The historians of Germany, to take the country with which comparison is made most often in these pages, find it difficult to write the modern story of their country, even its modern economic history, without frequent reference to the actions and opinions of the authorities, and with them, of the political constellations determining their stance. And indeed, while it may be possible to argue that the role of the German state in industrialization has been exaggerated[2] or even that it was negative, it is scarcely possible to argue that it was of no significant account at all.

Thus there seems to have been a rough correspondence between the historiographical tradition and the governing ideology and practice in each area. Where *laissez-faire* predominated in political philosophy and practice, historians have felt justified in ignoring the role of the State in the economy, whereas in the fortresses of *étatisme*, they have taken due account of its actions. Yet these neatly appropriate historiographical traditions may not do full justice to the complexities of real life. It may well be that, across the channel, the dominant philosophy exaggerated the actual functions of the State, and underrated the freedom

[1] Checkland (1983); MacDonagh (1977); also e.g. Aldcroft (1964–65), 133.
[2] Bowen (1950), 69–81.

and independence of the entrepreneurial classes, just as, on this side, it may have closed its eyes to the steady encroachment of authority on the free play of the capitalist market. Certainly, for the period 1870–1914, foreign observers have had no difficulty in registering a significant and active role for the political authorities in Britain in economic, and specifically in industrial life, which was not all that dissimilar from the continental experience.[3] Perhaps the time has come to re-examine the question of the influence of the State on economic life in Victorian Britain.

Our purpose here is much more limited than this. Here we are concerned merely with the question whether the policies pursued by the authorities contributed to the slowing down of economic growth, the loss of momentum and the falling behind in various fields of industrial technology in Great Britain.

At one time, the very formulation of the question in this form would have led to the raising of numerous eyebrows. Did not Britain form the classical example of a country where the bourgeoisie was in undisputed power, a country where, according to Engels as early as 1858,

> this most bourgeois of all nations is apparently aiming ultimately at the possession of a bourgeois aristocracy and a bourgeois proletariat as well as a bourgeoisie.[4]

How was it conceivable that a Government would act against the interests of the very classes which it represented?

We shall begin by examining this assumption and its ramifications. Who governed Britain in the later Victorian period? How large was the influence of industry over the economic policies of the British State?

II Political Power and Economic Policy to 1870

The traditional picture bears something like the following outline: the 'glorious Revolution' of 1688 led to dominance by the landed aristocracy, allied to city merchants and financiers, within British society. Their economic philosophy might be characterized as a form of Mercantilism, which, despite significant changes over time, was designed to benefit the two groups in power, the agrarians and the City. Their one-sided protectionism reached its zenith with the Corn Law of 1815 which protected the landlords at the expense of all consumers. Thereafter their control over policy was increasingly challenged by the manufacturers, whose growing economic power enabled them to press successfully for policies which would benefit them. The Reform Act of 1832 marked their political victory, and they achieved their goal of free trade, completely reversing the preceding economic policy, with the repeal of the Corn Laws in 1846 and of the Navigation Acts in 1849. Free trade was finally consolidated with the budget of 1860. To quote Engels once more, this time writing in 1892:

---

[3] Medick (1974).
[4] Engels to Marx, 7 October 1858, in Marx/Engels, *On Britain* (1954), 537.

The Reform Bill of 1831 had been the victory of the whole capitalist class over the landed aristocracy. The Repeal of the Corn Laws was the victory of the manufacturing capitalists not only over the landed aristocracy, but over those sections of capitalists, too, whose interests were more or less bound up with the landed interest – bankers, stock-jobbers, fundholders, etc. Free Trade meant the readjustment of the whole home and foreign, commercial and financial policy of England in accordance with the interests of the manufacturing capitalists – the class which now represented the nation.[5]

The allying in this passage of the City and of commerce with the landlords, rather than the manufacturers, is of interest, and we shall return to it. While Engels was by no means alone in his opinion that from the mid-nineteenth century, capitalist manufacturers dominated British society and determined its official policies, and in this respect may be said to have echoed the consensus of contemporaries, Marx and Engels were well aware that even in the second half of the nineteenth century, the bourgeoisie had by no means captured the formal centres of political power. Marx spoke of the 'antiquated compromise', in which the aristocracy ruled officially, while the bourgeoisie ruled 'over all the various spheres of civil society in reality', and Engels for his part noted that 'society became more and more bourgeois, while the political order remained feudal'. The reason for this was, he explained on another occasion, that

> The middle class of that time [1832] were as a rule, quite uneducated upstarts, and could not help leaving to the aristocracy those superior Government places where other qualifications were required than mere insular narrowness and insular conceit, seasoned by business sharpness.

Above all, it seems, the middle classes were ignorant of French, while Cabinet Ministers 'moved in a society where French was at least as necessary as English.'[6] This was difficult enough to reconcile with the Marxist assumption that political control derived from economic power; it was even more difficult to square with the facts. Recent research has challenged many of the certainties of the Victorians on this score, including those of Marx and Engels. The traditional account of the political role of the Victorian bourgeoisie, and of its industrial segment in particular, is in need of revision.

Let us return to the eighteenth century. There can be no doubt that it was indeed a period in which Mercantilist policies predominated, but it was Mercantilism with a difference. For one thing, in strong contrast to the absolutist States on the continent, which attempted to use that policy to foster manufacturing, in Britain a weak State was driven by its ruling agrarian and mercantile classes to support overseas trade and agriculture. What Cain and Hopkins have called 'the alliance . . . forged between the city, southern investors and the landed interest which was to play a leading role in Britain's overseas expansion',[7] favoured the kind of mercantilism, including a number of wars in which trading and colonial rivalry played a major part, and which Adam Smith attacked so persuasively.

[5] Preface to the new edition of F. Engels, *The Condition of the Working Class in England in 1844* (1968), XII.
[6] Quoted in Giddens (1974), 3, 8; also Mayer (1981), 131; Simon (1974), 279–80; Ingham (1984), 2–3, 16–17, 25–6, 83–8; Longstreth (1979), 158.
[7] Cain and Hopkins (1980), 496.

216

The voices of industry that were heard occasionally were largely those of the putting-out entrepreneurs, who were still merchants rather than manufacturers.

There were some measures which, indeed, conformed to the classical mercantilist pattern. One was the support of the woollen industry – but that was closely linked to agrarian interests. Another was the 'Board of Trustees for the Improvement of Fisheries and Manufactures', and the road building programme in the North – but both of these were confined to Scotland. There were import duties, but they were for revenue, to finance the wars of the period, not for protection, as is evident from the many export duties.[8] As far as the fate of the actual producer was concerned, it has been said with a great deal of justification, that at the time,

> most of the legislation which took note of the [entrepreneur] was designed to inhibit him rather than positively to help those who worked for him, not to speak of helping him. The significant difference between the industrial revolution in England and elsewhere in Europe was the indifference of central government, its failure for a long time to see any but undesirable consequences in what was happening – the ruin of agriculture.[9]

Yet it was among these politically insignificant small producers, emerging within the interstices of a society governed lightly but by people favouring privilege, monopoly and restrictionism, that the foundations were laid for the phase of economic expansion which has become known as the industrial revolution.

Did the hegemony of the old orders end in 1832? Was it true, as Engels put it, that the Reform Act represented the 'victory of the whole capitalist class over the landed aristocracy'? It was indeed the case that up to then, as the Birmingham Political Union complained in 1830.[10]

> The landed interest, the church, the law, the moneyed interest – all these have engrossed, as it were, the House of Commons into their own hands. . . . *But the interests of industry and trade have scarcely any representatives at all!* These, the most vital interests in the nation, the source of all its wealth and all its strength, are comparatively *unrepresented.*

Modern research has confirmed this accusation. Of 5,034 MPs of the period 1734–1832, there had only been 29 manufacturers – one half of one per cent. The maximum number in the House at any one time was 13, in a total of well over 600.[11]

But it would be quite wrong to assume that those who forced through the Reform Act were mainly concerned to remedy that particular imbalance. The motives which induced the unreformed house to vote out of existence the conditions under which it had been itself elected, were in fact mixed. As far as the Grey Ministry and its leading supporters are concerned, it seems most reasonable to summarize their varied and complex reasoning by supposing that they

[8] Davis (1966), 307; Schmoller (1899), 12; also Holland (1913), 9; Fielden (1969), 79.
[9] Nettl (1965), 23–4.
[10] Resolution of 25 January 1830, quoted in Read (1964), 86.
[11] Judd (1955) IV, 89, pp. 69–71.

wanted to avoid revolution by changing the 'modes of political action', but not the relative power of the different interests, and particularly not to increase the power of the urban middle classes as against the aristocracy.

Even the abolition of the rotten boroughs and their replacement by the larger real existing towns, looks only superficially like a strengthening of the influence of the urban bourgeoisie. Had that been the object, then the large cities would have been given much stronger representation compared with the smaller towns. Rather, the reform of the borough constituencies was designed at least as much to enhance the power of the higher nobility who controlled many of them, and remove large numbers of urban voters from the county register, helping the traditional county families to come into their own once more. The reform of the county constituencies, particularly by the Chandos clause, immensely strengthened the political influence of the landlords and reduced the power of urban capitalists to buy voters there. After the Act, many urban leaders retired from politics.[12]

Overall, then, the Act rather enhanced the power of the higher nobility, while changing only marginally the social composition of the House itself. In the House of Commons of 1833, some 246 members (nearly 40%) belonged to the higher aristocracy (baronets and above), while altogether 52.3% of members were concerned with the land, and 20.4% with commerce and finance, but only 5.0% with industry. In the Parliament that repealed the Corn Laws, there were in 1841, 45 industrialists (who had become 38 in 1847), plus 10 brewers and distillers (3), as against 495 landholders.[13] The one major change lay in the creation of blocks of middle-class voters in many boroughs who could, if they chose, exert pressure on their MP. In solidly industrial urban constituencies, as in the cotton districts of Lancashire, the industrial voters could even send their own men into Parliament.[14]

Bernard Cracroft no doubt exaggerated in the heat of the moment in 1867, when this phase was about to come to an end:

> So vast is their [sc. the aristocrats' and landowners'] traditional power, so broadly does it sit over the land, so deep and ancient are its roots, so multiplied and ramified everywhere are its tendrils, and creepers, and feelers, that the danger is never lest they should have too little, but always lest they should have too much power. . . . The 1832 Reform Bill . . . has left class ascendancy quite untouched. . . . Under any Reform Bill, the same classes who wield political power now will continue to wield it. . . . The parliamentary frame is kneaded together almost out of one class; it has the strength of a giant and the compactness of a dwarf.[15]

But the point he was making was a valid one. The wholesale transfer of political power from one class to another, postulated by Engels and others, simply did not take place. The middle classes, and *a fortiori* the industrial middle classes, had not been put in power by the Reform Act of 1832.

[12] Moore (1976), 229–40; and Moore (1961–62), and Moore (1966); Arnstein (1973), 215; Hill (1985), 226–230; Adelman (1984); Holland (1913), 57; Hanham (1968), 3, 11–13; Fry (1979), 111.
[13] Aydelotte (1962–63), 148; Greaves (1919), 176; Thomas (1929), 56–7; Thomas (1939), 4–7; Clark (1962), 294–7; Clark (1951), 7; Beckett (1986), 432–3.
[14] Howe (1984), 91, 112, 130–2; Fraser (1976), 180; Creenall (1974), 43.
[15] Quoted in Thompson (1984), 198.

It would be equally wrong to present the drive towards free trade as solely a middle-class movement. While the tariff reductions from the 1820s (and the easing of the export of machinery) were set in train by Tory Governments,[16] the impetus behind the repeal of the Corn Laws in 1846 has often been misrepresented.

Certainly, many industrialists pressed for repeal and many agrarians opposed it. It is equally true that the Irish famine provided the trigger, and that much dogma and doctrine was used by both sides to the debate. But recent research has revealed that voting on the Corn Laws in the House of Commons had little to do with economic interests;[17] that the Tory Prime Minister, Peel, as well as other leading agrarians saw the many benefits, even to their own interests, to be derived from free trade in corn; and that all were united in trying to alleviate the politically dangerous poverty arising from high grain prices.[18] The State subsidies and loans for drainage and improvements, which followed the repeal, make it clear that the large agrarian proprietors were still quite capable of looking after their interests in Parliament, and that they had in no way abdicated power to the industrial classes.[19]

Three years after the Corn Laws, the Navigation Acts were repealed, and five years later the restrictions on coastal navigation were removed; the budgets of 1852 and 1860 completed the free-trade edifice of Victorian Britain. Did free trade abroad also bring *laissez-faire*, the abdication of political action in favour of the market, at home? And if so, did this betoken the dominance of the manufacturing middle classes?

There is no doubt that many members of the industrial and commercial middle classes were opposed to the State and were urgently concerned to limit its actions. But it must be remembered that what they objected to, was not so much the State in the abstract, but their particular State, even though, like most interest groups, they found it easy to turn immediate concern into high principles.

For the contemporary State with which they were concerned was seen by them not as their State at all, but as a corrupt, expensive, parasitical organization of the landed and other privileged classes who were battening on the productive part of the nation. *Laissez-faire* principles found an echo among the middle classes precisely because they were not in control of the political power, distrusting, in Farnie's words, 'a landlord-dominated Government and [fearing] an inevitable administrative bias against the distant north.' 'Cobden's Liberalism', as Sontag averred correctly, 'took its rise in the needs of rising

---

[16] The highest rate of duty on the net imports was reached in 1821–25, at an average rate of 53.1%, or, omitting corn, of 53.6%. By 1836–40, this had fallen to 30.9%. Imlah (1958), 121; Hilton (1977), 109 ff, 173 ff; Brown (1958), 182 ff; Cordon (1979); Musson (1972b); Berg (1979), 36–7; Farnie (1979), 40, 42–3; Cain (1980), 18–20; Platt (1968), XXX–XXIV; Marrison (1983), 149; Hill (1985), 212–13.

[17] Clark (1951), 116; Aydelotte (1967b), 47–60; Aydelotte (1966), 95–114; Aydelotte (1972), 219–46; Thompson (1959), Spring (1953–4), 287–304; McCord (1968).

[18] Fay (1932), 196, 209; Fairlie (1965), 572; Gash (1965), 47–50; Gash (1979), 238; Walker-Smith (1933), 16, 39–40, 64; Moore (1965), 545–6; Moore (1976), 327–8; Chambers and Mingay (1966), 197, 157–8; Fairlie (1969); Vamlew (1980), 382–95; Thorold Rogers (1909), 43–4; Barnes (1965), 265; Hyde (1934), 28–47; Sill (1984); Ward (1971); Beckett (1968), ch. 7–9.

[19] Anderson (1964), 32; Cannadine (1977), 642 ff; Spring (1963), 149–54.

industrialism to free itself from the cramping bonds of a state which was the tool of the aristocracy.'[20]

This battle against corruption and parasitism which united many of the non-privileged middle, middling and working classes in a common political movement was not a battle against the social structure as such, but against particular political abuses. When it was won, which it largely was by the mid-century, the middle classes woke up to find that while they had cleared the way for *laissez-faire* in principle, a whole phalanx of new State powers had been raised up which were by no means always on their side. These powers were to continue to grow without interruption for the rest of the century.

The legislation establishing these powers had many and various origins. In numerous cases, social problems had arisen which cried out for political remedies, because the market did not provide any. In other cases, the selfish actions of a few did so much widespread harm to the many that they had to be curbed. In others still, traditional privileges had become wholly unacceptable. The new powers might be either coercive or enabling, and they might be exercised through the central authorities, through the local authorities or through *ad hoc* bodies created for special purposes. But in every case, they seemed to be set on a relentless path of growth. Cadres of officials and professionals were formed who had no difficulty in showing at each step that, to be effective, the legislation would have to be extended. Similarly, the wider public soon came to take each reform for granted and was ready to see it turned into a base from which to ask for something better.

Significantly, much of the new legislation went against the immediate interests of the middle classes, and especially the manufacturers. The attitude of Parliament seemed to be that industry had to be controlled rather than encouraged. Among the best-known examples were the Factory Acts beginning in 1833, the Mines Acts beginning in 1842 and the Chimney Sweep Acts, beginning in 1834: all three were continuously extended throughout the century, to form at its end a tight and complex system of protection to an extent which the early reformers could scarcely have envisaged. Then there were the Passenger Acts, to protect travellers at sea, and there was a growing body of legislation to limit the freedom of the railway companies, beginning in 1840, to protect passengers and merchants on land.

The Poor Law Amendment Act of 1834 was not compatible with a strict *laissez-faire* philosophy, and in the same vein there arose a large body of public health legislation, as well as Acts to prevent the adulteration of food in 1860, 1872 and 1875, and an Act establishing compulsory vaccination in 1853, strengthened in 1867. Income tax, resented by the middle classes, was reintroduced in 1842. The widening range of municipal enterprise also offended against the spirit of competitive private enterprise. The London police was established in 1829 and the Registrar General in 1836 in England and in 1854 in Scotland. In 1851 and 1875 there came legislation on working-class housing, in 1876 Plimsoll's Merchant Shipping Act, and the Government took over the electric telegraphs in 1869 and bought the Suez canal shares in 1875. Trade

[20] Sonntag (1938), 15 and quotations, 12; also MacDonagh (1977), 5, 17; Farnie (1979), 37; Boyson (1970), 85, 158, 207, 234; Eccleshall (1973), 191–2; Rubinstein (1983); Bourne (1986), 16–21.

Union Acts were passed in 1871 and 1875, and the Licensing Act in 1872. State action on education underwent a particularly interesting development from the minute subsidy of 1833 to the Act of 1870, when the public authorities created a means for filling the educational gaps in elementary education left by private institutions. Finally, from 1826 the Government began to interfere in the money supply, also playing the market to keep down the interest it paid on the public debt. The Bank Acts of 1833 and 1844 left monetary policy still in private hands, but tried, though as it turned out with indifferent success, to circumscribe the freedom and power of the Bank of England.[21]

The victory of *laissez-faire* was thus almost as circumscribed as the alleged hegemony of the middle classes. Besides, as we have seen, weak government was a tradition dating from the eighteenth century when it was maintained, if not actually introduced, by the landed aristocracy. It could therefore by no means be described as simply a plank of middle-class policy.

The question arises, and has often been asked, why the middle classes, and especially the industrial middle classes, failed to capture power on the basis of the growing economic superiority of the commercial and industrial sectors as against the agrarian, having made a first step in the reform programme of the 1830s. A number of answers have been given. Schumpeter wondering why 'the aristocratic element continued to rule the roost *right to the end of the period of intact and vital capitalism*' (his italics), thought that one major reason was that the bourgeoisie did not want to assume power. Moreover, he held it to be unheroic, lacking mystical glamour and burdened by too much rationalism to engage in popular politics. He also hinted that it was too weak on its own, always requiring protection or stiffening by some non-bourgeois group. Bagehot also considered the matter and came to the conclusion that merchants and manufacturers were

> a motley race. . . . Traders have no bond of union, no habit of intercourse; their wives, if they care for society, want to see not the wives of other such men, but 'better people', as they say – the wives of men certainly with land, and, if Heaven help, with the titles.

Another explanation focuses on the skill with which the upper classes used the elite educational institutions, above all the reformed public schools and the reformed ancient universities, managed to incorporate at least the leading sector of the middle classes into their system of values and their structure of social leadership. The latter, according to some, were only too eager for the aristocratic embrace, because they were afraid of the threat from below.[22]

There was also the argument that the middle classes lacked the leisure for parliamentary life and/or that they held the notion of politics as a party game,

[21] Checkland (1983), 67–9; Parris (1960), 17–37; Parris (1965), 13 ff; Perkin (1974), 439–43; Grove (1962), 14 ff; Paz (1980); Falkus (1977), 134–61; Davidson (1982), 159–83; Brebner (1948); Fry (1979); Dingle (1982); Bellini (1981), 60; Taylor (1977) stresses that the breaches in *laissez-faire*-principles were for social rather than economic reasons.
[22] Schumpeter (1979), 136–8; Camplin (1978), 19; quoting Bagehot; Arnstein (1973), 234–5; Perkin (1974), 365–6; Nairn (1977), 29–30. See also the interesting statement of a Lancashire manufacturer in Best (1971), 242; Cannon (178). Also chapter 3, esp. pp. 169–206, and notes 182–84 and 298 above.

open only to men not otherwise employed, while real decisions could always be influenced by *ad hoc* pressure groups and other tactics impinging on a pliable legislature. Yet another explanation, examined below, was that the ambitions of the middle classes were diverted successfully away from imperial politics into local government. There is some evidence to support each of these explanations. The argument which fits the developments in 1870–1914 best rests on the recognition, also supported by the sketch of events up to 1870, that it may be misleading to see in the 'middle classes' a single unified interest group: For an understanding of the political mechanism, they have to be divided into at least two separate groupings, the industrial sector, and the commercial-financial sector.

Before turning to examine this view further, it is worth while, to end this section, to pursue one of the more plausible current suggestions: namely that the provincial industrial middle classes were rendered harmless by being diverted into local politics. To test this hypothesis, it is necessary to begin by stressing that Britain at the time, unlike other countries and unlike Britain today, had no hierarchical structure of local government. Authorities were not subordinate and coordinated with each other, but existed side by side, sometimes overlapping, sometimes leaving gaps, with no obligation to consider each other, let alone to collaborate. In many cases not even central government could be considered to be hierarchically above them, though of course Parliament remained supreme as legislature. Much of this anarchy was the result of deliberate action or omission in the eighteenth century by the then ruling agrarian oligarchy.

As far as the towns were concerned, they were, at the beginning of the nineteenth century, administered in one of two ways. Most had no formal town government of any kind and were subject, inasmuch as they were subject to any authority at all, to the surviving manorial jurisdiction. There were also, secondly, numerous boroughs with chartered forms of self-government. The large majority of them had subsided into private fiefs exploited by corrupt, self-appointed and non-accountable oligarchies. These were, in fact, part of Old Corruption which was under attack in the first half of the century, and most of them were swept away by the Municipal Corporations Act of 1835, as part of the same set of reforms which also led to the electoral reform in 1832. The councils of small and non-existent boroughs were abolished by this Act; the governments of the larger towns were reformed in the sense of being made responsible to a legally defined body of electors; and large towns hitherto without government, which included many of the major new industrial centres and conurbations, could apply for incorporation on the same terms. In fact, to the original 178 boroughs, 22 new ones were added in this way by 1856, and over 60 by the late 1870s.

The franchise in the newly defined municipal corporations was based on households. Mostly this gave a somewhat larger electorate than the parliamentary franchise based on the £10 annual rating, but in some cases it turned out to be even more restricted. Moreover, ward boundaries, determining the balance of councillors and aldermen in the councils, were drawn in part not so much to equalize the number of voters as to equalize the rateable value. The richer wards were thus overrepresented. The upshot was that the voting strength lay with the lower middle class of shopkeepers, independent artisans and publicans, even in the mainly industrial boroughs. Factory and larger workshop owners, as well as the professional classes were well represented, but could never be more than a small minority. The working classes were once more largely without a vote, except where they merged into the independent artisan class, as in the metal districts of Birmingham, the West Midlands and Sheffield.

Borough politics in the nineteenth century have received a good deal of attention lately, but the interest has focused largely on two questions: the relationship of the political process in the towns to the national Party structure, and the struggle for supremacy within the towns between the lower middle class 'shopocracy' and the 'professionals'.[23] The first of these, the party political see-saw, is of limited interest in this context; we may learn something from the second.

In most towns the small artisans and shopkeepers, the earlier core of radicalism, came to be identified with parties and movements preaching 'economy' in municipal expenditure. Against them were ranged, not only the 'professionals' like doctors and borough engineers who stood to gain directly by higher expenditure, but also larger merchants and manufacturers with wider views, who were more concerned with public health and the provision of basic facilities and civic dignity for their towns. They also brought to Council affairs more business acumen, and greater experience in handling larger sums.[24]

The sequence in which these groups followed each other in the political control of the boroughs was not everywhere the same. Thus in Liverpool, an old borough ruled before Reform by a Tory-Anglican merchant oligarchy, there followed a brief Whig-Dissenter interval, but the former leading group was soon back in control, to be replaced after some years, from the early 1850s onwards, by the small tradesmen. In Leeds, another former Tory-Anglican stronghold, the same class remained in power at first, though the political complexion changed, but from the 1860s onwards the lower middle classes gained control until the 1890s, when the fortunes were reversed again. Similar developments may be traced in Bradford and in the North-East.

Birmingham, formerly unincorporated, showed a contrary development. It was a city in which skilled artisans were of some influence and made common cause with the small masters, helping a Liberal-Radical alliance to sweep into power in 1839. Thus the council became dominated by 'small tradesmen, shopkeepers and clerks' pursuing pettiness and 'economy', while it was shunned by the local elite. Only in the 1870 did the latter rouse itself under Chamberlain and other larger manufacturers to set in motion Birmingham's civic renaissance. The story of Sheffield was very similar. Early on the council, made up mostly of members of the lower middle classes, was economical, inactive and 'unattractive to the town's business elite'.

In 1864, the *Sheffield Independent* could write, in a rather uncharacteristic vein of snobbery:

[23] E.g. Fraser (1979); Garrad (1983), 45, 212–13.
[24] Fraser (1979), 139, 159 and Fraser (1976), 130; Smith (1982), 17 ff; Edsall (1973); 103–6; Bechhofer and Elliot (1976), 83; Hassan (1985), 541–2; Hennock (1973), 116–19; Checkland (1977), 14; Marshall (1940), 150–1.

The main reason for the degradation of the Council has been that the intellect and property of the town has stood aloof from it. . . . The Town Council has had no self-respect . . . there is now time for the men of intelligence and public spirit to lay their heads together and devise the means of making the Town Council equal to the new demands upon it.

The advice was not heeded at once, for in 1871 Mundella could still describe the Council membership as 'mean, petty and narrow in the extreme'[25] but broader views emerged some time later.

Who then were these two local class groupings, the 'shopocracy' and the elite 'professionals'? To some extent, they were both made up of the kind of local service trades possessed by all towns: among the lower middle classes, they included shopkeepers, publicans, cobblers and tailors, and small builders: among the elite, there were the larger wholesale merchants and the members of the professions who were about to emerge, after some struggle, as a recognized part of the upper middle classes: doctors, lawyers, perhaps also accountants, architects, apothecaries, music teachers, and owners of proprietary schools.

The line between them is not easy to draw, and it was shifting over time. Thus Zangerl, in his statistics on the distribution of urban JPs, included among the 'middle classes', the following: bankers, merchants, manufacturers, surgeons, solicitors, grocers and brewers. 'Others', above them, consisted of such as barristers and above, including judges, and physicians. Squires, gentlemen and clergy, incidentally, held the remainder of magistrates' appointments, 51.4% in 1841 and 23.9% in 1885.[26]

By most definitions the middle class would be made up of those who furnished the Radical impetus of the early years of the century, the class who worked but was distinguished from the workers by having some capital, and distinguished from the capitalists by having but very little of it. Its members were people who largely relied on local markets and local connections, and who generally had little to do with advanced technology. It has been observed that in the course of the century they shifted politically to the right, from Radicalism to Liberalism or even to Conservatism. While their hostility to the 'landlords' remained, it is ironic that many acquired small blocks of working-class housing property as 'safe' investments, and thus not only ended up by owning real estate, but also became what in popular parlance were called 'landlords' themselves.[27]

In addition to those supplying local markets among this group, as also among the elite, there were economic interests which varied according to the main occupations of the locality, being the suppliers of external markets. Thus in Liverpool and Bristol, the elite was one of overseas merchants. In the manufacturing parts of Lancashire the elite contained industrialists and in the coal districts of the North-East it contained coal masters, while Sheffield and Birmingham had large numbers of those who directly depended on local manufactures among their lower middle classes.

[25] These paragraphs are based largely on Hennock (1973), Fraser (1979) and L. Jones (1983); quotations from Fraser (1979), 96, 147, 148.

[26] Zangerl (1971), 115 and Table 4.3. below.

[27] Neale (1981), 135–6, 147–8; 174; Bechhofer and Elliot (1976); Nossiter (1975); Fraser (1976), 21–2.

Table 4.1 *Membership of councils (averages of years), in %.* *

	Salford			Bolton			Rochdale		
	1845–50	1866–70	1876–80	1843–45	1866–70	1876–80	1856–60	1866–70	1876–80
Manufacturers	53	37	39	51	43	37	55	45	51
Merchants	7	10	10	—	—	2	10	8	7
Shopkeepers, dealers	8	14	13	28	34	21	19	25	26
Builders, other bus	7	20	14	5	8	15	6	8	6
Total Business	75	81	76	84	85	75	91	86	90
'Gentlemen'	18	6	12	15	6	12	6	10	8
Professionals	6	13	12	1	8	13	3	4	3

* It is assumed that most 'merchants' are those connected with the local textile industries, and that the first two lines cover larger capitalists, and the next two, the smaller businesses. 'Gentlemen' are likely to have been, in part, retired wealthier businessmen. There was not, over the 25–35 years covered in any of the three towns, a single councillor outside the categories named.

In the larger cities none of these manufacturing groups was in a position to dominate the politics of its borough completely or continuously. In the smaller purely industrial towns, on the other hand, where they were numerically dominant (see Table 4.1), their power was constantly circumscribed by the County, especially by the magistrates and the police authority.[28] But even if we assume that the middle classes held power in the towns, that would still be a very limited field of political authority on the part of the industrial interests to compensate for the failure to share in the political power in the centre. If that was the bargain, it was a very poor one for the industrialists.

The countryside was governed in a manner very different from the towns. Until the 1880s, no breath or suggestion of any democratic influence was permitted there. It remained purely the preserve of the rule of the privileged landed and titled upper classes.

In an age which prided itself so frequently and volubly on its democratic progress, this survival of oligarchic hegemony is surely astonishing; but even more astonishing is the fact that it excited remarkably little comment or opposition at the time. Only in the 1870s, after the second Reform Act, did the demand for control of county government by the ratepayers become significant and ultimately irresistible.

Until then, the magistrates had been the effective local government in the counties as well as forming the judiciary. Magistrates, locally or in Quarter Session, had traditionally controlled the prisons, the asylums, the poor law, the roads, and they also had the task of maintaining public order. Even when new *ad hoc* authorities were created, like Poor Law Guardians and the Highway Boards, magistrates were *ex officio* represented. In due course, increasingly functional authorities came into being, especially in public health and education, which had a more democratic constitution. As for their legal powers,

28 That, indeed, is one of the major conclusions of Garrad's study (1983); Table 4.1. based on it pp. 14–20; Vincent (1968), 21; Nossiter (1975), 36 ff; Howe (1984), 116–17, 136 *passim*; Joyce (1980), 40, 209 ff and Table 4.3. below.

magistrates used them, as always, in line with their own sense of fairness: thus poachers and embezzlers of working materials could expect most severe treatment; those who violated the Factory Acts, in areas where manufacturers sat on the bench, could count on risible fines, at most.[29]

The magistrates were the 'County': By tradition, they were made up of aristocracy, gentry and other large landed proprietors, and clergy of the Established Church. They were appointed by the Lords Lieutenant, who saw to it that neither tradesmen nor dissenters were admitted to the county bench. It remained a unique, narrowly class-based centre of power for the ruling agrarian elite.[30]

Things changed somewhat after the 1830s. For one thing, a modest number of new Whig appointments were made: it is partly for that reason that the proportion of clerical appointees, almost all Tories, was reduced from that time onward.[31] For another, growing urban populations began to spill over into rural county territories, and leading merchants and manufacturers began to settle in large country houses, occasionally buying up estates from ancient families or mixing socially with others. In that case they had to be considered for appointment. This tendency was strengthened by the fact that it was the urban population which formed the growing sector that had to be provided with additional magistrates.

As a result, commercial and industrial magistrates were to be found in increasing numbers in the heavily urbanized or industrialized counties, like Lancashire, Cheshire, the West Riding or the Black Country.

The Black Country showed the following changes in the structure of the magistracy (in %):

Table 4.2 *The Black Country magistracy, 1836–60*

Appointees in years:	Before 1836	1836–48	1849–53	1854–60	Still in office in 1859
Gentry/Clergy	74.0	30.6	26	20.0	27.9
Trade	21.7	51.0	70	62.9	62.5
Professional	4.3	14.3	2	11.4	7.7
Unknown	—	4.1	2	5.7	1.9

Those in 'trade' were mainly coal and ironmasters, as well as merchants and bankers. Other manufacturers were hardly represented at all.[32]

Elsewhere, however, the county bench remained a stronghold of the landed classes and of the other privileged groups which were traditionally recruited from their families, such as clergy and military officers. Zangerl's figures of the social structure of the magistracy show the bias.[33]

---

[29] Brundage (1972), 27; Moir (1969), 143–8; Midwinter (1969).

[30] Armstrong (1973), 270; Nossiter (1975), *passim*; but see O'Gorman (1984).

[31] Zangerl (1971), 117–18; Philips (1975), 171; Quinault (1974), 185–7.

[32] Lee (1953), 7–16; Philips (1975), 166.

[33] Zangerl (1971), 115; also see Trainor (1982), 70–132; Joyce (1980), 6–7; Davie (1975), 9–14; Foster (1974).

Table 4.3 *Social composition of the magistracy, 1841–87*

% of magistrates		Aristo-cracy	Squire-archy	Gentle-men	Clergy	Total of these four	Middle classes	Others	N
Boroughs:	1841	0.0	45.0	5.7	0.7	51.4	43.4	5.2	730
	1885	0.0	11.6	12.1	0.2	23.9	71.5	4.6	1349
Counties:	1842	8.4	77.1	0.0	13.4	98.9	0.0	1.2	3090
	1887	6.2	68.1	0.0	5.3	79.6	14.9	5.4	2570

Something had changed between the 1840s and the 1880s, but it was changing very slowly in the counties.

It is perhaps worth noting that the City of London managed to preserve its privileged undemocratic constitution with, if anything, even greater tenacity than the rural counties. The result was that London's government had to remain chaotic and ineffective until the City had made sure that it would remain outside the newly constituted London County Council of 1888.

'The record of the City Corporation', wrote W.A. Robson, 'in delaying, obstructing of defeating legislation aimed at the reform of London government between 1835 and 1880 was one of unbroken success from their point of view.'[34]

It is perhaps equally worthy of comment that when the new County Councils were elected in 1888, much the same classes as before were found to be in control. In some counties, as many as one-half of the newly elected councillors were members of the magistracy who had ruled under the traditional constitution, and continued to hold power under the new.[35]

III Class and Power, 1870–1914

We may now turn to the period after 1870, the centre of our interest. At its beginning, as we have seen, the political control of the traditional landed elite was still unimpaired, and the influence of the manufacturing interest weak and uncertain. How was this constellation of power affected by the continuing decline of the economic contribution of agriculture to national economic welfare, and the continuing rise of the economic significance of the other sectors?

There is no doubt as to the decline of the economic role of the agrarian sector in those years, accelerated in the years of the Great Depression of 1873–96 which was not least an agricultural depression. In terms of the numbers employed, and the contribution to GNP, agriculture was becoming a relatively minor sector compared with manufacturing.[36]

[34] The violence, chicanery, deliberate lying propaganda and dirty 'tricks' employed by the gentlemen of the City to stave off (successfully) the bill of 1884 remind one uncannily of the methods of the Nixon administration at the time of Watergate. Robson (1948), 76–9; also Finer (1933).
[35] Arnstein (1973), 213; Moir (1969), 154.
[36] Matthews, Feinstein, Odling-Smee (1982), 222–3.

Table 4.4 *Shares of some major economic sectors, 1856–1913.*

	Agriculture, forestry fishing			Manufacturing		
	1856	1873	1913	1856	1873	1913
Share of output (constant prices)	18.4%	13.5%	6.4%	22.2%	24.6%	26.6%
Share of labour	29.6	21.4	11.5	32.5	33.5	32.1
Share of capital	19.1	15.4	6.2	12.9	14.6	18.5

Nevertheless, it was one of the most marked characteristics of the age that the leading role of the one, and the political weakness of the other, survived until 1914 and beyond, albeit with some modifications.

The landed classes, titled and with a firm territorial base, clearly still formed the very top of the social pyramid. Their social round was 'Society' *tout court*, their leisure activities were the envy and target for imitation of all the other classes, their employment, if any, was to occupy the top positions in the State and its institutions.

> 'The attitudes and values of . . . society', to quote Sir Henry Phelps Brown, 'had remained those of a society ruled by country gentlemen. Business men in the nineteenth century had not made much money and when they did, went out and bought land with it. The great fortunes were those of landowners and bankers.'

Indeed, the gentlemanly ideal, the ideal of those born to rule, experienced a new revival in this period, while the middle-class business ideal, though in some ways highly regarded, failed to acquire any social prestige.[37] Middle-class social climbing consisted of attempts to enter the ranks of the landed classes, to buy an estate and engage in the rustic pursuits of landed gentlemen, like hunting or sitting on county benches.[38] The reverse process was unthinkable: scions of noble families might wish to reap the monetary reward of entering commerce or industry, but there was always an element of condescension in so doing. Much the same phenomenon was observable in this period in the other advanced countries of Europe, including France, Belgium and Germany – not to mention Austria-Hungary and Russia:

> In most European countries the social and political pre-eminence of pre-industrial ruling groups continued even when their economic fortunes declined, and the subordinate social and political role of the 'middle classes' continued even when their economic fortunes rose.

Everywhere, State pomp and ceremonies were derived from, and upheld the standards of the traditional ruling classes. So did uniforms, titles and decorations. Emperors and kings were above all landowners and surrounded themselves with other landowners.[39] It follows that attempts to seek causes as well as

[37] Phelps Brown (1981), 252; Warwick (1985), 126–7; Heyck (1982), 21; Ingham (1984), 18–19; Lambert (1984), p. 234, note 59 below.
[38] Perkin (1974), 374; Joyce (1980), 28; Francis (1980), 4; Best (1971), 227, 243. Of course, social objectives may be as stong an incentive for active entrepreneurship as the profit motive: Payne (1974), 25–6. But see L. and J. Stone (1986).
[39] Bendix (1970), 302; Mayer (1981), 21, 80, 95, 136 ff; Schumpeter (1951), 122–3; Clark (1984), 140–7; McCagg (1972); but see Ingham (1984), 134.

consequences of this survival in purely British social constellations are *ab initio* implausible.

In England, the public schools as powerful agents for the absorption by the business elite of aristocratic patterns of thought, may well have been influenced in their peculiar characteristics by the existence of a vast Empire and the need to administer it, as far as its higher echelons were concerned, by members of the landed aristocracy.[40] To that extent the British process of social climbing on the part of the middle classes had some distinctive features. But social climbing itself was a universal European phenomenon.

It is true that the Liberal revival of the 1870s and the decades which followed saw several sustained onslaughts on many of the privileges of the landed classes. The Act of 1884, giving the vote to the rural workers, and the Act of 1888, creating elected County Councils, together with the Act of 1894 establishing Rural District and Parish Councils, destroyed the political hegemony of the landowner in the counties. Harcourt's inheritance tax of 1894 and Lloyd George's 'People's Budget' of 1909 affected the inheritance of his property. The Ground Game Act of 1880 gave tenants the right to get rid of hares and rabbits. Tenants were strengthened against their landlords by the Acts of 1875, 1882 and 1883 in Britain, 1886, 1897 and 1911 in the crofting counties in Scotland, and 1870, 1881 and 1885 in Ireland. Finally, the Allotment Act of 1889 and the Smallholding Acts of 1892, 1907 and 1908 also improved the bargaining position of the rural labourer and smallholder.[41]

Yet none of these was proof of a strengthening of the industrialist's political position *vis-à-vis* the landlords. On the contrary, they were a reflection of the shift of power within the Liberal Party away from the privileged of all sectors and towards the lower middle and working classes.

Nor must it be assumed that even economically, the land was played out. The value of land had risen until the 1870s. Thereafter there was still a further rise in the price of urban and mineral land, and in land required by the railways, though a severe fall in the value of land let for arable farming. Above all, a main characteristic of landed property was its immense concentration, a concentration linked to title and status. Thus in 1873, some 7,000 persons owned 80% of all privately owned land in the United Kingdom; the 525 peers owned 15 million acres, the 28 dukes alone 1.5 million acres. Even in 1914, 4,000 owners held 50% of all privately owned land. 1,500 of the nobility and gentry held an average of 8,000 acres each, equalling 40% of the total.[42] The leading landowners were thus immensely rich by contemporary standards, and especially by the standards of the industrialists. Perhaps even more significantly, the wealthy individuals outside the landed classes were to be found in London, in commerce and finance, rather than in the industrial provinces, in manufacturing. W.D. Rubinstein's recent painstaking work showed that, within the highest class of the 124 millionaires who died between 1880 and 1914, no fewer than 61, or just under half, came from London; of the 311 half-millionaires, it

---

[40] Warwick (1985), 123; Mayer (1981), 258–9; Armstrong (1973), 111; and see notes 52 and 58 below and chapter 3, p. 206, note 298 and this chapter note 22 above.

[41] Checkland (1983), 186 ff; Soldon (1974), 209; Orwin and Whetham (1971), 289–96.

[42] Bateman (1883); Lindert (1983); Offer (1981), 102–3; Cannadine (1977b), 77–9; Rubinstein (1986), 69–70, 90; Richards (1979), 45–6.

was 127, still 41%. By contrast, Greater Manchester, West and South Yorkshire and the West Midlands, with a very much larger population between them, furnished only 12 millionaires and 53 half-millionaires. Commercial cities like Liverpool, Glasgow and Bristol had significantly more wealthy men than the manufacturing centres.

The same structure emerges when we classify the richest estates (all of which exclude landed wealth) by the economic sector in which the fortune had been acquired. Sixty-one of the known 132 cases of millionaires were in finance and commerce, 28 in food, drink and tobacco (mostly the brewers), but only 42 in all other industries put together. Similarly with half-millionaires, 157 were in commerce, only 119 in all manufacturing, of which 45 in food, drink and tobacco. If we go down in wealth and income into lower levels, the predominance of finance and commerce – together with the land – remains. Industry was simply overshadowed by them. The total profits gained in cotton spinning and weaving, the Chancellor of the Exchequer reported in his budget speech in 1892, were less than the earnings of the medical profession; all of coal mining gained less than the legal profession. All productive industry together, including brewing and distilling, made less surplus than distribution.[43]

Other data confirm the impression conveyed by these figures that the manufacturing sector, in spite of its overwhelmingly important contribution to output and employment, lacked financial power compared with the City.[44] It was even more deficient in political punch. Overseas merchant houses and the segment of the banking world connected with them, mostly in London, had kept the foothold in the political and social hierarchy which they had gained in the eighteenth century. As the political and economic power of the landlords began to be undermined in the last two or three decades of the nineteenth century, it was in the first instance the 'City', and not the provincial industrialists, who filled the gap. 'There has never been any real doubt about the position of the banking community at the top of the social hierarchy [in 1890–1914]'.[45]

This is evident not least in the top echelons of the political world. Of the 111 landowners with over 50,000 acres, 59 sat in the House of Commons in 1868. In the House of 1865, 325 members were connected with the aristocracy and a further 100 with the land. In 1880, 170 MPs were the sons of peers and baronets, and as late as 1885, some 60 families supplied one-third of the members of Parliament, as they had done for generations. Of the 670 members in 1895, 420 were gentlemen of leisure, country squires, retired army officers and barristers. The House of 1897 contained 149 aristocrats and that of 1905, still 139. Measured differently, of the MPs of 1900, 23% had interests in finance and commerce and 15½% in the land, together 38½%, while the whole of the manufacturing and mining sector, including brewing, could muster only 16.3%.[46] In the Liberal landslide parliament of 1906 almost half the members

[43] Rubinstein (1977a), 605–10; 615–18; Rubinstein (1981), 61 ff, 182–5; Rubinstein (1977b) 111; Hansard, 1892, vol. 3 Goschen, 11 April 1892, cols. 1163–4.
[44] Harris and Thane (1984) 215 and the literature cited there.
[45] Cassis (1985), 212, also Ingham (1984), 9–10, 26–8; Escott (1973), 14, 113; Longstreth (1979), 160–1. A contrary view is put forward by Chapman (1986).

were connected with finance and insurance, one-fifth were landowners.

The differences were greater still in the elevation to the peerage, which represented the very peak of the social elite, not to mention a vote in the House of Lords. The House of Lords was politically still a most active body, blocking among other measures a whole range of progressive social legislation and legislation relating to Ireland, and exercising its veto over the ending of religious discrimination in Oxford, Cambridge and in the House of Commons.

Between 1837 and 1885, the heyday of the industrial revolution and after, a total of 241 new peerages were created. Practically all of these were landed or had connections with the land. Only seven new peers had mainly commercial or industrial interests without being of noble or gentle origin: three were bankers, three were merchants and there was one solitary industrialist, Edward Strutt. Thereafter, things changed somewhat. Whereas in the 10 years to 1886, there had been only 4 peerages for men of commerce and industry, in the 10 years following there were 18; there were similar changes in knighthoods and baronetcies. In 1886 itself there were no fewer than three new peerages for industrialists: two inevitable brewers (wits spoke of the 'beerage') and one iron-master, who had already been a baronet. Of the 570 members of the House of Lords of 1911, only 35 came from commerce and industry without any landed connections, and most of them were made barons only, the lowest rank. By another count, there were 147 landowners in the House of Lords in 1909, 35 bankers and 35 railway directors as against 39 'captains of industry'. Of the 1,700 knights in 1914, only 3.6% came from business. Within the 'business' group, the industrialists, in turn, formed a minority.[47]

Finally, the political *crème de la crème*, the members of the Cabinet. Selection here reflected not only family connections, but also schools and universities, political weight and service to the party. In the cabinets of 1885–1900, 43% of the membership consisted of peers, 21% of lesser aristocrats and 36% of commoners, many of whom, however, were related to the peerage: these proportions were not very different from those relating to the cabinets of 1830–1900 where the ratios were 47%, 24%, 29%. The Cabinet of 1895 of Lord Salisbury who 'detested the new plutocracy of industrial and financial wealth'[48] contained nine members of the House of Lords and 10 from the House of Commons, of whom nine were baronets, squires or were related to the peerage. Joseph Chamberlain, the Birmingham manufacturer and would-be tariff reformer, was indeed the odd man out. Of all the 101 cabinet ministers of 1886–1916, 47 were landowning, 32 had a legal and professional background, 3 were miscellaneous, and only 12 came from commerce, finance and industry. The first prime minister not from a landed family was H.H. Asquith in 1908.[49]

[46] Thomas (1939), 14–17; Raybould (1973), 432–3; Arnstein (1973), 212; Camplin (1978), 18–19, 114, 128; Guttsman (1974), 35; Best (1971), 240; Vaughan (1984), 6; Bernstein (1986), 14; Turner (1984), 3–6; Barker (1901), 268. The loss of time involved kept even the more successful manufacturers from entering Parliament: Boyson (1970), 236–7. 'Fortunes' were usually required before businessmen could enter Parliament; e.g. "Fortunes made in business" (1884–87 3 vols.) I, 113, 122–7, 437, III, 30, 210, 275, 429, 438.

[47] Pumphrey (1959); Thomas (1972); Greaves (1929); Hanham (1959–60), 278.

[48] Checkland (1983), 161.

[49] Guttsman (1951), 130; Arnstein (1973), 209–11, 221 ff.

These figures indicate the need to separate out the commercial and financial interests, the 'City', from manufacturing industry. There had been in the later nineteenth century a shift in the social structure of the two main political parties, symbolized by the split in the Liberal Party in 1886 over Gladstone's Irish policies. Whereas originally the Tory Party could be associated with the land and the Church of England, particularly the High Church, the Whigs contained, beside the more liberally-minded landowners, the Dissenters and the Low Churchmen, also most of the commercial classes. But by the 1880s there was a migration of virtually all the leaders of commerce and finance into the Conservative Party,[50] leaving the Liberals to represent increasingly the lower and less privileged orders.

But within Toryism it was high finance, together with commerce, rather than manufacturing industry, which now joined the landed interest as the dominant influence. While the City increasingly merged with the nobility and its agrarian base, industry continued to find not only the official, but also most of the unofficial channels of power closed to it. It was therefore not entirely surprising that some of the industrial leaders repeatedly flirted with the Labour Party, or looked for a producers' alliance with their workers against the rule by finance and landed nobility.[51] Only the brewers and distillers, because of their particular link with the land, seemed to enjoy easy access to the charmed circle of the social as well as the political elite.

One point of interaction, as noted above, was the public school, in which the boys originating from the commercial and financial world not only imbibed the manners and the world outlook of the landed classes, but also made friends and established personal contacts which eased the two-way traffic later. A recent study of the leading bankers of the period 1890–1914 found that of those whose educational background was known, 63% had been to public schools (44% of the whole sample, including those unknown), and 53% (37%) had been to Oxford or Cambridge. Of those who went to Public Schools, 45% went to Eton, 26% to Harrow and many of the remaining 29% to other top schools such as Rugby. The proportions were particularly high for private bankers, merchant bankers and directors of the Bank of England – often the same people. Especially significant was the recent rise in those proportions.[52]

Table 4.5 *Bankers' education, nineteenth century*

Age cohorts, Dates of birth	Attendance at Public School and/or Oxford or Cambridge (%)		
	Merchant bankers	Merchants	All bankers
1800–20	0	0	10
1821–40	30	34	44
1841–60	48	39	52
1961–80	69	66	72

It is intriguing to note that the same educational privilege helped to turn one of the superficially most bourgeois of reforms, the opening of the higher Civil

[50] Ensor (1949).
[51] Davenport-Hines (1984), 56, 62–3, 73.
[52] Cassis (1984), 109, 122. Also Lisle-Williams (1984), 346.

Service between 1855 and 1870 to entry by merit tested by examination, into its opposite. For the Civil Service Examinations, with their emphasis on the Classics, on Pure Mathematics and similar subjects, favoured, as indeed they were meant to do, those who had been expensively educated for a life of leisure rather than for a productive life, and this bias was increased by the personal interviewing of candidates which favoured those with the right social background. As late as 1905–14, 75% of the 283 entrants to the administrative class of the Civil Service came from the nine Clarendon public schools, an even higher proportion of them having Oxford or Cambridge degrees. Of those in the higher positions in the Civil Service above the rank of Assistant Secretary in 1929, no fewer than 68.2% came from families in which the father belonged to the landed classes, the army, the professions or the civil service itself; sons of manufacturers and of manufacturing managers numbered only 6.5%.[53]

Among other forms of interpenetration the intermarriages between the nobility and the City have often been remarked upon.[54] There was also the aristocratic lifestyle of the landed proprietor, which was now adopted by the 'Squires of Change Alley', the successful bankers or City merchants. Beside a luxurious city establishment they bought country houses and country estates; engaged in hunting, opened local events and gave generously to local charities; accepted local honours and duties; belonged to the best London Clubs; had their daughters 'coming out' in London and ultimately also achieved honorary court appointments.

By the end of our period, merchant bankers were given not only baronetcies and peerages, but also occupied positions of High Sheriff, Lord Lieutenant or Deputy Lord Lieutenant of counties – among the last bastions of privilege of the landed elite.[55]

Interpenetration occurred also in business relationships. Because of their territorial interests, landed proprietors were naturally found on the boards of railway and mining companies, and in 1896, 167 noblemen, over one quarter of the peerage, held company directorships. If the younger sons of landed families had to earn a living outside the traditional fields of the Church and the Army, they chose the City as the most gentlemanly occupation – and no doubt, as needing the least practical knowledge and requiring the least number of hours attending to business. They lost a great deal less caste thereby than if they had entered, say, the offices of a rolling mill or a cotton spinning enterprise. Conversely, boys from industrialists' homes learnt very quickly that to rise in the world meant to leave the realm of production and enter that of the professions, of trade or finance. 'City institutions monopolized the outstanding talents and energies of the business class'. The social and personal interlinking of City firms and the superior 'independent professional status in the city' meant, further, that 'in this whole financial structure of the City there was no place for industry'. Indeed, the ease with which the land could raise capital on

[53] Kelsall (1955), 139, 150–1; Black (1970); Hughes (1949), 72; Hart (1972); Barnett (1972), 41–3; Anderson (1974), 262–88; Bourne (1986), 31–40.
[54] Cassis (1984), 243 and Cassis (1985c), 217 ff; Lisle-Williams, (1984b), 337, 353–4; Offer (1981), 94 ff; Rubinstein (1974), 195, 203; Thompson (1963), 60 ff.
[55] Lisle-Williams (1984) *passim* and Lisle-Williams (1984a), 256; Camplin (1978), 87 ff; Davenport-Hines (1984), 71; Spring (1951), 12.

mortgage, and the 'intimate connection between land and social position . . . may have retarded industrial capital mobilization'.[56]

There was also a geographical dimension to this power structure. In contrast to the poorly provided north-western half of England, together with Scotland and Wales, the Britain of the Industrial Revolution, it was the South-East which had the cathedrals, the public schools, the country houses, and the permanent conservative majorities, then as now.[57] Towards the end of our period, as if to underline the switch from land to finance, the outstanding regional change was the growth of London,[58] whether measured in population, income tax returns or employment. London, among its other attractions, became the location of the head offices of firms as well as of pressure groups.

Exactly there lay one of the weaknesses of the manufacturing sector. For while the banks and the merchant firms could exert their influence and make their wishes known in numerous informal discussions, almost within the family, the manufacturers from the provinces found it hard, with some exceptions, to have any social contacts even with the local landed elites, let alone the centres of national power in the capital. Significantly, there never was a Department, or Ministry, for Industry or Manufacture.

This isolation from the power base was due not least to the same public schools and the ancient universities which had helped the consolidate the ruling landed/financial elite. Their glorification of upper-class values could not tolerate the recognition of skill and technical competence as signs of superiority. From the point of view of their own ethos, as well as from the point of view of the future careers of their charges, they had to be determinedly anti-industrial. They did not, as Hobsbawm stressed correctly, 'discourage money making, only technological and scientific professionalism'. Conversely, against this, the British 'bourgeoisie of manufacture and trade . . . never developed an educational project of its own.' 'The weight of the homogeneous British elite formed *after* industrialization was simply too strong for the entrepreneurs to be able to resist the aristocratic bias of the new education.'[59] Manufacture lacked not only power but prestige.

This weakness was aggravated by the scattered locations and the divergent interests of productive industry, compared with the concentrated and single-minded representations of the City where, in addition, a Central Association of Bankers, replacing earlier specialist organizations, was formed in 1895. A National Chamber of Trade had been set up as early as 1881, but the local Chambers of Commerce had mixed memberships and were mostly concerned with local affairs. Unlike its German counterpart, industry proper found it extremely difficult to organize on a national level, with the exception of employers' organizations, of which there were some 1,200 in 1914, to counteract the trade unions. An Employers' (or British) Parliamentary Council was set

[56] Read (1979), 30; Perkin (1974), 435; Armstrong (1973), 111; Cassis (1985c), 226; Davis (1966), 261; Cain (1985), 15; Ingham (1984), 134–6, 151, 230; Nairn (1977), 23; Warwick (1985), 116; also see p. 232 and Table 4.5. above.
[57] Rubinstein (1986), 105–7; Rubinstein (1974), 102ff; Thompson (1963), 30;
[58] Lee (1980), 254–74.
[59] Mayer (1981), 257; Armstrong (1973), 144–5; Hobsbawm (1968), 185; and see p. 228, note 37 above.

up in 1898 to monitor and act on bills relating to trade, freedom of contract, labour and similar issues, but most businesses stayed aloof. Dudley Docker's 'Business League' operated essentially in the Midlands only, while Sir Charles Macara's Employers' Parliamentary Association of 1912 was dominated by Lancashire free traders. The manufacturers' national organization, the FBI was not set up until 1916, to meet demands made by war conditions, and then it remained weak, because divided over the issue of protection, for at least another 20 years.[60] It seemed as though the manufacturers themselves accepted that it was not their place to try and exert a unified influence on the decisions of the British Government and its agencies. The voices of complaint seemed to be crying in the wilderness:

> The industrial interests, the interests of the humble toiler who produces wealth, have been sacrificed to all other interests. The financiers, the minor capitalists, the bankers, the merchants, the international traders, all have been admitted to a voice in the direct government of the country before any of the industrial class were admitted to its secret councils. That is the reason for the decay of British industry.

Consequently, British economic policy 'roughly corresponded with the general interest of the City of London, often apparently at the expense of industry when these interests came into conflict'.

> The City has . . . largely set the parameter of economic policy and its interests have generally predominated since the late nineteenth century.[61]

The following section will make an attempt to investigate this charge.

IV Policies on Industry, 1870–1914

The country, as we have seen, entered the period 1870–1914 with a tradition of minimal positive action in aid of British manufacturing but much to hamper it. Members of Government, of Parliament and of other ruling elites had little or no contact with industry, little interest in it and little regard for it, while manufacturers, in their turn, had only very limited access to the centres of power and were unable to form organizations to improve that position. None of this means that British policies would necessarily be hostile or detrimental to manufacturing industry; it merely opens out the possibility that they might be. How, in fact, did the 'State' act towards industry in this period? Did it have a share in the responsibility for the slowing down of industrial growth in Britain in the decades before World War I?

The economic crisis years of the 1870s brought it home to Britain for the first time that she was no longer without rivals, and that at least two powerful new industrial nations, Germany and the United States, were likely to catch up and ultimately even overtake her. In the following decades, contemporaries noted

[60] Redford *et al.* (1934) I, 125; Cassis (1985b), 118–19; Davenport-Hines (1984), 70–1, 104–17; Holland (1981), 287–300; Grant and Marsh (1977), 19–20; Garside and Gospel (1982), 104; Yarmie (1980); Kaelble (1967); Turner (1984), 33–49; Zeitlin (1987), 176.
[61] 'Artifex and Opifex' (1907) quoted in Hoffman (1964), 98. Also see Barker (1901), 797.

that Britain was losing one market after another, and that in certain crude tonnage measures, such as the output of iron and steel, she was falling behind the other two countries. A substantial literature,[62] underlined by periodic panicking in the press, bears witness to the widespread concern over these developments. Governments could therefore not plead ignorance of the relative weakening of the manufacturing sector of the economy and above all its export branches. Even if it is granted that an industrial nation which dominates every market needs no Government aid, under the new more adverse conditions it might have been expected that Government would take some initiatives in favour of British industry. The record shows that that expectation would have been misplaced.

Most other countries, including Germany in 1879, reacted to the deep depression by reimposing or heightening their tariff barriers. In Britain, similar policies were advocated in the 1880s by the industries most affected – Bradford woollens, Sheffield steel goods, silk – and by the members of Parliament representing the constituencies in which they were located, but their pleas fell on deaf ears. Free trade suited not only most other industries, but also the commercial and financial world of the City. Moreover, the agitation came at an awkward time for the Conservative Party, the natural home for protectionists, since it was just then about to seek common ground with the Liberal Unionists who would certainly oppose any deviation from the free-trade path.[63] The report of a Royal Commission on the depression, published in 1886, did not envisage any major new initiatives on the part of the State. Smoothing the peaks and troughs of the trade cycle was not, in the current view, one of the tasks of a British government. One sentence of its final Report is worth repeating: complaints, it averred, came mainly from

> those who may be said to represent the producer . . . especially from the employer of labour. On the other hand, those classes of the population who derive their income from foreign investments or from property not directly connected with productive industries, appear to have little ground for complaint: on the contrary, they have profited, by the remarkably low prices of many commodities.[64]

The distinction between these two groups was perceptively made, but the very form in which it was couched leaves no room for doubt whose interests the Commission thought to be the more significant. This disregard of the producer is an attitude that would not have been found in any other contemporary industrial country. Everywhere else in Europe, the bourgeoisie took its cue from its productive sections, to make common cause with the older agrarian ruling

[62] Cassis (1985c), 210, 228; Longstreth (1979), 161; A. Mayer (1981), 93; Cain and Hopkins (1986); Cain and Hopkins (1987); Cain (1985), 9, 16; Hoffman (1964); Williamson (1894); McKenzie (1902); Williams (1896); Shadwell (1906). Some early warnings came even before the collapse of 1873. In 1870, Sir Edward Sullivan complained, that free trade had benefited only those on fixed pensions and annuities, 'it has been a source of wealth to the commercial class, the bankers, brokers, merchants and shipowners . . . it has caused great depression, and threatened absolute ruin, in many of our industries, to the operatives, the small householders and tradesmen of the manufacturing districts', in: Sullivan (1870), 44.
[63] Brown (1943); Lord Penzance (1886); Zebel (1940), 161–85; Kennedy (1980), 52–3; Jennings (1881), 271–306; Sigsworth and Blackman (1968); Sigsworth (1958) 105–6.
[64] R.C. (1886) XXIII,C.4893, p. XI, also XXXIV, XLIV to LXVII.

circles in erecting tariff barriers that would protect both. In Britain, it is notable that even in their heyday the Fair Traders had argued for protection not as a principle but merely as a method of dealing with particular temporary losses and, as their coy name implied, as a means of retaliation in order to force others back onto a more liberal path.

If protection had no chance in Britain, neither had bimetallism, and for much the same reasons. The argument regarding a bi-metallic base for the currency, which is now all but forgotten, became a major issue of economic policy debate in the last quarter of the nineteenth century. Much of it was technical, but it was not too difficult to discern the economic interests which stood behind the two opposing points of view.

The key to the debate is to be sought in the fact that France, whose bi-metallic system had hitherto kept the relative prices of gold and silver stable, had been forced to abandon it in 1873. There followed a rapid fall in the price of silver in terms of gold, accompanied by a general tendency of prices to fall. Some thought that the rising value of gold was caused, at least in part, by the decision of several countries, notably Germany, the USA, the Netherlands, Japan, Norway and Sweden, to change to a gold standard between 1867 and 1874. It was not too difficult to argue that as a result, there was a relative 'scarcity' of gold in the world which drove prices in gold-standard countries down and caused depression and unemployment in industry.

Both evils, it was argued, could be remedied by an agreement of the major nations, including Britain, to use both gold and silver, in a fixed ratio to each other, as backing for their currencies. This would increase the quantity of monetized metal and thus raise prices, as well as ending the uncertainties of the rates of exchange between currencies based on gold and those based on silver.

Assuming that these causes and effects really operated (which was widely denied then and is considered unlikely now) it was the producers, above all the manufacturers, who wanted to change to a bi-metallic base in order to bring about reflationary conditions:

> 'The factory owner, the mine-owner, the ship-owner,' declared Samuel Smith, a bi-metallist Member of Parliament, 'who thought it safe 20 years ago to borrow half the value of his plant in order to find active capital for his business, now finds that the mortgagee is virtual owner.'

The active class, he alleged, was being robbed in favour of the 'lending capitalist' class. Fluctuating gold and silver exchange rates, echoed Sir W.H. Houldsworth, MP, in a memorable three-day debate in the Manchester Chamber of Commerce in April–May 1892 which ended in a narrow vote of 164:156 for bimetallism, harmed the producers and consumers, but far less the bankers, merchants and middlemen:

> The merchant can sometimes, as it were, jump from ledge to ledge while the earthquake is going on, while the producer has to stand where he is, and face the catastrophe as best he can.

Only those who did not suffer but profited by the ruin of their neighbours, Lombard Street, 'a few antiquated banks scattered up and down the country', and Mr Gladstone, he added, were opposed to bimetallism.

Robert Barclay, supporting him, commented that

> the merchants can make profits with declining markets as well as with advancing markets. And so it is not so much a merchants' question as a manufacturers' question in this city. It is the industries of the country that we hold have suffered . . . but if we go to London, on the Stock Exchange, all industries are very much counters in the estimation of those who deal in them. A mine in Spain or a mill in Russia is the same thing for a speculator as a mine in England or a mill in Lancashire.

The issue, thought Isaac Hoyle, MP, was one of 'merchants and distributors' versus 'producers'.[65]

Those who opposed the bimetallist proposals occasionally made use of the argument that falling prices benefited the working classes, since money wages tended to fall more slowly than prices, so that real wages rose: this argument also weighed heavily with Alfred Marshall. Any possible advantage of bimetallism, stated a *Memorial of Certain Merchants and Bankers of the City of London Against Monetary Reform* in 1895, 'would be at the expense of all those who invest, of all who save, and of all who earn wages'. It was not difficult to discern, however, that these particular memorialists were more troubled by the first two groups than by the third. London, as the financial hub of the world, depended 'in great manner' according to the Gold and Silver Commission, on the certainty that debts would be discharged in a known metal. Indeed, it was argued that as a creditor nation Britain stood to gain by falling prices. To this was added the convenient Liberal argument that it was not the job of the Government to regulate the currency in the first place.[66]

With the forces ranged against each other in this manner, industry versus finance, there was of course no doubt as to the line which the British Government would take. Bimetallism was never seriously considered; British opposition killed whatever chance the scheme might have had by international agreement in 1891; and Harcourt had no difficulty in rejecting in 1892 the request from Lancashire for bimetallism with the same contempt with which he rejected any request for protection.[67]

By the turn of the century, most of the advanced world, including Germany and the United States, experienced rapid economic expansion. In Britain alone, economic growth in general and industrial growth in particular, far from accelerating, came to a virtual standstill for a while. The problems of British industry were evidently more serious than had been thought in the 1880s. Many more industries were affected by foreign competition, and the protectionist campaign in consequence received more powerful support. It did, in fact, become a major political issue in Britain between 1903 and the General

[65] Smith (1887), 90–1; Triffin (1964), 17–19; Manchester Chamber of Commerce (1892), 6–8, 17, 35–6, 73; R.C. (1888), XLV,C.5512; Final Report par. 95 ff, part III, paras. 12 ff, 20–6. 41–2; First Report R.C. (1887), XXII,C.5099, Ev., Barclay, QQ.2230 ff, Titman, QQ.2834–6, Gibbs, QQ.3092–3; Prof. Nicholson, QQ.4028 ff, Smith *passim*.
[66] Bimetallic League (1895), 1; R.C. (1888), XLV,C.5248. Evidence, Raphael, Q.6918, Fielden, Q.7612; Final Report par. 1444, Comber, QQ.6374 and 8200 and Appendix 222, Letter by Rothschild, R.C. (1888a) evid., Marshall, Q.9751; Giffen (1899); Cassis (1985b), 121; Sir Ernest Cassel the financier, was a bimetallist – but then he had interests in silver-producing countries. Thane (1986), 89.
[67] Harris and Thane (1984), 223. For a theoretical survey see Chen (1972), 89–112.

Election of 1906, and the dominant issue within the Conservative Party in those years.

That the protectionist drive took on such a predominantly political dimension was due largely to one man, Joseph Chamberlain, the Colonial Secretary. At the time of entering upon his office in 1895 he had felt his way forward to some form of imperial customs union, but in 1903 this was changed to a demand for 'Tariff Reform' which was to combine protection for British industry with imperial preference and a strengthening of economic links within the Empire. The core proposal was a general tariff of 10% or perhaps even 20% on imports into Britain.

This programme met with a mixed response within the Conservative Party, and Chamberlain had to resign from the Cabinet in order to be free to engage in agitation for its acceptance. The battle for Tariff Reform had several distinct, though interconnected aspects. First, the conflict over policy, inevitably, became overlaid by personal antagonisms and, in the end, by a battle for the control of the Party, between Chamberlain, fighting for protection, the Duke of Devonshire, representing both the Whig and the free-trade Liberal Unionist elements in Conservatism, and Balfour, the party leader, who wavered along a central path between the two extreme positions in an effort to hold the party together.

As Chamberlain took his campaign into the country to woo the electorate in a series of mass rallies, backed by the powerful propaganda campaign of his Tariff Reform League, the programme had, secondly, to be elaborated into specific measures and promises for different sections of the electorate, including the working classes and the farming community. This has tended to hide the basic direction of the tariff reform programme behind a screen of political opportunism and electoral calculation.

In the literature, thirdly, the tariff reform movement is usually seen as an imperialist drive to consolidate the Empire, providing glory for some,[68] and an increase of strength in the international diplomatic game. Fourthly, the tariff receipts would provide funds to deal with working-class grievances and ameliorate the widely recognized and deplored effects of poverty and hardship in Edwardian Britain.[69]

At its roots, however, the appeal was to yet a fifth aim, to preserving jobs and to preserving the British industries under threat, by protecting them. The tariff reform campaign was, in essence, a manufacturers' campaign. The fear was that 'England could not remain the workshop of the world; she is fast becoming its creditor, its mortgagee, its landlord'.[70]

The range of industries clamouring for protection this time included iron and steel, most textiles inclusive of some cotton, chemicals, glass and food processing among others. If we may take membership of the Tariff Commission, established early in 1904 to 'enquire' into the need for industrial protection, as

---

[68] Davis and Huttenback have argued convincingly that the costs of Empire exceeded its benefits for the British economy, but while the middle classes largely paid the costs, in taxes, the upper classes received the benefits. Davis and Huttenback (1986), 251–2.

[69] Semmel (1968); Scally (1975), Chapter 3; Marrison (1977), 214–41.

[70] Ashley (1911), 112–13.

a sign of potential or actual support, we find that of the 59 original members, 47 were industrial, mostly from the secondary manufacturing sector. The large landlords were conspicuous by their absence. Even the more widely based Tariff Reform League had recruited only two leading landlords. One, the Duke of Sutherland, was also a coal and iron master; the other, the Duke of Westminister, had become rich on the basis of urban land.

More remarkable still was the absence of prominent bankers from the Tariff Commission. This gap, together with the lack of accredited labour representatives, was felt by Chamberlain himself to be its major weakness. The members of leading City houses who were canvassed declined the invitation to join. Those who did join, Charles Allen, Vice-president of the Hallamshire Bank, but also managing director of the Ebbw Vale Steel Co., or Vincent Caillard, Chairman of the London Committee of the National Bank of Egypt, but also a director of Vickers, could hardly be called representatives of the banking community. In the end, two not very prominent bankers, V. Gibbs and R. Littlejohn, were recruited.[71] These lacunae are all the more surprising in view of the fact that one might have expected to find even within the ruling elite of the landlords and bankers, at least some who were convinced by the protectionist arguments on abstract reasoning, irrespective of their personal economic interests.

Industries which, on the whole, remained staunchly free-trade were those still selling successfully abroad: above all coal, shipbuilding and shrinking parts of the cotton industry. The Tariff Reform Movement could be described, not entirely inaccurately, as 'Birmingham's protest against the tenets of Manchester'.[72]

A vigorous double-pronged campaign for tariff reform within the Party and among the electorate, was led by Chamberlain between 1903 and 1906. One element he stressed was reciprocity, and the power to retaliate against those who raised tariffs against British exports. The country should be able to discriminate in favour of the colonies and of 'those who treat us well'. Chamberlain declared that he did not believe that 'one of our duties is to buy in the cheapest market without regard to where we can sell'. The objective, on the contrary, was to increase the sales of our manufactures both at home and abroad. But in recent decades of free-trade policies, contrary to what was expected when Mr Cobden preached his doctrine, 'we are sending less and less of our manufactures to foreign countries, and they are sending more and more of their manufactures to us.'

Addressing himself particularly to the working classes, Chamberlain asserted in his Greenock speech of 7 October 1903 that this foreign industrial growth had benefited the British middle-class consumers and those who invested abroad. But for those who sought employment at home, 'sugar has gone; silk has gone; iron is threatened: wool is threatened; the turn of cotton will come!'

[71] Mock (1982), 121 ff, 263–70, 386–93; Semmel (1968), 103; Marrison (1983), 149–57.
[72] Bérard (1973), 75–6; Ingham (1984), 152–3, 158; Redford (1934) I, 104–7; Clarke (1972); Beresford (1951), 116–19; Gamble (1981), 138–9. The foundation of the FBI has been described as marking 'the ascendancy of Birmingham opinion over Manchester in British industrial policy'. Quoted in Davenport-Hines (1984), 110.

It was idle for free traders to tell middle-aged, unskilled workers to move to a new growing industry when their own declined. The chances were that they would have to subside into unemployment instead. A general tariff system would create both more employment and higher wages at home, and protect the British from the competition of low wages abroad and from dumped goods. The choice, Chamberlain told his Liverpool audience, lay between 'the demon of cheapness and high wages'. The most telling slogan later was: 'Tariff Reform Means Work for All'.[73]

Within the parliamentary Tory party, Chamberlain was pushing against many open doors. There was a great deal of sympathy for his programme particularly among the members affected by foreign competition. This support was substantially increased by the tariff-reform campaign itself, and after the landslide losses at the 1906 election, a large majority within the rump left in the House of Commons favoured some protectionist measures.[74]

Chamberlain suffered a stroke in 1906 which took him out of politics, and the impetus for Tariff Reform was consequently weakened. Yet protectionism lingered on as an acceptable Conservative creed, and many in the City now swung over in support of it. As an interest group, the City remained attached to free trade: international commerce, capital exports and the international bill of exchange were still its lifeblood. But there were individuals who joined the main trend in the Party even among the merchant bankers. Bankers were to be found among the hundreds of vice-presidents of the Tariff Reform League, though significantly, there was none on the Executive Committee. By contrast, there were more City men in the Free Trade Union and other free-trade organizations.[75]

Yet much of the leadership of the Conservative Party, in the Commons as well as the Lords, remained solidly opposed to Chamberlain and his campaign. This is puzzling at first sight. Why did at least the large landlords among them not follow the practically universal example of their European colleagues and favour agricultural protection, accepting industrial protection as a reasonable price to pay for it? Why was the Conservative Establishment so implacably hostile to Tariff Reform?

There are several explanations. One obvious one was that by linking tariff reform with imperial preference, Chamberlain was explicitly trying to quicken the interdependence between the mother country and the colonies, with the former as the supplier of manufactures, the latter as specializing in the export of food and raw materials. It seemed difficult to square preference for Canadian or Australian farmers with protection for British agrarians. One way out, namely to use imported grain, maize or husks as feeding stuff in British cattle, pig and chicken farms was open to farmers even without Empire preference. Landlords might well have felt that there was little in it for them.

More serious was the contemplation of Chamberlain's Radical past, and his standard promise that protection was to benefit the working man, while the

[73] Jay (1981), 271–5, 287–9, 297; Read (1973), 146; Hoffman (1964), 97, 101, 252; Corden (1976), 216–18; Amery (1969), 470 ff.
[74] Fraser (1962), 154; Scally (1975), 112–13.
[75] Cassis (1984), 357–64; Mock (1982), 292–5.

revenue raised by it would be made to serve social amelioration. The objects of the general tariff, according to *Outlook*, Chamberlain's propaganda paper, of 10 February 1906, were to 'broaden the basis of national finance; for revenue; for the security of capital invested in the country; for more employment; to make tariff reform the basis of social reform.'[76] It was not a programme that was likely to commend itself to the more senior members of the Conservative hierarchy.

Equally unwelcome was Chamberlain's manner of seeking acceptance for his programme. His campaign was directed at the constituencies, at the grass roots of the party, and it was from there that more and more demands for its implementation reached Head Office. By capturing the Liberal Unionist organization, and by his populist approach, Chamberlain was undermining the very structure of the Conservative party. Contrary to the Liberal practice, in which political directions might come upwards from the membership, the Tory traditions were that the leadership, made up of gentlemen who could be trusted to consult the national interest rather than their own selfish ends, would initiate and pursue policies which their followers would recognize as being correct and desirable and would be eager to support.

Worse still,

> Churchill and the Cecil connection shrewdly perceived that Chamberlain's plans threatened to transform the old landed Anglican Tory party into what they described as a 'secular, materialistic' (i.e. middle-class, business) party in which their ancestry would no longer be at a premium.

Chamberlain, after all, was the odd man out – he was a manufacturer; he was, in Hugh Cecil's less than perfectly elegant aristocratic phrase, an 'alien immigrant' in the Tory party, which the Cecils had ruled, almost like their own fief, for quite a number of years; and they disliked his 'materialism and pragmatism'.[77]

There was yet a further cause for hostility of the Establishment within the Conservative Party to Chamberlain's programme. Behind its overt, short-term provision there lay a different view 'over Britain's industrial future, and over the need for direct Government intervention' to reverse Britain's otherwise 'inevitable decline into an aged industrial backwater'.[78]

The ruling elite, on the other hand, landowners and the City alike, wanted no Government initiatives which might carry the danger of a redistribution of wealth and power. They were concerned, instead, to keep London as the centre of the world's financial exchanges, with the pound sterling as the leading international currency. Even those ministers who took an interest in economic matters and were disturbed by signs of Britain's decline, spoke of the loss of 'trade', never of the relative decline of her productive power or of technical backwardness. Manufacturing industry was simply taken for granted. By contrast, Chamberlain, the Birmingham manufacturer, understood the plight of industry, and knew instinctively that a country which does not produce, will have nothing to sell, and therefore will not be able to have any 'trade'.

[76] Summary in Fraser (1962), 153.
[77] Fraser (1962), 150–1; Jay (1981), 274; Scally (1975); Balfour (1985), 279.
[78] Jay (1981), 290–1. Also Newton and Porter (1988), 15–22.

Taking it all in all, Chamberlain had managed to offend, at the same time, both the economic beliefs and the political foundations of the hierarchy of his party. For the world view as seen from the City, he had substituted the world view as seen from the position of a provincial manufacturer. He was threatening an established oligarchy with the introduction of democracy. And – a final irony – he was not thereby improving the party's electoral chances.

Technically, the protectionist programme with which the Conservative party entered the election, half-hearted though it was, was defeated by the electorate at the polls in 1906. In reality it had no chance from the beginning, since it was opposed by the powers that really mattered, banking, finance, overseas merchanting and shipping, together with the top civil service trained for generations to look to the interests of these groups for guidance. It had been a bold bid by a substantial section of manufacturing industry, but it was only too obvious that manufacturing industry had no power base in Westminster, in Whitehall – or in the Conservative Party. The Liberal party, increasingly leaning on the electoral support of the lower middle and the working classes, was wedded to its traditional doctrine of looking to low-cost imports of food and of other commodities, while, like the Conservatives, taking productive industry for granted. Three generations of unchallenged success of British industry in world markets had accustomed the elites of both parties to take British 'technical virtuosity as given'[79] and to cherish the belief that industry could always look after itself and would never need any Government support.

In the end, it is never the plausibility of a policy in the abstract, but the power of those who think they will benefit directly from it, which matters in politics. It is interesting to speculate what would have happened, had the position been reversed, and a break with traditional policy been in the interests of the City: how long would the Establishment and the media have needed to bring round public opinion?

The question remains, how much all this mattered. Would a more vigorous forward trade policy, including industrial protection, have helped to stem the relative decline of British industry in that period? The books and articles on that theme would fill a library, but have not led to any agreement, and the argument cannot be pursued in any detail here. Modern multisectoral econometric tests have suggested that Chamberlain's Tariff Reform had a better chance of getting higher growth rates than the actual policies pursued. As for Germany, tariffs-cum-cartels may well have contributed to the vigorous growth of her steel industry. For the period 1841–81, McCloskey calculated that Britain sustained a loss by switching to free trade, but that it could not have exceeded 4% of national income. In our period, most British imports still consisted of food and raw materials only, so that industrial protection could not have made much difference one way or the other.[80]

However, no one looking through the debate at the time can believe that the manufacturers' main argument, that it was better to preserve industrial power for the future, as opposed to enjoying a high level of real incomes through cheap

---

[79] Rostow (1960), 69.
[80] Thomas (1985), 460–2; Webb (1980); McCloskey (1970–1); McCloskey (1971–2); McCloskey (1980); Capie (1983); Balfour (1985), 286–91.

imports today, received adequate consideration, though it was not entirely neglected. Capital, alleged W.J. Ashley, 'pursues an immediate gain without any regard to the ultimate effect on national prosperity,' and Balfour, as usual seeing both sides of the question, admitted that

> the majority of economists hold (I think rightly) that it [sc. free trade] may sacrifice the future to the present, and delay what may ultimately have proved to be the most productive distribution of capital and labour.[81]

Adverting to the tendency, mentioned several times in these pages, of British exports going increasingly to 'soft' overseas markets rather than into the 'hard' developed countries, B.S. Saul, writing as late as 1954, could still see it as a positive development within the world trading pattern, allowing Britain to balance her books, without considering the implied weakness of British industry. Only more recently, within the aura of British 'decline' has this been seen as a threat to industrial effort.

The difference in viewpoint is not affected by the fact that the tendency has been imperfectly observed, and that it affected all advanced nations, since the overseas world was growing and Europe was raising its tariffs, while British exports remained successful in Scandinavia, Spain, Portugal, Greece and France, by no means 'soft' markets:[82]

Table 4.6 *Destinations of the exports of the UK, France and Germany, 1860–1910*

Share of exports going to:	1860		1880			1910		
	UK	France	UK	France	Germany	UK	France	Germany
Europe	33.9%	65.1%	35.5%	71.7%	91.3%	35.0%	69.8%	73.9%
N. America	16.5	10.2	15.8	9.2	6.6	11.6	7.4	8.9
Total, 'hard markets'	50.4	75.3	51.3	80.9	97.9	46.6	77.2	82.8
Rest of world	49.6	24.7	48.7	19.1	2.1	53.4	22.8	17.2

Thus manufacture lost its bid for protection. Commercial policy, inasfar as it existed, was meant to safeguard 'trade' and the City investor and banker. The actual productive sector was simply taken for granted and did not otherwise figure in the calculations of the ruling elite.

Next to tariff policy, the maintenance of the gold standard was probably the most significant contribution of the authorities to economic policy-making. At that time, Britain, although credited with having invented the modern central bank, possessed no governmental bank at all – the Bank of England was a private enterprise, which still had, even in this period, the maximization of the

[81] Ashley (1911), 75; Balfour (1903), 9; Mock (1982), 117.
[82] Saul (1954–5), 65–6; Saul (1957), 190; Bairoch (1977), 42–3; Without coal, the proportion going to the hard markets would have been smaller; Kindleberger (1961–62), 296; Hilgerdt (1943), 398; also see Introduction, notes 17–18 Table 1.30.

profits of its proprietors as one of its main aims.[83] Moreover, it lacked a competent permanent senior professional bureaucracy, being run, in effect, by a temporary Governor and Deputy Governor. Nominal control lay in the hands of a board whose places were filled from time to time by co-option so that it was, to all intents and purposes, self-appointed.

The composition of this board, which after all had it in its power to decide the monetary policy of Great Britain, was possibly the most astonishing feature of all. Of the 35 firms represented on the Board of the Bank of England between 1890–1914, 13 (37%) were merchant bankers, 17 (49%) were merchants, and 5 operated in other spheres: two were breweries, one was a distillery, one was a hosiery firm (J. & B. Morley), and one was in the armaments industry (Vickers), though its representative entered only in 1910. It was not without irony for an organization with such far-reaching powers over the economic fate of the nation that seven of the members of the Board of the Bank of England were of recent foreign origin – though even that count reckons Baring's as being British.[84]

Not only industrialists, but also bankers dealing mainly with British industry and thus having a possible indirect interest in the productive sector at home, were carefully kept away. The *Bankers' Magazine*, eyeing with misgivings the tendency to replace the formerly dominant merchants with some bankers, pontificated in 1894:[85]

> Circumstances are certain to arise in the course of time when the interests of the Bank of England and those of the private banks represented by those gentlemen will not be identical, and this consideration would counsel caution before adopting this new departure.

The implication is clear. The interests of merchants, in contrast to those of bankers, would *always* correspond to those of the Bank of England; and this, in turn, must be because the Bank of England would always act simply and directly in the interests of the merchants, which were, of course, identical with those of the nation.

Reality, unfortunately, did not entirely correspond to that complacent view. As Jacob Viner put it in 1945 in a review of Clapham's history of the Bank of England:

> 'The directors were . . . limited to London merchants and merchant bankers, could rise to the highest Bank offices largely by seniority and financial respectability without need of other more intellectual qualifications, and as directors were not expected to suspend any of their other business activities even when these were such – as they often were – as to bring into direct conflict their personal interests and the interests and responsibilities of the Bank as a central bank. No one, I am sure', he added drily, 'would today even dream of setting up a new central bank on such a pattern.'[86]

Certain it is that the Bank used its immense prestige to prop up in the first instance the credit and credibility of the merchant bankers. The most striking

---

[83] Goodhart (1972); Sayers (1976, 3 vols) I, 2–4, 17–27; Sayers (1967), 10; Bagehot (1962), 18. Recent research by Dieter Ziegler of Bielefeld University confirms the continuous preoccupation of the Bank with the maximization of its own profits.
[84] Cassis (1984), 108–9 and Cassis (1985c), 214–15.
[85] Quoted in Cassis (1984), 107; also see Anonymous (1894).
[86] Viner (1945), 62.

example of this occurred in 1890, when Baring's, possibly the leading merchant bankers of the day, had by reckless speculation bordering on fraud manoeuvred itself into a position where, despite its huge resources, it faced total collapse. This was a case in which the Bank of England was not slow to look after its own: it mounted a successful rescue operation involving its own resources and those of other leading City houses. Nothing of the kind took place when other important firms, like Overend Gurney in 1866 and the City of Glasgow Bank in 1878, collapsed with large losses to numerous investors.[87]

The Government had no direct access to the decision making of the Bank of England whatever, and 'tended to treat the financial institutions as a separate independent power, rather than as a subordinate one'. Instead of setting the tone, the Government asked for and frequently took the advice of the Bank and the City on questions of monetary policy and related issues. Gladstone in his day resented the

> position of subserviency (for the State) which . . . it became in the interest of the Bank and City to prolong . . . I was reluctant to acquiesce, and I began to fight against it.

He set about tapping popular savings directly through the Post Office Savings Bank founded in 1861, and sought to strengthen the Treasury's independent command over money.[88] He had been the last Chancellor of the Exchequer to attempt to free himself from that dependence.

This unbelievable construct for the central bank of a major industrial nation had, according to its own pronouncements, but one overriding object of policy: the protection of its gold reserve, with which was linked the maintenance of the international value of the pound sterling. The mechanism was believed to be that a loss of gold would lead to a rise in the bank rate, which would attract foreign funds and discourage foreign lending, and/or at the same time cut prices and activity at home, improve the trade balance and thus bring gold back in.

That target, however, was hampered at every step by the fact that the Bank of England kept a ludicrously low gold reserve, and the gold reserve was kept low, in turn, in order to keep the profits of the Bank proprietors high.

In 1881 its bullion reserve was only 14.3% of the reserves of the British, French and German Central Banks and the US Treasury combined. In 1885 this had dropped to 9.2%, in a centre boasting that it was the financial hub of the world. Yet, curiously, no one thought of removing this incubus from the British economy by forcing the Bank to increase its reserve. Some members of the money market who saw the problem but would not have dreamt of burdening the Bank with a policy which might reduce the dividends of its proprietors, even suggested that 'it would pay the country to pay the Bank of England to keep a better reserve in order to create confidence in the stability of our enormous mass of credit.'[89]

[87] Clapham (1944) II, 329–39; Checkland (1957), 275; Fearns (1953), 71; de Cecco (1974), 82; Lisle-Williams (1984a), 256 and Lisle-Williams (1984b), 342.
[88] Pressnell (1968), 171, quoting John Morley (1903) I, 650–1; Harris and Thane (1984), 223; Wright (1972), 195–226; Thane (1985), 80.
[89] R.C. (1888b), Evidence Fowler QQ.7709, 7713, also Marshall (1888a), Evidence QQ.10198–1020; Lewis (1978a), 56; Viner (1945), 63. Also see chapter 2, page 89, note 12 above.

That the low gold reserve was the cause of the violent fluctuations in the Bank's monetary stance which destabilized the rest of the economy, contemporaries had no doubt. The joint-stock banks were particularly hard hit by these uncertainties, and in the last years before 1914, in despair, set up their own private gold reserves, thus substituting for what the central bank should have done, but because it was run for private profit, was unwilling to do. In 1915 Sir Edward Holden estimated that British banks held at least £50 million in gold, of which the Midland Bank alone held some £8 million.[90]

The Reichsbank, by contrast, made it its duty to see that the German banks had 'virtually unlimited access' to its resources in times of stringency. It thus tended to smoothe out the course of the trade cycle, while the Bank of England, more concerned with its own gold reserve than the fate of home business, cut its credits at precisely those times, thus reinforcing the effects of the trade cycle. Since the Bank of England's period of stringency were frequently caused by foreign rather than home trading conditions, the reductions in lending struck the British banks not only as harmful, but also as capricious. Schumpeter believed that this uncertainty as to their central bank's behaviour contributed to the British banks' reluctance to lend to industry as was the practice with German banks. The Reichsbank was not, of course, playing the game according to the 'rules'[91] – but then, the rules had been invented by the bank of England to protect its own inadequate gold holdings.

Apart from rationing the other banks, the Bank of England operated by changes in the Bank Rate, and these were remarkably frequent: there were 285 between 1851 and 1885, or one every six weeks, and 195 between 1880 and 1913, or one every two months on average. Between January 1904 and December 1914, British bank rate changed 49 times, the rate of the Banque de France 8 times, and that of the Reichsbank 37 times.

> One cannot dismiss the possibility that British economic activity may have been inhibited between 1875 and 1880, and again between 1885 and 1890, by the Bank of England's constant juggling with Bank Rate,

according to Sir Arthur Lewis, though he added that 'this can hardly have been a major factor'.[92]

What was particularly harmful was the raising of rates for the sake of the inadequate gold reserve, 'even when internal conditions were not "booming" by any means.' In 1890, and certainly once more in 1907, all the rates followed the Bank Rate upward, exerting an 'understandable deflationary pressure by the Bank on the English national economy'.

> The export industries . . . suffered, while it was the Bank of England and the City of London which were relatively unscathed.[93]

The records confirm that while long-term capital, as one might have expected, was considerably cheaper in London than in Paris, the Bank of England yet managed to keep its own rates well above those of the Banque de

---

[90] Beach (1935), 89; De Cecco (1974), 209–11.
[91] Schumpeter (1939) I, 430–5; Bowen (1950), 78; Seeger (1968), 128. But see Eistert (1970), 191.
[92] Yeager (1976), 303; Foreman-Peck (1983b), 168–9; Walker (1933), 199, 206; Lewis (1978a), 56; R.C. (1888), 208, Appendix XVI.
[93] Beach (1935), 120–1, 165; Viner (1945), 63; Ford (1964), 24.

France, and increasingly so, as soon as the French had got over the war and the German indemnity of the 1870s:[94]

Table 4.7 *Average cost of capital, 1870–1913*

	Long term					
	Consols London	Rentes Paris	Difference*	Railways		
				London	Paris	Difference*
1870–79	3.18%	4.63%	−1.45%	4.00%	5.76%	−1.76%
1880–89	2.99	3.68	−0.69	3.43	4.24	−0.81
1890–99	2.68	3.02	−0.34	2.79	3.59	−0.80
1900–13	2.98	3.10	−0.12	3.29	4.06	−0.77
	Short term					
	Bank of England	Banque de France	Difference*	Market rates		
				London	Paris	Difference*
1870–79	3.53	3.87	−0.34	3.23	3.53	−0.30
1880–89	3.31	3.18	+0.13	2.77	2.75	+0.02
1890–99	2.98	2.57	+0.39	2.23	2.14	+0.09
1900–13	3.72	3.16	+0.56	3.26	2.67	+0.59

* A minus sign means that London rates were lower, and vice versa.

That higher or fluctuating rates may have harmed industry cut no ice whatever with the Bank of England. Nor was it in the least troubled by the labour unrest of 1911–12 which indicated that the deflationary adjustments forced periodically on the whole economy, might no longer work without considerable social tension and social costs. The Government, too, would have been surprised to be told that this was any of its business, though in the end it was the Government which had to contain the consequences of the social unrest. Nor, significantly, was there anywhere 'an effective challenge (by) anyone opposed to the general subordination of national economic policy to international economic events'. No powerful debtor group emerged to fight the periodic deflation.[95] The Bank, for its part, would not have dreamt of rectifying the recurring presumed adverse balance of payments by the relatively simple device of restricting capital exports rather than harming real output and real employment at home. That, after all, would have affected its friends, the firms of the Bank's directors themselves.

Significantly, the central banks of France and Germany congratulated themselves on their ability to manage their affairs without having to engage in the damaging operations which the British central bank had to resort to so frequently.[96] The priorities of these banks and of their governments were evidently ordered in a different manner.

There are some signs that the Bank of England was reluctant to harm trade, as distinct from industry, and it may well be that the full effects of interest

[94] Based on Lévy-Leboyer (1977b); also see R.C. (1888), 207, Appendix XVI.
[95] Tomlinson (1981), 31–2; Checkland (1983), 170.
[96] Yeager (1976), 303; Inglis-Palgrave (1903), 98–91, 204–5, 219–21; Bagehot (1962), 23; Lévy-Leboyer (1977c), 138.

changes, imposed for external reasons, were cushioned for the home banks, and through them for industry, particularly after 1890.[97] But the lack of interest in, and understanding for, productive industry was an unmistakeable characteristic of the Bank parlour. In the numerous histories and accounts of the Bank of England and of the money market one will look in vain for any link with or concern for provincial manufacturing.

What effects the Bank's exclusive preoccupation with its own profits and the fortunes of its narrow circle of friends, had on total British economic performance or on the industrial slow-down cannot be measured. They may well have been marginal only, and confined to a few years. On the other hand, they may have played a vital, perhaps even a crucial part in setting the later Victorian and Edwardian markets into a pattern which discouraged innovation and enterprise on the part of productive industry, particularly that part of it which required large doses of outside capital. Government's part in this would be merely a passive one, of letting it happen, but the Government, in turn, was programmed to do so by the political, social and economic composition of the ruling elite.

The rest of the banking field may be divided into three broad groupings: merchant bankers, private bankers and the joint-stock banks. There was clearly little to hope for by industry from the first two; only the joint-stock banks, with their roots in the provinces, were likely to transmit some resources from the financial sector to industry.

Traditionally, the joint-stock banks and the country banks which had preceded them and out of which several of them had been formed, had always provided short-term loans for the trading purposes of productive firms, as many had seen themselves as bankers to support commerce. But equally traditionally and firmly they took great care never to be drawn into supplying long-term capital to industry, as was done for example by the contemporary German banks. Most of the handful of cases known to have occurred to the contrary arose out of the inability of borrowing firms to repay their loans to their banks, or out of the regularity of renewals of short-term loans to the point where they took on the guise of long-term financing.

The lack of contact between the banking sector and the industrial (as against commerce, insurance and other more favoured occupations) is brought out also by Cassis's statistical data on British bankers in 1890–1914. 'Bankers', defined as directors of joint-stock banks and partners in private banks, had seats on the boards of other companies in this period as follows:

Insurance	49 %
Investment Trusts	31
Railways	24
Colonial banks	19
Shipping	12
Mines (mostly overseas)	8
Electricity, water, gas	7
Industry	7
Miscellaneous	28

[97] Goodhart (1972), 206–13; Sayers (1976), 43; Bagehot (1962), 147 ff; Cottrell (1980), 207; Dutton (1984).

The insignificant proportion for 'industry' included oil, again a foreign resource worked abroad, and breweries. By another calculation it appears that only 5% of 'bankers' had mainly industrial interests as against 69.5% in finance, commerce and shipping. Similarly, while 56% of the fathers of bankers were in banking and 17% in commerce, only 2% had been in industry.[98]

The few links with manufacture were concentrated in a very small handful of banks. In leading position, reflecting its Birmingham origins, was the Midland Bank of whose directors 39% were in manufacture and 22% were shipowners. Lloyd's and Parr's were other banks with a fair industrial representation on their boards. Altogether, even among joint-stock bank directors, only 7% had manufacturing interests. Elsewhere industrialists were quite exceptional or unheard of.[99] It was therefore not entirely surprising that it was the Midland Bank which repeatedly took the lead in criticizing the heedless and damaging policies of the Bank of England.

The possibility that the lack of access to finance at critical times may have retarded the growth of British manufacturing, particularly of firms in new, fast-growing industries, has been discussed in chapter 2 above. The question here must be: could and should the Government have intervened to realign the London money market and other sources of possible finance for the benefit of industry?

There is no doubt that it could. The Government never hesitated to introduce legislation, including substantial changes to the Charter of the Bank of England, if it felt that important national interests were at stake. But the very posing of the question in this form shows its essential absurdity. In the minds of successive Governments the national economic interest, apart from the Government's own tax base and revenue, was symbolized by the welfare of the City and its institutions. To sacrifice any of them for the sake of some provincial manufacturer would simply not have been within the realm of practical politics inside the charmed circle of the ruling elite. As far as the provision of finance for industry was concerned, Victorian and Edwardian Governments washed their hands of any interest whatever.

Further examples of sheer neglect of the needs of industry on the part of Governments could easily be multiplied. Unlike other European Governments, the British did not subsidize the building of canals to cheapen the costs of transport to producers and users of bulky goods or to open up for economic development regions far from sea and rivers. It did not help to finance the extensions of the railway system, as was done on the Continent, and thereby neglected the chance, taken by Germany, France, Belgium and other countries, of freeing potential capital for industry.[100] The failure to use the consular and diplomatic staff to push British exports was put down widely to upper-class disdain for commercial pursuits. There was, of course, no Ministry for Industry, no Ministry for Science, no Government policy of buying British. Parliament laughed out of court the pleas of industrialists for decimalization.[101]

[98] Cassis (1984), 116, 186 ff, 212 and Cassis (1985b), 112.
[99] Cassis (1984), 68, 79–80; Cassis (1985a), 301–15.
[100] Carli (1981), 240.
[101] Platt (1968), XVII–XVIII–XXXV, 108–12, 360; Bryce (1923), 285–6; Balfour Report (1918), 13–15.

Beyond the sheer neglect, cases are not wanting of actual harm done to industrial progress. It is not suggested that Government, Parliament or other public authorities simply set out to damage the interests of British industry. Rather, the harm arose as a by-product of the observed need to protect the public, out of political dogmatism or out of sheer incompetence. Among the ingredients of the worst mistakes, however, were also generally a lack of understanding of industrial processes and the pervading notion that it was not the task of the State to make things easy for productive industry. To this day, British politicians and public authorities fail to grasp as a rule that successful industrial production may take years to prepare, that timing is important, and that unlike Governments which can simply order people to do what they want them to do, manufacturing firms operate in a bitterly competitive environment in which a lost chance or inflated costs will lead to grievous loss of markets, often to foreign competitors who have been aided and subsidized by their Governments.

One of the best-known examples of damage done in this way concerns the electrical engineering and supply industries, then in their critical initial expansion phase. Virtually all observers are agreed that at the beginning of the 1880s, Britain was still among the leaders in the field, yet by the end of the decade that lead had been lost, and Britain remained hopelessly outclassed by Germany and the USA. There is no agreement, however, on the causes of this change of fortune. Neither British inventors, scientists and university teachers in electrical engineering, nor British entrepreneurs had any need to fear comparison with their foreign counterparts.

On the other hand, the reversal of the 1880s may easily be brought into connection with legislation in Britain and with the actions of local authorities; but whether these were due to an 'incompetent and amateurish State', as a hostile critic maintained,[102] or had perfectly valid causes and whether the public authorities were the major, or only a contributing factor, may well be subject to debate.

Their single most important damaging action was the Electric Lighting Act of 1882. It followed in many important respects the pattern of the Tramways Act of 1870, which had given local authorities the option to buy out the proprietors of private companies at written-down values at the end of an 21-year period. Since no one could be certain of having amortized his investment in a new field in that space of time, this Act fatally inhibited initiative and capital investment.

Although a further Act of 1888 extended the option period to 42 years, the main damage had been done: these were precisely the key years in which American and German firms had broken through into mass markets and mass production.[103] By the outbreak of war in 1914, British consumption of electricity, use of electric lighting and electric power were fully comparable with those of the two main competitors, but her production and her exports of the more advanced products had dropped far behind. Most surviving British firms

---

[102] Wieser (1919), 439; chapter 3, notes 293–95 above.
[103] Wieser (1919), 439–40; Byatt (1979), 9, 18 ff, 199; Garcke (1907); Sakamoto (1980), 54; D.C. (1918b), 18–21; Hughes (1962), 27 ff, 54; Ballin (1946), 4 ff; for a contrary view, Hannah (1979), 5 ff; Parsons (1939), 186–92; Whyte (1930), 19, 21.

were, in fact, branches of German or American firms or, like the British GEC, they had German staff in key positions and used continental licences.[104]

The same legislation also favoured municipal as against private enterprise. But since many municipalities ran their own gas works, they were not in any hurry to install electric lighting[105] – an interesting example of the clogging effect of early technical superiority in Britain. Moreover, municipal limits meant, before long, enterprises that were much too small for efficiency. Britain was condemned to tiny power stations whereas efficiency and low costs lay with ever larger ones. Further, there was an unholy jumble of suppliers, voltages, frequencies and systems, sometimes within one area where the licensing authorities had licensed two rival suppliers.

Worst of all were conditions in London, where they should have been easiest, since a large and wealthy population lived close together. Two major electricity supply companies had been formed in 1887, but numerous small ones also existed, and after a public enquiry in 1889–90, Parliament divided up the territory among 16 local authority and 14 private suppliers, of whom five were duplicated in their own area. By 1908, there were 72 electricity authorities in London, supplying power from 66 stations with an average capacity of only 3,000 HP each. For the country as a whole, there were still, as late as 1934, after 20 years of reform, beside the Central Electricity Board, three joint electricity authorities, 635 licenced undertakers and five joint boards of local authorities using 40 different voltages.[106]

Meanwhile, from around 1900 onwards, new methods of transmitting multiphase HT current had removed obstacles to long-distance supplies, making the more efficient larger units economically feasible, but they could not be built in Britain because local authorities refused to give up their independence out of civic pride and private companies were not allowed to amalgamate. Parliament at no time set out to devise an optimal system. Only in the North-East was there a successful area constructed. In consequence, mass production of equipment and the supply of efficient large units were both impossible in the home market, and without them British firms were unable to match the Germans and Americans either in their production or the tendering abroad.[107]

The licensing system for new construction or extensions of generating capacity had some similarity with the early stages of railway building in Britain, when the motor of private initiative was braked by official licensing through Acts of Parliament. This increased costs and helped to create a network that was anything but logical. However, at that time Britain had a monopoly of railway building and could bear the losses implicit in a system of an uninhibited search for profit coupled with widespread political corruption and chicanery; in any case there were compensating advantages. In the case of electric power stations, foreign competitors stood ready to profit from British mistakes and the penalties were immediate.

[104] Saul (1960), 33; Byatt (1979), 161–4, 194 and Byatt (1968), 239, 255.
[105] Byatt (1979), 3, 105, 217; Checkland (1983), 201.
[106] Hennessey (1972), 35; Aldcroft and Richardson (1969), 211; Ballin (1946), 18–19, 40, 69 ff, 84; Parsons (1939), 136 ff; Hughes (1962), 38 ff.
[107] Byatt (1979), 69; Singer, Holmyard, Hall and Williams (1954–8) VI, 284–5 (1978); Brittain (1974), 114.

The Board of Trade was the licensing authority for private proposals, and the Local Government Board or the London County Council were the authorities for those coming from the municipalities. Authorization by the former was dependent on adequate measures 'primarily to secure the safety of the public, and secondarily to ensure a proper and sufficient supply of electricity'. The latter confined themselves 'mainly to a consideration of the financial position of the local authority, and the financial record of the undertaking, or to questions affecting lands, and have little regard to the efficiency or suitability of the projected expenditure.' In both, as the Departmental Committee of 1918 delicately put it, 'local considerations, owing to the exercise of parliamentary pressure, may become the determining factor in the action of the authorities.'[108] The Liberal Government, using the somewhat incongruous defence of *laissez-faire*, blocked private schemes in favour of municipal ones and at the same time refused to oblige these latter to collaborate, even in London.

To sum up. The range of agenda which Government set itself in the electricity industry included protection of the public, of shareholders, and of the City financiers. It did not include protection of manufacturers, or aiding their technical progress, or even preventing their efficiency and international competitiveness from being blocked and hamstrung by the action of the public authorities themselves. Industry was something to be watched, limited, controlled: never anything to be fostered.

The story of the 'Red Flag Act' has entered folklore and hardly needs to be repeated here in detail. To have a motor vehicle preceded by a man on foot and to keep to 4 m.p.h. even after 1878 will not have retarded progress in motor engineering in Britain by very much. The restriction after 1896 effectively to 12 m.p.h. by Local Authority fiat will have done more damage,[109] but only in the short term. By 1914 two of the other three leading European nations, Germany and Italy were no more advanced than Britain, only France having made greater progress.

The chemical industry complained of at least two adverse official measures. One was the heavy taxation of industrial alcohol, a key element in the costs of the dyestuffs industry which might exceed all other costs put together. The other was the Patent Law, which allowed foreign companies to register a patent in Britain and then block it by not using it, as had happened with Caro's famous alizarin dye. After some agitation, the Patent Act of 1907 attempted to remedy the latter weakness and although it was later made inoperative by legal decision, it was significant that immediately on its passing some German chemical firms hastened to open productive branches in the United Kingdom, as did the American Shoe Machinery Co.[110]

These well-known episodes illustrate three major features of the legislation and/or administrative interference hampering British industry in that period, quite apart from confirming the overriding impression of the British Government's general lack of interest in industrial progress. The first is, that no single

[108] D.C. (1918a), paras. 18–21.
[109] Singer *et al.* (1958) V, 429; Michie (1981b), 154; Rolt (1970), 270; Saul (1960b), 29–30; and Saul (1963), 40; Clapham (1963) III, 139–40; Wilson and Reader (1958), 53.
[110] See chapter 1, note 100 and chapter 3, p. 158, note 148. Also Saul (1960b), 20 and Heerding (1986), 28–31; Alford (1964–65), 108; D.C. (1918a), III–2; Schomerus (1952), 177.

Act by itself, not even the Electric Lighting Act of 1882, was likely to have had any significant adverse consequence, or can be given any significant responsibility for Britain's retardation. At the same time, this does not mean that the sum total of all the Government's measures together, may not have had a considerable, and perhaps decisive influence in delaying the key investments, the emergence of mass production, the introduction of the latest technology and the employment of a sufficient number of trained technologists and scientists, beyond the point when catching up in that period became impossible, at least in the three leading 'new' industries of the age, electrical engineering, motor cars and chemicals.

Secondly, there emerges a clear picture of the fatal consequences of the total ignorance of applied science and technology prevalent in the ruling circles, including members of the Government, their leading Civil Service advisers, and the national press. What utter lack of technical understanding or technical imagination, what total ignorance even of the historical experience of how a new technology develops, was implied by the 'Red Flag Act', which assumed that not only the technical possibilities, but even the speed, of the road vehicle would remain those of the very early prototypes.

Thirdly, a *laissez-faire* Government, while it would abstain from aiding industry, could on the same principle also be expected to abstain from harming it; if it did so, nevertheless, it was because it considered other factors to be more important than free markets, and these included the protection of the public at large, and of shareholders, customers or workers employed. The Factory and Workshop Acts, the Alkali and Nitroglycerine Acts, the Coal Mines Acts and the Food and Drugs Acts were clearly of that character, and while they put extra burdens on industry, they have to be accounted among the more positive contributions of successive Governments. Private profit-making capitalism, after all, was and was again likely to become, red in tooth and claw in Britain as elsewhere.

In time, Governments abroad would introduce similar protective legislation, imposing similar costs and handicaps on their own industries. However, pressure for such legislation always takes time to develop. It is generally easier, and certainly was so in nineteenth-century Europe, to copy a cost-reducing technology than to copy the complex provisions which in due course become necessary to ensure that its harmful side effects are minimized. More newly industrializing countries thus have, for a time, a market advantage, though at an appropriate social cost. Britain, as the much older industrialized country at the time, had the corresponding competitive disadvantages while being ahead in shielding its population from the more rapacious of her entrepreneurs. Here was, in effect, yet another example of the time-shift arising from having been the first in the field.

This point, together with some others, is also illustrated by the treatment meted out to the railways in Britain. Britain was almost unique in Europe in possessing a railway system that was still wholly privately owned and run. The public attitude towards it was suspicious, and there was widespread fear of a railway monopoly that would be in a position to exploit traders and travellers. The most concrete expressions of that hostility were the Acts of 1888 and 1894, which severely limited the companies' power to raise rates, a limitation made virtually absolute by judicial decision later; and the Act of 1893, which raised labour and other costs by placing restrictions on the shift working system. Moreover, it was rates and taxes, i.e. the charges levied by the public authorities, which formed the most rapidly rising cost items for the railways, though they did not amount to a very significant part of the costs in absolute terms.[111]

The political authorities thus prevented the railways, almost alone of all organizations in Britain, from raising their charges in line with their costs in a period of rising prices from the mid-1890s. While profits were adversely affected thereby, it is not at all clear whether this constraint forced the railways to improve their technology, or whether it robbed them of the means of doing so. What is perhaps most interesting in this case, is that while the restrictions on raising charges were, as in our other examples, actually intended to constrain the powers of the entrepreneurs, in order to benefit the merchants and traders, a further consequence was to benefit the industrialists.

Among the major items in the cost structure of the railways, it was only labour costs, apart from rates and taxes, which rose substantially and consistently in this period. This was so in part because of easier work schedules and better conditions, and in part because wages rose much faster than labour productivity.[112]

Distributional changes of this kind are in general very difficult to document in spite of some recent heroic attempts to do so.[113] If they did occur, the cause may lie among the trade unions whose greater power and willingness, than was found among their contemporaries abroad, to delay or prevent technical and managerial progress has been noted elsewhere in this book.[114] It is noted here again because, in part, it was derived from legislative provisions on trade unions in Britain. This type of legislation belied the *laissez-faire* claim of the Government, for the Government's inaction amounted, as always, itself to a kind of action. British Governments, instead of regulating the labour market, allowed it to develop into a battle-ground, into a framework of conflict in which it merely held the ring, except in the very last years before 1914, when major conflicts threatened what became known as essential supplies and the Government had to step in, in the guise of the protector of consumers.[115] It might easily have pursued a different policy, had that been acceptable to public opinion and, above all, to the ruling elite.

Against this formidable and mixed array of actions harmful or at least indifferent to the needs of productive industry, Government measures to aid manufacture and its progress appear rare and of little significance. There was the Patent Act, mentioned above, as well as the Merchandise Marks Acts of 1862 and 1887, both in their different ways having as their object the ending of fraud and abuse by foreigners. There was the expansion of educational provisions,

---

111 Irving (1978), 51–2; Cain (1978), 87–99 and Cain (1972), 623–41; Aldcroft and Dyos (1974), 177–8; Parris (1965), 223–4, also see chapter 1, note 164.
112 Irving (1978), 58; Bagwell (1963).
113 Matthews, Feinstein and Odling-Smee (1982).
114 Also Lewchuk (1984), 361 and Carr and Taplin (1962), 162–3. Also Introduction, p. xv, note 19 chapter 1, p. 53, note 184.
115 Feldman and Steinisch (1980), 116; Hunt (1981), 225 ff; Charles (1973); Wrigley (1982b), 142 ff.

which had many objectives and where Government disinterest and delay may have harmed British industry, but in the end was bound to benefit it also.[116] There were other measures, such as the limitation on railway freight rates and the Joint-Stock Company Acts of 1855 and 1862, with later amending Acts, the expenditure on surveys and expeditions and the reform of the Consular Service, which were largely designed to help merchants and city firms, but incidentally also benefited the manufacturers.[117] Beyond these it is difficult to think of Governmental actions which showed any signs of understanding the problems of manufacturing industry in an age of rapidly mounting foreign competition, still less of any willingness to come to its aid.

In the nature of things, it is impossible to measure the total effect of all this, or even to guess whether it was insignificant, small, large or decisive. It depends on our assessment of the alternatives, and in this case econometric guesses of the counterfactuals will not help, for the really significant question must be how far a more positive initiative on the part of the Government might have changed, not merely this or that cost or market structure, but the whole milieu in which entrepreneurial decisions were made in the manufacturing sector. The question, in other words, is whether it would have been possible to lift the whole of the industrial sector onto a different growth path, and in view of the discontinuity involved such a question is intrinsically unanswerable.

V Some General Considerations

Three final considerations remain. The first concerns the general tendency for leading industrial countries to find themselves obliged, as other, low-wage areas begin to compete with them, to shift the weight of their operations within the international division of labour, away from industry first to commerce and ultimately to finance. The Dutch in their golden age, and before them possibly the Italian cities, might furnish earlier examples of this sequence.[118] Might it then have been correct, even if not chosen deliberately but by a kind of unconscious collective drive, to neglect the declining manufacturing sector in favour of the sectors of the future, commerce and finance? Voices were not lacking, then as well as among those who are presiding over the far more devastating period of decline of British manufacturing in the 1980s, to claim just such a prospect.

However, the argument remains just as unconvincing in the context of the Victorian and Edwardian as in that of the second Elizabethan age. First, it is clear that the favours extended by the Government to the financial/commercial sector were not due to the recognition of the new, but to the survival of the old. The City, as we have seen, had gained its initial foothold in the centres of power in the seventeenth and eighteenth centuries, and had kept it ever since, not so much by the economic significance of its contribution, but by the kind of social, familial and political links and by the snobbery with which the British ruling

---

[116] See chapter 3, pp. 208–9, note 304 above.
[117] Pollard (1959), 138–9; Grove (1962), 23; Payne (1974) 18, 20; Platt (1962–63), 494–512; also see note 111 above.
[118] See chapter 1, p. 57, note 190.

elite traditionally recruited itself. Next, a successful high-wage economy might well sustain itself by a shrinking manufacturing base and a growing tertiary sector, but only if the manufacturing sector which survives, remains technically up-to-date and able to sustain the high incomes consistent with the incomes realized in the financial sector and with the expectations of an advanced country.

It cannot be achieved by the kind of governmental neglect of industry characteristic for our period. Furthermore, such modest attention as was claimed by and granted to industry by the British Government, tended to be given to the old staples. The new high-tech, growing industries on which future development should have rested were, as noted above, treated with particular lack of understanding and helpfulness.

Thirdly, the argument for a major switch to the services neglects the enormous social costs of transferring half the British population from its north-western, formerly industrial base, to a new geographical and occupational environment. At least one generation would remain immobile among the kind of dereliction which is visible in northern Britain today, even if the following generation might possibly be willing and able to move. And lastly, the argument overestimates the employment possibilities of the tertiary sector, even if we make the totally unrealistic assumption that Britain, having failed to modernize her industries, retained a world monopoly of invisible exports. It might, conceivably, be a solution for a small country like Singapore or Switzerland, though even that is doubtful; it is certainly not conceivable for the 50 millions who have to be maintained in the British Isles.

A second consideration relates to the range of options and the width of the horizon of the individual entrepreneur, and the role of Government, particularly in a period of rapid change and industrial shift in a modern economy. The individual firm, as is well known, is not in a position to calculate the external economies and diseconomies of its actions, nor should it, whereas

> a policy guided by the national interest ought to consider all the various types of external economy. It cannot be expected that investors in one industry [say steel] should take into account the consequential benefits,

in part, because these depend on the decisions of others which depend, in turn, on their expectations of the decisions in steel. The marginal productivity schedule ultimately shifts upwards not because of a single autonomous decision, but because of the effects of numerous co-ordinated investment plans:

> One of the more plausible economic generalizations is that while market forces may be successful in achieving short-term marginal adjustments they contain no mecha-. nism for assessing long-term needs and initiating the movements of research, resources and capital investment to satisfy those needs.[119]

Since the fault of the British economy had become structural, the inter-relatedness of the decisions that would have to be made to overcome it was particularly clearly marked. Only the Government could have fostered more technical education or research earlier, could have enforced a public utilities policy more favourable to manufacturing industry, could have introduced specific protectionist measures for certain key infant industries, or forced firms

[119] Balogh and Streeten (1960), 216–17; Williams (1899), 4–7; Fox (1985), 228.

depending on Government orders to buy from British sources – all of which were done by Britain's more successful competitors. Conversely, it may be held that in a rearmament phase, such as the years to 1914, when the Government was using up an inordinate amount of the engineering capacity of the country, it should have made sure that other promising industries, like motor cars, were not starved of talent or resources.[120]

It is at least arguable that the duty of a Government is to look beyond the micro-economic decisions of individual firms and to foresee macro-economic developments. If industry is hamstrung by institutional constraints only the Government can be expected to alter the institutional framework.[121] British Governments failed all along the line to engage in as much steering as did other contemporary Governments, while frequently doing great harm to industries at home.

It is no doubt possible to trace this back to a failure in economic understanding. If it is permitted to speak of a 'liberal' and a 'national' political economy, there is no doubt that economic thinking in Britain was dominated too exclusively by the former, while remaining ignorant and disdainful of the latter. But, in the end, large countries are seldom governed by theories in the abstract. It is far more common for Governments to pick those of the current theories which will support what they intend to do in any case for wholly mundane reasons. In the case of the British Government of the day, it was simply not programmed, nor was it subject to any effective pressure group, to consider the present, let alone the future of manufacturing industry.

This brings us to our third and last point. The debate has generally been conducted, even in this chapter, in terms of the actions or the views of the 'Government' or the 'State', as if those were independent agencies, outside society and the economy. Of course they were not. The failures of British Governments, if any, reflected 'public opinion' as organized and manipulated by politicians and the media, together with the interests and views of the voters or those who might soon become such. The latter's views, in turn, may be derived from an inextricable mixture of a genuine understanding of their self-interest, various erroneous views regarding it, and ideological predispositions which, in turn, have many and mixed roots.

If 'Governments', therefore, acted in certain ways, it was, from one point of view, because they were expected to. Had they acted differently and intervened, let us say, in favour of certain new industries in the manner of the German Government, the 'public' would have objected, and punished them by not re-electing them next time. Yet, at the same time, these views and ideologies such as those current at the time, do not float in the air. They derive from actual needs and experiences of the main historical actors. If there was no great pressure of public opinion for positive interventionism, it was because there was no powerful lobby in whose interest it would have been to institute it, and therefore no one to influence the media and those in power in that direction.

---

[120] Irving (1975), 168–9; Kennedy (1978), 109–10; Payne (1978) VII, 210; Burchardt (1975a), 338. On the role of Government as manufacturer and customer of ships and armaments see Ashworth (1969); Pollard (1952), 98–115.
[121] Elbaum and Lazonick (1986b), 11; Mowry (1980), 190, 209; Burn (1940), 317–18.

This, then, is the puzzle. Here we have the manufacturing sector of what had only recently been the leading industrial power, still by most measures by far the most important economic sector in the British economy. It is losing out steadily against superior foreign competition, its growth rate is lower, its technical ability in many areas clearly falling behind. Yet it is unable to get the Government to help it, or even to stop harming it. It cannot even develop a convincing theoretical construct, such as was developed by economists abroad, to justify positive interventionism in its favour. How is this to be explained?

No doubt there were several explanations, untouched in these pages. But among them was the peculiar constellation of power in British political society, developed over the centuries and buttressed over the critical decades. The political Establishment was wholly dominated by a small financial and commercial elite, together with an agrarian elite whose economic significance had lain in the past but was now all but played out. By contrast, the largely provincial productive manufacturing sector was virtually excluded. The significance of this political structure, and of the consequential negative role of Government regarding the economic interests of Britain in this period, has been overlooked far too long in the literature.

5

Some Conclusions: Maturity or Senescence?

This study set out to discover whether there was a decline in the rate of growth of the British economy between 1870 and 1914, and if so, in what sense a decline might be said to have occurred. It was then to proceed to survey, in a number of separate essays, the debate on some of the alleged causes of this deceleration.

Of these two tasks, the factual account seemed at first sight to be much the easier. This turned out very soon not to be the case. For apart from the ambiguities of the statistics themselves, there is no obvious guide to our interpretation of them. It depends on the standards of comparison we choose. Some observers have argued that what occurred was merely the kind of deceleration in the rate of economic growth such as even successful economies might expect at that stage of development. Those who alleged that a failure had occurred, expressed this in one of at least two forms: either that the British growth rate became slower than it had been before and thus represented a failure to hold the standards of success achieved by earlier generations, or, alternatively, that the growth rate was slower than that of other contemporary countries and thus represented failure in international comparison. None of these concepts is without ambiguities; what is more, our judgement will depend on a prior expectation of the British economic performance.

It would, of course, be possible simply to record that the rate of growth had slowed down, absolutely or relatively, just as one might record that the metabolism of the human body had slowed down with age without assigning blame to anyone. But that is not how most historians saw the issue. For them, the important thing was to determine the causes of the deceleration, and these causes very easily fall into two groups, 'natural causes', such as the giving out of ore supplies or an alteration in the world's trade routes, and human or social causes which might be considered to have been more under social control. It was precisely this possibility of control by human agencies which has given rise to the notion of failure and the debate on guilt or responsibility for it. Since David Landes's pioneer study[1] this alleged failure has largely meant failure of entrepreneurship, but other human or social agencies, such as the Government or the Civil Service, have not escaped blame.

The debate has so far remained inconclusive and also, to some extent, rather

[1] Landes (1969), chapter 5; Saul (1980), 5.

unsatisfactory. The widespread feeling of dissatisfaction with it most likely derives from the fluid nature of the counter-factual assumptions which underlie the notion of blame or failure. When we say that something should have or could have been different, our choice of the counter-factual, or what might have been different from the actual historical sequence of events, appears very largely arbitrary and thus not necessarily very convincing to others. As an example, let us say that we might blame British employers for not devoting more resources to scientific study and research. But their neglect derived from the attitude towards science on the part of their schools, their environment created by other entrepreneurs, Governments and public opinion, as well as their own experience as employers, and it would be most unnatural and indeed almost inconceivable that they should, in large numbers, have acted against all these influences. It would surely be unreasonable of us to expect it. Are we then to blame the public schools and universities, among others, for these failings? But their teachers and councils were, in turn, behaving quite normally in terms of their training, experience, sense of priorities and self-interest. The chain could be continued into infinity. To 'blame' entrepreneurship seems all the more misplaced in the light of the fact that British profits were doing quite well at the time.

Alternatively, we might therefore merely record that entrepreneurs, Government agencies and others concerned acted in ways which were natural and unexceptionable in themselves, but happened unfortunately to produce slow growth. This view has found much favour, but it runs the danger of reducing human beings simply to playthings of their environment. We might get round this by saying that while most people will always follow tradition and routine, we would expect, in a healthy or successful society, to find some individuals who would break through these and grasp new opportunities. Of course, there were some who did just that in late Victorian and Edwardian Britain, but possibly there were not enough of them. What, then, is enough? How do we judge the adequacy of the number and power of innovators in a given situation? It is not surprising that not much agreement has been achieved on any of these shifting definitions.

Because of this, curiously enough, the question of decline or undue deceleration could not be settled by the statistics alone, but became intimately connected with the 'failure' or 'success' of the separate sectors and issues discussed in the other essays. Counterfactual assumptions and might-have-beens, which hovered constantly in the background of these and frequently obtruded on the front of the stage, would in the end also reflect on the judgement whether the overall growth rate might be considered satisfactory or whether it represented a decline.

There are, to simplify matters, basically two possible descriptive patterns. We might say that the development of the British economy suffered a definite, discernible and permanent change in direction. This view has been put succinctly by at least one student of the literature:

> Economic historians generally recognize that during the second half of the nineteenth century the British economy underwent a climacteric from which it has never recovered even today.[2]

[2] Beenstock (1983), 161; also Roderick and Stephens (1981d), 232–3; Payne (1968), 98.

261

The alternative viewpoint would be to recognize that the exceptional lead achieved by British manufacturing by the 1860s, in a small country endowed with but limited resources, could not be expected to last forever. When other countries began to catch up and to equal British industrial and economic prowess, as they did in our period, this need not imply that the British economy had in some sense failed, nor did it imply that British growth, once others had been allowed to catch up, would not then continue in step with them thereafter.

Variants of either of these two simplified patterns could easily be imagined and built in, but the decision as to which of them actually applied should not have been too difficult. Alas, as we have seen, things did not turn out to have been so easy.

Let us start with the statistical evidence, much of which was presented in chapter 1. Growth in total national income showed no decline over 1870–1914, but was slower than in the immediately preceding years – but these, in turn, were exceptional years, and over a longer period the years on which our interest is centred saw no change in direction or speed. In output per head, there was indeed a clear tendency downward in the early years of the twentieth century, but a sharp upward kink reversed this just before the outbreak of war. There had been similar short-term drops before, and there is no telling whether this one might have belonged to that category, or was part of a long-term downward change cut off by the war. The same drop, followed by a remarkable recovery, is found in the manufacturing output series, representing for many observers the key element in the British economic performance. Exports, of which the manufactured goods component was much the most important, suffered their dip earlier, but then showed a very clear successful recovery from the mid-1890s. The movements of export quantities and export values diverged sharply from each other, but this dip and recovery were common to both. The statistics are thus clearly compatible with a stable development, but also, though less convincingly, with a change-over to a lower growth path or even a decline.

If we turn to international comparisons, we find much stronger evidence for a decline in the British performance: annual growth rates, at any rate of some foreign industrializing countries, were distinctly faster throughout. But, equally clearly, these others failed to catch up with Britain in absolute terms. The single exception to this was the USA which, however, overtook Britain as early as the 1870s in many fields when there was no suggestion of British failure, and which of course enjoyed a much more favourable ratio of resources to men than British. 'The superiority of the United States over England', the *Economist* had declared as early as the year of the great British triumph, 1851, 'is ultimately as certain as the next eclipse'.[3]

In export performance the British lead over all others, in absolute terms and per head, was greater still, despite the tendency for the British share to drop. Clearly here, too, the gap was closing but had not yet closed.

Equally inconclusive is the evidence from individual industries. In some, Britain remained in the lead; in numerous others, the gap had been closed, or was about to close; and in some, one or other foreign country was leading, but there were few total British failures.

[3] *Economist*, 8 March 1851; Abramovitz (1986), 393, 397.

How is this varied evidence to be interpreted? There is no doubt that growth can proceed very fast in the early phases of industrialization. In Jánossy's terms this is the phase of 'extensive' growth, when industrialization spreads to ever more sectors of the economy. In the following, 'intensive' growth phase, all sectors are industrialized and can grow only at the rate of their internal technical progress, so that overall growth must slow down.[4] According to an alternative theory, the advanced economy lies on the technological frontier and can only grow as fast as new discoveries allow, whereas the catching-up economies can make up for lost time by jumping over phases of growth in one go and can also still make use of switches in resource allocation.[5] It is therefore not in the least remarkable that other economies, in their earlier growth stages, were growing faster than the British, and indeed the kind of faster rates of growth of others after 1870 had been achieved by the United Kingdom earlier, when it was in a similar growth phase:[6]

Annual growth rates:	Germany	Great Britain
1860–80	1.55%	*1.65%*
1880–1913	*1.65*	1.10

Afterwards it slowed down, but this would have to happen to other economies also in due course. Of course, the absolute growth figures in tens of £millions might still be higher in many cases for Britain, because of the higher starting level, though its rate of increase had slipped below that of the followers-on.[7]

It was possible also to hold the alternative view. According to this, the 'British dominance and British industrialization belonged to an earlier phase in the development of the world economy'. Moreover, once a certain 'frame of mind' or 'momentum' had fixed the economy in a lower growth path it would stay on it and, worst of all, Britain from the early 1870s experienced a sharper rate of retardation than that which could normally be expected.[8] Britain, in this view, was not merely being caught up, but overtaken and left behind, to drop ever further behind the leaders, and perhaps eventually to meet the fate of Italy, Spain or Portugal in earlier ages.

If overall statistics offer no conclusive evidence to allow us to choose between these alternatives, since they are compatible with both, where could we look for additional information? Some of our more detailed indices may be quoted in favour of the proposition that a long-term reversal of fortune had set in and that Britain was dropping below the line of technical potentiality. In several key industries that were to become highly significant in the future she had a weak hold only, or else her plants were founded, managed or financed by foreigners. Among these, as noted in chapter 1, were chemicals and electrical engineering.

[4] Jánossy (1966); Aldcroft and Richardson (1969), 105.
[5] Abramovitz (1986); Edelstein (1982), 216–17; Musson (1962–63), 531–2; Platt (1968), 106.
[6] Goldsmith (1969), 406–7; Rathgen (1913), 5. Growth for the whole of the period 1856/60 to 1911/13 was also similar: 1.64% p.a. for Germany, 1.64% p.a. for Germany, 1.65% for Britain: Feldenkirchen (1980), 81–2.
[7] Musson (1962–63), 533; Medley (1896), 32 ff. Also Introduction, pp. xii–xiii, note 4.
[8] Aldcroft and Richardson (1969), 102; Saville (1963), 69; Lewis (1957), 587; Gamble (1981), 84. For Saul's recantation on this issue, cf. Saul (1980) p. 30.

More seriously, in other industries, including the staples that formed the backbone of Britain's industrial strength, Britain seemed to be very slow to adopt the latest technology. This was true of cotton and wool, of iron and steel, of coal mining and even of shipbuilding, where Britain still totally dominated world markets.[9] For each of these, there might be a perfectly good individual explanation, but the coincidence that in each case it always turned out to be Britain in which the new technology was not appropriate seemed too great to be entirely fortuitous. Even if Britain continued to score market and export successes, this might well be due to the earlier momentum and could evaporate very rapidly. By contrast, the industries in which Britain was in a genuine technical lead were few. Britain was also backward in industrial organization and in modern forms of internal management.

At this point the other essays might be brought into the argument. The exceptionally large amounts of capital sent abroad, as discussed in chapter 2, might, on certain assumptions, be considered to have been at the expense of investment and innovation at home, and thus explain the slow-down in Britain as well as the particular form it took. The evidence that that is indeed what had taken place is, however, by no means clear-cut. It is equally possible to argue that foreign investment was a welcome alternative to shrinking home opportunities, that returns at home would have been low while returns abroad were high, and benefited not only the investors, but the whole economy by developing parts of the world which supplied Britain with the cheap food and raw materials that helped to raise real standards of living at the time. Capital exports were part of the pattern which kept down industrial output below what it might have been otherwise, but by the same token raised incomes, and the output of the tertiary sector.

Chapter 3, concerned with the teaching and research in science and technology, left the issue equally uncertain. It was not difficult to show that formal teaching was, in organization and quantity, well below the German level and that teachers, students and researchers were numerically but a fraction of those found in Germany and the USA. Dangerous and inhibiting as this position was before 1914, its real menace lay in the likelihood of its cumulation in the future: few teachers meant few graduates in the next generation, few employers capable of understanding the contribution which formal science could make, and ultimately a complete loss of contact with the most advanced work done elsewhere. But equally, there was no sign of a shortage of scientists and technologists from the point of view of industry; a vast network of informal training at all levels exceeded that offered abroad and might have been more appropriate to British needs and traditions; and far from losing contact with the best, British scientists were still clearly in the lead in many fields in 1914. Moreover, the kind of arguments and accusations brought forward by the science lobby could be duplicated by the propaganda from equally interested parties in other countries, including Germany, at the time.

Another possible weakness lay in the role played by the Government in the widest sense, discussed in chapter 4. The most prominent failing lay not so much in what the Government did, but in what it omitted to do. Many of the

---

[9] Musson (1962–63), 533; Saul (1965), 17; Schulze-Gaevernitz (1906), 256–7.

necessary functions of a modern state had not yet been taken on but left to self-interested private initiative, including even financial policy and monetary control. Other functions the State was not yet in a position to undertake for lack of the necessary staff, or, more seriously, because it lacked the will or the sense of responsibility to do so. The negative stance towards industry was not simply an indiosyncracy of Government but was shared by wide sections of public opinion, including some of the victims of industry itself. But, put differently, this might be taken to mean that the need for State intervention was not yet keenly felt and therefore not a dire necessity. Moreover, the most successful economy of the day, that of the United States, was similarly lightly governed. Yet the social constellation of political influence there was very different from the British, and it might well be the case that because of the political weakness of industry in Britain, the political will to aid it was lacking, and this was both a cause and consequence of industrial decline.

By no means all the possible causes and symptoms of the British 'decline' or slow-down in that period have been discussed here. The list is a long one, and ours is but intended as a selection, to emphasize the ambiguities, but not to be capable of furnishing a definitive answer. Possibly other issues might have offered a more clear-cut and satisfactory indicator of relative decline, or relative success.

The topic most conspicuously missing in this collection of essays is the alleged weakness or failure in entrepreneurship. Apart from the fact that this volume did not set out to offer a comprehensive set of causes, there are several reasons for that particular omission. One is that it has been very widely debated, and therefore is less in need of a further airing. A second, more fundamental cause, is that it in fact pervades all the other issues and a separate airing would do little more than duplicate what has been said elsewhere. Thus the decision to send capital abroad instead of investing it at home, the decisions of individual industrial firms on new technologies or their attitudes to markets, the appointment of trained scientists as against the preference for apprenticed men – all these and many more are the kind of questions commonly discussed under the heading of entrepreneurship. In much of the debate it is but a substitute for rational decision-making.

Above all, however, the debate on entrepreneurship in much of the literature is fundamentally misconceived. Great Britain was not a backward country steeped in traditionalism which had to wait for its entrepreneurs to awaken it to its economic opportunities. It was the most advanced industrial country of the day, the country in which the breakthrough to the modern economy had occurred first, in which, therefore, certain inhibiting elements of traditionalism had the weakest hold in Europe. There was no lack of commercial spirit in Britain: on the contrary, from the nobility downwards, all were keen to make money. In the services, such as banking, insurance or shipping, Britain led the world. Modern consumer industries, from daily newspapers for the masses to chocolates and cigarettes, had been pioneered in Britain. Even in some of the staples she dominated the world markets still. If there was a lack, it was in certain sectors only, a failure to reach particular decisions, in particular contexts, for particular reasons, not a failure in entrepreneurship as a weakness in British society.

Another topic omitted here, apart from some oblique references, is the issue of free trade versus protection. Among contemporaries, it was the leading topic of economic policy debate, and the literature is enormous. Alas, it is not conclusive and there seemed little value in adding to it. Other topics which might have deserved extended treatment and have been mentioned here either briefly or not at all were the labour market, the decline in the raw material sources or a shift in their significance, the costs of Empire, and the debate on eugenics or racial decline.

At the same time, the view that a cumulative downward trend had established itself in 1870–1914, at least in a relative sense of a falling behind the possibilities and the levels achieved by other countries, was not the only interpretation possible of the data available. There was nothing like a failure along the whole front, a lack of ability to compete with the best that could be produced and developed abroad. On the contrary, while there were evident weaknesses, many of which were signs of old age, or the 'early start', these were scattered and indeed cause for comment and surprise, rather than being typical. The decades to 1913 had, in fact, seen an enormous number of changes, new beginnings, transformations and adaptations in the British economy.[10] The economy was not clinging blindly to the old, even if it might not be clear that it was looking for the new in the right direction. When free-traders spoke of continuous growth, flexibility and competitiveness, they were not merely making propaganda. There were many areas of economic life in which British practitioners would have been surprised to be told that they were on a downward path, however defined. True, the overwhelming superiority over the rest, still visible in the early 1870s, had gone for good; but failures and successes were scattered patchily over the economy, and it was by no means easy to say which was dominant or determinant.

It must not be forgotten that the path for other countries was by no means smooth either. The United States, much the richest and most progressive economy of the day, benefiting among other factors from the large immigration of able-bodied young men and women, and from the enormous wealth of its land and natural resources, yet had much unemployment, suffered from severe cyclical crises and monopolistic restrictions, and some of its major initiatives, like the attempt to corner the major Atlantic shipping routes in the International Mercantile Marine, or to conquer the British cigarette market, went badly astray. Germany had to contend with a Government dominated by a landed class showing little sympathy for industry and keeping the price of food well above world prices, and with a system of cartels and protection favouring the basic producers against the interests of the manufacturers of finished goods. Among other handicaps, she also had the difficult task of the late-comer of breaking into established British markets overseas and in the colonies. Other countries faced difficulties of at least equal import and much of the rest of the world, even the rest of Europe, was in fact so far behind Britain that no valid comparisons were possible. No one registered untarnished 'success': on a world-wide basis, signs of 'convergence' to the level of the handful of leaders were still very weak before 1913.[11]

---

[10] Ashworth (1960), 80, *passim*, and Ashworth (1966), 24–6; Crouzet (1978), 368.
[11] Abramovitz (1986), 394–5.

What would a world look like in which others were catching up on the leader, but the leader himself was advancing quite satisfactorily? We would expect to see a rather ragged front line, in which each country had some strong sectors and some weak ones, making a spurt forward here and falling temporarily behind there, but possibly also keeping in the van with some specialisms over longer periods. We would expect an international division of labour dominated by resource endowment and a Heckscher–Ohlin factor distribution. As a first approximation, such a picture of mixed strengths and weaknesses among the leading countries was remarkably close to reality in the years to 1913.[12] The international division of labour arising therefrom was particularly clearly marked in the relationship between Britain and Germany, especially in the textile and iron and steel industries, but also in such esoteric specialisms as German subsidized sugar as base for British biscuit exports.[13]

To come closer still to reality, however, our model must be modified in at least one important respect: Britain's main competitors had introduced protective tariffs with the express intention, in most cases, of achieving precisely the degree of catching up which had become evident in the years before 1913. That they harmed thereby some of the key British industries which had hitherto supplied their home market, and that they fostered their own key industries in the short and medium term, there is no doubt. In particular, by a careful 'scientific' tariff, at least Germany and the USA were better able to concentrate resources in 'strategic areas for rapid development at moments crucial to the evolution of new products and new techniques'. They could also achieve greater stability of sales,[14] from which derived a powerful incentive to invest, while the free-trade economy of Britain was left to bear more than its fair share . of the fluctuations.

Britain's free-trade policies, precisely as theory would lead one to expect, provided cheaper food and other low-priced imports and thus a higher standard of living at a given level of home productivity than was enjoyed by comparable contemporary societies,[15] but at the expense of disorienting certain productive sectors and subjecting them to the effects of foreign dumping and/or monopolistic competition. It was therefore as one-sided to deplore only the losses incurred by free-trade policies, as it was, conversely, to stress their gains without counting the costs. Some industries in which experience, skill, resources and market dominance counted, would no doubt survive in such conditions, and the shipbuilding industry might furnish an example for this, but under pressure from foreign tariffs imposed by economies which were increasingly similar, one would expect a tendency for Britain's comparative advantages to shift to the commercial and financial sector and to invisibles in

---

[12] Musson (1959), 207–8; Aldcroft (1968b), 34–5; Dispatch from Chamberlain (1897), LX,C.8449, pp. 579 ff; Ashworth (1960), 260–1; Saul (1980), 28–9; Barker (1972) I, pp. 54 ff.

[13] Buchheim (1986), 31–5; Crammond (1914), 794–5 and Paish in discussion, 810; Walker (1980), 7; Medley (1896), 39, 43; Pope and Hoyle (1985), 30; Saul (1980), 8; Wengenroth (1986), 289–90.

[14] Kennedy (1976), 156; also Chapman (1904) I, 65; Hirsch (1967), 2; Krassner (1975–76), 318–19; Semmel (1970), 36; Wengenroth (1986), 295–6. Introduction, note 12.

[15] Crafts and Thomas (1986), 642, in their typically negative way, paraphrased this by saying that at any given level of national income, British manufacturing output was lower than that of others. Also Ashworth (1965), 69–70.

general, where her early start, her longer experience and her consequent high reputation would continue to give her an edge over the later arrivals. Indeed, it was precisely her free-trade policies which were the basis of success in those fields, as was noted by Robert Giffen as early as 1903:

> Only a free-trade country, or rather a free import country, can be the centre of the world's international commerce, as we are, which brings us an enormous business and gain, whatever special disadvantages it *may* have in the shape of 'dumping' and so on.[16]

As shown in chapter 4, this was not the least reason why protection for British key industries had no chance in this period.

The tendency for the leading industrial economy to shift, at the height of its power, to commerce and ultimately finance and foreign investment has been observed in earlier centuries also, particularly among the Italian cities and later in the case of the Netherlands. The Dutch, who furnish the closest parallel, had in the seventeenth and eighteenth centuries, like the British in the nineteenth and twentieth, also suffered from tariffs raised against their exports by other countries, and from accusations that their workmen's wages were too high and that their entrepreneurs had become too lethargic.[17] But whether this switch was a sign of weakness[18] or of strength, a symbol of leadership or of decline, is precisely the point at issue. The matter is discussed at some length in chapter 2 and towards the end of chapter 4.

In a similar light has also to be seen the unusual concentration of British exports to the less developed and the colonial world, while other European industrial nations, above all Germany, held the dominant share in the more developed European markets. This did not necessarily imply a weaker sales effort on the part of British suppliers; more significantly, it helped to strengthen Britain's position as the fulcrum of world trade, and once again, indicated a shift from production to commerce and finance. Thus it helped to keep the British payments surplus and capital export surplus in balance. In turn, a stable world trading and payments system was a vital necessity for Britain's lucrative international financial business, lucrative not least because it was conducted with a cheap minimal gold reserve. But being cheap, it was also vulnerable and desperately required stability to survive.[19]

When some of Britain's chief export and staple industries were, like agriculture before them, sacrificed to the advantages of free trade, the stakes were therefore higher than merely gaining the advantages of an international division of industrial labour, by importing freely cheap goods for which foreign makers had cost advantages, to help such industries as still enjoyed comparative advantages in Britain. The more significant gain consisted in channelling the world's shipping to British lines and its financial business to the City of London. But if Britain's specialism increasingly lay in the commercial and

---

[16] Underlined in the original. Letter to Chamberlain in Coats (1968), 207. Also see chapter 1, pp. 1, 17 and 50, notes 236 and 167 above.

[17] See chapter 1 p. 57, note 190 above.

[18] Kindleberger (1978), 220; Cain (1979), 42; Gilpin (1976), 46–7.

[19] Saul (1954–55), esp. 57–9, 65–9 and Saul (1980), 24–5; Kindleberger (1961–2), 294; Introduction, p. xv, notes 17–18.

financial sectors, the exclusive concern with industrial performance in the discussion on decline or retardation becomes highly questionable.

. Moreover, this unique stance was not without effect on the structure of Britain's industries and her internal service sectors themselves. The higher standard of living achieved by industrial growth and progress, but also by the international specialization in the tertiary sector, had brought changes in British consumption patterns and the market provisions for them. This was the period of much new housing, of new school buildings, of faster and more comfortable trains, of the rise of seaside resorts – all of them, incidentally, objects requiring a great deal of capital without immediate visible effects on output or 'productivity'. It was also the period of a shopping revolution with better and costlier shopping facilities at all social levels. Mass-production industries and commodities of a new type, most of them pioneered in Britain, catered for the higher available incomes, especially for the working and the lower middle classes. These included soap, chocolates, tobacco, newspapers, pharmaceuticals and drugs, and ready-made clothing and footwear. Other typical British innovations were mass spectator sports and the long week-end, while the practices of an increasingly costly social insurance system were taken over from Germany.[20] It was this switch of production resources, including investments, from the staple export industries to the consumption sector, much of it in the form of services, which created the difficulties for the Rostow stage theory as applied to Britain, according to which a large and unexplained gap of over 80 years had opened up between 'maturity' around 1850 and the age of mass consumption, by which Rostow apparently meant motor cars and electrical gadgets, around 1935.[21]

It might be argued that such indulgence in higher consumption was premature and that it was precisely the sybaritic quest for leisure and comfort to be found among all classes in Britain, from the top entrepreneurs down to the meanest labourer, which allowed other countries to catch up and possibly overtake the formerly leading economy. To be sure, every economy makes decisions about consumption or investment for consumption later, and a market economy does it by means of myriads of independent decisions. The British, because they had reached higher levels of national income earlier, also began to enjoy higher consumption earlier than other Europeans. But there is no way of determining whether this was 'too early', and how many more generations should have invested frugally in ever better productive equipment before enjoying its fruits.

Sooner or later, every economy will translate its higher output into higher income. How that is distributed, and especially whether it benefits largely the poorer and working classes, who will consume most of it, or the capital-owning classes, who will save a larger share, will depend on social, political, organizational and many other factors within society and cannot be predicted from purely economic data. There certainly was a tendency, because of her relatively liberal political structure, for Britain to be early in the field with strong unions (though rather late with State social welfare services) and thus an early

[20] Chapter 1, note 2 and note 167.
[21] Kindleberger (1964), 309.

269

distribution in favour of wage earners. The tendency for rising incomes, generated by better industrial performance, to be accompanied by similar liberalizing social and political changes, is no doubt widespread, but can by no means be taken for granted. It may well be that newly industrializing nations find it easier to transfer the technology of the pioneer(s) than the freedom for trade unions and the social legislation which ensure the fairer distribution of its fruits, so that, for a time, they enjoy the 'advantage' of using similar technology at lower wages than the leading economies.

It is considerations of this kind which have led to the development of the thesis of the 'product cycle', associated with Raymond Vernon's pathbreaking work, but foreshadowed earlier by H. Frankel and M.V. Posner.[22] According to this theory, the advanced country will have the advantage in new commodities or processes, especially if they require much capital or complex technological knowledge and experience, but once the initial stages of research, development and pioneer production are over, it may well be cheaper to transfer production to less developed countries, with lower wage and other costs and perhaps more unspoilt resources, and, when the product or process has reached a mass-production basis, to transfer it further to even more backward countries.

Thus to keep its own productive equipment going, the leading (high income and high wage) country has to be forever one step ahead, at least until such time as other catching up economies have, by building up a similar industrial base, reached the same level of incomes. In a pessimistic version of this theory, the peripheral countries will regularly undercut the industrial output of the core countries and cause a major crisis there, such as the 'Great Depression' of 1873–95, before the latter recover again by renewed major effort.[23] Even without such extreme pessimism, the danger at least of balance of payments difficulties, caused not by dropping behind but simply by not keeping ahead of the rest, always exists for the leading country.

In all of this, the *a priori* model of a formerly leading economy with no particular resource advantages which was being caught up technically by others similarly endowed conforms remarkably closely to what happened to the British economy in its international setting in our period. This must be a strong argument for taking the catching up, rather than the climacteric senescence model, as the more appropriate one.

There is, however, an even stronger argument for doubting the decline thesis, and it turns on the ability of the British economy to react to stimuli and to overcome crises in the following period. We have seen, in chapter 3, how astonishingly rapidly Britain was able to build up its science and technology teaching and research in the last few years before the war, when the need seemed to be widely accepted. Starting from almost nowhere, in a few years the figures began to approach German levels, when the war intervened. One is reminded of the American reaction to the Russian Sputnik in more recent years. While the Russian satellite represented an astonishing achievement and a clear

---

[22] Vernon (1966), 190–207; Frankel (1943), 188–201; Hufbauer (1966); Posner (1961), Grubel and Lloyd (1975), 113; Burenstam Linder (1961); Vernon (1979), 255; Hirsch (1967), 16–41; Jahrreisz (1984), 21–2; Gilpin (1976).
[23] Beenstock (1983), 162 ff.

sign of technical leadership in one specific field, the American capacity for high-technology production was so much more solid and more advanced that even in the one strong point of its competitor it was able in a few years not only to catch up, but to lead at will, so as even to be able to put a man on the moon. In the years to 1913 the British economy was not only still the most productive in Europe, but also flexible and possessing hidden reserves at least the equal of any other. Nowhere had it lost contact with the best, or made irremediable mistakes. More significant still in this context was its ability to install and operate successfully a whole range of industries hitherto hardly known in Britain or dependent on Germany, as soon as war-time needs made this imperative. Examples cited in chapter 1 range from chemicals and optical glassware to aircraft and motor vehicles.

It is not difficult to see why the thesis that there was a downturn in the British economy somewhere near the end of the nineteenth century, and that the relative decline has continued ever since, should have enjoyed such popularity in recent years, at least among British authors. That there was a change at that time is undisputed: this was the change-over from solitary pre-eminence in industrial and mining production to being one of several industrialized countries, each of which had access to similar capital resources, technical equipment and scientific know-how. It was a traumatic experience for many British citizens, and one which they had scarcely fully absorbed even half a century later when the devastation left by the Second World War in Europe made it possible once again to think of a built-in British superiority over the European continent in industrial matters.

When, however, in the later post-war years, evidence of Britain's real relative decline had become only too obvious, it shook British self-assurance all the more. What lies closer than to hark back to that earlier trauma and assume that the decline had set in then? At least in that way the full blame for the sorry current performance might be diverted from the living generation.

Yet, to quote S.B. Saul, the

> shifting comparative advantages . . . [and] shifting patterns . . . make it very dangerous to look back before 1914 to determine the long roots of Britain's current industrial problems.[24]

Edwardian Britain is not to be confused with the managed economy of the past 40 years. Though there were signs of weakness, of mistaken policies and false assumptions, of snobbery in the schools and of short-sightedness in the City, the economy was fundamentally sound. As events were to prove, it was capable of acting as the launching pad for astonishing industrial progress and technical, scientific and organizational pioneering efforts under much more difficult conditions than those which had tested its mettle before 1914. The faults of the decline after 1945 are not to be shuffled off to earlier generations; they remain firmly the responsibility of those who controlled Britain's economic fortunes in those years.

[24] Saul (1980), 30.

Bibliography

Official Publications

Balfour Committee (1918), Committee on Commercial and Industrial Policy after the War, *Report*, Parl.P. 1918,XIII. C.9035.

Balfour Committee (1929), Committee on Industry and Trade, *Final Report* Cmd.3282, 1929. *Factors in Industrial and Commercial Efficiency* (1927); *Survey of Textile Industries* (1928).

Children's Employment Commission (1842). *Appendix to First Report of Commissioners* (Mines), *Part I: Reports and Evidence from Sub-Commissioners*. Parl.P. 1842.XVI.(301).

D.C. (1906), D.C. on Royal College of Science. *Final Report with Appendix* I, Parl.P. 1906.XXXI, Cd.2872, Vol.II, Minutes of Evidence, Appendices, Cd.2956.

D.C. (1916), D.C. Board of Trade, *Report on Financial Facilities for Trade*, Parl.P. 1916.XV.Cd.8346.

D.C. (1918a), D.C. on Textile Trades after the War, *Report*, Parl.P. 1918.XIII. Cd.9070.

D.C. (1918b), D.C. Board of Trade to Consider the Position of the Electrical Trades after the War, *Report*, Parl.P. 1918, Cd.9072.

Diplomatic and Consular Officers (1899), *Opinion of H.M. Diplomatic and Consular Officers on British Trade Methods*, Parl.P. 1899.XCVI. C.9078.

Diplomatic and Consular Reports (1901), *Germany*, Parl. P. 1901.LXXXV. Cd.430–16.

O.E.C.D. (n.d.), Study Group in the Economics of Education, *The Residual Factor and Economic Growth*, Paris.

R.C. (Newcastle) (1861) *The State of Popular Education in England*. Vol. 1, Parl.P. 1861.XXI.(2704.1); Reports of Assistant Commissioners, Parl.P. 1861.XXI.(2794.IV).

R.C. (Clarendon) (1864) *On the Revenues and Management of Certain Colleges and Schools, Report*. Parl.P. 1864.XX.(3288).

R.C. (Devonshire) (1972–5), *On Scientific Instruction and the Advancement of Science. First and Second Reports*, Parl.P. 1872.XXV.c.536;
  Third Report, Parl.P. 1873.XXVII.c.868.
  Fourth Report, 1874.XXII.c.884
  Fifth Report, 1874.XXII.c.1087
  Sixth Report, 1875.XXVIII.c.1279
  Seventh Report, 1875.XXVIII.c.1279
  Eighth Report, 1875.XXVIII.c.1298.

R.C. (Samuelson) (1882–4), *On Technical Instruction. First Report*, Parl.P. 1882.XXVII.c.3171; *Second Report*, Parl.P. 1884.XXIX and XXXI, c.3981.

R.C. (1886) *On the Depression in Trade and Industry, Report*, Parl.P. 1886.XXIII.c.4893.

R.C. (Gold and Silver) (1887–8), *On the Recent Changes in the Relative Values of the Precious Metals, First Report*, Parl.P. 1887.XXII.c.5099; *Second Report*, 1888.XLV.c.5248; *Final Report* 1888.XLV.c.5512.

R.C. (Bryce) (1895), *On Secondary Education, Report*, Parl.P. 1895.XLIII,XLIV,XLV, XLVI,XLIX, c.7862.

R.C. (1905), *On the Supply of Food and Raw Material in Time of War, Report*, Parl.P. 1905.XXXIX.Cd.2643.

S.C. (Samuelson) (1867–8), *On the Provisions for giving Instruction in Theoretical and Applied Science to the Industrial Classes. Report*. Parl.P. 1867–8.XV. (432).
S.C. (1875), *On Loans to Foreign States, Report.*, Parl.P. 1875.XI.367.
S.C. (1877), *On the Companies Acts 1862 and 1867, Report*, Parl.P. 1877.VIII.365.
Trade Statistics. Parl.P. 1896.LXXVI.C.8211.
United Nations, Department of Economic and Social Affairs, (1955) *Foreign Capital in Latin America*, New York.
United Nations, Department of Economic Affairs, (1949) *International Capital Movements during the Inter-War Period*, Lake Success.
Visit to Germany (1897), *Report*, Parl.P. 1897.LXXXVIII.C.8301.

Other Publications

Abramovitz, M. (1956), 'Resource and Output Trends in the United States Since 1870'. *A.E.R.* 46.
—— (1962), 'Economic Growth in the United States', *A.E.R.* 52.
—— (1968), 'The Passing of the Kuznets Cycle', *Economica* 35.
—— (1986), 'Catching up, Forging Ahead, and Falling Behind', *J.Ec.H.* 46.
Adams, R.N. (1982), *Paradoxical Harvest. Energy and Explanation in British History, 1870–1914*, Cambridge.
Adelmann, G. (1979), 'Die berufliche Aus- und Weiterbildung in der deutschen Wirtschaft 1871–1918', in Hans Pohl (ed.), *Berufliche Aus- und Weiterbildung in der deutschen Wirtschaft seit dem 19. Jahrhundert*, Wiesbaden.
Adelmann, P. (1984), *Victorian Radicalism. The Middle Class Experience 1830–1914*.
Adler, D.R. (1970) *British Investment in American Railways 1834–1898*, Charlottesville.
Adler, J.H. (1968), 'Internationale Kapitalbewegungen', in *Enzyklopädisches Lexikon für das Geld-, Bank- und Börsenwesen*, vol. 2, Frankfurt/M.
—— (ed.) (1970), *Capital Movements and Economic Development*.
Ady, Peter (ed.), (1971a), *Private Foreign Investment and the Developing World*, New York.
—— (1971b), 'Private Overseas Investment and the Developing Countries', *Ibid.*
Ahlström, G. (1982), *Engineers and Industrial Growth. Higher Technical Education and the Engineering Profession During the Nineteenth and Early Twentieth Centuries: France, Germany, Sweden and England.*
Akerlof, G.A. (1970), 'The Market for "Lemons": Quality Uncertainty and the Market Mechanism', *Q.J.E.* 84.
Albu, A. (1980), 'British Attitudes to Engineering Education: a Historical Perspective', in Pavitt.
Aldcroft, D.H. (1964–5), 'The Enterpreneur and the British Economy, 1870–1914', *Ec.H.R.* 17.
—— (1966), 'Technical Progress and British Enterprise 1875–1914', *Bus.H.* 8.
—— (1967), 'Economic Growth in Britain in the Inter-War Years: A Re-assessment', *Ec.H.R.* 20.
—— (1967–68), 'The Efficiency and Enterprise of British Railways, 1870–1914', *Expl.Ent.H.*
—— (ed.) (1968a), *The Development of British Industry and Foreign Competition, 1815–1914, Studies in Industrial Enterprise.*
—— (1968b), 'British Industry and Foreign Competition 1875–1914', in Aldcroft.
—— (1974), 'McCloskey on Victorian Growth: A Comment', *Ec.H.R.* 27.
—— (1975), 'Investment in – and Utilization of Manpower: Great Britain and her Rivals, 1870–1914', in Ratcliffe.
—— (1981), 'The Economy, Management and Foreign Competition', in Roderick and Stephens.
—— and H.J. Dyos (1974) *British Transport. An Economic Survey from the Seventeenth Century to the Twentieth.*
—— and P. Fearon (eds.) (1972), *British Economic Fluctuations 1790–1934.*
—— and H.W. Richardson (1969), *The British Economy 1870–1939.*
Alford, B.W.E. (1973), *W.D. + H.O. Wills and the Development of the UK Tobacco Industry 1786–1965.*
—— (1964–5), 'Government Expenditure and the Growth of the Printing Industry in the Nineteenth Century', *Ec.H.R.* 17.
—— (1965), 'Business Enterprise and the Growth of the Commercial Letterpress Printing Industry, 1850–1914', *Bus.H.* 7.

—— (1977), 'Penny Cigarettes, Oligopoly and Entrepreneurship in the UK Tobacco Industry in the late 19th century', in Supple.

Allen, G.C. (1929), *The Industrial Development of Birmingham and the Black Country, 1860–1927.*

—— (1976), *The British Disease.*

Allen, Robert C. (1977), 'The Peculiar Productivity History of American Blast Furnaces, 1840–1913' *J.Ec.H.* 37.

—— (1979), 'International Competition in Iron and Steel 1850–1913', *J.Ec.H.* 39.

—— (1981), 'Entrepreneurship and Technical Progress in the Northeast Coast Pig Iron Industry: 1850–1913', *Res.Ec.H.* 6.

—— (1983), 'Recent Developments in Production, Cost and Index Number Theory, with an Application to International Differences in the Cost and Efficiency of Steelmaking 1907/09', in Fremdling and O'Brien.

Alter, P. (1978), 'Staat und Wissenschaft in Großbritannien vor 1914' in Helmut Berding *et al.*, *Vom Staat des Ancien Regime zum modernen Parteienstaat.* Festschrift für Theodor Schieder, Munich-Vienna.

—— (1982), *Wissenschaft, Staat, Mäzene, Anfänge moderner Wissenschaftspolitik in Großbritannien 1850–1920*, Stuttgart.

Amery, J. (1969), *Joseph Chamberlain and the Tariff Reform Campaign. The Life of Joseph Chamberlain*, vol. 5.

Ames, E. and N. Rosenberg (1963), 'Changing Technical Leadership and Industrial Growth', *E.J.* 73.

—— (1970), 'The Enfield Arsenal in Theory and History', in Saul.

Anderson, C.A. and M.J. Bowman (eds.) (1963a), *Education and Economic Development*, Chicago.

—— (1963b), 'Literacy and Schooling', *ibid.*

Anderson, O. (1974), 'The Administrative Reform Association 1855–1857', in Hollis, Patricia (ed.), *Pressure from Without in Early Victorian England.*

Anderson, P. (1964), 'Origins of the Present Crisis', *New Left Review* 23.

Anderson, R.D. (1983a), *Education and Opportunity in Victorian Scotland. Schools and Universities*, Oxford.

—— (1983b) 'Education and the State in Nineteenth Century Scotland', *Ec.H.R.* 36.

—— (1985b), 'Secondary Schools and Scottish Society in the 19th Century', *P&P* 109.

—— (1985a), 'In Search of the "Lad of Pairts": the Mythical History of Scottish Education', *History Workshop* 19.

Andre, D. (1971), *Indikatoren des technischen Fortschritts. Eine Analyse der Wirtschaftsentwicklung in Deutschland von 1850 bis 1913*, Göttingen.

Angell, J.W. (1926), *The Theory of International Prices. History, Criticism and Restatement*, Cambridge, Mass.

—— (1928) 'Equilibrium in International Trade: The United States, 1919–1926', *Q.J.E.* 42.

Annan, N.G. (1969), 'The Intellectual Aristocracy', in Plumb (1969).

Anonymous (1909), 'Investment, Exports and Employment', *Bankers' Magazine* 88.

Anonymous (1982), 'Personal Recollection of the Cotton Industry in Lancashire', *Three Banks Review* 134.

Anonymous (1894), 'The Recent Criticism of the Bank of England', *E.J.* 4.

Argles, M. (1964), *South Kensington to Robbins. An Account of English Technical and Scientific Education Since 1851.*

Armstrong, John A. (1973), *The European Administrative Elite.*

Armytage, W.H.G. (1945), 'A.J. Mundella and the Hosiery Industry', *Ec.H.R.* 15.

—— (1955), *Civic Universities. Aspects of a British Tradition.*

—— (1961), *A Social History of Engineering.*

—— (1965), *The Rise of the Technocrats. A Social History.*

—— (1969), *The German Influence on English Education.*

Arndt, P. (1912), 'Wesen und Zweck der Kapitalanlage im Auslande', *Zeitschrift für Sozialwissenschaft*, Neue Folge III.

—— (1915), 'Neue Beiträge zur Frage der Kapitalanlage im Auslande', *Ibid.*, N.F. VI.

Arnold, M. (1874), *Higher Schools and Universities in Germany.*

Arnstein, W.L. (1973), 'The Survival of the Victorian Aristocracy', in Jaher, F.C., *The Rich, the Wellborn and the Powerful*, Urbana.

Arrow, K.J. (1969), 'The Economic Implications of Learning by Doing', *Rev.Ec.Studies* 29.

Artifex and Opifex (1907) *The Causes of Decay in British Industry*.
Ashby, E. (1958), *Technology and the Academics. An Essay on Universities and the Scientific Revolution*.
— (1974), *Adapting Universities to Technological Society*, San Francisco.
Ashley, F.co. (1958), *Technology and the Academics. An Essay on Universities and the Scientific Revolution*.
Ashley, W.J. (ed.) (1907), *British Industries*.
— (1911), *The Tariff Problem*.
Ashworth, W. (1960), *An Economic History of England 1870-1939*.
— (1965), 'Changes in the Industrial Structure: 1870-1914', *Yorkshire Bulletin* 17.
— (1966), 'The Late Victorian Economy', *Economica* 33.'
— (1969), 'Economic Aspects of Late Victorian Naval Administration', *Ec.H.R.* 22.
Atkin, J.M. (1977), *British Overseas Investment, 1918-1931*, New York.
— (1970), 'Official Regulation of British Overseas Investment, 1914-1931', *Ec.H.R.* 23.
Aukrust, O. (1971), 'Investment and Economic Growth', in Kiker.
Aydelotte, W.O. (1962-63), 'Voting Patterns in the British House of Commons in the 1840's', in *Comp.Stud.Soc.H.* 5.
— (1966), 'Parties and Issues in Early Victorian England', in *J.Brit.S.* 5.
— (1967a), 'The Conservative and Radical Interpretations of Early Victorian Social Legislation', in *Victorian Studies*, 11.
— (1967b), 'The Country Gentlemen and the Repeal of the Corn Laws', *E.H.R.*, 82.
— (1972), 'The Disintegration of the Conservative Party in the 1840's' in W.O. Aydelotte *et al.*, *The Dimensions of Quantitive Research in History*, Princeton.
Babbage, Ch. (1837), *Economy of Machinery and Manufactures*.
— (1968), *The Exposition of 1851*.
Bachmann, H. and E. Heuss (1956), 'International Kapitalbewegungen', in *Handwörterbuch der Sozialwissenschaften* vol. 5.
Bagehot, W. (1962), *Lombard Street. A Description of the Money Market*, Homewood.
Bagwell, Ph.S. and G.E. Mingay (1970), *Britain and America 1850-1939: a Study of Economic Change*.
Bagwell, P. (1963). *The Railwaymen*.
Balley, J.D. (1959-60), 'Australian Borrowing in Scotland in the Nineteenth Century', *Ec.H.R.* 12.
Bairoch, P. (1976a), *Commerce extérieur et développement économique de l'Europe au XIXe siècle*, Paris-Hague.
— (1976b), 'Europe's Gross National Product 1800-1975', *J.Europ.Ec.H.* 5.
— (1977), 'La place de la France sur les marchés internationaux', in Levy-Leboyer.
— (1982), 'International Industrialisation Levels from 1750 to 1980', *J.Europ.Ec.H.* 11.
Baker, W.J. (1970), *A History of the Marconi Company*.
Balfour, A.J. (1903), *Economic Notes on Insular Free Trade*.
Balfour, M. (1985), *Britain and Joseph Chamberlain*.
Ballin, H.H. (1946), *The Organisation of Electricity Supply in Great Britain*.
Ballod, K. (1916), 'Review of A. Hesse and H. Großmann, 'Englands Handelsleistung und die chemische Industrie', in *Schmollers Jahrbuch* 40.
Balogh, T. (1982), *The Irrelevance of Contemporary Economics*.
— and P.P. Streeten (1960). 'Domestic versus Foreign Investment', *Bull.Ox.U.Inst.Stat.* 22.
Bamford, T.W. (1961), 'Public Schools and Social Class, 1801-1850', *Brit.J.Sociology* 12.
— (1967), *Rise of the Public Schools. A Study of Boys' Public Boarding Schools in England and Wales from 1837 to the Present Day*.
Barbour, V. (1976), *Capitalism in Amsterdam in the 17th Century*, Ann Arbor.
Barker, J.E. (1901), 'The Economic Decay of Great Britain', *Contemporary Review*.
Barker, T.C. (1960), *Pilkington Brothers and the Glass Industry*.
— (1977), *The Glassmakers. Pilkington: the Rise of an International Company 1826-1976*.
— (1968), 'Glass Industry', in Aldcroft.
— (1972), 'History: Economic and Social', in C.B. Cox and A.E. Dyson (eds.), *The Twentieth Century Mind 1. 1900-1918*.
Barnett, C. (1972), *The Collapse of British Power*.
— (1986), *The Audit of War. The Illusion and Reality of Britain as a Great Nation*.

Bibliography

Barratt, Brown, M. (1973), *After Imperialism*.

Bartlett, C.J. (1969), *Britain Pre-Eminent. Studies in British World Influence in the Nineteenth Century*.

Basalla, G. (1968), *The Rise of Modern Science. External or Internal Factors?*, Lexington, Mass.

——, Coleman, W., and Kargon, R. (eds.) (1970), *Victorian Science. A Self-Portrait from the Presidential Addresses of the British Association for the Advancement of Science*, New York.

Baster, A.J.S. (1933), 'A Note on the Colonial Stocks Acts and Dominion Borrowing', *Economic History*, 2.

Bateman, J. (1883), *Great Landowners of England and Wales*.

Bataille, L. (ed.) (1976), *A Turning Point for Literacy. Adult Education for Development. The Spirit and Declaration of Persepolis*, Oxford.

Baudis, D. (1981), 'Deutschland und Großbritannien in der Zeit des Ersten Weltkrieges. Versuch einer vergleichenden Betrachtung einiger Aspekte der wirtschaftlichen und sozialen Entwicklung', *Jahrbuch für Wirtschaftsgeschichte* III.

Bauer, M. and Cohen, E. (1982), 'Les Limites du savoir des cadres: L'organisation savante homme moyen de déqualification', *Sociologie du Travail* 24.

Baugh, D.A. (1975), *Aristocratic Government and Society in Eighteenth Century England. The Foundations of Stability*. New York.

Baumgart, P. (ed.) (1980), *Bildungspolitik in Preussen zur Zeit des Kaiserreichs*, Stuttgart.

Beach, W.E. (1935), *British International Gold Movements and Banking Policy 1881–1913*, Cambridge, Mass.

Bechhofer, F. and Elliot, B. (1976), 'Persistence and Change: the Petite Bourgeoisie in Industrial Society', *Archives européennes de Sociologie* XVII.

Becker, G.S. (1975), *Capital. A Theoretical and Empirical Analysis, with Special Reference to Education*. New York.

Becket, J.V. (1986), *The Aristocracy in England 1660–1914*, Oxford.

Beenstock, M. (1983), *The World Economy in Transition*.

Beer, J.J. (1959), *The Emergence of the German Dye Industry*, Urbana.

Behrman, J.N. (1962). 'Foreign Associates and their Financing', in Mikesell.

Beland, F. (1976), 'Du paradoxe professionel: medecins et ingenieurs des années 1800', *Archives Européennes de Sociologie* 17.

Bell, S.P. (ed.) (1974), *Victorian Lancashire*. Newton Abbot.

Ben-David, J. (1968), *Fundamental Research and the Universities. Some Comments on International Differences*. Paris.

—— (1971), *The Scientist's Role in Society. A Comparative Study*. Englewood Cliffs, N.J.

—— (1977), *Centers of Learning. Britain, France, Germany, United States*, New York.

—— (1960), 'Scientific Productivity and Academic Organisation in Nineteenth-Century Medicine', *Amer. Soc. R.* 25.

—— (1968–69), 'The Universities and the Growth of Science in Germany and the United States', *Minerva* 7.

—— and Zloczower (1972), The Growth of Institutionalised Science in Germany, *European J. of Sociology* 3.

Bendix, R. (1970), *Embattled Reason. Essays on Social Knowledge*, Oxford.

Berard, D. and Victor, M. (1973), *Britain, Imperialism and Commercial Supremacy*, New York.

Beranek, W. Jr. and Ranis, G. (eds.), (1978), *Science, Technology, and Economic Development. A Historical and Comparative Study*, New York.

Berck, P. (1978), 'Hard Driving and Efficiency: Iron Production in 1890', *J.Ec.H.* 38.

Beresford, M.W. (1951), *The Leeds Chamber of Commerce*, Leeds.

Berg, M. (ed.), (1979), *Technology and Toil in Nineteenth Century Britain*.

Berg, W. (1984), *Wirtschaft und Gesellschaft in Deutschland und Großbritannien in Übergang zum 'organisierten Kapitalismus'. Unternehmer, Angestellte, Arbeiter und Staat im Steinkohlenbergbau des Ruhrgebieis und von Südwales, 1850–1914*, Berlin.

Berman, M. (1978), *Social Change and Scientific Organisation. The Royal Institution 1799–1844*, Ithaca, N.Y.

—— (1975), 'Hegemony and the Amateur Tradition in British Science', *J.Soc.H.* 8.

Bernstein, G.L. (1986), *Liberalism and Liberal Politics in Edwardian England*, Boston.

Best, G. (1971), *Mid Victorian Britain: 1851–75*.

Best, M.H., and Humphries, J. (1986), 'The City and Industrial Decline', in Elbaum and Lazonick.

Beveridge, Sir W. (1944), *Full Employment in a Free Society.*
Bill, E.G.W. (1973), *University Reform in Nineteenth-Century Oxford: A Study of Henry Halford Vaughan 1811-1885,* Oxford.
Bimetallic League (1985), *Reply to the Memorial of Certain Merchants and Bankers.*
Birch, A., (1967), *The Economic History of the British Iron & Steel Industry 1784-1879.*
Black, E.C. (1970), *British Politics in the Nineteenth Century.*
Black, J. and Winters, L.A. (1983), *Policy and Performance in International Trade.*
Blaich, F. (1982), 'Absatzstrategien deutscher Unternehmer im 19. und in der ersten Hälfte des 20. Jahrhunderts', in Hans Pohl (ed.), *Absatzstrategien deutscher Unternehmer,* Wiesbaden.
Blainey, G. (1984), 'The History of Multinational Factories in Australia', in Okochi and Inoue.
Blankerts, H. (1969), *Bildung im Zeitalter der großen Industrie. Pädagogik, Schule und Berufsbildung im 19. Jahrhundert,* Hanover.
Blaug, M. (ed.), (1968), *Economies of Education: 1. Selected Readings,* Harmondsworth.
— (1960), 'Technical Change and Marxian Economies', *Kyklos* 13.
— (1960-1), 'The Productivity of Capital in the Lancashire Cotton Industry During the Nineteenth Century', *Ec.H.R.* 13.
— (1963), 'A Survey of the Theory of Process-Innovations' *Economica* 30.
Bloomfield, A.I. (1950), *Capital Imports and the American Balance of Payments 1934-39. A Study in Abnormal International Capital Transfers,* Chicago.
— (1963), *Short-Term Capital Movements under the Pre-1914 Gold Standard,* Princeton.
— (1968), *Patterns of Fluctuation in International Investment. Before 1914,* Princeton.
Boch, R. (1983), *Solinger Lokalgewerkschaften und deutscher Metallarbeiterverband. Eine Fallstudie zur krisenhaften Ablösung alter durch neue Arbeiterschichten 1871-1914,* Diss. Bielefeld.
— (1985), *Handwerker-Sozialisten gegen Fabrikgesellschaft,* Göttingen.
Böhme, G. *et al.* (1972), 'Alternative in der Wissenschaft', in Pohrt, W. (ed.).
Böhme, G., van den Daele, W., and Krohn, W. (1978), 'The "Scientification of Technology" ', in Krohn *et al.*
Böhme, H. (1974), 'Bankenkonzentration und Schwerindustrie 1873-1896. Bemerkungen zum Problem des organisierten Kapitals', in Wehler.
Boggs, T. 1914-15, 'Capital Investments and Trade Balances within the British Empire', *Q.J.E.* 29.
Booth, A.E. and Glyn S. (1975), 'Unemployment in the Interwar Period: A Multiple Problem', *J.Contemp.H.* 10.
Borchardt, K. (1965), 'Zum Problem der Erziehungs- und Ausbildungs- investitionen im 19. Jahrhundert', in Hermann Aubin, *et al.* (ed.) *Beiträge zur Wirtschafts- und Stadtgeschichte. Festschrift Hektor Amman,* Wiesbaden.
Bordo, M.D. (1984), 'The Gold Standard: The Traditional Approach', in Bordo and Schwartz.
— (1977), 'The Income Effects of the Sources of New Money: A Comparison of the United States and the United Kingdom, 1870-1913', *Expl.Ec.H.* 14.
— and Schwartz, A.J. (eds.) (1984), *A Retrospective on the Classical Gold Standard, 1821-1931,* Chicago.
Born, K.E. (1983), *International Banking in the 19th and 20th Centuries.* Stuttgart.
Borscheid, P. (1976a), *Naturwissenschaft, Staat und Industrie in Baden (1848-1914),* Stuttgart.
— (1976b), 'Fortschritt und Widerstand in den Naturwissenschaften. Die Chemie in Baden und Württemberg 1850-1865', in Engelhardt *et al.*
Borts, G.H. (1964), 'A Theory of Long-Run International Capital Movements', *J.P.E.* 72.
Bourne, J.M. (1986), *Patronage and Society in Nineteenth Century England.*
Bowen, R.H. (1950), 'The Roles of Government and Private Enterprise in German Industrial Growth, 1870-1914', *J.Ec.H.,* 10.
Bowker, B. (1928), *Lancashire under the Hammer.*
Bowley, A.L. (1920), *The Change in the Distribution of the National Income 1880-1913,* Oxford.
Bowman, M.J. *et al.* (1971), *Readings in the Economics of Education,* Paris.
— (1969), 'The Costing of Human Resource Development', in Robinson, and Vaizey.
— and Anderson, C.A. (1971), 'Concerning the Role of Education in Development', in Bowman *et al.*
Boyce, G. (1986), 'The Growth and Dissolution of a Large-Scale Business Enterprise: The Furness Interest, 1892-1919', *J.Ec.H.* 46.
Boyson, R. (1970), *The Ashworth Cotton Enterprise. The Rise and Fall of a Family Firm 1818-1880,* Oxford.

Bibliography

Brealey, R.A. (1969), *In Introduction to Risk and Return from Common Stocks*, Cambridge, Mass.

Brebner, J.B. (1948), 'Laissez-Faire and State Intervention in 19th Century Britain', *J.Ec.H.* 8.

Brehony, K. (1985), 'Popular Control or Control by Experts? Schooling Between 1880 and 1902', in Langan and Schwarz.

Brewster, D. (1830), 'Reflexions on the Decline of Science in England', *Quarterly Review* 86.

Brittain, J.E. (1974), 'The International Diffusion of Electrical Power Technology, 1870–1920', *J.E.H.* 34.

Brittan, S. (1982), 'A Transformation of the English Sickness', in R. Dahrendorf (ed.), *Europe's Economy in Crisis*.

Broadberry, S. (1986), 'ESRC Quantitative Economic History Study Group 1985. Conference at University College, Cardiff', *J.Europ.Ec.H.* 15.

Brock, W.H. (1976), 'The Spectrum of Science Patronage', in Turner.

Brocke, B. von (1980), 'Hochschule und Wissenschaftspolitik in Preußen und im Deutschen Kaiserreich 1882–1907. Das System Althoff', in Baumgart.

Brooks, H. (1965), 'The Interactions of Science and Technology: Another View', in Warner *et al.*

Brown, B.H. (1943), *The Tariff Reform Movement in Great Britain, 1881–1895*, New York.

Brown, A.J. (1965) 'Britain in the World Economy 1870–1914', *Yorkshire Bulletin* 17.

Brown, E.H.P. and Browne, M.H. (1968), *A Century of Pay*.

Brown, L. (1958), *The Board of Trade and the Free Trade Movement 1830–1842*, Oxford.

Brundage, A. (1972), 'The Landed Interest and the New Poor Law: a Reappraisal of the Revolution in Government', *E.H.R.* 87.

Brunner, E. (1949), 'The Origins of Industrial Peace: the Case of the British Boot and Shoe Industry', *O.E.P.* 1.

Brunschwig, H. (1974), *Englightenment and Romanticism in Eighteenth-Century Prussia*, Chicago.

Bryce, J. (1923), *International Relations*.

Buchanan, N.S. (1945), *International Investment and Domestic Welfare*, New York.

Buchanan, R.A. (1985), 'Institutional Proliferation in the British Engineering Profession, 1847–1914', *Ec.H.R.* 38.

—— (1976), 'The Promethean Revolution: Science, Technology and History', *History of Technology* 1.

Buchheim, C. (1986), *Deutsche Gewerbexporte nach England in der zweiten Hälfte des 19. Jahrhunderts*, Ostfildern.

—— (1981), 'Aspects of XIXth Century Anglo-German Trade Rivalry Reconsidered', *J.Europ.Ec.H.* 10.

Buckley, P.J. and Roberts, B.R. (1982), *European Direct Investment in the USA Before World War I*.

Bud, R.F. (1974), 'The Royal Manchester Institute', in Cardwell.

—— and Roberts, G.K. (1984), *Science versus Practice. Chemistry in Victorian Britain*, Manchester.

Buer, M.C. (1921), 'The Trade Depression following the Napoleonic Wars', *Economica* I.

Bulwer, E.L. (1971), *England and the English*.

Burchardt, L. (1975a), *Wissenschaftspolitik im Wilhelminischen Deutschland*, Göttingen.

—— (1975b), 'Deutsche Wissenschaftspolitik an der Jahrhundertwende. Versuch einer Zwischenbilanz', *Geschichte in Wissenschaft und Unterricht* 26.

—— (1976), 'Wissenschaft und Wirtschaftswachstum: Industrielle Einflußnahme auf die Wissenschaftspolitik im Wilhelminischen Deutschland', in Engelhardt *et al.*

—— (1977), 'Halbstaatliche Wissenschaftsförderung im Kaiserreich und in der frühen Weimarer Republik', in Mann and Winau.

—— (1977/78), 'Die Ausbildung des Chemikers im Kaiserreich', *Zeitschrift für Unternehmensgeschichte* 23.

—— (1983), 'Die Förderung schulischer Ausbildung und wissenschaftlicher Forschung durch deutsche Unternehmen bis 1918', in Hans Pohl (ed.). *Wirtschaft, Schule und Universität*, Wiesbaden.

Burn, D.L. (1940), *The Economic History of Steelmaking 1867–1939. A Study in Competition*, Cambridge.

—— (1970), 'The Genesis of American Engineering Competition 1850–1870', in Saul.

Burnham, T.H., and Hoskins, G.O. (1943), *Iron and Steel in Britain 1870–1930. A Comparative Study of the Causes which limited the Economic Development of the British Iron and Steel Industry Between the Years 1870 and 1930*.

Burton, H. and Corner, D.C. (1968), *Investment and Unit Trusts in Britain and America*.

Butlin, N.G. (1964), *Investment in Australian Economic Development 1861–1900*, Cambridge.

278

Buxbaum, B. (1921), 'Die englischen Werkzeugmaschinen und Werkzeugbau im 18. und 19. Jahrhundert', *Beiträge zur Geschichte der Technik und Industrie* 19.

Buxton, N.K. (1978), *The Economic Development of the British Coal Industry From the Industrial Revolution to the Present Day.*

—— (1981), 'The Coal Industry', in Roderick and Stephens.

Byatt, I.C.R. (1968), 'Electrical Products', in Aldcroft.

—— 1979, *The British Electrical Industry 1875-1914. The Economic Returns to a New Technology*, Oxford.

Byres, T.J. (1967), 'Entrepreneurship in the Scottish Heavy Industries 1870-1900', in P.L. Payne (ed.), *Studies in Scottish Business History.*

Cahen, L. (1939), Une nouvelle interpretation du traité Franco-Anglais de 1786-1787, in *Revue Historique* 64.

Cain, L.P. and Paterson, D.G. (1981), 'Factor Bias and Technical Change in Manufacturing: The American System, 1850-1919' *J.Ec.H.* 41.

Cain, P.J. (1972), 'Railway Combination and Government 1900-1914', *Ec.H.R.* 25.

—— (1973), 'Traders versus Railways. The Genesis of the Railway and Canal Traffic Act of 1894', *J. Transp. Hist.* N.S.II.

—— (1978), 'The British Railway Rates Problem 1894-1913', *Bus.H.* 20.

—— (1979), 'Political Economy in Edwardian England: The Tariff Reform Controversy', in O'Day.

—— (1980), *Economic Foundations of British Overseas Expansion, 1815-1910.*

—— (1981), 'Hobson's Developing Theory of Imperialism', *Ec.H.R.* 34.

—— (1985), 'J.A. Hobson, Financial Capitalism and Imperialism in Late Victorian and Edwardian England', in Porter and Hollander.

—— and Hopkins, A.G. (1980), The Political Economy of British Expansion Overseas 1750-1914, *Ec.H.R.* 33.

—— (1986), 'Gentlemanly Capitalism and British Expansion Overseas. I. The Old Colonial System', *Ec.H.R.* 39.

Cairncross, A.K. (1953), *Home and Foreign Investment 1870-1913*, Cambridge.

—— (1958), 'English Capital Market Before 1914', in *Economica* 25.

Cairncross, F. (1981), *Changing Perceptions of Economic Policy. Essays in Honour of the Seventieth Birthday of Sir Alec Cairncross.*

Campbell, F. (1970), 'Latin and the Elite Tradition in Education', in Musgrave.

Campbell, R.H. (1971), *Scotland Since 1707. The Rise of an Industrial Society*, Oxford.

—— (1980), *The Rise and Fall of Scottish Industry, 1707-1939*, Edinburgh.

Camplin, J. (1978), *The Rise of the Plutocrats. Wealth and Power in Edwardian England.*

Cannadine, D. (ed.), (1982), *Patricians, Power and Politics in Twentieth-Century Towns*, Leicester.

—— (1977a), 'Aristocratic Indebtedness in the 19th Century: The Case Re-opened', *Ec.H.R.* 30.

—— (1977b), 'The Landowner as Millionaire', *Ag.H.R.* 25.

Cannon, J. (1984), *Aristocratic Century. The Peerage of Eighteenth-Century England*, Cambridge.

Cannon, S.F. (1978), *Science in Culture: the Early Victorian Period*, New York.

Capie, F. (1983), 'Tariff Protection and Economic Performance in International Trade', in Black and Winters.

Cardwell, D.S.L. (1957), *The Organisation of Science in England. A Retrospect.*

—— (ed.) (1974), *Artisan to Graduate. Essays to commemorate the Foundation in 1824 of the Manchester Mechanics' Institution in 1974*, Manchester.

—— (1976), 'The Patronage of Science in the 19th Century', in Turner.

—— (1978), 'Science, Technology and Economic Development: the British Experience', in Beranek and Ranis.

Carli, G. (1981), 'Are the British so different', in Cairncross.

Carr, I.C. and Taplin, W. (1962), *History of the British Steel Industry*, Cambridge, Mass.

Carr-Saunders, A.M. and Wilson, P.A. (1933), *The Professions*, Oxford.

Carter, A. (1953), 'Dutch Foreign Investment, 1738-1800', *Economica* 20.

Carter, C.F. and Williams, B.R. (1957), *Industry and Technical Progress.*

Cassel, G. (1928), 'The International Movements of Capital', in Cassel *et al.*

—— (1928), *Foreign Investments*, Chicago.

Cassis, Y. (1984), *Les Banquiers de la City à l'époque Eduardienne (1840-1914)*, Geneva.

—— (1985a), 'Management and Strategy in the English Joint-Stock Banks, 1890-1914', *Bus.H.* 27.

—— (1985b), 'The Banking Community of London 1890-1914: A Survey', in Porter/Hollander.

279

— (1985c), 'Bankers in English Society in the Late Nineteenth Century', *Ec.H.R.* 38.

Casson, M. (1979), *Alternatives to the Multinational Enterprise.*

Catherwood, H.F.R. (1966), *Britain with the Brakes off.*

Caves, R.E. (1960), *Trade and Economic Structure*, Cambridge, Mass.

Cecco, M. de (1974), *Money and Empire. The International Gold Standard 1890–1914*, Oxford.

Chaloner, W.H. (1963), *People and Industries.*

Chamberlain, J. (1897), *Dispatch from Mr. Chamberlain to the Governors of Colonies . . . on the Trade of the British Empire and Foreign Competition and the Replies thereto.*

Chambers, J.D. (1961), *The Workshop of the World.*

— and Mingay, G.E. (1966), *The Agricultural Revolution 1750–1880.*

Chapman, S.D. (1984), *The Rise of Merchant Banking.*

— (1979), 'British Marketing Enterprise. The Changing Role of Merchants, Manufacturers and Financiers, 1700–1860', *Bus.H.R.* 53.

— (1981), 'The Textile Industries', in Roderick and Stephens.

— (1982), 'The Evolution of Merchant Banking in Britain in the Nineteenth Century', *8. International Economic History Congress Budapest 1982*, vol. B.10.

— (1985), 'British-based Investment Groups before 1914', *Ec.H.R.* 38.

— (1986), 'Aristocracy and Meritocracy in Merchant Banking', *Brit.J.Sociology*, 37.

Chapman, S.J. (1904), *Work and Wages*, vol. I.

— and Ashton, T.S. (1914), 'The Sizes of Business, mainly in the Textile Industries', *J.R.S.S.* 77.

Charles, R. (1973), *The Development of Industrial Relations in Britain 1911–1939.*

Chatterton, D.A. (1972), 'State Control of Public Utilities in the Nineteenth Century: the London Gas Industry', *Bus.H.* 14.

Checkland, S.G. (1964), *The Rise of Industrial Society in England 1815–1885.*

— (1977), *The Upas Tree. Glasgow 1875–1975*, Glasgow.

— (1983), *British Public Policy 1776–1939. An Economic, Social and Political Perspective*, Cambridge.

— (1952–53), 'Economic Altitudes in Liverpool, 1793–1867', *Ec.H.R.* 5.

— (1957), 'The Mind of the City 1870–1914', *O.E.P.* 9.

Chen, Ch.-N. (1972), 'Bimetallism: Theory and Controversy in Perspective', *History of Political Economy* 4.

Chenery, H.B. (1970), 'Foreign Assistance and Economic Development', in J.H. Adler.

Chipman, J.S. (1972), 'The Theory of Exploitative Trade and Investment Policies', in Luis Eugenio di Marco, *International Economics and Development.*

Christie, J.R.R. (1975), 'The Rise and Fall of Scottish Science', in Crosland.

Church R.A. (1975a), *The Great Victorian Boom 1850–1873.*

— (ed.), (1980a), *The Dynamics of Victorian Business. Problems and Perspectives to the 1870's.*

— (1986), *The History of the British Coal Industry*, vol. 3, *1830–1913: Victorian Pre-eminence*, Oxford.

— (1970), 'Labour Supply and Innovation 1800–1960: The Boot and Shoe Industry', *Bus.Hist.* 12.

— (1971), 'The British Leather Industry and Foreign Competition, 1870–1914', *Ec.H.R.* 24.

— (1975b), 'Nineteenth-Century Clock Technology in Britain, the United States, and Switzerland', *Ec.H.R.* 28.

— (1977), Family and Failure: Archibald Kendrick & Sons Ltd. 1900–1950', in Supple.

— (1980b), 'Problems and Perspective', in Church.

— (1982), 'Markets and Marketing in the British Motor Industry Before 1914 with Some French Comparisons', *J.Transp.Hist.* 3.

Cipolla, C.M. (ed.) *The Economic Decline of Empires.*

— (1969), *Literacy and Development in the West*, Harmondsworth.

— (1952/53), 'The Decline of Italy. The Case of a Fully Matured Economy', *Ec.H.R.* 5.

— (1968),'The Economic Decline of Italy', in Pullan.

Cipriano, C. (1971), 'Hedging in the Labour Market', in Kiker.

Clapham, J.H. (1907), *The Woollen and Worsted Industries.*

— (1936), *The Economic Development of France and Germany 1815–1914*, Cambridge.

— (1944), *The Bank of England. A History*, 2 vols. Cambridge.

— (1963), *An Economic History of Modern Britain*, 3 vols. Cambridge.

Clark, C. (1951), *The Conditions of Economic Progress.*

Clark, G. (1986), 'British Labour in Britain's Decline', *J.Ec.H.* 46.
—— (1987), 'Why isn't the Whole World Developed? Lessons from the Cotton Mills, *J.Ec.H.* 47.
Clark, K. (1962), *The Making of Victorian England.*
—— (1951a), The Repeal of the Corn-Laws and the Politics of the Forties', *Ec.H.R.* 9.
—— (1951b), The Electorate and the Repeal of the Corn-Laws, in *T.R.H.S.* 5.
Clark, S. (1984), 'Nobility, Bourgeoisie and Industrial Revolution in Belgium', *P.&P.* 105.
Clarke, H. (1878), 'On the Debts of Sovereign and Quasi-Sovereign States, Owing by Foreign Countries, *J.R.S.S.* 46.
Clarke, M.L. (1959), *Classical Education in Britain 1500-1900,* Cambridge.
Clarke, P.F. (1972), 'The End of Laissez-Faire and the Politics of Cotton', *Hist.J.* XV.
Clarke, R.N. and Summers, L.H. (1980), 'The Labour Scarcity Reconsidered', *E.J.* 90.
Clarke, W.M. (1965), *The City in the World Economy.*
Clow, A. and Nan, L. (1972), 'Vitriol in the Industrial Revolution', in Musson.
Coats, A.W. (1968), 'Political Economy and the Tariff Reform Campaign of 1903', *Journal of Law and Economics* 11.
Colebrook, P. (1972), *Going International. A Handbook of British Direct Investment Overseas.*
Coleby, L.J.M. (1953), 'Richard Watson, Professor of Chemistry at the University of Cambridge, 1764-71', *Annals of Science* 9.
Coleman, D.C. (1969), *Courtaulds. An Economic and Social History.* 2 Vols., Oxford.
—— (1973), 'Gentlemen and Players', *Ec.H.R.* 26.
—— (1975), 'War and Industrial Supply: the Dope Scandal 1915-19', in Winter.
—— (1977), 'Courtaulds and the Beginning of Rayon', in Supple.
—— and MacLeod, C. (1986), 'Attitudes and New Techniques: British Businessmen, 1800-1950', *Ec.H.R.* 39.
Collins, J. (1972), 'The Bank of England at Liverpool 1827-1844', *Bus.H.* 14.
Collins, M. (1978), 'Monetary Policy and the Supply of Trade Credit 1830-1844', *Economica* 45.
—— (1986), 'Sterling Exchange Rates, 1847-80', *J.Europ.Ec.H.* 15.
Colmer, J.G. (1896), 'An Imperial Customs Union', *E.J.* 6.
Colls, R. (1981), 'Rejoinder to Critique', in Heesom and Duffy.
N.N. (1860), 'Commercial Relations of England and France', *The Edinburgh Review.*
Conant, J.B. (1971), *Science and Common Sense,* New Haven.
Constant, E.W.II. (1973), 'A Model for Technological Change Applied to the Turbojet Revolution', *Technology and Culture* 14.
Conrad, A.H. and Meyer, J.R. (1964), 'An Input-Output Approach to Evaluating British Industrial Production in the Late Nineteenth Century', in idem, *Slavery and Other Studies in Econometric History,* Chicago.
Conze, W. und Kocka, J. (eds.) (1985), *Bildungsbürgertum im 19. Jahrhundert. I. Bildungssystem und Professionalisierung in Internationalen Vergleichen,* Stuttgart.
Cooney, E.W. (1949), 'Capital Exports and Investment in Building in Britain and the USA 1856-1914', *Economica* 16.
—— (1960-61), 'Long Waves in Building in the British Economy of the Nineteenth Century', *Ec.H.R.* 13.
Copeland, M.T. (1909), 'Technical Development in Cotton Manufacturing since 1860', *Q.J.E.* 33.
Coppock, D.J. (1956), 'The Climacteric of the 1890's: A Critical Note', *Manchester School* 24.
—— (1961), 'The Cause of the Great Depression 1873-96', *Manchester School* 29.
—— (1964-65), 'British Industrial Growth During the 'Great Depression' (1873-96): a Pessimist's View', *Ec.H.R.* 17.
Corden, W.M. (1985), *Protection, Growth and Trade. Essays in International Economics,* Oxford.
—— (1967), 'Protection and Foreign Investment', *Economic Record* 43.
—— (1976), 'Conclusions on the Logic of Government Intervention', in Corden and Fels (1976b).
—— and Fels, G. (1976a), *Public Assistance to Industry Protection and Subsidies in Britain and Germany.*
—— (1976b), 'Public Assistance to Industry in Britain and Germany', *ibid.*
Corley, T.A.B. (1972), *Quaker Enterprise in Biscuits: Huntley and Palmer of Reading 1822-1972.*
Cornwall, J. (1977), *Modern Capitalism, its Growth and Formation.*
Correa, H. (1963), *The Economics of Human Resources,* Amsterdam.
—— and Tinbergen J. (1962), 'Quantitative Adaptation of Education to Accelerated Growth', *Kyklos* XV.

Bibliography

Cotgrove, S.F. (1958), *Technical Education and Social Change*.

Cottrell, P.L. (1975), *British Overseas Investment in the Nineteenth Century*.

—— (1980), *Industrial Finance 1830-1914. The Finance and Organisation of English Manufacturing Industry*.

Courtney, L.H. (1898), 'An Experiment in Commercial Expansion', *J.R.S.S.* 61.

Crafts, N.F.R. (1973), 'Trade as a Handmaiden of Growth: an Alternative View', *E.J.* 83.

—— (1979), 'Victorian Britain Did Fail', *Ec.H.R.* 32.

—— (1983), 'Gross National Product in Europe 1870-1910: Some New Estimates', *Expl.Ec.H.* 20.

—— and Thomas, M. (1986), 'Comparative Advantage in UK Manufacturing Trade, 1910-1935', *E.J.* 96.

Craig, J.E. (1983), 'Higher Education and Social Mobility in Germany', in Jarausch.

Crammond, E. (1913-14), 'The Economic Relations of the British and German Empires', *J.R.S.S.* 77.

Creasey, C.H. (1905), *Technical Education in Evening Schools*.

Crohn, H.F. (1915), 'Argentinien im deutsch-englischen Wirtschaftskampf', *Schmollers Jahrbuch* 39.

Crosland, M. (ed.) (1975), *The Emergence of Science in Western Europe*.

Crotty, J.R. (1983), 'On Keynes and Capital Flight', *J.Ec.Lit.* XXI.

Crowther, J.G. (1974), *The Cavendish Laboratory 1874-1974*.

Crouzet, F. (1978), *L'économie de la Grande-Bretagne Victorienne*, Paris.

—— (1985), *The First Industrialists. The Problem of Origins*, Cambridge.

Cruickshank, M.A. (1974), 'From Mechanics Institute to Technical School, 1850-92', in Cardwell.

—— (1979), 'The Anglican Revival and Education: A Study of School Expansion in the North-West of England, 1840-1850', *Northern History* 15.

Cunningham, W. (1911), *The Case against Free Trade*.

Curtis, S.J. (1963), *History of Education in Great Britain*.

Dahmen, E. (1963), 'Technology, Innovation and International Industrial Transformation', in L.H. Dupriez (ed.), *Economic Progress*.

Dale, R., Esland, G. and MacDonald, M. (eds.) (1976), *Schooling and Capitalism. A Sociological Reader*.

Darwin, M.L. (1897), *Bimetallism. A Summary and Examination of the Arguments Formed Against a Bimetallic System of Currency*.

Daumard, Adeline (1977), 'Diffusion et nature des placements à L'étranger dans les patrimoines des Français au XIX Siècle', in Lévy-Leboyer.

Davenport-Hines, R.P.T. (ed.) (1986), *Markets and Bagmen. Studies in the History of Marketing and British Industrial Performance 1830-1939*, Aldershot.

—— (1984), *Dudley Docker. The Life and Times of a Trade Warrior*, Cambridge.

David, Paul A. (1975), *Technical Choice, Innovation and Economic Growth. Essays on American and British Experience in the Nineteenth Century*, Cambridge.

—— (1971), 'The Landscape and the Machine', in McCloskey.

—— and Scadding, J.L. (1974), 'Private Savings; Ultrarationality, Aggregation and "Dennison's Law"', *J.P.E.* 82.

Davidson, Roger (1982), 'Government Administration', in Wrigley.

Davie, A.F. (1974), 'The Administration of Lancashire 1838-1889', in Bell.

Davie, G.E. (1961), *The Democratic Intellect. Scotland and Her Universities in the Nineteenth Century*, Edinburgh.

Davies, A.E. (1927), *Investments Abroad*, Chicago/New York.

Davis, C.B. (1982), 'Financing Imperialism: Britain and American Bankers as Vectors of Imperial Expansion in China, 1908-1920', *Bus.H.R.* 56.

Davis, Lance (1966), 'The Capital Markets and Industrial Concentration: the U.S. and U.K., a Comparative Study', *Ec.H.R.* 19.

—— and Huttenback, R.A. (1986), *Mammon and the Pursuit of Empire. The Political Economy of British Imperialism, 1860-1912*, Cambridge.

—— (1982), 'The Political Economy of British Imperialism: Measures of Benefits and Support', *J.Ec.H.* 42.

—— (1985), 'The Export of British Finance, 1865-1914', in Porter and Hollander.

Davis, Ralph (1966), 'The Rise of Protection in England 1689-1786', *Ec.H.R.* XIX.

Day, Alan (n.d.), *Evidence to Radcliffe Committee. Principal Memoranda of Evidence III*.

Deane, P. and Cole, W.A. (1967), *British Economic Growth 1688–1952*, Cambridge.

Dearle, N.B. (1914), *Industrial Training, with Special Reference to Conditions Prevailing in London*.

Debauvais, M. and Khoi, Le Thanh (1971), 'Literacy, Work and School Education in Economic Development', in Bowman *et al.*

Deerr, Noel (1950), *The History of Sugar*, Vol. II.

Denison, Edward F. (1962), *The Sources of Economic Growth in the United States and the Alternatives Before US*, New York.

— (1967), *Why Growth Rates Differ. Postwar Experience in Nine Western Countries*, Washington.

— (1974), *Accounting for United States Economic Growth 1929–1969*, Washington.

— (1966), 'Measuring the Contribution of Education to Economic Growth', in Robinson and Vaizey.

— (n.d.), 'Measuring the Contribution of Education (and the Residual) to Economic Growth', in *OECD*, Study Group in the Economics of Education.

Derry, T.K. (1931–2), 'The Repeal of the Apprenticeship Clauses of the Statute of Apprentices', *Ec.H.R.* 3.

— and Williams, T.I. (1960), *A Short History of Technology, from the Earliest Times to AD 1950*, Oxford.

Dibblee, G.B. (1902), 'The Printing Trade and the Crisis in British Industry', *E.J.* 12.

Digby, Anne and Searby, Peter (1981), *Children, School and Society in Nineteenth-Century England*.

Dingle, A.E. (1982), ' "The Monster Nuisance of All": Landowners, Alkali Manufacturers and Air Pollution, 1828–64', *Ec.H.R.* 35.

Dinwiddy, J.R. (1986), *From Luddism to the First Reform Bill. Reform in England 1810–1832*, Oxford.

Domar, Evsey D. (1950). 'The Effect of Foreign Investment on the Balance of Payments', *A.E.R.* 40.

— (1971), 'On Total Productivity and All That', in Bowman *et al.*

Donnachie, Ian (1979), *A History of the Brewing Industry in Scotland* , Edinburgh.

Douglas, P.H. (1929–30), 'An Estimate of the Growth of Capital in the U.K. 1865–1909', *J.Ec.&Bus.H.* 2.

Dumett, E.W. (1975), 'Joseph Chamberlain, Imperial Finance and Railway Policy in British West Africa in the Late 19th Century', *E.H.R.* XL.

Dunning, John H. (ed.) (1972a), *International Investment: Selected Readings*, Harmondsworth.

— (1970), *Studies in International Investment*.

— (1956), 'The Growth of U.S. Investment in U.K. Manufacturing Industry 1856/1940', *Manchester School* 24.

— (1972b), 'Capital Movements in the Twentieth Century', *ibid.*

Dunsheath, Percy (1962), *A History of Electrical Engineering*.

Durey, Michael (1983), 'Medical Elites, the General Practitioners and Patient Power in Britain During the Cholera Epidemic of 1831–32',in Inkster and Morell.

Dutton, H.I. (1984), *The Patent System and Inventive Activity During the Industrial Revolution 1750–1852*, Cambridge.

Dutton, J. (1984), 'The Bank of England and the Rules of the Game under the International Gold Standard: New Evidence', in Bordo and Schwartz.

Eaglesham, E.J.R. (1956), *From School Board to Local Authority*.

Easterlin, R.A. (1966), 'Economic-Demographic Interactions and Long Swings in Economic Growth', *A.E.R.* 56.

— (1981), 'Why isn't the Whole World Developed?', *J.Ec.H.* 41.

— *et al.* (1982), *Immigration*, Cambridge, Mass.

Eccleshall, R. (ed.) (1986), *British Liberalism. Liberal Thought from the 1640's to 1980's. Economist*, Weekly.

Eckaus, R.S. (1981), 'Education and Economic Growth', in Bowman *et al.*

Edgeworth, R.L. (1809), *Essays on Professional Education*.

Edding, F. (1958), *Internationale Tendenzen in der Entwicklung der Ausgabe für Schule und Hochschule*, Kiel.

Edding, F. (1966), 'Expenditure on Education: Statistics and Comments', in Robinson and Vaizey.

Edelstein, M. (1982), *Overseas Investment in the Age of High Imperialism. The United Kingdom, 1850–1914*.

— (1974), 'The Determinants of U.K. Investment Abroad, 1870–1913: The U.S. Case", *J.Ec.H.* 34.

—— (1976), 'Realized Rates of Return on U.K. Home and Overseas Portfolio Investment in the Age of High Imperialism', *Expl.Ec.H.* 13.

—— (1977), 'UK Savings in the Age of High Imperialism and After', *A.E.R.* 67.

Edsall, N.C. (1973), 'Varieties of Radicalism: Attwood, Cobden and the local Politics of Municipal Incorporation', *Hist.J.* 16.

Eichengreen, B.J. (1982), 'The Proximate Determinants of Domestic Investment in Victorian Britain', *J.Ec.H.* 42.

—— (1983a), 'Asset Markets and Investment Fluctuations in Late Victorian Britain', *Res.Ec.H.* 8.

—— (1983b), 'The Causes of British Business Cycles, 1833–1913', *J.E.Ec.H.* 12.

—— (1986), 'What have we learned from Historical Comparisons of Income and Productivity?', in O'Brien, P. (ed.).

Eicher, I.C. (1971), 'The Profitability of Human Investment', in Bowman *et al.*

Eistert, E. (1970), *Die Beeinflüssung des Wirtschaftswachstums im Deutschland von 1883 bis 1913 durch das Bankensystem*, Berlin.

Elbaum, B. (1986), 'The Steel Industry before World War I', in Elbaum and Lazonik.

Elbaum, B., and Lazonik, W. (1986a), *The Decline of the British Economy*, Oxford.

—— (1986b), 'An Institutional Perspective on British Decline', *ibid.*

—— (1984), 'The Decline of the British Economy: an Institutional Perspective', *J.Ec.H.* 44.

Ellis, A. (1985), *Educating our Masters. Influences on the Growth of Literacy in Victorian Working Class Children*, Aldershot.

Ellis, H.S. (1936), 'The Equilibrium Rate of Exchange', in *Explorations in Economics*, New York.

Ellison, T. (1886), *The Cotton Trade of Great Britain*.

Ellsworth, P.T. (1956), 'The Terms of Trade Between Primary-Producting Countries and Industrial Countries', *Inst.Am.Ec.Affairs*

Emmanuel, A. (1972), *Unequal Exchange. A Study of the Imperialism of Trade*, New York.

Engel, A.J. (1983a), *From Clergyman to Don. The Rise of the Academic Profession in Nineteenth Century Oxford*, Oxford.

—— 'Emerging Concepts of the Academic Profession at Oxford, 1800–1854', in Stone.

—— (1983b), 'The English Universities and Professional Education', in Jarausch.

Engelhardt, U. *et al.* (1976), *Soziale Bewegung und Politische Verfassung. Beiträge zur Geschichte der Modernen Welt*, Stuttgart.

Ensor, R.C.K. (1949), 'Some Political and Economic Interactions in Later Victorian England', *T.R.H.S.* 31.

Epstein, R.C. (1926), 'Industrial Invention: Heroic or Systematic?', *Q.J.E.* 40.

Erickson, C. (1959), *British Industrialists. Steel and Hosiery*, Cambridge.

Escott, T.H.S. (1973), *Social Transformation of the Victorian Age. A Survey of Court and Country*, Folcroft.

Evans, E.W. and Wiseman, N.C. (1984), 'Education, Training and Economic Performance: British Economists' Views 1868–1939', *J.Europ.Ec.H.* 13.

Fach, W. and Wessel, H.A. (1981), *Hundert Taler Preussisch Courant: Industriefinanzierung in der Gründerzeit*, Vienna.

Fahrländer, M. (1919), *Das Volksvermögen der Schweiz*, Basel.

Fairlie, S. (1965), 'The Nineteenth-Century Corn Law Reconsidered', *Ec.H.R.* 18.

—— (1969), 'The Corn-Laws and British Wheat Production 1829–76', *Ec.H.R.* 22.

Falise, M. and Lepas, A. (1970), 'Les Motivations de localisation des investissements internationaux dans l'Europe du Nord-Ouest', *Revue Economique* 21.

Falkus, M. (1977), 'The Development of Municipal Trading in the Nineteenth Century', *Bus. H.* 19.

Fanno, M. (1939), *Normal and Abnormal International Capital Transfers*, Minneapolis.

Farnie, D.A. (1979), *The English Cotton Industry and the World Market 1815–1846*, Oxford.

—— (1981), 'Platt Bros.&Co. Ltd of Oldham, Machine Makers to Lancashire and to the World: an Index of Production of Cotton Spinning Spindles, 1880–1914' *Bus.H.* XXIII.

Farrar, F.W. (ed.), *et al.* (1868), *Essays on a Liberal Education*.

Farrar, D.M. and Pacey, A.J. (1974), 'Aspects of the German Tradition in Technical Education', in Cardwell.

Farrar, Lord (1898), 'Does Trade Follow the Flag?', *Contemporary Review* 74.

Farrar, W.V. (1975), 'Science and the German University System 1790–1850', in Crosland.

Farrer, T.H. (1882), *Free Trade versus Fair Trade*.

Fay, C.R. (1932), *The Corn Laws and Social England*, Cambridge.

Fearon, P. (1974), 'The British Airframe Industry and the State, 1918–35', *Ec.H.R.* 27.
Feiler, A. (1935), 'International Movement of Capital', *A.E.R.* 15.
Feinstein, C.H. (1972), *National Income, Expenditure and Output of the United Kingdom, 1855-1965.*
—— (1978), 'Capital Formation in Great Britain', *The Cambridge Economic History of Europe* VII.
—— *et al.* (1981), 'The Timing of the Climacteric and its Sectoral Incidence in the UK, 1873–1913', in C.P. Kindleberger + G. di Tella (eds.), *Economics in the Long View.*
Feis, H. (1965), *Europe, the World's Banker 1870-1914*, New York.
Feldenkirchen, W. (1980), 'Die wirtschaftliche Rivalität zwischen Deutschland und England im 19. Jahrhundert', *Zeitschrift für Unternehmensgeschichte* 25.
—— (1981), 'The Banks and the Steel Industry in the Ruhr. Developments in Relations from 1873 to 1914', in Engels, W. and Pohl, H. (eds.), *German Yearbook of Business History*, Berlin, Heidelberg, New York.
Feldman, G.D. (1987), 'The Politics of Wissenschaftspolitik in Weimar Germany: a Prelude to the Dilemmas of Twentieth-Century Science Policy', in Maier, Charles S. *Changing Boundaries of the Political*, Cambridge.
—— and Steinisch, I.(1980), 'Notwendigkeit und Grenzen sozial-staatlicher Intervention', *Archiv für Sozialgeschichte* 20.
Fellner, W. (1971), 'Two Propositions in the Theory of Induced Innovations', in Rosenberg.
Ferber, C.v. (1965), *Die Entwicklung des Lehrkörpers der deutschen Universitäten und Hochschulen 1864-1954*, Göttingen.
Ferns, H.S. (1960), *Britain and Argentina in the Nineteenth Century*, Oxford.
—— (1950–1), 'Investment and Trade between Britain and Argentina in the Nineteenth Century, *Ec.H.R.* 3.
—— (1951–2), 'Beginnings of British Investment in Argentina', *Ec.H.R.* 4.
Fessner, M. (1985), 'Von der Gewerbeschule zur technischen Mittelschule: Die Entwicklung des gewerblich-technischen Schulwesens in Barmen bis 1914' in B. Dietz and H.F. Becker, (eds.), *Neues Bergisches Jahrbuch*, Vol. 2. Wuppertal.
Fetter, F.W. (1965), *Development of British Monetary Orthodoxy 1797-1875*, Cambridge, Mass.
Ffrench, Y. (1950), *The Great Exhibition, 1851.*
Field, A.J. (1979), 'Occupational Structure, Dissent, and Educational Commitment: Lancashire 1841', *Res.Ec.H.* 4.
—— (1983), 'Land Abundance, Interest/Profit Rates, and Nineteenth-Century American and British Technology', *J.Ec.H.* 43.
Fielden, K. (1969), 'The Rise and Fall of Free Trade', in Bartlett.
Fieldhouse, D.K. (1966), *The Colonial Empires. A Comparative Survey from the Eighteenth Century.*
Finch, D. (1951–2), 'Investment Service of Underdeveloped Countries', *I.M.F. Staff Papers* 2.
Finer, H. (1933), *English Local Government.*
Firth, J.F.B. (1976), *Municipal London.*
Fischer, W. (1978), 'The Role of Science and Technology in the Economic Development of Modern Germany', in Beranek and Ranis.
—— and Lundgreen, P. (1975), 'The Recruitment and Training of Administrative and Technical Personnel', in Charles Tilly (ed.) *The Formation of Nation States in Western Europe*, Princeton.
Fisher, H.A.L. (1918) *Educational Reform: Speeches*, Oxford.
Fisher, F.M. (1969), 'The Existence of Aggregate Production Functions', *Econometrica* 37.
Fishlow, A. (1966), 'Levels of Nineteenth-Century American Investment in Education', *J.Ec.H.* 26.
Fleischer, A. (1984), *Patentgesetzgebung und Chemisch-Pharmazeutische Industrie im deutschen Kaiserreich (1871-1918)*, Stuttgart.
Fletcher, T.W. (1960–1), 'The Great Depression in English Agriculture 1873–1896', *Ec.H.R.* 13.
Flett, J.S. (1937), *The First Hundred Years of the Geological Survey of Great Britain.*
Flick, C. (1978), *The Birmingham Political Union and the Movements from Reform in Britain 1830-1839*, Hamden, Conn.
Flinn, M.W. (1967), 'Social Theory and the Industrial Revolution', in T. Burns and S.B. Saul (eds.), *Social Theory and Economic Change.*
Floud, R.C. (1976), *The British Machine Tool Industry, 1850-1914*, Cambridge.
—— (1984), *Technical Education 1850-1914: Speculations on Human Capital Formation.*

—— (1974), 'The Adolescence of American Engineering Competition, 1860–1900', *Ec.H.R.* 27.

—— (1971), 'Changes in the Product of Labour in the British Machine Tool Industry, 1856–1900', in McCloskey (1971a).

—— and McCloskey, D. (1981), *The Economic History of Britain Since 1700*. Vol. 2: 1860 to the 1870's, Cambridge.

Floyd, J.E. (1969), 'International Capital Movements and Monetary Equilibrium', *A.E.R.* 59.

Flux, A.W. (1893), 'The Flag and Trade', *J.R.S.S.* 62.

—— (1897),'British Trade and German Competition', *E.J.* 7.

—— (1899), 'The Commercial Supremacy of Great Britain', *E.J.I.* 9

Foden, F. (1970), *Philip Magnus. Victorian Educational Pioneer*.

Foot, K.D.K.W. (1972), 'Balance of Payments in the Interwar Period', *Bank of England Quarterly Bulletin* 12.

Foote, G.A. (1954), 'Science and its Function in Early Nineteenth Century England', *Osiris* 11.

Forbes, I.L.D. (1978), 'German Informal Imperialism in South America Before 1914', *Ec.H.R.* 31.

Ford, A.G. (1962), *The Gold Standard 1880–1914. Britain and Argentina*, Oxford.

—— (1956), 'Argentina and the Baring Crisis of 1890', *O.E.P.* 8.

—— (1958–9), 'The Transfer of British Foreign Lending, 1870–1913', *Ec.H.R.* 11.

—— (1964), 'Bank Rate, the British Balance of Payment, and the Burdens of Adjustment', *O.E.P.* 16.

—— (1965), 'Overseas Lending and Internal Fluctuations: 1810–1914', *Yorkshire Bulletin* 17.

—— (1969), 'A Note on British Export Performance 1899–1913', *Ec.H.R.* 22.

—— (1971), 'British Investment in Argentina and Long Swings, 1880–1914', *J.Ee.H.* 31.

Foreman-Peck, J. (1983a), *History of the World Economy: International Economic Relations Since 1850*, Brighton.

—— (1982a), 'The American Challenge of the Twenties: Multinationals and the European Motor Industry', *J.Ec.H.* 42.

—— (1983b), 'Diversification and the Growth of the Firm. The Rover Company to 1914', *Bus.H.* 25.

Foreman, Paul (1973), 'Physics Circa 1900. Personnel, Funding, and Productivity of the Academic Establishments', *Hist. Studies in the Physical Sciences* 5.

Fortunes Made in Business (1884–1887), A Series of Original Sketches, Biographical and Anecdotic from the Recent History of Industry and Commerce. By Varous Writers. I. II. III.

Foster, D. (1974), 'Class and County Government in Early Nineteenth Century Lancashire', *Northern History* 9.

Foster, J. (1974), *Class Struggle and the Industrial Revolution. Early Industrial Capitalism in Three English Towns*.

Fox, Alan (1985), *History and Heritage. The Social Origins of the British Industrial Relations System*.

Fox, J.H. (1974), 'The Victorian Entrepreneur in Lancashire', in Bell.

Fox, Robert.(1984), 'Science, Industry and the Social Order in Mulhouse, 1798–1871', *Brit.J. of the History of Science* 17.

Foxwell, H.S. (1919), *Papers on Current Finance*.

—— (1917a), 'The Nature of Industrial Struggle', *E.J.* 27.

—— (1917b), 'The Financing of Industry and Trade', *E.J.* 27.

Francis, A. (1980), 'Families, Firms and Finance Capital: the Development of UK Industrial Firms with Particular Reference to their Ownership and Control', *Sociology* 14.

Frankel, H. (1943), 'Industrialisation of Agricultural Countries and the Possibilities of a New International Division of Labor', *E.J.* 53.

Frankel, M. (1957), *British and American Manufacturing Productivity*, Urbana.

—— (1955), 'Obsolescence and Technical Change in a Maturing Economy', *A.E.R.* 45.

—— (1965), 'Home versus Foreign Investment: A Case Against Capital Export, *Kyklos* 18.

Frankel, S.H. (1938), *Capital Investment in Africa. Its Cause and Effects*.

Fraser, D. (1976), *Urban Politics in Victorian England. The Structure of Politics in Victorian Cities*, Leicester.

—— (1979), *Power and Authority in the Victorian City*, Oxford.

Fraser, P. (1962), 'Unionism and Tariff Reform: the Crisis of 1906', *Hist.J.* 5.

Freeman, C. (1973), 'A Study of Success and Failure in Industrial Innovation', in Williams.

—— (1977), 'Economics of Research and Development', in Spiegel-Rösing and Price.

Fremdling, R. (1986), 'Commodity Output in Great Britain and Germany 1855–1913', in O'Brien.

—— and O'Brien, P. (eds.) (1983), *Productivity in the Economics of Europe*, Stuttgart.

—— and Tilly, R. (1976), 'German Banks, German Growth and Econometric History', *J.Ec.H.* 36.

French, M.J. (1987), 'The Emergence of a US Multinational-Enterprise: the Goodyear Tire and Rubber Company, 1910–1939', *Ec.H.R.* XL.

Fries, R.I. (1975), 'British Response to the American System: the Case of the Small-Arms Industry after 1850', *Technology and Culture* 16.

Frith, S. (1977), 'Socialization and International Schooling: Elementary Education in Leeds before 1870', in McCann.

Fritzsche, H. (1913), *Ausländische Anleihen auf dem deutschen Geldmarkte*, Leipzig.

Froude, W. (1955), *The Papers of William Froude 1816–1879*.

Fry, G.K. (1979), *The Growth of Government. The Development of Ideas about the Role of the State and the Machinery and Functions of Government in Britain Since 1780*.

Führ, C. (1980), 'Die preußischen Schulkonferenzen von 1890 und 1900', in Baumgart.

Gallagher, John and Robinson, Ronald (1953), 'The Imperialism of Free Trade', *Ec.H.R.* 6.

Galton, Francis (1874), *English Men of Science: Their Nature and their Nurture*.

Galtung, Johan (1976), 'Literacy, Education and Schooling – For What', in Bataille.

Gamble, Andrew (1981), *Britain's Decline. Economic Policy, Political Strategy and the British State*.

Garcke, E. (1907), *The Progress of Electrical Enterprise*.

Gardener, Phil (1984), *The Lost Elementary Schools of Victorian England. The People's Education*.

Garland, M.M. (1980), *Cambridge Before Darwin: The Ideal of a Liberal Education 1800–1860*, Cambridge.

Garrard, John (1983), *Leadership and Power in Victorian Industrial Towns 1830–80*, Manchester.

Garside, W.R.P. and Gospel, H.F. (1982), 'Employers and Managers: Their Organizational Structure and Changing Industrial Strategies', in Wrigley.

Garvin, J.L. (1909), *Tariff or Budget*.

Gash, Norman (1953), *Politics in the Age of Peel*.

—— (1965), *Reaction and Reconstruction in English Politics 1832–1852*, Oxford.

—— (1972), *Sir Robert Peel. The Life of Sir Robert Peel after 1830*.

—— (1979), *Aristocracy and People. Britain 1815–1865*.

Gastrell, William S.H. (1879), *Our Trade in the World in Relation to Foreign Competition 1885–1895*.

Geison, G.L. (1978), *Michael Foster and the Cambridge School of Physiology. The Scientific Enterprise in Late Victorian Society*, Princeton.

Gerschenkron, Alexander (1966), *Economic Backwardness in Historical Perspective*. Cambridge, Mass.

Gibbs, F.W. (1965), *Joseph Priestley, Adventurer in Science and Champion of Truth*.

—— (1972), 'Bryan Higgins and His Circle', in Musson.

Gibson, I.F. (1958), 'The Establishment of the Scottish Steel Industry', *Scott.J.Pol.Econ.* 5.

Giddens, Anthony (1974), 'Elites in the British Class Structure', in Stanworth and Giddens.

Giere, Ronald N. and Westfall, Richard S. (1973), *Foundations of Scientific Method. The Nineteenth Century*, Indiana/London.

Giffen, Sir Robert (1898), *The Case Against Bimetallism*.

—— (1878), 'Recent Accumulations of Capital in the United Kingdom', *J.R.S.S.* 41.

—— (1899), 'The Excess of Imports, *J.R.S.S.* 62.

Gilbart, J.W. (1905), *The History, Principles and Practice of Banking*. Vol. I.

Gilbert, Bentley B. (1973), *The Evolution of National Insurance in Great Britain. The Origins of the Welfare State*.

—— (1978), 'David Lloyd George; The Reform of British Landholding and the Budget of 1914', *Hist.J.* 21.

Gilbert, J.C. (1939), *A History of Investment Trusts in Dundee 1873–1938*.

Gilfillan, S.C. (1970), *The Sociology of Invention*, Cambridge, Mass.

—— (1945), 'Invention as a Factor in Economic History', *J.Ec.H.* 5 Suppl.

Gillespie, Charles C. (1969), *Genesis and Geology. A Study in the Relations of Scientific Thought, Natural Theology and Social Opinion in Great Britain, 1790–1850*, Cambridge, Mass.

—— (1972), 'The Natural History of Industry', in Musson.

Gilpin, Richard (1976), *U.S. Power and the Multinational Corporation. The Political Economy of Foreign Direct Investment*.

Gintis, Herbert (1971), 'Education, Technology and the Characteristics of Worker Productivity', *A.E.R.* 61.

Bibliography

Glass, David V. (1961), 'Education and Social Change in Modern England', in Halsey *et al.*

Goldsbrough, David J. (1979), 'The Role of Foreign Direct Investment in the External Adjustment Process', *IMF Staff Papers* 26.

Goldsmith, Raymond W. (1969), *Financial Structure and Development*, New Haven.

Goldstrom, J.M. (1977), 'The Content of Education and the Sozialization of the Working-Class Child 1830–1860', in McCann.

Gonner, E.C.K. (1912), 'The Economic History', in Rose et al.

Goodhart, C.A.E. (1972), *The Business of Banking 1891–1914*.

Gordon, Barry (1979), *Economic Doctrine and Tory Liberalism 1824–1830*.

Gordon, Donald F. (1956), 'Obsolescence and Technological Change: Comment', *A.E.R.* 46.

Goschen, Viscont (1932), *The Theory of the Foreign Exchanges*.

Gospel, Howard F. and Littler, Craig R. (eds.) (1983), *Managerial Strategies and Industrial Relations*.

Gourvish, T.R. (1978), 'The Performance of British Railway Management after 1860: The Railways of Watkin and Forbes', *Bus.H.* 20.

Gower, Barry (1972–73), 'Speculations in Physics: The History and Practice of Naturphilosophie', *Stud. Hist. & Philosophy of Science* 3.

Gowing, Margaret (1977–78), 'Science, Technology and Education: England in 1870', *Notes and Records of the Royal Society of London* 32.

Graaff, J. De V. (1957), *Theoretical Welfare Economics*, Cambridge.

Graff, H.J. (ed.) (1981a), *Literacy and Social Development in the West: A Reader*, Cambridge.

—— (1981b), 'Literacy, Jobs and Industrialization', *ibid.*

Graham, G.S. (1959), 'Imperial Finance, Trade and Communications, 1895–1914', *Cambridge History of the British Empire*, vol. 3., Chap. 12.

Grant, Wyn and Marsh, David (1977), *The Confederation of British Industry*.

Grassman, Sven and Lundberg, Eric (eds.) (1981), *The World Economic Order, Past and Prospect*, New York.

Gray, H. Peter (1972), *The Economics of Business Investment Abroad*.

Greasley, David (1982), 'The Diffusion of Machine Cutting in the British Coal Industry 1902–1938', *Expl.Ec.H.* 19.

—— (1986), 'British Economic Growth: The Paradox of the 1880's and the Timing of the Climacteric', *Expl.Ec.H.* 23.

Greaves, H.R.G. (1929), 'Personal Origins and Interrelations of the House of Parliament', *Economica* 9.

Green, Alan and Urquhart, M.C. (1976), 'Factor and Commodity Flows in the International Economy of 1870–1914: A Multi-Country View', *J.Ec.H.* 36.

Green, V.H.H. (1974), *A History of Oxford University*.

Greenall, R.L. (1974), 'The Making of the Borough of Salford 1830–1853', in Bell.

Gregory, Theodore E. (1928), 'Foreign Investments and British Public Opinion', in Cassel.

Griffin, Alan R. (1971), *Mining in the East Midlands 1550–1947*.

Griliches, Zvi (ed.) (1984), *R + D. Patents and Productivity*, Chicago.

—— (1957), 'Hybrid Corn: An Exploration in the Economics of Technological Change', *Econometrica* 25.

—— (1973), 'Research Expenditure and Growth Accounting', in Williams.

—— and Lichtenberg, Frank (1984), 'R + D and Productivity Growth at the Industry Level: Is there Still a Relationship?', in Griliches.

—— and Schmookler, Jacob (1963), 'Inventing and Maximising', *A.E.R.* LIII.

Grove, J.W. (1962), *Government and Industry in Britain*.

Grubel, Herbert G. and Lloyd, P.J. (1975), *Intra-Industry Trade. The Theory of International Trade in Differentiated Products*.

Gulhati, Ravi I. (1970), 'The Need for Foreign Resources, Absorptive Capacity and Debt Servicing Capacity', in Adler, H.

Gulvin, Clifford (1984), *The Scottish Hosiery and Knitwear Industry 1660–1980*, Edinburgh.

Gustman, Alan L. and Steinmeier, Thomas L. (1982), 'The Relation Between Vocational Training in High School and Economic Outcomes', *Industrial and Labour Relations Review* 36.

Gutmann, Franz (1956), 'Internationaler Kapitalverkehr', in *Handwörterbuch der Sozialwissenschaften*, Vol. 5, Göttingen.

Guttsman, W.L. (1951), 'The Changing Social Structure of the British Political Elite. 1886–1935', *Brit.J. of Sociology* 2.

—— (1954), 'Aristocracy and the Middle-Class in the British Political Elite 1886–1936', *Brit.J. of Sociology* 5.

—— (1974), 'The British Political Elite and the Class Structure', in Stanworth and Giddens.

Habakkuk, H.J. (1967), *American and British Technology in the Nineteenth Century: the Search for Labour-Saving Inventions*, Cambridge.

—— (1968), 'Fluctuations in House-Building in Britain and the United States, in the Nineteenth Century' in Hall.

—— (1972), 'Fluctuations in House-Building in Britain and the United States in the Nineteenth Century', in Aldcroft and Fearon.

Haber, L.F. (1958), *The Chemical Industry During the Nineteenth Century. A Study of the Economic Aspects of Applied Chemistry in Europe and North America*, Oxford.

—— (1971), *The Chemical Industry 1900–1930. International Growth and Technological Change*, Oxford.

—— (1980), 'From Alkalis to Petrochemicals: Economic Development and Technological Diffusion in the British Chemical Industry', in Okochi and Uchida.

Haines, G. (1969), *Essays on German Influence upon English Education and Science 1850–1919*, Hamden, Conn.

—— (1958), 'German Influence upon Scientific Instruction in England 1867–1887', *Victorian Studies*, I.

Haldane, R.B. (1902), *Education and Empire*.

Hall, A.R. (1963), *The London Capital Market and Australia*, Canberra.

—— (1968a), *The Export of Capital from Britain 1870–1914*.

—— (1957), 'A Note in the English Capital Market as a Source of Funds for Home Investment Before 1914', *Economica* 24.

—— (1958), 'The English Capital Market Before 1914 – a Reply', in *Economica* 25.

—— (1968b), 'Capital Imports and the Composition of Investment in a Borrowing Country', in Hall.

Hall, M.B. (1984), *All Scientists Now. The Royal Society in the Nineteenth Century*, Cambridge.

Hall, P.A. (1986), 'The State and Economic Decline', in Elbaum and Lazonick.

Halsey, A.H. (1961),'The Changing Functions of Universities', in Halsey *et al.*

—— and Trow, M.A. (1971) *The British Academics*.

—— *et al.* (1961), *Education, Economy and Society. A Reader in the Sociology of Education*, New York.

Haltern, Lutz (1971), *Die Londoner Weltansstellung von 1851. Ein Beitrag zur Geschichte der bürgerlich-industriellen Gesellschaft im 19. Jahrhundert*, Münster.

Hampson, N. (1982), *The Enlightenment*, Harmondsworth.

Handwörterbuch der Wirtschaftswissenschaft, (1977–83), Göttingen.

Hanham, H.J. (1968), *The Reformed Electoral System in Great Britain 1832–1914*.

—— (1959/60), 'The Sale of Honours in Late Victorian England', *Victorian Studies* 3.

Hannah, L. (1976), *The Rise of the Corporate Economy*.

—— (1979), *Electricity Before Nationalisation. A Study of the Development of the Electricity Supply Industry in Britain to 1948*.

—— (1974), Managerial Innovation and the Role of the Large-Scale Company in Inter-War Britain, *Ec.H.R.* 27.

Hanoch, G. (1971), 'An Economic Analysis of Earnings and Schooling', in Kiker.

Hans, N. (1951), *New Trends in Education in the Eighteenth Century*.

Hansard, *Parliamentary Reports*.

Hansen, B. (1983), 'Interest Rates and Foreign Capital in Egypt under British Occupation', *J.Ec.H.* 43.

Harbison, F. (1963), The Prime Movers of Innovation, in Anderson and Bowman.

—— (1969), 'Quantitative Indications of Human Resource Development', in Robinson and Vaizey.

Harbison, R. and Myers, C.A. (1964), *Education, Manpower and Economic Growth. Strategies of Human Resource Development*, New York.

Harcourt, G.C. (1969), 'Some Cambridge Controversies in the Theory of Capital', *J.Ec.Lit.* 7.

Hardie, D.W.F. (1972), 'The Macintoshes and the Origins of the Chemical Industry', in Musson.

Harley, C.K. (1971), 'The Shift from Sailing Ship to Steam Ship – a Study in Technical Change and Diffusion', in McCloskey.

—— (1973/74), 'Skilled Labour and the Choice of Technique in Edwardian Industry', *Expl.Ec.H.* 11.

—— (1977), 'The Interest Rate and Prices in Britain, 1873–1913: A Study of the Gibson Paradox', *Expl.Ec.H.* 14.

Harnack, A. (1970), *Geschichte der Königlichen Preußischen Akademie der Wissenschaften zu Berlin*, Hildesheim, New York.

Harney, K. (1985), 'The Emergence of the Technical School System in Prussia in the Nineteenth Century', in Inkster.

Harris, J.S. (1955), *British Government Inspection. The Local Services and the Central Departments.*

Harris, J.R. (1976), 'Skills, Coal and British Industry in the Eighteenth Century', *History* 61.

—— (1986), 'Michael Alcock and the Transfer of Birmingham Technology to France before the Revolution', *J.Europ.Ec.H.* 15.

Harris, Jose (1972), *Unemployment and Politics. A Study in English Social Policy 1886–1914*, Oxford.

—— and Thane, Pat (1984), 'British and European Bankers, 1880–1914: an "Aristocratic" Bourgeoisie', in Thane *et al.*

Harrison, A.E. (1969), 'The Competitiveness of the British Cycle Industry 1890–1914', *Ec.H.R.* 22.

—— (1981), 'Joint-Stock Company Flotation in the Cycle, Motor-Vehicle and Related Industries, 1882–1914' *Bus.H.* 23.

—— (1982), 'F. Hopper and Co. – The Problems of Capital Supply in the Cycle Manufacturing Industry, 1891–1914', *Bus.H.* 24.

Harrison, J.F.C. (1961), *Learning and Living 1790–1960. A Study in the History of the English Adult Movement.*

Harrod, R. (1963), 'Desirable International Movements of Capital in Relation to Growth of Borrowers and Lenders and Growth of Markets' in R. Harrod and D. Hague (eds.) *International Trade Theory in a Developing World.*

Harrod, R.F. (1951), *Life of John Maynard Keynes.*

Hart, J. (1972), 'The Genesis of the Northcote-Trevelyan Report', in Sutherland.

Hassan, J.A. (1985), 'The Growth and Impact of the British Water Industry in the Nineteenth Century', *Ec.H.R.* 38.

Hatton, T.J. (1982), Report on: 'Quantitative Economic History at the University of Essex', *J.Europ.Ec.H.* 11.

Hauser, H. (1917), *Germany's Commercial Grip on the World. Her Business Methods Explained.*

Hawkins, K.H. and Pass, C.L. (1979), *The Brewing Industry. A Study in Industrial Organisation and Public Policy.*

Hayek, F.A. (1937), 'Investment that Raises the Demand for Capital', *Rev.Ec.Statistics* 19.

Hays, T.N. (1983), 'The London Lecturing Empire, 1800–1850', in Inkster and Morell.

Head, P. (1968), 'Boots and Shoes' in Aldcroft.

Heathcote, H.L. (1909), 'The University Training of Industrial Chemists', *J.of the Society of Chemical Industry* 28.

Heerding, A. (1986), *The History of N.V. Philips' Gloeilampenfabrieken*, Cambridge.

Heesom, A.J. and Duffy, B. (1981),'Coal, Class and Education in the North-East', *P.&P.* 90.

Heggen, A. (1975), *Erfindungsschutz und Industrialisierung in Preußen 1793–1877*, Göttingen.

Heidhues, F. (1969), *Zur Theorie der internationalen Kapitalbewegungen. Eine kritische Untersuchung unter besonderer Berücksichtigung der Direktinvestitionen.* Tübingen.

Heindel, R.M. (1940), *The American Impact on Britain*, Philadelphia.

Helm, E. (1894), *The Joint Standard. A Plain Exposition of Monetary Principles and of the Monetary Controversy.*

—— (1892), 'The Alleged Decline of the British Cotton Industry'. *E.J.* 2.

Henderson, W.O. (1967), *The State and the Industrial Revolution in Prussia 1740–1870*, Liverpool.

Hennessey, R.A.S. (1972), *The Electrical Revolution*, Newcastle.

Hennock, E.P. (1973), *Fit and Proper Persons. Ideal and Reality in Nineteenth-Century Urban Government.*

Herford, C.H. (1912), 'The Intellectual and Literacy History', in Rose *et al.*

Hermann, A. (1977), 'Wissenschaftspolitik und Entwicklung der Physik im Deutschen Kaiserreich', in Mann and Winau.

Hessen, B.M. (1968), 'The Social and Economic Roots of Newtons' "Principia" ', in Basalla.

Hewins, W.R.S. (1901), 'Der Imperialismus und seine voraussichtliche Wirkung auf die Handelspolitik des Ver. Königreichs', *Schriften des Vereins für Sozialpolitik* 91.

Heyck, T.W. (1982), *The Transformation of Intellectual Life in Victorian England.*

Hickel, E. (1977), 'Das kaiserliche Gesundheitsamt und die chemische Industrie im zweiten Kaiserreich (1871–1914): Partner oder Kontrahenten', in Mann and Winau.

Hicks, J.R. (1936), 'Mr Keynes' Theory of Employment', *Ec.J.* 46.

— (1953), 'An Inaugural Lecture', *O.E.P.* 5.

Hidy, R.W. and Hidy, M.E. (1960), 'Anglo-American Merchant Bankers and the Railroads of the Old Northwest, 1848–1860', *Bus.H.R.* 34.

Hilgerdt, F. (1945), *Industrialization and Foreign Trade*, New York.

— (1943), 'The Case for Multilateral Trade', *A.E.R.* 23.

Hilken, T.J.N. (1967), *Engineering at Cambridge University 1783–1965*, Cambridge.

Hill, B.W. (1985), *British Parliamentary Parties 1742–1832. From the Fall of Walpole to the First Reform Act.*

Hill, Karl (ed.), (1964), *The Management of Scientists*, Boston.

Hilton, B. (1977), *Corn, Cash, Commerce: The Economic Policies of the Tory Governments 1815–1830*, Oxford.

Hinshaw, R. (1945), 'Foreign Investment and American Employment', *A.E.R.* 35.

Hirsch, B.P. and Hausman, W.J. (1983), 'Labour Productivity in the British and South Wales Coal Industry, 1874–1914', *Economica* 50.

Hirsch, S. (1967), *Location of Industry and International Competitiveness*, Oxford.

Hirst, F.W. (1932), *The Stock Exchange*.

— (1928), 'Kapital und Kapitalanlagen Großbritanniens seit dem Krieg', in Walther Lotz (ed.), *Die Auslandskredite*. 3. Teil. *Wissenschaftliche Gutachten*, Munich/Leipzig.

Hobhouse, C. (1950), *1851 and the Crystal Palace*.

Hobsbawm, E.J. (1968), *Industry and Empire. An Economic History of Britain Since 1750*.

Hobson, C.K. (1914), *The Export of Capital*.

— (1916), 'British Overseas Investments. Their Growth and Importance', in Kemmerer.

Hobson, J.A. (1968), *Imperialism. A Study*.

— (1911), 'An Economic Interpretation of Investment', *Financial Review of Reviews*.

Hoffman, Ross, J.S. (1964), *Great Britain and the German Trade Rivalry 1815–1914*, New York.

Hoffmann, Walther (1955), *British Industry 1760–1950*, Oxford.

Hohenberg, P.M. (1967), *Chemicals in Western Europe: 1850–1914. An Economic Study of Technical Change*, Chicago.

Hoke, D. (1986), 'Ingenious Yankees, the Rise of the American System of Manufacture in the Private Sector', *J.Ec.H.* 46.

— (1987), 'British and American Horology: Time to Test Factor-Substitution Models', *J.Ec.H.* 47

Holland, B. (1913), *The Fall of Protection 1840–1850*.

Holland, R.F. (1981), 'The Federation of British Industries and the International Economy 1929–39', *Ec.H.R.* 34.

Hollander, J.H. (1916/17), 'International Trade under Depreciated Paper', in Taussig.

Hollenberg, G. (1974), *Englisches Interesse am Kaiserreich. Die Attraktivität Preußen-Deutschlands für konservative und liberale Kreise in Großbritannien 1860–1914*, Wiesbaden.

Hollomon, T.H. (1965), 'Science and Civilian Technology', in Warner.

Holmes, G.M. (1976), *Britain and America. A Comparative Economic History 1850–1939*, Newton Abbot.

Hooykaas, R. (1966), 'Die Chemie in der ersten Hälfte des 19. Jahrhunderis', *Technikgeschichte* 33.

Hortleder, G. (1970), *Das Gesellschaftsbild des Ingenieurs. Zum politischen Verhalten der technischen Intelligenz in Deutschland*, Frankfurt a.M.

Houghton, W.E. (1970), *The Victorian Frame of Mind 1830–1870*, New Haven.

Hounshell, D. (1984), *From the American System to Mass Production, 1800–1932: The Development of Manufacturing Technology in the United States*, Baltimore.

Houston, H.J. (1925), *The Real Horatio Bottomley*.

Houthakker, H.S. (1959), 'Education and Income', *Rev.Ec.Statistics* 41.

Howard, E.D. (1907), *The Cause and Extent of the Recent Industrial Progress of Germany*.

Howarth, O.J.R. (1922), *The British Association for the Advancement of Science: A Retrospect 1831–1921*.

Howe, A. (1984), *The Cotton Masters 1830–1860*, Oxford.

Höweler, K. (1927), *Der Geld- und Kapitalmarkt der Schweiz*, Berlin.

Howson, S. (1974), 'The Origin of Dear Money, 1919–20', *Ec.H.R.* 27.

Bibliography

Hudson, D. and Luckhurst, K.W. (1954), *The Royal Society of Arts 1754–1954*.
Hufbauer, K. (1971), 'Social Support for Chemistry in Germany During the Eighteenth Century: How and Why Did it Change?, *Historical Studies in the Physical Sciences* 3.
Hughes, E. (1942), 'Civil Service Reform 1853–5', *History* 27.
—— (1949), 'Sir Charles Trevelyan and Civil Service Reform 1853–5', *E.H.R.* 64.
Hughes, J.T.R. (1971), Discussion, in McCloskey.
Hughes, T.P. (1962), 'British Electrical Industry Lag: 1882–1888', *Technology and Culture* 3.
—— (1969), 'Technological Momentum in History: Hydrogenation in Germany 1898–1933', *P.&P.* 44.
Hull, D.L. (1973), 'Charles Darwin and the 19th Century Philosophers of Science', in Giere and Westfall.
Hume, J.R. (1976), 'Shipbuilding Machine Tools', in John Butt and J.T. Ward (eds.).
Hunt, E.H. (1981), *British Labour History 1815–1914*.
Hurt, J.S. (1979), *Elementary Schooling and the Working Classes 1860–1918*.
—— (1971), 'Professor West on Early Nineteenth Century Education', *Ec.H.R.* 24.
Huxley, T.H. (1895), *Essays*. Vol. III. *Science and Education*.
Hyde, F.E. (1934), *Mr Gladstone at the Board of Trade*.
Hynes S. (1968), *The Edwardian Turn of Mind*, Princeton.
Imlah, A.H. (1958), *Economic Elements in the Pax Britannica. Studies in British Foreign Trade in the Nineteenth Century*, Cambridge, Mass.
—— (1952/53), 'British Balance of Payments and Export of Capital', *Ec.H.R.* 5.
Inglis Palgrave, R.H. (1903), *Bank Rate and the Money Market in England, France, Germany, Holland and Belgium*.
Ingham, G. (1984), *Capitalism Divided? The City and Industry in British Social Development*.
Inkster, Ian (ed.) (1985a), *The Steam Intellect Societies. Essays on Culture, Education and Industry circa 1820–1914*. Nottingham.
—— (1983), 'Introduction: Aspects of the History of Science and Science Culture in Britain, 1780–1850 and Beyond', in Inkster and Morrell.
—— (1985b), 'The Context of Steam Intellect in Britain',in Inkster.
—— (1985c), 'Conclusions: Hypotheses: Patterns in the Economic and Social History of Steam Intellect Prior to 1814', in Inkster.
—— and Morrell, J. (eds.), (1983), *Metropolis and Province. Science in British Culture, 1780–1850*.
Inove, T. (1984), 'A Comparison of the Emergence of Multinational Manufacturing by U.S., European and Japanese Firms', in Okochi and Inove.
Intriligator, M.D. (1965), 'Embodied Technical Change and Productivity in the United States 1929–58', *Rev. Econ.Stat.* 47.
Irving R.J. (1975), 'New Industries for Old? Some Investment Decisions of Sir W.G. Armstrong, Whitworth & Co., Ltd., 1900–1914', *Bus.H.* 17.
—— (1978), 'The Profitability and Performance of British Railways, 1870–1914', *Ec.H.R.* 31.
Isard, W. (1948), 'Some Locational Factors in the Iron and Steel Industry Since the Early Nineteenth Century', *J.P.E.* 56.
Islam, N. (1960), *Foreign Capital and Economic Development: Japan, India and Canada*, Rutland and Tokyo.
Iversen, C. (1958), *Economic Elements in the Pax Britannica. Studies in British Foreign Trade in the Nineteenth Century*, Cambridge, Mass.
—— (1967), *Aspects of the Theory of International Capital Movements*, New York.
Jack, M. (1968), 'The Purchase of the British Government's Shares in the British Petroleum Company 1912–1914', *P.&P.* 39.
Jahrreisz, W. (1984), *Zur Theorie der Direktinvestitionen im Ausland*, Berlin.
Janossy, F. (1966), *Das Ende der Wirtschaftswunder. Erscheinung und Wesen der wirtschaftlichen Entwicklung*, Hamburg.
Jansen, M. and Stone, L. (1966/67), 'Education and Modernization in Japan and England', *Comp.Stud.Soc.H.* IX.
Jarausch, K.H. (1983a), *The Transformation of Higher Learning in 1860–1930*. Stuttgart.
—— (1980), 'Frequenz und Struktur. Zur Sozialgeschichte der Studenten im Kaiserreich', in Baumgart.
—— (1983b), 'Higher Education and Social Change: Some Comparative Perspectives', in Jarausch.
Jasay, A.E. (1972), 'The Social Choice between Home and Overseas Investment', in Dunning.

Jay, R. (1981), *Joseph Chamberlain: A Political Study*.

Jeismann, K.H. (1974), *Das preussische Gymnasium in Staat und Gesellschaft*, Stuttgart.

Jenkins, D.T. and Ponting, K.G. (1982), *The British Wool Textile Industry 1770–1914*.

Jenkins, H. and Jones, C. (1950), 'Social Class of Cambridge University Alumni of the Eighteenth and Nineteenth Centuries', *Brit.J.Sociology* 1.

Jenks, L.H. (1927), *The Migration of British Capital to 1875*, New York.

—— (1944), 'British Experience with Foreign Investment', *J.Ec.H.* 4.

—— (1951), 'British and American Railway Development', *J.Ec.H.* 11.

Jennings, J.L. (1881), 'English Trade and Foreign Competition', *Quarterly Review*, 152.

Jeremy, D.J. (1984), *Dictionary of Business Biography. A Bibliographical Dictionary of Business Leaders Active in Britain in the Period 1860–1980*.

—— (1977), 'Damming the Flood: British Government Efforts to Check the Outflow of Technicians and Machinery 1780–1843', *Bus.H.R.* LI.

Jervis, F.R.J. (1947), 'The Handicap of Britain's Early Start', *Manchester School* 14.

Jevons, H.S. (1915), *The British Coal Trade*.

Jewkes, J. (1960), 'How Much Science?', *E.J.* 70.

——, Sawers, D. and Stillerman, R. (1969), *The Sources of Invention*.

Johnson, H.G. (1958), *International Trade and Economic Growth*.

—— (1965), 'An Economic Theory of Protectionism, Tariff Bargaining, and the Formation of Customs Unions', *J.P.E.* 73.

—— (1972), 'The Crisis of Aid and the Pearson Report', in di Marco, E.L., *International Economics and Development*, New York.

Johnson, R. (1970), 'Educational Policy and Social Control in Early Victorian England', *P.&P.* 49.

—— (1976), 'Notes on the Schooling of the English Working Class, 1780–1850', in Dale *et al.*

Jones, B. (1870), *The Life and Letters of Faraday.*

Jones, C.A. (1987), *International Business in the Nineteenth Century. The Rise and Fall of the Cosmopolitan Bourgeoisie*, Brighton.

—— (1980), 'Great Capitalists and the Direction of British Overseas Investment in the Late Nineteenth Century: The Case of Argentina', *Bus.H.* 22.

Jones, D.K. (1977), 'Socialization and Social Science: Manchester Model Secular School 1854–1861', in McCann.

Jones, G. (1982), 'Lombard Street on the Riviera: the British Clearing Banks and Europe 1900–1960', *Bus.H.* 24.

—— (1984a), 'The Growth and Performance of British Multinational Firms before 1939: The Case of Dunlop', *Ec.H.R.* 37.

—— (1984b), 'The Expansion of British Multinational Manufacturing 1890–1939', in Okochi and Inove (1984).

Jones, G.S. (1971) *Outcast London*, Oxford.

—— (1983), *Languages of Class. Studies in English Working-Class History 1832–1982*, Cambridge.

Jones, G.T. (1933), *Increasing Return*, Cambridge.

Jones, G.W. (1969), *Borough Politics. A Study of the Wolverhampton Town Council 1888–1964*.

Jones, L. (1983), 'Public Pursuit of Private Profit? Liberal Businessmen and Municipal Politics in Birmingham, 1865–1900', *Bus.H.* 25.

Jordan, D.W. (1985), 'The Key for Useless Knowledge – Education for a New Victorian Technology', *Proc.Inst.Elec.Engineers.*

Jorgensen, D.W. and Griliches, Z. (1974), 'Issues of Growth Accounting. A Reply to E.F. Denison', *Survey of Current Business* 5.

—— (1974), 'The Explanation of Productivity Change', *Rev.Ec.Studies* 34.

Joslin, D. (1963), *A Century of Banking in Latin America*, Oxford.

Joyce, P. (1980), *Work, Society and Politics. The Culture of the Factory in Later Victorian England*, Brighton.

Judd, G.P., IV. (1955), *Members of Parliament 1734–1832*, New Haven.

Kaelble, H. (1967), *Industrielle Interessenpolitik in der wilhelminischen Gesellschaft, Centralverband Deutscher Industrieller 1895–1914*, Berlin.

Kaestle, C. (1976), 'Elite Attitudes Toward Mass Schooling in Early Industrial England and America', in Stone.

Kafka, A. (1970), 'Economic Effects of Capital Imports', in Adler, J.H.

Bibliography

Kaku, S. (1980), 'The Development and Structure of the German Coal-Tar-Dyestuffs Firms', in Okochi and Uchida.

Kaldor, N. (1957), 'A New Model of Economic Growth', *E.J.* 67.

— (1961), 'Increasing Returns and Technical Progress – A Comment on Professor Hicks's Article', *O.E.P.* 13.

Kamarck, A.M. (1970), 'The Financial Experiences of Lenders and Investors', in Adler, J.H.

Karachi, Ministers (1971), 'The Economic Impact of Private Education', in Bowman *et al.*

Kargon, R.H. (1977), *Science in Victorian Manchester*, Baltimore.

Kaser, M.C. (1969), 'Education and Economic Progress: Experience in Industrialized Market Economies', in Robinson and Vaizey.

Katz, M.B. (1968), *The Irony of Early School Reform. Educational Innovation in Mid-Nineteenth Century Massachusetts*, Cambridge, Mass.

Kay, J. (1846), *The Education of the Poor in England and Europe.*

— (1850), *The Social Condition and Education of the People in England and Europe.*

Kellenberger, E. (1939–42), *Kapitalexport und Zahlungsbilanz*, 3 Vols., Bern.

Kelly, A.C. (1965), 'International Migration and Economic Growth in Australia, 1865–1935', *J.Ec.H.* 25.

Kelsall, K.R. (1955), *Higher Civil Service in Britain: From 1870 to the Present Day.*

Kemmerer, E.W. (1916), 'The Theory of Foreign Investment', *Annals of the American Academy of Political and Social Science* 68.

Kemp, B. (1961), 'Reflections on the Repeal of the Corn Laws', *Victorian Studies* V.

Kemp, M.C. (1964), *The Pure Theory of International Trade*, Englewood Cliffs.

— (1962), 'Foreign Investment and the National Advantage', *The Economic Review* 38.

— (1966), 'The Gain from International Trade and Investment: A Neo-Heckschen-Ohlin Approach', *A.E.R.* 56.

Kendrick, J.W. (1961), *Productivity Trends in the United States*, New York.

Kenen, P.B. (1976), 'International Capital Movements and the Integration of Capital Markets', in Machlup. F. (ed.), *Economic Integration: Worldwide, Regional, Sectoral.*

Kennedy, C. and Thirlwall, A.P. (1972), 'Surveys in Applied Economics: Technical Progress', *E.J.* 83.

Kennedy, P.A. (1980), *The Rise of Anglo-German Antagonism 1860–1914.*

Kennedy, W.P. (1978), *Economic Growth and Structural Change in the United Kingdom 1870–1914*, Essex.

— (1973/74), 'Foreign Investment, Trade and Growth in the United Kingdom, 1870–1913', *Expl.Ec.H.* 11.

— (1976), 'Institutional Response to Economic Growth: Capital Markets in Britain to 1914', in Hannah, L. (ed.) (1976), *Management Strategy and Business Development.*

— (1984), 'Notes on Economic Efficiency in Historical Perspective: The Case of Britain, 1870–1914', *Res.Ec.H.* 9.

Kent, M. (1975), 'Agent of the Empire? The National Bank of Turkey and British Foreign Policy', *Hist.J.* 18.

Kenwood, A.G. and Lougheed, A.L. (1982), *Technological Diffusion and Industrialisation before 1914.*

Keynes, J.M. (1930), *A Treatise on Money.*

— (1914a), 'The Prospect of Money', *E.J.* XXIV.

— (1914b), 'War and the Financial System', *E.J.* XXIV.

— (1929), 'Rejoinders', *E.J.* XXXIX.

— (1971), 'Great Britain's Foreign Investments', in *Collected Works*, 15.

— (1981), 'Foreign Investment and National Advantage', in *Collected Works*, 11.

— (1981), 'Home versus Foreign Investment', in *Collected Works*, 11.

— (1981), 'Some Tests for Loans to Foreign and Colonial Governments', in *Collected Works*, 11.

Keynes, M. (ed.) (1975), *Essays on John Maynard Keynes*, Cambridge.

Kiker, B.F. (ed.) (1971a), *Investment in Human Capital*, Columbia.

— (1971b) 'The Historical Rest of the Concept of Human Capital', *ibid.*

Killick, J.R. and Thomas, W.A. (1970), 'The Provincial Stock Exchanges 1830–1870', *Ec.H.R.* 23.

Kindleberger, C.P. (1958), *Economic Development*, New York.

— (1964), *Economic Growth in France and Britain 1851–1950*, Cambridge, Mass.

— (1968), *International Economics*, Homewood.

—— (1984), *A Financial History of Western Europe*.

—— (1961), 'Obsolescence and Technical Change', *Bull.Ox.U.Inst.Stat.* 23.

—— (1961/62), 'Foreign Trade and Economic Growth: Lessons from Britain and France, 1850–1913', *Ec.H.R.* 14.

—— (1972), 'Direct Investment in Less-Developed Countries: Historical Wrongs and Present Values', in di Marco, L.E. *International Economics and Development*, New York.

—— (1975), 'The Rise of Free Trade in Western Europe, 1820–1875', *J.Ec.H.* 35.

—— (1978), 'Germany's Overtaking of England, 1806–1914', in *Economic Response. Comparative Studies in Trade, Finance and Growth*, Cambridge, Mass.

Kirby, M.W. (1977), *The British Coalmining Industry, 1870–1946. A Political and Economic History*.

—— (1981), *The Decline of British Economic Power Since 1870*.

—— (1984), *Men of Business and Politics. The Rise and Fall of the Quaker Pease Dynasty of North-East England, 1700–1943*.

Kirchner, W. (1986), *Die deutsche Industrie und die Industrialisierung Russlands 1815–1914*, St Katharinen.

Kleinert, A. (1985), 'Mathematik und anorganische Naturwissenschaften', in Vierhaus, R. (ed.), *Wissenschaft im Zeitalter der Aufklärung*, Göttingen.

Knapp, J. (1942/43), 'The Theory of International Capital Movements and its Verifications', *Rev.Ec.Stud.* 10.

—— (1957), 'Capital Exports and Growth', *E.J.* 67.

Knight, D.M. (1975), 'German Science in the Romantic Period', in Crosland.

Kocka, J. (1981a), *Die Angestellten in der deutschen Geschichte 1850–1914*, Göttingen.

—— (1981b), 'Capitalism and Bureaucracy in German Industrialization before 1914', *Ec.H.R.* 34.

—— and Siegrist, H. (1979), 'Die hundert größten deutschen Unternehmen im späten 19. und frühen 20. Jahrhundert', in Horn, N. and Kocka, J. (eds.), *Law and the Formation of Big Enterprises in the Nineteenth and Early Twentieth Centuries*, Göttingen.

König, R. (1970), *Vom Wesen der deutschen Universität*, Darmstadt.

König, W. (1981), 'Die Ingenieure und der VDI als Großverein in der wilhelminische Gesellschaft', in Ludwig.

Komarov, V.E. (1971), 'The Scientification of Education', in Bowman *et al.*

Komlos, J. (1978a), 'The Kreditbanken and German Growth: A Postscript', *J.Ec.H.* 32.

—— (1978b), 'Rejoinders', *J.Ec.H.* 38.

Krätz, O. (1973), 'Der Chemiker in den Gründerjahren' in Schmauderer.

Kranzberg, M. and Pursell, C.W., Jr. (1967), *Technology in Western Civilization*, New York.

Krasner, S.D. (1975/76), 'State Power and the Structure of International Trade', *World Politics* 28.

Kreinin, M.E. (1979), *International Economcis. A Policy Approach*, New York.

Krohn, W., Layton, E.T. and Weingart, P. (eds.) (1978), *The Dynamics of Science and Technology, Social Values, Technical Norms and Scientific Criteria in the Development of Knowledge*, Dordrecht.

Kroker, E. (1975), *Die Weltausstellungen im 19. Jahrhundert*, Göttingen.

Kuczynski, T. (1982), 'Leads and Lags in an Escalation Model of Capitalist Development', *8th. International Economic History Congress*, Budapest.

Kullmer, H. and Krug, W. (1967), 'Beziehungen zwischen beruflicher Ausbildung und Nettoeinkommen der ausgebildeten Person', *Wirtschaft und Statistik*.

Kusamitsu, T. (1981), 'British Industrialization and Design before the Great Exhibition', *Textile History* 12.

—— (1985), 'Mechanics' Institute and Working Class Culture: Exhibition Movements 1830–1840s', in Inkster.

Kuznets, S. (1962), *Long Term Changes in National Income of the U.S. since 1869*, Cambridge.

—— (1966), *Modern Economic Growth. Rate, Structure and Spread*.

—— (1959/60), 'Quantitive Aspects of the Economic Growth of Nations: V. Capital Formation Proportions: International Comparisons for Recent Years', *Ec.Dev.Cult.C.* 8.

—— (1961), 'idem: VI. Long Term Trends in Capital Formation Proportions', *Ec.Dev.Cult.C.* 9.

—— (1967), 'idem: X. Level and Structure of Foreign Trade: Long Term Trends', *Ec.Dev.Cult.C.* 15.

Lachman, L.M. (1947), 'Complementarity and Substitution in the Theory of Capital', *Economica* 14.

—— (1948), 'Investment Repercussions', *Q.J.E.* 62.

Bibliography

Lambert, A. (1984), *Unquiet Souls. The Indian Summer of the British Aristocracy 1880–1918.*

Landmann, J. (1916), *Der schweizerische Kapitalexport*, Bern.

Langan, M. and Schwarz, B. (1985), *Crises in the British State 1880–1930.*

Laqueur, T.W. (1976a), *Religion and Respectability. Sunday Schools and Working Class Culture 1780–1850*, New Haven.

—— (1976b), 'Working-Class Demand and the Growth of English Elementary Education, 1750–1850', in Stone.

Latham, A.S.H. (1978), *The International Economy and the Underdeveloped World, 1865–1914.*

Landes, D.S. (1969), *The Unbound Prometheus.*

—— (1983), *Revolution in Time. Clocks and the Making of the Modern World*, Cambridge, Mass.

Laughlin, J.L. (1903), *The Principles of Money*, New York.

Laves, W.H.C. (1977), *German Governmental Influence on Foreign Investments 1871–1914*, New York.

Lavington, F. (1921), *The English Capital Market.*

—— (1922), 'Uncertainty in its Relation to the New Rate of Interest', *E.J.* 22.

Layton, D. (1973), *Science for the People. The Origins of the School Science Curriculum in England.*

Layton, E. (1977), 'Conditions of Technological Development', in Spiegel-Rösing and Price.

—— (1979a) 'Managers, Entrepreneurs and Choice of Technique: Rings and Mules in Lancashire', *Harvard Institute of Economic Research Paper* No. 726 (Cyclost.)

Lazonick, W. (1979a) 'Industrial Relations and Technical Change: The Case of the Self-Acting Mule', *Cambridge Journal of Economics* 3.

—— (1980) 'Industrial Organization and Technical Change: The Decline of the British Cotton Industry', *Harvard Institute of Economic Research Paper* No. 794, (Cyclost).

—— (1981a), 'Production Relations, Labor Productivity and Choice of Technique: British and U.S. Cotton Spinning', *J.Ec.H.* XLI.

—— (1981b), 'Industrial Organization and Technical Change: The Decline of the British Cotton Industry' (Cyclost.)

—— (1981c), 'Factor Costs and the Diffusion of Ring Spinning in Britain Prior to World War I.', *Q.J.E.* 96.

—— (1981d), 'Competition, Specialization and Industrial Decline', *J.Ec.H.* XL.

—— (1986a), 'Social Organisation and Productivity Growth: Britain and the United States', in O'Brien.

—— (1986b), 'The Cotton Industry', in Elbaum and Lazonick.

Lazonick, W., Saxonhouse, G. and Wright, G. (1987), Debate, *Ec.H.R.* 40.

Leary, H.B. (1945), 'The Domestic Effects of Foreign Investment', *A.E.R. P.&P.* 35.

Lecky, W.H.E. (1892), *A History of England in the Eighteenth Century*, 8 Vols.

Leclerc, M. (1894), *Les professions et al societé en Angleterre*, Paris.

—— (1899), *L'éducation des classes moyennes et dirigeantes en Angleterre*, Paris.

Lee, C.H. (1986), *The British Economy since 1700*, Cambridge.

—— (1980), 'Regional Structural Change in the Long Run: Great Britain 1841–1971', in Pollard, S., *Region und Industrialisierung*, Göttingen.

—— (1980), 'The Cotton Textile Industry', in Church.

—— (1981), 'Regional Growth and Structural Change in Victorian Britain', *Ec.H.R.* 34.

Lee, J.J. (1978), 'Labour in German Industrialization', *Cambridge Ec.H. of Europe.* VII.

Lee, J.M. (1963), *Social Leaders and Public Persons. A Study of County Government in Cheshire since 1880*, Oxford.

Le Guillou, M. (1981), 'Technical Education 1850–1914', in Roderick and Stephens.

Lehfeldt, R.A. (1913), 'Rate of Interest on British and Foreign Investment', *J.R.S.S.* 76.

—— (1914), idem, *J.R.S.S.* 77.

—— (1915), idem, *J.R.S.S.* 78.

Leibenstein, H. (1966), 'Allocative Efficiency versus X-Efficiency', *A.E.R.* 56.

Lenin, V.I. (1917), *Imperialism, the Highest Stage of Capitalism.*

Lenman, B. (1977), *An Economic History of Modern Scotland 1660–1976.*

—— and Donaldson, K. (1971), 'Partners' Incomes, Investment and Diversification in the Scottish Linen Area 1850–1921', *Bus.H.* 13.

Lenfant, J.H. (1951), 'Great Britain's Capital Formation 1865–1914', *Economica* 18.

Lenz, F. (1922), 'Wesen und Struktur des deutschen Kapitalexports vor 1914', *W.W. Archiv.* 18.

Leubuscher, C. (1917), 'Die ausländische Kapitalbeteiligung an der deutschen Industrie', *Schmollers Jahrbuch*, 41.

Levine, A.L. (1967), *Industrial Retardation in Britain 1880-1914*. New York.

Lévy-Leboyer, M. (ed.) (1977a) *La position internationale de la France. Aspects économiques et financiers XIXe-XXe Siècles*, Paris.

— (1977b), 'La capacité financière de la France au debut du XXe siècle', *ibid.*

— (1977c), 'La balance des payements et exportation des capitaux Français' *ibid.*

Lewchuk, W. (1984), 'The Role of the British Government in the Spread of Scientific Management and Fordism in the Interwar Years', *J.Ec.H.* XLIV.

— (1985), 'The Return to Capital in the British Motor Vehicle Industry 1849-1939', *Bus.H.* 27.

— (1986), 'The Motor Vehicle Industry', in Elbaum and Lazonick.

Lewis, C.M. (1983), *British Railways in Argentina 1857-1914. A Case Study of Foreign Investment*.

Lewis, J.P. (1965), *Building Cycles and Britain's Growth*.

Lewis, W.A. (1970), *The Theory of Economic Growth*.

— (1978a), *Growth and Fluctuations 1870-1913*.

— (1957), 'International Competition in Manufacturers', *A.E.R.* 47.

— (1971), 'Education and Economic Development', in Bowman *et al.*

— (1978b), 'The Rate of Growth of World Trade, 1830-1973', in Grassman, S. and Lundberg, E. (eds.), *The World Economic Order. Past and Prospects*.

Lexis, W. (1904), *Das Unterrichtswesen im Deutschen Reich*, Berlin.

Liberal Industrial Inquiry (1928), *Britain's Industrial Future*.

Lilley, S. (1973), 'Technological Progress and the Industrial Revolution. 1700-1914', in Cipolla, C. (ed.), *The Fontana Economic History of Europe. III. The Industrial Revolution*.

Lindert, P.H. (1969), *Key Currencies and Gold 1900-1913*, Princeton.

— (1983), *Who Owned Victorian England*, Davis (Cyclost).

— and Morton, P.J. (1987), *How Sovereign Debt has Worked*, Davis (Cyclost).

— and Trace, K. (1971), 'Yardsticks for Victorian Entrepreneurs', in McCloskey.

Lintner, J. (1965a), 'The Valuation of Risk Assets and the Selection of Risky Investments in Stock Portfolios and Capital Budgets', *Rev.Econ.Stat.* 47.

— (1965b), 'Security Prices, Risk and Maximal Gains from Diversification', *Journal of Finance* 20.

Lipson, C. (1985), *Standing Guard. Protecting Foreign Capital in the Nineteenth and Twentieth Centuries*.

Lisle-Williams, M. (1984a), 'Beyond the Market: the Survival of Family Capitalism in the English Merchant Banks', *British J. of Sociology* 35.

— (1984b), 'Merchant Banking Dynasties in the English Class Structure: Ownership, Solidarity and Kinship in the City of London, 1850-1960', *British J. of Sociology* 35.

Locke, R.R. (1984), *The End of Practical Man: Entrepreneurship and Higher Education in Germany, France and Great Britain, 1880-1940*.

— (1977), 'Industrialisierung und Erziehungssystem in Frankreich und Deutschland vor dem ersten Weltkrieg', *Hist.Z.* 225.

Lockyer, Sir N. (1903), 'The Influence of Brain-Power on History', *Nature* 68.

Lomax, K.S. (1969), 'Growth and Productivity in the United Kingdom', in Aldcroft, D.H. and Fearon, P., *Economic Growth in Twentieth-Century Britain*.

Longstrenth, F. (1979), 'The City, Industry and the State', in Crouch, C., *State and Economy in Contemporary Capitalism*.

Lorenz, E.H. (1984), 'Two Patterns of Development: the Labour Process in the British and French Shipbuilding Industries 1880 to 1930', *J.Europ.Ec.H.* 13.

Lorenz, E. and Wilkinson, F. (1986), 'The Shipbuilding Industry', in Elbaum and Lazonick.

Lowe, R. (1983), 'The Expansion of Higher Education in England', in Jarausch.

— (1985), 'English Elite Education in the Late Nineteenth and Early Twentieth Centuries', in Conze and Kocka.

Lowenfeld, H. (1909), *All about Investment*.

Ludwig, K.H. (1974) *Technik und Ingenieure im Dritten Reich*, Düsseldorf.

— (ed.) unter Mitwirkung von König, W. (1981), *Technik, Ingenieure und Gesellschaft. Geschichte des Vereins Deutscher Ingenieure 1856-1981*, Düsseldorf.

Lundgreen, P. (1973), *Bildung und Wissenschaftswachstum im Industrialisierungsprozess des 19. Jahrhunderts*, Berlin.

— (1975b), *Techniker in Preußen während der frühen Industrialisierung*, Berlin.

— (1970) 'Analyse Preußischer Schulbücher als Zugang zum Thema "Schulbildung und Industrialisierung"', *Int.R.Soc.H.* 15.

—— (1975a), 'Industrialization and the Educational Formation of Manpower in Germany', *J.Soc.H.*

—— (1981), 'Bildung und Besitz – Einheit oder Inkongruenz in der europäischen Sozialgeschichte?', *G.&G.* 7.

—— (1983), 'Differentiation in German Higher Education', in Jarausch.

—— (1984), 'Education for the Science-Based Industrial State. The Case for Nineteenth-Century Germany', *History of Education* 13.

—— (1985), 'Zur Konstituierung des Bildungsbürgertums – Berufs und Bildungsauslese der Akademiker in Preußen', in Conze and Kocka.

—— with Contr. by Thirlwall, A.P. (1976), 'Educational Expense and Economic Growth in Nineteenth Century Germany: a Quantitive Study', in Stone.

Luxemburg, R. (1913), *Die Akkumulation des Kapitals*, Berlin.

McCagg, W.O. (1972), 'Hungary's 'Feudalized' Bourgeoisie', *J.Mod.H.* 44.

McCann, P. (ed.) (1977a), *Popular Education and Socialization in the Nineteenth Century.*

—— (1977b), 'Popular Education, Socialization and Social Control: 1812–1824', *ibid.*

McClelland, C.E. (1980), *State, Society and University in Germany 1740–1914*, Cambridge.

—— (1976), 'The Aristocracy and University Reform in Eighteenth Century Germany', in Stone.

—— (1983), 'Professionalization and Higher Education in Germany', in Jarausch.

McCloskey, D.N. (ed.) (1971a), *Essays on a Mature Economy: Britain after 1840.*

—— (1973), *Economic Maturity and Entrepreneurial Decline: British Iron and Steel 1870–1913*, Cambridge, Mass.

—— (1981), *Enterprise and Trade in Victorian Britain.*

—— (1968), 'Productivity Change in British Pig Iron, 1810–1939', *Q.J.E.* 82.

—— (1970), 'Did Victorian Britain Fail?', *Ec.H.R.* 23.

—— (1970/71), 'Britain's Loss from Foreign Industrialization: A Provisional Estimate', *Expl.Ec.H.* 8.

—— (1971b), 'International Differences in Productivity? Coal and Steel in America and Britain before World War I.', in McCloskey.

—— (1974), 'Victorian Growth: a Rejoinder', *Ec.H.R.* 27.

—— (1979), 'No, It Did Not: A Reply to Crafts', *Ec.H.R.* 32.

—— (1980), 'Magnanimous Albion: Free Trade and British National Income, 1841–1881', *Expl.Ec.H.* 17.

—— and Sandberg, L.G. (1971/72), 'From Damnation to Redemption: Judgements on the Late Victorian Entrepreneur', *Expl.Ec.H.* 9.

McCord, N. (1968), *The Anti-Corn Law League 1838–1846.*

—— (1970), *Free Trade, Theory and Practice from Adam Smith to Keynes*, Newton Abbot.

McCormach, R. (1974), 'On Academic Scientists in Wilhelmian Germany', *Daedalus* 103.

MacDonagh, O. (1977), *Early Victorian Government 1830–1870.*

—— (1974/75), 'Government, Industry and Science in Nineteenth Century Britain: a Particular Study', *Hist.St.* 16.

MacDougall, G.D.A. (1966), 'The Benefits and Costs of Private Investment from Abroad: a Theoretical Approach', *Bull.Ox.U.Inst.Stat.* 22.

Machlup, F. (1932), 'Die Theorie der Kapitalflucht', *W.W. Archiv* 36.

Mack, E.C. (1973), *Public Schools and British Opinions since 1860*, New York.

McKendrick, N. (1973), 'The Role of Science in the Industrial Revolution: a Study of Josiah Wedgwood as a Scientist and Industrial Chemist', in Teich and Young.

—— (1982), 'The Consumer Revolution of Eighteenth-Century England', in McKendrick, N., Brewer, J. and Plumb, J.H. (1982), *The Birth of a Consumer Society. The Commercialization of Eighteenth-Century England.*

McKenzie, F.A. (1902), *The American Invaders.*

MacKinder, Sir H.J. (1922), *Britain and the British Seas*, Oxford.

MacKinnon, J. (1921), *The Social and Industrial History of Scotland. From the Union to the Present Time.*

McLaughlin, C.C. (1954), 'The Stanley Steamer: A Study in Unsuccessful Innovation', *Expl.Ent.H.* 7.

MacLaurin, W.R. (1950), 'The Process of Technological Innovation: the Launching of a New Scientific Industry', *A.E.R.* XL.

—— (1953), 'The Sequence from Invention to Innovation and its Relation to Economic Growth', *Q.J.E.* 67.

McLean, D. (1976), 'Finance and "Informal Empire" before the First World War', *Ec.H.R.* 29.

MacLean, I.W. (1976), 'Anglo-American Engineering Competition, 1870–1914: Some Third-Market Evidence', *Ec.H.R.* 29.

McLelland, D.C. (1966), 'Does Education Accelerate Economic Growth?', *Ec.Dev.Cult.C.* 14.

MacLeod, R.M. (1970), 'The X-Club. A Social Network of Science in Late-Victorian England', *Royal Society of London Notes and Records* 24.

— (1971a), 'The Royal Society and the Government Grant: Notes on the Administration of Scientific Research, 1849–1914', *Hist.J.* 14.

— (1971b), 'The Support of Victorian Science: The Endowment of Research Movement in Great Britain, 1868–1900', *Minerva* 4.

— (1972), 'Resources of Science in Victorian England: The Endowment of Science Movement 1868–1900', in Mathias.

— (1976), 'Science and the Treasury: Principles, Personalities and Policies, 1870–85', in Turner.

— (1983), 'Whigs and Saints: Reflections on the Reform Movement in Royal Society, 1830–48', in Inkster and Morell.

MacLeod, R. and K. (1975), 'War and Economic Development: Government and the Optical Industry in Britain, 1914–1918', in Winter.

MacRae, H. and Cairncross, F. (1973), *Capital City. London as a Financial Centre.*

Maddison, A. (1982), *Phases of Capitalist Development*, Oxford.

— (1959), 'Economic Growth in Western Europe 1870–1957', *Banca Nationale Di Lavoro Q.Rev.* 12.

— (1962), 'Growth and Fluctuation in the World Economy 1870–1960', *Banca Nationale Di Lavoro Q.Rev.* 15.

— (1979), 'Long Run Dynamics of Productivity Growth', *Banca Nationale Di Lavoro Q.Rev.* 32.

Madoc-Jones, B. (1977), 'Patterns of Attendance and their Social Significance: Mitcham National School 1830–39', in McCann.

Maizels, A. (1970), *Growth and Trade*, Cambridge.

Manchester Chamber of Commerce (1892), *International Bimetallism*. Manchester.

Manegold, K.H. (1970), *Universität, Technische Hochschule und Industrie*, Berlin.

— (1976), 'Das Verhältnis von Naturwissenschaft und Technik im Spiegel der Wissenschaftsorganisation', in Treue and Mauel.

— (1978), 'Technology Academised: Education and Training of the Engineer in the Nineteenth Century', in Krohn *et al.*

— (1981), 'Der VDI in der Phase der Hochindustrialisierung', in Ludwig.

Mann, G. und Winau, R. (eds.) (1977), *Medizin, Naturwissenschaft. Technik und das zweite Kaiserreich*, Göttingen.

Mansfield, E. (1968) *The Economics of Technical Change*, New York.

— (1971), 'Technical Change and the Rate of Imitation', in Rosenberg.

— (1973), 'Determinants of the Speed of the Application of New Technology', in Williams. B.R. (ed.).

Mare, M.L. and Quarrell, W.H. (1938), *Lichtenberg's Visits to England, as Described in his Letters and Diaries*, Oxford.

Marris, R. (1979), 'Britain's Relative Economic Decline', in Kramnick, I. (ed.), *Is Britain Dying? Perspectives on the Current Crisis*, Ithaca.

Marrison, A.J. (1975), 'Great Britain and the Rivals in the Latin American Piece Goods Market, 1880–1914', in Ratcliffe.

— (1977), 'The Development of a Tariff Reform Policy during Joseph Chamberlain's First Campaign, May 1903–February 1904', in Chaloner, W.H. and Ratcliffe, B.M. (eds.), *Trade and Transport. Essays in Economic History in Honour of T.S. Willan*, Manchester.

— (1983), 'Businessmen, Industries and Tariff Reform in Great Britain, 1903–1930', *Bus.H.* 25.

Marshall, A. (1923), *Industry and Trade. A Study of Industrial Technique and Business Specialization: and their Influence on the Conditions of Various Classes and Nations.*

— (1946), *Principles of Economics.*

Marshall, L.S. (1940), 'The Emergence of the First Industrial City: Manchester 1780–1850', in Ware, C.F. (ed.), *A Cultural Approach to History*, Port Washington.

Martin, A. and Lewis, W.A. (1956), 'Patterns of Public Revenue and Expenditure', *Manchester School* 24.

Martin, K. (1949), 'Capital Movements, the Terms of Trade and the Balance of Payments', *Bull.Oxf.U.Inst.Stat.* 11.

Bibliography

Martin, T. (1942), *The Royal Institution*.
— (1963), 'Origins of the Royal Institution', *Bri.J.Hist.Science* I.
— (1964), 'Early Years of the Royal Institution', *Brit.J.Hist.Science* 2.
Martins, S.W. (1980), *A Great Estate at Work. The Holkham Estate and its Inhabitants in the Nineteenth Century*. Cambridge.
Massel, B.F. (1964), 'Exports, Capital Imports, and Economic Growth', *Kyklos* 17.
Mathias, P. (ed.) (1972a), *Science and Society 1600–1900*, Cambridge.
— (1972b), 'Who Unbound Prometheus? Science and Technical Change, 1600–1800', *ibid.*
— (1983), *The First Industrial Nation. An Economic History of Britain. 1700–1914*.
Matthews, R.C.O. (1964–65) 'Some Aspects of Post-War Growth in the British Economy in Relation to Historical Experience', *Manchester Stat.Soc.*
— (1973), 'The Contribution of Science and Technology to Economic Development', in Williams, B.R. (ed.).
Matthews, R.C.O., Feinstein, C.H. and Odling-Smee, J.C. (1982), *British Economic Growth 1856–1973*, Oxford.
Mayer, A. (1981), *The Persistance of the Old Regime. Europe to the Great War*, New York.
Maynard, G. (1962), *Economic Development and the Price Level*.
Mayr, O. (1976), 'The Science – Technology Relationship as a Historiographical Problem', *Technology and Culture* 17.
Mayr, O. and Post, R.C. (eds.) (1981), *Yankee Enterprise: the Rise of the American System of Manufacture*, Washington.
Meade, J.E. (1955), *Trade and Welfare*.
Meadows, A.J. (1972), *Science and Controversy. A Biography of Sir Norman Lockyer*.
Medick, H. (1974), 'Anfänge und Voraussetzungen des organisierten Kapitalismus in Großbritannien', in Winkler, H.A., *Organisierter Kapitalismus*, Göttingen.
Medley, G.W. (1896) *The German Bogey: A Reply to 'Made In Germany'*.
Meier, G.M. (1952/53), 'Long Period Determinants of Britain's Terms of Trade, 1880–1913', *Rev.Econ.Studies* 20.
— (1953), 'Economic Development and the Transfer Mechanism: Canada 1895–1913', *The Canadian Journal of Economics and Political Science* 19.
— and Baldwin, R.E. (1969), *Economic Development. Theory, History, Policy*, New York.
Mendelsohn, E. (1964), 'The Emergence of Science as a Profession in Nineteenth-Century Europe', in Hill.
Menze, C. (1972), 'Grundzüge der Bildungsphilosophie Wilhelm von Humboldts', in Steffen.
Merttens, F. (1893/94), 'Hours and Cost of Labour in the Cotton Industry at Home and Abroad', *Manchester Stat.Soc.*
Merz, J.T. (1904), *A History of European Thought in the Nineteenth Century*, Vol. I., Edinburgh.
Messerschmidt, M. (1980), 'Die Bedeutung der Schulpolitik des Militärs', in Baumgart.
Meyer, F. (1976), *Schule der Untertanen. Lehrer und Politik in Preußen 1848–1900*, Hamburg.
Meyer, J.R. (1964), 'An Input-Output Approach to Evaluating British Industrial Production in Late Nineteenth Century', in Conrad, A.H. and Meyer, J.R., *The Economies of Slavery and Other Studies in Econometric History*, Chicago.
Miall, S. (1931), *A History of the British Chemical Industry*.
Michie, R.C. (1981a), *Money, Manias and Markets. Investment, Company Formation and the Stock Exchange in Nineteenth Century Scotland*, Edinburgh.
— (1979), 'The Social Web of Investment in the Nineteenth Century', *Revue Internationale d'Histoire de la Banque* 18.
— (1981b), 'Options, Concessions, Syndicates and the Provision of Venture Capital, 1880–1913', *Bus.H.* 23.
— (1985), 'The London Stock Exchange and the British Securities Market 1850–1914', *Ec.H.R.* 38.
Midwinter, E.C. (1969), *Social Administration in Lancashire 1830–1860. Poor Law, Public Health and Police*, Manchester.
Mikesell, R.F. (ed.) (1962), *U.S. Private and Government Investment Abroad*, Eugene.
— (1968), *The Economics of Foreign Aid*, Chicago.
— et al. (1971), *Foreign Investment in the Petroleum and Mineral Industries*, Baltimore.
Mill, J.S. (1848), *Principles of Political Economy with some of their Applications to Social Philosophy*, in *Collected Works*, Vol. 3, Toronto.

Miller, H.P. (1960), 'Annual and Lifetime Income in Relation to Education: 1939–1950', *A.E.R.* 50.
— idem, in Kiker.
Millerson, G. (1964), *The Qualifying Association. A Study in Professionalization.*
Millis, C.T. (1932), *Education for Trades and Industries.*
Milward, A.S. (1977), 'Les placements Français a L'étranger en les deux guerres mondiales', in Lévy-Leboyer (1977a).
Mincer, J. (1971), 'On the Job-Training: Costs, Returns and some Implications', in Kiker.
— idem, in Bowman.
Minchinton, W.E. (ed.) (1969), *Industrial South Wales 1750–1914.*
— (1957), *The British Tinplate Industry. A History,* Oxford.
— (1954/55), 'The Tinplate Makers and Technical Change', *Expl.Ec.H.* 7.
Mitch, D.F. (1984), 'Underinvestment in Literacy? The Potential Contribution of Government Involvement in Elemantary Education to Economic Growth in Nineteenth-Century England', *J.Ec.H.* 44.
— (1986), 'The Impact of Subsidies to Elementary Schooling on Enrolment Rates in Nineteenth-Century England', *Ec.H.R.* 39.
Mitchell, B.R. (1981), *European Historical Statistics 1750–1975.*
— (1984), *Economic Development of the British Coal Industry 1800–1914,* Cambridge.
— and Deane, P. (1962), *Abstract of British Historical Statistics,* Cambridge.
Mock, W. (1982), *Imperiale Herrschaft und nationales Interesse. Constructive Imperialism oder Freihandel in Großbritannien vor dem ersten Weltkrieg,* Stuttgart.
Moffatt, G.G. (1967), 'The Foreign Ownership and Balance-of-Payments Effects of Direct Investment from Abroad', *Australian Economic Papers* 6.
Moir, E. (1969), *The Justice of the Peace,* Harmondsworth.
Mommsen, W.J. (1979), *Der Europäische Imperialismus,* Göttingen.
— (1977), 'Europäischer Finanzimperialismus vor 1914', *Hist.Z.* 224.
Moody, T.W. 'The Irish University Question of the Nineteenth Century', *History* 43.
Moore, D.C. (1976), *The Politics of Deference. A Study of the Mid-Nineteenth Century English Political System,* Hassocks.
— (1965), 'The Corn Laws and High Farming', *Ec.H.R.* 18.
— (1966), 'Concession or Cure: The Sociological Premises of the First Reform Act', *Hist.J.* IX.
Moos, F. (1910), 'Die französischen Kreditinstitute und die französischen und englischen Kapitalanlagen im Ausland', *Jahrbücher für Nationalökonomie und Statistik.* III.
More, C. (1980), *Skill and the English Working Class.*
Morgan T. (1959), 'The Long Run Terms of Trade between Agriculture and Manufacturing', *Ec.Dev.Cult.C.* 8.
Morgan E.V. and Thomas, W.A. (1962), *The Stock Exchange. Its History and Function.*
Morrell, J.B. (1971), 'Individualism and the Structure of British Science in 1830', *Historical Studies in the Physical Science* 3.
— (1976), 'The Patronage of Mid-Victorian Science in the University of Edinburgh', in Turner.
— (1983), 'Economic and Ornamental Geology. The Geological and Polytechnical Society of the West Riding of Yorkshire', in Inkster and Morrell.
Morrell, J. and Thackray, A. (1981), *Gentlemen of Science. Early Years of the British Association for the Advancement of Science,* Oxford.
— (eds.) (1984), *Gentlemen of Science. Early Correspondence of the British Association for the Advancement of Science.*
Mosely Industrial Commission to the United States of America (1903), Report of the Delegates, Manchester.
Mosely Educational Commission to the United States of America (1904), Reports, Manchester.
Moss, M.S. (1983), 'William Todd Lithgow – Founder of a Fortune', *Scot.H.R.* 62.
Mosse, G.L. (1945), 'The Anti-League 1844–1846', *Ec.H.R.* 15.
Mottaz, C. (1984), 'Education and Work Satisfaction', *Human Relations* 37.
Mowery, D.C. (1986), 'Industrial Research', in Elbaum and Lazonick.
Müller, D.K. (1977), *Sozialstruktur und Schulsystem. Aspekte zum Strukturwandel des Schulwesens im 19. Jahrhundert,* Göttingen.
Müller, K. (1947), *Der Kapitalimport. Studie zur Theorie der internationalen Kapitalbewegungen,* St Gallen.

Muir, G. (1950), *John Anderson*, Glasgow.

Mundell, R.A. (1957), 'International Trade and Factor Mobility', *A.E.R.* 47.

Munting, R. (1978), 'Ransomes in Russia: An English Agricultural Engineering Company's Trade with Russia to 1917', *Ec.H.R.* 31.

— (1985), 'Agricultural Engineering and European Exports before 1914', *Bus.H.* 27.

Murphy, J.C. (1960–61), 'International Investment and the National Interest', *The Southern Economic Journal* 22.

Musgrave, P.W. (1967), *Technical Change, the Labour Force and Education. A Study of the British and German Iron and Steel Industries 1860–1964*, Oxford.

— (ed.) (1970a), *Sociology, History and Education. A Reader.*

— (1970b), 'A Model for the Analysis of the Development of the English Educational System from 1860', *ibid.*

— (1970c), 'The Definitions of Technical Education 1860–1910', *ibid.*

— (1970d), 'Constant Factors in the Demand for Technical Education, 1860–1960', *ibid.*

— (1970e), 'Metallurgy and the Department of Science and Art, 1870–1950', *ibid.*

— (1981), 'The Labour Force: Some Relevant Attitudes', in Roderick and Stephens.

Musgrove, F. (1959/60), 'Middle-Class Education and Employment in the Nineteenth Century', *Ec.H.R.* 12.

— (1963), *The Migratory Elite.*

— (1970), 'Middle-Class Families and School, 1780–1880: Interaction and Exchange of Functions between Institutions', in Musgrave.

Mushkin, S.J. (1966), 'Resource Requirement and Educational Obsolescence', in Robinson and Vaizey.

Musson, A.E. (1965), *Enterprise in Soap and Chemicals. Joseph Crosfield and Sons, Limited 1815–1965*, Manchester.

— (1972a), *Science, Technology and Economic Growth in the Eighteenth Century.*

— (1978), *The Growth of British Industry.*

— (1959), 'The Great Depression in Britain, 1873–1896. A Reappraisal', *J.Ec.H.* 19.

— (1962/63), 'British Industrial Growth during the "Great Depression" 1873–96': Some Comments', *Ec.H.R.* 15.

— (1964/65), 'British Industrial Growth 1873–96: a Balanced View', *Ec.H.R.* 17.

— (1972b), 'The Manchester School and Exportations of Machinery', *Bus.H.* 14.

— (1980), 'The Engineering Industry', in Church (1980a).

— and Robinson, E. (1969), *Science and Technology in the Industrial Revolution*, Manchester.

Myers, S. and Marquis, D.S. (1969), *Successful Industrial Innovations*, Washington.

Myint, H. 'The Gains from International Trade and the Backward Countries', *Rev.Ec.Studies* 21.

Nadiri, M.I. (1970), 'Some Approaches to the Theory and Measurement of Total Factor Productivity: A Survey', *J.Ec.Lit.* 8.

Nairn, (1977), *The Break-up of Britain. Crisis and Neo-Nationalism.*

Nash, B.D. (1924), *Investment Banking in England*, Chicago, New York.

Nash, R.L. (1881), *A Short Enquiry into the Profitable Nature of our Investments.*

Neale, R.S. (1981), *Class in English History*, Oxford.

Nebenius, C.F. (1833), *Über technische Lehranstalten in ihrem Zusammenhang mit dem gesammten Unterrichtswesen und mit besonderer Rücksicht auf die polytechnische Schule zu Karlsruhe*, Karlsruhe.

Neisser, H. (1929), 'Der Internationale Geldmarkt vor und nach dem Kriege, I. Vor dem Kriege 1.', *W.W. Archiv* 29.

— (1930), 'Der Internationale Geldmarkt vor und nach dem Kriege, II. Vor dem Kriege 2.', *W.W. Archiv* 32.

Nelson, R.R. (1959), 'The Economics of Invention: A Survey of the Literature', *Journal of Business* 32.

— (1971), 'The Simple Economics of Basic Economic Research', in Rosenberg.

—, Peck, M.J. and Kalachek, E.D. (1967), *Technology Economic Growth and Public Policy*, Washington.

Nettl, J.P. (1965), 'Consensus or Elite Domination: The Case of Business', *Political Studies* 13.

Neuburger, H. (1977), 'The Industrial Politics of the Kreditbanken, 1880–1914', *Bus.H.R.* 51.

— and Stokes, H.H. (1974), 'German Banks and German Growth, 1883–1913: an Empirical View', *J.Ec.H.* 34.

Neufeld, J.L. (1987), 'Price Discrimination and the Adoption of the Electricity Demand Charge', *J.Ec.H.* 47.

Newton, S. and Porter, D. (1988), *Modernization Frustrated. The Politics of Industrial Decline in Britain since 1900.*

Neymark, A. (1911), *Finances contemporaines*, Paris.

Nicholas, S.J. (1982a), 'British Multinational Investment before 1939', *J.Europ.Ec.H.* XI.

—— (1982b), 'Total Factor Productivity Growth and the Revision of Post-1870 British Economic History', *Ec.H.R.* 35.

—— (1983), 'Agency Contracts, Institutional Modes and the Transition to Foreign Direct Investment by British Manufacturing Multinationals before 1939', *J.Ec.H.* 43.

—— (1984), 'The Overseas Marketing Performance of British Industry, 1870–1914', *Ec.H.R.* 37.

—— (1985), 'Technical Education and the Decline of Britain', in Inkster.

Nicholson, J.S. (1890), 'The Living Capital of the United Kingdom', *E.J.* I.

Norris, J.M. (1958), 'Samuel Garbett and the Early Development of Industrial Lobbying in Great Britain', *Ec.H.R.* 10.

North, D.C. (1956), 'International Capital Flows and the Development of the American West', *J.Ec.H.* 16.

—— (1962), 'International Capital Movements in Historical Perspective', in Mikesell.

—— and Heston, A. (1960), 'The Estimation of Shipping Earnings in Historical Studies of the Balance of Payment', *Canadian J. of Economics and Political Science* 26.

Nossiter, T.J. (1975), *Influence, Opinion and Political Idioms in Reformed England. Case Studies from the North-East 1832–74*, Hassocks.

Nostitz, H. (1900), *Das Aufsteigen des Arbeiterstandes in England*, Jena.

Nugent, J.B. (1973), 'Exchange Rate Movements and Economic Development in the Late Nineteenth Century', *J.P.E.* 81.

Nurkse, R. (1935), *Internationale Kapitalbewegungen*, Vienna.

—— (1961), *Equilibrium and Growth in the World Economy*, Cambridge, Mass.

—— (1972), 'Causes and Effects of Capital Movements', in Dunning.

O'Boyle, L. (1968), 'Klassische Bildung und soziale Struktur in Deutschland zwischen 1750 und 1848', *Hist.Z.* 207.

—— (1970), 'The Problem of Excess of Educated Men in Western Europe 1800–1850', *J.Mod.H.* 42.

O'Brien, P. (ed.) (1986), *International Productivity Comparisons and Problems of Measurement, 1750–1939*, Berne.

O'Day, A. (ed.) (1979), *The Edwardian Age: Conflict and Stability 1900–1914.*

O'Day, R. (1982), *Education and Society 1500–1800. The Social Foundations of Education in Early Modern Britain.*

Offer, A. (1981), *Property and Politics 1870–1914*, Cambridge.

—— (1983), 'Empire and Social Reform: British Overseas Investment and Domestic Politics, 1908–1914', *Hist.J.* 26.

O'Gorman, F. 'Electoral Deference in Unreformed England: 1760–1832', *J.Mod.H.* 56.

O'Hagan, H.O. (1929), *Leaves from my Life*, 2 Vols.

Ohlin, B. (1929a), 'The Reparations Problem: A Discussion', *E.J.* 39.

—— (1929b), 'Rejoinder', *E.J.* 39.

—— (1937), 'International Capital Movements', *Nationaloekonomisk Tidsskrift* 75.

Okochi, A. and Inoue, T. (eds.) (1980), *Overseas Business Activities*, Tokyo.

Okochi, A. and Uchida, H. (1984), *Development and Diffusion of Technology*, Tokyo.

O'Leary, P.J. and Lewis, W.A. (1955), 'Secular Swings in Production and Trade, 1870–1913', *Manchester School* 23.

Olson, R. (1975), *Scottish Philosophy and British Physics 1750–1880*, Princeton.

Orange, A.D. (1973), *Philosophers and Provincials. The Yorkshire Philosophical Society from 1822 to 1844*, York.

—— (1971), 'The British Association for the Advancement of Science: the Provincial Background', *Science Studies* I.

—— (1972/73), 'The Origins of the British Association for the Advancement of Science', *Brit.J.Hist. Science* 6.

Orsagh, T.J. (1960–61), 'Progress in Iron and Steel: 1870–1913', *Comp.Stud.Soc.H.* 3.

Orwin, C.S. and Whetham, E.H. (1971), *History of British Agriculture 1846–1914*, Newton Abbot.

Bibliography

Oulton, N. (1976), 'Effective Protection for British Industry', in Corden and Fels.

Overy, R.J. (1976), *William Morris, Lord Nuffield*.

Page, A. (1966), 'Desirable Balance between General Education and Technical and Vocational Training', in Robinson and Vaizey.

Paish, F.W. (1951), 'The London New Issue Market', *Economica* 18.

Paish, G. (1909), 'Great Britain's Capital Investment in Other Lands', *J.R.S.S.* 72.

— (1911), 'Great Britain's Capital Investment in Individual Colonial and Foreign Countries', *J.R.S.S.* 74.

— (1914), 'The Export of Capital and the Cost of Living', *Statist* 79.

Pamuk, S. (1984), 'The Ottoman Empire in the "Great Depression" of 1873–1896', *J.Ec.H.* 44.

Papi, G.U. (1966), 'General Problems of the Economics of Education', in Robinson and Vaizey.

Pares, R. (1937), 'The Economic Factors in the History of Empire', *Ec.H.R.* 7.

Parker, W. (1971), 'Economic Development in Historical Perspective', in Rosenberg.

Parrini, C.P. and Sklar, M.J. (1983), 'New Thinking about the Market, 1896–1904: Some American Economists on Investment and the Theory of Surplus Capital', *J.Ec.H.* 43.

Parris, H. (1965), *Government and the Railways in Nineteenth-Century Britain*.

— (1960), 'The Nineteenth-Century Revolution in Government: A Reappraisal Reappraised', *Hist.J.* 3.

Parsons, R.H. (1939) *The Early Days of the Power Station Industry*, Cambridge.

Paterson, D.G. (1976), *British Direct Investment in Canada 1890–1914*, Toronto.

Patterson, Sir R.L. (1907), 'The British Flax and Linen Industry', in Ashley (1907).

Paulsen, F. (1889), *Das Realgymnasium und die humanistische Bildung*, Berlin.

— (1902), *Die deutschen Universitäten und das Universitätsstudium*, Berlin.

— (1906), *Das deutsche Bildungswesen in seiner geschichtlichen Entwicklung*, Leipzig.

— (1921), *Geschichte des gelehrten Unterrichts auf den deutschen Schulen und Universitäten vom Anfang des Mittelalters bis zur Gegenwart*, 2 Vols., Leipzig.

Pausenberger, E. *et al.* (1980), 'Entscheidungsprozesse bei Auslandsinvestitionen', *Zeitschrift für betriebswissenschaftliche Forschung* 32.

Pavitt, K. (ed.) (1980), *Technical Innovations and British Economic Performance*.

— and Soete, L. (1980), 'Innovative Activities and Export Shares: Some Comparisons between Industries and Countries', in Pavitt.

— with Ward, S. for OECD. (1971), *The Conditions for Success in Technological Innovation*, Paris.

Payne, P.L. (1967a), *Studies in Scottish Business History*.

— (1974), *British Entrepreneurship in the Nineteenth Century*.

— (1979), *Colvilles and the Scottish Steel Industry*, Oxford.

— (1980), *The Early Scottish Limited Companies 1856–1895*, Edinburgh.

— (1967b), 'The Emergence of the Large-Scale Company in Great Britain 1870–1914', *Ec.H.R.* 20.

— (1968), 'Iron and Steel Manufactures', in Aldcroft.

— (1978), 'Industrial Entrepreneurship and Management in Great Britain', in Mathias, P. and Postan, M. (eds.) (1978), *Cambridge Economic History of Europe* VII.

Paz, D.G. (1980), *The Politics of Working Class Education in Britain. 1830–1850*, Manchester.

Pazos, F. (1970), 'The Role of International Movements of Private Capital in Promoting Development', in Adler.

Pearce, I.F. and Rowan, D.C. (1966), *A Framework of Research into the Real Effects of International Capital Movements*.

Penrose, E.T. (1956), 'Foreign Investment and the Growth of the Firm', *E.J.* 66.

Penzance, Lord (1886), 'The Collapse of the Free Trade Argument', *Nineteenth Century* 20.

Perkin, H.J. (1969), *Key Profession. The History of the Association of University Teachers*.

— (1974), *The Origins of Modern English Society, 1780–1880*.

— (1961–62), 'Middle Class Education and Employment in the Nineteenth Century: A Critical Note', *Ec.H.R.* 14.

— (1983), 'The Patterns of Social Transformation in England', in Jarausch.

Perren, R. (1970), 'The Landlord and Agricultural Transformation, 1870–1900', in Perry (1970).

Perry, J. (1903), 'Oxford and Science', *Nature*, 21. Dec.

Perry, P.J. (ed.) (1973), *British Agriculture 1875–1914*.

Pesmazoglou, J.S. (1951), 'A Note on the Cyclical Fluctuations of British Home Investment, 1870–1913', *O.E.P.* 3.

Pethick-Lawrence (1904), 'The Taxation of Foreign Investments', *Contemporary Rev.* 85.

Pfetsch, F.R. (1974), *Zur Entwicklung der Wissenschaftspolitik in Deutschland 1750–1914*, Berlin.

Phelps, E.S. (1962), 'A New View of Investment: a Neo-Classical Analysis', *Q.J.E.* 76.

Phelps-Brown, E.H. (1972), 'Then and Now: The British Problem of Sustaining Development, 1900's and 1960's, in Peston, M. and Corry, B. (eds.) (1972), *Essays in Honour of Lord Robbins*.

— and Handfield-Jones, S.J. (1952), 'The Climacteric of the 1890's: A Study of the Expanding Economy', *O.E.P.* 4.

— and Weber, B. (1953), 'Accumulation, Productivity and Distribution in the British Economy, 1870–1938', *E.J.* 63.

Philips, D. (1975), 'The Black Country Magistracy 1855–60. A Changing Elite and the Exercise of its Power', *Midland History* III.

Phillips, W.H. (1981), 'The Economic Performance of Late Victorian Britain: Traditional Historians and Growth'. (unpbl.)

— (1982a), 'Induced Innovation and Economic Performance in Late Victorian Britain', *J.Ec.H.* 42.

— idem, in Eichengreen (1982).

Phillipson, N.T. (1975), 'Culture and Society in the Eighteenth Century Province: The Case of Edinburgh and the Scottish Enlightenment', in Stone.

Pigou, A.C. (1952), *Economics of Welfare*.

— (1932), 'The Effect of Reparations on the Ratio of International Interchange', *E.J.* 42.

Platt, D.C.M. (1968), *Finance, Trade and Politics in British Foreign Policy 1815–1914*, Oxford.

— (1984), *Foreign Finance in Continental Europe and the USA 1815–1870*.

— (1986), *Britain's Investment Overseas on the Eve of the First World War*.

— (1962–63), 'The Role of the British Consular Service in Overseas Trade 1825–1914', *Ec.H.R.* 15.

— (1973), 'Further Objections to an "Imperialism of Free Trade", 1830–1860', *Ec.H.R.* 36.

— (1973–74), 'The National Economy and British Imperial Expansion before 1914', *J. of Imperial and Commonwealth History* 2.

— (1980), 'British Portfolio Investment Overseas before 1870: Some Doubts', *Ec.H.R.* 33.

— (1985), 'Canada and Argentina: The First Preference of the British Investor, 1904–14', in Porter and Hollander.

Pollard, S. (1959), *A History of Labour in Sheffield*, Liverpool.

— (1984), *The Neglect of Industry: A Critique of British Economic Policy since 1870*, Rotterdam.

— (1950), 'The Decline of Shipbuilding on the Thames', *Ec.H.R.* 3.

— (1952), 'Laissez-Faire and Shipbuilding', *Ec.H.R.* 5.

— (1957), 'British and World Shipbuilding, 1890–1914: A Study in Comparative Costs', *J.Ec.H.* 17.

— (1966), 'Die Bildung und Ausbildung der industriellen Klassen Großbritanniens im 18. Jahrhundert', *Jahrbuch für Wirtschaftsgeschichte* IV.

— and Robertson, P. (1979), *The British Shipbuilding Industry, 1870–1914*, Cambridge, Mass.

Pollins, H. (1971), *British Railways: an Industrial History*, Newton Abbot.

Poole, J.B. and Andrews, K. (eds.) (1972), *The Government of Science in Britain*.

Pope, R. and Hoyle, B. (1985), *British Economic Performance 1880–1980*.

Pope, W.J. (1917), 'The National Importance of Chemistry', in Seward.

Porter, A.N. and Hollander, R.F. (eds.) (1985), *Money, Finance and Empire 1790–1960*.

Porter, B. (1975), *The Lion's Share. A Short History of British Imperialism 1850–1970*.

Porter, R. (1973), 'The Industrial Revolution and the Rise of the Science of Geology', in Teich and Young.

Posner, M. (1961), 'International Trade and Technical Change', *O.E.P.* 13.

Postan, M.M. (1935), 'Recent Trends in the Accumulation of Capital', *Ec.H.R.* 6.

Prais, S.J. (1981), 'Vocational Qualifications of the Labour Force in Britain and Germany', *National Institute Economic Review* 95.

Prandy, K. (1965), *Professional Employees. A Study of Scientists and Engineers*.

Pratt, E.A. (1904), *Trade Unionism and British Industry*.

Pratten, C.F. (1972), 'The Reasons for the Slow Economic Progress of the British Economy', *O.E.P.* 24.

Pressnell, L.S. (1968), 'Gold Reserves, Banking Reserves, and the Banking Crisis of 1890', in Whittlesley and Wilson J.S.G. (eds.), *Essays in Money and Banking in Honour of R.S. Sayers*, Oxford.

305

Price, D. (1965), 'Is Technology Historically Independent of Science? A Study in Statistical Historiography', *Technology and Culture* 6.
—— (1972), 'Science and Technology: Distinctions and Interrelationships', in Barnes.
Price, R. (1983), 'The Labour Process and Labour History', *Social History* 8.
—— (1984), 'Structures of Subordination in Nineteenth-Century British Industry', in Thane et al.
Pullan, B. (1968), *Crisis and Change in the Venetian Economy in the Sixteenth and Seventeenth Centuries.*
Pumphrey, R.E. (1959), 'The Introduction of Industrialists into the British Peerage,' *A.H.R.* LXV.
Purdue Faculty (1967), *Papers in Economic History 1956–1966*, Homewood.
Quinault, R. (1974), 'The Worchestershire County Magistracy and Public Order, c.1830–1870', in R. Quinault and J. Stevenson (eds.), *Popular Protest and Public Order.*
Rabi, I.I. (1965), 'The Interactions of Science and Technology', in Warner *et al.*
Rae, John B. (1960), 'The Know-How Tradition: Technology in American History', *Technology and Culture* 1.
Ranis, Gustav (1978), 'Science, Technology and Development: a Retrospective View' in Beranek and Ranis.
Ratcliffe, Barrie M. (ed.) (1975), *Great Britain and her World 1750–1914*, Manchester.
Rathgen, Karl (1896), 'Über den Plan eines Britischen Reichszollvereins', *Preussische Jahrbücher* 26.
—— (1901), 'Die englische Handelspolitik am Ende des 19. Jahrhunderts', *Verein für Sozialpolitik, Beiträge zur neuesten Handelspolitik Deutschlands*, vol. 2, Leipzig.
—— (1913), 'Deutschland und England auf dem Weltmarkt', *Schmollers Jahrbuch* 37.
Ray, G.F. and Nabseth, L. (1974), *The Diffusion of New Industrial Process: an International Study*, Cambridge.
Raybould, T.J. (1973), *The Economic Emergence of the Black Country. A Study of the Dudley Estate*, Newton Abbot.
Read, Donald (1973), *Documents from Edwardian England 1901–1915.*
—— (1979), *England 1868–1914. The Age of Urban Democracy.*
—— (1964), *The English Provinces, c.1760–1960. A Study in Influence.*
Reader, W.J. (1966), *Professional Men. The Rise of the Professional Classes in Nineteenth-Century England.*
—— (1970), *Imperial Chemical Industries. A History. Vol.I. The Forerunners 1870–1926.*
Reddaway, W.B. *et al.* (1967), *Effects of UK Direct Investment Overseas. An Interim Report*, Cambridge.
Redford, Arthur *et al.* (1934), *Manchester Merchants and Foreign Trade*, vol. 1, Manchester.
Redlich, Fritz (1914), *Die Volkswirtschaftliche Bedeutung der Deutschen Teerfarbenindustrie*, Munich, Leipzig.
Ricardo, David (1951a), *The High Price of Bullion. A Proof of the Depreciation of Bank Notes, Works* vol. 3, Cambridge.
—— (1951b), *On the Principles of Political Economy and Taxation, Works* vol. 1, Cambridge.
Rich, Eric (1970), *The Education Act 1870. A Study of Public Opinion.*
Richards, Eric (1979), 'An Anatomy of the Sutherland Fortune: Income, Consumption, Investments and Returns, 1780–1880', *Bus.H.* 21.
Richardson, H.W. (1965), 'Over-Commitment in Britain Before 1930', *O.E.P.* 17.
—— (1962), 'The Development of the British Dyestuffs Industry Before 1939', *Scot.J.Pol.Ec.* 9.
—— (1968), 'Chemicals', in Aldcroft.
—— (1972), 'British Emigration and Overseas Investment, 1870–1914', *Ec.H.R.* 25.
—— and Bass, J.M. (1965), 'The Profitability of Consett Iron Company Before 1914', *Bus.H.* 7.
Riden P.J. (1980), 'The Iron Industry', in Church.
Riedler, A. (1898), *Unsere Hochschulen und die Anforderungen des Zwanzigsten Jahrhunderts*, Berlin.
Riese, R. (1977), *Die Universität Heidelberg und das Badische Hochschulwesen 1860–1914*, Stuttgart.
Riesser, J. (1910), *Die deutschen Grossbanken und ihre Konzentration im Zusammenhang mit der Entwicklung der Gesamtwirtschaft in Deutschland*, Jena.
Riley, James C. (1980), *International Government Finance and the Amsterdam Capital Market 1740–1815*, Cambridge.
Ringer, Fritz K (1969), *The Decline of the German Mandarins. The German Academic Community, 1890–1933*, Cambridge, Mass.
—— (1979), *Education and Society in Modern Europe*, Bloomington.

—— (1967), 'Higher Education in Germany in the Nineteenth Century', *J. Contemp. H.* 2.

Rippy, J. Fred (1959), *British Investments in Latin America, 1822–1949. A Case Study in the Operations of Private Enterprise in Retarded Regions*, Minneapolis.

Ritortus (1899), 'The Imperialism of British Trade', *Contemp. Rev.* 76.

Roach, John (1971), *Public Examinations in England 1850–1900*, Cambridge.

Roberts, David (1960), *Victorian Origins of the British Welfare State*, New Haven.

Roberts, G. (1975), 'The Establishment of the Royal College of Chemistry: An Investigation of the Social Context of Early Victorian Chemistry', *Hist.Stud. in Physic. Sciences* 7.

Roberts, R.O. (1958), 'Bank of England Branch Discounting 1826–59', *Economica* 25.

Robertson, A.J. (1970), 'The Decline of the Scottish Cotton Industry 1860–1914', *Bus.H.* 12.

Robertson, D.H. (1931a), 'Notes on International Trade', in Pigou and Robertson.

—— (1931b), 'The Terms of Trade', in Pigou and Robertson.

—— (1931c), 'The Transfer Problem', in Pigou and Robertson.

—— (1948), 'New Light on an old Story', *Economica* 15.

Robertson, Paul (1984), 'Scottish Universities and Industry, 1860–1914', *Scottish Economic and Social History* 4.

——, 'Technical Education in British Shipbuilding and Marine Engineering Industries', *Ec.H.R.* 27.

Robinson, E.A.G. and Vaizey, J.E., (eds.) (1966). *The Economics of Education.*

Robinson, Harry J. (1961), *The Motivation and Flow of Private Foreign Investments*, Menlo Park.

Robinson, Joan (1947), *Essays on the Theory of Employment*, Oxford.

—— (1946–47), 'The Pure Theory of International Trade', *Rev.Ec.Studies* 14.

Robinson, R. (1957), *The Cotton Industry in Britain.*

Robson, W.A. (1948), *The Government and Mis-Government of London.*

Roderick, G.W. (1967), *The Emergence of a Scientific Society in England 1800–1965.*

—— and Stephens, Michael D. (1972), *Scientific and Technical Education in Nineteenth-Century England*, Newton-Abbot.

—— (1978), *Education and Industry in the Nineteenth-Century: The English Disease?*

—— (1981a), *Where Did We Go Wrong? Industrial Performance, Education and the Economy in Victorian Britain*, Lewes.

—— (1981b), 'The Universities', in idem.

—— (1982), *The British Malaise. Industrial Performance, Education and Training in Britain Today*, Lewes.

—— (1985), 'Steam Intellect Created. The Educational Role of the Mechanics Institutes', in Inkster.

Rogers, E.M. (1962), *Diffusion of Innovations*, New York.

Rogers, Thorold (1909), *The Industrial and Commercial History of England.*

Rolt, L.T.C. (1976), *Victorian Engineering.*

Roepke, Wilhelm (1930), 'Zum Transferproblem bei Internationalen Kapitalbewegungen', *Jahrbücher für Nationalökonomie und Statistik 13.*

Roscoe, Sir Henry (1901), 'The Outlook for British Trade', *Monthly Rev.*

Rose, Hilary and Steven (1969), *Science and Society.*

Rose J. (1908), 'The Franco-British Commercial Treaty 1786', *E.H.R.* 23.

Rose, J.H. (1912), *Germany in the Nineteenth Century*, Manchester.

Rose, Mary B. (1986), *The Gregs of Quarry Bank Mill. The Rise and Decline of a Family Firm, 1750–1914*, Cambridge.

Rosenberg, Nathan (1969) (ed.), *The American System of Manufacture*, Edinburgh.

—— (ed.) (1971), *The Economics of Technological Change*, Harmondsworth.

—— (1972), *Technology and American Growth*, New York.

—— (1976), *Perspectives on Technology*, Cambridge.

—— (1982), *Inside the Black Box*, Cambridge.

—— (1963), 'Technological Change in the Machine Tool Industry 1840–1910', *J.Ec.H.* 23.

—— and Vincenti, Walter (1978), *The Britannia Bridge: The Generation and Diffusion of Technological Knowledge*, Cambridge, Mass.

Rosenberg, W. (1961) 'Capital Inputs and Growth. The Case of New Zealand – Foreign Investment in New Zealand, 1840–1958', *E.J.* 71.

Ross, Sidney (1962), 'Scientist: The Story of a Word', *Annals of Science* 18.

Rostow, Walt W. (1948), *British Economy of the Nineteenth-Century*, Oxford.

—— (1960a), *The Stages of Economic Growth*, Cambridge.

Bibliography

—— (1960b), *The Process of Economic Growth*, Oxford.

—— (1950), 'The Terms of Trade in Theory and Practice', *Ec.H.R.* 3.

—— (1951–52), 'The Historical Analysis of the Terms of Trade', *Ec.H.R.* 4.

Rothbarth, E. (1946), 'Causes of the Superior Efficiency of U.S.A. Industry as Compared With the British Industry', *E.J.* 56.

Rothblatt, Sheldon (1968), *The Revolution of the Dons. Cambridge and Society in Victorian England*, New York.

—— (1975), 'The Student Subculture and the Examination System in Early 19th. Century Oxbridge', in Stone.

—— (1983), 'The Diversification of Higher Education in England', in Jarausch.

Rothstein, Th. (1904), 'Der Niedergang der britischen Industrie', *Neue Zeit*.

Routh, Guy (1980), *Occupation and Pay in Great Britain 1906–1979*.

Royal Institute of International Affairs (1937), *The Problem of International Investment*.

Rubinstein, David (1977), 'Socialization and the London School Board 1870–1904, Aims, Methods and Public Opinion' in McCann.

Rubinstein, W.D. (1981), *Men of Property. The Very Wealthy in Britain Since the Industrial Revolution*.

—— (1986), *Wealth and Inequality in Britain*.

—— (1974), 'Men of Property: Some Aspects of Occupation, Inheritance and Power Among Top British Wealthholders', in Stanworth and Giddens.

—— (1977a), 'The Victorian Middle Class: Wealth, Occupation and Geography', *EcH.R.* 30.

—— (1977b), 'Wealth, Elites and the Class Structure of Modern Britain', *P.&P.* 76.

—— (1983), 'The End of "Old Corruption" in Britain 1780–1860', *P.&P.* 101.

Ruegg, Walter (1972), 'Bildung und Gesellschaft im 19. Jahrhundert', in Steffen.

Ruerup, R. (ed.) (1979), *Wissenschaft und Gesellschaft. Beiträge zur Geschichte der technischen Universität Berlin, 1879–1979*, Berlin, Heidelberg.

Rule, John (1981), *The Experience in Eighteenth-Century Industry*.

Ruske, W. (1976), 'Wissenschaft am Beispiel der Chemischen Industrie Berlins im 19. Jahrhundert', in Treue und Mauel.

Russell, Colin A. (1983), *Science and Social Change 1750–1900*.

Russell, C.A. and Goodman D.C. (ed.) (1972), *Science and the Rise of Technology since 1800*, Bristol.

Rymes, Thomas K. (1971), *On Concepts of Capital and Technical Change*, Cambridge.

Sadler, M.E. (1908) (ed.), *Moral Instruction and Training in Schools. Report of an International Inquiry*.

Sakamoto, Takuji (1980), 'Technology and Business in the British Electrical Industry 1880–1914', in Okochi and Uchida.

Salant, Walter S. (1950), 'The Domestic Effect of Capital Export under the Point Four Programme', *A.E.R.*, 40.

Salter, Sir Arthur (1951), *Foreign Investment*, Princeton.

—— (1960), *Productivity and Technical Change*, Cambridge.

Samuelson, Paul A. (1962), 'The Transfer Problem and Transport Costs: The Terms of Trade When Impediments Are Absent', *E.J.* 62.

Sandberg, Lars G. (1974), *Lancashire in Decline. A Study in Entrepreneurship, Technology and International Trade*, Columbus Ohio.

—— (1968), 'Movements in the Quality of British Cotton Textile Exports', *J.Ec.H.* 28.

—— (1970), 'American Rings and English Mules. The Role of Economic Rationality', in Saul (1970a).

Sanderson, Michael (1972a), *The Universities and British Industry 1850–1970*.

—— (1967), 'Education and the Factory in Industrial Lancashire, 1840–1880', *Ec.H.R.* 20.

—— (1968), 'Social Change and Elementary Education in Industrial Lancashire, 1780–1840', *Northern History* 3.

—— (1972b), 'The University of London and Industrial Progress. 1880–1914', *J.Contemp.H.* 7.

—— (1978), 'The Professor as Industrial Consultant: Oliver Arnold and the British Steel Industry, 1900–14', *Ec.H.R.* 31.

—— and Laqueur, T.W. (1972), 'Literacy and Social Mobility in the Industrial Revolution in England, *P.&P. 56* and Debate, *ibid. (1974)*, 64.

Sartorius von Waltershausen, A. (1907), *Das Volkswirtschaftliche System der Kapitalbewegungen im Auslande*, Berlin.

Saul, B.S. (1960a), *Studies in British Overseas Trade 1870–1914*, Liverpool.

—— (1970a), *Technological Change: The United States and Britain in the Nineteenth-Century.*
—— (1980), *Industrialization or De-Industrialization? The Interactions of the German and British Economies before the First World War.*
—— (1954–55), 'Britain and World Trade, 1870–1914', *Ec.H.R.* 7.
—— (1957), 'The Economic Significance of Constructive Imperialism', *J.Ec.H.* XVII.
—— (1960b), 'The American Impact on British Industry 1895–1914', *Bus. H.* 3.
—— (1962–63), 'House Building in England 1890–1914', *Ec.H.R.* 15.
—— (1963), 'The Motor Industry to 1914', *Bus.H.* 5.
—— (1965), 'The Export Economy', *Yorkshire Bulletin* 17.
—— (1967), 'The Market and the Development of the Mechanical Engineering Industry in Britain, 1860–1914', *Ec.H.R.* 20.
—— (1968a), 'The Machine Tool Industry in Britain to 1914', *Bus.H.* 10.
—— (1968b), 'The Engineering Industry', in Aldcroft.
—— (1970b), 'The Market and the Development of the Mechanical Engineering Industry in Britain, 1860–1914', in Saul (1970a).
—— (1979), 'Research and Development in British Industry from the End of the Nineteenth Century to the 1960's', in T.C. Smout, *The Search for Wealth and Stability. Essays in Economic and Social History Presented to M.W. Flinn.*
Saville, John (1954), 'A Comment on Professor Rostow's British Economy of the 19th. Century', *P.&P.* 6.
—— (1961), 'Some Retarding Factors in the British Economy Before 1914', *Yorkshire Bulletin* 13.
—— (1963), 'Mr Coppock on the Great Depression: A Critical Note', *Manchester School* 31.
—— (1970), 'The Development of British Industry and Foreign Competition 1875–1914', *Bus.H.* 12.
Saxonhouse, Gary and Wright, Gavin (1984a), 'New Evidence on the Stubborn English Mule and the Cotton Industry, 1878–1920', *Ec.H.R.* 37.
—— (1984b), 'Rings and Mules around the World: A Comparative Study in Technological Choice, in *idem, Technique, Spirit and Form in the Making of the Modern Economies. Essays in Honor of William N. Parker. Research in Economic History, Suppl.3*, Greenwich.
—— (1987), 'Stubborn Mules and Vertical Integration: The Disappearing Constraint?', *Ec.H.R.* 40.
Sayers, R.S. (1965), *The Vicissitudes of an Export Economy: Britain since 1880*, Sydney.
—— (1967), *Central Banking after Bagehot*, Oxford.
—— (1976), *The Bank of England, 1891–1944, 3 vols.*
Scally, Robert J. (1975), *The Origins of the Lloyd George Coalition. The Politics of Social Imperialism, 1900–1918*, Princeton.
Scammel, W.M. (1965), 'The Working of the Gold Standard', *Yorkshire Bulletin* 17.
Schelsky, Helmut (1963), *Einsamkeit und Freiheit. Idee und Gestalt der deutschen Universität und ihrer Reform*, Reinbek.
Schieder, Theodor (1977), 'Kultur, Wissenschaft und Wissenschaftspolitik im deutschen Kaiserreich', in Mann und Winau.
Schiersmann, Christine (1979), *Zur Sozialgeschichte der Preussischen Provinzialgewerbeschule im 19. Jahrhundert*, Weinheim und Basel.
Schimank, Hans (1961), *Der Ingenieur. Entwicklungsweg eines Berufes bis Ende des 19. Jahrhunderts*, Cologne.
—— (1973), 'Der Chemiker im Zeitalter der Aufklärung und des Empire', in Schmauderer.
Schlote, Werner (1976), *British Overseas Trade. From 1700 to the 1930's*, Oxford.
Schmauderer, E. (ed.) (1973), *Der Chemiker im Wandel der Zeiten. Skizzen zur Geschichtlichen Entwicklung des Berufsbildes*, Weinheim.
—— (1976), *Die Stellung des Wissenschaftlers.*
Schmidt, Gustav (1974), 'Landed Interests und Organisierte Arbeiterschaft 1850–1880. Ein deutsch-englischer Vergleich.', in Wehler.
Schmiechen, James A. (1975), 'State Reform and the Local Economy: an Aspect of Industrialization in Late Victorian and Edwardian London', *Ec.H.R.* 28.
Schmitz, Andrew and Helmberger, Peter (1970), 'Factor Mobility and International Trade: The Case of Complementarity', *A.E.R.* 60.
Schmookler, Jacob (1966), *Invention and Economic Growth*, Cambridge, Mass.
—— (1952), 'The Changing Efficiency of the American Economy, 1869–1938', *Rev. Econ. Stat.* 34.
—— (1971), 'Economic Sources of Inventive Activity', in Rosenberg.

Bibliography

—— (1972), *Patents, Invention and Economic Change. Data and Selected Essays*, Cambridge.

Schofield, Robert (1963), *The Lunar Society of Birmingham. A Social History of Provincial Science and Industry in Eighteenth-Century England*, Oxford.

—— (1968), 'The Measurement of Literacy in Pre-Industrial England', in Jack Goody (ed.), *Literacy in Traditional Societies*, Cambridge.

—— (1972–73), 'Dimensions of Illiteracy, 1750–1850', *Expl.Ec.H.* 10.

—— (1981), '*idem*', in Graff.

Scholl, Lars U. (1981), 'Der Ingenieur in Ausbildung, Beruf und Gesellschaft 1856–1881', in Ludwig.

Schomerus, Friedrich (1952), *Geschichte des Jenaer Zeisswerkes 1846–1946*, Stuttgart.

Schramm, Percy Ernst (1951), 'Englands Verhältnis zur deutschen Kultur zwischen der Reichsgründung und der Jahrhundertwende', in Werner Conze (ed.), *Deutschland und Europa. Festschrift für Hans Rothfels*, Düsseldorf.

Schroeder, Juergen (1978), 'Internationale Kapitalbewegungen', in *Handwörterbuch der Wirtschaftswissenschaft*.

Schoeder-Gudehues, Brigitte (1977), 'Science, Technology and Foreign Policy', in Spiegel-Roesing and Price.

Schultz, Theodore W. (1960), 'Capital Formation by Education', *J.P.E.* 68.

—— (1961), 'Investment in Human Capital', *A.E.R.* 51.

—— (1962), 'Reflections on Investment in Man', *J.P.E.* 70.

Schulze-Gaevernitz, G. von (1892), *Der Grossbetrieb, ein wirtschaftlicher und sozialer Fortschritt*, Leipzig.

—— (1906), *Britischer Imperialismus und englischer Freihandel*, Leipzig.

Schumpeter, Joseph A. (1939), *Business Cycles. A Theoretical Historical and Statistical Analysis of the Capitalist Process*, 2 vols., New York.

—— (1951), *Imperialism and Social Classes*, New York.

—— (1979), *Capitalism, Socialism and Democracy*.

Schuster, George (1909), 'The Patents and Design Act 1907', *E.J.*, XIX.

Schwartz, Anna (1984), 'Introduction', in Bordo and Schwartz.

Schwartzman, David (1968),'The Contribution of Education to the Quality of Labour 1929–1963', *A.E.R.* 58.

"Science in Schools" (1867), *Quarterly Review*, 123.

Scott, J.D. (1958), *Siemens Brothers 1858–1958. An Essay in the History of Industry*.

—— (1962), *Vickers. A History*.

Scoville, Warren, C. (1972), *Revolution in Glassmaking*, New York.

Searle, G.R. (1971), *The Quest for National Efficiency. A Study in British Politics and Political Thought 1899–1914*, Berkeley.

Seeger, Manfred (1968), *Die Politik der Reichsbank 1876–1914 im Lichte der Spielregeln der Geldwährung*, Berlin.

Seeley (1968), 'Liberal Education in Universities', in Farrar.

Segal, H. and Simon, Matthew (1961), 'British Foreign Capital Issues, 1865–1894', *J.Ec.H.* 21.

Selowsky, Marcelo (1969), 'On the Measurement of Education's Contribution to Growth', *Q.J.E.* 83.

Semmel, Bernhard (1968), *Imperialism and Social Reform. English Social-Imperial Thought, 1895–1914*, New York.

—— (1970), *The Rise of Free Trade Imperialism. Classical Political Economy, the Empire of Free Trade and Imperialism, 1750–1850*, Cambridge.

Senger, Juergen (n.d.), 'Ökonomische Aspekte des Forschungs- und Entwicklungsprozesses', in Pohrt, W. (ed.), *Wissenschaftspolitik – von wem, für wen, wie?*, Munich.

Seward, A.C. (1917), *Science and the Nation. Essays by Cambridge Graduates*, Cambridge.

Seymour, Charles (1970), 'Electoral Reform in England and Wales. The Development and Operation of the Parliamentary Franchise, 1832–1885'.

Shadwell, Arthur (1906), *Industrial Efficiency: A Comparative Study of Industrial Life in England, Germany and America*.

—— (1908), *England, Deutschland und Amerika. Eine vergleichende Studie ihrer industriellen Leistungsfähigkeit*, (Industrial Efficiency), Berlin.

Shannon, H.A. (1932), 'The First Five Thousand Limited Companies and Their Duration', *Economic History* 2.

— (1932–4), 'The Limited Companies of 1866–1883', *Ec.H.R.* 4.

Shapin, Steven and Barnes, Barry (1976), 'Science, Nature and Control: Interpreting Mechanics' Institutes', in Dale, Esland, MacDonald.

Shapin, Steven and Thackeray, Arnold (1974), 'Prosopography as a Research Tool in History of Science: The British Scientific Community 1700–1900', *History of Science* 12.

Shapiro, Seymour (1967), *Capital and the Cotton Industry in the Industrial Revolution*, Ithaca, N.Y.

Sharpe, William F. (1964), 'Capital Asset Prices: A Theory of Market Equilibrium under Conditions of Risks', *Journal of Finance* 19.

Shepherd, David, Silberston, Aubrey and Strange, Roger (1985), *British Manufacturing Investment Overseas*.

Shonfield, Andrew (1958), *British Economic Policy Since the War*, Harmondsworth.

Short, P.J. (1974), 'The Municipal School of Technology and the University 1890–1914', in Cardwell.

Sigsworth, Eric M. (1958), *Black Dyke Mills. A History*, Liverpool.

— (1964–5), 'Science and the Brewing Industry', *Ec.H.R.* 17.

— and Blackman, J.M. (1968), 'The Wollen and Worsted Industries', in Aldcroft.

Sill, M. (1984), 'Landownership and Industry: the East Durham Coalfield in the Nineteenth Century', *Northern History* 20.

Silver, Harold (1977), 'Ideology and the Factory Child: Attitudes to Half-time Education', in McCann.

Silverman, A.G. (1931), 'Some International Trade Factors for Great Britain, 1880–1913', *Rev.Ec.Stat.* 13.

Simon, Brian (1965), *Education and the Labour Movement 1870–1920*.

— (1974), *The Two Nations and the Educational Structure 1780–1870*.

Simon, Matthew (1966–67), 'The Enterprise and Industrial Composition of New British Portfolio Foreign Investment, 1865–1914', *J.of. Devel. Stud.* 3.

— (1970), 'New British Investment in Canada, 1865–1914', *Canad.Journ.Ec.* III.

— (1968), 'The Pattern of New British Portfolio Foreign Investment, 1865–1914', in Hall.

Simpson, Paul B. (1962), 'Foreign Investment and the National Economic Advantage: A Theoretical Analysis', in Mikesell.

Sims, Geoffrey (1981), 'Engineering', in Roderick and Stephens.

Sinclair, W.A. (1959), 'The Growth of the British Steel Industry in the Late Nineteenth Century', *Scot.J.Polit.Ec.* 6.

Singer, H.W. (1950), 'The Distribution of Gains Between Investing and Borrowing Countries', *A.E.R.* 40.

Singer, Charles *et al.* (1954–58), *A History of Technology*, (5 vols.), Oxford.

Singh, Aji (1978), *UK Industry and the World Economy: A Case of De-Industrialization?*, Cambridge.

Skidelsky, Robert (1976), 'Retreat from Leadership: The Evolution of British Economic Foreign Policy, 1870–1939', in Benjamin M. Rowland (ed.), *Balance of Power: The Interwar Monetary System*, New York.

Slaven, Anthony (1975), *The Development of the West of Scotland: 1750–1960*.

— (1980), 'The Shipbuilding Industry', in Church.

Smith, Dennis (1982), *Conflict and Compromise. Class Formation in English Society. A Comparative Study of Birmingham and Sheffield*.

Smith, Roland (1961), 'An Oldham Limited Liability Company 1875–1896', *Bus.H.* 4.

Smith, Samuel (1887), *The Bimetallic Question*.

Smout, T.C. (1969), *A History of the Scottish People 1560–1830*.

Soedersten, Bo (1964), *A Study of Economic Growth and International Trade*, Stockholm.

Soldon, N. (1974), 'Laissez-Faire as Dogma: The Liberty and Property Defence League, 1882–1914', in Kenneth D. Browne, *Essays in Anti- Labour-History. Responses to the Rise of Labour in Britain*.

Solo, R. (1971), 'The Capacity to Assimilate an Advanced Technology', in Rosenberg.

Solomou, Solomos (1986), 'Non-Balanced Growth and Kondratieff Waves in the World Economy 1850–1914', *J.Ec.H.* 46.

Solow, Robert M. (1971a), *Capital Theory and the Rate of Return*, Amsterdam.

— (1957), 'Technical Change and the Aggregate Production Function', *Rev. Econ. Stat.* 39.

— (1971b), 'Investment and Economic Growth: Some Comments', in Bowman *et al.*

Bibliography

Sonnemann, Rolf (1963), *Der Einfluss des Patentwesens auf die Herausbildung von Monopolen in der deutschen Teerfarbenindustrie (1877-1904),* Halle-Wittenberg.

Sontag, Raymond James (1938), *Germany and England. Background of Conflict 1848-1894,* New York.

Sparrow, John (1967), *Mark Pattison and the Idea of a University,* Cambridge.

Spence, Charles C. (1958), *British Investment and the American Mining Frontier 1860-1901,* Ithaca, N.Y.

Spencer, Herbert (1893), *Education. Intellectual, Moral and Physical.*

Spiegel-Rösing, Ina und Price, Derek de Solla (1977), *Science, Technology and Society. A Cross-Disciplinary Perspective.*

Spohr, Wilfried (1977), *Weltmarktkonkurrenz und Industrialisierung Deutschlands 1870-1914,* Berlin.

Spring, David (1963), *The English Landed Estate in the 19th Century,* Baltimore.

— (1952), 'The English Industrial Estate in the Age of Coal and Iron, 1830-1880', *J.Ec.H.* XI.

— (1955-54), 'Earl Fitzwilliam and the Corn Laws', *A.H.R.* LIX.

Sraffa, Piero (1926), 'The Laws of Returns under Competitive Conditions', *E.J.* 36.

Staley, Eugene (1935), *War and the Private Industry,* New York.

Stanworth, Philip and Giddens, Anthony (1974), *Elites and Power in British Society,* Cambridge.

Stauffacher, Werner (1929), *Der Schweizerische Kapitalexport unter Besonderer Berücksichtigung der Kriegs- und Nachkriegsperiode,* Glarus.

Steffen, Hans (1972), *Bildung und Gesellschaft. Zum Bildungsbegriff von Humboldt bis zur Gegenwart,* Göttingen.

Stein, Herbert (1969), *The Fiscal Revolution in America,* Chicago.

Stephens, Michael D. and Roderick, Gordon W. (1972), 'Science, the Working Class and Mechanics Institutes', *Annals of Science* 29.

Stewart, Rosemary (1966), 'The Socio-Cultural Setting of Management in the United Kingdom', *International Labour Review* 94.

Stimson, Dorothy (1968), *Scientists and Amateurs. A History of the Royal Society,* Greenwood.

Stock, Alfred (1929), *Die Technische Hochschule am Scheideweg,* Karlsruhe.

A 'Stock-Broker' (1912), 'The Development of British Home Investments', *E.J.* 22.

Stone, Irving (1968), 'British Long-Term Investment in Latin America, 1865-1913', *Bus.H.R.* 42.

— (1971), 'Financial Panics: Their Implications For the Mix of Domestic and Foreign Investments of Great Britain, 1880-1913', *Q.J.E.* 85.

— (1977), 'British Direct and Portfolio Investment in Latin America before 1914', *J.Ec.H.* 37.

Stone, Lawrence (ed.) (1975a), *The University in Society,* Princeton.

— (ed.) (1976), *Schooling and Society. Studies in the History of Education,* Baltimore, London.

— (1969), 'Literacy and Education in England 1640-1900, *P.&P.* 42.

— (1975b), 'The Size and Composition of the Oxford Student Body 1580-1909', in idem.

— and Stone, Jeanne C. Fawtier (1986), *An Open Elite, England 1540-1880,* Oxford.

Stopford, John M. (1974), 'The Origins of British Based Multinational Manufacturing Enterprises', *Bus.H.R.* 48.

Strassmann, W. Paul (1968), *Technological Change and Economic Development. The Manufacturing Experience of Mexico and Puerto Rico,* Ithaca, N.Y.

Straub, Hans (1975), *Die Geschichte der Bauingenieurskunst,* Basel/Stuttgart.

Streeten, Paul (1961), *Economic Integration. Aspects and Problems,* Leyden.

— (1971), 'New Approaches to Private Overseas Investment', in Ady.

Sturmey, S.G. (1958), *The Economic Development of Radio.*

Sullivan, Sir Edward (1870), *Protection of Native Industry.*

Sullivan, Richard J. (1985), 'The Timing and Pattern of Technological Development in English Agriculture 1611-1850', *J.Ec.H.* 45.

Supple, Barry (ed.) (1977a), *Essays in British Business History,* Oxford.

— (1977b), 'A Framework for British Business History', *ibid.*

Sussman, Herbert L. (1968), *Victorians and the Machine. The Literary Response to Technology,* Cambridge, Mass.

Sutherland, Gillian (ed.) (1972), *Studies in the Growth of Nineteenth-Century Government.*

— (1973), *Arnold on Education,* Harmondsworth.

Svedberg, Peter (1978), 'The Portfolio- Direct Composition of Private Foreign Investment in 1914 Revisited', *E.J.* 88.

— (1981), 'Colonial Enforcement of Foreign Direct Investment', *Manchester School* 49.

—— (1982), 'The Profitability of UK Foreign Direct Investment under Colonialism', *J. of Development Econ.* 11.

Svennilson, Ingvar (1954), *Growth and Stagnation in the European Economy*, Geneva.

—— (1966), 'Education, Research and Other Unidentified Factors in Growth', in Robinson and Vaizey.

Sviedrys, Romualdas (1970), 'The Rise of Physical Science at Victorian Cambridge', *Hist. Stud.in Phys. Sciences* 2.

Sylla, Richard (1977), 'Financial Intermediaries in Economic History', in Robert E. Gallman (ed.), *Recent Developments in the Study of Business and Economic History. Essays in Memory of Hermann E. Kroos,* Greenwich.

Symons, Julian (1955), *Horatio Bottomley.*

Tacke, Gerd (1933), *Kapitalausfuhr und Warenausfuhr. Eine Darstellung ihrer unmittelbaren Verbindung*, Jena.

Tanner, J. Ernst and Bonomo, Vittorio (1968), 'Gold, Capital Flows and Long Swings in American Business Activity', *J.P.E.* 76.

Tariff Commission (1904), *Reports*, vols. 1 and 2.

Taussig, F.W. (1927), *International Trade*, New York.

—— (1906), 'Wages and Prices in Relation to International Trade', *Q.J.E.* 20.

—— (1916/17a), 'International Trade under Depreciated Paper: A Contribution to Theory.' *Q.J.E.* 31.

—— (1916/17b), 'Comment', *ibid.*

—— (1916/17c), 'A Rejoinder', *ibid.*

—— (1925), 'The Change in Great Britain's Foreign Trade Terms after 1900.' *E.J.* 35.

Taylor, A.J. (1977), *Laissez-Faire and State Intervention in Nineteenth-Century Britain.*

—— (1961/62), 'Labour Productivity and Technological Innovation in the British Coal Industry, 1850–1914', *Ec.H.R.* XIV.

—— (1968), 'The Coal Industry', in Aldcroft.

—— (1975), 'County College and Civic University: An Introductory Essay', in P.J. Gosden and A.J. Taylor (eds.), *Studies in the History of a University 1874–1984*, Leeds.

Taylor, F. Sherwood (1952), 'The Teaching of Science in Oxford in the Nineteenth Century', *Annals of Science* 8.

Teich, Mikulas and Young, Robert (eds.) (1973), *Changing Perspectives in the History of Science. Essays in Honour of Joseph Needham*, Dordrecht.

Temin, Peter (1966a), 'Labour Scarcity and the Problem of American Industrial Efficiency in the 1850's', *J.Ec.H.* 26/3.

—— (1966b), 'The Relative Decline of the British Steel Industry 1880–1913', in Henry Rosovsky (ed.), *Industrialization in Two Systems: Essays in Honor of Alexander Gerschenkron*, New York.

Thackeray, Arnold (1970), 'Science and Technology in the Industrial Revolution', *History of Science* 9.

—— (1974), 'Natural Knowledge in Cultural Context: The Manchester Model', *A.H.R.* 79.

Thane, Pat (1986), 'Financiers and the British State: the Case of Sir Ernest Cassel', *Bus.H.* 28.

—— (1978), 'Non-Contributory versus Insurance Pension 1878–1908', in idem (ed.), *The Origins of British Social Policy.*

——, Crossick, Geoffrey and Floud, Roderick (1984), *The Power of the Past. Essays for Eric Hobsbawm*, Cambridge.

Thomas, Brinley (1972a), *Migration and Urban Development. A Reappraisal of British and American Long Cycles.*

—— (1973), *Migration and Economic Growth. A Study of Great Britain and the Atlantic Economy*, Cambridge.

—— (1968), 'Migration and International Investment', in Hall.

—— (1970), 'The Historical Record of International Capital Movements to 1913', in Adler, J.H.

—— (1972b), 'The Historical Record of International Capital Movements to 1913', in Dunning, J.H.

Thomas, David (1972), 'The Social Origins of Marriage Partners of the British Peerage in the 18th/19the Century', *Population Studies* XXVI.

Thomas, J.A. (1939), *The House of Commons*, Cardiff.

—— (1929), 'The Repeal of the Corn Laws 1846', *Economica* 9.

313

Bibliography

Thomas, Mark (1985), 'An Input-Output Approach to the British Economy 1890–1914', *J.Ec.H.* 45.

Thomas, W.A. (1973), *The Provincial Stock Exchanges*.

—— (1978), *The Finance of British Industry 1918–1976*.

Thompson, E.P. (1963), *The Making of the English Working Class*.

—— (1965), 'The Peculiarities of the English', in Ralph Milliband and John Saville, *The Socialist Register*.

Thompson, F.M.L. (1963), *Landed Society in the 19th Century*.

—— (1959), 'Whigs and Liberals in the West Riding 1830–1860', *E.H.R.* 124.

—— (1984), 'English Landed Society', in Thane *et al*.

Thoms, David and Donnelly, Tom (1985), *The Motor Car Industry in Coventry Since the 1890's*.

Thorner, Daniel (1951), 'Great Britain and the Development of Indian Railways', *J.Ec.H.* 11.

Thyssen, Simon (1954), *Die Berufsschule in Idee und Gestaltung*, Essen.

Tilly, Richard (1966), *Financial Institutions and Industrialization in the Rhineland, 1815–1870*, Madison.

—— (1983), 'Financing Industrial Enterprise in Great Britain and Germany in the Nineteenth Century: Testing Ground for Marxist and Schumpeterian Theories', Münster, (cyclost).

—— (1984), 'Zur Finanzierung des Wirtschaftswachstums in Deutschland und Grossbritannien 1880–1913', in Ernst Helmstaedter (ed.), *Die Bedingungen des Wirtschaftswachstums in Vergangenheit und Zukunft. Gedenkschrift für Walther G. Hoffmann*, Tübingen.

Timmons, George (1983), 'Education and Technology in the Industrial Revolution', *Hist. of Technology* 8.

Tinbergen, Jan (1951), *Business Cycles in the United Kingdom 1870–1914*, Amsterdam.

—— and Bos, H.C. (n.d.), 'A Planning Model for the Educational Requirement of Economic Development', in *O.E.C.D.*

Tipton, Frank B.Jr. (1976), *Regional Variations in the Economic Development of Germany during the Nineteenth Century*, Middletown.

Titze, Hartmut (1983), 'Enrollment Expansion and Academic Overcrowding in Germany', in Jarausch.

Tolley, Brian (1981), 'Technical Education and the University College of Nottingham', in Roderick and Stephens.

Tomlinson, Jim (1981), *Problems of British Economic Policy 1870–1945*.

Torrance, John (1978), 'Social Class and Bureaucratic Innovation: The Commissioners for Examining the Public Accounts 1780–1787', *P.&P.* 78.

Trace, Keith (1981), 'The Chemical Industry', in Roderick and Stephens.

Trainor, Richard (1982), 'Peers on Industrial Frontiers: the Earls of Dartmore and Dudley in the Black Country', in Cannadine.

Trebilcock, Clive (1977), *The Vickers Brothers. Armaments and Enterprise 1854–1914*.

—— (1982), *The Industrialization of the Continental Powers 1780–1914*.

—— (1969), ' "Spin-off" in British Economic History: Armaments and Industry, 1760–1914', *Ec.H.R.* 22.

—— (1970), 'Legends of the British Armament Industries 1890–1914: A Revision', *J.Contemp.H.* 5.

—— (1973), 'British Armaments and European Industrialization, 1880–1914', *Ec.H.R.* 26.

—— (1975), 'War and the Problem of Industrial Mobilisation 1899–1914', in Winter.

Treue, Wilhelm (1964), 'Das Verhältnis der Universitäten und Technischen Hochschulen zueinander und ihre Bedeutung für die Wirtschaft', in F. Luetge (ed.), *Die wirtschaftliche Situation in Deutschland und die Wende vom 18. zum 19. Jahrhundert*, Stuttgart.

—— (1966), 'Die Bedeutung der chemischen Wissenschaft fuer die chemische Industrie', *Technikgeschichte* 33.

—— (1967), 'Ingenieur und Erfinder. Zwei Sozial und Technikgeschichtliche Probleme', *V.S.W.G.* 54.

—— und Mauel, Kurt (1976), *Naturwissenschaft, Technik und Wirtschaft im 19. Jahrhundert*, Göttingen.

Trickovic, Vidosard (1973), 'Science Policy and Development Strategy in Developing Countries', in Williams, B.R.

Triffin, Robert (1964), *The Evolution of the International Monetary System: Historical Reappraisal and Future Perspectives*, Princeton.

314

Troitzsch, Ulrich (1970), 'Die Rolle des Ingenieurs in der Frühindustrialisierung – ein Forschungsproblem', *Technikgeschichte* 37.

Tropp, A. (1970), 'The Changing Status of the Teacher in England and Wales', in Musgrave.

Tucker, G.S.L. (1960), *Progress and Profits in British Economic Thought 1650-1850*, Cambridge.

— (1970), 'The Application and Significance of Theories of the Effect of Economic Progress on the Rate of Profit, 1800-1850', in A.G.L. Shaw (ed.), *Great Britain and the Colonies 1815-1865*.

— Turnbull, Geoffrey (1951), *A History of the Calico Printing Industry of Great Britain*, Altrincham.

— Turner, Doris Mabel (1927), *History of Science Teaching in England*.

Turner, G.L.E. (1976), *The Patronage of Science in the Nineteenth Century*, Leyden.

Turner, Henry Ashby (1985), *German Big Business and the Rise of Hitler*, New York.

Turner, John (ed.) (1984), *Businessmen and Politics. Studies of Business Activity in British Politics, 1900-1945*.

Turner, R. Steven (1971), 'The Growth of Professorial Research in Prussia, 1818 to 1848 – Causes and Context', *Historical Studies in Physical Sciences*, 3.

— (1975), 'University Reformers and Professorial Scholarship in Germany', in Stone.

— (1980), 'The Bildungsbürgertum and the Learned Profession in Prussia, 1770–1830: The Origins of a Class', *Histoire Sociale – Social History 13*.

Tweedale, Geoffrey (1983), 'Sheffield Steel and America: Aspects of the Atlantic Migration of Special Steelmaking Technology, 1850–1930', *Bus. H. 25*.

Tylecote, Mabel (1957), *The Mechanics Institutes of Lancashire and Yorkshire Before 1851*, Manchester.

— (1974), 'The Manchester Mechanics Institute, 1824–50', in Cardwell.

Tyson, R.E. (1967), 'Scottish Investment in American Railways: the Case of the City of Glasgow Bank, 1856–1881', in Payne.

— (1968), 'The Cotton Industry', in Aldcroft.

Tyszynski, H. (1951), 'World Trade in Manufactured Commodities, 1899–1950', *Manchester School* 19.

Utton, M.A. (1972), 'Some Features of the Early Merger Movements in British Manufacturing Industry', *Bus.H. 14*.

Vaizey, John (1960), *The Brewing Industry 1886-1951. An Economic Study*.

— (1962), *The Economics of Education*.

— (1974), *The History of British Steel*.

— (n.d.), 'Towards a New Political Economy', in *O.E.C.D.*

— (1966), 'Criterions for Public Expenditure on Education', in Robinson and Vaizey.

Vaizey, John and Debauvais, Michael (1961), 'Economic Aspects of Educational Development', in Halsey *et al.*

Vallance, Aylmer (1955), *Very Private Enterprise*.

Vamplew, Wray (1971), 'Nihilistic Impressions of British Railway History', in McCloskey.

— (1980), 'The Protection of English Cereal Producers: the Corn Laws Reassessed', *Ec.H.R.* 33.

Vaughan, W.E. (1984), *Landlords and Tenants in Ireland 1848-1904*, Dundalgan.

Veblen, Thorstein (1964), *Imperial Germany and the Industrial Revolution*, New York.

Vernon, Raymond (1966), 'International Investment and International Trade in the Product Cycle', *Q.J.E.* 80.

— (1979), 'The Product Cycle Hypothesis in a New International Environment', *Oxford Bull. of Econ. Stat.* 41.

Vincent, J.R. (1968), *Pollbooks. How Victorians Voted*, Cambridge.

Viner, Jacob (1924), *Canada's Balance of International Indebtedness, 1900-1913. An Inductive Study in the Theory of International Trade*, Cambridge, Mass.

— (1937), *Studies in the Theory of International Trade*, New York.

— (1958), *The Long View and the Short. Studies in Economic Theory and Policy*, Glencoe.

— (1945), 'Clapham on the Bank of England', *Economica* 12.

Vinovskis, Maris (1970), 'Horace Mann on the Economic Productivity of Education', *New English Quarterly* 43.

de Vries, Jan (1985), 'The Population and Economy of the Pre-Industrial Netherlands', *J. of Interdisciplinary History* 15.

Bibliography

Wadsworth, A.P. (1974), 'The First Manchester Sunday Schools', in M.W. Flinn and T.C. Smout, *Essays in Social History*, Oxford.

Walder-Heene, E. (1918), *Die Schweizerischen Kapitalinteressen in In- und Auslande und ihr Schutz*, St Gallen.

Walker, Charles (1933), 'The Working of the Pre-War Gold Standard', *Rev. Ec. Stud.* 1.

Walker, W.B. (1982), 'Britain's Industrial Performance 1850–1950: A Failure to Adjust', in Keith Pavitt (ed.), *Technical Innovation and British Economic Performance*.

Walker-Smith, Derek (1933), *The Protectionist Case in the 1840's*, Oxford.

Walter, François (1982), 'La France et les emprunements de la Confédération Helvétique', *Revue Suisse d'Histoire* 32.

Walters, Rhodri (1975), 'Labour Productivity in the South Wales Steam-Coal Industry, 1870–1914', *Ec.H.R.* 28.

Wandel, Eckard (1978), 'Internationale Kapitalbewegungen, I. Geschichte', in *Handwörterbuch der Wirtschaftswissenschaft*.

Ward, David (1967), 'The Public Schools and Industry in Britain after 1870', *J.Contemp. H.* 2.

Ward, J.T. (1971), 'Landowners and Mining', in J.T. Ward and R.G. Wilson (eds.), *Land and Industry. The Landed Estate and the Industrial Revolution*, Newton Abbot.

Wardle, David (1970), *English Popular Education*, Cambridge.

Ware, Fabian (1901), *Educational Foundations of Trade and Industry*.

Warner, Aaron W., Morse, Dean and Eichner, Alfred S. (eds.) (1965), *The Impact of Science on Technology*, New York.

Warren, Kenneth (1970), *The British Iron and Steel Industry Since 1840. An Economic Geography*.

—— (1976), *The Geography of British Industry Since 1800*.

—— (1980), *Chemical Foundations. The Alkali Industry in Britain to 1926*, Oxford.

Warwick, Paul (1985), 'Did Britain Change? An Inquiry into the Causes of National Decline', *J. Contemp.H.* 20.

Webb, R.K. (1971), *The British Working Class Reader 1790–1848. Literacy and Social Tension*, New York.

—— (1949), 'Working Class Readers in Early Victorian England', *E.H.R.* 64.

—— (1954), 'Literacy among the Working Classes in Nineteenth-Century Scotland', *Scot.H.R.* 33.

Webb, Sidney (1902), 'London University: A Policy and a Forecast', *Nineteenth Century and After* 51.

Webb, Sidney and Beatrice (1923), *The Decay of Capitalist Civilization*.

Webb, Steven B. (1980), 'Tariffs, Cartels, Technology and Growth in the German Steel Industry, 1879–1914', *J.Ec.H.* XL.

Wehler, Hans Ulrich (ed.) (1974), *Sozialgeschichte Heute. Festschrift für Hans Rosenberg zum 70. Geburtstag.*, Göttingen.

Weiher, Sigfrid von (1980), 'The Rise and Development of Electrical Engineering and Industry in Germany in the 19th Century', in Okochi and Uchida.

Weindling, Paul (1983), 'The British Mineralogical Society – a Case Study in Science and Social Improvement', in Inkster and Morell.

Weingart, Peter (1978), 'The Relation between Science and Technology – a Sociological Explanation', in Krohn *et al.*

Weir, R.B. (1980), 'The Drink Trades', in Church.

Weisbrod, Burton A. (1972), 'Education and Investment in Human Capital', in Kiker.

Welch, B.F. (1971), 'Education in Production', in Kiker.

Wellens, J. (1970), 'The Anti-Intellectual Tradition in the West', in Musgrave.

Wengenroth, Ulrich (1986), *Unternehmensstrategien und Technischer Fortschritt. Die Deutsche und die Britische Stahlindustrie, 1865–1895*, Göttingen.

West, E.G. (1965), *Education and the State. A Study in Political Economy*.

—— (1970), 'Resource Allocation and Growth in Early Nineteenth-Century British Education', *Ec.H.R.* 23.

—— (1971), 'The Interpretations of Early Nineteenth-Century-Education Statistics', *Ec.H.R.* 24.

—— (1975), 'Educational Slowdown and Public Intervention in 19th Century England. A Study in the Economics of Bureaucracy', *Expl.Ec.H.* 12.

—— (1978), 'Literacy and the Industrial Revolution', *Ec.H.R.* 31.

—— (1981), 'Progress in Artisan Literacy from 1790', in Roderick and Stephens.

—— (1983), 'Nineteenth-Century Educational History: The Kiesling Critique', *Ec.H.R.* 36.

Whale, P. Barrett (1930), *Joint Stock Banking in Germany. A Study of the German Creditbanks Before and After the War.*

— (1936), 'The Theory of International Trade in the Absence of an International Standard', *Economica* 3.

— (1937), 'The Working of the Pre-War Gold Standard', *Economica* 4.

— (1939), 'International Short-Term Capital Movements', *Economica* 6.

Whipp, Richard (1983), *Potbank and Union: A Study of Work and Trade Unionism in the Pottery Industry, 1900–1924*, Warwick, Diss.

White, Harry D. (1933), *The French International Accounts 1880–1913*, Cambridge, Mass.

Whittlesey, Charles R. (1936), 'Foreign Investment and the Terms of Trade', *Q.J.E.* 46.

Whyte, Adam Gowans (1930), *Forty Years of Electrical Progress. The Story of the GEC.*

Wicksell, Knut (1916/17), 'International Freights and Prices', in Taussig (1916/17a).

Wiener, Martin J. (1981), *English Culture and the Decline of the Industrial Spirit*, Cambridge.

Wieser, Carl Wolfgang Freiherr von (1919), *Der Finanzielle Aufbau der Englischen Industrie* (ed. Ernst Herzenberg), Jena.

Wiles, P.J.D. (1951), 'Notes on the Efficiency of Labour', *O.E.P.* 3.

Wilken, Paul H. (1979), *Enterpreneurship: A Comparative and Historical Study*, Norwood.

Wilkinson, Rupert (1964), *The Prefects. British Leadership and Public School Tradition. A Comparative Study in the Making of Rulers.*

— (1962), 'Political Leadership and the Late Victorian Public School', *Brit.J.Sociology* XIII.

— (1970), 'The Gentlemen Ideal and the Maintenance of a Political Elite', in Musgrave.

Williams, B.R. (1967), *Technology, Investment and Growth.*

— (ed.). (1973), *Science and Technology in Economic Growth.*

Williams, David (1968), 'The Evolution of the Sterling System', in E.R. Whittlesey and J.S.G. Wilson (eds.), *Essays in Money and Banking in Honour of R.S. Sayers*, Oxford.

Williams, E.E. (1896), *Made in Germany.*

— (1899), *The Case for Protection.*

Williams, J.H. (1920), *Argentine International Trade under Inconvertible Paper Money 1880–1920*, Cambridge, Mass.

Williams, L. Pearce (1973), 'Kant, Naturphilosophie and Scientific Method', in Giere and Westfall.

Williams, Trevor Illtyd (1972), *The Chemical Industry. Past and Present*, Wakefield.

Williamson, A. (1894), *British Industry and Foreign Competition.*

Williamson, Jeffrey G. (1964), *American Growth and the Balance of Payments, 1820–1913*, Chapel Hill.

— (1968), 'The Long Swing. Comparisons and Interactions Between British and American Balance of Payments, 1820–1913', in Hall.

— (1982), 'The Structure of Pay in Britain, 1710–1911', *Res.Ec.H.* 7.

Wilson, Charles (1954), *The History of Unilever. A Study in Economic Growth and Social Change.* 2 vols.

— (1965), 'Economy and Society in Late Victorian Britain', *Ec.H.R.* 18.

— and Reader, William (1958), *Men and Machines. A History of D. Napier and Sons, Engineers, Ltd. 1908–1958.*

Wilson, Huntington (1916), 'The Relation of Government to Foreign Investment', in Kemmerer.

Wilson, J.M. (1868), 'On Teaching Natural Science in Schools', in Farrar.

Wilson, P.M.G. (1959), 'The Routes of Entry of New Members of the British Cabinet, 1868–1958', *Political Studies* 7.

Wilson, Roland (1931), *Capital Imports and the Terms of Trade.* Melbourne.

Winch, David (1969), *Economics and Policy.*

Winston, A.P. (1927), 'Does Trade "Follow the Dollar"?', *A.E.R.* 17.

Winter, J.M. (ed.) (1975), *War and Economic Development. Essays in Memory of David Joslin*, Cambridge.

Witte, S.N. (1954), 'Report of the Minister of Finance to His Majesty, 1899', *J.Mod.H.* 26.

Wood, G.H. (1909), 'Real Wages and the Standard of Comfort Since 1850', *J.R.S.S.* 72.

Woodbury, Robert S. (1960), 'The Legend of Eli Whitney and Interchangeable Parts', *Technology & Culture* I.

Woodruff, William (1966), *Impact of Western Man. A Study of Europe's Role in the World Economy 1750–1960.*

Bibliography

Wrigley, Chris (ed.) (1982a), *A History of British Industrial Relations, 1875–1914*, Brighton.

— (1982b), 'The Government and Industrial Relations', *ibid.*

Wrigley, Julia (1986), 'Technical Education and Industry in the Nineteenth Century', in Elbaum and Lazonick.

Wright, J.F. (1981), 'Britain's Inter-War Experience', *O.E.P.* 33.

Wright, Maurice (1972), 'Treasury Control, 1854–1914', in Sutherland.

Wulf, Juergen (1968), *Der Deutsche Aussenhandel seit 1850. Entwicklung, Strukturwandlungen und Beziehungen zum Wirtschaftswachstum*, Diss. Basel, Repro. Stuttgart.

Yang, Tien-Yi (1984), 'Foreign Business Activities and the Chinese Response', in Okochi and Inoue.

— (1980), 'Employers' Organization in Mid-Victorian England', *Int. R. Soc. H.* 25.

Yarmie, Andrew H. (1984), 'British Employers' Resistance to 'Grandmother's Government, 1850–80', *Soc.H.* 9.

Yeager, Leland B. (1976), *International Monetary Relations: Theory, History and Policy*, New York.

Young, Allyn A., 'Increasing Return and Economic Progress', *E.J.* 38.

Zangerl, Carl H.E. (1971), 'The Social Composition of the County Magistracy in England and Wales, 1831–1887', *J.Brit.S.* 11.

Zebel, Sydney H. (1940), 'Fair Trade: An English Reaction to the Breakdown of the Cobden Treaty-System', *J.Mod.H.* XII.

Zeitlin, Jonathan (1983), 'The Labour Strategies of British Engineering Employers 1890–1922', in H.F. Gospel and Craig R. Littler (eds.), *Managerial Strategies and Industrial Relations*.

— (1987), 'From Labour History to the History of Industrial Relations', *Ec.H.R.* XL.

Zimmermann, Louis and Grumbach, F. (1953), 'Saving, Investment and Imperialism. A Reconsideration of the Theory of Imperialism', *W.W. Archiv*, 71.

Zloczower, A. (1981), *Career Opportunities and the Growth of Scientific Discovery in Germany*, New York.

Zollinger, Walter (1914a), *Die Bilanz der Internationalen Wertübertragungen. Eine Studie über die Zahlungsbilanz und die Ausländische Kapitalanlage in der Schweiz*, Jena.

— (1914b), 'Die Bilanz der Internationalen Wertübertragungen' *W.W.Archiv* 3.

Zunkel, Friedrich (1962), *Der Rheinisch-Westfälische Unternehmer 1834–1879. Ein Beitrag zur Geschichte des deutschen Bürgertums im 19. Jahrhundert*, Cologne.

Zweig, Konrad (1928), 'Die Internationalen Kapitalwanderungen vor und nach dem Kriege', *W.W.Archiv* 27.

— (1929), 'Strukturwandlungen und Konjunkturschwingungen im Englischen Aussenhandel der Vorkriegszeit', *W.W.Archiv* 30.

List of Abbreviations

A.E.R.	American Economic Review
Ag.H.R.	Agricultural History Review
A.H.R.	American Historical Review
Amer.Soc.R.	American Sociological Review
Archiv.Soz.	Archiv für Sozialgeschichte
Brit.J.Sociology	British Journal of Sociology
Bull.Ox.U.Inst.Stat.	Bulletin of the Oxford University Institute of Statistics
Bus.H.	Business History
Bus.H.R.	Business History Review
Comp.Stud.Soc.H.	Comparative Studies in Society and History
D.C.	Departmental Committee
Ec.Dev.Cult.C.	Economic Development and Cultural Change
Ec.H.R.	Economic History Review (1948 onward: 2nd Series)
E.H.R.	English Historical Review
E.J.	Economic Journal
Expl.Ec.H.	Explorations in Economic History
Expl.Ent.H.	Explorations in Entrepreneurial History
G. & G.	Geschichte und Gesellschaft
Hist.J.	Historical Journal
Hist.St.	Historical Studies
Hist.Z.	Historische Zeitschrift
Int.R.Soc.H.	International Review of Social History
J.Brit.S.	Journal of British Studies
J.Contemp.H.	Journal of Contemporary History
J.Ec.H.	Journal of Economic History
J.Ec.Lit.	Journal of Economic Literature
J.Europ.Ec.H.	Journal of European Economic History
J.Mod.H.	Journal of Modern History
J.P.E.	Journal of Political Economy
J.R.S.S.	Journal of the Royal Statistical Society
J.Soc.H.	Journal of Social History
J.Transp.Hist.	Journal of Transport History
O.E.P.	Oxford Economic Papers
P. & P.	Past and Present
Q.J.E.	Quarterly Journal of Economics
R.C.	Royal Commission
Res.Ec.H.	Research in Economic History
Rev.Econ.Stat.	Review of Economics and Statistics
Rev.Ec.Studies	Review of Economic Studies
S.C.	Select Committee
Scot.Ec.S.H.	Scottish Economic and Social History
Scot.H.R.	Scottish Historical Review
Soc.H.	Social History
T.R.H.S.	Transactions of the Royal Historical Society
V.S.W.G.	Vierteljahrschrift für Sozial-und Wirtschaftsgeschichte
W.W.Archiv	Weltwirtschaftliches Archiv
Yorkshire Bulletin	Yorkshire Bulletin of Economic and Social Research

Index

Agriculture machinery 19, 21
Amalgamations 49, 54
American system of manufacture 19
American technology 26, 28, 38, 39, 40
Andersonian Institution, Glasgow 127, 177
Apprenticeship 127, 200–2
Argentina 67–8, 103, 105
Armaments industry 19, 22, 23, 51, 102
Arnold, Matthew 119, 207
Artificial silk 43
Australia 67
Autonomous foreign investment 67, 108–9, 110

Babbage, Charles 116, 139
Balance of payments 107–10
Baldwin, Stanley 106
Balfour Committee (1918) 50
Bank of England 70, 88, 89, 106, 221, 232, 244–9
Bank rate 247–8
Banks 94–5, 100, 237, 249–50; German 96–7
Baring crisis 246
Bessemer, Henry 129, 173, 204
Bethlehem Steel Co. 22
Bicycles 21, 23, 44, 51, 52, 98
Bimetallism 237–8
Birmingham local government 224; trades 98, 231; University 26
Biscuit making 46
Boot and shoe industry 43–4, 52
Bottomley, Horatio 96
Bradford worsted trade 42, 236
Brazil 103
Brewing industry 46

British Association 118, 146, 189, 192, 195–6, 203, 209, 211
Brunner Mond 95
Bryce Commission 173
Building industry 47, 96
Bullion 69

Canada 67, 68, 103
Capital exports 58f., 264; flight 72
Cartels xiii, 30, 96
Central schools 167–8, 207
Chamberlain, Joseph 48, 85, 231, 239–43
Chemical industry 32–4, 51, 98, 124–5, 128, 200, 239, 253, 263, 271; German 130, 157–60, 162, 199
Chemistry (science) 124, 125, 128, 130; German 129–30, 157–8, 162, 200
China 103, 105, 106
Church of England 122, 169, 182, 226, 233
City (of London), see London capital market
City and Guilds of London Institute 173–4, 177, 179, 185, 207, 213
Civil service 209, 233, 260
Clarendon Commission 118, 119, 169, 170, 208
Classical education 169
Clocks and watches 19, 44–5, 52
Coal cutting machinery 24; mining see Mining; viewers 127, 140
Coking plants 24
College of Chemistry, Royal 175, 185
Colonies xiv-xv, 60, 77, 94, 104–5, 107, 268
Colt, Colonel Samuel 19

Commerce, Chambers of 233, 237
Commercial correspondence 199
Commons, House of 217–18, 230, 231
Comsumer goods industries 51, 52, 55, 269
Continuation schools 147
Corn Laws 215, 216, 219
Cotton industry 35–41, 51, 55, 239, 264
Courtauld's 43
Craft traditions 51
'Crowding out' of investment 65, 99
Crystal Palace 116
Cutlery industry 45
Cycles of capital exports 63–5, 78, 79

Department of Science and Art 171–3, 174, 176, 181, 193, 207
Depression, great xi, 13, 85, 99, 140, 227, 236, 270
Design 51, 171
Devonshire Commission 118, 119, 122, 170, 197, 208
Diesel engines 23
Diffusion of innovations 136
Direct investments 63, 102
Distilling 45
Dividends and interest from abroad 61–2, 68–70
Division of labour, international 30, 101, 110, 267
Dumping xiv, 31, 267
Dutch foreign investments 62; *also see* Netherlands
Dyes, synthetic 33, 130
Dynamic of growth 82, 101

Early start 51, 55, 83, 266, 268
East India Company 126, 180
East Midland iron ore 52
Economist 98
Edelstein, M. 77–8, 80–1, 112
Education 115f.; Act 117, 166; British, unorganized 142, 181, 201–2, 210–12; compulsory, German 147; differences Britain–Germany 151–2, 161–2, 181–2, 194, 195–7, 200, 205, 207–11, 270; elementary 163–7; and growth 136f., 264; secondary 168
Electric traction 48
Electrical engineering 21–2, 23, 51, 97, 128, 203, 204, 251, 263
Electricity supply 47–8, 251–2, 254
Empire, *see* Colonies

Engels, Friedrich 215, 216, 217
Engineering contracting 98; industry 19–23, 202
Engineers, graduate or qualified 120–1, 142, 199, 201
Entrepreneurial spirit 56
Entrepreneurship xiii, 27, 40, 44, 257, 261, 265, 268
Eton College 119, 232
Evening classes 179, 195
Examinations, civil service 233; schools 171, 172–3, 193
Exhibitions 116–17
Exports 3, 6–8, 11–15, 36–7, 52, 109, 244; cotton 41; cutlery 45; woollens 42–2

Fachschulen 148
Factory Acts 220, 254
Fair trade 85
Faraday, Michael 21, 119, 124, 134
Finsbury Technical College 174, 179
Foreign bondholders 106
Foreign investment, *see* Capital exports
Foreign Office 106
Foremen and education 141
France, competition 3, 21, 42
Free trade, *see* Protection

Gas industry 47
Geology 122, 126, 175, 188
George, David Lloyd 72, 86
Germany, competition xi, 3, 21, 24, 28, 32, 56, 84, 235, 266; education system 116, 143f., 199; role of government 214
Gerschenkron A. 96–7
Gewerbeschulen 148
Glass industry 35, 239
Gold reserve 247; standard 86, 89, 244f.
Government, British 113, 122, 208, 214f., 249f., 264–5; Chemist 188; expenditure on education 194, 209, 210; loans 60, 76–7, 81, 106; School of Mines (later Royal School of Mines) 175–6, 185, 197
Grain milling 45
Grammar schools 125–6, 170–1
Greenwich Observatory 188
Growth, economic 1f., 49–50, 131, 260, 262–3
Gymnasium 145, 149–51, 154, 197, 207, 212

321

Habakkuk, H. J. 50
Harrow School 119, 232
Hayek, F. A. von 82
Hicks, Sir John 82, 101
Hobson, J. A. 73, 104, 105, 108
Hofmann, A. W. 129, 146, 157, 175, 200, 208
Hooley, E. T. 96
Hopper, Fred 98-9
Hosiery industry 43
Human capital 137-8
Humboldt, Alexander von 143; Wilhelm von 143, 144, 145, 157
Huxley, Thomas Henry 119, 120, 121, 134

Idealism 144
Imperial College 176, 185, 197, 213
Imperialism 104-5; imperialists 117
India 37, 77, 107
Industrialization, early x
Industrialists and education 138, 140-1, 156, 197-8
Industries 18f., 262-3
Interchangeable parts 19, 203
Interrelatedness xi, 52, 83
Inventions 134-5
Investment 58, 60, 64, 250
Investor 68, 74, 81, 105, 111
Iron and Steel industry 27-31, 51, 98, 129, 199, 264
Italian cities 57, 263

Joint-stock organization 54, 256
Jute industry 43

Kelvin, 1st Baron 21, 123, 133, 134, 184, 204
Kew Observatory 122
Keynes, J. M. 73, 81, 86, 87, 89, 90, 100, 104, 108
Krupp armaments Co. 22
Kuznets, Simon 64, 80, 109

Labour costs 50
Labour-saving equipment 50-1
Lancashire 40
Landed classes 228 f., 242, 259
Latin America 67, 79, 105
Learned Societies 126-7, 189-93; German 128, 146
Leather industry 44, 51
Lenin, V. I. 104, 105

Lever, William Hesketh (Lord Leverhulme) 35, 95
Liebig, Justus von 157, 175
Linen industry 42-3
Literacy rates 125, 137, 139, 147, 163, 206
Local government and politics 222f.
Location, industrial xiii, 56
Locomotives 20, 23, 51
London capital market 58, 91f., 215, 216, 230, 232f. 242, 256; electricity supply, 252, exhibition 116; local government 227; region 52

Machine tools 19-20, 52, 128
Magistrates 225-7
Management, scientific 54
Manchester Colleges 177; University 186, 200
Manufacturing, growth 8-15, 17; influence 234, 242 f., 256, 259
Marconi, G. 135, 204
Markets, 'soft' xv, 37, 52, 244
Marshall, Alfred 98, 140, 238
Marx, Karl 216
Mass production 51, 52, 269
Mathematics teaching 118, 119, 126
Maxim, Sir Hiram Stevens 22
Mechanics' Institutes 127, 139, 172, 176, 177-9
Medical Research Council 189, 197
Merchandise Marks Acts 255
Metallurgy 204
Mexico 81
Mill, John Stuart 140
Mines, School, *see* Government School of Mines
Mining 25-7, 51, 55, 98, 264
Motor industry 21, 51, 97, 203, 253, 271

National Physical Laboratory, 188, 197, 210, 213
Nature 117, 118
Naturphilosphie 145-6, 157
Netherlands 113, 256, 268
Newcastle Commission 118, 163
Newcastle University 26
Noble, Alfred 22, 33

Old and new industries 50, 55, 257
Oldham Limiteds 40, 95
Optical glassmaking 45-6, 51, 124, 271; German 160, 199, 271

Overend Gurney crash 92, 246
Overhead capital 82–3

Palmerston, Viscount 105
Parsons, Sir Charles A. 135, 203
Patent legislation 34, 158, 253
Perkin, W. H. 129, 157, 208
Physical-Technical-Institute (PTR), Berlin 154–5, 188
Pilkington's 35
Platt, D. C. M. 63, 71
Playfair, Lyon 116, 119, 133
Polytechnics 180, 181, 196
Poor Law Amendment Act 220
Portfolio investment 59, 102
Post Office Savings Bank 246
Printing industry 46
Product cycle 110, 142, 270
Professors 121; German 145, 155, 160
Promoters 95
Protection xiv, 30, 42, 44, 53, 102, 236–7, 238–44, 257, 266, 267–8
Public opinion 258, 261
Public Schools 116, 169–70, 212, 229, 232
Public utilities 60
Pupillage, *see* apprenticeship
Push and pull, capital exports 65–6, 108–9

Radio 135, 204
Railways 47–8, 79, 104, 254–5; foreign 60; investment 77
Raw material producers 91, 101, 112
Realgymnasium 150–1; *Realschulen* 150–1, 154, 212
Red Flag Act 253, 254
Reform Act 215, 216, 217–18, 223
Reparations 87
Research 120, 132, 205; and development (R & D) 135, 212
Residual, among growth factors 130, 136
Revised code 166
Risk 76–81, 112
Rothschild, Lord 72
Royal Society 191
Rubber industry 35, 204
Rugby School 119
Russia 75, 81, 106

Salesmanship 56
Samuelson, Bernard 195

Samuelson Commission 118; Committee 118
Savings, rate of 58, 64, 99, 111
Science 115 f., based industries x; discovery 132 f.; in the industrial revolution 123 f.; in industry 199, 270; lecturers 175; publications 192–3; in schools 165–7, 206; training xiii
Scientists 121, 198, 209, 264
Scotland cotton industry, 40, 98; education 125, 163, 165; investments 62; steel industry 28
Service industries 52, 265, 267–9
Sewing machines 19
Sheffield Chamber of Commerce 141; cutlers 45, 139; local government 223–4; silver-plating 45; steel 29–30, 204, 236
Shipbuilding industry 23–5, 31, 51–2, 55, 98, 264, 267
Shipyards xiii, 51
Shortsightedness 113
Short-term capital 71
Silver plating 45
Size of firms 55–6, 57
Soap industry 34–5, 55
Society of Arts, Royal 117, 126, 173, 174
Solvay process 33
South Africa 103
South Kensington 174, 176, 185
State, role of, *see* Government
Steam engines 20
Steel industry, *see* iron and steel industry
Student numbers 120, 153–4, 156, 176, 187, 193, 196, 197
Swan, Sir Joseph Wilson 21, 203
Swiss watchmaking 45, 52

Tariffs, *see* Protection
Taussig, F. W. 90
Taunton Commission 118, 119, 170
Taxation 100
Technical education, German 148–9; Technical Instruction Act 117, 171; training 44, 200, 257; Technical Universities (*Technische Hochschulen*), German 120, 152–4, 208
Technologies, new 56, 202, 264
Technology and growth 83, 115 f., 130 f., 205

Telegraphy 124, 128, 220
Telephone 203
Terms of Trade 87, 89–91
Textile industry 36–43; machinery 20, 23, 51
Thomas, Sidney Gilchrist 30, 129, 204
Tied loans 103–4
Tinplate 31
Tobacco industry 44, 46–7, 52, 266
Total factor productivity 14–16, 30, 131
Trade cycle 84, 89
Trade schools 181
Trade unions xv, 53–4, 84, 220–1, 255, 269
Training colleges 165, 167, 172
Transfer costs 86, 89, 112
Turkey 81
Turning point 16–17, 261
Typewriters 19

Unemployment 75, 84–6, 112
United Alkali 95, 199
United States, competition xi, 3, 19–20, 21, 24, 28, 44, 56, 235, 262, 266
Universities, ancient 116, 117, 118, 122, 124, 126, 127, 182–4, 194, 205, 209, 213, 231, 232; German 120, 143, 146, 155–6, 160–1; other British 118, 184–8, 213; Scottish 118, 120, 126, 184

Value systems xiv, 115, 228
Verein Deutscher Ingenieure 154
Verdoorn effect 83
Vickers Ltd 22, 93, 95, 204

Wage level 50, 53
Wealthy classes 229–30
Wheatstone, Sir Charles 21, 128
Whitney, Eli 19
Whitworth, Sir Joseph 174, 202
Woollen and worsted industry 41–2, 55, 264
Woolwich Arsenal 124
World War I 57, 102, 271